Lecture Notes in Computer Science　11342

Commenced Publication in 1973
Founding and Former Series Editors:
Gerhard Goos, Juris Hartmanis, and Jan van Leeuwen

More information about this series at http://www.springer.com/series/7409

Guojun Wang · Jinjun Chen
Laurence T. Yang (Eds.)

Security, Privacy, and Anonymity in Computation, Communication, and Storage

11th International Conference
and Satellite Workshops, SpaCCS 2018
Melbourne, NSW, Australia, December 11–13, 2018
Proceedings

 Springer

Editors
Guojun Wang
Guangzhou University
Guangzhou, China

Laurence T. Yang
St. Francis Xavier University
Antigonish, NS, Canada

Jinjun Chen
Swinburne University of Technology
Melbourne, Victoria, Australia

ISSN 0302-9743   ISSN 1611-3349   (electronic)
Lecture Notes in Computer Science
ISBN 978-3-030-05344-4   ISBN 978-3-030-05345-1   (eBook)
https://doi.org/10.1007/978-3-030-05345-1

Library of Congress Control Number: 2018962985

LNCS Sublibrary: SL3 – Information Systems and Applications, incl. Internet/Web, and HCI

This Springer imprint is published by the registered company Springer Nature Switzerland AG
The registered company address is: Gewerbestrasse 11, 6330 Cham, Switzerland

Preface

A very warm welcome to the proceedings of the 11th International Conference on Security, Privacy and Anonymity in Computation, Communication, and Storage (SpaCCS 2018), held in Melbourne, Australia, December 11–13, 2018. SpaCCS 2018 was organized by Swinburne University of Technology, Melbourne, Australia.

The SpaCCS 2018 main conference and its associated symposia/workshops provided a forum for international scholars to gather and share their research findings, achievements, innovations, and perspectives in cyberspace security research. Previous SpaCCS conferences were successfully held in Guangzhou, China (2017), Zhangjiajie, China (2016), Helsinki, Finland (2015), Beijing, China (2014), Melbourne, Australia (2013), Liverpool, UK (2012), and Changsha, China (2011).

The conference program this year consisted of the main conference and seven symposia/workshops covering a broad range of research topics on security, privacy, and anonymity in computation, communication, and storage:

(1) The 11th International Conference on Security, Privacy, and Anonymity in Computation, Communication, and Storage (SpaCCS 2018)
(2) The 4th International Symposium on Sensor-Cloud Systems (SCS 2018)
(3) The 4th International Symposium on Dependability in Sensor, Cloud, and Big Data Systems and Applications (DependSys 2018)
(4) The 10th International Symposium on UbiSafe Computing (UbiSafe 2018)
(5) The 7th International Symposium on Security and Privacy on Internet of Things (SPIoT 2018)
(6) The 9th International Workshop on Trust, Security, and Privacy for Big Data (TrustData 2018)
(7) The 10th International Workshop on Security in e-Science and e-Research (ISSR 2018)
(8) The 8th International Symposium on Trust, Security, and Privacy for Emerging Applications (TSP 2018)

The SpaCCS 2018 main conference and its associated symposia/workshops attracted 120 submissions from different countries and institutions. All submissions were reviewed by at least three reviewers through a high-quality review process. Based on the recommendations of the reviewers and Program Committee members' discussions, 45 papers were selected for oral presentation at the conference and inclusion in this Springer volume (i.e., an acceptance rate of 37.5%).

We would like to thank the symposium and workshop organizers for their hard work in soliciting high-quality submissions, assembling the Program Committee, managing the peer-review process, and planning the symposium and workshop agenda. We would also like to acknowledge the strong support of the Organizing Committee of SpaCCS 2018, and in particular the honorary chairs, Robert Deng and Colin Fidge, the general chairs, Willy Susilo, and Kui Ren, and the program chairs, Hua Wang,

Ron Steinfeld, and Tianqing Zhu. Without their support and guidance, this event would not have been possible. We are also grateful to the experts who volunteered their time to act as reviewers and session chairs. Thanks also go to: symposium/workshop chairs, Dr. Tian Wang, Dr. Md Zakirul Alam Bhuiyan, Dr. Shuhong Chen, Dr. Marios Anagnostopoulos, Dr. Georgios Kambourakis, Dr. Qin Liu, Dr. Shaobo Zhang, and Dr. Wenjun Jiang.

Last, but not the least, we would like to thank all the authors, participants, and session chairs for their valuable contributions. Many of them traveled a long distance to attend this conference and contribute to the success of SpaCCS 2018.

October 2018

Guojun Wang
Jinjun Chen
Laurence T. Yang

SpaCCS 2018 Organizing and Program Committees

Honorary Chairs

Robert Deng	Singapore Management University, Singapore
Colin Fidge	Queensland University of Technology, Australia

General Chairs

Willy Susilo	University of Wollongong, Australia
Kui Ren	State University of New York at Buffalo, USA

Program Chairs

Hua Wang	Victoria University, Australia
Ron Steinfeld	Monash University, Australia
Tianqing Zhu	Deakin University, Australia

Program Committee

Arcangelo Castiglione	University of Salerno, Italy
Sudip Chakraborty	Valdosta State University, USA
Josep Domingo-Ferrer	Universitat Rovira i Virgili, Spain
Subrata Dutta	Haldia Institute of Technology, India
Ugo Fiore	University of Naples Federico II, Italy
Felix J. Garcia Clemente	University of Murcia, Spain
Yao Guo	Peking University, China
Selena He	Kennesaw State University, USA
Abdessamad Imine	Lorraine University, France
Vana Kalogeraki	Athens University of Economics and Business, Greece
Zaheer Khan	University of the West of England, UK
Xin Li	Nanjing University of Aeronautics and Astronautics, China
Giovanni Livraga	Università degli Studi di Milano, Italy
Guazzone Marco	University of Piemonte Orientale, Italy
Asad Masood Khattak	Zayed University, United Arab Emirates
Ilaria Matteucci	Istituto di Informatica e Telematica CNR, Italy
Vincent Roca	Inria, France
Traian Marius Truta	Northern Kentucky University, USA
Omair Uthmani	Glasgow Caledonian University, UK
Yong Yu	Shaanxi Normal University, China
Sherali Zeadally	University of Kentucky, USA
Mingwu Zhang	Hubei University of Technology, China
Kalman Graffi	Heinrich-Heine-Universität Düsseldorf, Germany

Dimitrios Karras   Sterea Hellas Institute of Technology, Greece
Mirco Marchetti   University of Modena and Reggio Emilia, Italy
Juan Pedro Munoz-Gea   Universidad Politécnica de Cartagena, Spain
Thinagaran Perumal   Universiti Putra Malaysia, Malaysia
Antonio Ruiz-Martínez   University of Murcia, Spain
Jorge S. A. Silva   University of Coimbra, Portugal
Saratha Sathasivam   Universiti Sains Malaysia, Malaysia
Junggab Son   Kennesaw State University, USA

Steering Committee

Guojun Wang (Chair)   Guangzhou University, China
Gregorio Martinez   University of Murcia, Spain
  (Chair)
Jemal H. Abawajy   Deakin University, Australia
Jose M. Alcaraz Calero   University of the West of Scotland, UK
Jiannong Cao   Hong Kong Polytechnic University, SAR China
Hsiao-Hwa Chen   National Cheng Kung University, Taiwan
Jinjun Chen   Swinburne University of Technology, Australia
Kim-Kwang Raymond   University of Texas at San Antonio, USA
  Choo
Robert Deng   Singapore Management University, Singapore
Mario Freire   The University of Beira Interior, Portugal
Minyi Guo   Shanghai Jiao Tong University, China
Weijia Jia   Shanghai Jiao Tong University, China
Wei Jie   University of West London, UK
Georgios Kambourakis   University of the Aegean, Greece
Ryan Ko   University of Waikato, New Zealand
Constantinos Kolias   George Mason University, USA
Jianbin Li   Central South University, China
Jie Li   University of Tsukuba, Japan
Jianhua Ma   Hosei University, Japan
Felix Gomez Marmol   University of Murcia, Spain
Geyong Min   University of Exeter, UK
Peter Mueller   IBM Zurich Research Laboratory, Switzerland
Indrakshi Ray   Colorado State University, USA
Kouichi Sakurai   Kyushu University, Japan
Juan E. Tapiador   The University Carlos III of Madrid, Spain
Sabu M. Thampi   Indian Institute of Information Technology
                              and Management, India
Jie Wu   Temple University, USA
Yang Xiao   The University of Alabama, USA
Yang Xiang   Swinburne University of Technology, Australia
Zheng Yan   Aalto University, Finland
Laurence T. Yang   St. Francis Xavier University, Canada
Wanlei Zhou   University of Technology Sydney, Australia

Sponsors

Contents

The 4th International Symposium on Dependability in Sensor, Cloud and Big Data Systems and Applications (DependSys 2018)

The 10th International Symposium on UbiSafe Computing (UbiSafe 2018)

**The 7th International Symposium on Security and Privacy
on Internet of Things (SPIoT 2018)**

**The 9th International Workshop on Trust, Security and Privacy
for Big Data (TrustData 2018)**

**The 10th International Workshop on Security in e-Science
and e-Research (ISSR 2018)**

The 8th International Symposium on Trust, Security and Privacy for Emerging Applications (TSP 2018)

The 11th International Conference on Security, Privacy and Anonymity in Computation, Communication and Storage (SpaCCS 2018)

Protecting Your Smartphone from Theft Using Accelerometer

Huiyong Li[1](✉), Jiannan Yu[1](✉), and Qian Cao[2](✉)

[1] School of Computer Science, Beihang University, Beijing 100000, China
{lihuiyong,zy1706139}@buaa.edu.cn
[2] Department of Computer and Information Engineering,
Beijing Technology and Business University, Beijing 100000, China
caoqian125@126.com

Abstract. In recent years, there have been many studies using the data generated by the built-in sensors of mobile phones for authentication and the selection of features is involved in the use of sensor data. This article discusses the method of biological feature selection by taking the mobile phone acceleration sensor as an example. 30 participants were invited to walk with their mobile phones for data collection to obtain data set 1. Several characteristics were evaluated from multiple aspects to select a number of effective features. 15 participants were invited to collect data set 2 under the condition of simulating dialy life. A feature-based authentication method is proposed and a success rate of 93.6% is obtained on data set 1. On the data set 2, 91.90% of the recognition success rate was obtained.

Keywords: Authentication · Biological feature · Accelerometer
Feature evaluation

1 Introduction

Traditional authentication methods such as pictures and passwords require explicit unlocking operations each time. Besides, the passwords need to be remembered which is inconvenient [1,2] and vulnerable to various attacks [3–5]. Authentication methods based on human biological features such as fingerprint, iris, voice have the advantages of no memory. However, such methods also have their shortcomings. (1) The above biological authentication process requires the user to explicitly perform the authentication operation [6]. For example, if the fingerprint is used, the mobile phone needs to be placed and put finger on the fingerprint recognition area. Face recognition needs to turne on the camera and look at it. People often need to use their mobile phones frequently and most of them are not used for a long time [7,8]. Frequently ask users for authentication will be annoying [9–11]. (2) The authentication speed is slow, such as the fingerprint recognition process often exceeds one second. (3) Security is difficult to guarantee. For example, face recognition, which is very common nowadays, can

© Springer Nature Switzerland AG 2018
G. Wang et al. (Eds.): SpaCCS 2018, LNCS 11342, pp. 3–14, 2018.
https://doi.org/10.1007/978-3-030-05345-1_1

often be attacked by using a photo of the user. Therefore, it is very important to design a secure and easy-to-use authentication method.

Compared with the above authentication methods, authentication with user behavior such as gait has unique advantages. (1) Convenience. This type of authentication is usually based on a certain user behavior pattern in daily life such as walking, running, going upstairs, etc. User no longer need to authenticate frequently. (2) High security. Each person's behavior has a unique pattern that is different between different people. Taking gait as an example, Muaaz et al. [12] proved that the acceleration sensor data generated while walking can be used for authentication and even if the attacker is a professional, such as a dancer, it is impossible to improve attack success rate significantly by imitating the user's walking posture. (3) Easy to implement. The data used for authentication comes from mobile phone sensors, which are already available on most mobile phones and require no additional equipment to complete the authentication.

In the process of authentication with sensor data, it is necessary to extract features from sensor data to characterize the specific user. The quality of these selected biological features directly affects the final authentication result. Existing methods are quite similar in the selection of features (See Table 1). They are often based on observations in daily life. In the actual process of authentication, the impact of each feature on the final result of authentication is hard to know. The usual practice is to select a number of features for authentication and then observe the results then adjust the features according to the result. Based on the above considerations, this paper analyzes various features and selects effective features from various aspects by analyzing the acceleration sensor data generated by 30 people. The main contributions of this article are:

Table 1. Selected feature in some research. Common features (1. mean, 2. median, 3. average synthetic acceleration, 4. cross-correlation, 5. peak number, 6. peak spacing, 7. average absolute error, 8. standard deviation, 9. kurtosis, 10. Touch screen features, 11. Sensor data changes, 12. Maximum change 13. Variance 14. Skewness 15. Correlation coefficient 16. Distribution)

Research	Selected feature	Accuracy (%)
Thingom Bishal Singha [13]	1 2 3 4 5 6 7	96
Attaullah Buriro [14]	1 8 9 14	95
Zdenka Sitova [15]	1 8 10 11 12	90
Hongzi Zhu [16]	Custom feature	98
Attaullah Buriro [17]	10	-
Yonggang Lu [18]	1 3 8 9 13 14 15	-
Jennifer R. Kwapisz [19]	1 3 6 7 8 16	100

1. We analyzed the data of mobile phone sensors and proposed a method to quantify the performance of biological feature in authentication.

2. An algorithm for comparing two features is proposed to rank all features. The best features are selected according to the ranking for authentication. Experiments were performed using selected features and classification algorithms.

3. The validity of the selected features was verified by experiments and the performance of authentication was tested under various conditions.

2 Related Work

There are many kinds of identity authentication based on user behavior. Here we discuss some of the most relevant researches in our work. At the same time, we will focus on the features selected during the processing of raw data.

In [13], a scheme for authentication using acceleration sensor is proposed. Feature extraction was performed using the data of acceleration sensor. Then the random forest classifier was used for authentication, achieving a 96% success rate. The considerations for selecting features are not described in this article. The features used include mean, median, average combined acceleration, correlation coefficient of the sensor's three axes, number of peaks per gait cycle, peak spacing, and mean absolute error.

In [14], a scheme that uses the data from user touch screen for identification is proposed. User's sensor data on the screen of the mobile phone is used for identity recognition and a success rate of about 95% is achieved. The features used were average, data standard deviation, kurtosis and skewness of the data and then the four features were mixed to yield 16 features.

An identification scheme using a variety of new biological behavioral feature is proposed in [15]. These biological behavioral feature take into account how the user grabs the handset when using the handset and how to enter it on the screen, identifying the data of the handset sensor as the user completes these actions. A success rate of about 93% and 90% was achieved in the walking state and the sitting state, respectively.

In [16], a scheme for identity recognition by shaking a mobile phone is proposed. Achieved an average success rate of 98.8%. Instead of using simple statistics, the authors used three simple data structures that are more suitable for shaking mobile phone identification (the tangential speed when shaking the phone, the angular velocity when shaking the phone and the sway radius). It can be seen that this complex feature can help us to understand more deeply the principle of using sensor data for identification and also achieve a satisfactory success rate.

In [17], a scheme for authentication with only the data touched by the user is proposed. Specific features include the location where the user clicks on the screen of the mobile phone, the interval at which the screen of the mobile phone is clicked and the others.

An unsupervised motion recognition scheme is proposed in [18]. The biggest innovation is that there is no need to collect a large amount of tagged training data in advance. The entire process is fully automated, using features such as mean, combined acceleration, standard deviation of the data, kurtosis of the data, skewness, variance of the data, and correlation coefficients.

A motion recognition scheme is proposed in [19]. The features used are the mean, the average combined acceleration, the peak spacing of the data, the average absolute error of the data, the standard deviation of the data, and the overall distribution of the data. Similarly, the author did not give the reason for this choice.

3   Feature Selection

3.1   Data Preprocessing

Before feature extraction, the continuous sensor data is first periodically divided to generate corresponding features for each cycle. In order to preserve biological significance, this cycle usually uses the cycle of gait. We use the periodic division method in [12] to divide the original data, that is, take a segment in the middle of the data [20, 21] as a template, calculate the Euclidean distance between the entire data and the template. Then obtain the gait cycle by periodically dividing the euclidean distance cycle. The results of the division are shown in Fig. 1.

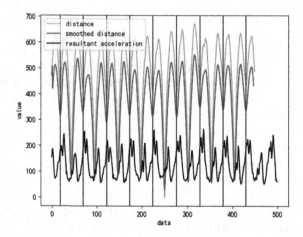

Fig. 1. Schematic diagram of cycle division. Black is the resultant acceleration, yellow is the distance between the template and the synthetic acceleration during the sliding process, red is the result of the smoothing of the distance, and blue is the period of the division. (Color figure online)

3.2   Feature Evaluation

For the selection of features, we evaluate from the following four aspects.

– The degree of difference. The degree of difference in features means that features can effectively distinguish different people. It is this difference that

4.2   Experiment Result

30 volunteers were invited to hold the mobile phone with right hand and walked on a flat road of about 100m. In addition, another 15 volunteers were invited to carry mobile phones to simulate the use of mobile phones in daily life as data set 2. In the process of authentication, we use the selected features as input data to characterize different people. We use svm in weka[1] for classification to get the result. When classifying, we use one class svm with default parameter for classification because the number of negative samples is much larger than the positive samples. That is, the test data is classified into two categories to achieve the purpose of authentication. On data set 1, the authentication success rate reached 93.6%. Due to space limitations, we only showed the authentication result of 5 people as shown in Table 3. The data of the i-th row and the j-th column represents the authentication result of testing the data of the j-th person (attacker) by using the data of the i-th person (user) as the training data. If i is equal to j, the value represents the proportion of successful authentication of the test data to the user, a total of 30 results with an average accuracy of 67.4%. Otherwise the value represents the proportion of successful identification of the test data as an attacker, a total of 870 results with an average accuracy of 94.5%.

Table 3. Dataset 1 authentication accuracy result (%)

U	A										
	1	2	3	4	5	...	26	27	28	29	30
1	89.74	100.00	100.00	100.00	99.64	...	100.00	100.00	100.00	100.00	98.55
2	100.00	65.82	100.00	100.00	100.00	...	64.88	100.00	100.00	100.00	100.00
3	100.00	100.00	92.16	100.00	100.00	...	100.00	94.10	99.48	100.00	100.00
4	64.55	90.22	100.00	46.82	100.00	...	100.00	100.00	100.00	100.00	100.00
5	100.00	100.00	100.00	100.00	14.98	...	100.00	100.00	100.00	100.00	100.00
...	...	...	...	...	...	...	...	...	...	...	...
26	100.00	100.00	100.00	100.00	100.00	...	15.00	100.00	100.00	100.00	100.00
27	100.00	100.00	10.47	100.00	100.00	...	100.00	100.00	99.48	100.00	100.00
28	100.00	100.00	98.65	99.39	100.00	...	100.00	100.00	39.74	89.23	97.83
29	100.00	100.00	100.00	100.00	100.00	...	100.00	100.00	88.57	100.00	98.19
30	100.00	100.00	100.00	100.00	100.00	...	100.00	100.00	100.00	100.00	10.87

Next, We conducted an experiment with the simulated real scene. When simulating the real scene, the volunteers can perform any kind of action because the volunteers are not required to keep walking when collecting the test data. A 91.00% authentication success rate is achieved on this data set.

---

[1] https://www.cs.waikato.ac.nz/ml/weka/.

4.3 Phone Placement Analysis

When the mobile phone is in different positions, the value of the generated acceleration sensor data is also very different. In actual daily life, the phone may be placed in a different location. Therefore, the accuracy of identity authentication in different locations also needs to be considered. In three different locations (trouser pocket, hip, bag), we achieved an accuracy of 92.03%, 78.39%, and 95.72%, respectively. Experiment result shows that even if the mobile phone is placed in a different position, the regular periodicity is still present in the process of walking. Among them, the mobile phone has achieved more than 90% recognition success rate in the pocket of the trousers and the pocket of the bag, mainly because the mobile phone is fixed in a relatively stable position and has a relatively stable periodicity during the walking process. When the mobile phone is in the pocket of the buttocks, the overall swing amplitude of the mobile phone is small, and some components of the gait vector appear weakly, resulting in a decrease in the authentication success rate (Tables 4, 5 and 6).

Table 4. Authentication success rate (phone in trouser pocket)

Volunteer	Attacker		
	Attacker1	Attacker2	Attacker3
Volunteer1	44.82%	98.54%	100.00%
Volunteer2	95.27%	97.07%	100.00%
Volunteer3	100.00%	99.64%	92.96%

Table 5. Authentication success rate (phone in hip pants pocket)

Volunteer	Attacker		
	Attacker1	Attacker2	Attacker3
Volunteer1	90.33%	99.44%	99.39%
Volunteer2	98.90%	85.74%	65.58%
Volunteer3	90.33%	69.61%	6.31%

Table 6. Authentication success rate (phone in bag)

Volunteer	Attacker		
	Attacker1	Attacker2	Attacker3
Volunteer1	88.97%	100.00%	89.20%
Volunteer2	100.00%	98.60%	91.42%
Volunteer3	100.00%	100.00%	93.32%

5 Summary

This paper proposes a method of how to select features in the process of using the acceleration sensor for authentication. The features are evaluated from multiple aspects such as difference and stability to select the most effective features. Based on the selected effective features, an acceleration sensor based authentication scheme is performed. The user can complete the identification process while holding the mobile phone.

In the next step, we will explore further the selected features. Try to optimize the certification process based on ensuring the success rate of recognition.

Acknowledgments. This work was supported in part by National Natural Science Foundation of China (61602024, 61702018).

References

1. Böhmer, M., Hecht, B.J., Schöning, J., Krüger, A., Bauer, G.: Falling asleep with angry birds, Facebook and kindle: a large scale study on mobile application usage. In: Proceedings of the 13th International Conference on Human Computer Interaction with Mobile Devices and Services, pp. 47–56 (2011)
2. Lee, W.-H., Lee, R.B.: Implicit sensor-based authentication of smartphone users with smartwatch. In: Proceedings of the Hardware and Architectural Support for Security and Privacy 2016, p. 9 (2016)
3. Consumer Reports 2013: Keep your phone safe: how to protect yourself from wireless threats. Consumer reports, Technical (2013)
4. Harbach, M., Von Zezschwitz, E., Fichtner, A., De Luca, A., Smith, M.: It's a hard lock life: a field study of smartphone (un)locking behavior and risk perception. In: Symposium On Usable Privacy and Security (SOUPS 2014), pp. 213–230 (2014)
5. Shi, E., Niu, Y., Jakobsson, M., Chow, R.: Implicit authentication through learning user behavior. In: Burmester, M., Tsudik, G., Magliveras, S., Ilić, I. (eds.) ISC 2010. LNCS, vol. 6531, pp. 99–113. Springer, Heidelberg (2011). https://doi.org/10.1007/978-3-642-18178-8_9
6. Schaub, F., Deyhle, R., Weber, M.: Password entry usability and shoulder surfing susceptibility on different smartphone platforms. In: Proceedings of the 11th International Conference on Mobile and Ubiquitous Multimedia, p. 13 (2012)
7. Spencer, B.: Mobile users can't leave their phone alone for six minutes and check it up to 150 times a day. http://www.dailymail.co.uk/news/article-2276752/Mobile-users-leave-phone-minutes-check-150-times-day.Html
8. Falaki, H., Mahajan, R., Kandula, S., Lymberopoulos, D., Govindan, R., Estrin, D.: Diversity in smartphone usage. In: Proceedings of the 8th International Conference on Mobile Systems, Applications, and Services, pp. 179–194 (2010)
9. Weir, M., Aggarwal, S., De Medeiros, B., Glodek, B.: Password cracking using probabilistic context-free grammars. In: 2009 30th IEEE Symposium on Security and Privacy, pp. 391–405 (2009)
10. Bonneau, J.: The science of guessing: analyzing an anonymized corpus of 70 million passwords. In: 2012 IEEE Symposium on Security and Privacy, pp. 538–552 (2012)
11. Kelley, P.G., et al.: Guess again (and again and again): measuring password strength by simulating password-cracking algorithms. In: 2012 IEEE Symposium on Security and Privacy, pp. 523–537 (2012)

12. Muaaz, M., Mayrhofer, R.: Smartphone-based gait recognition: from authentication to imitation. IEEE Trans. Mob. Comput. **16**(11), 3209–3221 (2017)
13. Singha, T.B., Nath, R.K., Narsimhadhan, A.V.: Person recognition using smartphones' accelerometer data (2017)
14. Buriro, A., Crispo, B., Delfrari, F., Wrona, K.: Hold and sign: a novel behavioral biometrics for smartphone user authentication. In: 2016 IEEE Security and Privacy Workshops (SPW), pp. 276–285 (2016)
15. Sitova, Z., et al.: HMOG: new behavioral biometric features for continuous authentication of smartphone users. IEEE Trans. Inf. Forensics Secur. **11**(5), 877–892 (2016)
16. Zhu, H., Jingmei, H., Chang, S., Li, L.: Shakein: secure user authentication of smartphones with single-handed shakes. IEEE Trans. Mob. Comput. **16**(10), 2901–2912 (2017)
17. Buriro, A., Crispo, B., Del Frari, F., Wrona, K.: Touchstroke: smartphone user authentication based on touch-typing biometrics. In: Murino, V., Puppo, E., Sona, D., Cristani, M., Sansone, C. (eds.) ICIAP 2015. LNCS, vol. 9281, pp. 27–34. Springer, Cham (2015). https://doi.org/10.1007/978-3-319-23222-5_4
18. Lu, Y., Wei, Y., Liu, L., Zhong, J., Sun, L., Liu, Y.: Towards unsupervised physical activity recognition using smartphone accelerometers. Multimedia Tools Appl. **76**(8), 10701–10719 (2017)
19. Kwapisz, J.R., Weiss, G.M., Moore, S.A.: Cell phone-based biometric identification. In: 2010 Fourth IEEE International Conference on Biometrics: Theory, Applications and Systems (BTAS), pp. 1–7 (2010)
20. Alvarez, D., González, R.C., López, A., Alvarez, J.C.: Comparison of step length estimators from weareable accelerometer devices. In: Conference Proceedings: Annual International Conference of the IEEE Engineering in Medicine and Biology Society. IEEE Engineering in Medicine and Biology Society. Annual Conference, vol. 1, pp. 5964–5967 (2006)
21. Sekine, M., et al.: Assessment of gait parameter in hemiplegic patients by accelerometry. In: Proceedings of the 22nd Annual International Conference of the IEEE Engineering in Medicine and Biology Society (Cat. No. 00CH37143), vol. 3, pp. 1879–1882 (2000)
22. Hemminki, S., Nurmi, P., Tarkoma, S.: Accelerometer-based transportation mode detection on smartphones. In: Proceedings of the 11th ACM Conference on Embedded Networked Sensor Systems, p. 13 (2013)
23. Reddy, S., Mun, M., Burke, J., Estrin, D., Hansen, M., Srivastava, M.: Using mobile phones to determine transportation modes. ACM Trans. Sensor Netw. **6**(2), 13 (2010)

SOS - Securing Open Skies

Savio Sciancalepore$^{(\boxtimes)}$ and Roberto Di Pietro

Division of Information and Computing Technology,
College of Science and Engineering, Hamad Bin Khalifa University, Doha, Qatar
{ssciancalepore,rdipietro}@hbku.edu.qa

Abstract. Automatic Dependent Surveillance - Broadcast (ADS-B) is
the next generation communication technology selected for allowing commercial and military aircraft to deliver flight information to both ground
base stations and other airplanes. Today, it is already on-board of 80%
of commercial aircraft, and it will become mandatory by the 2020 in
the US and the EU. ADS-B has been designed without any security
consideration—messages are delivered wirelessly in clear text and they
are not authenticated.

In this paper we propose Securing Open Skies (SOS), a lightweight
and standard-compliant framework for securing ADS-B technology wireless communications. SOS leverages the well-known μTESLA protocol,
and includes some modifications necessary to deal with the severe bandwidth constraints of the ADS-B communication technology. In addition,
SOS is resilient against message injection attacks, by recurring to majority voting techniques applied on central community servers. Overall, SOS
emerges as a lightweight security solution, with a limited bandwidth overhead, that does not require any modification to the hardware already
deployed. Further, SOS is standard compliant and able to reject active
adversaries aiming at disrupting the correct functioning of the communication system. Finally, comparisons against state-of-the-art solutions
do show the superior quality and viability of our solution.

Keywords: ADS-B · Security · Authentication · Avionics
Tesla · Experimentation

1 Introduction

For years, the surveillance of air traffic has been performed through a combination of legacy radar technologies and human control [1]. Communication systems
such as the Secondary Surveillance Radar (SSR) leverage on ground-based stations, that periodically interrogate transponders on-board of the aircraft to get
information about the current status of the flight [2].

Starting from 2020, a new communication technology, namely Automatic
Dependent Surveillance - Broadcast (ADS-B), will become mandatory on all the
commercial and military aircraft in the US and EU, by following specifications

© Springer Nature Switzerland AG 2018
G. Wang et al. (Eds.): SpaCCS 2018, LNCS 11342, pp. 15–32, 2018.
https://doi.org/10.1007/978-3-030-05345-1_2

published by International Civil Aviation Organization (ICAO) and Radio Technology Commission Aeronautics (RTCA) [3]. Anticipatory to the regulations, a few companies (e.g., Qatar Airways, American Airlines and British Airways) have already adopted the ADS-B standard.

ADS-B uses the same frequency spectrum of the previous SSR technology, but the communications are initiated by the aircraft, that periodically broadcasts messages reporting position, speed and other airplane-related information [4]. On the one hand, ADS-B provides a lot of advantages, both from the system perspective and from the costs side. On the other hand, it poses a lot of concerns regarding communication security. In fact, messages are delivered in clear text and without any inherent mechanism to guarantee their authenticity. This paves the way to a huge variety of threats, such as the one introduced by the capillary diffusion of cheap Software Defined Radios (SDRs), able to inject custom-made packets in the air without requiring specific skills by operating entities [2].

Dealing with security issues in the context of avionic operations is a challenging task. In fact, avionic firms are often very slow to implement changes in their routines, due to business and regulatory concerns. In addition, the task is further complicated by both constraints in the communication bandwidth and the high message loss experienced on the single link due to obstacles and congestion [5]. In the last years, with the approaching of the cited deadline, researchers from both academia and industry started formulating solutions to overcome these vulnerabilities. While a part of them focused on non-cryptographic security solutions, others still pushed for cryptography-based approaches. However, these latter contributions did not maintain compatibility with the latest standards, requiring substantial modifications to the message size, the available bandwidth, or the hardware to be used on-board of equipped aircraft (see Sect. 2 for a detailed overview).

Contributions. Our contributions are manifold. First, we propose Securing Open Skies (SOS), a standard-compliant framework integrating the well-known Timed-Efficient Streamed Loss Tolerant Authentication (TESLA) protocol and allowing the verification of the authenticity of ADS-B messages on a time-slot basis, without resorting to resource-demanding public-key cryptography solutions. Second, the integration is carried out in a standard compliant fashion. Third, the framework allows for a joint processing of all the received packets on dedicated community servers, thus overcoming limitations due to the distributed nature of the network and the not negligible message loss on standalone receiving antennas. Moreover, SOS does not require hardware modification of the ADS-B receivers already deployed, thus being easy to integrate through a simple software update. Finally, a thorough evaluation of SOS against competing solutions allows to establish its superior performance in terms of bandwidth overhead and provided security.

Roadmap. The paper is organized as follows: Sect. 2 reviews the recent literature on the topic; Sect. 3 introduces the preliminary details about the ADS-B technology, the TESLA protocol and the adversary model; Sect. 4 provides the details of SOS, while Sect. 5 analyzes the performance of the proposed solution and provides a comparison against state-of-the-art approaches, showing the superiority of our solution. Finally, Sect. 6 tightens conclusions and draws future work.

2 Related Work

The huge amount of work dealing with security in the context ADS-B technology can be divided in two main branches. From one side, grounding on the consideration that the scarce amount of bytes available in a ES1090 packet (see Sect. 3.1 for more details) does not allow for the inclusion of reliable cryptography solutions, many contributions focused on providing security services through additional system-level approaches. To provide an example in this direction, the authors in [5] propose a two-stage location verification scheme. During an offline stage it creates a fingerprint of a particular aircraft, leveraging both Time Difference of Arrival (TDoA) values and deviations from nominal behavior. Then, in the online phase, it compares the received values with the fingerprint and evaluates the feasibility of the received data. In another work by the same authors [6], they propose an intruder detection algorithm based on the received signal strength, combining the measurements at the two antennas on board of an ADS-B aircraft. Also, privacy issues are investigated in [7].

From the opposite side, other contributions still strive for cryptography based approaches, contextualizing their adoption in the severe constraints of the ADS-B technology. Authors in [8] use a Staged Identity Based Encryption (IBE) (SIBE) scheme to provide confidentiality in ADS-B communications. In their scheme, an aircraft uses the public key of a specific ground station to encrypt a message containing a random symmetric key. The ground station is the only entity able to decrypt the message with its private key, and then all subsequent communications use this new symmetric key. Even if the proposal is valuable, authors are converting a broadcast communication channel in a unicast communication channel, thus heavily modifying the logic and the functioning of the ADS-B technology. Authors in [9] propose a three-level Hierarchical Identity Based Signature (IBS) (HIBS) scheme, in which each aircraft, associated to a given airlines recognized by a root authority (as ICAO or EUROCONTROL) is able to sign its ADS-B OUT messages by using keys generated according to its identity. Upon reception of a given signed message, a ground controller is able not only to identify the generating aircraft, but also its relationship with a given airline, approved by the root authority. However, being rooted on bilinear pairings, this scheme incurs a very high message fragmentation and overhead, thus being very hard to really be implemented in commercial aircrafts (more details will be provided in Sect. 5.2). In [10] and [11] the authors propose to use the Hashed Message Authentication Code (HMAC) technique to assure integrity and authenticity of ADS-B messages. To reduce the message overhead of their solution, they split the cryptographic value between several concatenated messages, and verify the cryptographic validity of the HMAC value only when all the portions are correctly received. However, the digests are computed over each single message, generating a very high communication overhead. In addition, they change the computation of the Cyclic Redundancy Check (CRC) field, thus making their proposal not standard compliant.

As for the adoption of the TESLA authentication scheme in the ADS-B technology, only few previous contributions have discussed its feasibility. While [2] briefly highlights potential benefits and drawbacks of such an approach, recent work [12] and [13] delved into details, providing also an initial implementation of the solution using SDR. However, these approaches are not standard compliant and they did not consider the constraints of the communication technology, neither with regards to the message size nor with respect to the severe bandwidth requirements highlighted in Sect. 3.1. In addition, their integration in a complete security framework, as well as their interaction with a set of community receivers, is not considered.

To sum up, by considering both branches of the current literature discussed above, we highlight that cryptography-based solutions are the only possible way to secure the ADS-B system in a fully reliable fashion. However, a standard compliant solution that is able to integrate security services while maintaining the full compatibility with the standard and guaranteeing a tolerable overhead on the communication side is still missing. In this context, SOS emerges a standard-compatible approach, that integrates cryptography in the ADS-B communications by requiring a limited amount of additional packets to be exchanged on the wireless channel.

3   Preliminaries and Adversary Model

3.1   ADS-B in a Nutshell

Despite its mandatory adoption on-board of commercial flights has been scheduled for the 2020, the ADS-B technology was born in the late 1980s, in correspondence with the introduction of the satellite technology, and it was originally designed to work aside with legacy communication technologies such as Primary Surveillance Radar (PSR) and SSR [11].

The system has been designed to be *Automatic*, given that it just needs to be turned on to work as intended, *Dependant* because it requires dedicated operating airborne equipment, *Surveillance*, because it is used as the primary surveillance method for controlling aircraft worldwide, and finally *Broadcast*, due to the particular operational mode, in which the information is sent in broadcast [2]. The reference communication model is depicted in Fig. 1.

An aircraft equipped with the ADS-B technology is able to obtain its position through satellites; then, it broadcasts its position via dedicated ADS-B messages. The wireless operations can take place at two different frequencies: the 1090 MHz frequency band, namely Extended Squitter - 1090 MHz (ES1090), is used when the aircraft is above the height of 18,000 ft (about 5.5 km), while below this threshold the communications take place using the 978 MHz frequency band, referred to as Universal Access Transceiver (UAT), to avoid further congestion on the ES1090 frequency band (due to the operation of previous technologies). In

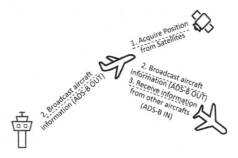

Fig. 1. Overview of the ADS-B communication model.

both cases, the dedicated channel bandwidth is 50 kHz. The information delivered by the aircraft can be both received by Air Traffic Control (ATC) ground stations, that can use them as a replacement or as a validation source for SSR, or by other aircrafts.

The advantages deriving by the adoption of the ADS-B technology are manifold. First, ADS-B can improve pilots *situation awareness*. In fact, pilots become able to receive traffic information about surrounding ADS-B enabled aircraft, weather reports, and temporary flight restrictions. In addition, the cost of installing ADS-B ground stations is significantly cheaper with respect to installing and operating the PSR and SSR systems previously used. Moreover, ADS-B provides better visibility to the aircraft with respect to legacy radar technologies, being able to guarantee an acceptable transmission range also in harsh regions (about 250 Nautical Miles, i.e., 450 km). At the data-link level, the ADS-B message is encapsulated in Mode-S frames. As such, ADS-B uses Pulse-Position Modulation (PPM) and the replies/broadcasts are encoded by a certain number of pulses, each pulse being 1 μs long [14].

From the system perspective, ADS-B consists of two different subsystems, *ADS-B OUT* and *ADS-B IN*. *ADS-B OUT* is the service that allows the aircraft to periodically broadcasts information about the aircraft itself, such as identification information, current position, altitude, and speed, through a dedicated on-board transmitter. The *ADS-B IN* service, in parallel, allows for the reception of Flight Information Service - Broadcast (FIS-B), Traffic Information Service - Broadcast (TIS-B) data and other ADS-B messages by the aircraft, as a result of a direct communication from nearby aircraft.

UAT and ES1090 have different payload requirements. The UAT technology dedicates 272 bits (34 bytes) to the payload, while 36 and 112 bits are allocated for synchronization information (SYNC) and forward error correction parity information (FEC PARITY), respectively [3]. As for ES1090, the structure of the packet is showed in Fig. 2.

While the preamble is used for synchronization purposes, the Downlink Format (DF) field provides an indication of the transmission encoding, the Capability field is used to report the capability of an ADS-B transmitting installation that is based on a Mode-S transponder, the ICAO Address Field is reserved to

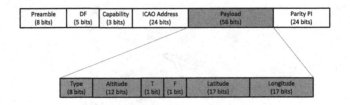

Fig. 2. ADS-B ES1090 message format.

the unique identification of the aircraft, while the Parity Information (PI) field provides error detection. A total number of 56 bits are reserved for the payload, where the Type field (8 bits) identifies the specific type of the payload message, the type T flag is used for synchronization purposes, the Subfield F flag indicates if the following position data are the even (0) or the odd (1) part of the message, while Altitude, Latitude and Longitude are reserved for data about the actual position of the aircraft.

Finally, we highlight that the standard currently recommends (without forcing it) an overall maximum transmission rate of 6.2 messages per seconds, averaged over 60 s time interval.

3.2   Security Considerations

The ADS-B protocol does not include any security mechanism. Indeed, messages are transmitted in clear-text, allowing anyone equipped with a compatible receiver to decode their content and easily access to the information contained therein. This choice was done in the 80 s to boost message availability. However, nowadays it is the cause of dreadful threats associated with the operation of the ADS-B technology. In fact, the wide availability of cheap Commercial Off-The-Shelf (COTS) SDRs opens the possibility to easily inject custom-made ADS-B messages on the wireless communication channel. Thus, it is very easy to perform a number of message injection attacks, including Aircraft Spoofing, Ghost Aircraft Injection/Flooding, Aircraft Disappearance, and Trajectory Modification, to name a few [2, 15].

However, the public availability of aircraft's data has the potential to strengthen the control on the avionic traffic and help establishing open initiatives to maintain the security of the sky navigation. In fact, the openness of the system inspired the rise of many collaborative networks, such as the *OpenSky-Network* project [16]. OpenSky-Network is a community-based receiver network, which continuously collects ADS-B data delivered from operational airplanes. In addition, OpenSky-Network makes data accessible to researchers worldwide for experimentation and testing.

As it will clearly emerge from the discussion in the following sections, the SOS protocol leverages a community-oriented approach on the receiver side, inspired by the presence of projects such as the OpenSky-Network. This allows the overall system to be inherently able to overcome limitations such as the potential loss of messages and the limited computational capabilities of single receiver antennas.

3.3 Adversary Model

In this work we assume a very powerful attacker, characterized by both passive and active features. The adversary is able to eavesdrop all the communications on the 1090 MHz frequency band, by assuming the use of COTS devices such as a SDR [17]. Moreover, it is also able to inject fake messages over the wireless communication channel, by pretending to be a legitimate aircraft. This is indeed possible thanks to the presence of cheap SDRs, held at the ground level, able to forge fake messages and deliver them on the wireless communication channel. We also assume that the adversary, in order to stay stealthy, follows the constraints of the ADS-B technology on the transmission rate: thus, it injects packets with a transmission rate within the limits imposed by the standard. Finally, we assume that the adversary is able to carry on the attack only for a reduced portion of the area covered by the flight, i.e., it is static and does not move with the aircraft.

3.4 The TESLA Protocol

The Timed-Efficient Streamed Loss Tolerant Authentication (TESLA) protocol was initially proposed in [18] to authenticate media streams in a lightweight and time-efficient way, without resorting to resource-consuming public key cryptography solutions. In TESLA the time is divided in *epochs*, with each epoch i having a well-defined starting and ending time. It also assumes a loose synchronization between the communicating parties. To provide authentication of broadcast messages, the entity that generates the messages is equipped with an initial secret, namely the *root key*, shared only with a well-known authority, known to all the parties. At the boot-up of the system, the authority provides an initial key, namely *key chain commit*, generated by hashing the root key a number n of consecutive times. This element is shared on the communication channel and it is known to all the parties involved in the communication. A message, i.e., m_i, is authenticated by appending a HMAC generated through a key K_i, obtained by hashing the initial *key chain commit* exactly $n - i$ times.

The security of the scheme lies in the fact that the key used to generate the HMAC in the epoch i is not shared before the ending of the epoch itself. Thus, the receiving entities simply store the messages received in the slot, but they cannot verify them immediately (because of the lack of knowledge about the symmetric key). Only after a disclosure lag d in epochs, the key is disclosed (in broadcast) on the communication channel and included in all the packets generated exactly d epochs after, allowing the verification of all the messages delivered by the transmitting entity exactly d epochs before. Note that the key disclosed by the transmitting entity is assumed to be genuine only if it allows, by i consecutive hashing operations, to obtain exactly the *key chain commit*. In this way, because of the one-way features of the hashing operation, the authenticity is guaranteed. Despite its success and wide adoption, TESLA was not designed for severe constrained environments. To cope with this limitation, in μTESLA the key is not disclosed in each packet, but only once per epoch [19]. In addition, taking care of the constraints in the size of the memory of sensors, μTESLA also restricts the number of authenticated senders, thus limiting the memory footprint of the protocol.

As it will emerge in the following sections, the proposed framework leverages the core logic of the μTESLA protocol, even if it provides further modifications necessary to deal with the limited payload size of ADS-B messages.

4   The SOS Framework

4.1   Preliminary Considerations

The system scenario assumed hereby involves the following actors:

- *Aircraft.* It is an ADS-B equipped plane, emitting standard-compliant ADS-B messages.
- *Avionics Authority.* It is a super-parties authority, whose responsibility is to assign cryptography materials and unique addresses to operating aircraft. It is assumed to be online at least for a small amount of time during the operation of the aircraft. This role is the one natively assumed by ICAO and EUROCONTROL.
- *Receiver Antennas.* They are a set of ADS-B receivers, distributed over a large area, able to receive and successfully decode the messages delivered by the aircraft. In addition, they are supposed to forward the received messages to a remote server. This role is actually played by OpenSky Receiver Antennas.
- *Community.* It represents a set of general-purpose servers that receive messages from the distributed antennas and provide additional computing intelligence to validate their authenticity and web-oriented services. This role is actually played by the OpenSky-network project.

In the following we assume that the legitimate ADS-B-equipped aircraft has already taken off from an airport, and it has exceeded the altitude of 5,500 meters. Thus, it switches from UAT to ES1090 mode, and starts emitting standard ADS-B messages. The set of wireless receivers in its communication range, equipped with ADS-B decoders, are able to detect and decode the messages. Next, they deliver all the messages to the servers community. The aim of the SOS framework is to provide authentication of the messages that have been effectively transmitted by the transmitting plane.

We also assume that the receivers and the transmitter are loosely synchronized with a common clock source, such as the UTC or the GPS system. In addition, the time is divided in time-slots of a given duration d_i. Assuming t_0 is the time of the boot-up of the aircraft, the time-slot t_i will trigger at the absolute value $t_i = t_0 + \sum_{j=0}^{i-1} d_j$. Finally, without loss of generality, we assume that legitimate aircraft deliver ADS-B messages at a constant rate of 6 packet/s, in line with constraints defined by the standard for the maximum allowed transmission rate for each aircraft [3].

4.2 Extending the ADS-B Protocol

SOS provides the authentication of broadcast messages by leveraging symmetric cryptography techniques, without modifying the legacy structure of ADS-B messages. To this aim, we extend the ADS-B technology, while pursuing standard-compliance, by adding new type of messages dedicated to the delivering of cryptography elements.

The security messages are included in the ADS-B packet as a part of the payload, leveraging the sub-field *Type* of the message and specific values whose meaning is reserved for future use by the standard. A sample picture of the structure of security packets is provided in Fig. 3.

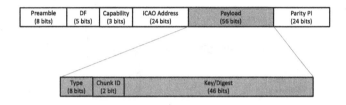

Fig. 3. The content of verification packets transmitted by adopting SOS.

The following two verification messages are defined:

- Verification Digest, $Type = 25$. This message is used to allow for the transmission of a message digest at the end of a slot by an aircraft.
- Verification Key, $Type = 32$. This message is used to transmit a verification key used in the previous slot, allowing the verification of the full batch of messages.

When the *Type* field in the payload is either 25 or 32, the following part of the payload includes the following sub-fields:

- Chunk ID (2 bits). It specifies the unique identifier of the portion of the following content included in this message.
- Content (46 bits). It contains the effective payload of the verification message. In case the *Type* field was 25, it contains the portion of the digest. Otherwise, in case the *Type* field was 32, it includes the specified segment of the verification key for the previous slot.

4.3 Details of the SOS Framework

SOS provides messages authentication leveraging delayed hash chains. While it is inspired by the μTESLA protocol proposed in [19], it presents several modifications made in order to adapt the protocol to the more severe constraints of the ADS-B technology.

Overall, an ADS-B receiver system that runs the SOS framework can work in two modes:

- *Unsecured Mode*: The receiver does not verify the authenticity of packets received through the receiver antenna. Thus, as soon as the packet is correctly decoded, the information are processed. The new ADS-B messages having the Payload Type Field equal to 25 or 32 are simply discarded.
- *Secured Mode*. As soon as the messages are decoded, they are buffered until the related verification digest and verification code are received. Only if the pool of messages is verified through the procedure described below, the information contained therein are further processed.

From now on, we will assume that the Community Server (or, equivalently, the computational unit behind the receiver antennas) works in the *Secured Mode*. The SOS scheme, depicted in Fig. 4, can be divided in three distinct phases, that are the *Setup Phase*, the *Online Phase* and the *Verification Phase*.

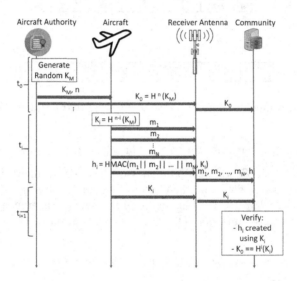

Fig. 4. The SOS scheme.

The steps performed in each of these phases are reported in the following.

- **Setup Phase.** It is executed at the bootstrap of the flight by the Avionics Authority (i.e., a prominent authority, such as ICAO or EUROCONTROL). Specifically, the Aircraft Authority equips the aircraft with the following elements:
  - a master key, K_M, that is a K bit key uniquely assigned to the particular aircraft for the duration of the flight;
  - an integer n, that is a large integer number representing the length of the hash chain.

  Specifically, starting from the above two parameters, the root key K_0 of the aircraft is computed as:

  $$K_0 = H(H(\ldots(H(K_M)\ldots))) = H^n(K_M), \tag{1}$$

where $H^n(K_M)$ refers to the execution of the hashing function H on the input value K_M for n consecutive times. At the end of this phase, the Aircraft Authority makes public the following parameters:

- the ICAO address of the flight, that is the unique identifier of the aircraft during the present flight;
- the absolute value of t_0, that represents the boot-up time of the flight, i.e., the time in which the aircraft was equipped with the previous materials;
- the root key K_0 of the aircraft, representing the key used by the aircraft to authenticate messages broadcast at the first useful slot.

All these parameters are shared through a publicly available server, that is supposed to be online at least for some time during the duration of the flight.

- **Online Phase.** Let us focus on the operation of the aircraft during the time-slot t_i, with $i > 0$, and assume the aircraft actually delivers N messages, $[m_1, m_2, \ldots, m_n, \ldots, m_N]$, $N \geq 1$, during the time-slot t_i.

At some point in time, before the end of the slot, the aircraft computes the key for the current time-slot t_i, according to the following Eq. 2:

$$K_i = H^{n-i}(K_M). \tag{2}$$

The key K_i is used by the aircraft to authenticate all the messages delivered during the time-slot t_i. To this aim, the aircraft generates a message digest h_i, by using a HMAC function and the key K_i, as in the following Eq. 3:

$$h_i = HMAC(m, K_i) = H((K_i' \oplus opad)||H((K_i' \oplus ipad)||m)), \tag{3}$$

where K_i' is another secret key generated from the key K_i, the symbol $||$ refers to the concatenation operation, while $ipad$ and $opad$ are the well-known hexadecimal inner and outer constants, respectively [20].

The digest h_i is the element that allows for the verification of the pool of messages delivered within the time-slot t_i. Given that all the messages sent in that time-slot should be verified together, the aircraft delivers this message as the last of its pool, within the time-slot t_i.

Note that the receivers decode and store all the messages received by the aircraft. However, they still cannot validate them, given that they miss the information about the key K_i used to generate the digest h_i. Thus, they temporarily store the messages in a buffer.

- **Verification Phase.** This final phase is dedicated to the verification of the messages delivered within the slot t_i, and it takes place at the beginning of the following slot, namely the $i + 1$-th slot.

From the aircraft perspective, it consists in the delivery of a single-message, containing the key K_i used by the aircraft to build the digest h_i and to authenticate the messages sent in the time-slot t_i. The verification message is delivered by specifying a Payload Sub-Type field equal to 32.

When the ground stations receive the message, provided that they have received all the messages delivered by the aircraft in that time slot, they can verify the authenticity of all the messages received within the time-slot

t_i. However, this is more likely to happen on the central server of the community controlling the particular receiver. Indeed, while some packets can be lost by some receivers hardly reached by the aircraft messages, it is very unlikely that a message is lost by all the receivers, since they enjoy a loose location correlation. This is further discussed in Sect. 5.1.

This phase can be further divided in two sub-phases: the *Normal Mode* and the *Recovery Mode*.

Normal Mode. In this sub-phase the verifier (either the single receiving sensor or the community server) checks the following conditions:

- It is possible to obtain the root key K_0 by hashing exactly i times the key K_i, thus $K_0 = h^i(K_i)$;
- The received hash h_i' is equal to the hash computed over all the messages received in the time-slot t_i, by using the key K_i; thus, $h'i = HMAC(m, K_i)$.

In this way, the set of community receivers can be confident that the messages were authenticated using the key K_i, and that the key could only be generated by the target aircraft, given that it is the only entity that could have generated it. Otherwise, if the second check is not verified for any of the active airplanes, it means that the target aircraft is under message injection attack. Thus, the *recovery mode* is triggered.

Recovery Mode. The aim of this phase is to make an attempt to recover the set of legitimate messages. Specifically, the messages can be discarded, or an attempt to recover them can be performed as discussed below:

- Assume $M = N + J$ distinct messages have been received by the community server in the time-slot from a given aircraft, where N is the number of legitimate messages and J is the number of malicious messages. Note that N is known to the Community Server, given that the number of messages between two consecutive *Verification Key* messages is fixed.

  The time within the time-slot bounds is further divided in a number S of smaller sub-slots, each containing L messages, Within the sub-slot, the community server takes a decision based on majority voting. Thus, it selects the messages whose position is validated by the majority of the anchors. After applying the majority voting within all the slots, the community server ends up with a total of T messages, with $T < M$.

- On the selected T messages, assuming N of these are legitimate messages, the community server tries all the possible combinations of messages, with the aim of finding the legitimate pool. Specifically, it evaluates all the possible groups of N messages, checking that the digest computed through the verification key k_i and the selected pool of messages is equal to the value h_i previously delivered by the aircraft. Thus, the maximum number of hash operations and comparisons required by the community server to find the correct sequence of messages is $\Delta = \binom{T}{N}$. If a valid pool is found, these are the authentic messages. Otherwise, no authentic messages are found for the time-slot t_i and the messages are discarded.

It is worth noting that the strategy implemented in the *Verification Phase* of SOS is indeed effective against an adversary that injects fake position messages of the target aircraft, being this position totally different from the real one. In addition, realistic adversaries emit their messages with a SDR that is located at the ground-level. Being the ADS-B technology very sensitive to the presence of obstacles [16], the expected number of receivers for the fake messages is lower than the legitimate ones, that are emitted at greater altitudes, with a reduced probability to find obstacles and thus higher chances to be received by a greater pool of anchors. Otherwise, if the attacker is able to force the reception of the fake message by many anchors (i.e., by using ADS-B equipped drones), the maximum benefit it can expect is to cause a Denial of Service (DoS) on the system, given that none of the authentic messages will be accepted.

5 Performance Assessment

5.1 Benign Scenario

In this section we evaluate the performances of SOS in a benign scenario, with the aim of gaining more insights on its bandwidth and computational requirements in standard operational conditions.

In Fig. 5 we illustrate the bandwidth overhead of SOS with respect to the size of the verification digest and the duration of the time-slot, by assuming a fixed 128-bit verification key. As the length of the verification digest increases, both the security provided to the messages and the message overhead increase, given that more messages need to be delivered over the radio interface. At the same time, the overhead lowers as the time-slot duration increases, given that more messages are authenticated using the same digest. It is worth noting that the same considerations are valid if we increase the key size, while fixing a specific digest size. As the security of SOS lies in the size of both the verification key and verification digest, a compromise between the bandwidth overhead and the security level is required. In general, assuming both a key length and a verification digest of 128 bits, and assuming to fix a 2 s long time-slot, the bandwidth overhead introduced by SOS is 47.58%, that is we use roughly the 50% of the

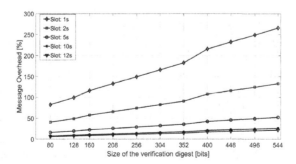

Fig. 5. Overhead derived by the adoption of SOS, by considering different lengths of the verification digest and different duration of the time slot.

messages to authenticate the batch of messages sent within the time-slot. Note that this overhead can be considered both as included in the actual through-put of a peer-to-peer communication, or added as an additional overhead to the actual rate of the ADS-B technology. In the second case, this leads to an increase of the maximum packets rate from 6.2 to 9.14 packets/s. Given that the ICAO standard envisions situations in which the maximum recommended rate can be exceeded, this is not a violation of the standard.

5.2   Comparison and Discussion

Still assuming a benign scenario, in this section we compare the performance of SOS with closely related work, by considering the size of the cryptography materials (keys and digest size), the bandwidth overhead, and the compliance to the standard of all the solutions. The main results have been reported in Table 1.

Table 1. Comparison with security approaches published in [12,13] and [9].

Scheme	Key size [bits]	Digest size [bits]	Crypto parameters soundness	Slot duration	Std. compliance	Overhead [%]
SOS	128	128	✔	2 s	✔	47.58
SAT [12]	128	16	✗	5 s	✗	22.9
LHCSAS [13]	80	128	✔	1 msg.	✗	500
HIBS [9]	N/A	1,024	✔	-	✔	2,200

SAT [12] is based on the TESLA authentication primitive, but it is not standard-compliant. In fact, its authors include the digest of each message within the related ADS-B packet just before the PI field, thus modifying the message length imposed by the standard. In addition, every 30 s the protocol recommends the broadcast of a certificate including a key of 128 bits, signed through a public key of 512 bits and the Elliptic Curve Digital Signature Algorithm (ECDSA) technique. Finally, independently from the particular hashing algorithm used, SAT constrains the digest to be 16-bits long, hence jeopardizing the security of the proposed scheme. Assuming that the certificate is generated through the well-known *openssl* tool, it results in a minimum overhead of 22.9%.

LHCSAS [13] still breaks the compatibility with the standard: in fact, it modifies the mandatory *subType* field, replacing it with cryptography data. In addition, the aircraft delivers cryptography elements for each message, thus generating 5 additional packets for every ADS-B message.

HIBS [9] adopts robust cryptography properties. In fact, packets are authenticated through a digest of 1024 bits. However, a digest of such a size is generated for each packet, resulting in an enormous bandwidth overhead. By assuming to work with the extended version of the scheme and maintaining the size of the message imposed by the standard, 22 additional messages are necessary for each payload to be authenticated, resulting in a dramatic bandwidth increase of 2200%. Instead, SOS integrates authentication services based on symmetric encryption within the ADS-B payload in a standard-compliant fashion. The resulting overhead, as per what discussed in the previous subsection, is 47.58/%. This slight higher overhead, however, is compensated by the enhanced security level provided to the ADS-B technology.

SOS, as all the other solutions that do require packet fragmentation, is vulnerable to packet loss. In fact, if a single packet delivered within the whole time-slot is not received by any of the ground receivers, all the packets within the same slot cannot be verified [21]. In general, the deployment of a large number of antennas improves the probability that at least one of them receives a packet. Even if packet loss is theoretically always possible, it is worth noting that an high level of packet loss disrupts also the correct functioning of the other computing solutions discussed above. Neglecting not standard-compliant approaches and assuming different values of the slot duration of SOS, Fig. 6 evaluates the probability to successfully receive all the elements necessary to carry out the authenticity check, both with SOS and with [9], with an increasing loss probability on the overall system.

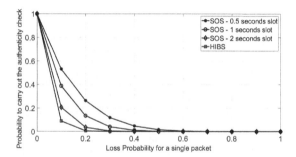

Fig. 6. Loss probability for a single packet.

SOS cannot verify the authenticity of a single packet if at least a message transmitted in the time-slot of duration 2 s is lost. Assuming a default transmission rate of 6 packet/s, the loss could occur in any of the 12 messages sent within the time-slot, or in the 3 messages delivered in the next slot and containing the verification key. Thus, there would be at least a single packet loss in 15 messages. However, HIBS requires the correct reception of 23 messages to evaluate the authenticity of the information. Thus, the packet loss would be more disruptive in the proposal by [9] than in the SOS scheme. This is still true also in case packet losses happen in burst, given that SOS could provide, under reasonable assumptions, intermittent connectivity with the community server.

5.3   Scenario with a Malicious Adversary

In this section we evaluate the performance of SOS and the contribution in [9] in the presence of a malicious active adversary.

During a given time-slot, the adversary injects fake packets in the wireless communication medium, with the aim of confusing the receivers about the current position occupied by the legitimate aircraft. In case of an active attack, the second check performed in the verification phase of SOS fails. Specifically, the digest computed over all the messages received by the community server from the target aircraft, through the key K_i of the current slot t_i, will not be equal to the verification digest h_i. In this situation, the community server triggers the *Recovery Mode*. Thus, it first adopts an approach based on majority voting, by discarding messages claiming a given position but received by the minority of the anchors within a given sub-slot. On the remaining messages, the community server checks for the pool of messages that verifies the authenticity check. This is indeed possible thanks to the fixed number of packets between two consecutive digests. The performance of SOS and HIBS in this situation are showed in Fig. 7, assuming the maximum transmission rate by the legitimate aircraft of 6 pkts/s.

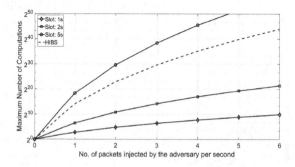

Fig. 7. Number of required computations by SOS and [9] on the community servers, under the hypothesis of attack by a malicious adversary.

Focusing on the performance of SOS, the figure shows that the shorter the time-slot, the less the maximum number of operations that are required on the community server's side. Assuming a short duration of the time-slot, i.e., 1 s, and that the adversary injects malicious packets with a rate of 6 pkts/s, the number of operations required by the community server would be equal to about 924, indeed a tolerable amount of HMAC for the community server. Of course, the higher the rate of transmission by the adversary, the higher the computational overhead by the aircraft. This becomes an issue by assuming an higher duration of the time-slot, resulting in an unmanageable maximum number of comparisons when the duration of the slot is equal or higher to 5 s. The same issue emerges with the usage of the HIBS protocol. Assuming the transmission rate of 6 packets/s, HIBS requires almost 4 s to deliver a single information packet, along with all the security material. If the attacker injects packets at a rate of 6 pkts/s, this would result in more than 2^{42} maximum computations, indeed a very resource-consuming task. By looking at results showed in Sect. 5.1, the time-slot duration of the SOS protocol must be carefully selected in order to trade-off between the bandwidth overhead and the number of comparisons to deal with in case of attack. For instance., by assuming to work with a time-slot duration of 2 s, in case the adversary injects 6 packets, the community-server will require about a maximum number of 2^{21} hashes and comparisons to find the authentic pool of messages. According to latest measurement with dedicated hardware (https:// gist.github.com/epixoip/a83d38f412b4737e99bbef804a270c40), about 2.25 s are necessary to find the legitimate pool of messages. Other measurements with non-dedicated hardware can be obtained through public data (https://en.bitcoin.it/ wiki/Non-specialized_hardware_comparison).

6   Conclusions and Future Work

Inspired by its mandatory adoption on board of all commercial aircraft by the 2020, and pressed by its anticipated adoption by major airlines (e.g., Qatar Airways, American Airlines and British Airways), in this paper we proposed SOS, a lightweight and standard-compliant framework designed to guarantee the authenticity of the communications in the ADS-B technology. The framework integrates the μ-TESLA protocol in ADS-B communications, allowing to batch-verify all the messages originated by an airplane in a given time-slot. In addition, the framework leverages a majority voting filtering stage in the message reception phase and it is suitable for deployment on community-oriented services, as the emerging OpenSky-Network community. Moreover, it is resilient to active attacks attempting to poisoning the message authentication process. Finally, comparisons with state of the art solutions do show that SOS is the winning solution in terms of provided security and achieved performance.

Future research activities include refining the packet loss hypothesis (studying packet burst loss model) and the implementation of the proposed framework using commercial Software Defined Radios.

References

1. Lim, Y., Bassien-Capsa, V., Ramasamy, S., et al.: Commercial airline single-pilot operations: system design and pathways to certification. IEEE Aerosp. Electron. Syst. Mag. **32**(7), 4–21 (2017)
2. Strohmeier, M., Lenders, V., Martinovic, I.: On the security of the automatic dependent surveillance-broadcast protocol. IEEE Commun. Surv. Tuts. **17**(2), 1066–1087 (2015)
3. Radio-Technology-Commission-Aeronautics: Minimum Operational Performance Standards for 1090 MHz Extended Squitter Automatic Dependent Surveillance – Broadcast (ADS-B) and Traffic Information Services – Broadcast (TIS-B). Technical report (2014)
4. Strohmeier, M., Schäfer, M., Lenders, V., Martinovic, I.: Realities and challenges of NextGen air traffic management: the case of ADS-B. IEEE Commun. Mag. **52**(5), 111–118 (2014)
5. Strohmeier, M., Lenders, V., Martinovic, I.: Lightweight location verification in air traffic surveillance networks. In: Proceedings of ACM Workshop on Cyber-Physical System Security, pp. 49–60 (2015)

6. Strohmeier, M., Lenders, V., Martinovic, I.: Intrusion detection for airborne communication using PHY-layer information. In: Proceedings of International Conference on Detection of Intrusions and Malware, and Vulnerability Assessment, pp. 67–77 (2015)

7. Alhazbi, S., Sciancalepore, S., Di Pietro, R.: A hole in the sky: de-anonymizing OpenSky receivers. T.R. 2018-2 (2018). https://cri-lab.net/wp-content/uploads/2018/10/Alhazbi_PERCOM2019.pdf

8. Baek, J., Hableel, E., Byon, Y., et al.: How to protect ADS-B: confidentiality framework and efficient realization based on staged identity-based encryption. IEEE Trans. Intell. Transp. Syst. **18**(3), 690–700 (2017)

9. Yang, A., Tan, X., Baek, J., Wong, D.S.: A new ADS-B authentication framework based on efficient hierarchical identity-based signature with batch verification. IEEE Trans. Serv. Comput. **10**(2), 165–175 (2017)

10. Kacem, T., Wijesekera, D., Costa, P.: Integrity and authenticity of ADS-B broadcasts. In: IEEE Aerospace Conference, pp. 1–8, March 2015

11. Kacem, T., Wijesekera, D., Costa, P., Barreto, A.B.: Secure ADS-B framework: ADS-Bsec. In: IEEE International Conference on Intelligent Transportation Systems (ITSC), pp. 2681–2686, November 2016

12. Berthier, P., Fernandez, J.M., Robert, J.M.: SAT: security in the air using Tesla. In: IEEE/AIAA Digital Avionics Systems Conference, pp. 1–10, September 2017

13. Yang, H., Yao, M., Xu, Z., Liu, B.: LHCSAS: a lightweight and highly-compatible solution for ADS-B security. In: IEEE Global Communications Conference, pp. 1–7, December 2017

14. Calvo-Palomino, R., Ricciato, F., Repas, B., et al.: Nanosecond-precision time-of-arrival estimation for aircraft signals with low-cost SDR receivers. In: Proceedings of ACM/IEEE International Conference on Information Processing in Sensor Networks, pp. 272–277 (2018)

15. Di Pietro, R., Chessa, S., Maestrini, P.: Computation, memory and bandwidth efficient distillation codes to mitigate DoS in multicast. In: International Conference on Security and Privacy for Emerging Areas in Communications Networks, pp. 13–22, September 2005

16. Schäfer, M., Strohmeier, M., Lenders, V., Martinovic, I., Wilhelm, M.: Bringing up OpenSky: a large-scale ADS-B sensor network for research. In: Proceedings of International Symposium on Information Processing in Sensor, pp. 83–94, April 2014

17. Tuttlebee, W.: Software Defined Radio: Enabling Technologies. Wiley, Hoboken (2002)

18. Perrig, A., Canetti, R., Tygar, J.D., Song, D.: Efficient authentication and signing of multicast streams over lossy channels. In: Proceedings of the IEEE Symposium on Security and Privacy, pp. 56–73 (2000)

19. Perrig, A., Szewczyk, R., Tygar, J.D., Wen, V., Culler, D.E.: SPINS: security protocols for sensor networks. Wirel. Netw. **8**(5), 521–534 (2002)

20. Krawczyk, H., Bellare, M., Canetti, R.: HMAC: keyed-hashing for message authentication. In: RFC 2104, February 1997

21. Alhazbi, S., Sciancalepore, S., Di Pietro, R.: Reliability of ADS-B communications: novel insights based on an experimental assessment. T.R. 2018-1 (2018). https://cri-lab.net/wp-content/uploads/2018/10/AlHazbi_SAC2019_noanonym.pdf

DNS Traffic of a Tor Exit Node - An Analysis

Michael Sonntag$^{(\boxtimes)}$ (iD)

Institute of Networks and Security, Johannes Kepler University Linz,
Altenberger Strasse 69, Linz 4040, Austria
michael.sonntag@ins.jku.at

Abstract. The DNS traffic of a large-bandwidth Tor exit node is investigated for anomalies and compared to domain name registrations. From the results we can conclude what people are using the Tor network for. Some national anomalies can be identified - websites in China (.cn) and Russia (.ru/.su), and to some degree in Ukraine (.ua), are used differently through Tor than e.g. websites under the top-level domain of Germany (.de).

Keywords: Anonymization · Tor · DNS · Traffic statistics · ccTLDs gTLDs

1 Introduction

The institute of networks and security (INS) operates a high bandwidth (max. 200 MBit/s) exit node (tor2e.ins.tor.net.eu.org) within the Tor anonymization network [1]. For research purposes we investigated the exit traffic [2] and provided statistics regarding bandwidth, services contacted, and target countries based on GeoIP [3]. The investigation was then extended to include the DNS traffic of this exit node. As there is no other use of this system except anonymization, all DNS requests and the associated replies stem from the Tor exit traffic. This data was obtained by installing a DNS relay server (dnsmasq), pointing it to a university DNS server, and configuring the Tor exit node to use this relay server for name resolution. Query logs from the DNS relay server then contain all the information needed: what domain name was requested plus the response, i.e. the IP address (not used here and ignored) or an error. Additionally, any direct (timestamps remain) relation to connections/Tor circuits is broken. To ensure as detailed data as possible, the DNS timeout values the relay returns to the exit node is set to a very low value of 1 min. Note that this is only partially effective, as Tor itself sets the timeout to 5 min for very small timeouts it receives (and 60 min to longer ones) to protect against attacks (DefecTor: [4]). This limitation was seen as acceptable for the investigation and reasonably retains privacy.

1.1 Ethical Considerations

What is investigated here is traffic intended to be anonymous, and the first priority of any research in this area must be to keep this promise. Note that the DNS name alone usually does not tell anything about the user visiting this site (domain name only, not the full URL), but this is not necessarily true for every domain name. Also, together

© Springer Nature Switzerland AG 2018
G. Wang et al. (Eds.): SpaCCS 2018, LNCS 11342, pp. 33–45, 2018.
https://doi.org/10.1007/978-3-030-05345-1_3

with the exact time of the request the domain name could potentially be useful for correlation attacks against anonymization. To avoid imperiling anonymity the recorded data is additionally stored in 1-h chunks and the exact time of requests/replies is removed at the earliest opportunity - and not used anyway. As we observed a minimum of 3,698 DNS requests per hour, this results in approximately one query per second (average over all 1-h periods: 18 requests/second; maximum: 81/s during a single period). As the precision of timestamps is typically one second, this lower value is perilously close to being able to identify individual connections, so all evaluations took place over aggregations in 1-h periods.

Note that this information is not confidential anyway: DNS requests are usually sent to the next server in full. Even when passing it on (iterative resolution), typically the whole name is passed on, not merely the necessary subpart (see QNAME minimisation for privacy improvements: RFC 7816 [5]). Therefore, third parties may observe parts or all of the data anyway, so more complex schemes to collect statistics and preserve privacy as e.g. described in [6] are not necessary.

1.2   Related Work

Main directions of Tor research are hidden services (see [7, 8]) and malicious behavior through Tor [9] or by exit nodes [10]. In contrast to this we focus on the "normal" (and typically legal) use by ordinary end users: illegal behavior does exist and for some persons anonymity is important, so they use Tor. But for some groups Tor might be much more important and we try to identify whether this is the case and if these groups can be more clearly identified/located/described.

Always interesting to many parties are methods to de-anonymize users (individually or generally; see [11, 12] as examples). This is investigated here indirectly and to a smaller degree: DNS information of Tor traffic is mostly public (see above). We contribute to this by investigating how much information can be collected from this data and whether the exit traffic show differences between groups of users - which at least allow a reduction in the number of persons that might be the source of some traffic. A proposal to improve DNS privacy is described by [13], although outside Tor. Based on our results this might be a worthwhile addition.

1.3   External Data Sources

To classify domains, we employ external services. As we cannot disclose to them when a specific domain name (DN) was accessed (or that it was accessed at all, esp. as we don't know in advance whether there will be a match), only free lists available for offline use were considered. This excluded e.g. various "safe-browsing" APIs.

- Alexa Top 1 million [14]: The list of the one million most visited web sites during the last three month. We check whether a DN appears on the list (+rank) or not.
- Shalla's Blacklists [15]: These lists provide categorizations of URLs. With a count of 1.7 million entries they are quite comprehensive. These lists contain both DN and URLs. While it is easy to extract domains from the URLs, this would be problematic. E.g. download links of the microsoft.com website are classified as

"download", but this does not mean that the whole of "microsoft.com" is a download site.

- Finally, a list of known mal- or adware sites is used [16]. This is a compilation of several other lists with duplicates removed, containing slightly below 60,000 DN. Variants with more categories (fake news, gambling, porn...) exist, but we avoided them, especially because many extensions are legal in most countries or are already covered by the blacklists classification (previous item).

After preliminary testing it turned out that the website ranking (Alexa) needs special treatment: counting DNS requests e.g. for "google.com" does not make sense because of caching (the number of DNS requests is not identical to the number of users visiting this website or the number of connections to it), and because it is a single domain and not a class of sites. Also, most websites at the top of the list were visited during almost every observation period. It is rather more informative to identify which websites were *not* visited during the observation periods. Small numbers are of no interest (even very popular sites will by chance not be visited by anyone during some 1-h period), but as shown below, certain sites are practically completely absent.

2 Top-Ranked Websites NOT Visited

Websites from the Alexa Top 1 Million list which have *not* been visited is one of the investigations performed. These can be broadly classed in sites, that are sometimes not visited during a 1-h period, sites that are often missing, and those very rarely or never visited at all via our exit node. Only the top 100 sites of the whole list were checked. The first group (almost always visited) consists of (increasing visit count): twitch.tv, 360.cn, sina.com.cn, aliexpress.com, wikia.com, livejasmin.com, weibo.com, ebay.com, google.co.uk, yahoo.co.jp, alipay.com, netflix.com, t.co, linkedin.com, bongacams.com, tumblr.com, baidu.com, wikipedia.org, reddit.com, pornhub.com, google.fr, and xhamster.com. These are absent between 6.7% of all 1-h periods (twitch.tv) and ≈0% (not occurring merely in one single hour over five month; the last six of the list above). Twenty sites from the top 100 were visited in every single monitoring period.

The second group is absent between 29.8% and 12.8%: google.com.br, amazon.co. jp, sohu.com, jd.com, imdb.com, google.co.in, and naver.com

The third and most often missing group is absent between 100% (never occurring) and 53.7% missing periods (note: no websites between 29.8% and 53.7% respectively 6.7% and 12.8%!), where merely 9 sites are below 99% absence. This means, 42 of the top 100 sites were *not* observed even once in at least 99% of all 1-h periods. Because of large bandwidth, random exit node selection, 5-month long observation window, and the huge popularity of these sites, this is quite unexpected and was investigated in more detail. Based on rank, the highest ones missing more often are tmall.com (rank 9; 62.2% absent), google.co.in (13; 14.5%), sohu.com (15; 19.6%), jd.com (17; 18.9%), google.co.jp (22; 53.7%), and login.tmall.com (25; 99.6%).

If we classify the missing DN (from the two least visited groups, i.e. at least 12.8% absence; 58 sites), we find the following categories:

- "National versions" of main sites (e.g. google.co.in vs google.com): These are 14 Google and 3 Amazon sites. This can tentatively be explained in two ways: preferentially visiting the "main" site via Tor, and that these sites might perform a GeoIP lookup and redirect you to national versions based on your location - which would not work correctly (or be deactivated) for Tor exit nodes. This is therefore to be expected and may not say much about users or their activities.
- "Huge files" are sites with large downloads, like video streaming. These are less suited for Tor, as the bandwidth through the system is still limited and delays increase, and so probably less often visited. In this group there are 8 sites.
- "Shopping" sites (7 occurrences) are a bit more problematic. Buying things is mostly not anonymous there (delivery address, payment methods…), so Tor makes less sense. However, at least for some of them it is known that prices change based on search&surfing behavior. Anonymization would therefore be useful. Four of them are "tmall" sites (Taobao mall), a very large Chinese shopping portal. Compare this to amazon.com too, which was observed in every single 1-h period.
- The "News" sites category contains 6 domain names, with five virtually never being visited (thestartmagazine.com, bbc.com, bbc.co.uk, and tribunnews.com), while msn.com was slightly more often queried for (85.2%) and sohu.com fared much better (19.0% absence rate). It seems that for the former sites it is not necessary to remain anonymous - or there is no desire for this with the groups using Tor. Together with the next section below (country code TLDs), however the Chinese website sohu.com is interesting: it provides (according to itself) information, entertainment and communication (apparently in Chinese only). The much lower level of absence as compared to the broadly similar msn.com points to it being more important for its users to remain anonymous.
- "Social" web sites (7 domain names) are probably rare, because they require users to login. However, facebook.com is not on the list (visited during every single 1-h period) and it provides practically nothing without login - and despite of offering access as a hidden service (but which would not show up as a DN query). Some can be explained (whatsapp.com - used mostly as App and not via the web; requires identification). Interesting to compare is pixnet.net and csdn.net: the former is Korean (absence rate 100%), while the latter is Chinese (missing in 62.6%), reinforcing the trend identified above. Note, that csdn.net is SW-developer focused and less "private", so anonymity might be of less interest there - or these users emphasize anonymity because of technical knowledge. However, stackoverflow.com (100% absence) and github.com (99.9%; but not classed as "social" site) are practically never visited anonymously - there the social aspect is even less pronounced.
- Web sites of companies are easy to explain (4 sites): If interested in Apple, Adobe, or Microsoft (including office.com), browsing via Tor is rarely a necessity. The same should apply to developer websites (github.com) too.
- Ads: These consist of three sites: popads.net and cobalten.com, as well as craigslist.org. The first two sites' absence is obvious: these are pure advertisement sites with no own content. As the "NoScript" and "uBlock Origin" extensions are part of the (typ. used for anonymous web surfing) Tor browser, they reduce/prevent contacts to these websites, which happen typically through advertisements shown as banners,

iFrames or other indirect ways. Craigslist.com (classified ads) is more difficult, as browsing there might be of use anonymously (replying/buying probably not).

- Six other DN do not easily fit the classification: hao123.com is completely absent. As it is often classed as malware, this could also be seen as part of the "Ad" category. So.com and soso.com (ranks 85/67; both 100% missing) are Chinese search engines. The site naver.com (54; 12.8%) is also a search engine but focused on Korea. Here the pattern seen above is inverted (but see below). Github.com has been discussed above already. Wordpress.com (99.7% absence) is not interesting in itself: it hosts many small individual sites below this domain name. So while it scores high on Alexa (which aggregates subsites), most of the separate subsites would probably not be on the list at all, so not showing up here as often is understandable. But note that wikia.com, a somewhat similar site, is visited practically all the time (merely 0.6% absence).

3 Country-Code TLDs Queried

The evaluation regarding countries shows some anomalies too. When excluding all generic Top-Level-Domains (TLDs), the distribution regarding the TLDs of the DN queried for depicts an extreme distribution (see Fig. 1): 29% of all country-code Top-Level-Domains (ccTLD) queries are for domains under .ru, and 12.5% refer to .de. The next ones (.fr/.nl) are already at 4.27% resp 4.04%. In total each of the top 25 countries achieves more than 1% and together they account for 86.9% of all queries. In comparison [17], under .ru there are 4,976,168 domains registered, while under .de there are 14,572,649, i.e. almost three times as many. This means that in direct comparison .ru is overrepresented to .de by a factor of 6.8. An even more pronounced result can be seen with .su (former Soviet Union; still existing as TLD and administered by/primarily used in Russia), which produced 4.7 times as many queries during the five months than domain names exist (note: repetitions; the same domain name can be queried for many times!). A similar spike exists for Ukraine (.ua) - where state censorship of website access exists [18]. The peaks of .io and .tv can be explained by the fact that unlike the other country-code TLDs their DN have nothing to do with the territory and are registered for the name itself (.io → computer science term, used especially for start-ups; . tv → television).

From this we can conclude for which ccTLDs accessing them anonymously is more important for users: Russian websites are "only" accessed anonymously, but "nobody" cares whether German websites know who the surfer is. However, there exists a counterexample: China. China has strict rules regarding web access, so Tor could be very important. However, it has a very large number of domains registered, but only comparatively few queries. This could be explained by the fact that most Chinese websites (in the sense of registered under the China-TLD) are hosted in China, i.e. their content is under political control, and the real name of the owner is strictly verified. Accessing them anonymously is therefore useless, as critical or undesirable content cannot be expected. The importance for Tor lies for Chinese users at least partly in accessing foreign web sites - but we cannot identify such activities here, as we lack all

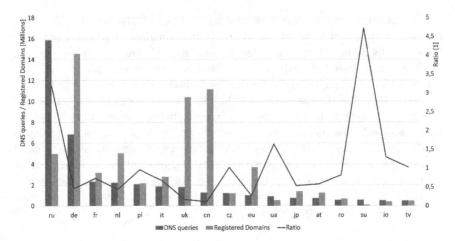

Fig. 1. Domain name queries compared to domain names registered

"source" information. Russians/Ukrainians on the other hand have comparatively little (but see censorship) difficulties accessing foreign web sites but might want to remain anonymous against their own country and unsupervised "local" sites.

The results are similar regarding the amount of traffic, i.e. Bytes transferred to these countries (see Fig. 2; traffic data has been collected as described in [3]), based on GeoIP of the destination IP address. Some countries show again large spikes: Russia, France, Netherlands, United Kingdom, China, and Austria; Notably missing, i.e. less or normal are Ukraine, Soviet Union, and Indian Ocean. So while they may have lots of DN queries related to their TLD, the actual traffic to these countries is much less. Note that .su, .io, and .tv are zero, as these do not represent an actual hosting location (.su domains are probably hosted in Russia; Indian Ocean/Tuvalu likely have no significant "local" hosting facilities at all).

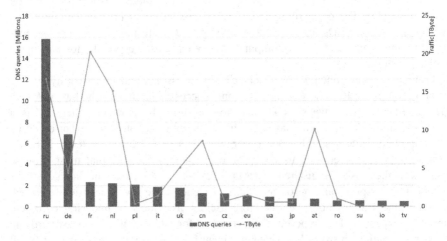

Fig. 2. DNS queries compared to traffic from/to these countries

However, a better measurement is the ratio of bytes per flow (see Fig. 3; traffic data again from our own collection cited above), i.e. the average size of a connection to these sites. Here we can observe that exceptions are .fr, .nl, .cn, .at, and .ro. The large amount of traffic (and the large ratio) to Austria is easy to explain with the location of the exit node: especially large-scale traffic, like video, will be directed to "close" servers, resp. for such traffic distributed hosting with GeoIP lookup is most rewarding. France, the Netherlands and Romania are comparable - they have numerous hosting centers for TLDs from everywhere. This leaves China as the only exception: few popular sites targeted at other countries are likely to be hosted physically within China. A possible explanation is that Chinese users are "forced" to use Tor, even when it is suboptimal (remote exit node, large files etc.).

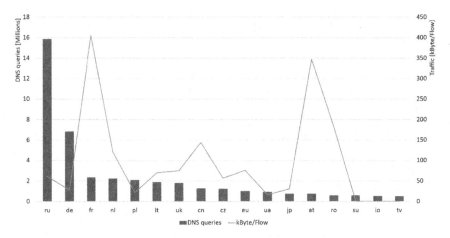

Fig. 3. kBytes per flow for destination countries

4   Second-Level Domain Results

We then investigated which second-level domains (ignoring "intermediate SLDs" like ".co.uk" or ".com.cn") are accessed how frequently for each country and how often each TLD is queried for, producing an interesting list. The top TLDs are .uk (average of 58.7 visits per SLD), then .ua (18.6), .io (8.24), .kr (8.23), .cn (6.12), and .jp (5.64). These extreme differences were further investigated:

- The most common SLDs for .uk are "adskeeper" (80,655), "amazon" (76,020), "google" (50,133), "bbci" (37,236), "dailymail" (27,114), "bbc" (22,172), and "vitalfootball" (31,792, with the next one below 20,597). Apart from advertisements on the top position, two companies and two news agencies score high. Vitalfootball is a sports network site with subsites for individual clubs, i.e. a kind of "hosting". As they are solely from England/Scotland and typically do not cover any special content, visiting them via Tor seems peculiar.
- For Ukraine (.ua) the list is only partly similar: "at" (191,232), "google" (143,687), "yandex" (65,805), "in" (55,871), "ucoz" (47,470), and "kiev" (31,296; next one:

18,427). Especially interesting here is Yandex, which is simple to explain: Yandex is a Russian social network, which is very much in use in Ukraine. However, for political reasons this DN was blocked by government orders to ISPs. People probably do not want to lose access to their social network, so visits via Tor to circumvent these restrictions is important and borne by the numbers. "at" and "ucoz" belong together and are, like vitalfootball, merely a header for subsites. Here, however, no topical restrictions apply. This might also explain the enormous count (238,702, which is almost twice that of the national version of Google).

- The TLD .io (British Territories in the Indian Ocean, but mostly used for its name) differs from this, as practically no generic or special SLDs occur. This is to be expected, as the rules for that TLD state, that such domains are only available to residents of the territory - but no civilian population exists at all (Population: approx. 3,500 military person; mostly USA nationals on Diego Garcia). In essence, this should be treated as a generic TLD. The SLDs require 25 domain names to drop from 44,347 down to below 10,000. The most popular SLD are liftoff (44,347), intercom (43,878), onthe (42,590), 1rx (37,497), and 1dmp (36,628).

- The Korean .kr shows the following SLDs: "www" (17,257), "auction" (12,533), "gmarket" (11,249), "hosting" (9,949), "dotname" (8,531) and "11st" (6,178; next 4,936). Again, hosting services figure prominently.

- The Russian ".ru" starts with "mail" (1,292,387), "yandex" (729,591), "ucoz" (525,895), "imgsmail" (452,312), "fastpic" (420,176), "rambler" (291,963), and "ok" (240,715; next is 202,709). Communication sites and search engines/portals top the list.

- The Soviet Union .su contains "clan" (184,272), "rolka" (63,475), "moy" (44,406), "rambler" (44,127), "fsin" (17,784) and "ipb" (16,189; next is 12,548). A strong concentration is visible, with the top being again occupied by hosting services.

- The Chinese .cn TLD shows several anomalies. Like .io it seems to be very balanced, as the top 50 only drop from 88,147 to 15,571. However, this is misleading, as many of these domain names start with "360" and very likely belong to the same company. If accounting for this, "360*" tops the list with 912,209 DN queries, followed by 373,209 for "022*" and 131,702 for "sin*" on place three. As a consequence, queries to China are concentrated to few, but huge, companies: Number four on the list (123*; 91,525) is only one tenth the size of the first one. Compare this to other countries: in the UK only the 17th falls below 10%, for Ukraine it is the 7th, Japan, 21st, io the 50th and Korea the 18th. The most prominent sites are sina.cn (infotainment portal), uc.cn (mobile web browser - proxy for faster loading; could be used on top of Tor to improve speed), 12306.cn (Chinese Railways - this is very curious and hard to explain; perhaps to circumvent measures against webscraping software/automated ticket buying), weibo.cn (Blogging site), 3g.cn (portal for mobile users) and 360.cn (search engine, security services, customized browser). Search engines, portals, and infotainment dominate, with hosting playing a smaller part. A very large share are sites affiliated to Qihoo 360 Inc (360. cn), an internet security company which is sometimes classified as malware, cheating customers, or a privacy problem.

- In Japan (.jp) the list begins with "yahoo" (107,763), and then follow "ne" (100,410), "ameba" (97,002), "ameblo" (63,095), "naver" (61,210), "amazon"

(54,261), "shinobi" (50,874), and "rakuten" (32,554). Yahoo/Naver are large search engine/social networks, while ne.jp is intended for network providers, i.e. a kind of hosting domain, but for large companies. Ameba/ameblo/shinobi are social networks respectively blogging, sites, i.e. a kind of hosting. Rakuten is a shopping site. Japan therefore partly resemble China with its focus on social networking sites/large portals, but with a much smaller concentration, i.e. many other sites, especially hosting, are important for Tor users there too.

From this we can conclude that "hosting" sites figure prominently in many countries. In some (Russia, Ukraine), communication sites are important too. But only China shows a strong focus on infotainment portals, railways and security sites at the top.

How many Second-Level-Domains were queried for how often was investigated too. In many countries a very large share of second-level domain names was asked for only once during the full five months (see Table 1). Korea tops the list: 73% of all queries were to SLDs that were never seen again. This is a large difference to Ukraine, where such queries only account for 26% - i.e. a query for some .ko DN is three times as likely to never be seen again than one under .ua. Such queries do not seem to show real user interest (even small sites would probably be visited more often than once in 5 month), or they could be a sign of extensive scans for domain names (for which some actual evidence not discussed here was found). Note that this does not take into account "hosting" sites as identified above, as e.g. vitalfootball.co.uk would be seen (and counted) multiple times, but the subsite "bournemouth.vitalfootball.co.uk" might have been queried for only once, but would not show up in this table under that heading as only the third-level domain is different.

Table 1. Share of SLDs queried once

TLD	Once	All	Queried once
kr	44,334	60,375	73.43%
jp	65,480	102,913	63.63%
cn	163,988	271,463	60.41%
uk	223,663	387,837	57.67%
ru	1,073,882	2,023,506	53.07%
se	52,602	108,856	48.32%
de	426,272	916,636	46.50%
it	115,031	256,900	44.78%
su	22,547	52,673	42.81%
pl	89,579	224,792	39.85%
ro	32,200	83,046	38.77%
nl	110,051	290,117	37.93%
fr	112,552	369,117	30.49%
io	6,375	21,932	29.07%
ua	14,166	54,229	26.12%

These results were investigated in more detail by calculating average values and standard deviations for the number of queries per second-level domain - with the restriction of only taking SLDs into account that were queried for at least twice during the whole five months observation period to exclude automated scans (see Table 2). The "average" value tells us how often all SLDs under a given TLD were queried for during the whole five months. High values mean that either all sites are asked for often, or that there are a few sites queried for very often and most of the rest rarely. This measurement is enhanced by the standard deviation: if it is large, a wide diversity of visit counts exists, like some sites visited several hundred times and some thousands of times etc. over five months. A low standard deviation however means that few different query counts other than the average occurred (i.e. all SLDs were queried for the same number of times during five month). The thresholds for "high" and "low" have been determined according to the numeric results. For the average this was set to 27 - the middle value (excluding .io), while for standard deviation this is where a strong drop occurs between 564 (.cn) and 900 (.io).

Table 2. Visits per TLD

TLD	Average	Std. deviation
Russia (.ru)	29.9884	1,609.1124
Ukraine (.ua)	35.9571	1,147.4791
Soviet Union (.su)	26.6181	1,023.9960
Japan (.jp)	36.8108	984.5983
Indian Ocean (.io)	75.6114	900.6163
China (.cn)	40.1727	564.0314
Italy (.it)	17.6033	525.6812
Poland (.pl)	25.6187	465.0291
France (.fr)	15.9863	447.6316
United Kingdom (.uk)	14.6441	316.8021
Germany (.de)	19.7816	259.4667
Sweden (.se)	19.9829	248.2967
Korea (.kr)	23.4048	207.2832
Netherlands (.nl)	17.0734	195.1083
Romania (.ro)	15.0148	94.0264

Group 1 (high average and high standard deviation) consists of Russia, Ukraine, and Japan (plus .io). These countries show frequent queries for a wide range of query counts of DN. Access via Tor seems to be important for low, medium, and high-traffic sites. For Russia and Ukraine this can be explained by fears of monitoring traffic on the end-user side. This does not apply to Japan, where censorship etc. does not seem to be an issue.

Group 2 (high avg., low std. dev.; few sites queried for very often, while others are rarely asked for) contains only China. This is similar to the previous group, but some very popular sites dominate. With aggregating SLDs belonging together (e.g. 360*), this would be enhanced even more (see above). Chinese domains are therefore predominantly large portals with very high query counts, and access to comparatively few other SLDs. This can perhaps be explained by wanting to remain anonymous with respect to these sites, i.e. monitoring access on the sites themselves: anonymously accessing "other" sites (general surfing anonym.) seems to be a lesser priority.

Group 3 (low avg., high std.dev.) consists of the Soviet Union: Many sites are of interest, with low, medium, and high visit count, but generally the number of visitors per SLD is lower. Note that here the difference to group 1 is small, as the average is just barely below the limit.

Group 4 (low avg., low std.dev.) shows the rest of the countries investigated: Italy, Poland, France, UK, German, Sweden, Korea, Netherlands, and Romania. Here visits are not so common and few sites with a very high count of visits exist. These can best be characterized as generally surfing anonymously, except perhaps the "high-profile" sites. Anonymity seems to be valued more in general terms than for specific sites.

5 Conclusions

Internet use in/regarding websites differs according to the countries, in some aspects to a very large degree. Especially countries where censorship exists or is an actual concern show differences.

We could tentatively identify three large groups of countries: "normal" countries where anonymization is used generally for web surfing, both for visiting small sites as well as large ones, but e.g. shopping sites being visited (in comparison to their importance/non-anonymized visits) less often.

Countries like Russia and Ukraine are in a different group, because websites are visited more often anonymously. This happens across a very wide share of less to very commonly visited sites. I.e., anonymization seems to be used most of the time. This is enhanced by accessing "communication sites" (E-Mail, messaging, etc.) anonymously, which is rare in the first group.

The third "group" is China, which stands out in several aspects

- No anonymization for sites, where this is not possible anyway: Amazon is encountered in every single 1-h period, but tmall.com is practically completely absent. It can be accessed via Tor, but nobody seems to bother. As buying most things is not possible anonymously because of physical delivery, Chinese persons (and nobody/few else are probably interested, as it seems to be a Chinese only site - no language-switch could be found) seem to avoid visiting it anonymously.
- Some very high-ranking websites like the search engines so.com, soso.com, and hao123.com are (almost) completely missing and not visited via Tor, while e.g. google.com was queried for in every single 1-h period. This could be because of active countermeasures, as while they can be accessed via Tor, all tests to access them were extremely slow with hao123.com, while so.com was barely reachable at all (and all were quick outside Tor).
- Second-level-domains visits in China via Tor are strongly concentrated, with a large share pertaining to 360*.cn sites. As these sites perhaps often coincide with locally

installed software (the company's main products are anti-virus, a customized web-browser, an own app store etc.), anonymity is potentially endangered. Tor only provides anonymization on the network level, hiding the IP address from the communication partner and intermediate entities, while locally installed software can typically communicate with the Internet directly as well if it wants to.

- For both news and social websites, the prevalence in DNS queries is higher for such sites directly targeting China than those of other countries or a worldwide audience, see e.g. sohu.com vs msn.com or pixnet.net vs csdn.net (see above). This either means that such sites are more important for Chinese people and therefore more often visited, or that anonymization is used by a larger share of their users.
- Despite a huge number of domains under the TLD .cn, comparatively very few of them are queried for via Tor, which strongly differs e.g. for Russia, Ukraine, or Soviet Union. Such a low ratio is not completely uncommon, it is shared e.g. with the United Kingdom and Brazil. Still, it is one more hint for a concentration towards selected/few domains being accessed via Tor.
- Unlike the other countries where a large amount of traffic is transferred per connection, China is not known for hosting "foreign" ccTLDs or generic TLD websites. So either Chinese content is generally larger (potentially because of the language - but more bytes might be compensated by more "meaning" for a single ideogram), or users of Chinese content access even "large" data via Tor, although this is commonly slower.

So while no definite conclusions can be derived from monitoring the DNS data, evidence points to a significantly different use depending on the Top-Level Domain that is accessed. We will monitor these trends and verify, whether longer observation can confirm these findings.

References

1. Dingledine, R., Mathewson, N., Syverson, P.: Tor: the second-generation onion router. In: Proceedings of the 13th Conference on USENIX Security Symposium (SSYM 2004), vol. 13. USENIX Association, Berkeley (2004)
2. Sonntag, M., Mayrhofer, R., Hörmanseder, R.: Technical and legal determinants of implementing a Tor exit node. In: 33rd GEANT Networking Conference - TNC17 (2017). https://tnc17.geant.org/core/presentation/32
3. Sonntag, M., Mayrhofer, R.: Traffic statistics of a high-bandwidth Tor exit node. In: Mori, P., Furnell, S., Camp, O. (eds.) Proceedings of 3rd International Conference on Information Systems Security and Privacy, pp. 270–277. SCITEPRESS (2017)
4. Greschbach, B., Pulls, T., Roberts, L.M., Winter, P., Feamster, N.: The effect of DNS on Tor's anonymity. In: NDSS 2017. Internet Society, San Diego (2017)
5. Bortzmeyer, S.: DNS query name minimisation to improve privacy. RFC 7816. https://tools.ietf.org/html/rfc7816
6. Jansen, R., Johnson, A.: Safely measuring Tor. In: Proceedings of the 2016 ACM SIGSAC Conference on Computer and Communications Security (CCS 2016), pp. 1553–1567. ACM, New York (2016)

7. Biryukov, A., Pustogarov, I., Thill, F, Weinmann, R.-P.: Content and popularity analysis of Tor hidden services. In: ICDCSW 2014, Proceedings of the 2014 IEEE 34th International Conference on Distributed Computing Systems Workshops, pp. 188–193. IEEE, New York (2014)
8. Loesing, K., Sandmann, W., Wilms, C., Wirtz, G.: Performance measurements and statistics of Tor hidden services, applications and the internet. In: 2008 International Symposium on Applications and the Internet, SAINT 2008, pp. 1–7. IEEE, New York (2008)
9. Ling, Z., Luo, J., Wu, K., Yu, W., Fu, X.: TorWard: discovery, blocking, and traceback of malicious traffic over Tor. IEEE Trans. Inf. Forensics Secur. **10**(12), 2515–2530 (2015)
10. Winter, P., et al.: Spoiled onions: exposing malicious Tor exit relays. In: De Cristofaro, E., Murdoch, Steven J. (eds.) PETS 2014. LNCS, vol. 8555, pp. 304–331. Springer, Cham (2014). https://doi.org/10.1007/978-3-319-08506-7_16
11. Johnson., A., Wacek, A., Jansen, R., Sherr, M., Syverson, P.: Users get routed: traffic correlation on tor by realistic adversaries. In: Proceedings of the 2013 ACM SIGSAC Conference on Computer & Communications Security (CCS 2013), pp. 337–348. ACM, New York (2013)
12. Manils, P., Abdelberi, C., Blond, S.L., Kâafar, M.A., Castelluccia, C., Legout, A., Dabbous, W.: Compromising Tor anonymity exploiting P2P information leakage. CoRR (2010). arXiv:1004.1461
13. Federrath, H., Fuchs, K.-P., Herrmann, D., Piosecny, C.: Privacy-preserving DNS: analysis of broadcast, range queries and mix-based protection methods. In: Atluri, V., Diaz, C. (eds.) ESORICS 2011. LNCS, vol. 6879, pp. 665–683. Springer, Heidelberg (2011). https://doi.org/10.1007/978-3-642-23822-2_36
14. Alexa Top 1 Million. http://s3.amazonaws.com/alexa-static/top-1m.csv.zip
15. Shalla's Blacklists. http://www.shallalist.de/
16. Black, S.: Unified Hosts File with Base Extensions. https://github.com/StevenBlack/hosts
17. Domaintools: Domain Count Statistics for TLDs. https://research.domaintools.com/statistics/tld-counts/
18. Freedom House: Freedom on the Net 2017: Ukraine Country Profile. https://freedomhouse.org/report/freedom-net/2017/Ukraine

SDN-Based Secure VANETs Communication with Fog Computing

Muhammad Arif[1], Guojun Wang[1(✉)], Tian Wang[2], and Tao Peng[1]

[1] School of Computer Science and Technology, Guangzhou University,
Guangzhou 510006, Guangdong, China
arifmuhammad36@hotmail.com, csgjwang@gmail.com
[2] Department of Computer Science and Technology, Huaqiao University,
Xiamen 361021, Fujian, China
cs_tianwang@163.com

Abstract. We present a new VANETS architecture, which is a composition of two modules, software defined network (SDN), and Fog computing. The SDN-based framework gives the scalability, flexibility, programming capability, and the global information, while the Fog computing delivers delicate and locations-aware services that can meet the future demands of VANETs. The proposed framework can address the main problems of VANETs by providing vehicles communications (V2V), vehicle to infrastructures (V2I). We used hybrid SDN architecture and addition od security plane, proposed secure mechanism for communication. In addition, our proposed framework provides a textual awareness system that automatically and intelligently provides possible traffic safety and provides secure and fast communications. Results indicates that the proposed system provides the best results in terms of both type of communication in VANETs.

Keywords: VANETs · SDN · Vehicles · Fog computing
Cloud computing · Communication · Infrastructure

1 Introduction

VANETs have attracted a considerable attention in the modern era [10]. This potentially active and progressive area is designed to improve the road safety, increase traveling and traffic and efficacy, and give the comfort and convenience to the travelers and drivers [8]. V2I, and V2V communications are expected to increase in demand by increasing the growth of mobiles and onboard unite (OBUs) devices [6,11,30]. For providing the better services on the roads, VANETs can be very useful in provision of safety and the non safety programs [5,9]. For example, management and safety services for vehicles, social services, cloud services, and monitoring service. The VANETs is now a phenomena and supports a diversity of new protocols, and services [4,19], the traditional VANETs architecture for communication is illustrated in Fig. 1. Such as

© Springer Nature Switzerland AG 2018
G. Wang et al. (Eds.): SpaCCS 2018, LNCS 11342, pp. 46–59, 2018.
https://doi.org/10.1007/978-3-030-05345-1_4

traffic alert, route planning, background information and mobile cloud services, unbalanced traffic between multi-router topologies, and inappropriate network utilization [1,18,22,29].

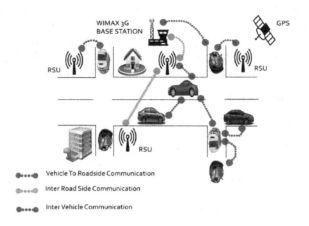

Fig. 1. VANETs architecture and communication [4].

Some challenges are unresolved with the latest framework, such as increasing the connected devices, the use of effective resources and irregular traffic,privacy, security, geographical address, delays due to excessive traffic and unreliable connections, and QoS [7,15]. Even if, self-organized, distributed networks mode, such as MANETs, can be used to resolve the problems [26,28]. In these cases, the absence of a enthusiastic methods for connections and resource management makes the some services inaccessible. Therefore, open and flexible architecture of vehicles is a key requirement that allows testers to conduct their testing in production of environment, and improve the network resource management, applications, and the users [7,16]. To handle the above mentioned challenges, we look at the Software Defined Networks (SDN) and Fog computing. Today, SDN has emerged as a commonly used SDN protocol as a flexible method for controlling the networks in a free flow and in efficient way [18]. SDN Flexibility is an interesting method that can be used to meet the concerns of the VANETs. For employing the SDN policies and rules to VANETs, there is plenty of planning and flexibility available in today's wireless distribution network [14]. For enabling the V2I and V2V applications and services and facilitate the network management [20].

In this article, we focus on using SDN and Fog Commuting (FC) for secure communication. In particular, we have attention on the framework, services, operations and communication of the software-defined VANETs with FC.

The reminder of the paper is organized as follows. Section 2, is about the overview of the system design and architecture. Section 3, is about results, discussion, and performance analysis, and the last section is about the conclusion.

2   Overview of the System and Design

The flow of the proposed framework is illustrated in the Fig. 2, for the secure communication among the vehicles and the cloud and transportation servers, we used SDN controller (SDNC) and FC. We used hybrid SDNC with security plane as shown in Fig. 3 for scalability, flexibility, security, programmability, and for the global information. While, the FC provide location-awareness and delay-sensitive services, for satisfying the demand of the future VANETs. The main components we used in our system are given below,

- SDNC is a logical essential intelligence entity of our framework. The SDNC controls the actions of the whole network.
- SDN wireless node: this node is controlled by SDNC, also receive the instructions from SDNC to execute the processes.
- SDN RSUs: the SDN RSU also controls by the SDNC, and they are fixed alongside the roads, and used for forwarding the data, All RSUs works as fog devices.
- SDN Roadside Controllers (RSUC): A group of the RSUs connect to the RSUC priors to approaching the SDNC to bandwidth connections. RSUC Open Flow is enable and control by SDNC. In addition to data transmission responsibility, RSUC also stores road information and provides emergency and necessary services. All RSUC works as fog devices under the orchestration of SDN controller.
- Fog Computing: Fs acts as an intermediate tier between SDNC and the cloud server to provide the secure transmission of communication in VANETs.

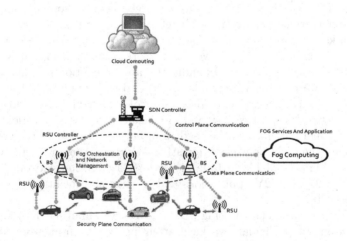

Fig. 2. VANETs architecture based on SDN controller and fog computing.

2.1   Software Defined Networks

The main idea behind SDN is the collision between the control and the data planes [13]. In the SDN, the network devices like switches and the routers are based on the policies and rules. These rules are created or changed before being sent to network devices. The overall behaviours of the network is only determined by the control logic [21]. This new network paradigm has many advantages correlated with the traditional distribution methods. First, the network is being developed and deployed in applications, functions and protocols. In the SDNC, it is very simple to program, modify, manipulates and configures a centralized protocols, without the need for independent access and configuration of network hardware across the networks [21].

Second, SDN-based architectures are network-based controllers that have global knowledge of network status that can control the network infrastructure independently of the vendor. These network devices simply accept control policies without understanding and enforcing the standards of different network protocols and directly controls, programs, synchronize, and managed the network resources in SDNC. For SDNC, the communication protocol is the main requirement for control and the data planes.

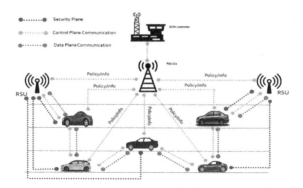

Fig. 3. Software defined VANETs architecture and communication.

2.2   Fog Computing (FC)

Recently, FC has become an active cloud-related research area. It was incorporated by the Cisco in 2012 [23,27]. It is extended paradigm of the cloud computing where network edge is employed for data processing and services on contrary to the existing technique in which it is completely done in the cloud. It offers many advantages in comparison with traditional systems as location awareness, mobility support and low latency can be achieved by using fog architecture which eventually places it closer to end-users. FC also incorporates core cloud services. It also changes conventional data centres into heterogeneous and distributed platforms [24,25]. Therefore, the FC support the applications of IOT in vehicular network, actors/sensor networks and the industrial automations that require the processing of contexts awareness and sensitive delays [12,17].

Privacy in Fog Computing. The most concerning problem of user is the risk of privacy leakage in VANETs. In fog computing, the algorithms of privacy preserving are run among FC nodes and cloud, because there is no problem of computation, processing, and storage for the both sides, and these are sufficient. And the running algorithms are resources barricade at end devices level, they usually collect the data for the end devices for the privacy preservation at the fog nodes the homomorphic encryption is used for the preservation of the privacy without the decryption. For the statistical and aggregation differential privacy is applied to validation of non exposure of privacy of an arbitrary and conflicting single entrance in data set.

2.3 Basic Operations

The communication of SDNC in proposed framework are composed on three parts, the security, control, and the data planes. We used hybrid control mode of SDN with little modification of security plane in it, to provide the better security for vehicles communication as shown in Fig. 3. Data control communications are for flow of rules and policies regulations, while, data plan communication is for data transfer. The security control plane send the security keys to the RSUs, where the RSUCs collect all the keys, combined them and send to the SDNC as illustrated in Fig. 3. By using of the FC, we select the mode with the hybrid control, because in this mode the controller does not have complete controls over the network, but it propagate the policies and rules with the RSUCs through RSUs. For example, in preference of providing specific flow rules and policies, SDN provides an abstract policy called policy information, where the particular behaviours are determined by the RSUs and RSUCs, its depends on their local information. RSUC data is then sent to the Fog server via SDNC for the global and continuous goals. To manage the network topology, the link layer structure in any vehicle can be used for tracking accessible messages continuously to learn neighbouring knowledge. This knowledge, contains the vehicle traffic information, route map, speed, position, and the sensor information.

SDNC not only receives the vehicles information from the RSUs and RSUCs, but, also transmits information from the RSUs and RSUCs to the vehicles. So, it can create a global connected graph of the SDN, RSUCs and RSUs, and other information essentials for the different services. The RSUCs also receive traffic knowledge from an RSUs, so they can process some supervisory information without full knowledge of the SDNC. RSUs and RSUCs provide local and appropriated information with short-term awareness and location features. These RSUCs and RSUs merge the sub quires and security keys and then send to the SDNC.

In the FC, both the edge devices and the data centers, support indirect sources and services. The RSUs and RSUCs, send the information through SDNC to the Fog server, also share resources for vehicle control. To enabled the FC architecture in the software defined VANETs, SDNC, RSUCs and RSUs provide not only the SDN capabilities but also Virtualization to enable Fog and cloud services [2,3]. Hence, a hyper visor, which is a small-level middle-ware, must be run on these physical devices to support virtual machine abstraction (VM). Services are hosted on these VMs that allow the transmission and re-service of the service.

2.4   V2V and V2I Communication Mechanism with Security Plane

In this section we only provide the secure communication mechanism for V2V and V2I communication in the VANETs, by using SDN and Fog computing.

For the secure communication plan we used three types of data plan in our proposed system, namely, security plan, control plan and data plan. Where the security plane is used to forward the encrypted keys. An active switch also acts as a secures channel for communication to the SDNC, which allows data packets and remote streaming packets are sent through the SDNC by using free stream protocols [13]. SDNC have the responsibility for deciding whether to add, remove, and modify the policies, rules, and actions in the flow of traffic through free flow, thus enabling scheduling to automatically configures the VANETs networks. SDN services and applications communicate directly to their needs and network activities through the North-bound (NBI) user interface APIs to the SDNC.

The software component required to construct a SDN architecture to ensure the cooperation of integration. The SDN function and the fog calculation enter the vehicular network. The RSUs and the BS can match the Mayor Orchestration is based on MANO architecture. In this way, BS and RSUs need a management mechanisms to allow data transfer the information and rules to the managed services. Fog node must acknowledge the dissimilar decisions, for example, quality of service (QoS), quality of experience (QoE), network technology,topology, operators, to determine its location and time.

Request Generation Process. The anonymous inquiry process is generated by the vehicle V, which intend to approach the service giving by the transportation server or cloud server. There is no communication overhead for the V in execution of inquired queries for communication process, V commitments to firstly define M as message and the k as privacy preferences. Then, V added the M identity mid and transmit the M into the k data movement generating the set of messages $\{m1, m2, \ldots, mk\}$ and set of keys $K = \{k_1, k_2, \ldots, k_m\}$. The encrypted messages are distributed among the vehicles communication range in the VANETs, and the derived keys are sent to the RSUs through security plane, where the RSUCs collect all the keys and send to the SDNC. Distinctive methods (it depends on the position of the vehicles or the state of the network) can be implemented for the broadcasting of messages in the vehicles. Here in our method, we use a easy approach for the sharing of messages among the vehicles in VANETs. Our broadcasting method for communication among the vehicles performs as follows. The initiator V encrypts all the encrypted messages mi using the set of keys Ks shared among vehicles and RSUs, Fs and the affix mid, that $\{mi = \{EKs(mi)\|mid\}\}$ for every $\{i = 1, k\}$. Due to the, existence of the id of the message mid in all the messages, allow the vehicles to recognize the dissimilar sub-messages associated to the same M. Query initiator V randomly chose $k - 1$ vehicles Vs in his communications ranges, then send the messages from $\{m1 \Rightarrow mk\}$to each of them. It then send these messages to SDNC via Fs, RSUs and RSUCs, where these RSUs and RSUCs works as fog devices. Upon accepting the messages mi from the every vehicle in the communication range, then $V1$ first checks the mid. If the vehicle is already acknowledged to send the message with same mid, $\{mid \in Sent\}$, $V1$ transmit mi to next vehicle $V2$ in the communications range. After the transmission process every selected vehicle V separately sends the encrypted messages received by the SDNC. These encrypted messages from all the vehicles are forwarded to SDNC through RSUCs and the FS. Now SDNC can decrypt the each message incrementally, reconstruct the messages and sends it to the cloud server.

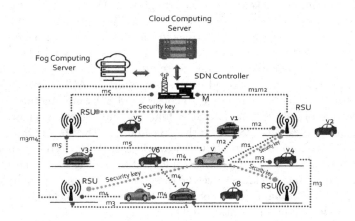

Fig. 4. Anonymous request based on SDN and fog computing.

Figure 4 shows an example of communication among the vehicles. Where, the vehicle V generate and forward a encrypted message to the next neighbouring vehicles, while the selected vehicles in the communication range sends the encrypted messages to the SDNC through RSUs and RSUCs. In the given example, the inquired V describe $k = 5$ then distribute M into the five sub-messages $\{m1, \ldots, m5\}$. Messages are then encrypted with the ABE method, generated the set of keys $K = \{k_1, k_2, \ldots, k_m\}$ and shared between V and SDNC, and mid is appended with each of the sub messages. The set of keys are directly forwarded by the particular V to the all nearest RSUs, from there the RSUCs collect all keys and send to the SDNC through FS. The inquired vehicle V sends the encrypted message $m1$ to SDNC and transmits the remaining $k - 1$ messages to other vehicles in communications ranges. Categorically, the sub-message $m2$ and the $m5$ are forwarded to the vehicles $V1$ and $V3$ that forward these messages to the Fs. Considering $v4$ not accept for transmit sub-message $m3$, sub-message $m3$ then gets a route $V4 \Longrightarrow V7$. The sub-message $m4$ gets a route $V6 \Longrightarrow V7 \Longrightarrow V9$ because, when the sub-message is acknowledged by $V7$ and $V7$ considers that it has already get sub-message $(m3)$ with same $mids$, then it forward sub-message $m4 \Rightarrow V9$. Lastly, vehicles $V, V1, V3, V7$, and $V9$ sends the sub-message to SDNC via FS, RSUs and RSUCs.

Response Generation Process. The response generation process is anonymous, because of encryption and decryption, and no one can track the original vehicle by tracking the communication process. If in the case, the cloud or transportation server, compromised no one can track the communication, because they did not know the exact query or information of the vehicles.

Figure 5 represent an illustration of anonymous feedback to the query in Fig. 5. Encrypted Queries Mr are broadcast to all the vehicles utilized in Fig. 5, that are, $\{V, V1, V3, V7, V9\}$. When V collects the message, he can decrypt it with keys Ks shared by the SDNC. The auxiliary vehicles deleted this message Mr, because they do not have the key.

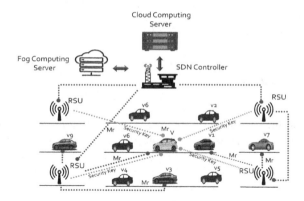

Fig. 5. Anonymous response based on SDN and fog computing.

3   Experiments, Results and Discussion

3.1   Experimental Setup and Simulation

For the simulation, we used Veins model for simulation along with SUMO and OMNet++ environment. The parameters we used in simulations are presented below in the Table 1.

Table 1. Description of the parameters

Parameter	Value
Simulation framework	OMNet++, Sumo and Veins
Area	$50-100\,\mathrm{km}^2$
Vehicles	100–200
No of RSU	25–50
Transport protocol	UDP
Propagation model	Nakagami
Speed	15, 20, 25, 30 m/s
Maximum acceleration	6 m/s
Maximum deceleration	4 m/s
Channel bandwidth	12 MHz
OBU receiver sensitivity	−80.0dBm
Antenna height	1–1.5 m
Type of the antenna	Omnidirectional
Network layer	802.11p and IEEE 1609.4
ROI size	$9\,\mathrm{km}^2$
Transmission range	500 m

3.2   Security Analysis

Our secure communication method provides complete privacy protection because it guarantees the privacy of the vehicle and the anonymity of the link in terms of both the vehicle and the server. Our approach preserves the communication privacy of vehicles and protects against privacy breaches by using secure communication methods as well as SDNC and FC. In order to check the privacy of the vehicle, through our proposed method, when establishing a new communication session with the cloud or transport server, the vehicle always generates a set of keys for its own message. Therefore, it is computationally impossible for a vehicle or group of vehicles to notice the true identification of other vehicles and to link different communication sessions or authentication *mids* to the same vehicle.

For both types of communication (V2V and V2I), the cloud and transport server does not know the real information about the communication due to encrypted communication. The desired result produced by the cloud or transport server is the user result of all vehicles within the communication range, not the enemy, nor the cloud server, knowing that the result is returned to the active user. Therefore, they cannot access location information related to the vehicle. The fog server was unable to know the original query information for each vehicle because we had performed encryption through the vehicle driver and SDNC.

The communication and location information from every vehicle to the Fog server is encrypted queries and information. The decryption function parameters are only known by the vehicles Vs and SDNC. The trusted entity could not find the original query information about the communication. Even if the SDNC or fog server is attacked by an enemy, the information of the vehicle will not be revealed due to the fog server privacy.

The vehicles does not know the queries of the other vehicle while communicating with each other. The FS accurately obtains the expected results for every vehicle, and everyx vehicle can easily obtain their own results without knowing the identity of other vehicles. Even if some malicious cars cooperate, they can't understand other problems with trusted vehicles.

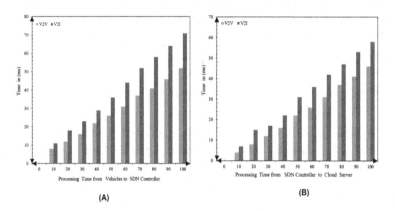

Fig. 6. (A) Processing time from vehicle to SDNC, (B) Processing time from SDNC to cloud server

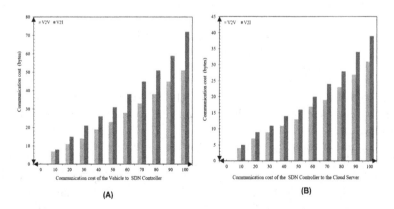

Fig. 7. (A) Communication cost from vehicles to SDNC, (B) Communication cost from SDNC to cloud server.

3.3   Performance Analysis

There are four entities in our proposed scheme, and we calculate the cost of computation of these four entities, the complexity of vehicle is the $O(N + mk)$, where N, and m, and ks are the numbers of the vehicles, messages, and security plan respectively. The ruining time of SDNC is the $O(N + m + K)$, where the N shows the vehicles and m are the messages, and K is the set of security keys, because the SDNC is only responsible to collect the messages from the vehicle encrypt them and forward to the Fog server. The running time of the fog server is the $O(N + logm)$, where N are the vehicles and m are the messages. The complexity of cloud server is $O(N + logm + mr)$, where the N are vehicles and m are messages and r are the required results. The total complexity of proposed system is given below.

$O(N + m + K + N + logm + N + logm + mr)$.
$O(3N + 2m + k + 2logm + mr)$.
we excluded the constant, so the final computational cost is given below.
$O(N + m + k + logm + mr)$.

The communication cost among the vehicles and the SDNC becomes $O(Ck+D)$, where C and D are the constants, and we reduce it as $O(k)$. The communication cost between the SDNC and the Fog server is $O(Ak + B)$. Lastly, we examine the communication cost between the SDNC and the cloud server. So, the communication cost is $O(KC * mD)$, where C and D are the constants. So the total cost among the vehicles and the cloud server is $O(k + AK * mB)$.

Mainly the complexity of the framework depends on its algorithms. To evaluate and analyse the complexity, we perform some simulations, in simulations we calculated the communication cost and time complexity.

Figure 6(a, b), shows the time of processing for vehicles in our proposed method. The x-axis and Y-axis contain the vehicles and time information respectively.

The Fig. 6(a, b) contain the processing time of the vehicles with SDNC and cloud computing. to achieve this goal, we simulate approximately 100 vehicles, and it is clearly shown that, if the all vehicles are in the communication range, then the processing time is very low. Figure 6(a, b) shows the time of processing from the Vehicles to the SDNC and from the SDNC to the cloud server, from the Figs, we can clearly analyse that the time of processing for this environment is also very low.

The communication cost (CC) of the proposed system is shown in the Figs. 7(a, b). The information about vehicles and memory (bytes) is listed on x-axis and Y-axis respective. the CC is represented in Fig. 7(a), when vehicles start the communication through RSUs or by others vehicles that are available in the communication range. Figure 7(b) represents the CC from SDNC to the cloud server.

The results from the Figs shows that our proposed scheme have very low CC, when all vehicles are in the communication range. From the Fig. 8, the execution time required by the OBU to generate the messages for the communication between V2V and V2I is very low. It is seems that in very short time span the maximum numbers of the messages are communicated between the vehicles.

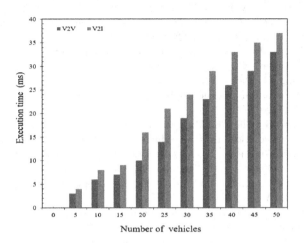

Fig. 8. Execution time of messages

4 Conclusion

In our proposed approach, we preserve the communication privacy in VANETs. There are two types of communications in VANETs V2V and V2I. In order to preserve communication privacy for V2V and V2I, we provide the trusted communication among the vehicles and infrastructure. In V2V and V2I communication privacy, primarily, we used SDNC along with Fog computing. In SDNC, we used security, data, and control planes, for sending the keys and data to the RSUs generated by the vehicle. Fs operated as and intermediate tier between SDNC and cloud server to provide the secure transmission of communication in VANETs. We create encrypted messages at initial level from the user side and send to the SDNC, where the SDNC combined the keys as well as the messages, decrypt the message. After this, we send all these information to the cloud server for the desired results, after getting the results the SDNC transmit all the results to the vehicles through FS and RSUC, RSU, where the vehicle driver received the results with keys and decrypt the results.

Acknowledgment. This work was supported in part by the National Natural Science Foundation of China under Grant 61632009 and Grant 61472451, in part by the Guangdong Provincial Natural Science Foundation under Grant 2017A030308006, and in part by the High-Level Talents Program of Higher Education in Guangdong Province under Grant 2016ZJ01.

References

1. Arif, M., Alam, K.A., Hussain, M.: Application of data mining using artificial neural network: survey. Int. J. Database Theory Appl. **8**(1), 245–270 (2015)
2. Arif, M., Mahmood, T.: Cloud computing and its environmental effects. Int. J. Grid Distrib. Comput. **8**(1), 279–286 (2015)
3. Arif, M., Shakeel, H.: Virtualization security: analysis and open challenges. Int. J. Hybrid Inf. Technol. **8**(2), 237–246 (2015)
4. Arif, M., Wang, G., Balas, V.E.: Secure VANETs: trusted communication scheme between vehicles and infrastructure based on fog computing. Stud. Inform. Control **27**(2), 235–246 (2018)
5. Arif, M., Wang, G., Chen, S.: Deep learning with non-parametric regression model for traffic flow prediction. In: Proceedings of IEEE 16th International Conference on Dependable, Autonomic and Secure Computer, 16th International Conference on Pervasive Intelligence and Computer, 4th International Conference on Big Data Intelligence and Computer, and 3rd Cyber Science and Technology Congress, pp. 681–688. IEEE, August 2018
6. Arif, M., Wang, G., Peng, T.: Track me if you can? query based dual location privacy in VANETs for V2V and V2I. In: 2018 17th IEEE International Conference On Trust, Security And Privacy In Computing And Communications/12th IEEE International Conference On Big Data Science And Engineering (TrustCom/BigDataSE), pp. 1091–1096. IEEE (2018)
7. Ghosal, A., Halder, S.: Building intelligent systems for smart cities: issues, challenges and approaches. In: Mahmood, Z. (ed.) Smart Cities. CCN, pp. 107–125. Springer, Cham (2018). https://doi.org/10.1007/978-3-319-76669-0_5
8. Guerrero-Ibáñez, J., Zeadally, S., Contreras-Castillo, J.: Sensor technologies for intelligent transportation systems. Sensors **18**(4), 1212 (2018)
9. Klingler, F., Cohen, R., Sommer, C., Dressler, F.: Bloom hopping: bloom filter based 2-hop neighbor management in VANETs. IEEE Trans. Mob. Comput., 1 (2018)
10. Li, H., Lu, R., Misic, J., Mahmoud, M.: Security and privacy of connected vehicular cloud computing. IEEE Netw. **32**(3), 4–6 (2018)
11. Ligo, A.K., Peha, J.M.: Cost-effectiveness of sharing roadside infrastructure for internet of vehicles. IEEE Trans. Intell. Transp. Syst. **19**, 2362–2372 (2018)
12. Liu, Q., Wang, G., Liu, X., Peng, T., Wu, J.: Achieving reliable and secure services in cloud computing environments. Comput. Electr. Eng. **59**, 153–164 (2017)
13. Naman, A.T., Wang, Y., Gharakheili, H.H., Sivaraman, V., Taubman, D.: Responsive high throughput congestion control for interactive applications over sdn-enabled networks. Comput. Netw. **134**, 152–166 (2018)
14. Nobre, J., et al.: Vehicular software-defined networking and fog computing: integration and design principles. Ad Hoc Netw. **82**, 172–181 (2018)
15. Peng, S., Wang, G., Zhou, Y., Wan, C., Wang, C., Yu, S.: An immunization framework for social networks through big data based influence modeling. IEEE Trans. Dependable Secure Comput. (2017)
16. Peng, T., Liu, Q., Meng, D., Wang, G.: Collaborative trajectory privacy preserving scheme in location-based services. Inf. Sci. **387**, 165–179 (2017)
17. Rahmani, A.M., et al.: Exploiting smart e-health gateways at the edge of healthcare internet-of-things: a fog computing approach. Future Gener. Comput. Syst. **78**, 641–658 (2018)

18. Rego, A., Garcia, L., Sendra, S., Lloret, J.: Software defined networks for traffic management in emergency situations. In: 2018 Fifth International Conference on Software Defined Systems (SDS), pp. 45–51. IEEE (2018)

19. Singh, G.D., Tomar, R., Sastry, H.G., Prateek, M.: A review on VANET routing protocols and wireless standards. In: Satapathy, S.C., Bhateja, V., Das, S. (eds.) Smart Computing and Informatics. SIST, vol. 78, pp. 329–340. Springer, Singapore (2018). https://doi.org/10.1007/978-981-10-5547-8_34

20. Teniou, A., Bensaber, B.A.: Efficient and dynamic elliptic curve qu-vanstone implicit certificates distribution scheme for vehicular cloud networks. Secur. Priv. 1(1), e11 (2018)

21. Truong, N.B., Lee, G.M., Ghamri-Doudane, Y.: Software defined networking-based vehicular adhoc network with fog computing. In: 2015 IFIP/IEEE International Symposium on Integrated Network Management (IM), pp. 1202–1207. IEEE (2015)

22. Wang, F., Jiang, W., Li, X., Wang, G.: Maximizing positive influence spread in online social networks via fluid dynamics. Future Gener. Comput. Syst. 86, 1491–1502 (2018)

23. Wang, T., et al.: Data collection from WSNs to the cloud based on mobile fog elements. Future Gener. Comput. Syst. (2017, in press). https://doi.org/10.1016/j.future.2017.07.031

24. Wang, T., Zhang, G., Bhuiyan, M.Z.A., Liu, A., Jia, W., Xie, M.: A novel trust mechanism based on fog computing in sensor-cloud system. Future Gener. Comput. Syst. (2018, in press). https://doi.org/10.1016/j.future.2018.05.049

25. Wang, T., et al.: Fog-based storage technology to fight with cyber threat. Future Gener. Comput. Syst. 83, 208–218 (2018)

26. Xing, X., Wang, G., Li, J.: Collaborative target tracking in wireless sensor networks. Adhoc Sens. Wirel. Netw. 23, 117–135 (2014)

27. Yi, S., Li, C., Li, Q.: A survey of fog computing: concepts, applications and issues. In: Proceedings of the 2015 Workshop on Mobile Big Data, pp. 37–42. ACM (2015)

28. Zhang, Q., Liu, Q., Wang, G.: PRMS: a personalized mobile search over encrypted outsourced data. IEEE Access 6, 31541–31552 (2018)

29. Zhang, S., Wang, G., Bhuiyan, M.Z.A., Liu, Q.: A dual privacy preserving scheme in continuous location-based services. IEEE Internet of Things J. 5, 4191–4200 (2018)

30. Zhou, Z., Dong, M., Ota, K., Wang, G., Yang, L.T.: Energy-efficient resource allocation for D2D communications underlaying cloud-RAN-based LTE-A networks. IEEE Internet of Things J. 3(3), 428–438 (2016)

Wearable Device Data for Criminal Investigation

Sarah Mcnary and Aaron Hunter[✉]

School of Computing and Academic Studies,
British Columbia Institute of Technology,
3700 Willingdon Avenue, Burnaby V5G 3H2, Canada
etmcnary@hotmail.com, aaron_hunter@bcit.ca

Abstract. Wearable devices collect and share data through social networks accessed by a smartphone. We can therefore view the smartphone carried by a criminal suspect as a central repository of information that may be useful in a criminal investigation. But it is not clear how this information can be used to deduce conclusive, legally admissible evidence. The challenges here are not only technological, but practical. In this paper, we discuss the challenges faced when we try to abstract criminal data from wearable devices. We also present a case study involving a wearable fitness tracker. In particular, we try to determine if a phone synced with a fitness tracker can provide evidence related to the execution of a violent act. While the approach presented here opens up a new area for investigators to look for evidence, our results suggest that it can actually be difficult to obtain concrete digital evidence in this manner.

Keywords: Wearable devices · Forensic investigation
Information retrieval · Experimental methods · Information security

1 Introduction

Wearable devices collect information about the behaviour of the user. In principle, this information can be used as evidence in criminal investigations. However, there are technical, legal and practical issues that make this challenging. In this paper, we consider the potential of such devices for forensic investigation. We focus primarily on wearable fitness trackers. These are simple devices that track the movement of the wearer to help them achieve certain fitness goals. Users can share progress online, which is normally done by syncing the fitness tracker to their phone and then using the phone to communicate data over the Internet. As such, there may be a great deal of data about a user involved in a crime that is being shared and stored for analysis.

Before fitness trackers can be used effectively in an investigation, we first need to understand exactly what information is being stored and synced. Wearable fitness trackers such as Fitbits are relatively new and can offer a wealth of information to investigators as the device constantly monitors the physical status of

© Springer Nature Switzerland AG 2018
G. Wang et al. (Eds.): SpaCCS 2018, LNCS 11342, pp. 60–71, 2018.
https://doi.org/10.1007/978-3-030-05345-1_5

its wearer. There are vast amounts of information that can be extracted from these devices, including geolocation data, distance traveled, heart rate data, and activity time. There is great value in this data as it can describe the state of the person wearing the Fitbit during physically violent moments.

Although various fitness trackers have been tested for their accuracy in the field of health sciences, little information about the forensic applications of these devices is available. As such, we need to determine if commercial fitness trackers are actually collecting and sharing data that can be useful in identifying criminal activity.

This paper makes several contributions to existing literature on social network forensics. While there is a great deal of technical documentation and health related information about fitness trackers, this paper is unique in that we explicitly consider the challenges faced when using the data for investigating purposes. Moreover, to the best of our knowledge, this paper includes the first experimental study that attempts to use a fitness tracker to identify when a violent attack has been perpetrated. Methodologically, our paper is distinct in the computing literature as we advocate for the importance of physical experimentation with wearable devices; this is an important step towards correlating the actions with the data being stored.

2   Preliminaries

2.1   Challenges

Fundamentally, the information collected and stored through a fitness tracker may be useful in a criminal investigation. But several issues need to be addressed:

1. *Legal*: What information can be stored, and where can it be maintained?
2. *Technical*: How easily can we obtain stored information from the device, or from a paired smartphone?
3. *Empirical*: How do we demonstrate conclusively that the information on the device is evidence that a given behaviour has occurred?

This challenges are all related. In this paper we focus primarily on the third, and only remark on the first two challenges as they relate to identifying behaviours.

2.2   Related Work

With all the different sensors built into a wearable device, there is a lot of data being collected, and therefore a lot of ways the data can be useful. For example, we can try to identify the activities being performed based on the data. This has been done for various forms of exercise [2], but other activities can be detected as well. One novel application of wearable devices comes from [5]. In this study, the police officers, construction workers, members of the general population each wore a wearable device to compare whether the detection of gunshots was accurate or if the device would confuse a gunshot with the usage of construction equipment, for example. The results found 98.9% of gunshots were correctly identified, and only 0.4% of non-gunshots were misidentified as gunshots. In this study, the AX3 Watch was used as a wearable device; the data was obtained from an accelerometer.

Several studies have tested the accuracy, validity, and reliability of fitness trackers as they measure energy expenditure, physical activity, and heart rate [7,9]. In one study, participants engaged in an hour routine of running and cycling with some time to rest between the exercises. The results found that although the fitness trackers produce poor estimates of energy expenditure, they all accurately measure heart rate [10]. The same conclusion was drawn in [6]. It is worth noting that these two studies differed in several respects, including the physical placement of the wearable devices. Note, for example, that a Fitbit worn on the wrist will detect arm motion more accuratelly than one worn on the hip. This must be taken into account when setting up new experiments for activity detection.

In terms of measuring physical activity, [8] tested a Fitbit on 25 university students performing a variety of activities such as treadmill walking, incline walking, jogging, and stair stepping. This study concluded that the Fitbit had "moderate" validity in identifying activities. Roughly speaking, the Fitbit is able to be used to identify certain kinds of exercise, but it is not useful for activities such as climbing stairs.

In stark contrast with [10] regarding heart rate measurements, [3] concluded that the Fitbit Charge failed to accurately measure heart rate during more intensive physical activities, but the device still could adequately measure heart rate during rest and recovery. There are many differences between these two studies. First of all, the test equipment was slightly different. Second, the exercise protocols were not the same. In order to validate the data obtained through the use of wearable tech to monitor physical activity, other studies have used statistics to interpret the results and draw conclusions. For example, [1] measures the range of motion using three different apparatus which all measuredchanges in joint angles and reach distance. To interpret the results, means and standard deviations were calculated for each set of data to perform an analysis of variance. Going further, coefficients of determination were computed between two pairs of apparatus for all the movements to be able to determine how much variability can be explained by the model used. Loeffler [5] calculated feature statistics for each spike in that data that could potentially be a gunshot. Furthermore, a logistic regression model was used to predict the identification or misidentification of a gunshot. All of the statistical features for the potential gunshot detections were entered into this model to support the predicted classifications of whether the spike was a gunshot or not.

3 Stored Data

3.1 Sensors

Although fitness trackers vary in terms of the actual embedded sensors, the following are standard:

- *Accelerometer*: Senses device acceleration.
- *Gyroscope*: Senses angular velocity.
- *Heart Rate*: Senses the heart rate of the user.
- *Orientation*: Senses orientation of the device.

In principle, these sensors can give a great deal of information about the activities being carried out by the user.

3.2 Where is the Data?

In general, the data is stored in three locations:

- *The Device*: Information gathered is stored for a short term on the device before syncing. For Fitbit trackers, for example, information is stored for 7 days.
- *Local Machine*: Information is synced with a local PC or smart phone.
- *Remote storage*: Information is stored on the cloud indefiinitely.

Information stored on the device or locally should be useful for criminal investigation. There is a legal issue surrounding remote storage, however. In many countries, privacy laws dictate that information can only be stored for a specified purpose. Obtaining this information for investigative purposes may therefore be problematic. For this reason, we focus on the first two storage locations in this paper.

The data gathered by fitness trackers is stored in a way that allows the user to track their activity, and overall health. This is quite different than the way we would store information to identify particular activities. For this reason, it is an open question how useful the data will actually be in a criminal investigation. In order to make such a determination, we actually need to look at specific activities and determine if they can be associated with particular stored profiles.

4 A Case Study

4.1 Motivation

Having specified the sensors and the storage locations for information, we now describe a case study intended to demonstrate how data gathered may be used in a criminal investigation. Ther purpose of this case study is not necessarily to give precise, legally admissible results. Instead, the purpose is to show a methodology that can be used to evaluated the utility of fitness trackers to identify particular behaviours.

We remark that the primary contribution of this case study is actually methodological. By setting up a precise scenario, we hope to demonstrate how a controlled experiment can be useful in determining which kinds of physical activity a fitness tracker can be used to identify. But this is a preliminary paper on work in progress; at present we are actually refining the methodology and studying teh data available on different devices. As such, the results to date have not been particularly useful. Nevertheless, this report will describe our general methodology in order to start a useful discussion about the value of activity detection through fitness tracker data.

4.2 Equipment

Our case study uses a commercial fitness tracker, a rooted Android smart phone, and digital forensic tools for investigation. We list the hardware and software that was used in our work.

- **Cellebrite UFED**: Hardware designed for mobile device forensics that can take an image of the internal digital storage of many different mobile devices.
- **EnCase**: A professional digital forensic software toolkit designed to analyze a multitude of digital information including disk images, memory dumps, and individual files.
- **Fitbit**: A brand of wearable fitness tracker devices that can measure the wearer's fitness levels, heart rate, steps taken, distance traveled, length of time spent being physically active or inactive, hours of sleep, and so on. Throughout this paper, "Fitbit" will refer to the Fitbit Charge 2 which is the specific device that we used.

The Fitbit Charge 2 used in this study came fresh out of the box with the absolute minimum amount of setup completed for the device to function. Fitbit was selected as the brand due to its popularity in the marketplace.

5 The Experiment

In this study, a participant wore the Fitbit Charge 2 and let it sync with an Android smartphone via the official Fitbit app in real time. The procedure for one run of the experiment began with Wi-Fi and Bluetooth being turned on and the Fitbit app was run so the phone can sync with the Fitbit in real time. The participant wore the Fitbit on their dominant hand.

The main steps of each run were as follows:

1. The participant walked for 30 min. During this phase the Fitbit collected data about the participant during a normal, non-violent state.
2. After 30 min, the participant stopped at a designated, safe location.
3. The participant kneeled on the ground and used a rock to hit the ground in front of them 10 times.
4. The participant then walked for a second round of 30 min.

Fig. 1. Experiment flowchart

Following these steps, the fitbit was removed and placed in a safe location (with the paired smartphone) until the next trial. The experiment was repeated three times to ensure consistency in the resulting fitness data.

After the experiment had been performed three separate times with adequate time for the participant to recover in between the tests, the rooted smartphone with the synced Fitbit data on it was analyzed with EnCase sofware. This involved several steps to complete the acquisition process, which was repeated twice for the sake of consistency in the data. The two images were each hashed through two separate hashing algorithms, MD5 and SHA1, to check if the images matched each other.

The images were imported into a free forensic toolkit called Autopsy 4.0.0 and a case insensitive keyword search was conducted on both images for files and folders containing the text "fitbit". Matching files and folders appeared in many places throughout the Android system:

```
/CarvedFiles/
/app/
/app-lib/
/dalvik-cache/
```

```
/data/com.android.browser/
/data/com.android.providers.downloads/
/data/com.android.vending/
/data/com.fitbit.FitbitMobile/
/data/com.google.android.gms/
/data/com.google.android/.../shared_prefs/
/data/com.samsung.InputEventApp/share_prefs/
/data/com.samsung.android/databases/
/data/com.samsung.klmsagent/databases/
/data/com.sec.android.app.launcher/databases/
/data/com.sec.android.app.memo/shared_prefs/
/log/dumpstate_app_error.txt.gz/
/log/dumpstate_app_native.txt.gz/
/media/0/Android/data/com.fitbit.FitbitMobile/
/system/
```

Of these, the most important location was the Fitbit app's data directory located at "/data/com.fitbit.FitbitMobile/".

For both images, the folder for the Fitbit app was exported using Autopsy and all the files in the two exports had their write permissions removed. Because the hashes of the two images did not match, all the files from the two exports had their SHA1 hashes computed, saved to a file and the files were compared. At this point, we need to manually look at the data to determine if the fitbit had stored any evidence on the smartphone that could be used as evidence of a violent act. A complete flow chart for the case study experiment is given in Fig. 1.

Note that there are other methods of recovering the Fitbit data directly. These methods include Joint Test Action Group (JTAG) which would have someone partially disassembling the Fitbit device to expose its circuits. Wires would be soldered to the right places for special hardware to read a bit-by-bit copy of the device's digital storage. Alternatively, a Chip-off could be performed where the device's flash memory chips are physically removed and read with specialized equipment. These methods were not attempted in this experiment; our focus was solely on obtaining information from the disc image. We are envisioning a scenario where the fit bit itself may have been damaged or unavailable, hence the one way to retrieve information is through the phone.

5.1 Results

The exported Fitbit app data contains cache directories, a preferences directory, a database directory, and several other miscellaneous directories, as shown in Fig. 2.

The cache directories contain plaintext files, JSON files, images, and videos. The videos range from only 37 kilobytes in size to a little over 1 megabyte. Inside the "shared_prefs" folder are XML files, almost all of which are less than a kilobyte in size. The "files" directory contains unrecognizable content. The only

Name	▼	Size	Type	Date Modified
app_MixpanelAPI.Images.DecideChecker		4.1 kB	folder	2017-02-25 19:10:26
app_MixpanelAPI.Images.ViewCrawler		4.1 kB	folder	2017-02-25 19:10:26
app_webview		4.1 kB	folder	2017-02-25 19:10:26
cache		4.1 kB	folder	2017-02-25 19:10:26
code_cache		4.1 kB	folder	2017-02-25 19:10:26
databases		4.1 kB	folder	2017-02-25 19:10:26
files		4.1 kB	folder	2017-02-25 19:10:26
shared_prefs		4.1 kB	folder	2017-02-25 19:10:26
lib		39 bytes	unknown	2017-02-25 19:08:07

Fig. 2. Directories in Fitbit app data

file with content that makes sense to a human is the plaintext file "gaClientId" which holds a 36 character hyphen-separated hexadecimal string.

The last and most notable directory is "databases". This directory contains pairs of files where one file is an SQLite3 database and the other contains the name of the database file with the text "-journal" appended to the end of the file name. Some of the names of these SQLite3 databases are as follows: "activity_db", "exercise_db", "fitbit_db", "heart_rate_db", and "mobile_track_db". The full listing of the database directory is in Fig. 3.

The names of columns in the tables of the databases indicate that the databases hold metadata. There are several columns for timestamps including creation time, time updated, start time, and stop time. Other columns hold various identification values such as server ID, session ID, and UUID. Some of the tables also include information about certain kinds of activities, such as thresholds. For example, Fig. 4 shows the contents of "activity_db".

Similarly, "heart_rate_db" contains thresholds for differing levels of activity, except "heart_rate_db" actually has data describing the amount of time spent in each of the ranges and the amount of calories burned, but it is unclear why several records contain duplicate ranges with different times spent in the ranges. There are no associated timestamps with the records to possibly explain this as different results for different days.

Manual investigation of all database files indicates that none of the databases contains any information about the actual times when different levels of activity were recorded. As such, there is no information on the phone that allows us to determine when vigorous activity occurred.

5.2   Discussion

It is not immediately clear why the phone contains no useful data about the actual activities performed by the user. Given that the fitbit itself does in fact have the activity data, there are several possibilities. It may be the case that the Fitbit app simply does not store such data on the phone by default. Instead,

Name	▼	Size	Type	Date Modified
activity_db		57.3 kB	SQLite3 database	2017-02-25 19:08:06
activity_db-journal		53.9 kB	unknown	2017-02-25 19:08:06
challenges		323.6 kB	SQLite3 database	2017-02-25 19:08:06
challenges-shm		4.1 kB	unknown	2017-02-25 19:08:06
challenges-wal		0 bytes	plain text document	2017-02-25 19:08:06
com.fitbit.FitbitMobile.devmetrics		24.6 kB	SQLite3 database	2017-02-25 19:08:06
com.fitbit.FitbitMobile.devmetrics-journal		62.1 kB	unknown	2017-02-25 19:08:06
exercise_db		77.8 kB	SQLite3 database	2017-02-25 19:08:06
exercise_db-journal		78.5 kB	unknown	2017-02-25 19:08:06
fibit-swap-db		32.8 kB	SQLite3 database	2017-02-25 19:08:06
fibit-swap-db-journal		29.2 kB	unknown	2017-02-25 19:08:06
fitbit_analytics		24.6 kB	SQLite3 database	2017-02-25 19:08:06
fitbit_analytics-journal		29.2 kB	unknown	2017-02-25 19:08:06
fitbit-db		196.6 kB	SQLite3 database	2017-02-25 19:08:06
fitbit-db-journal		209.8 kB	unknown	2017-02-25 19:08:06
food_db		929.8 kB	SQLite3 database	2017-02-25 19:08:06
food_db-journal		524.3 kB	unknown	2017-02-25 19:08:06
google_analytics_v4.db		28.7 kB	SQLite3 database	2017-02-25 19:08:06
google_analytics_v4.db-journal		8.7 kB	unknown	2017-02-25 19:08:06
heart_rate_db		20.5 kB	SQLite3 database	2017-02-25 19:08:06
heart_rate_db-journal		25.1 kB	unknown	2017-02-25 19:08:06
logging_db		77.8 kB	SQLite3 database	2017-02-25 19:08:06
logging_db-journal		74.4 kB	unknown	2017-02-25 19:08:06
mixpanel		65.5 kB	SQLite3 database	2017-02-25 19:08:06
mixpanel-journal		58.0 kB	unknown	2017-02-25 19:08:06
mobile_track_db		24.6 kB	SQLite3 database	2017-02-25 19:08:06
mobile_track_db-journal		21.0 kB	unknown	2017-02-25 19:08:06
social_db		163.8 kB	SQLite3 database	2017-02-25 19:08:06
social_db-journal		156.5 kB	unknown	2017-02-25 19:08:06

Fig. 3. Database directory

this data may bestored on Fitbit's servers, and the phone app is only used to retrieve simple metadata about activities.

It could also be the case that rooting the device caused synced data to be damaged or overwritten. With some models of phone, it is actually possible to use the Cellebrite UFED to obtain application data form an unrooted device. However, that approach did not work in our test case.

In any event, using standard mobile forensic tools, we were unable to find any useful data on the phone for an investigation. It may be the case that this is not true for other brands on wearable fitness trackers. It may also be the case that the Fitbit data could in fact be retrieved through JTAG or Chip-off.

Despite the results of this case study, we certainly expect that, for some phones and some wearable fitness trackers, we will be able to obtain useful data about activity levels with timestamps. The point of this study is not, therefore, to reject the utility of this approach. Instead, the point of this paper is to demonstrate a viable methodology for studying the investigative potential of fitness tracker data for activity detection. The methodology here is experimental: we need to first produce behaviour that replicates a criminal activity, and then we use forensic tools to dtermine if that behaviour can be detected. Once we are able to detect our "fake" criminal activity, then we can try to determine how closely our fake activity resembles a real violent act. As such, this is a long term project, and we are just at the outset.

Fig. 4. Database directory

6 Activity Detection

6.1 Revisiting the Case Study

The case study presented here failed for technological reasons, as the phone did not record activity from the device. However, even if the phone had collects the data, there is an empirical question about the degree of granularity that we can expect from the device. Activity recognition on the Fitbit basically operates by matching the information recorded with an "expected" profile for different activities. For example, *aerobic* activity can be distinguished from *sport* activity by looking at fluctuating heart rates and accelerations.

Activity matching in this manner requires a characteristic set of a data for a given activity. We can then compare the sensed movements with the characteristic set; if it is close, then we can conclude that the given activity was taking place. There are two problems here. First, the precise notion of "close" for activity recognition is not clear. Second, we essentially need to know the activity that we are looking for in advance.

The notion of determining "closeness" is actually a question of statistical variation; there are known methods for addressing this problem. The second problem is an empirical one. If we want to get a profile for a given activity, how can we do it? The case study here suggests a simple solution: we simply replicate the action on a new device.

6.2 A Methodology for Investigation

The preceding discussion suggests a methodology for using Fitbit data in a criminal investigation. Given that an event has taken place, involving a suspect wearing a Fitbit:

1. Retrieve all available data from the suspect's device and paired hardware.
2. Generate a hypothesis *h* about what actually occurred in the crime under investigation.

3. Recreate the physical activity described in h, with a collection of actors wearing the same Fitbit.
4. Perform a similarity comparison between the suspect's device data and the data obtained from the actors.

At step (1), we address all technological and legal issues related to gathering the activity data collected by the wearable device. Step (2) is essentially traditional investigation; based on any available information about the crime, we come up with a possible explanation. Step (3) is essentially what we have outlined in our case study. By replicating the physical performance of a given crime, we can get an activity profile for that crime. The final step is a statistical matching. The evidence provided by this step is similar to DNA evidence, in a sense. We are able to conclude some level of certainty in the activity matching, based on the data.

We remark that repeatedly performing recreations of physical acts is a difficult process. It would certainly be better over time to collect activity profiles for different criminal acts that are resilient to small variation. In this manner, we would be able to use device data to identify activity without the costly recreation process. Better yet, using Machine Learning techniques, we should be able to learn the profiles for different activities without specifically labelling them. However, this requitres a great deal of data that is not currently available. Moreover, in terms of a criminal investigatino, it would be more convincing to demonstrate close correlation with a specific story rather than a complicated mathematical explanation.

7   Conclusion

This study attempted to find potential forensic evidence originating from a Fitbit tracker that was worn during a simulated attack. The reason for this study was to contribute to the field of digital forensics and benefit forensic investigators by exploring the potentials for new digital devices such as fitness trackers to provide data that is useful as evidence in an investigation. To acquire the data from the Fitbit, an Android smartphone synced with the fitness tracker via the official Fitbit app and the Android device was rooted and forensically imaged with EnCase. The Fitbit app data located at "/data/com.fitbit.FitbitMobile/" was exported from the images and the files contained within were analyzed. Among the exported files were preferences saved in XML format, cache files, and SQLite 3 databases. Although the SQLite database files were named appropriately for some given tracking feature of the Fitbit, they did not contain very useful information or sometimes did not contain any information at all. Therefore, this study finds no useful evidence present on the Android smartphone.

While the case study experiment did not obtain useful information, in future work in this area could extract the data straight from the Fitbit by performing a Chip-off or JTAG technique to skip using a smartphone entirely and give the best chances at obtaining the device data. In addition, other Fitbit trackers could be tested since several different types are available and this study used one of the higher-end models. A final area of further study would be analyzing other brands of fitness trackers as other companies would most likely design their product differently and other kinds of data could be extracted and the success of syncing with a smartphone to obtain data may be different with these other brands as well.

Significantly, the case study suggests an approach to using wearable devices in an investigation. By replicating criminal activities and performing statistical analysis, we should be able to determine with great confidence if the wearer of a device was performing a given activity. This information could surely be useful in a criminal investigation.

References

1. Adams, P.S., Keyserling, W.M.: Three methods for measuring range of motion while wearing protective clothing: a comparative study. Int. J. Ind. Ergon. **12**(3), 177–191 (1993)
2. De Pessemier, T., Martens, L.: Heart rate monitoring, activity recognition, and recommendation for e-coaching. Multimed. Tools Appl. **77**(18), 23317–23334 (2018)
3. Jo, E., Lewis, K., Directo, D., Kim, M.J., Dolezal, B.A.: Validation of biofeedback wearables for photoplethysmographic heart rate tracking. J. Sports Sci. Med. **15**(3), 540–547 (2016)
4. Kanitthika, K., Soochan, K., Kaewkannate, K., Kim, S.: A comparison of wearable fitness devices. BMC Public Health **16**, 1–16 (2016)
5. Loeffler, C.E.: Detecting gunshots using wearable accelerometers. PLoS One **9**(9), 1–6 (2014)
6. Sasaki, J.E., et al.: Validation of the Fitbit wireless activity tracker for prediction of energy expenditure. J. Phys. Act Health **12**(2), 149–154 (2015)
7. Shcherbina, A., et al.: Accuracy in wrist-worn, sensor-based measurements of heart rate and energy expenditure in a diverse cohort. J. Pers. Med. **7**(2), 3 (2017)
8. Sushames, A., Edwards, A., Thompson, F., McDermott, R., Gebel, K.: Validity and reliability of fitbit flex for step count, moderate to vigorous physical activity and activity energy expenditure. PLoS One **11**(9), 1–14 (2016)
9. Thiebaud, R.S., et al.: Validity of wrist-worn consumer products to measure heart rate and energy expenditure. Digit. Health **4** 2018
10. Wallen, M.P., Gomersall, S.R., Keating, S.E., Wisloff, U., Coombes, J.S.: Accuracy of heart rate watches: implications for weight management. PLoS One **11**(5), 1–11 (2016)

Authentication of Skyline Query over Road Networks

Xiaoyu Zhu[1], Jie Wu[2], Wei Chang[3], Guojun Wang[4(✉)], and Qin Liu[5]

[1] School of Information Science and Engineering, Central South University,
Changsha 410083, China
[2] Center for Networked Computing, Temple University, Philadelphia, PA 19122, USA
[3] Department of Computer Science, Saint Joseph's University, Philadelphia,
PA 19131, USA
[4] School of Computer Science and Technology, Guangzhou University,
Guangzhou 510006, China
csgjwang@gmail.com
[5] School of Computer Science and Electronic Engineering, Hunan University,
Changsha 410082, China

Abstract. With the increase of location-aware and Internet-capable mobile handset devices, location-based services (LBSs) have experienced an explosive growth in recent years. To scale up services, location-based service providers (LBSPs) outsource data management to third-party cloud service providers (CSPs), which in turn provide data query services to users on behalf of LBSPs. However, the CSPs cannot be trusted, which may return incorrect or incomplete query results to users, intentionally or not. Skyline query is an important kind of query, which asks for the data that is not spatially dominated by any other data. Therefore, enabling users to authenticate skyline query results is essential for outsourced LBSs. In this paper, we propose an authentication solution to support location-based skyline query. By embedding each data with its skyline neighbors in the data's signature, our solution allows users to efficiently verify the soundness and completeness of location-based skyline query results. Through theoretical analysis, we demonstrate the effectiveness of our proposed solution.

Keywords: Data outsourcing · Query authentication
Skyline query · LBSP · Road network

1 Introduction

With the explosive growth of mobile handset devices, such as smartphones and tablet computers, location-based services (LBSs) attract increasing attention from both research and industry communities. Mobile users carrying location-aware and Internet-capable mobile devices are able to perform queries to learn about points of interests (POIs) anywhere and at any time. As the adoption of cloud computing increases, which provides LBSs an efficient way to outsource

© Springer Nature Switzerland AG 2018
G. Wang et al. (Eds.): SpaCCS 2018, LNCS 11342, pp. 72–83, 2018.
https://doi.org/10.1007/978-3-030-05345-1_6

POI datasets and various data queries to third-party cloud service providers (CSPs). Outsourcing POI searching to third-party CSPs provides a cost-effective way to support large scale data storage and query processing.

As one important class among various types of location-based queries, location-based skyline queries (LBSQs) [1–3] ask for the POIs that are not dominated by any other POI with respect to a given query position, and we say one POI dominates another if the former is both closer to the query position and preferable in the numeric attribute of interest. In Fig. 1, a POI is characterized by a location and a price, such as o_1's location and price are 1 and 2, respectively. We say one POI dominates another if the former is both cheaper. For example, o_4 dominates o_3 because o_4 is both closer to q and cheaper than o_3. We can observe that the LBSQ results are unpredictable, because as the query position moves, the POIs' distance to the query position changes.

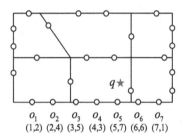

$$
\begin{array}{ccccccc}
o_1 & o_2 & o_3 & o_4 & o_5 & o_6 & o_7 \\
(1,2) & (2,4) & (3,5) & (4,3) & (5,7) & (6,6) & (7,1)
\end{array}
$$

Fig. 1. An example of road network.

Due to security concerns, query-result integrity needs be protected against possibly dishonest CSPs. The CSPs may return incorrect results for a variety of reasons. For example, the CSPs may manipulate LBSP's POI dataset or return biased results in favor of POIs willing to pay. In addition, the CSPs may opt to return incomplete results in order to save computation resources, or they may return overly large results so that the CSPs can charge fees for the communication bandwidth. Hence, it is vital to provide users a capability to authenticate query results to ensure the authenticity and completeness. Results are authentic if every result appears in the original POI datasets and are complete if all the skyline POIs are included in the query results.

Most recently, Chen et al. [4] proposed a LBSQ authentication method in which the POIs are modeled as distributed over a road network. However, Chen's solutions still have several limitations. Firstly, the data preprocess is complex. The LBSP needs to preprocess the dataset, generate the skyline neighbor set and skyline neighbor range, and then generate MHT for query verification. Secondly, the query process has a high computation overhead. The dataset is first divided into two subsets, then CSP do skyline query three times on the dataset and its two subsets respectively. Finally, the size of the verification object is large, each skyline result contains an auxiliary set for verification.

In this paper, we propose a novel method to solve the LBSQ authentication problem: our method enables simple data preprocess, efficient skyline query and lower communication overhead.

The contributions of this paper are summarized as follows:

- We propose a novel authentication solution to verify skyline query in road network. Our method supports efficient skyline neighbor generation process and each record is chained with its distance neighbors and skyline neighbors.
- Our method supports efficient data query process and small communication overhead from LBSP to CSP and from CSP to user.
- We give the performance analysis, which shows the effectiveness and efficiency of our method.

The remains of the paper is organized as follows: Sect. 2 summarizes the related work. Section 3 presents the problem formulation. Section 4 describes the details of our proposed solution. Section 5 presents the security analysis and overhead analysis. Finally, Sect. 6 concludes our paper.

2   Related Work

Query authentication has been studied extensively. Most studies [5–8] are based on either Merkle Hash Tree (MH-tree) [5] or signature chain [6]. In signature chain, each data in the dataset is signed by the data owner, while the signatures of results and non-result boundaries are returned to the client. Various types of queries have been studied, including range queries [9,10], spatial top-k queries [11–13], multi-dimensional top-k queries [14,15], kNN queries [8,16], shortest-path queries [17], skyline queries [4,18,19] etc. It is common to let the data owner outsource both its dataset and its signatures of the dataset to the service provider, which returns both the query result and a VO computed from the signatures for the querying user to verify query integrity.

The skyline query can be widely adopted in information retrieval [20–22], searchable encryption [23–25], system monitoring [26], resource allocation [27], and etc. References [4,18,19,28] are the most related work targeting verifiable outsourced skyline query processing via untrusted CSPs. In [18,19], Lin et al. presented several schemes based on a data structure called Merkle Skyline R-tree assumed that the POIs are distributed in a general 2D plane. Recently, Chen et al. [4] proposed a LBSQ authentication method which is more practical in real situations, the POIs are modeled as distributed over a road network rather than a 2D plane. However, their work returns large verification objects, incurs high communication overhead. Our work aims at decreasing the communication cost in LBSQ authentication methods.

3   Models and Problem Formulation

In this section, we introduce our system model, the definition of LBSQ, and problem formulation.

3.1   System Model

Our system model involves three types of parties: LBSP, CSP, and data user. The general setting works as follows: First, the LBSP makes some pre-computation on the POI dataset and computes the dataset's signatures S. Second, the LBSP uploads the POI dataset and their signatures to the CSP. Third, a user sends a skyline query to the CSP, and the CSP computes the results, a verification object and sends both of them back to the user. Finally, the user verifies the soundness and completeness.

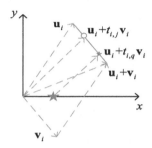

Fig. 2. Representation of a road segment. (Color figure online)

The dataset $\mathcal{O}$ contains a set of POIs of the same category, e.g., hotel, and each POI is characterized by its location and one numeric attribute (e.g., price). We adopt the similar settings with Chen's [4]. As shown in Fig. 1, the POIs reside in a road network is represented by a planar graph $G = (\mathbb{V}, \mathbb{E})$, where $\mathbb{V}$ is the set of vertices, and $E = \{e_1, \cdots, e_m\}$ is the set of road segments. The representative red road segment and POI are e_i and $o_{i,j}$, and the query position is denoted as q. As shown in Fig. 2, we use $\{e_i = u_i + t v_i\}$ to denote the segment, where $\boldsymbol{u}_i, \boldsymbol{v}_i \in \mathbb{R}^2$ are two reference vectors, $\boldsymbol{u}_i$ and $\boldsymbol{u}_i + \boldsymbol{v}_i$ are two end points.

The dataset is denoted as $\mathcal{O} = \bigcup_{i=1}^m \mathcal{O}_i$, where $\mathcal{O}_i$ is the set of POIs in road segment e_i. Assume there are n_i POIs in road e_i, and we use $o_{i,j}$ to denote the jth POI in road e_i. Each POI can be represented as $o_{i,j} = \{t_{i,j}, \lambda_{i,j}\}$, where $t_{i,j}$ is $o_{i,j}$'s relative position with respect to road e_i, $\lambda_{i,j}$ is the numeric attribute of interest. The query q can be projected on segment e_i and its relative position is denoted as $t_{i,q}$. We assume that a POI only belongs to one road segment, and the POIs are at different positions and have different numerical values.

3.2   Location-Based Skyline Query

Assuming that a lower numeric attribute (e.g., price) is preferable, we now give the definitions for spatial dominance and location-based skyline query.

Definition 1 (Distance). For any two POIs $o_{i,j}$ and $o_{i',j'}$ in one road segment e_i, the distance between $o_{i,j}$ and $o_{i',j'}$ is denoted as $d(o_{i,j}, o_{i',j'}) = |t_{i,j} - t_{i',j'}|$.

Definition 2 (Query distance). For a POI $o_{i,j}$ in road segment e_i, the query distance between query position q and POI $o_{i,j}$ is denoted as $d(q, o_{i,j}) = |t_{i,j} - t_{i,q}|$.

Definition 3 (Dominance). For any two POIs $o_{i,j}$ and $o_{i',j'}$ in one road segment e_i, we say $o_{i,j}$ spatially dominates $o_{i',j'}$ with respect to query position q if and only if $d(q, o_{i,j}) \leq d(q, o_{i',j'})$ and $\lambda_{i,j} \leq \lambda_{i',j'}$ but the two equalities do not both hold.

Definition 4 (Location-based skyline query). A location-based skyline query $sky(O|q)$ asks for the POIs that are not spatially dominated by any other POI in O with respect to q.

3.3   Problem Formulation

Assume a user submits a LBSQ query $\langle q, I \rangle$ to the CSP where $q \in \mathbb{R}^2$ is the query position and $I \subseteq \{1, \cdots, m\}$ is a set of indexes of road segments $E = \{e_1, \cdots, e_m\}$. After receiving $\langle q, I \rangle$ from the user, the CSP returns the results $sky(O|q)$, where $O = \bigcup_{i \in I} \mathcal{O}_i$.

The LBSP is assumed trusted; however, the CSP is considered untrusted due to a variety of reasons. For example, the CSP may modify LBSP's POI dataset, forge non-existent POI records, return some results that are not skyline records, or omit some skyline records.

Our security goal is to offer approaches for authenticating LBSQ queries. In our setting, we consider the CSP is dishonest and may present to the user a tampered result. Our proposed solutions can allow the user to verify the soundness and completeness of the query results.

Soundness: The user can verify that all qualifying data records returned are correct. They have not been tampered with nor have spurious data records been introduced.

Completeness: The user can verify that the results covers all the qualifying skyline POI records.

4   Basic Solution

In this section, we introduce the basic solution for verifiable LBSQ processing via an untrusted CSP.

4.1   Properties of LBSQ

We adopt Proposition 1 from [4].

Proposition 1. Let $\mathcal{O}$ be the set of POIs distributed along road segment $e = \{u + tv\}$. For any query position $q \in \mathbb{R}^2$, we have

$$sky(\mathcal{O}|q) = sky(\mathcal{O}|t_q). \tag{1}$$

In other words, $sky(\mathcal{O}|q)$ is determined by the query q's relative position t_q, where t_q is defined as

$$t_q = \frac{v^T(q-u)}{||v||_2^2} \tag{2}$$

Figure 3(a) shows 7 POIs on a road segment, where all POIs are distributed along a road segment, and the x- and y-coordinates represent each POI's relative position and numeric attribute, respectively. Each POI o_i can be represented by its numerical value λ_i and relative position t_i. For example, $o_1 = (1,2)$, where 1 and 2 are the o_1's relative position and numerical value, respectively. The query position's relative position is $t_q = 5$. Figure 3(b) shows the LBSQ results for q, where $d(q, o_i) = |t_i - t_q|$ represents the query distance, and the LBSQ results are $sky(\mathcal{O}|q) = \{o_5, o_4, o_7\}$. The other POIs are dominated by the POI in $sky(\mathcal{O}|q)$, for example, o_6 is dominated by o_4, o_3 is dominated by o_7.

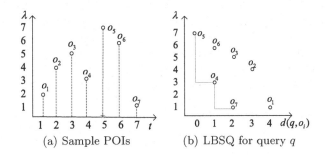

(a) Sample POIs   (b) LBSQ for query q

Fig. 3. LBSQ results.

We give a formal description of the properties of LBSQ. Without loss of generality, for a given query q, we assume that there are u results $\{o_1, o_2, \cdots, o_u\}$, where $o_i = (t_i, \lambda_i)$ is the ith result. Which are ordered by query distance $d(q, o_1) < d(q, o_2) < \cdots < d(q, o_u)$. The LBSQ results have the following properties:

- The LBSQ results can also be ordered based on the numerical attribute, $\lambda_1 > \lambda_2 > \cdots > \lambda_u$.
- o_1 should be a POI with the smallest query distance for all $o_i \in \mathcal{O}$.
- o_u should be the POI with the smallest numerical value for all $o_i \in \mathcal{O}$, and it has no skyline neighbors.
- For every adjacent pair (o_x, o_{x+1}), $x \in [1, u-1]$, o_{x+1} is the closest POI towards the query position in the subset under o_x, represented as $d(q, o_{x+1}) \le d(q, o_j)$ for all o_j in $\mathcal{O}_x^- = \{o_i | \lambda_i < \lambda_x, o_i \in \mathcal{O}\}$.

Based on these properties, for each POI o_i, our method finds the first skyline result by finding the POI having the smallest query distance, and then continue to find the next result, the next result's numerical value is smaller and its query distance is smallest in all candidate POIs.

In the following subsection, we define distance neighbor to find the closest POI to the query position, which has smallest query distance. We define skyline neighbor to find the next skyline result, which has smallest query distance in all POIs whose numerical value is smaller than the previous result.

4.2   Distance and Skyline Neighbor

Definition 5 (Distance neighbor). For any $o_i \in \mathcal{O}$, we define that its left (or right) distance neighbor with respect to relative position denoted by $N_l(o_i)$ (or $N_r(o_i)$), as the closest POI $o_j \in \mathcal{O}$ with $t_j < t_i$ (or $t_j > t_i$).

For each POI o_i, its distance neighbors are two POIs having smallest distance with o_i on its left and right sides. For each POI $o_i \in \mathcal{O}$, o_i's query distance is computed as $d(q, o_i) = |t_i - t_q|$.

We define the closest POI towards the query position on this segment as o_{min} if $d(q, o_{min}) = min\{d(q, o_i) | o_i \in \mathcal{O}\}$. The left and right distance neighbor of o_{min} are denoted as $N_l(o_{min})$ and $N_r(o_{min})$, respectively.

Note that only the closest POI o_{min}'s query distance is not larger than its both left and right distance neighbors' query distance for all POIs in the same road segment, which is described as $d(q, o_{min}) \leq d(q, N_l(o_{min}))$ and $d(q, o_{min}) \leq d(q, N_r(o_{min}))$.

For each POI o_i, we divide $\mathcal{O}$ into two subsets according to t_i as

$$
\begin{aligned}
\mathcal{O}_l^- &= \{o_j | o_j \in \mathcal{O}, \lambda_j < \lambda_i, t_j < t_i\} \\
\mathcal{O}_r^- &= \{o_j | o_j \in \mathcal{O}, \lambda_j < \lambda_i, t_j > t_i\}
\end{aligned} \tag{3}
$$

Definition 6 (Skyline neighbor). For any $o_i \in \mathcal{O}$, we define its left (or right) skyline neighbor in subset $\mathcal{O}_l^-$ (or $\mathcal{O}_r^-$), denoted by $N_l^-(o_i)$ (or $N_r^-(o_i)$), as the closest POI $o_j \in \mathcal{O}_l^-$ (or $o_j \in \mathcal{O}_r^-$) according to relative position.

For each POI o_i, its skyline neighbors are two POIs chosen from POIs with a numeric attribute smaller than o_i's numerical attribute, meanwhile the skyline neighbors have smallest distance with o_i on its left and right sides.

4.3   Data Preprocessing

The LBSP preprocesses its POI dataset $\mathcal{O} = \{o_i | 1 \leq i \leq n\}$ before outsourcing it to the CSP, where $o_i = (t_i, \lambda_i)$. Without loss of generality, we assume that $t_1 < t_2 < \cdots < t_n$.

For every POI record $o_i, i \in [1, n]$, the LBSP computes the distance neighbors $N_l(o_i), N_r(o_i)$ and skyline neighbors $N_l^-(o_i), N_r^-(o_i)$. If the left or right neighbor does not exist, then assign null as its neighbor.

LBSP creates a signature for $o_i, i \in [1, n]$ by chaining o_i with its four neighbors:

$$
\begin{aligned}
s(o_i) = &Sig(H(H(o_i)|H(N_l(o_i))|H(N_r(o_i)) \\
&|H(N_l^-(o_i))|H(N_r^-(o_i))))
\end{aligned} \tag{4}
$$

Here, $H(\cdot)$ is a hash function, and Sig is a signature generation algorithm. The total number of signatures is n. Then LBSP sends the POI dataset $\mathcal{O}$ and signatures S to the CSP.

4.4   Query Processing

Assume that the user issues an LBSQ $sky(\mathcal{O}|t_q)$. The CSP constructs the query result as follow.

- Compute t_q from q as in Eq. (1).
- For every $o_i \in \mathcal{O}$, find the closest POI point o_{min} with query position, which has the minimum distance $d(q, o_{min})$; Select o_{min} as the first skyline result, put o_{min} into $sky(\mathcal{O}|t_q)$, set the skyline result o_j equal to o_{min}. If there are two POIs having the minimum distance, then choose the one with a smaller numerical value.
- Put the skyline result o_j into $sky(\mathcal{O}|t_q)$, find the next skyline result from o_j's two candidate skyline neighbors; Select the POI with a smaller query distance from $N_l^-(o_j)$ and $N_r^-(o_j)$ and set it as the next result o_j. If two skyline neighbors have the same distances, then choose the one with a smaller numerical value, as the skyline neighbor with smaller numerical value dominates the other one.
- Repeat the previous step until o_j has no skyline neighbor.
- For each $o_i \in sky(\mathcal{O}|t_q)$, the CSP returns its neighbors $N_l^-(o_i)$, $N_r^-(o_i)$, $N_l(o_i)$ and $N_r(o_i)$ and its signature $s(o_i)$.

4.5   Query Result Verification

On receiving the query results from the CSP, the user verifies the results' authenticity and completeness. Without loss of generality, assume that the query results are $\{o_1, \cdots, o_u\}$, where $d(q, o_1) < d(q, o_2) < \cdots < d(q, o_u)$. The verification object contains all the signatures of results, $\{s(o_1), \cdots, s(o_u)\}$, and the distance and skyline neighbors of results, $\{N_l(o_1), N_r(o_1), N_l^-(o_1), N_r^-(o_1), \cdots\}$.

During authenticity verification, for each $x \in [1, u]$; since its neighbors are in the query result, the user uses them to compute its signature $s(o_x)$. If the query result is authentic, the user proceeds to check the completeness of the query result in the following three steps.

First, user checks whether o_1 is the closest POI to query position by checking if $d(q, o_1) \leq d(q, N_l(o_1))$ and $d(q, o_1) \leq d(q, N_r(o_1))$, as only the closest POI's distance to query position is not greater than its both neighbors' distance. If there are two same minimum distances, then check the numerical value. If $d(q, o_1) = d(q, N_l(o_1))$, then $\lambda_1 < \lambda(N_l(o_1))$. If $d(q, o_1) = d(q, N_r(o_1))$, then $\lambda_1 < \lambda(N_r(o_1))$. Second, user verifies that o_u is the last POI by checking whether o_u's numeric value λ_u is equal to λ_{min}.

Third, user checks every pair of adjacent POIs in $\{o_1, \cdots, o_u\}$ are indeed skyline neighbors of each other with respect to query position t_q using its neighbors. Specifically, for every $o_x, x \in [1, u-1]$, the user checks its next neighbor o_{x+1} with its skyline neighbors $N_l^-(o_x)$ and $N_r^-(o_x)$. If $N_l^-(o_x)$ is equal to o_{x+1}, then check if $d(q, N_l^-(o_x)) < d(q, N_r^-(o_x))$, or if $d(q, N_l^-(o_x)) = d(q, N_r^-(o_x))$ and $\lambda(N_l^-(o_1)) < \lambda(N_r^-(o_1))$. If $N_r^-(o_x)$ is equal to o_{x+1}, then check if $d(q, N_r^-(o_x)) < d(q, N_l^-(o_x))$, or if $d(q, N_l^-(o_x)) = d(q, N_r^-(o_x))$ and $\lambda(N_r^-(o_1)) < \lambda(N_l^-(o_1))$. If any POI does not pass the verification, the query result is considered incomplete. If all the verifications succeed, the user considers the query result as complete and incomplete otherwise.

5   Performance Analysis

In this section, we study the performance of the proposed solutions through security, comparison with Chen's and overhead analysis.

5.1   Security Analysis

We prove that the proposed skyline query authentication scheme can achieve the security goals as follows. Let $sky(\mathcal{O}|t_q) = \{o_1, \cdots, o_u\}$ be the query results, where $d(q, o_1) < d(q, o_2) < \cdots < d(q, o_u)$.

We first discuss the case in which $sky(\mathcal{O}|t_q)$ is not sound: As for an adversary, in order to change the value of a record, he must be able to generate the corresponding signature. However, it is computationally infeasible without knowing the private key of LBSP.

Then we discuss three cases in which $sky(\mathcal{O}|t_q)$ is not complete:

Case 1: If the initial result o_1 is forged, then the adversary must forge a fake POI o_1', its distance neighbors $N_l(o_1')$ and $N_r(o_1')$ and its signature $s(o_1')$, which satisfy $d(q, o_1') < d(q, N_l(o_1'))$ and $d(q, o_1') < d(q, N_r(o_1'))$. However, there is only one record o_1 in the road segment which satisfies this requirement; it is computationally infeasible to compute $s(o_1')$ without knowing the private key of LBSP.

Case 2: The end result o_u is forged. The adversary must forge a fake POI o_u' whose numerical attribute is λ_{min} and its signature $s(o_u')$. It is computationally infeasible to compute $s(o_u')$ without knowing the private key of LBSP.

Case 3: Two contiguous records o_x and o_{x+1} in $sky(\mathcal{O}|t_q)$ are not skyline neighbors. Since every o_x, $x \in [1, u - 1]$, its signature $s(o(x))$ contains its candidate skyline neighbors $\{N_l^-(o_x), N_r^-(o_x)\}$, the adversary cannot forge a fake POI $o_{x+1}' \notin \{N_l^-(o_x), N_r^-(o_x)\}$. Suppose $o_{x+1} = N_l^-(o_x)$, the user can further check if $d(q, o_{x+1}) < d(q, N_r^-(o_x))$. Any fake o_{x+1}' will be detected by the user.

5.2   Comparison with Chen's

We illustrate the processes of the benchmark method in [4] (denoted by Chen's) using Fig. 3(a) as an example.

In data preprocessing process, for each POI, the LBSP needs to issue a LBSQ to obtain the POI's skyline neighbor set, and each POI binds with its candidate skyline neighbors.

In query process, if $t_q = t_5$, the CSP issues three LBSQs and obtains results $sky(\mathcal{O}^-|t_q) = \{o_1, o_4, o_5\}$, $sky(\mathcal{O}^+|t_q) = \{o_6, o_7\}$ and $sky(\mathcal{O}|t_q) = \{o_4, o_5, o_7\}$. Then it returns $\bigcup_{o_i \in sky(\mathcal{O}^-|t_q) \cup sky(\mathcal{O}^+|t_q)} \mathcal{T}_i$, where $\mathcal{T}_i$ is the set of non-leaf nodes required along with the leaf node o_i to compute the Merkle root hash.

In query result verification process, for each $o_i \in \{o_1, o_4, o_5, o_6, o_7\}$, the user uses $\mathcal{T}_i$ to compute the Merkle root hash. The user also needs to check whether all the results are indeed skyline neighbors, in addition, it checks that every $o_i \in \{o_1, o_6\}$ is indeed dominated by some other returned POI, and every $o_i \in \{o_4, o_5, o_7\}$ is indeed not dominated by any other returned POI.

We can observe from the examples that Chen's methods have some limitations. Each POI record is bound with its candidate skyline neighbors which can up to $n - 1$, while our method's neighbors is 4. Meanwhile, Chen's needs 3 skyline query in query process, while our method is much simpler, meanwhile our results and verification object are smaller than theirs.

5.3 Overhead

We analyze the overhead introduced by the proposed technique on the LBSP, the CSP, and the user side, respectively, and we compare our methods with Chen's methods.

(1) LBSP Overhead: In the data preprocess, Chen's methods need to generate skyline neighbor set and skyline neighbor range for each POI, which takes $O(n)$ skyline query operations, and the skyline query incurs high computation overhead. While our methods do not need to do the skyline query in data preprocess and our skyline neighbor generation process is simpler than Chen's methods.

In addition, in Chen's methods, the LBSP generates a MHT as the authentication structure, which needs 1 signature generation and $O(n)$ hash computation, then the LBSP outsources 1 signature and $O(n)$ digests to CSP. Our solution's main cost is related to the number of the signatures, which is proportional to the cardinality of POI dataset n. The computation and communication cost of our solution is $O(n)$. Since MHT and signature chain are two different authentication structures.

(2) CSP Overhead: In our methods, the CSP compares n POI's distance to the query position and chooses the minimum one as the first result. Then it finds the next skyline neighbor subsequently, which takes $o(n)$ comparisons. The remaining cost comes from constructing the verification object and sending it to users. The verification object contains $O(k)$ signatures and $4k$ neighbors, where k is the number of query results. In Chen's, the CSP needs to do 3 skyline query for n POI, which takes $o(n^2)$ comparisons. The verification object contains 1 signature and $k' log n$ digests, where k' is the number of query results, which is larger than k. Thus, Chen's query cost and VO size are larger than our solution.

(3) User Overhead: In our methods, user takes k signature verify operation in verification process, while Chen's takes 1 signature verify operation and $k' log n$ hash computations.

6 Conclusion

In this paper, we consider the problem of authenticating location-based skyline queries. We propose novel solutions that allow users to verify if the query results are sound and complete. By embedding skyline neighbors with each POI to its signature, our solutions achieve better performance in query process and communication overhead compared with the existing scheme. We prove that without knowing the private key of the data owner, it is computationally infeasible for an adversary to forge query results without being detected. Our extensive performance evaluation shows the proposed solutions are practical and can be used in real-world applications.

Acknowledgments. This work is supported in part by the National Natural Science Foundation of China under Grants 61632009 & 61472451, in part by the Guangdong Provincial Natural Science Foundation under Grant 2017A030308006 and High-Level Talents Program of Higher Education in Guangdong Province under Grant 2016ZJ01, in part by NSF and CSC grants CNS 1629746, CNS 1564128, CNS 1449860, CNS 1461932, CNS 1460971, CNS 1439672, in part by the China Scholarship Council under Grant 201606370141, in part by Hunan Provincial Natural Science Foundation 2017JJ2333.

References

1. Zheng, B., Lee, K.C.K., Lee, W.-C.: Location-dependent skyline query. In: Proceedings of the 9th International Conference on Mobile Data Management, pp. 148–155 (2008)
2. Lee, K.C.K.: Efficient evaluation of location-dependent skyline queries using non-dominance scopes. In: Proceedings of the 2nd International Conference on Computing for Geospatial Research & Applications, p. 14 (2011)
3. Goncalves, M., Torres, D., Perera, G.: Making recommendations using location-based skyline queries. In: Proceedings of the 23rd International Workshop on Database and Expert Systems Applications (DEXA), pp. 111–115 (2012)
4. Chen, W., Liu, M., Zhang, R., Zhang, Y., Liu, S.: Secure outsourced skyline query processing via untrusted cloud service providers. In INFOCOM, pp. 1–9 (2016)
5. Devanbu, P., Gertz, M., Martel, C., Stubblebine, S.G.: Authentic data publication over the internet. J. Comput. Secur. **11**(3), 291–314 (2003)
6. Pang, H.H., Jain, A., Ramamritham, K., Tan, K.-L.: Verifying completeness of relational query results in data publishing. In: ACM SIGMOD, pp. 407–418 (2005)
7. Ku, W.-S., Hu, L., Shahabi, C., Wang, H.: Query integrity assurance of location-based services accessing outsourced spatial databases. In: Mamoulis, N., Seidl, T., Pedersen, T.B., Torp, K., Assent, I. (eds.) SSTD 2009. LNCS, vol. 5644, pp. 80–97. Springer, Heidelberg (2009). https://doi.org/10.1007/978-3-642-02982-0_8
8. Yiu, M.L., Lo, E., Yung, D.: Authentication of moving KNN queries. In ICDE, pp. 565–576 (2011)
9. Yang, Y., Papadopoulos, S., Papadias, D.: Authenticated indexing for outsourced spatial databases. VLDB J. **18**(3), 631–648 (2009)
10. Hu, H., Xu, J., Chen, Q., Yang, Z.: Authenticating location-based services without compromising location privacy. In: ACM SIGMOD, pp. 301–312 (2012)

11. Zhang, R., Zhang, Y., Zhang, C.: Secure top-k query processing via untrusted location-based service providers. In: INFOCOM, pp. 1170–1178 (2012)
12. Chen, Q., Hu, H., Xu, J.: Authenticating top-k queries in location-based services with confidentiality. Proc. VLDB Endow. **7**(1), 49–60 (2013)
13. Zhang, R., Sun, J., Zhang, Y., Zhang, C.: Secure spatial top-k query processing via untrusted location-based service providers. IEEE Trans. Dependable Secure Comput. **12**(1), 111–124 (2015)
14. Yang, G., Cai, Y., Hu, Z.: Authentication of function queries. In: ICDE, pp. 337–348 (2016)
15. Zhu, X., Wu, J., Chang, W., Wang, G., Liu, Q.: Authentication of multi-dimensional top-k query on untrusted server. In: Proceedings of the IEEE/ACM International Symposium on Quality of Service (IWQoS) (2018)
16. Hu, L., Ku, W.-S., Bakiras, S., Shahabi, C.: Spatial query integrity with Voronoi neighbors. IEEE Trans. Knowl. Data Eng. **25**(4), 863–876 (2013)
17. Yiu, M.L., Lin, Y., Mouratidis, K.: Efficient verification of shortest path search via authenticated hints. In: ICDE, pp. 237–248 (2010)
18. Lin, X., Xu, J., Hu, H.: Authentication of location-based skyline queries. In: Proceedings of the 20th ACM International Conference on Information and Knowledge Management, pp. 1583–1588 (2011)
19. Lin, X., Xu, J., Hu, H., Lee, W.-C.: Authenticating location-based skyline queries in arbitrary subspaces. IEEE Trans. Knowl. Data Eng. **26**(6), 1479–1493 (2014)
20. Liu, Q., Wu, S., Pei, S., Wu, J., Peng, T., Wang, G.: Secure and efficient multi-attribute range queries based on comparable inner product encoding. In: 2018 IEEE Conference on Communications and Network Security (CNS), pp. 1–9. IEEE (2018)
21. Zhang, S., Wang, G., Bhuiyan, Md.Z.A., Liu, Q.: A dual privacy preserving scheme in continuous location-based services. IEEE Internet Things J. **5**(5), 4191–4200 (2017)
22. Liu, Q., Wang, G., Li, F., Yang, S., Jie, W.: Preserving privacy with probabilistic indistinguishability in weighted social networks. IEEE Trans. Parallel Distrib. Syst. **28**(5), 1417–1429 (2017)
23. Zhang, Q., Liu, Q., Wang, G.: PRMS: a personalized mobile search over encrypted outsourced data. IEEE Access **6**, 31541–31552 (2018)
24. Zhu, X., Liu, Q., Wang, G.: A novel verifiable and dynamic fuzzy keyword search scheme over encrypted data in cloud computing. In: Trustcom/BigdataSE/ISPA, pp. 845–851 (2017)
25. Liu, Q., Wang, G., Liu, X., Peng, T., Wu, J.: Achieving reliable and secure services in cloud computing environments. Comput. Electric. Eng. **59**, 153–164 (2016)
26. Zheng, H., Chang, W., Wu, J.: Coverage and distinguishability requirements for traffic flow monitoring systems. In: IEEE/ACM 24th International Symposium on Quality of Service, pp. 1–10 (2016)
27. Chang, W., Wu, J.: Progressive or conservative: rationally allocate cooperative work in mobile social networks. IEEE Trans. Parallel Distrib. Syst. **26**(7), 2020–2035 (2015)
28. Lo, H., Ghinita, G.: Authenticating spatial skyline queries with low communication overhead. In: Proceedings of the third ACM Conference on Data and Application Security and Privacy, pp. 177–180 (2013)

A Service Oriented Healthcare Architecture (SOHA-CC) Based on Cloud Computing

Syed Qasim Afser Rizvi, Guojun Wang$^{(\boxtimes)}$, and Jianer Chen

School of Computer Science and Technology, Guangzhou University,
Guangzhou 510006, Guangdong, China
csgjwang@gmail.com

Abstract. Healthcare systems are designed to facilitate the end users in order to maintain the good health and predicting the future trends for safety measures. Most of the systems running right now are assisting the users with the number of services like m-health, e-health. Although, many of the systems are operative, but still a lot of problems are to be addressed. The data related to healthcare industry is extremely sensitive, that could not be altered or edited by any source, and likely many problems of privacy and security are still maintained in the current systems. Though, many systems are still working on the security challenges but they are struggling to resolve the related issues. To secure patients data is the biggest deal to solve. We will try to overcome the problem related to security by proposing a framework, named as Service Oriented Architecture for Health care based on cloud computing (SOHA-CC). This framework contains four layers, specifically, Application layer, Cloud application and Service layer, Network computing layer and, finally Healthcare layer.

Keywords: Healthcare · Cloud computing · Security · Privacy
Architecture

1 Introduction

Health is an important issue to consider, and so is the fabrication of healthcare systems is being done. The healthcare systems are devised to analyse and fix the healthcare issues growing in the environment [26]. They deal with the betterment of the health services such as improving the quality of service, reducing the delay time, early access to emergency situations, reducing the cost. A lot of researches are going on for providing the better health services, but there are lot of diverse issues in the systems that are not related to the health service only [21, 26].

Despite of much difficulties, a lot of systems have been designed in the past and a bunch is running. Healthcare is acquiring importance day by day with the advancement in the information technology [1, 21, 26] modern technologies are being integrated with the traditional systems to make them more efficient.

© Springer Nature Switzerland AG 2018
G. Wang et al. (Eds.): SpaCCS 2018, LNCS 11342, pp. 84–97, 2018.
https://doi.org/10.1007/978-3-030-05345-1_7

Cloud computing and Big Data Analytic are couple of the rising tides currently and in the near future [3,4,14]. Substantial, systems are presently running comprising of the cloud computing and Big Data Analytic for securing the data [21,27]. With amplifying medical data from gigabytes through tera bytes to peta bytes along with a lot of heterogeneity in it, manipulating and analysing such gigantic data is not an easy task. Privacy and security is a great threat with this abundance of the data [8]. This acceleration in the volume and velocity of data disposing it to the extent of big data. Now for analysing and processing such a huge amount of heterogeneous data big data analytic is being utilized [14].

The proposed system is designed to deliver the healthcare services, in the consideration of improving the services to the users. Most of the systems are delivering the services part, but, still considerable issues are dwelling. To overcast these issues of services, we have proposed a framework that emphasizes on refining the services provided to the user. In this framework, we have tried to address this matter at hand by proposing a model constituting of four layers. These layers are designed in a way that it manages the data in a well-organized manner that delivers the services to the end user in a most promising fashion.

This paper is organized in five sections, on-wards with related work progressively next section is the proposed framework leading to analysis and discussion and finally ending with conclusion.

2   Related Work

Bunch of smart system have been developed posterior to the dawn of the information technology. For instance, the National Centre for Bio-computation (NCBC) in alliance with Stanford University School of Medicine and the Department of Surgery, collectively, initiated a project avowed as smart health monitoring system (SHMS) in order to proper a motile tele-medicine mechanism conductive to physiological, experimental and environmental inspection for facilitating NASAs consignment to anthropoid probes [23]. In USA, in 2004 a non-profit Health Information Exchange (HIE), Indiana Health Information Exchange (IHIE) had developed a system which facilitates the hospitals to share the data in order to provide better health support and to provide the secure channel for sharing the patient data [11].

Furthermore, only in 2004 another web-based application was developed in USA known as PatientsLikeMe, this was a platform in which patient shares their experience so that others can improve based on their experience data [25]. In 2005, Sermo was developed as a social networking for the physicians acting as a virtual lounge for the doctors in order to provide pervasive treatment [9]. Furthermore, in 2005, cancer predictive and diagnostic system was derived which had amended the bio-diagnostic decisions but lacks in data integration. Onwards, by Hande et al. [12] a system was created for monitoring ECG, BP (Blood Pressure) and pulse-oximeters remote position. In another system developed by [17] for observing the personalized heart utilizing smart phones and wireless bio sensors. In a while in 2008, an organization, Hong Kong smart health developed a system for decision making and data integration but having shortcomings in the privacy and security. Two systems in UK had executed a collaborative project, specifically, NHS Harefield Hospital and NHS Royal Brompton Hospital [5], deployed a system comprises of SMART Bridgit Collaboration Servers in addition to touch empowered LCDs and software system. This system was designed to provide secure and worthy data collaboration [7]. In 2010, Mayo Clinic implemented an algorithm for image processing in order to analyse brain aneurysms which shows 95% efficiency and substantially enhance the patient outcomes. For such work Mayo clinic was also presented by the reward of leading neurosurgery and neurology hospital in 2016. Another system was designed in China, by the We Doctor Group. It was China's utmost online platform designed for facilitating the users with the online registration, treatment and medical services [13]. It was a great accomplishment simplifying for the patient as they dont have to waste time for consultation and managing to reach the hospital due to the reason that, by gaining the popularity a lot of hospitals nearly 1900 key hospitals embrace the system along with 270 million consultants [13].

Health service improvement system is developed in USA in 2010 proposed by Health Data Initiative (HDI), the main aspiration is to disseminate the medical data and to educate the external users about the value of data, harnessing the potential of the data for improving the healthcare services HDI (2010). A treatment system was designed in Italy, for understanding the clinical divergence within families IOR (2011). In 2011, a collaborative effort was produce by two organizations specifically, AstraZeneca and Healthcare, for experimental analysis regarding chronicle illness that improved the research and development community a lot CAH (2011). A program was initiated by Blue Cross Blue Shield of Massachusetts (BCBSMA), in order to control the over dose of opioid and to precisely analyse the hazardous problems BCBSMA (2011).

Imminently, smart system was designed for monitoring health of elderly persons wherein a call is connected through server computer using wireless mobile, this call grant the access of the graphical chart using wireless mobile (Maki et al. 2011). Additionally, Italian Medicines Agency (AIFA) developed a web portal for improving clinical research. This system is designed for medical analysis [22]. Further, a smart approach is used by the kids hospital (SickKids) to avert nosocomial disease. It applies analytic to the data aggregated from the different devices to determine the probable indication of the infection to take preventive measures (IBM software, 2015).

3   Proposed Architecture

We have designed an architecture that concentrates to deal with the services issues presently. We can observe from the Fig. 1, that it contains four layers specifically, Cloud Real time application layer, Service layer, Cloud Infrastructure layer and finally the essential part of our system is Healthcare system layer as shown in Fig. 1. From these four layers the Service layer is having two sub layers namely, Cloud Service layer and Web Service layer. These layers are described in the next part.

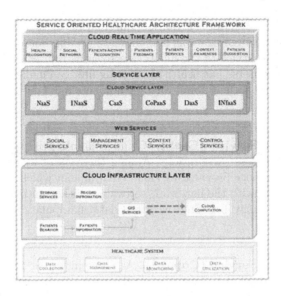

Fig. 1. Service Oriented for Healthcare Framework (SOHA).

3.1 Cloud Real Time Application

Being aware of the real-time circumstances should be the primeval focus for the healthcare organizations. The envisioned theme is to implement an interface for the medical organizations, in order to examine real time position of the patient. The first component of this layer considers the exact situation of the patient. By accessing the instant update of the patient, its easy to analyse the condition and to take action according to the circumstances. Physician, can examine the activities any of his patient and can warn him/her, if the situation is getting injurious to the patient.

3.2 Cloud Real Time Application

The services to be provided are the necessity for any system. For healthcare, different services are available and the services, we are utilizing in our system are described below.

Network as a Service (NaaS). Almost everyone in the world is utilizing the internet, but the important part is that no one is facilitating the resources effectively. For overcome this problem an architecture was proposed by [18] as a Network as A Service (NaaS). This architecture address the issue of properly utilizing the network resources. In our architecture this service is included for the same reason.

Information as a Service (INaaS). Information as a Service being used by excessive business organizations and they are getting bounteous results. We can implement this service to the healthcare towards improving the healthcare services for the end users. The health monitoring unit can make use of INaaS for updating the remote patient about any amendments made by the doctor about him/her.

Computing as a Service (CaaS). Cloud computing is providing a lot of facilities to the business corporations. Among these on of the facility is CaaS. CaaS is a type of service provided by cloud environment which allows any organization to facilitate with the hardware/software utilities renting form the cloud providers and can easily benefited with the data manipulation for the desired results.

Cooperation as a Service (CopaaS). As name indicates, this service is utilizing the experience of the other fabricated systems for making precautionary measures as proposed by Hajar Moussaieff et al. in [20] for VANETS. In healthcare environment number of systems are running, we can utilize the experience of these systems for safety measures.

Data as a Service (DaaS). In Data as a service (DaaS), the data from the organizations is made available to the user or organization for convenience, and is independent of the geographical area, which is an important factor to consider.

Infrastructure as a Service (INaaS). Infrastructure as a service (INaaS), is a service provided by the cloud environment as to avail the computing infrastructure through internet. The best part is that it reduces the trouble of handling hardware installation and the cost overhead also.

3.3   Web Services

Social networking is one of the common platforms right now for ever field [4]. The extraction of the data is also on a high trend from these platforms. We can deal with these platforms too, to get the useful information.

Social Services. Social networking is becoming most prevailing platform for research institutions for scrutinizing the concealed patterns. Healthcare environments are also engaging for disclosing the power of data present on the social networking sites. We can utilize these platforms to discover new patterns or changes in the different environments and can apply these changes to the current areas.

Context Information Services. Context information services could be respective to the user. The patients or users connected to the medical organization are usually in regular contact to the organizations, now the information related to the user exist in the organizations history and this data is useful for transmitting the updates to the patient regarding the disease he/she is suffering from.

Control Services. The name specified the working, this service usually controls the activity of all the services. This service actually look over the running services, and direct the service.

Management Services. The managing services used to manage all the other services. It connects the flow of services on the basis of service call. The service which is called, is directed by the management service and look over the resources available to make a possible connection.

3.4 Cloud Infrastructure Layer

Cloud storage systems are widely used updated technology. Also cloud computing provides analytic tools for managing and manipulating the data. In healthcare, the data accumulated is hard to process due to its complexity and heterogeneity. The cloud Infrastructure Layer contains two modules which are as follows:

GIS Services. These services are concerned with medical records. The patients records is extremely essential entity for the healthcare organizations. To manage the patient information in a convenient manner should be the intent of the organization. So this service manages the patients information before its gets manipulated with in the cloud storage.

Cloud Computation. Cloud computing is the robust and updated technology in the present situation. To facilitate the business world cloud computing is one of the powerful mechanism. We have utilized cloud computation to manipulate the accumulated data form different sources. As we are using the cloud storage, all the data collected is stored on the cloud and to perform analysis to make the data precise.

3.5 Healthcare Layer

The healthcare layer comprises of four modules, as Data Collection, Data Management, Data Monitoring and Data Utilization respectively, having specific functionality. These modules are defined in Fig. 2.

Fig. 2. Health care architecture.

Data Collection. Data is the main entity for any organization. In healthcare, there are diverse sources of data. Most of the organizations are practising Electronic Health Record (EHR). But the data could be gathered from different sources including social network for analysing it in a proper manner as depicted in Fig. 3. Most of the data produced in healthcare domain is in the forms of images, such images includes different dimensionality depending upon the type of tool used for capturing the image and also there format are different too.

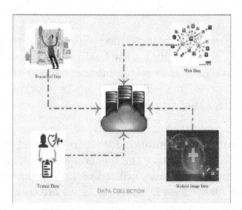

Fig. 3. Data collection in healthcare architecture.

Data Management. The managing part is also important because, it includes depositing, securing and evaluating the data. Figure 4 depicts the life cycle of the Data Management process. After the collection of data processing is the next step, currently, cloud computing are popular schemes where we can rent space and store the data. Cloud computing is providing the tools for managing the data which abolishes the complexity of the organizations to handle the data. Big data analytical techniques are the recent trend for making the data work. Due to the complexity of the data, analysing it also difficult, since it contains structured, unstructured data [10].

Fig. 4. Data management in healthcare architecture.

Data Monitoring. The data organized in the healthcare organizations is extremely important, hence to maintain the data quality is one of the important measures. This monitoring should provide a great essence to the data present or gathering in the repository. Figure 5 sketches the functionality of the Data Monitoring unit, the data monitoring unit of the organization scrutinize the data at regular basis, if any of the data accumulated signals to be doubtful, its prompt a warning indicating the flaws in the data to the management unit in order to notify the monitoring unit [19].

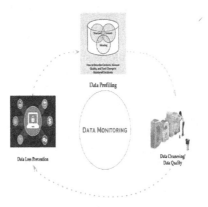

Fig. 5. Data monitoring in healthcare architecture.

Data Utilization. After collecting, monitoring and managing the data, the essential part is the utilization of the assembled data. Now after refining the data, how to use this data is the significant phase. As depicted in Fig. 6 before utilization it requires three steps to make the data utilized, these three phases aims to make the data in such format that it could be utilized. For healthcare domain using this data is quite complicated part also, due to its diversified type.

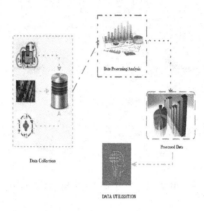

Fig. 6. Data utilization in healthcare architecture.

4   Security Mechanism for Data Sharing in Proposed Framework

We are using the AES algorithm for encrypting the data to make the patient data more secure. AES is the algorithm that runs on block cipher works iteratively. The basic block of the AES is of 128 bit and cloud be of 192 and 256 bits. The key is also having the length of 128, 192 and 256 bits. The number of rounds is 10, 12 and 14 depending on the block size. The Key depending on the key length, the key is represented by an array of matrix consisting of 4 rows and Nk columns, where Nk = Key length/32, means for 128 bits it is 4 columns and so on. The block size is also calculated as same, means it also depends upon the length of the block. It contains the same 4 rows and Nb columns, where Nb = Block Length/32, for 128 bits it will be 4 rows. The AES algorithm follows four basic steps during each cycle namely, Sub-bytes, Shift-Rows, Mix Columns, Add Round Key.

4.1   Substitute Byte Transformation

The first step required bytes from every block state is substituted with the S-Box mapped byte as shown in Fig. 7.

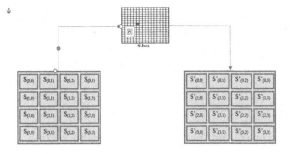

Fig. 7. Byte transformation.

4.2   Shift Rows Transformation

After being byte transformed the succeeding step is the Shifting of the rows. This concept runs on the transformation of rows from left to right without moving the first row circularly. The first row is shifted 1 byte towards left, the second row is shifted two bytes toward left and the last row is shifted 3 bytes towards left circularly [24]. The size of the new stat is not changed but just the position of the indexed of the elements will be changed.

4.3   Mix Columns Transformation

The consecutive step is the Mix Column. In this step matrix multiplications takes place, each row of the transformation is multiplied by the column of the row. Forwardly, these multiplications are XORed to form the new state matrix.

4.4   Add Round Key Transformation

This stage is most important stage in the AES. Both the state (input data) and the key are accommodated in the 4×4 matrix. Here the input data is the transformed matrix which is the cipher [15]. The output of the Add Round key is fully depends upon the key specified by the user [2,6] as shown in the Fig. 8

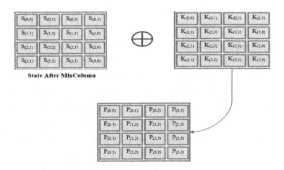

Fig. 8. Round key transformation.

Yet sub key is also used and combined with the state in the stages. For deriving the sub keys, the main key is utilized incorporating Rijndaels key schedule. Size of the state and the sub key is same. Now, the sub key is added by integrating every element of the state with the element of the sub key utilizing bit wise XOR [16].

4.5 Decryption

Decrypting the received information is the process to uncover the original information [2–4]. In AES the decryption process is just reverse of the encryption. The same key is used to decrypt the data as that used in the encryption. The last cycle of the decryption includes the same components in the reverse order InvShiftRows, InvSubBytes and Add Round Key. InvMixColumn depicted in the Fig. 9.

Along with the AES, we are using the Base64 to make the data more secure. Because we are using 128 bits key in the AES algorithm, although the algorithm itself is strong towards attack but still is having some vulnerabilities.

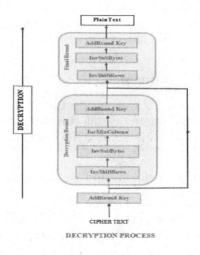

Fig. 9. Decryption process.

BASE64. The Base64 is an encoding process that use to encode the binary data into the ASCII based on the base 64. It includes A—-Z, a—z, 0—9 and two symbols +, /. The algorithm works in the manner that it divides the incoming bytes into 3 bytes. Continually, it divides the input into 4 parts of 6 bits each and replace each 6 bits patch with the corresponding Base64 character set. Padding is used if it does not makes the multiple of three if one byte is missing then two 0's are appended with the input bytes and if 2 bytes are missing then number of 0's are appended according to the condition a to make the octet complete and in the output string = is replaced in the place of 0's in pair.

5   Analysis and Discussion

Our algorithm utilizes the benefits of AES first and the output of the AES is then transformed using the Base 64. The key used in the AES is transferred to the requested end to make the decryption. First of all the data obtained on the requested site will be decoded by the Base64 and then the output is considered as the input for the AES algorithm for decrypt the original data.

Currently, the conditions for data utilization are becoming more suitable with the advent of innovative technologies. From the systems which were designed up to now, a lot of systems had used up-to-date technologies but still they lacks in various sections, especially, in providing the services, either on the part of the user or from the organizations point-of-view. Data is the fundamental entity for the organizations to act upon and extract meaningful information to provide service. Cloud computing and Big Data Analytic are the major contributor currently towards enhancing the technologies potential to higher extent for transforming the data into valuable asset. The organizations needs appropriate tools to process the data in order to utilize it to the maximum extent.

In our framework, the second layer Service Layer, reap the benefits of the most of the members of as a service family that maintains the service part of the system. It provides the sublime strength to the designed system for maintaining the durability of the data over time. These services definitely have reformed the information maintained on the cloud as they are equipped with the recent mechanism to govern the data in a proper manner. As an analogy, consider the Information as a Service service, thats trades on right information at right time, improves the condition a lot for the recent systems and many of the live systems are relying on the said service for avoiding miscalculated information that leads to inferior conclusions.

The proposed architecture SOHA, incorporates four layers among which the functionality of fourth layer is responsible for making an association between the healthcare corporations to the cloud warehouse, and making the data analysed by the clinical experts to make conclusions from the data. Also, the first three layers are processing the data collected in the cloud from different sources to make it in structured format, because the data accumulated is in structured, un-structured and semi-structured formats. These different formats cant be integrated easily, in contrast with, we have worked on the collected data in different layers to make it in a precise format for analysis. This processed data is easy to analyze by the physicians and the organizations productivity definitely improves to prosper the service to the user or patient. So deductively, we can say that this system incorporates the integrative influence of cloud-computing mechanism along with some Big data Analytics and smart systems, that makes it precise and distinctive model. Although, it is having advantages but none of the system is perfect, likewise this designed model also suffers from the issues related to security and privacy and we will try to figure out and minimize these issues in the next turn.

6 Conclusion

We conducted reviews on the design of health care systems, according to our best knowledge, these systems have some limitations in terms of security, privacy, and data communication. We can say that, we have tried our best to overcome some of the problems inclined to the healthcare services. We have tried to focus on the medical services and to develop an architecture to deliver the solutions for the healthcare organizations. In our architecture we have proposed a healthcare services layer, which is the main component from the services perspective. And this proposed architecture will improve the functionality of the clinical industry.

Acknowledgment. This work was supported in part by the National Natural Science Foundation of China under Grant 61632009, Grant 61472451 and Grant 61872097, in part by the Guangdong Provincial Natural Science Foundation under Grant 2017A030308006, and in part by the High-Level Talents Program of Higher Education in Guangdong Province under Grant 2016ZJ01.

References

1. Arif, M., Abdullah, N.A., Phalianakote, S.K., Ramli, N., Elahi, M.: Maximizing information of multimodality brain image fusion using curvelet transform with genetic algorithm. In: 2014 International Conference on Computer Assisted System in Health (CASH), pp. 45–51. IEEE (2014)
2. Arif, M., Wang, G., Balas, V.E.: Secure vanets: trusted communication scheme between vehicles and infrastructure based on fog computing. Stud. Inform. Control **27**(2), 235–246 (2018)
3. Arif, M., Wang, G., Chen, S.: Deep learning with non-parametric regression model for traffic flow prediction. In: Proceedings of IEEE 16th International Conference on Dependable, Autonomic & Secure Computing, 16th International Conference on Pervasive Intelligence & Computing, 4th International Conference on Big Data Intelligence & Computing, and 3rd Cyber Science & Technology Congress, pp. 681–688. IEEE, August 2018
4. Arif, M., Wang, G., Peng, T.: Track me if you can? Query based dual location privacy in VANETs for V2V and V2I. In: 2018 17th IEEE International Conference on Trust, Security and Privacy in Computing and Communications/12th IEEE International Conference on Big Data Science And Engineering (TrustCom/BigDataSE), pp. 1091–1096. IEEE (2018)
5. Bate, S.P., Robert, G.: Knowledge management and communities of practice in the private sector: lessons for modernizing the national health service in England and Wales. Public Adm. **80**(4), 643–663 (2002)
6. Benvenuto, C.J.: Galois field in cryptography. University of Washington (2012)
7. Blumenthal, D., Hsiao, W.: Privatization and its discontents the evolving Chinese health care system (2005)
8. Conti, M., Lal, C.: A survey on context-based co-presence detection techniques. arXiv preprint arXiv:1808.03320 (2018)
9. DeCamp, M.: Physicians, social media, and conflict of interest. J. Gen. Intern. Med. **28**(2), 299–303 (2013)
10. Ginter, P.M., Duncan, W.J., Swayne, L.E.: The Strategic Management of Health Care Organizations. Wiley, Hoboken (2018)

11. Grannis, S.J., Stevens, K.C., Merriwether, R.: Leveraging health information exchange to support public health situational awareness: the Indiana experience. Online J. Public Health Inform. **2**(2), 335–344 (2010)

12. Hande, A., Polk, T., Walker, W., Bhatia, D.: Self-powered wireless sensor networks for remote patient monitoring in hospitals. Sensors **6**(9), 1102–1117 (2006)

13. Hao, H.: The development of online doctor reviews in China: an analysis of the largest online doctor review website in China. J. Med. Internet Res. **17**(6), e134 (2015)

14. Javaid, Q., Arif, M., Shah, M.A., Nadeem, M., et al.: A hybrid technique for denoising multi-modality medical images by employing cuckoo's search with curvelet transform. Mehran Univ. Res. J. Eng. Technol. **37**(1), 29 (2018)

15. Kretzschmar, U.: Aes128-ac implementation for encryption and decryption. TI-White Paper (2009)

16. Lee, H., Lee, K., Shin, Y.: AES implementation and performance evaluation on 8-bit microcontrollers. arXiv preprint arXiv:0911.0482 (2009)

17. Leijdekkers, P., Gay, V.: Personal heart monitoring and rehabilitation system using smart phones. In: International Conference on Mobile Business, ICMB 2006, p. 29. IEEE (2006)

18. Mai, L., et al.: NetAgg: using middleboxes for application-specific on-path aggregation in data centres. In: Proceedings of the 10th ACM International on Conference on Emerging Networking Experiments and Technologies, pp. 249–262. ACM (2014)

19. Manogaran, G., Varatharajan, R., Lopez, D., Kumar, P.M., Sundarasekar, R., Thota, C.: A new architecture of internet of things and big data ecosystem for secured smart healthcare monitoring and alerting system. Future Gen. Comput. Syst. **82**, 375–387 (2018)

20. Mousannif, H., Khalil, I., Al Moatassime, H.: Cooperation as a service in VANETs. J. UCS **17**(8), 1202–1218 (2011)

21. Muhammad, A., Guojun, W.: Segmentation of calcification and brain hemorrhage with midline detection. In: 2017 IEEE International Symposium on Parallel and Distributed Processing with Applications and 2017 IEEE International Conference on Ubiquitous Computing and Communications (ISPA/IUCC), pp. 1082–1090. IEEE (2017)

22. Piai, S., Claps, M.: Bigger data for better healthcare. IDC Health Insights (2013)

23. Pramanik, M.I., Lau, R.Y., Demirkan, H., Azad, M.A.K.: Smart health: big data enabled health paradigm within smart cities. Expert Syst. Appl. **87**, 370–383 (2017)

24. Selmane, N., Guilley, S., Danger, J.L.: Practical setup time violation attacks on AES. In: Seventh European Dependable Computing Conference, EDCC 2008, pp. 91–96. IEEE (2008)

25. Wicks, P., et al.: Sharing health data for better outcomes on PatientsLikeMe. J. Med. Internet Res. **12**(2), e19 (2010)

26. Zhang, Y., Qiu, M., Tsai, C.W., Hassan, M.M., Alamri, A.: Health-CPS: healthcare cyber-physical system assisted by cloud and big data. IEEE Syst. J. **11**(1), 88–95 (2017)

27. Zhu, C., Wang, G., Sun, K.: Cryptanalysis and improvement on an image encryption algorithm design using a novel chaos based S-Box. Symmetry **10**(9), 399 (2018)

Processing Analysis of Confidential Modes of Operation

Yasir Nawaz[⊠], Lei Wang, and Kamel Ammour

School of Electronic Information and Electrical Engineering,
Shanghai Jiao Tong University, Shanghai 200240, China
my_nawaz@sjtu.edu.cn

Abstract. This paper analyzes the processing of cryptographic confidentiality block cipher operation modes on "Advance Encryption Standard" recommended by the National Institute of Standards and Technology. The block cipher operation modes that are under consideration for analysis are Electronic Code Book mode, Cipher Block Chaining mode, Cipher Feedback mode, Output Feedback mode, Counter mode, and XEX-based tweaked-codebook mode. The processing analysis of each block cipher operation modes are based on encryption time and decryption time with variable sizes of the data file when implemented in MATLAB. The result of each experiment of the operation mode is summarized in the graphical representation to help to make an instructional decision about operation mode processing when choosing for different applications with secret key ciphers.

Keywords: Cryptography · Block cipher · Advance Encryption Standard
Modes of operation · Encryption algorithms

1 Introduction

The block cipher is an elementary and important component in the design of security protocol, an encryption protocol, and cryptographic protocol. Block cipher extensively used to perform encryption of sizeable data and process the input text on a fixed length of bits (block size) and the length of each input text is exactly the same as another block. A block cipher only appropriate for the secure encryption and decryption of one block. On the other hand, if data larger than a block then for securely transform a mode of operation are used, some sort of mode used for feedback and some sort for simple operation. The modes of operation divided into three categories (I) confidentiality (II) authenticity (III) authenticated encryption [1].

In this paper, we analyze the processing of confidentiality operation modes and these modes recommended by the National Institute of Standards and Technology (NIST) [2, 3]. There are six confidentiality operation modes in which Cipher Block Chaining mode (CBC), Cipher Feedback mode (CFB), Output Feedback mode (OFB), Counter mode (CTR), and XEX-based tweaked-codebook mode (XTS-AES) have initialization vector (IV) where IV is either a random value, nonce, or tweak but in Electronic Code Book mode (ECB) mode IV is not present. The processing analysis of these confidentiality modes is based on the following two metrics: (I) Encryption Time

G. Wang et al. (Eds.): SpaCCS 2018, LNCS 11342, pp. 98–110, 2018.
https://doi.org/10.1007/978-3-030-05345-1_8

(II) Decryption Time, with different size of data file. On the other hand, the Advance Encryption Standard (AES) algorithm is used for block encryption with 128-bit block size and 128-bit the size of encryption key it has been standard by NIST in 2001. The results show that the operation modes are not appreciably different in term of processing time with a high confidence level. The significant difference between the operation modes is relatively small for the small size of data files and for sizeable data files there is a visible difference in term of encryption time and decryption time among these modes.

The rest of this paper is organized as follows. Section 2 describes the background and related work. Section 3 introduces block cipher mode of operation proposed by NIST. The methodology of our study explains in Sect. 4. Section 5 describes the results and analysis. The comparison of each operation mode and contribution of our study describe in discussion Sect. 6. Section 7 concludes this paper.

2   Background and Related Work

In 1997 NIST was realized that Data Encryption Standard (DES) is not secure enough because computer processing power increase, so in order to replace the DES. In 2001 NIST introduce another data encryption algorithm that is AES. After the recommendation of AES, there are numbers of data encryption algorithm introduce, they have its own pros and cons [4, 5]. Today, AES is one of the most used algorithms for block encryption. In 2001 NIST recommend five confidentiality modes of operation that are: ECB mode, CBC mode, CFB mode, OFB mode, and CTR mode. Each operation mode has its own functionalities and own parameters and these modes are important to provide the necessary security for confidentiality. In 2010 NIST recommend another confidential mode XTS-AES mode that has an extra input a tweak instead of initialization vector (IV).

Diedon and Erke [6] investigate the confidential mode of operation that is recommended by NIST. The modes analyzed in this paper are the following: ECB mode, CBC mode, CFB mode, OFB mode, and CTR mode. These operation modes are analyzed and compared in terms of their efficiency, security, and performance when implemented in MATLAB. The result of this analysis show CTR mode is the most efficient, secure, and fastest way of doing encryption and decryption.

Blazhevski et al. [7] this paper describes all recommended modes operation and their strengths and weaknesses and for a proper AES implementation demand the parameters that are necessary to guarantee security. In addition, the analysis shows that in CTR mode each block encrypts or decrypt independently, so due parallel encryption and decryption, there is no propagation of error occur from one block to other blocks.

Almuhammadi and Al-Hejri [8] in this paper describes the comparison of the NIST recommended block cipher operation mode (ECB mode, CBC mode, CFB mode, OFB mode, and CTR mode) on AES on the bases of encryption time, decryption time and throughput. The analysis shows that ECB mode takes small time for encryption and decryption than the other operation modes. The difference between the operation modes is relatively small for small files. However, with big size of data files a visible difference in the performance among these operation modes.

A new block cipher mode of operation proposed named counter chaining by El-Semary and Abdel-Azim [9]. The proposed counter chaining mode integrates the CBC mode with the CTR mode. To achieves the better encryption time than CBC mode and CTR mode, conduct experimental result in a multi-processor environment. the CTR mode provides a similar encryption time with the advantage of providing message authentication.

3 Block Cipher Modes of Operation

This section describes and illustrate six confidential operation modes that are recommended by NIST.

3.1 Electronic Codebook Mode (ECB)

The ECB mode is a confidential mode that is simplest and fastest mode than other modes. The ECB mode is defined as follows:

$$C_i = E_k(P_i) \quad for \ i = 1 \ldots n. \quad (Encryption)$$
$$P_i = D_k(C_i) \quad for \ i = 1 \ldots n. \quad (Decryption)$$

In ECB mode the Encryption/Decryption algorithm is applied independently and directly to each block of the input text. The input text divided into blocks $P = (P_1, P_2, P_3, \ldots, P_n)$, where each divided input text encrypted separately. The resulting sequence of each block is the ciphertext $C = (C_1, C_2, C_3, \ldots, C_n)$, respectively resultant ciphertext decrypt separately. If the input text size is larger than a block, then the last block filled with padding. If there is an error appear in any block, then ECB mode not propagated to the other block because each block encrypts or decrypt independently. So, the processing time of ECB mode is higher than other modes of operation due to independent block encryption/decryption.

3.2 Cipher Block Chaining Mode (CBC)

The CBC mode is a confidential mode in which a chain appears between the successive encryption/decryption blocks. The CBC mode is defined as follows:

$$C_1 = E_k(P_1 \oplus IV) \qquad (Encryption)$$
$$C_i = E_k(P_i \oplus C_{i-1}) \qquad for \ i = 2 \ldots n.$$
$$P_1 = D_k(C_1) \oplus IV \qquad (Decryption)$$
$$P_i = D_k(C_i) \oplus C_{i-1} \qquad for \ i = 2 \ldots n.$$

The encryption, as well as decryption of each block, significantly depend on previous block ciphertext or input text. Its XORed with the previous block output before encrypting the block of the input text. On the other hand, in first block initialization vector XORed with input text. If the same input text encrypted number of times the resulting ciphertexts are distinct due to use of IV. The IV must be unpredictable and need not be secret. Due to the chaining mechanism, CBC mode takes more processing time than ECB mode.

Cipher Feedback Mode (CFB)

The CFB mode is a confidential mode requires an initial input block IV and must be unpredictable like CBC mode and need not be secret. The CFB mode is defined as follows:

$$
\begin{aligned}
C_1 &= (E_k(IV) \oplus P_1) & &(Encryption) \\
C_i &= (E_k(C_{i-1}) \oplus P_i) & &for\ i = 2\ldots n. \\
P_1 &= (D_k(IV) \oplus C_1) & &(Decryption) \\
P_i &= (D_k(C_{i-1}) \oplus C_i) & &for\ i = 2\ldots n.
\end{aligned}
$$

The CFB mode runs a block cipher as a stream cipher at the first block the encryption algorithm performed by using a key and IV then resulting XORed with input text and for other blocks encryption and decryption depend on the output/ciphertext of the previous blocks and XORed with corresponding input text. In CFB mode the encryption and decryption operation are the same. If the error occurs in any block, then it propagates to the next block due to depending on the previous block.

3.3 Output Feedback Mode (OFB)

The OFB mode is a confidentiality mode that is quite similar to the CFB mode and also runs a block cipher as a stream cipher. The OFB mode is defined as follows:

$$
\begin{aligned}
S_1 &= E_k(IV);\ C_1 = (S_1 \oplus P_1) & &(Encryption) \\
S_i &= E_k(S_{i-1});\ C_i = (S_i \oplus P_i) & &for\ i = 2\ldots n. \\
S_1 &= E_k(IV);\ P_1 = (S_1 \oplus C_1) & &(Decryption) \\
S_i &= E_k(S_{i-1});\ P_i = (S_i \oplus C_i) & &for\ i = 2\ldots n.
\end{aligned}
$$

The OFB mode generates a keystream block then it XORed with input text or ciphertext to get resultant input text or ciphertext. Each block depends on all previous block expect the first block if there is an error propagate in any block during the encryption or decryption operation it will influence a part of the input text or cipher text that will result from that block.

3.4 Counter Mode (CTR)

The CTR mode is a confidential mode that uses a block cipher as its stream generator, whose input is a counter value. The value of the counter changes every time a new key stream is generated and the counters for a given message are divided into chunks of counters. The CTR mode is defined as follows:

$$
\begin{aligned}
C_i &= (E_k(IV)\|CTR_i) \oplus P_i) & &(Encryption) \\
P_i &= (E_k(IV)\|CTR_i) \oplus C_i) & &(Decryption)
\end{aligned}
$$

The value of the counter is independent of the output of the previous block, so if an error occurs in one block then there is no effect of other blocks. Considering the independence of the blocks and parallelism in the encryption operation and the decryption operation facts show that CTR mode takes less processing time than other mode including CBC mode, CFB mode, OFB mode.

3.5   XTS-AES Mode

The XTS-AES mode is a confidentiality mode use for full disk encryption. The XTS-AES is the two-key version of XEX construction [10]. The XTS mode is defined as follows:

$$C_i = E_k(P_i, T, N) \quad for\ i = 1...n. \quad (Encryption)$$
$$P_i = D_k(C_i, T, N) \quad for\ i = 1...n. \quad (Decryption)$$

The XTS-AES cipher takes an input a key 128-bit, a tweak 128-bit, block inside the data unit is 128-bit and the input text 128-bit. The whole construction and working of XTS-AES mode [10–12]. The XTS-AES mode is a relatively new mode that is a relatively complex design. it involves a multiplication in a Galois Field, two ECB-AES encryptions, and two XORed operations. This mode work with fixed-size data units, for instance, logical disk blocks, and each data block processed separately and independently of another data block.

4   Methodology

This is a quantitative research used in our analysis. In our experimental analysis, we used MATLAB R2014a to do the processing evaluation of all block cipher modes. These modes wrapping with the AES-128 algorithm (Standardized by NIST). Whereas the size of the used encrypted key is 128-bits.

We used core i5 with 2.30 GHz CPU, 8 GB RAM and a hard disc of 1 TB for this technique. The different size of data files with different ranges used like 3 MB to 200 MB. Our experiment with different size of data file has achieved a different processing time. We discuss the processing of each operation modes (ECB mode, CFB mode, OFB mode, CBC mode, CTR mode, and XTS-AES mode). The processing evaluation of each operation mode are based on the Encryption time and Decryption time. The processing time of each operation mode is calculated one by one.

5   Results and Analysis

This section shows that the processing of each operation modes, which are obtained by running the simulation of each mode using different size of data file. The processing (encryption time and decryption time) of each operation mode (ECB mode, CFB mode, OFB mode, CBC mode, CTR mode, and XTS mode) are shown in graphical representation.

5.1   ECB Processing

In our first experiment, we implement ECB mode using AES, it takes the different size of the data file using implemented ECB mode and yields different processing time Fig. 1 shows the processing of ECB mode and summarizes the results of encryption time and decryption time with the different size of data file.

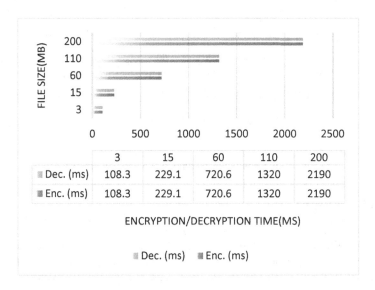

Fig. 1.   Encryption & decryption time of ECB mode

Our analysis observed that ECB mode take less processing time (encryption time and decryption time) as compared to the other operation modes because different data block encrypted by different encryption unit in parallel.

5.2   CBC Processing

In our second experiment for analysis of CBC mode processing, we implement CBC mode using AES, it takes different size of data file using implemented CBC mode and yield different processing time Fig. 2 shows the processing of CBC mode in term of encryption time and decryption time and summarizes the results of encryption time and decryption time with different size of data file.

Our analysis observed that CBC mode takes much processing time (encryption time and decryption time) than ECB mode because the input block of each encryption algorithm depends on the result of the previous block. So due to chaining of each block with other blocks the processing time more than ECB mode encryption and decryption.

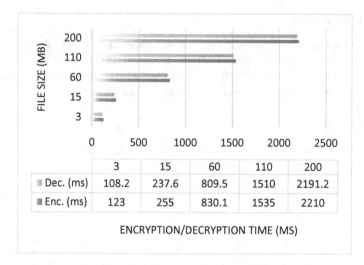

Fig. 2. Encryption & decryption time of CBC mode

5.3 CFB Processing

In our third experiment for analysis of CFB mode processing, we implement CFB mode using AES and takes the different size of the data file using implemented CFB mode and yield different processing time Fig. 3 shows the processing of CBC mode and summarizes the results of encryption time and decryption time with the different size of data file.

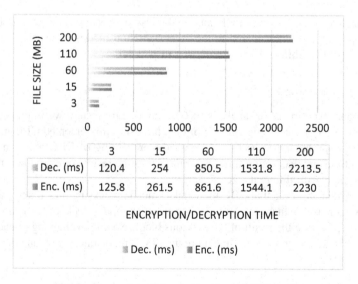

Fig. 3. Encryption & decryption time of CFB mode

Our analysis observed that CFB mode take almost the same processing time (encryption and decryption time), like CBC mode encryption and decryption each input block depends on the result of the previous block output. The encryption and decryption block cannot perform in parallel, so, the processing time almost like CBC mode.

5.4   OFB Processing

In processing analysis of OFB mode, we implement OFB mode using AES and takes the different size of the data file using implemented CFB mode and yield different processing time Fig. 4 shows the processing of CBC mode and summarizes the results of encryption time and decryption time with the different size of data file.

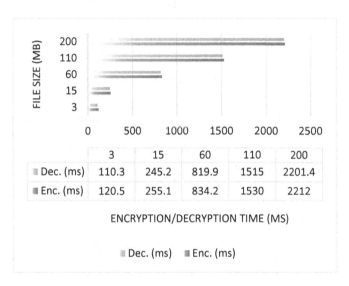

	3	15	60	110	200
Dec. (ms)	110.3	245.2	819.9	1515	2201.4
Enc. (ms)	120.5	255.1	834.2	1530	2212

ENCRYPTION/DECRYPTION TIME (MS)

Dec. (ms)   Enc. (ms)

Fig. 4. Encryption & decryption time of OFB mode

Our analysis observed that OFB mode take less processing time than CBC mode and CFB mode because the input block to each encryption algorithm takes the output of the previous block before XORed with input text. The processing time is less than the CBC mode and CFB mode due to the get immediately output of previous encryption algorithm (before XORed with input text).

5.5   CTR Processing

In our CTR mode processing experiment, we implement CTR mode using AES and takes the different size of the data file using implemented CTR mode and yield different processing time Fig. 5 shows the processing of CTR mode and summarizes the results of encryption time and decryption time with the different size of data file.

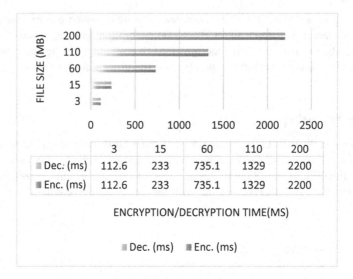

Fig. 5. Encryption & decryption time of CTR mode

In CTR mode, the encryption, as well as decryption, performed independently each input text encrypt or decrypt through block separately and yield corresponding ciphertext or input text. So, due to parallel encryption or decryption of input text or cipher text the CTR modes have less encryption and decryption time than CBC mode, CFB mode and OCB mode.

5.6   XTS-AES Processing

In our last experiment, we implement XTS-AES mode, it takes the different size of the data file using implemented XTS-AES mode and yield different processing time Fig. 6 shows the processing of XTS-AES mode in term of encryption time and decryption time and summarizes the results of processing time with the different size of data file.

Our analysis observed that XTS-AES mode take more processing time than all another confidential mode. The XTS-AES mode is a relatively recent operation mode that is a relatively complex. it involves two ECB mode encryptions, two XORed operations and a multiplication in a Galois Field. This mode has been designed to work with fixed-size data units, for instance, logical disk blocks, and each data unit must be processed separately and independently of other data units.

6   Discussion

Our study deeply analyzes the processing in term of encryption time and decryption time of each operation mode (ECB mode, CBC mode, CFB mode, OFB mode, CTR mode and XTS-AES mode) and plotted the encryption time and decryption time of these operation modes with variable size of data file. We observed that significant

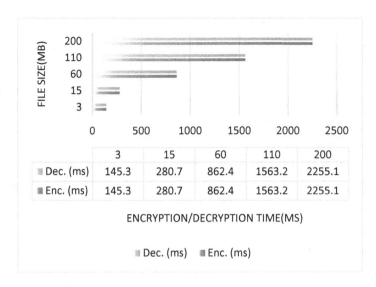

	3	15	60	110	200
▨ Dec. (ms)	145.3	280.7	862.4	1563.2	2255.1
▨ Enc. (ms)	145.3	280.7	862.4	1563.2	2255.1

ENCRYPTION/DECRYPTION TIME(MS)

▨ Dec. (ms)   ▨ Enc. (ms)

Fig. 6. Encryption & decryption time of XTS-AES mode

different between the operation modes is relatively small for the small size of data files and for sizeable data files there is a visible difference in term of encryption time among these modes. Table 1 comparatively summarizes the results of the encryption time analysis with different size of data file among all these operation modes.

Table 1. Encryption time comparison

File size	ECB	CBC	CFB	OFB	CTR	XTS-AES
3	108.3	123	125.8	120.5	112.6	145.3
15	229.1	255	261.5	255.1	233	280.7
60	720.6	830.1	861.6	834.2	735.1	862.4
110	1320	1535	1544.1	1530	1329	1563.2
200	2190	2210	2230	2212	2200	2255.1
Aveg. 388	Aveg. 4568 (ms)	Aveg. 4953.1 (ms)	Aveg. 5023 (ms)	Aveg. 4951.8 (ms)	Aveg. 4609.7 (ms)	Aveg. 5106.7 (ms)

We also noticed that the decryption time for these operation modes are almost the same. Generally, the differences between the modes are negligible. Table 2 comparatively summarizes the results of the decryption time analysis with different size of data file among all these operation modes.

We conduct our analysis on the most popular encryption algorithm AES. Our analysis fills the gaps in the existing operation modes analysis on AES. On the other hand, our work first-time analyze the processing of XTS-AES mode. The study

Table 2. Decryption time comparison

File size	ECB	CBC	CFB	OFB	CTR	XTS-AES
3	108.3	108.2	120.4	110.3	112.6	145.3
15	229.1	237.6	254	245.2	233	280.7
60	720.6	809.5	850.5	819.9	735.1	862.4
110	1320	1510	1531.8	1515	1329	1563.2
200	2190	2191.2	2215.5	2201.4	2200	2255.1
Aveg. 388 (MB)	Aveg. 4568 (ms)	Aveg. 4856.5 (ms)	Aveg. 4972.2 (ms)	Aveg. 4891.8 (ms)	Aveg. 4609.7 (ms)	Aveg. 5106.7 (ms)

Table 3. Comparison with existing analysis

Sr. #	Operation mode	Performance analysis	References
1	ECB	Encryption time, CPU time, CPU clock cycle, battery power	[13]
2	ECB, CBC, CFB	Encryption time, decryption time, throughput	[14]
3	ECB, CBC, CFB, OFB	Execution time	[15]
4	ECB, CBC	Data transfer cost, throughput	[16]
5	ECB	Execution time, throughput, memory usage	[17]
6	CBC, ICBC	Encryption time, decryption time	[18]
7	CBC	Encryption time	[19]
8	ECB, CBC, CFB, OFB, CTR, XTS-AES	Encryption time, decryption time	This paper

provides additional insights into the processing of recommended modes. Table 3 summarizes the operation mode and the performance analysis of all existing studies, and compares them to our work.

7 Conclusion

This paper experimentally analyzed the processing of confidential operation modes on AES in term of encryption time and decryption time. The block cipher operation modes that analyzed in our experiments are: ECB mode, CBC mode, CFB mode, OFB mode, CTR mode and XTS-AES mode. Previous studies have reported the processing analysis on modes recommended by NIST 2001. However, this paper presents the analysis on the processing of XTS-AES mode recommended by NIST 2010, in addition to the five confidential modes recommend by NIST 2001. Our study provides additional insights into the processing of recommending modes. The results show that the operation modes are not appreciably different in term of processing time with a high confidence level. The significant different between the operation modes is relatively small for the small size of data files as well as for sizeable data files there is a visible difference in term of encryption time and decryption time among these modes. On the basis of current understanding of processing analysis of confidential modes, we intend to analyze the processing of other authenticate modes as well as authenticated encryption mode in the future.

Acknowledgements. I would like to express my special appreciation and sincere gratitude to my supervisor Professor Lei Wang for his guidance, patience and support. I would like to thank you for encouraging my research and advice on both research as well as on my career have been invaluable.

References

1. Rogaway, P.: Evaluation of Some Blockcipher Modes of Operation. Cryptography Research and Evaluation Committees (CRYPTREC) for the Government of Japan (2011)
2. Dworkin, M.: Recommendation for Block Cipher Modes of Operation. Methods and Techniques. National Institute of Standards and Technology (2001)
3. Dworkin, M.J.: Recommendation for Block Cipher Modes of Operation: The XTS-AES Mode for Confidentiality on Storage Devices. National Institute of Standards and Technology (2010)
4. Bhanot, R., Hans, R.: A review and comparative analysis of various encryption algorithms. Int. J. Secur. Appl. **9**, 289–306 (2015)
5. Agrawal, M., Mishra, P.: A comparative survey on symmetric key encryption techniques. Int. J. Comput. Sci. Eng. **4**, 877 (2012)
6. Bujari, D., Aribas, E.: Comparative analysis of block cipher modes of operation. In: International Advanced Researches & Engineering Congress-2017, pp. 1–4 (2017)
7. Blazhevski, D., Bozhinovski, A., Stojchevska, B., Pachovski, V.: Modes of operation of the AES algorithm. In: The 10th Conference for Informatics and Information Technology, pp. 212–216 (2013)
8. Almuhammadi, S., Al-Hejri, I.: A comparative analysis of AES common modes of operation. In: 2017 IEEE 30th Canadian Conference on Electrical and Computer Engineering (CCECE), pp. 1–4. IEEE (2017)
9. El-Semary, A.M., Abdel-Azim, M.M.: Counter chain: a new block cipher mode of operation. J. Inf. Process. Syst. **11**, 266–279 (2015)
10. Rogaway, P.: Efficient instantiations of tweakable blockciphers and refinements to modes OCB and PMAC. In: Lee, P.J. (ed.) ASIACRYPT 2004. LNCS, vol. 3329, pp. 16–31. Springer, Heidelberg (2004). https://doi.org/10.1007/978-3-540-30539-2_2
11. Liskov, M., Rivest, R.L., Wagner, D.: Tweakable block ciphers. In: Yung, M. (ed.) CRYPTO 2002. LNCS, vol. 2442, pp. 31–46. Springer, Heidelberg (2002). https://doi.org/10.1007/3-540-45708-9_3
12. Liskov, M., Rivest, R.L., Wagner, D.J.: Tweakable block ciphers. J. Cryptol. **24**, 588–613 (2011)
13. Elminaam, D.S.A., Abdual-Kader, H.M., Hadhoud, M.M.: Evaluating the performance of symmetric encryption algorithms. Int. J. Comput. Sci. Netw. Secur. **10**, 216–222 (2010)
14. Singhal, N., Raina, J.: Comparative analysis of AES and RC4 algorithms for better utilization. Int. J. Comput. Trends Technol. **2**, 177–181 (2011)

15. Thakur, J., Kumar, N.: DES, AES and Blowfish: symmetric key cryptography algorithms simulation based performance analysis. Int. J. Emerg. Technol. Adv. Eng. **1**, 6–12 (2011)
16. Li, Q., Zhong, C., Zhao, K., Mei, X., Chu, X.: Implementation and analysis of AES encryption on GPU. In: 2012 IEEE 14th International Conference on High Performance Computing and Communication and 2012 IEEE 9th International Conference on Embedded Software and Systems (HPCC-ICESS), pp. 843–848. IEEE (2012)
17. Ramesh, A., Suruliandi, A.: Performance analysis of encryption algorithms for information security. In: 2013 International Conference on Circuits, Power and Computing Technologies (ICCPCT), pp. 840–844. IEEE (2013)
18. Desai, A., Ankalgi, K., Yamanur, H., Navalgund, S.S.: Parallelization of AES algorithm for disk encryption using CBC and ICBC modes. In: 2013 Fourth International Conference on Computing, Communications and Networking Technologies (ICCCNT), pp. 1–7. IEEE (2013)
19. Saraf, K.R., Jagtap, V.P., Mishra, A.K.: Text and image encryption decryption using advanced encryption standard. Int. J. Emerg. Trends Technol. Comput. Sci. **3**, 118–126 (2014)

The 4th International Symposium on Sensor-Cloud Systems (SCS 2018)

SCS 2018 Organizing and Program Committees

Honorary Chairs

Jiannong Cao   The Hong Kong Polytechnic University, Hong Kong
Weijia Jia   Shanghai Jiaotong University, China

Advisory Chairs

Guojun Wang   Guangzhou University, China
Qing Li   City University of Hong Kong, Hong Kong

Steering Chairs

Xiaojiang Chen   Northwest University, China
Kim-Kwang Raymond Choo   The University of Texas at San Antonio, USA
Mianxiong Dong   Muroran Institute of Technology, Japan
Wei Dong   Zhejiang University, China
Xiao-Jiang Du (James)   Temple University, USA
Guangjie Han   Hohai University, China
Kuan-Ching Li   Providence University, Taiwan
Limin Sun   Institute of Information Engineering, Chinese Academy of Sciences, China
Hongyi Wu   Old Dominion University (ODU), USA
Yang Xiao   The University of Alabama, USA

General Chairs

Tian Wang   Huaqiao University, China
Chunsheng Zhu   The University of British Columbia, Canada
Md. Zakirul Alam Bhuiyan   Fordham University, USA

Program Chairs

Sheng Wen   Deakin University, Australia
Zhangbing Zhou   China University of Geosciences (Beijing), China and TELECOM SudParis, France

Program Committee

A. M. A. Elman Bashar	Plymouth State University, USA
Yonghong Chen	Huaqiao University, China
Siyao Cheng	Harbin Institute of Technology, China
Lin Cui	Jinan University (Guangzhou), China
Haipeng Dai	Nanjing University, China
Weiwei Fang	Beijing Jiaotong University, China
Zhitao Guan	North China Electric Power University, China
Xiali (Sharon) Hei	Delaware State University, USA
Qiangsheng Hua	Huazhong University of Science and Technology, China
Patrick Hung	University of Ontario Institute of Technology, Canada
Yongxuan Lai	Xiamen University, China
Feng Li	Shandong University, China
Guanghui Li	Jiangnan University, China
Jianxin Li	University of West Australia, Australia
Junbin Liang	Guangxi University, China
Wanyu Lin	University of Toronto, Canada
Zhen Ling	Southeast University, China
Anfeng Liu	Central South University, China
Chi (Harold) Liu	Beijing Institute of Technology, China
Kai Liu	Chongqing University, China
Liang Liu	Beijing University of Posts and Telecommunications, China
Peng Liu	Hangzhou Dianzi University, China
Xiao Liu	Deakin University, Australia
Xuxun Liu	South China University of Technology, China
Kai Peng	Huaqiao University, China
Zhen Peng	College of William and Mary, USA
Rajesh Prasad	Saint Anselm College, USA
Yiran Shen	Data61, CSIRO, Australia
Rui Tan	Nanyang Technological University, Singapore
Shaolei Teng	Howard University, USA
Jiliang Wang	Tsinghua University, China
Weigang Wu	Sun Yat-Sen University, China
Yong Xie	Xiamen University of Technology, China
Wenzheng Xu	Sichuan University, China
Guisong Yang	University of Shanghai for Science and Technology, China
Dongxiao Yu	Huazhong University of Science and Technology, China
Yong Yu	Shanxi Normal University, China
Dong Yuan	Sydney University, Australia
Shigeng Zhang	Central South University, China
Chunsheng Zhu	The University of British Columbia, Canada
Yanmin Zhu	Shanghai Jiao Tong University, China

Journal Special Issue Chairs

Kim-Kwang Raymond Choo   University of Texas at San Antonio, USA
James Xi Zheng   Deakin University, Australia

Publicity Chairs

Zeyu Sun   Luoyang Institute of Science and Technology, China
Xiaofei Xing   Guangzhou University, China
Zenghua Zhao   Tianjin University, China

Coordination Chairs

Zhen Peng   College of William and Mary, USA
Yang Liu   Beijing University of Posts and Telecommunications, China

Web Chair

Guangxue Zhang   Huaqiao University, China

Matching Sensor Ontologies Through Compact Evolutionary Tabu Search Algorithm

Xingsi Xue[1,2,3,4(✉)] and Shijian Liu[1,3]

[1] College of Information Science and Engineering, Fujian University of Technology,
Fuzhou 350118, Fujian, China
jack8375@gmail.com
[2] Intelligent Information Processing Research Center,
Fujian University of Technology, Fuzhou 350118, Fujian, China
[3] Fujian Provincial Key Laboratory of Big Data Mining and Applications,
Fujian University of Technology, Fuzhou 350118, Fujian, China
[4] Fujian Key Lab for Automotive Electronics and Electric Drive,
Fujian University of Technology, Fuzhou 350118, Fujian, China

Abstract. Although sensor ontologies are regarded as the solution to data heterogeneity on the Semantic Sensor Web (SSW), these sensor ontologies themselves introduce heterogeneity by defining the same entity with different names or in different ways. To solve this problem, it is necessary to determine the semantic identical entities between heterogeneous sensor ontologies, so-called sensor ontology matching. Due to the complexity of the sensor ontology matching process, Evolutionary Algorithm (EA) can present a good methodology for determining ontology alignments. To overcome the EA-based ontology matcher's shortcomings, i.e. premature convergence, long runtime and huge memory consumption, this paper present a Compact Evolutionary Tabu Search algorithm (CETS) to efficiently match the sensor ontologies. The experiment utilizes Ontology Alignment Evaluation Initiative (OAEI)'s bibliographic benchmark and library track, and two pairs of real sensor ontologies test CETS's performance. The experimental results show that CETS is both effective and efficient when matching ontologies with various scales and under different heterogeneous situations, and comparing with the state-of-the-art sensor ontology matching systems, CETS can significantly improve the ontology alignment's quality.

Keywords: Semantic Sensor Web · Sensor ontology matching
Compact evolutionary algorithm · Tabu search

1 Introduction

The linking of elements from semantic web technologies with sensor networks is called Semantic Sensor Web (SSW), whose main feature is the use of sensor

G. Wang et al. (Eds.): SpaCCS 2018, LNCS 11342, pp. 115–124, 2018.
https://doi.org/10.1007/978-3-030-05345-1_9

ontologies. A sensor ontology is defined as 3-tuples (C, P, R), where C, P and R are respectively the set of classes, properties and relationships. In general, class, property and relationship can also be called ontology entities. Sensor ontology can capture information about sensor capabilities, performance, and the conditions in which it can be used, allowing the discovery of data for different purposes and in different contexts [1]. Sensor ontologies are regarded as the solution to data heterogeneity on the SSW, and in recent years, such sensor ontologies as CSIRO sensor ontology[1], SSN ontology[2] and MMI Device ontology[3] have been developed. However, these sensor ontologies themselves introduce heterogeneity by defining the same entity with different names or in different ways. To solve this problem, we need to use the ontology matching technique to determine the semantic identical entities between heterogeneous sensor ontologies. The obtained sensor ontology alignment A is a correspondence set, and each correspondence inside is a 4-tuple (e_1, e_2, n, r), where e_1 and e_2 are the entities of two sensor ontology, respectively, $n \in [0, 1]$ is a confidence value holding for the correspondence between e_1 and e_2, r is the relation existing between e_1 and e_2, which refers to equivalence.

Due to the complexity of the ontology matching problem (large-scale optimal problem with lots of local optimal solutions), Evolutionary Algorithm (EA) can present a good methodology for determining ontology alignments [12]. Recently, Xue et al. [10,11] have utilized EA to match the sensor ontologies and obtained good alignments. However, the premature convergence, long runtime and huge memory consumption are three main shortcomings of EA-based matchers, which make them incapable of effectively searching the optimal solution for sensor ontology matching problems. In this paper, a Compact Evolutionary Tabu Search algorithm (CETS) is proposed, which makes use of a probabilistic representation of the population to perform the optimization process, and introduces the Tabu Search algorithm (TS) [6] as a local search strategy into EA's evolving process. In particular, a similarity measure on sensor concept is proposed to calculate the similarity value of two sensor concepts, an optimal model for sensor ontology matching is constructed, and CETS is presented to efficiently solve the sensor ontology matching problem.

The rest of the paper is organized as follows: Sect. 2 presents the single objective optimal model for ontology meta-matching problem; Sect. 3 gives the details of CETS; Sect. 4 shows the experimental results; finally, Sect. 5 draws the conclusions.

---

[1] https://www.w3.org/2005/Incubator/ssn/wiki/SensorOntology2009.
[2] https://www.w3.org/TR/vocab-ssn.
[3] https://marinemetadata.org/.

2 Sensor Ontology Matching Problem and Similarity Measure

2.1 Sensor Ontology Matching Problem

Based on the observations that the more correspondences found and the higher mean similarity values of the correspondences are, the better the alignment quality is [2], we utilize the following metric to measure the quality of a sensor ontology alignment:

$$f(A) = \frac{\phi(A) \times \frac{\sum_{i=1}^{|A|} \delta_i}{|A|}}{\alpha \times \phi(A) + (1 - \alpha) \times \frac{\sum_{i=1}^{|A|} \delta_i}{|A|}} \tag{1}$$

where $|A|$ is the number of correspondences in A, ϕ is a function of normalization in $[0, 1]$, δ_i is the similarity value of the ith correspondence in A, and α is a parameter used to tradeoff the instance alignments characterized by high recall [3] (with the decreasing of α) or high precision [3] (with the increase of α). In general, the value of α is set to 0.5 to prefer neither recall nor precision.

On this basis, given two sensor ontologies O_1 and O_2, the optimal model of sensor ontology matching problem can be defined as follows:

$$\begin{cases} min & F(X) \\ s.t. & X = (x_1, x_2, \cdots, x_{|O_1|})^T \\ & x_i \in \{1, 2, \cdots, |O_2|\}, i = 1, 2, \cdots, |O_1| \end{cases} \tag{2}$$

where $|O_1|$ and $|O_2|$ respectively represent the cardinalities of two entity sets of O_1 and O_2, $x_i, i = 1, 2, \cdots, |O_1|$ represents the ith pair of correspondence, and $F(X)$ calculates X's corresponding alignment's quality.

2.2 Similarity Measure on Sensor Concept

The similarity measure on concept is the foundation of ontology matching [5]. In this work, a profile-based similarity measure is utilized to calculate the similarity value between two sensor concepts. First, for each sensor class, a profile is constructed by collecting the label, comment, and property information from itself and all its direct descendants. Then, the similarity of two sensor concepts c_1 and c_2 is measured based on the similarity of their profiles p_1 and p_2:

$$sim(c_1, c_2) = \frac{\sum_{i=1}^{f} \max_{j=1 \cdots g} (sim(p_{1i}, p_{2j})) + \sum_{j=1}^{g} \max_{i=1 \cdots f} (sim(p_{1i}, p_{2j}))}{f + g} \tag{3}$$

The similarity value of two profile elements is calculated by N-gram distance [13], which is the most performing string-based similarity measure for the biological ontology matching problem, and a linguistic measure, which calculate a synonymy-based distance through Wordnet [8]. Given two words w_1 and w_2, the similarity $sim(w_1, w_2)$ is calculated according to the following formula:

$$sim(w_1, w_2) = \begin{cases} 1, & \text{if two words are synonymous} \\ N - gram(w_1, w_2), & \text{otherwise} \end{cases} \tag{4}$$

3   Compact Evolutionary Tabu Search Algorithm

In this work, a Compact Evolutionary Tabu Search algorithm is presented to solve the problem of sensor ontology matching. The Evolutionary Tabu Search algorithm (ETS) is an optimization algorithm composed of an evolutionary framework which contains and launches in each generation one or more local search components. This marriage between global search and local search is helpful to reduce the possibility of the premature convergence and increasing the convergence speed. To save the runtime and memory consumption, we present a compact version of ETS, i.e. CETS. CETS simulates the behaviour of population-based TES by employing the probabilistic representation of the population. Thus, a run of CETS is able to highly improve the performance of solving large scale matching problem in terms of both runtime and memory consumption.

3.1   Chromosome Encoding

In this work, the genes are encoded through the binary coding mechanism to represent the correspondences in the alignment. Given the total number of classes in source ontology and target ontology O_1 and O_2, the first part of a chromosome (or PV) consists of O_1 gene segments, and the Binary Code Length (BCL) of each gene segment is equal to $\lfloor \log_2(O_2) + 0.5 \rfloor$, which ensures each gene segment could present any target ontology class's index. While, the second part of a chromosome (or PV) has only one gene segment, whose BCL is equal to $\lfloor \log_2(\frac{1}{numAccuracy}) + 0.5 \rfloor$, which can ensure this gene segment could present any threshold value under the numerical accuracy $numAccuracy$. Thus, the total length of the chromosome (or PV) is equal to $n_s \times \lfloor \log_2(n_t) + 0.5 \rfloor + \lfloor \log_2(\frac{1}{numAccuracy}) + 0.5 \rfloor$. Given a gene $gene = \{geneBit_1, geneBit_2, \cdots, geneBit_n\}$ where $geneBit_i$ is the ith gene bit value of the gene segment, we decode it to obtain a decimal number whose value is equal to $\sum_{i=1}^{n} 2^{geneBit_i}$. In particular, the decimal numbers obtained represent the indexes of the target classes, where 0 means the source instance is not mapped to any target ontology's class.

3.2   Probability Vector

In this work, we use one Probability Vector (PV) to characterize the entire population. The number of elements in PV is equal to the number of individual's gene bits and each element's value is in $[0, 1]$. Since each element's value in PV represents the probability of being one, we can use PV to generate various solutions. In addition, PV can be updated based on the better solution in terms of its fitness value, with the aim to move the PV toward the better solution. Here is an example of generating a new solution through PV $(0.1, 0.8, 0.5, 0.9)^T$. First, generate four random numbers, such as 0.4, 0.5, 0.8 and 0.1. Then compare the numbers with the elements in PV accordingly to determine the new generated individual's gene values, For example, since $0.4 > 0.1$, the first gene bit's value of the new solution is 0, and similarly, the remaining gene bits' values are 1, 0 and 1, respectively. In this way, the new solution we obtain is 0101. By repeating this procedure, we can obtain various individuals. In addition, if 0101 is the best solution in the current generation, i.e. elite, PV should be updated according to its information. Given the PV update value *updateValue*, say 0.1, if the gene value of the elite is 0, the corresponding element of PV will decrease by *updateValue*, otherwise increase by *updateValue*. In this way, the updated PV is $(0.0, 0.9, 0.4, 1.0)^T$.

3.3   Local Search Process

The local search strategy performs iterative search for optimal solution in the neighborhood of a candidate. In order to tradeoff between the local search and the global search, the local search process in our work is designed according to the following rules:

- the local search is applied within each evolutionary cycle,
- the local search is executed after crossover and mutation,
- the local search is applied to the best individual of population,
- the local search method is the tabu search algorithm.

Tabu search concerns with imposing restrictions to guide a search process to negotiate otherwise difficult regions, where the restrictions can operate by direct exclusion of search alternatives classed as "forbidden" [6]. Given a tabu matrix $TM = [TV_1, TV_2, \cdots, TV_{|O_1|}]$ where the ith tabu list $TV_i = (tv_1, tv_2, \cdots, tv_{tLength})^T$, $i = 1, 2, \cdots, |O_1|$, $tv_j \in 0, 1, 2, \cdots, |O_2|$, the pseudocode of tabu search process is given as follows:

During the EA's evolving process, if $soluiton_{elite}$ keep unchanged for $\delta = 20$ generations, each $tv_j^i \in TV_i$, whose corresponding class in C_{tgt} has the highest similarity value with c_i, will be removed.

4   Experimental Results and Analysis

In the experiments, the bibliographic benchmark and library track in the Ontology Alignment Evaluation Initiative (OAEI)[4] and two pairs of real sensor ontologies, i.e. CSIRO sensor ontology vs SSN ontology and MMI Device ontology vs SSN ontology, are used to test the performance of our approach. The obtained alignments are assessed by means of the standard evaluation metrics, i.e. recall, precision and f-measure [3], and the symbols r, p and f in the tables are respectively referred to recall, precision and f-measure. In particular, our approach's results are the average of ten independent runs.

---

[4] http://oaei.ontologymatching.org/2016.

Algorithm 1. Local Search Process

$iterNum = 0$;
while $iterNum < maxIterNum$ **do**
  for $neighborNum = 0; neighborNum < neighborScale; neighborNum + +$ **do**
    $solution_{new} = solution_{elite}.copy()$;
    for $i = 0; i < solution_{new}.length; i + +$ **do**
      if $random(0, 1) < localSearchMutationProbability$ **then**
        $solution_{new}[i] = random(\{0, 1, \cdots, |C_{tgt}|\} - \{tv_j^i \in TV_i\})$;
      end if
    end for
    append $solution_{new}[i]$ into $neiborPopulation$;
  end for
  $solution_{localElite} = $ selectBestSolution($neiborPopulation$);
  compete($solution_{Elite}, solution_{localElite}$);
  if $winner == solution_{localElite}$ **then**
    for each $TV_i \in TM$ **do**
      if TV_i is not full **then**
        append $solution_{localElite}[i]$ to TV_i;
      else
        replace $tv_j^i \in TV_i$, whose corresponding class in C_{tgt} has the lowest similarity value with c_i, with $solution_{localElite}[i]$;
      end if
    end for
    $iterNum + +$;
  else
    break;
  end if
end while

4.1 Experiment Configuration

In our work, CETS uses the following parameters which represent a trade-off setting obtained in empirical way to achieve the highest average alignment quality on all testing cases. Through the configuration of parameters chosen in this way, it has been justified by the experiments that parameters chosen are robust for all the heterogeneous problems presented in the testing cases, and it is hopeful to be robust for the common heterogeneous situations in the real world.

- Tabu list length = 10,
- Local search population scale = 15,
- Local search iteration number = 5,
- Local search mutation probability = 0.5,
- Termination condition = 3000 generations.

The hardware configurations used to run the algorithms are as follows:

- Processor: Intel Core i7-4600U CPU,
- CPU speed: 2.10 GHz,
- RAM capacity: 15G.

4.2   OAEI Datasets

Bibliographic Benchmark. Bibliographic benchmark consists of a set of small scale ontologies which are built around a seed ontology and many variations of it. The brief description of bibliographic benchmark is presented in Table 1, and Table 2 shows the average recall, precision, f-measure, runtime and f-measure provided per second of all test cases in bibliographic benchmark.

Table 1. Brief description of bibliographic benchmarks. 1XX, 2XX and 3XX stands for the test case whose ID beginning with the prefix digit 1, 2 and 3, respectively.

ID	Brief description
1XX	The ontologies are the same
2XX	The ontologies have different lexical, linguistic or structure features
3XX	The ontologies are real world cases

Table 2. Comparison of CETS with OAEI participants on bibliographic benchmark. The symbols r, p and f in the table stand for recall, precision and f-measure, respectively.

Systems	r	p	f	Runtime (second)
AML	0.24	1.00	0.38	120
CroMatch	0.83	0.96	0.89	1,100
Lily	0.83	0.97	0.89	2,211
LogMap	0.39	0.93	0.55	194
LogMapLt	0.50	0.43	0.46	96
PhenoMF	0.01	0.03	0.01	1,632
PhenoMM	0.01	0.03	0.01	1,743
PhenoMP	0.01	0.02	0.01	1,833
XMap	0.40	0.95	0.56	123
LogMapBio	0.24	0.48	0.32	454,439
CETS	0.86	0.95	**0.90**	**82**

As can be seen from Table 2, the results of CETS outperform all the participants in OAEI in terms of f-measure and runtime. Therefore, for small-scale ontology matching problem, CETS is both effective and efficient.

Library Track. The library track is also a large ontology matching task which is about matching two real world thesauri: STW (economics) and TheSoz (social sciences). Despite being from two different domains, these two thesauri have huge overlapping areas, and moreover, they have roughly the same size, are both originally developed in German, are both multilingual, both have English translations. To be specific, the STW Thesaurus for economics provides more than 6,000 standardized subject headings and 19,000 additional keywords in both language, and TheSoz contains overall about 12,000 keywords, from which 8,000 are standardized subject headings (in English and German) and 4,000 additional keywords.

Table 3. Comparison of CETS with OAEI participants on library track. The symbols r, p and f in the table stand for recall, precision and f-measure, respectively.

Systems	r	p	f	Runtime (second)
AML*	0.78	0.82	0.80	68
AML	0.75	0.72	0.73	71
LogMap*	0.68	0.74	0.71	222
LogMap	0.65	0.78	0.71	73
LogMapLite	0.77	0.64	0.70	93
XMap2	0.89	0.51	0.65	12,652
MaasMatch	0.66	0.50	0.57	14,641
LogMap-C	0.26	0.48	0.34	**21**
RSDLWB	0.04	0.78	0.07	32828
CETS	0.80	0.81	**0.80**	62

As can be seen from Table 3, although CETS's f-measure is equal to AML, which are the best among all competitors, the runtime needed by our approach is less than AML. Thus, CETS is able to effectively handle such ontology including a huge amount of concepts and additional descriptions. To conclude, experimental results on OAEI testing cases show that CETS is both effective and efficient when matching ontologies with various scales and under different heterogeneous situations.

4.3   Real Sensor Ontologies

In this section, we test CETS on two pairs of real sensor ontologies, i.e. CSIRO sensor ontology vs SSN ontology and MMI Device ontology vs SSN ontology. Since SSN is the most used global reference ontology that has been developed in the domain of sensor networks, the goal of this experiment is to align the CSIRO sensor ontology and MMI Device ontology to SSN ontology. Table 4 shows the comparative results of CETS and the state-of-the-art sensor ontology matching systems ASMOV [7], CODI [4], SOBOM [9], FuzzyAlign [1] and CCEA [11], on two pairs of real sensor ontologies in terms of recall, precision and f-measure. Table 4 shows the experimental results of CETS and five state-of-the-art sensor ontology matching systems on two pairs of real sensor ontologies.

Table 4. Comparison of CETS with the state-of-the-art sensor ontology matching systems on two pairs of real sensor ontologies. The symbols r, p and f in the table stand for recall, precision and f-measure, respectively.

Systems	CSIRO vs SSN			MMI device vs SSN		
	r	p	f	r	p	f
ASMOV	0.78	0.72	0.75	0.65	0.84	0.73
CODI	0.78	0.81	0.79	0.83	0.78	0.80
SOBOM	0.81	0.76	0.78	0.74	0.81	0.77
FuzzyAlign	0.82	0.95	0.88	0.84	0.92	0.88
CCEA	0.89	0.96	0.92	0.86	0.94	0.90
CETS	0.94	0.96	0.94	0.90	**0.95**	**0.92**

As can be seen from Table 4, the values of recall, precision and f-measure obtained by CETS all outperform other approaches, which demonstrates the effectiveness of it when matching sensor ontologies. Despite high recall obtained, there are still a few mappings undetected because some very specific terms in sensor networks domain, e.g. hygrometer and humistor, are not found in Word-Net databases, so it would be desirable to use a specialized sensor thesaurus instead of WordNet.

5   Conclusion

In this paper, a Compact Evolutionary Tabu Search Algorithm is proposed to efficiently address the sensor ontology heterogeneity problem. CETS makes use of a probabilistic representation of the population to perform the optimization process, and introduces the Tabu Search algorithm as a local search strategy to overcome the algorithm's premature convergence, long runtime and huge consumption. The experimental results show that CETS is both effective and efficient when matching ontologies with various scales and under different heterogeneous situations, and comparing with the state-of-the-art sensor ontology matching systems, CETS can significantly improve the ontology alignment's quality.

Acknowledgments. This work is supported by the National Natural Science Foundation of China (No. 61503082), Natural Science Foundation of Fujian Province (Nos. 2016J05145 and 2017H0003), Scientific Research Foundation of Fujian University of Technology (Nos. GY-Z17162 and GY-Z15007, GY-Z160130 and GY-Z160138), Fujian Province Outstanding Young Scientific Researcher Training Project (No. GY-Z160149) and Project of Fujian Education Department Funds (JK2017029).

References

1. Fernandez, S., Marsa-Maestre, I., Velasco, J.R., Alarcos, B.: Ontology alignment architecture for semantic sensor web integration. Sensors **13**(9), 12581–12604 (2013)
2. Gulić, M., Vrdoljak, B., Banek, M.: CroMatcher: an ontology matching system based on automated weighted aggregation and iterative final alignment. Web Semant.: Sci. Serv. Agents World Wide Web **41**, 50–71 (2016)
3. Hand, D., Christen, P.: A note on using the F-measure for evaluating record linkage algorithms. Stat. Comput. **28**(3), 539–547 (2018)
4. Huber, J., Sztyler, T., Noessner, J., Meilicke, C.: CODI: combinatorial optimization for data integration–results for OAEI 2011. Ontol. Matching **134** (2011)
5. Otero-Cerdeira, L., Rodríguez-Martínez, F.J., Gómez-Rodríguez, A.: Ontology matching: a literature review. Expert Syst. Appl. **42**(2), 949–971 (2015)
6. Smutnicki, C., Bożejko, W.: Tabu search and solution space analyses. The job shop case. In: Moreno-Díaz, R., Pichler, F., Quesada-Arencibia, A. (eds.) EUROCAST 2017. LNCS, vol. 10671, pp. 383–391. Springer, Cham (2018). https://doi.org/10.1007/978-3-319-74718-7_46
7. Stojanovic, N., Bradley, R.M., Wilkinson, S., Kabuka, M.R., Shironoshita, E.P.: Web-based ontology alignment with the GeneTegra alignment tool. In: SIMBig, pp. 127–132 (2017)
8. Wei, T., Lu, Y., Chang, H., Zhou, Q., Bao, X.: A semantic approach for text clustering using WordNet and lexical chains. Expert Syst. Appl. **42**(4), 2264–2275 (2015)
9. Xu, P., Wang, Y., Cheng, L., Zang, T.: Alignment results of SOBOM for OAEI 2010. In: Proceedings of the 5th International Conference on Ontology Matching, vol. 689. pp. 203–211. CEUR-WS.org (2010)
10. Xue, X., Chen, J.: A preference-based multi-objective evolutionary algorithm for semiautomatic sensor ontology matching. Int. J. Swarm Intell. Res. (IJSIR) **9**(2), 1–14 (2018)
11. Xue, X., Pan, J.S.: A compact co-evolutionary algorithm for sensor ontology meta-matching. Knowl. Inf. Syst. **56**(2), 335–353 (2018)
12. Xue, X., Pan, J.S.: An overview on evolutionary algorithm based ontology matching. J. Inf. Hiding Multimed. Signal Process **9**, 75–88 (2018)
13. Yeh, J.F., Chang, L.T., Liu, C.Y., Hsu, T.W.: Chinese spelling check based on N-gram and string matching algorithm. In: Proceedings of the 4th Workshop on Natural Language Processing Techniques for Educational Applications, NLPTEA 2017, pp. 35–38 (2017)

Event-Triggered Fault-Detection Filter Using Coordinate Transformation Approach for Time-Varying Stochastic Systems

Yunji Li[1], Li Peng[1(✉)], Xuefang Zhu[2], and Wen Li[3]

[1] Engineering Research Center of Internet of Things Technology Applications
(Ministry of Education), Jiangnan University, Wuxi 214122, China
jnpengli@126.com
[2] Wuxi High Electromechanical Technology Vocational School, Wuxi 214028, China
[3] School of Mechanical Engineering, Jiangnan University, Wuxi 214122, China

Abstract. In this paper, an event-triggered fault-detection filter design for reducing communication actions in networked time-varying stochastic systems over a finite-time horizon is proposed. A coordinate transformation approach is exploited to achieve the purpose that the fault-detection residual is only sensitive to system faults while robust to additive unknown disturbances. This approach can transform the considered system into two subsystems, and the disturbances are removed from one of the subsystems. Furthermore, the optimal gain for each filter is derived, which applies to the optimization criteria of unbiasedness and minimum mean-square estimation error.

Keywords: Networked fault detection · Event-triggered protocol
Coordinate transformation · Stochastic system · Time-varying system

1 Introduction

In this work, a novel event-triggered fault-detection strategy for time-varying stochastic systems is proposed. We consider the problem of model-based fault detection based on the measurements taken by a battery-powered sensor. The remote fault-detection module can receive the sensor information through a wireless channel. It is supposed that the transmission itself will consume more energy than computation, which is a reasonable assumption because the energy consumed by the wireless transmission module is always much more than the computing module in practice [1,2]. Thus, an event-triggered sensor data transmission scheme is designed for reducing communication actions [3–6].

The presented coordinate transformation approach for event-triggered fault detection is one common approach in fault diagnosis literature [7–9], where can transform the system into two subsystems. One of the subsystems is free from

© Springer Nature Switzerland AG 2018
G. Wang et al. (Eds.): SpaCCS 2018, LNCS 11342, pp. 125–135, 2018.
https://doi.org/10.1007/978-3-030-05345-1_10

disturbances, but subject to system faults. Consequently, a fault-detection residual based on the derived filter for this subsystem can only sensitive to faults. However, to the best of the authors' knowledge, coordinate transformation approach has not been considered for event-triggered fault detection.

In particular, this article makes the following main contributions: two separated event-triggered optimal filters for each subsystem based on coordinate transformation approach are synthetically designed so that the fault-detection residual is sensitive only to faults while insensitive to disturbances. The gain of each filter is derived by the optimization criteria of unbiasedness and minimum-variance.

Nomenclature: The terms state observer and state estimator are used synonymously in this paper. $\mathbb{N}$ and $\mathbb{R}$ denote the sets of natural and real numbers, respectively. $\mathbb{R}^{m \times n}$ denotes the sets of m by n real-valued matrices, whereas $\mathbb{R}^n$ is short for $\mathbb{R}^{n \times 1}$. $\mathbb{R}_+^{n \times n}$ and $\mathbb{R}_{++}^{n \times n}$ are the sets of $n \times n$ positive semi-definite and positive definite matrices, respectively. When $X \in \mathbb{R}_+^{n \times n}$, it is simply denoted as $X \geq 0$ or $X > 0$ if $X \in \mathbb{R}_{++}^{n \times n}$. For $X \in \mathbb{R}^{m \times n}$, X^{T} denotes the transpose of X. A diagonal matrix is denoted by $diag\,[\cdot]$. In symmetric block matrices, "*"is used as an ellipsis for terms induced by symmetry. I denotes a identity matrix with appropriate dimensions. Furthermore, $\mathbb{E}[\cdot]$, $Var(\cdot)$ and $tr(\cdot)$ denote the mathematical expectation, variance and the trace of a matrix, respectively.

2 Problem Statement

2.1 System Model

Consider the following discrete stochastic time-varying system defined on $k \in [0, L]$:

$$
\begin{aligned}
x_{k+1} &= A_k x_k + B_k u_k + D_{w,k} w_k + F_k f_k + D_{d,k} d_k \\
y_k &= C_k x_k + D_{v,k} v_k
\end{aligned}
\tag{1}
$$

In above equations, the subscript "k" is a discrete-time index, system state x_k is a m-dimensional vector, u_k is a n-dimensional control input, y_k is a p-dimensional sensor's measurement. The noise process $\{w_k\}$, $\{v_k\}$ and the initial state x_0 are assumed mutually independent, white, zero-mean with known variance: $\mathbb{E}\left(w_k w_k^T\right) = Q_{w,k} \geq 0$, $\mathbb{E}\left(v_k v_k^T\right) = R_{v,k} > 0$ and $\mathbb{E}\left(x_0 x_0^T\right) = P_{0,k} > 0$, respectively. The additional terms, fault signal f_k is a q-dimensional vector, and d_k represents bounded uncertainties/disturbances with s-dimension. It is assumed that the time-varying matrices A_k, B_k, C_k, F_k, $D_{w,k}$, $D_{d,k}$ and $D_{v,k}$ with appropriate dimensions are known.

When y_k is obtained in sensors, the event-triggered data transmission scheme is supposed to decide on whether it is sent it to the remote fault-detection filter or not. Let γ_k be the decision variable: $\gamma_k = 1$ indicates that y_k is sent out and otherwise $\gamma_k = 0$. As a result, only when $\gamma_k = 1$, the filter knows the exact value y_k.

Roughly speaking, we develop a novel fault-detection strategy with event-triggered data scheme for the above system (1) so that the fault-detection residual is still able to contain the characteristics of sensibility and real-time capacity. To achieve this goal, we first introduce two assumptions.

Assumption 1: [4]

$$rank\left(C_k \times D_{d,k}\right) = rank\left(D_{d,k}\right) \tag{2}$$

Assumption 2: [5]

For every complex number ζ with nonnegative real part,

$$rank\left(\begin{bmatrix} A_k - \zeta I & F_k & D_{d,k} \\ C_k & 0 & 0 \end{bmatrix}\right) = n + rank\left(F_k\right) + rank\left(D_{d,k}\right) \tag{3}$$

2.2 Transforming of the System into Two Subsystems

Inspired by [4,5] and [6], we adopt the coordinate transformation approach to transform the system into two subsystems: the first subsystem is free from disturbances, but subject to system faults. For the first subsystem, a fault-detection residual based on the derived filter will only sensitive to faults; conversely, the designed estimator of the second subsystem includes disturbances and system faults, which can robust to the disturbances. The transformation results are briefly presented below.

According to [4], Assumption 1 is equivalent to the existence of a set of non-singular matrices T_k and S_k such that

$$x = T_k^{-1}\begin{bmatrix} \tilde{x}^1 \\ \tilde{x}^2 \end{bmatrix}, \text{ and } y = S_k^{-1}\begin{bmatrix} \tilde{y}^1 \\ \tilde{y}^2 \end{bmatrix} \tag{4}$$

respectively. The system (1) can be accordingly transformed into

$$\begin{aligned}
\tilde{x}_{k+1}^1 &= \tilde{A}_{11,k}\tilde{x}_k^1 + \tilde{A}_{12,k}\tilde{x}_k^2 + \tilde{D}_{w,k}^1 w_k + \tilde{F}_k^1 f_k + \tilde{B}_{1,k}u_k \\
\tilde{x}_{k+1}^2 &= \tilde{A}_{22,k}\tilde{x}_k^2 + \tilde{A}_{21,k}\tilde{x}_k^1 + \tilde{D}_{w,k}^2 w_k + \tilde{F}_k^2 f_k + \tilde{D}_{d,k}d_k + \tilde{B}_{2,k}u_k \\
\tilde{y}_k^1 &= \tilde{C}_{11,k}\tilde{x}_k^1 + \tilde{D}_{v,k}^1 v_k \\
\tilde{y}_k^2 &= \tilde{C}_{22,k}\tilde{x}_k^2 + \tilde{D}_{v,k}^2 v_k
\end{aligned} \tag{5}$$

where

$$T_k A_k T_k^{-1} = \begin{bmatrix} \tilde{A}_{11,k} & \tilde{A}_{12,k} \\ \tilde{A}_{21,k} & \tilde{A}_{22,k} \end{bmatrix}, \ T_k B_k = \begin{bmatrix} \tilde{B}_{1,k} \\ \tilde{B}_{2,k} \end{bmatrix}, \ T_k D_{w,k} = \begin{bmatrix} \tilde{D}_{w,k}^1 \\ \tilde{D}_{w,k}^2 \end{bmatrix} \tag{6}$$

$$T_k F_k = \begin{bmatrix} \tilde{F}_{1,k} \\ \tilde{F}_{2,k} \end{bmatrix}, \ T_k D_{d,k} = \begin{bmatrix} 0 \\ \tilde{D}_{d,k} \end{bmatrix},$$

$$S_k C_k T^{-1} = \begin{bmatrix} \tilde{C}_{11,k} & 0 \\ 0 & \tilde{C}_{22,k} \end{bmatrix}, \ S_k D_{v,k} = \begin{bmatrix} \tilde{D}_{v,k}^1 \\ \tilde{D}_{v,k}^2 \end{bmatrix} \tag{7}$$

Thus, two subsystems given by (5) can be rewritten separately as

The 1st subsystem:

$$\tilde{x}_{k+1}^1 = \tilde{A}_{11,k}\tilde{x}_k^1 + \tilde{A}_{12,k}\tilde{x}_k^2 + \tilde{D}_{w,k}^1 w_k + \tilde{F}_k^1 f_k + \tilde{B}_{1,k} u_k$$
$$\tilde{y}_k^1 = \tilde{C}_{11,k}\tilde{x}_k^1 + \tilde{D}_{v,k}^1 v_k \tag{8}$$

The 2nd subsystem:

$$\tilde{x}_{k+1}^2 = \tilde{A}_{22,k}\tilde{x}_k^2 + \tilde{A}_{21,k}\tilde{x}_k^1 + \tilde{D}_{w,k}^2 w_k + \tilde{F}_k^2 f_k + \tilde{D}_{d,k} d_k + \tilde{B}_{2,k} u_k$$
$$\tilde{y}_k^2 = \tilde{C}_{22,k}\tilde{x}_k^2 + \tilde{D}_{v,k}^2 v_k \tag{9}$$

Obviously, the disturbances are not included in the 1st subsystem, and the 2nd subsystem contains both. For each subsystem, we will derive the corresponding event-triggered fault-detection filter in the next section.

3   Design of Event-Triggered Fault-Detection Filter

Now we proceed to develop the recursive equations of fault-detection filter for each subsystem. For each $i = 1$ and 2, define the state estimation error e_k^i as

$$e_k^i = \hat{\tilde{x}}_k^i - \tilde{x}_k^i \tag{10}$$

where $\hat{\tilde{x}}_k^i$ indicates estimated state value for each $i = 1$ and 2, and the corresponding error covariance P_k^i is defined as follows

$$P_k^i = \mathbb{E}\left[\left(\hat{\tilde{x}}_k^i - \tilde{x}_k^i \right) \left(\hat{\tilde{x}}_k^i - \tilde{x}_k^i \right)^T \right] \tag{11}$$

The main result on the filter of the 1st subsystem will be presented in the following theorem.

Theorem 1. *For the 1st subsystem given by the formula (8), the optimal event-triggered filter $\hat{\tilde{x}}_k^1$ satisfies:*

$$\hat{\tilde{x}}_{k+1}^1 = \begin{cases} \tilde{A}_{11,k}\hat{\tilde{x}}_k^1 + \tilde{A}_{12,k}\hat{\tilde{x}}_k^2 + \tilde{B}_{1,k} u_k + K_k^1 \left(\tilde{y}_{k+1}^1 - \tilde{C}_{11,k}\tilde{A}_{11,k}\hat{\tilde{x}}_k^1 \right. \\ \left. -\tilde{C}_{11,k}\tilde{A}_{12,k}\hat{\tilde{x}}_k^2 - \tilde{C}_{11,k}\tilde{B}_{1,k} u_k \right) & \text{if } \gamma_k = 1 \\ \tilde{A}_{11,k}\hat{\tilde{x}}_k^1 + \tilde{A}_{12,k}\hat{\tilde{x}}_k^2 + \tilde{B}_{1,k} u_k & \text{if } \gamma_k = 0 \end{cases} \tag{12}$$

where

$$\begin{cases} K_k^1 = O_k^1 \tilde{C}_{11,k}^T \left(\tilde{C}_{11,k} O_k^1 \tilde{C}_{11,k}^T + R_k^1 \right)^{-1} \\ O_k^1 = \tilde{A}_{11,k} P_k^1 \tilde{A}_{11,k}^T + \tilde{D}_{w,k}^1 Q_{w,k} \left(\tilde{D}_{w,k}^1 \right)^T + \tilde{A}_{12,k} P_k^2 \tilde{A}_{12,k}^T \\ P_{k+1}^1 = \left(I - K_k^1 \tilde{C}_{11,k} \right) O_k^1 \left(I - K_k^1 \tilde{C}_{11,k} \right)^T + K_k^1 R_k^1 \left(K_k^1 \right)^T \\ R_k^1 = \tilde{D}_{v,k}^1 R_{v,k} \left(\tilde{D}_{v,k}^1 \right)^T \end{cases} \tag{13}$$

Proof. If $\gamma_k = 1$, a linear filter structure is considered as follows

$$
\begin{aligned}
\hat{\tilde{x}}^1_{k+1} = {}& \tilde{A}_{11,k}\hat{\tilde{x}}^1_k + \tilde{A}_{12,k}\hat{\tilde{x}}^2_k + \tilde{B}_{1,k}u_k + K^1_k\Big(\tilde{y}^1_{k+1} - \tilde{C}_{11,k}\tilde{A}_{11,k}\hat{\tilde{x}}^1_k \\
& -\tilde{C}_{11,k}\tilde{A}_{12,k}\hat{\tilde{x}}^2_k - \tilde{C}_{11,k}\tilde{B}_{1,k}u_k\Big)
\end{aligned}
\tag{14}
$$

We need to find the gain matrix K^1_k that minimizes $tr\left(P^1_k\right)$ and the corresponding error dynamics of the 1st subsystem without system faults are calculated as

$$
\begin{aligned}
e^1_{k+1} = {}& \hat{\tilde{x}}^1_{k+1} - \tilde{x}^1_{k+1} \\
= {}& \tilde{A}_{11,k}\hat{\tilde{x}}^1_k + \tilde{A}_{12,k}\hat{\tilde{x}}^2_k + K^1_k\Big(\tilde{y}^1_{k+1} - \tilde{C}_{11,k}\tilde{A}_{11,k}\hat{\tilde{x}}^1_k - \tilde{C}_{11,k}\tilde{A}_{12,k}\hat{\tilde{x}}^2_k \\
& -\tilde{C}_{11,k}\tilde{B}_{1,k}u_k\Big) - \tilde{A}_{11,k}\tilde{x}^1_k - \tilde{A}_{12,k}\tilde{x}^2_k - \tilde{D}^1_{w,k}w_k \\
= {}& \left(I - K^1_k\tilde{C}_{11,k}\right)\left(\tilde{A}_{11,k}e^1_k + \tilde{A}_{12,k}e^2_k - \tilde{D}^1_{w,k}w_k\right) + K^1_k\tilde{D}^1_{v,k}v_{k+1}
\end{aligned}
\tag{15}
$$

By the formulae (15) and (11), the expression for the estimation error covariance matrix can be expanded as

$$
\begin{aligned}
P^1_{k+1} = {}& \mathbb{E}\left[\left(\hat{\tilde{x}}^1_{k+1} - \tilde{x}^1_{k+1}\right)\left(\hat{\tilde{x}}^1_{k+1} - \tilde{x}^1_{k+1}\right)^T\right] \\
= {}& \mathbb{E}\left[\left(\left(I - K^1_k\tilde{C}_{11,k}\right)\left(\tilde{A}_{11,k}e^1_k + \tilde{A}_{12,k}e^2_k - \tilde{D}^1_{w,k}w_k\right) + K^1_k\tilde{D}^1_{v,k}v_{k+1}\right) \right. \\
& \left. \times\left(\left(I - K^1_k\tilde{C}_{11,k}\right)\left(\tilde{A}_{11,k}e^1_k + \tilde{A}_{12,k}e^2_k - \tilde{D}^1_{w,k}w_k\right) + K^1_k\tilde{D}^1_{v,k}v_{k+1}\right)^T\right]
\end{aligned}
\tag{16}
$$

Now, the indicated expectation is performed and nothing that the estimation errors e^1_k are uncorrelated with the system noise w_k and the measurement noise v_{k+1}, and then w_k is independent to v_{k+1}. Thus we have

$$
\begin{aligned}
P^1_{k+1} = {}& \left(I - K^1_k\tilde{C}_{11,k}\right)\Big(\tilde{A}_{11,k}P^1_k\tilde{A}^T_{11,k} + \tilde{A}_{12,k}P^2_k\tilde{A}^T_{12,k} \\
& +\tilde{D}^1_{w,k}Q_{w,k}\left(\tilde{D}^1_{w,k}\right)^T\Big)\left(I - K^1_k\tilde{C}_{11,k}\right)^T + K^1_k\tilde{D}^1_{v,k}R_{v,k}\left(\tilde{D}^1_{v,k}\right)^T\left(K^1_k\right)^T
\end{aligned}
\tag{17}
$$

Notice that the first and second terms are quadratic in K^1_k. The matrix differentiation formula may be applied to formula (17). Now differentiate $tr\left(P^1_{k+1}\right)$ with respect to K^1_k. The result is

$$
\begin{aligned}
\frac{\partial\left(tr\left(P^1_{k+1}\right)\right)}{\partial\left(K^1_k\right)} = {}& \left(I - K^1_k\tilde{C}_{11,k}\right)\Big(\tilde{A}_{11,k}P^1_k\tilde{A}^T_{11,k} + \tilde{A}_{12,k}P^2_k\tilde{A}^T_{12,k} \\
& +\tilde{D}^1_{w,k}Q_{w,k}\left(\tilde{D}^1_{w,k}\right)^T\Big)\tilde{C}^T_{11,k} - K^1_k\tilde{D}^1_{v,k}R_{v,k}\left(\tilde{D}^1_{v,k}\right)^T
\end{aligned}
\tag{18}
$$

We assume the derivative equal to zero. The optimal gain is given as follows

$$
K^1_k = O^1_k\tilde{C}^T_{11,k}\left(\tilde{C}_{11,k}O^1_k\tilde{C}^T_{11,k} + R^1_k\right)^{-1}
\tag{19}
$$

where $R_k^1 = \tilde{D}_{v,k}^1 R_{v,k} \left(\tilde{D}_{v,k}^1 \right)^T$ and $O_k^1 = \tilde{A}_{11,k} P_k^1 \tilde{A}_{11,k}^T + \tilde{D}_{w,k}^1 Q_{w,k} \left(\tilde{D}_{w,k}^1 \right)^T + \tilde{A}_{12,k} P_k^2 \tilde{A}_{12,k}^T$.

Remark 1. Theorem 1 provides the optimal gain K_k^1 without system faults, which is a similar form to the discrete-time standard Kalman filter [2]. When the 1st subsystem is healthy, the mean-square estimation error is minimized so as to ensure accurate state estimation. Otherwise, the estimation error become larger for achieving the purpose of fault alarming.

Parallel to the event-triggered state estimator (12) for the 1st subsystem, the following estimator form for the 2nd subsystem can also be considered as follows

$$
\hat{\tilde{x}}_{k+1}^2 =
\begin{cases}
\tilde{A}_{22,k} \hat{\tilde{x}}_k^2 + \tilde{A}_{21,k} \hat{\tilde{x}}_k^1 + \tilde{B}_{2,k} u_k + K_k^2 \left(\tilde{y}_{k+1}^2 - \tilde{C}_{22,k} \tilde{A}_{22,k} \hat{\tilde{x}}_k^2 \right. \\
\left. \quad -\tilde{C}_{22,k} \tilde{A}_{21,k} \hat{\tilde{x}}_k^1 - \tilde{C}_{22,k} \tilde{B}_{2,k} u_k \right) & \text{if } \gamma_k = 1 \\
\tilde{A}_{22,k} \hat{\tilde{x}}_k^2 + \tilde{A}_{21,k} \hat{\tilde{x}}_k^1 + \tilde{B}_{2,k} u_k & \text{if } \gamma_k = 0
\end{cases}
\tag{20}
$$

Similar to Theorem 1, the gain K_k^2 can be derived such that the state estimation error satisfies unbiasedness, and then the mean-square estimation error is minimized in the following theorem.

Theorem 2. *The event-triggered filter for the 2nd subsystem (9) with the formula (20) has the following optimal gain:*

$$
K_k^2 = O_k^2 \tilde{C}_{22,k}^T \tilde{O}_k^2 + \left(\tilde{D}_{d,k} - O_k^2 \tilde{C}_{22,k}^T \left(\tilde{O}_k^2 \right)^{-1} \tilde{C}_{22,k} \tilde{D}_{d,k} \right)
$$
$$
\times \left(\tilde{D}_{d,k}^T \tilde{C}_{22,k}^T \left(\tilde{O}_k^2 \right)^{-1} \tilde{C}_{22,k} \tilde{D}_{d,k} \right)^{-1} \tilde{D}_{d,k}^T \tilde{C}_{22,k}^T \left(\tilde{O}_k^2 \right)^{-1}
\tag{21}
$$

where

$$
\begin{cases}
O_k^2 = \tilde{A}_{22,k} P_k^2 \tilde{A}_{22,k}^T + \tilde{D}_{w,k}^2 Q_{w,k} \left(\tilde{D}_{w,k}^2 \right)^T + \tilde{A}_{21,k} P_k^1 \tilde{A}_{21,k}^T \\
\tilde{O}_k^2 = \tilde{C}_{22,k} \left(\tilde{A}_{22,k} P_k^2 \tilde{A}_{22,k}^T + \tilde{D}_{w,k}^2 Q_{w,k} \left(\tilde{D}_{w,k}^2 \right)^T \right) \tilde{C}_{22,k}^T + R_k^2 \\
P_{k+1}^2 = \left(I - K_k^2 \tilde{C}_{22,k} \right) O_k^2 \left(I - K_k^2 \tilde{C}_{22,k} \right)^T + K_k^1 R_k^2 \left(K_k^1 \right)^T \\
R_k^2 = \tilde{D}_{v,k}^2 R_{v,k} \left(\tilde{D}_{v,k}^2 \right)^T
\end{cases}
\tag{22}
$$

Proof. Let $\mathbb{E}\left[\hat{\tilde{x}}_k^2 - \tilde{x}_k^2\right] = 0$. When $\gamma_k = 1$, the error dynamics of the 2nd subsystem with unknown disturbances can be obtained as

$$
\begin{aligned}
e_{k+1}^2 &= \hat{\tilde{x}}_{k+1}^2 - \tilde{x}_{k+1}^2 \\
&= \tilde{A}_{22,k}\hat{\tilde{x}}_k^2 + \tilde{A}_{21,k}\hat{\tilde{x}}_k^1 + K_k^2\left(\tilde{y}_{k+1}^2 - \tilde{C}_{22,k}\tilde{A}_{22,k}\hat{\tilde{x}}_k^2 - \tilde{C}_{22,k}\tilde{A}_{21,k}\hat{\tilde{x}}_k^1\right. \\
&\quad \left. -\tilde{C}_{22,k}\tilde{B}_{2,k}u_k\right) - \tilde{A}_{22,k}\tilde{x}_k^2 - \tilde{A}_{21,k}\tilde{x}_k^1 - \tilde{D}_{w,k}^2 w_k - \tilde{D}_{d,k}d_k \\
&= \left(I - K_k^2\tilde{C}_{22,k}\right)\left(\tilde{A}_{22,k}e_k^2 + \tilde{A}_{21,k}e_k^1 - \tilde{D}_{w,k}^2 w_k\right) + K_k^2\tilde{D}_{v,k}^2 v_{k+1} \\
&\quad + \left(K_k^2\tilde{C}_{22,k}\tilde{D}_{d,k} - \tilde{D}_{d,k}\right)d_k
\end{aligned}
\tag{23}
$$

Unbiasedness is viewed as the first optimization criterion. So, the estimator must satisfy

$$
\begin{aligned}
&\mathbb{E}\left[\hat{\tilde{x}}_{k+1}^2 - \tilde{x}_{k+1}^2\right] = 0 \\
&\mathbb{E}\left[\left(I - K_k^2\tilde{C}_{22,k}\right)\left(\tilde{A}_{22,k}e_k^2 + \tilde{A}_{21,k}e_k^1 - \tilde{D}_{w,k}^2 w_k\right) + K_k^2\tilde{D}_{v,k}^2 v_{k+1}\right. \\
&\quad \left. + \left(K_k^2\tilde{C}_{22,k}\tilde{D}_{d,k} - \tilde{D}_{d,k}\right)d_k\right] = 0 \\
&\left(I - K_k^2\tilde{C}_{22,k}\right)\left(\tilde{A}_{22,k}e_k^2 + \tilde{A}_{21,k}e_k^1\right) + \left(K_k^2\tilde{C}_{22,k}\tilde{D}_{d,k} - \tilde{D}_{d,k}\right)d_k = 0
\end{aligned}
\tag{24}
$$

which leads to the following constraint

$$
K_k^2\tilde{C}_{22,k}\tilde{D}_{d,k} - \tilde{D}_{d,k} = 0
\tag{25}
$$

The second optimization criterion that we presented is also selected as the minimum mean-square estimation error, which is similar to the optimization indicator of Theorem 1. Recall from the definition of error covariance P_k^2 in formula (11), P_k^2 can be derived as follows

$$
\begin{aligned}
P_{k+1}^2 &= \mathbb{E}\left[\left(\hat{\tilde{x}}_{k+1}^2 - \tilde{x}_k^2\right)\left(\hat{\tilde{x}}_{k+1}^2 - \tilde{x}_k^2\right)^T\right] \\
&= \mathbb{E}\left[\left(\left(I - K_k^2\tilde{C}_{22,k}\right)\left(\tilde{A}_{22,k}e_k^2 + \tilde{A}_{21,k}e_k^2 - \tilde{D}_{w,k}^2 w_k\right) + K_k^2\tilde{D}_{v,k}^2 v_{k+1}\right)\right. \\
&\quad \left. \times\left(\left(I - K_k^2\tilde{C}_{22,k}\right)\left(\tilde{A}_{22,k}e_k^2 + \tilde{A}_{21,k}e_k^2 - \tilde{D}_{w,k}^2 w_k\right) + K_k^2\tilde{D}_{v,k}^2 v_{k+1}\right)^T\right] \\
&= \left(I - K_k^2\tilde{C}_{22,k}\right)\left(\tilde{A}_{22,k}P_k^2\tilde{A}_{22,k}^T + \tilde{A}_{21,k}P_k^1\tilde{A}_{21,k}^T + \tilde{D}_{w,k}^2 Q_{w,k}\left(\tilde{D}_{w,k}^2\right)^T\right) \\
&\quad \times\left(I - K_k^2\tilde{C}_{22,k}\right)^T + K_k^2\tilde{D}_{v,k}^2 R_{v,k}\left(\tilde{D}_{v,k}^2\right)^T\left(K_k^2\right)^T
\end{aligned}
\tag{26}
$$

Now it has become an optimization problem to find the estimator gain K_k^2 that minimizes $tr\left(P_{k+1}^2\right)$ subject to the constraint formula (25). The Lagrangian function is constructed as follows.

$$tr\left(P_{k+1}^2\right) = tr\left(\left(I - K_k^2\tilde{C}_{22,k}\right)O_k^2\left(I - K_k^2\tilde{C}_{22,k}\right)^T + K_k^2 R_k^2 (K_k^2)^T\right)$$
$$- tr\left(\left(K_k^2\tilde{C}_{22,k}\tilde{D}_{d,k} - \tilde{D}_{d,k}\right)(\theta_k^2)^T\right) \tag{27}$$

where θ_k^2 is a Lagrangian operator and $O_k^2 = \tilde{A}_{22,k}P_k^2\tilde{A}_{22,k}^T + \tilde{D}_{w,k}^2 Q_{w,k}\left(\tilde{D}_{w,k}^2\right)^T + \tilde{A}_{21,k}P_k^1\tilde{A}_{21,k}^T$. Some further matrix manipulations lead to

$$tr\left(P_{k+1}^2\right) = tr\left(K_k^2\tilde{O}_k^2(K_k^2)^T - 2O_k^2\tilde{C}_{22,k}^T(K_k^2)^T + O_k^2\right)$$
$$- tr\left(\left(K_k^2\tilde{C}_{22,k}\tilde{D}_{d,k} - \tilde{D}_{d,k}\right)(2\theta_k^2)^T\right) \tag{28}$$

where $\tilde{O}_k^2 = \tilde{C}_{22,k}\left(\tilde{A}_{22,k}P_k^2\tilde{A}_{22,k}^T + \tilde{D}_{w,k}^2 Q_{w,k}\left(\tilde{D}_{w,k}^2\right)^T\right)\tilde{C}_{22,k}^T + R_k^2$. Now assume the derivative of $tr\left(P_{k+1}^2\right)$ with respect to K_k^2 equals to zero, which combines the formula (25) into equations below:

$$\begin{cases} \frac{\partial\left(tr\left(P_{k+1}^2\right)\right)}{\partial\left(K_k^2\right)} = \tilde{O}_k^2(K_k^2)^T - \tilde{C}_{22,k}O_k^2 - \tilde{C}_{22,k}\tilde{D}_{d,k}(\theta_k^2)^T = 0 \\ K_k^2\tilde{C}_{22,k}\tilde{D}_{d,k} - \tilde{D}_{d,k} = 0 \end{cases} \tag{29}$$

In this paper, we concern that $\tilde{D}_{d,k}$ has full column rank, i.e., its columns are linearly independent, where this condition is required for the existence of a solution of the formula (29) satisfying constraint formula (25). Thus, the gain K_k^2 is recursively computed as follows

$$K_k^2 = O_k^2\tilde{C}_{22,k}^T\tilde{O}_k^2 + \left(\tilde{D}_{d,k} - O_k^2\tilde{C}_{22,k}^T\left(\tilde{O}_k^2\right)^{-1}\tilde{C}_{22,k}\tilde{D}_{d,k}\right)\left(\tilde{D}_{d,k}^T\tilde{C}_{22,k}^T\left(\tilde{O}_k^2\right)^{-1}\right)$$
$$\times\tilde{C}_{22,k}\tilde{D}_{d,k}\right)^{-1}\tilde{D}_{d,k}^T\tilde{C}_{22,k}^T\left(\tilde{O}_k^2\right)^{-1} \tag{30}$$

where $O_k^2 = \tilde{A}_{22,k}P_k^2\tilde{A}_{22,k}^T + \tilde{D}_{w,k}^2 Q_{w,k}\left(\tilde{D}_{w,k}^2\right)^T + \tilde{A}_{21,k}P_k^1\tilde{A}_{21,k}^T$, and

$$\tilde{O}_k^2 = \tilde{C}_{22,k}\left(\tilde{A}_{22,k}P_k^2\tilde{A}_{22,k}^T + \tilde{D}_{w,k}^2 Q_{w,k}\left(\tilde{D}_{w,k}^2\right)^T\right)\tilde{C}_{22,k}^T + R_k^2 \tag{31}$$

Remark 2. In the above filter design, the filter (12) of the 1st subsystem is derived, which is dependent of disturbances; on the contrary, the filter (20) of the 2nd subsystem contains disturbances. Therefore, the proposed fault-detection residual of the 1st subsystem is only robust to faults. Furthermore, it is noted that the filter design for reduce-order system can improve the computational efficiency.

4 Design of Event-Triggered Fault-Detection Strategy Based on the Observer of the 1st Subsystem

Prior to presenting a novel fault-detection strategy, the state estimation error dynamics of the 1st subsystem can be obtained as follows

$$e^1_{k+1} = \left(I - K^1_k \tilde{C}_{11,k}\right)\left(\tilde{A}_{11,k} e^1_k + \tilde{A}_{12,k} e^2_k - \tilde{D}^1_{w,k} w_k\right) + K^1_k \tilde{D}^1_{v,k} v_{k+1} - \tilde{F}^1_k f_k \tag{32}$$

Let us define a fault-detection residual as

$$r^1_k = \mathbb{E}\left\|\tilde{y}^1_k - \hat{\tilde{y}}^1_k\right\|_2 = \mathbb{E}\left\|\tilde{C}_{11,k} e^1_k\right\|_2 \tag{33}$$

where $\hat{\tilde{y}}^1_k = \tilde{C}_{11,k}\left(\tilde{A}_{11,k}\hat{\tilde{x}}^1_k + \tilde{A}_{12,k}\hat{\tilde{x}}^2_k\right)$. To achieve both the satisfactory robustness against disturbances and the satisfactory sensitivity to faults, we suggest the following event-triggered fault-alarming algorithm.

Algorithm 1. Event-triggered fault-detection

In each time instant, the following steps are implemented:

1: **while** $r^1_k < \delta_f$ **do**

2:    **if** $\left(\left(\hat{\tilde{y}}^1_k - \tilde{C}_{11,k}\hat{\tilde{x}}^1_k\right)^T \left(\hat{\tilde{y}}^2_k - \tilde{C}_{22,k}\hat{\tilde{x}}^2_k\right)^T\right) H_b$

3:    $\times \left(\left(\hat{\tilde{y}}^1_k - \tilde{C}_{11,k}\hat{\tilde{x}}^1_k\right)^T \left(\hat{\tilde{y}}^2_k - \tilde{C}_{22,k}\hat{\tilde{x}}^2_k\right)^T\right)^T > \delta_{e,k}$ **then**

4:        $\gamma_k = 1$, the remote filter can receive the measurements,
         $\hat{\tilde{x}}^1_{k+1} = \tilde{A}_{11,k}\hat{\tilde{x}}^1_k + \tilde{A}_{12,k}\hat{\tilde{x}}^2_k + \tilde{B}_{1,k} u_k$

5:        $+ K^1_k \left(\tilde{y}^1_{k+1} - \tilde{C}_{11,k}\tilde{A}_{11,k}\hat{\tilde{x}}^1_k - \tilde{C}_{11,k}\tilde{A}_{12,k}\hat{\tilde{x}}^2_k - \tilde{C}_{11,k}\tilde{B}_{1,k} u_k\right)$,
         $\hat{\tilde{x}}^2_{k+1} = \tilde{A}_{22,k}\hat{\tilde{x}}^2_k + \tilde{A}_{21,k}\hat{\tilde{x}}^1_k + \tilde{B}_{2,k} u_k + K^2_k \left(\tilde{y}^2_{k+1} - \tilde{C}_{22,k}\tilde{A}_{22,k}\hat{\tilde{x}}^2_k\right.$

6:        $\left. - \tilde{C}_{22,k}\tilde{A}_{21,k}\hat{\tilde{x}}^1_k - \tilde{C}_{22,k}\tilde{B}_{2,k} u_k\right)$.

7:    **else**

8:        $\gamma_k = 0$, the remote filter cannot receive the measurements to achieve energy-saving,

9:        $\hat{\tilde{x}}^1_{k+1} = \tilde{A}_{11,k}\hat{\tilde{x}}^1_k + \tilde{A}_{12,k}\hat{\tilde{x}}^2_k + \tilde{B}_{1,k} u_k$,

10:       $\hat{\tilde{x}}^2_{k+1} = \tilde{A}_{22,k}\hat{\tilde{x}}^2_k + \tilde{A}_{21,k}\hat{\tilde{x}}^1_k + \tilde{B}_{2,k} u_k$.

11:    **end if**

12: **end while**

13: $r^1_k \geq \delta_f$, declaring that a fault has happened. For the purpose of detecting fault immediately, the current sensor measurement is sent to the remote fault-detection filter without entering the event-triggered decision.

Remark 3. Based on the proposed event-triggered fault-alarming algorithm, the system is free from system faults when $r_k^1 < \delta_f$. Thus, the event-triggered data transmission scheme can be utilized to achieve energy conversation. Whereas, if $r_k^1 \geq \delta_f$, it is claimed that the system is faulty. The current sensor measurement is sent to the remote estimator immediately without entering event-triggered decision. The time-delay issue on fault detection can be effectively solved, although such strategy may reduce working-life of battery slightly. Furthermore, the thresholds H_b and $\delta_{e,k}$ in Algorithm 1 are assumed to be known, which greatly simplifies our design. The problem about how to determine the event threshold will appear in the near future.

5   Conclusion

A coordinate transformation approach for removing additive unknown disturbances from the one of subsystems was utilized in this work. For each subsystem, the optimal event-triggered filter was constructed using the optimal criteria of unbiasedness and minimum variance. A reduced-order Kalman-like filter was designed for the 1st subsystem without faults to generate a fault-detection residual. When any system faults occurred, the residual would exceed the predetermined threshold. The current measurement information would be sent to the remote filter immediately without entering the event-triggered decision. Such fault-alarming strategy can guarantee the sensitivity of fault-detection residual. The derived filters also reduced the computational complexity because they were based on reduced-order subsystems.

References

1. Li, Y., Peng, L.: Event-triggered sensor data transmission policy for receding horizon recursive state estimation. J. Algorithm Comput. Technol. **11**, 178–185 (2017)
2. Li, Y., Li, P., Chen, W.: An energy-efficient data transmission scheme for remote state estimation and applications to a water-tank system. ISA Trans. **70**, 494–501 (2017)
3. Wang, Y.L., Lim, C.C., Shi, P.: Adaptively adjusted event-triggering mechanism on fault detection for networked control systems. IEEE Trans. Cybern. **47**, 2299–2311 (2017)
4. Li, H., Chen, Z., Wu, L., Lam, H.-K., Du, H.: Event-triggered fault detection of nonlinear networked systems. IEEE Trans. Cybern. **47**, 1041–1052 (2017)
5. Li, Y., Peng, L.: Event-triggered fault estimation for stochastic systems over multi-hop relay networks with randomly occurring sensor nonlinearities and packet dropouts. Sensors (Switzerland) **18**, 731 (2018)
6. Gao, Y., Li, Y., Peng, L., Liu, J.: Design of event-triggered fault-tolerant control for stochastic systems with time-delays. Sensors (Switzerland) **18**, 1929 (2018)
7. Chen, W., Chen, W.T., Saif, M., Li, M.F., Wu, H.: Simultaneous fault isolation and estimation of lithium-ion batteries via synthesized design of Luenberger and learning observers. IEEE Trans. Control Syst. Technol. **22**, 290–298 (2014)

8. Li, Y., Wu, Q., Peng, L.: Simultaneous event-triggered fault detection and estimation for stochastic systems subject to deception attacks. Sensors (Switzerland) **18**, 321 (2018)
9. Chen, W., Chowdhury, F.N.: A synthesized design of sliding-mode and Luenberger observers for early detection of incipient faults. Int. J. Adapt. Control Signal Process. **24**, 1021–1035 (2010)

Indoor Interference Classification Based on WiFi Channel State Information

Zhuoshi Yang[1], Yanxiang Wang[1], Lejun Zhang[2], and Yiran Shen[1,3(✉)]

[1] Harbin Engineering University, Harbin 150001, China
{yangzhuoshi,wangyx}@hrbeu.edu.cn
[2] Yangzhou University, Yangzhou 211400, China
zhanglejun@yzu.edu.cn
[3] Data61, CSIRO, Brisbane 4069, Australia
yiran.shen@csiro.au

Abstract. Wireless communication channels around 2.4 GHz are shared by a number of popular wireless protocols, such as WiFi, Bluetooth, Zigbee, implemented on off-the-shelf devices. The fast increasing number of internet-of-things (IoTs) devices introduce serious challenge on reliable communication due to the problem of cross-technology interference. While, the interference problem can be mitigated if the type of the interference source is known so that the sophisticated interference avoidance method can be facilitated to improve the communication quality. In this paper, we focus on the cross-technology interference problem in indoor environment. We propose to use Channel State Information (CSI) to detect and classify the type of the interference. According to our evaluation on dataset collected from real-world experiments, our proposed CSI-based approach achieved significant performance gain compared with existing RSSI-based approach when using different classification methods including Nearest Neighborhood (NN), Supportive Vector Machine (SVM) and Sparse Representation Classification (SRC).

Keywords: 2.4 GHz interference · IoTs interference detection
Sparse Representation Classification · Channel state inference
Received Signal Strength Indicator

1 Introduction

The internet-enabled devices or Internet-of-Things (IoTs) are booming in last decade with the fast development of wireless communication technologies [1,17]. In which, the IEEE 802.15.4 protocols, such as WiFi, Bluetooth, Zigbee are popularly used. These wireless communication technologies are pervasive in our indoor environment. They enable smart devices providing comprehensive services for our living, working and education, and these services are becoming the basic needs for human beings' modern life.

However, the penetration of internet-enabled devices within indoor environment also bring severe cross-technology interference which significantly degrades

© Springer Nature Switzerland AG 2018
G. Wang et al. (Eds.): SpaCCS 2018, LNCS 11342, pp. 136–145, 2018.
https://doi.org/10.1007/978-3-030-05345-1_11

the performance of services. The interference may bring higher package loss or even high probability of connection failure due to the fact that the different wireless technologies may share the same frequency band [8]. For example, WiFi and Bluetooth devices are pervasive in indoor environment. There sometimes exist multiple of such devices running simultaneously in a very limited indoor space however they have to request same frequency band, i.e., 2.4 GHz.

To solve the interference problem, different interference mitigation approaches have been proposed recently [4–6,8]. However, the interference mitigation approaches are technology-dependent, understanding the source of the interference can be essential for fully utilising the existing interference mitigation approaches.

The interference classification approaches are proposed to determine the type of the interference based on the cutting-edge machine learning techniques, e.g., using Supportive Vector Machine (SVM) to classify the interference basing on Received Signal Strength Indicator (RSSI) readings [5].

In this paper, we facilitate another important wireless channel property, i.e., Channel State Information (CSI) as the reference to classify different types of interference (WiFi, Bluetooth and Microwave) using frequency band around 2.4 GHz which are common in our daily life and working environment. Compared with RSSI, CSI provides more prolific information with detailed wireless sub-channel states, i.e., 30 subchannels in our experiment. We then apply Sparse Representation Classification (SRC) to classify different types of interference and fully utilising the information from multiple channels by fusing the multi-channel CSI by Sparse Fusion [12]. The contributions of this paper can be summarised as follows,

- We propose to use CSI to classify different types of 2.4 GHz interference. As our knowledge, this is the first work concerning using CSI for interference classification.
- We propose to use SRC for CSI-based interference detection and incorporating Sparse Fusion to better facilitate the multi-channel state property of CSI.
- We conduct real-world interference experiments to collect CSI datasets and evaluate the performance of different types of classifiers.
- The results from extensive evaluations show that CSI-based interference classification is superior than RSSI-based approach and the SRC with Sparse Fusion improves the classification accuracy significantly compared with other traditional classifiers, i.e., SVM and KNN.

The rest of the paper is organised as follows. We first describe the experiment setting and the approach to classify different types of interference in Sect. 2 then evaluate it and compare with state-of-the-art approaches with real-world dataset in Sect. 3. The related work is reviewed in Sect. 4. Finally the whole paper is concluded in Sect. 5.

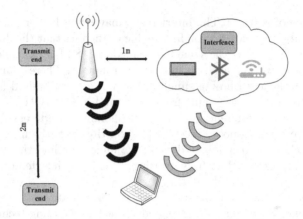

Fig. 1. Experiment deployment for interference classification

2   CSI-based Interference Classification via SRC

2.1   Experiment Setup and CSI Data Collection

The experiment setup is shown in Fig. 1. We use a Dell INSPIRON N4050 laptop equipped with Intel WiFi Link 5300 network chip as the receiver and a Netgear R7000 WiFi router as transmitter to build the interference classification system. We only use single antenna for both transmitter and receiver which provides 30 sub-channels. The laptop samples the CSI of each sub-channels at 400 Hz which produces observation matrix with 30×400 CSI elements for every second. We place two WiFi or Bluetooth enabled devices and transmit large video files to build wireless communication link as interference. We use the microwave oven to generate the Microwave interference source. We conduct the experiments in a classroom around 100 square meters and collect trainingset and testset for further evaluation. The testset is collected two weeks after the trainingset to include sufficient variance.

We present examples of the CSI time series from 30 sub-channels for 0.1 s of three types of interferences and non-interference in Fig. 2. From the figures we can observe that, different types of interference will produce different patterns of CSI time-series which can be used to train a machine learning model to automatically classify current interference so that most effective interference mitigation strategy can be applied accordingly.

2.2   SRC for Interference Classification

In this paper, we model the CSI-based interference classification as a sparse representation problem and incorporating sparse fusion [12] to fuse the CSI time series from multiple channels (30 in our experiment).

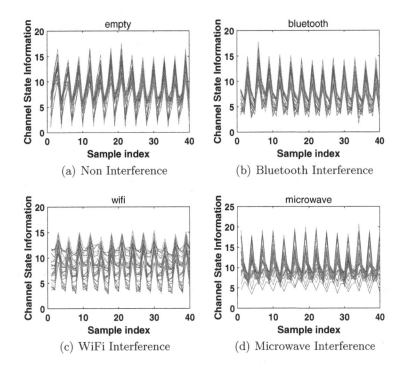

Fig. 2. Samples of CSI time series influenced by different types of interferences

Dictionary Building. The first step of modelling a sparse representation problem is to build a appropriate dictionary from the training data. Different from the traditional approaches used in [10, 11, 13, 15, 16], we build multiple sub-dictionaries for the CSI data, i.e., one sub-dictionary for each CSI sub-channel, as we consider the CSI sub-channels as providing intermediate results independently. We denote the set of sub-dictionary as $\mathcal{D} = \{D_1, D_2, D_3, ..., D_i..., D_C\}$, where C is the number of sub-channels of CSI and D_i consists of time-series of the amplitudes of CSI from the i_{th} channel with the same length.

Sparse Representation for CSI Time-Series. When a new matrix of CSI observation $Y = \{y_1, y_2, y_3.., y_i.., y_C\}$ are acquired, the sparse representations for each sub-channel observation vector y_i can be obtained by solving the linear equation,

$$y_i = D_i \theta_i \tag{1}$$

where θ_i is the representation of y_i under sub-dictionary D_i. When the representation vector θ_i is sparse, i.e., only few elements are non-zeros or dominant, the sparse representation problem can be solved by ℓ_1 optimisation,

$$\min_{\theta_i} \frac{1}{2}||y_i - D_i\theta_i||_2^2 + \lambda||\theta_i||_1 \tag{2}$$

where the ℓ_1-norm accounts for the sparseness of the representation and ℓ_2 penalty controls the accuracy of the representation under dictionary D_i.

Sparse Fusion. After multiple sparse representations from different sub-dictionaries are obtained, sparse fusion is applied to reduce the inaccuracy caused by random noises so that the classification accuracy can be improved. The approach of sparse fusion can be expressed as,

$$\theta = \Sigma_{i=1}^{C} \omega_i \theta_i \tag{3}$$

where ω_i is the weight determined by the quality of the sparse representation of the i_{th} channel. The quality of sparse representation is defined in [15], which is

$$SCI(\theta_i) = \frac{P \cdot \max_{j=1}^{P} \|\delta_j(\theta_i)\|_1 / \|\theta_i\|_1 - 1}{P - 1} \tag{4}$$

where P is the number of classes, i.e., the total types of interferences considered in the system. Then the weights can be computed as,

$$\omega_i = SCI(\theta_i) / \Sigma_{j=1}^{C} SCI(\theta_j) \tag{5}$$

Besides fusing the sparse representation vectors, the SCI observation vectors and sub-dictionaries are also required to combined using the weights determined above and the weighted observation vector and the dictionary is expressed as,

$$y = \Sigma_{i=1}^{C} \omega_i y_i, D = \Sigma_{i=1}^{C} \omega_i D_i \tag{6}$$

Class Residues for Interference Classification. After sparse fusion, the residues for each classes are computed to determine the type of the interference. The residue for the j_{th} class is,

$$r_j = \|y - D^j \theta^{(j)}\|_2 \tag{7}$$

Finally, the classification results are obtained by finding the class having the minimal residue, i.e.,

$$\hat{j} = \arg\min_{i=1,2,...P} r_j, \tag{8}$$

3   Evaluation Results

In this section, we evaluate our proposed approach, sparse representation classification for CSI-based interference classification, termed as SRC-CSI using the dataset collected from our real-world experiments. To demonstrate its performance, we compare it with other baseline approaches by varying the wireless channel properties, i.e., CSI v.s. RSSI and machine learning models, i.e., KNN, SVM and SRC. Therefore, five competing approaches are considered in our evaluations.

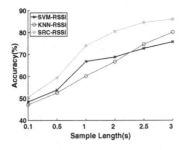

Fig. 3. Classification accuracy using RSSI

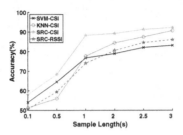

Fig. 4. Classification accuracy using CSI

3.1 Overall Classification Accuracy

We first evaluate the overall accuracy of interference classification approaches based on RSSI or CSI. We gradually change the length of the time series from 0.1 to 3 s and compute the corresponding classification accuracy. The results are shown in Figs. 3 and 4. In Fig. 3 SRC-RSSI demonstrates the best performance on classification accuracy compared with KNN-RSSI and SVM-RSSI. For CSI-based approaches, different from SRC-CSI, SVM-CSI and KNN-CSI apply majority voting to fuse the classification results from different sub-channels. We also include the SRC-RSSI as the baseline because it achieves highest accuracy among RSSI-based approaches. From the results in Fig. 4, we can observe that our proposed approach, SRC-CSI, outperforms other CSI-based and RSSI-based approaches significantly. The classification accuracy increases with the growth of the signal length then becomes level when the sample length is over 1 s. Therefore, we set the sample length as 1 s for the following evaluations.

3.2 Classification Results for Different Types of Interferences

We then further investigate the performance of the proposed approaches on each specific type of interference, i.e., the classification accuracy on WiFI, Bluetooth and Microwave respectively. The length of the sample is set as 1 s and the results are shown in Fig. 5. From the results we can see that SRC-CSI always achieves the best performance on every interference type and the CSI-based approach produces higher classification accuracy than RSSI-based approach when using the same classifier. Another observation is that detecting WiFi interference tends to be more difficult (i.e., lower classification accuracy). An intuitive explanation is the CSI time series are extracted from WiFi probes which can be easily mixed together with WiFi interference and corrupted.

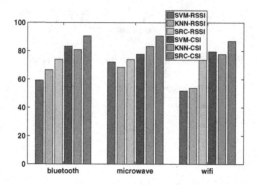

Fig. 5. Classification accuracy for different interference sources

At last, we plot the confusion matrices of different classification approaches to investigate which classes are easily confused. The results are presented in Fig. 6, where the vertical labels are groudtruth and the horizontal labels are predicted. The darkness of the small blocks represents the percentage of the classification results falling in the corresponding category. According to the definition, a confusion matrix with dark blocks on the diagonal but light blocks for the rest is desirable. From the confusion matrices, we can see that the correct classifications are dominant for most of the approaches especially the CSI-based approaches which means the CSI-based classifiers are able to distinguish different interferences better than RSSI-based ones.

4   Related Work

In this section, we will review the related work to interference classifications and some interference mitigate strategies. Recently,the number of wireless signals operating in the 2.4 GHz frequency bands is steadily increasing, numerous prior works have been done to investigate the interference. A rich literature focus on using RSSI to analyze signal components. In [18], the author sample the signals and compute the RSSI and they focus on FFT of RSSI to evaluate the accuracy of prediction. A approach based on spectrum sampling is proposed by Bloessl et al. [2], they determine the interference by the spectrogram of RSSI. However, This method does not work well in high frequency signal aliasing such as microwave and bluetooth. [9] use commercial WiFi hardware to detect WiFi access points and other non-WiFi devices. However, their approach relies on device-specific

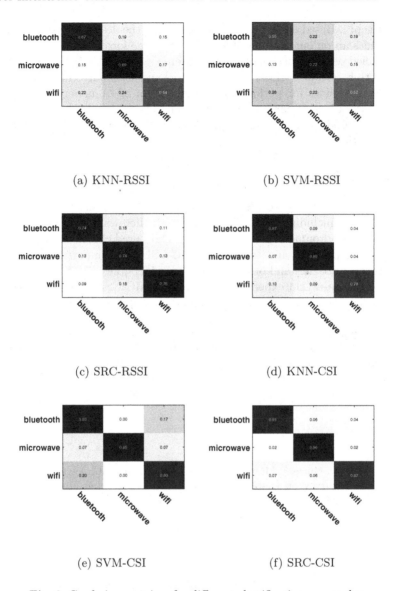

(a) KNN-RSSI

(b) SVM-RSSI

(c) SRC-RSSI

(d) KNN-CSI

(e) SVM-CSI

(f) SRC-CSI

Fig. 6. Confusion matrices for different classification approaches

WiFi functionality and involves computationally intensive processing such that it is not feasible for resource-constrained wireless device or human activity.

RSSI provides the coarse information of the received signal strength, while CSI data contain numerous information from 30 wireless sub-channels. In [19], the authors propose a classification model to predict human activity.Hand gestures Identification can also use CSI data in [7]. In [14], the authors present a novel deep-learning-based indoor fingerprinting system using CSI data, which is termed DeepFi. Based on three hypotheses on CSI, the designed system architecture includes an offline training phase and an online localization phase. [3] propose a unified performance analysis of interference alignment (IA) over multiple-input-multiple-output (MIMO) interference channels, finally they obtain some important guidelines for performance optimization of IA under imperfect CSI data. Our work in this paper is different from papers above, we prove that CSI data can be used for interference classification and signal component analysis for the first time.

5   Conclusion

In this paper, we propose to CSI-based approach to differentiate different types of interferences including WiFi, Bluetooth and Microwave which are common within indoor environment. We formulate the CSI-based classification as a sparse representation problem and term it as SRC-CSI. We compare SRC-CSI with RSSI-based approaches and other common classifiers, i.e., SVM and KNN. The evaluation on real-world experiments show that SRC-CSI achieves significantly higher classification accuracy than its competing approaches.

Acknowledgements. This work is partially supported by National Natural Science Foundation of China under Grant 61702132 and 61702133, Natural Science Foundation of Heilongjiang province under grant QC2017069 and QC2017071, the Fundamental Research Funds for the Central Universities under Grant HEUCFJ160601, the China Postdoctoral Science Foundation under Grant 166875 and Heilongjiang Postdoctoral Fundation under grant LBH-Z16042.

References

1. Al-Fuqaha, A., Guizani, M., Mohammadi, M., Aledhari, M., Ayyash, M.: Internet of things: a survey on enabling technologies, protocols, and applications. IEEE Commun. Surv. Tutor. **17**(4), 2347–2376 (2015)
2. Bloessl, B., Joerer, S., Mauroner, F., Dressler, F.: Low-cost interferer detection and classification using TelosB sensor motes, pp. 403–406 (2012)
3. Chen, X., Yuen, C.: On interference alignment with imperfect CSI: characterizations of outage probability, ergodic rate and SER. IEEE Trans. Veh. Technol. **65**(1), 47–58 (2016)
4. Hauer, J.-H., Willig, A., Wolisz, A.: Mitigating the effects of RF interference through RSSI-based error recovery. In: Silva, J.S., Krishnamachari, B., Boavida, F. (eds.) EWSN 2010. LNCS, vol. 5970, pp. 224–239. Springer, Heidelberg (2010). https://doi.org/10.1007/978-3-642-11917-0_15
5. Iyer, V., Hermans, F., Voigt, T.: Detecting and avoiding multiple sources of interference in the 2.4 GHz spectrum. In: Abdelzaher, T., Pereira, N., Tovar, E. (eds.) EWSN 2015. LNCS, vol. 8965, pp. 35–51. Springer, Cham (2015). https://doi.org/10.1007/978-3-319-15582-1_3
6. Iyer, V., Woehrle, M., Langendoen, K.: Chrysso–a multi-channel approach to mitigate external interference. In: 2011 8th Annual IEEE Communications Society Conference on Sensor, Mesh and Ad Hoc Communications and Networks (SECON), pp. 449–457. IEEE (2011)

7. Li, S., Sen, S., Koutsonikolas, D., Kim, : K.H.: WiDraw: enabling hands-free drawing in the air on commodity WiFi devices. In: International Conference on Mobile Computing and Networking, pp. 77–89 (2015)

8. Liang, C.J.M., Priyantha, N.B., Liu, J., Terzis, A.: Surviving Wi-Fi interference in low power ZigBee networks. In: Proceedings of the 8th ACM Conference on Embedded Networked Sensor Systems, pp. 309–322. ACM (2010)

9. Rayanchu, S., Patro, A., Banerjee, S.: Catching whales and minnows using WiFiNet: deconstructing non-WiFi interference using WiFi hardware. In: Usenix Conference on Networked Systems Design and Implementation, p. 5 (2012)

10. Shen, Y., Hu, W., Yang, M., Wei, B., Lucey, S., Chou, C.T.: Face recognition on smartphones via optimised sparse representation classification. In: Proceedings of the 13th International Symposium on Information Processing in Sensor Networks, pp. 237–248. IEEE Press (2014)

11. Shen, Y., Luo, C., Yin, D., Wen, H., Daniela, R., Hu, W.: Privacy-preserving sparse representation classification in cloud-enabled mobile applications. Comput. Netw. **133**, 59–72 (2018)

12. Shen, Y., et al.: GaitLock: protect virtual and augmented reality headsets using gait. IEEE Trans. Dependable Secure Comput. (2018)

13. Shen, Y., Yang, M., Wei, B., Chou, C.T., Hu, W.: Learn to recognise: exploring priors of sparse face recognition on smartphones. IEEE Trans. Mob. Comput. **12**(6), 1705–1717 (2017)

14. Wang, X., Gao, L., Mao, S., Pandey, S.: CSI-based fingerprinting for indoor localization: a deep learning approach. IEEE Trans. Veh. Technol. **66**(1), 763–776 (2017)

15. Wright, J., Yang, A.Y., Ganesh, A., Sastry, S.S., Ma, Y.: Robust face recognition via sparse representation. IEEE Trans. Pattern Anal. Mach. Intell. **31**(2), 210–227 (2009)

16. Xu, W., Shen, Y., Bergmann, N., Hu, W.: Sensor-assisted multi-view face recognition system on smart glass. IEEE Trans. Mob. Comput. **17**(1), 197–210 (2018)

17. Yang, Q., Shen, Y., Yang, F., Zhang, J., Xue, W., Wen, H.: HealCam: energy-efficient and privacy-preserving human vital cycles monitoring on camera-enabled smart devices. Comput. Netw. **138**, 192–200 (2018)

18. Zacharias, S., Newe, T., O'Keeffe, S., Lewis, E.: Identifying sources of interference in RSSI traces of a single IEEE 802.15.4 channel. In: The Eighth International Conference on Wireless and Mobile Communications, pp. 408–414 (2012)

19. Zeng, Y., Pathak, P.H., Mohapatra, P.: Analyzing shopper's behavior through WiFi signals, pp. 13–18 (2015)

Secure and Privacy Preserving RFID Based Access Control to Smart Buildings

Ahmed Raad Al-Sudani[1]([✉]) [iD], Shang Gao[1], Sheng Wen[2],
and Muhmmad Al-Khiza'ay[1]

[1] School of Information Technology, Faculty of Science, Engineering and Built
Environment, Deakin University, Geelong, Australia
{aralsuda,shang.gao,malkhiza}@deakin.edu.au
[2] School of Information Techonolgy, Swinburne University, Hawthorn, Australia
swen@swin.edu.au

Abstract. With the emergence of Internet of Things (IoT), there is
exponential growth in the usage of smart applications that exhibit
machine-to-machine and device-device interactions. As IoT integration
with applications like healthcare became a reality, it is inevitable to
leverage RFID authentication systems with privacy preserving features.
Unless RFID system guarantees a strong meaning of privacy, the technology cannot be used by people without apprehensions. To address
aforementioned issues, in this paper, we first investigate the privacy concerns in RFID authenticated systems. We define privacy and its probable
occurrences in such systems. Then we propose and implement a framework for secure and privacy preserving RFID based access control to
smart buildings. We evaluate it with an attack model that focuses on
privacy related attacks. Our prototype application demonstrates proof
of the concept. Our empirical results reveal the utility of the proposed
system for leveraging privacy while authenticating requests to access
smart buildings.

Keywords: RFID · Smart buildings · Privacy preservation · Security

1 Introduction

Radio Frequency Identification (RFID) is the technique used to identify objects
and help them to participate in computing. Unlike barcodes that are tradition-
ally used to identify objects and to have data about objects, As RFID became a
popular means of identifying objects uniquely, it is used for authentication process. RFID and sensor networks are active participants in the vision of Internet
of Things (IoT), a technology used to integrate physical and digital world, evolution [1]. RFID tags carry information required for authentication. In all kinds of
RFID based authentication systems, there is every possibility of privacy issues.
The tag information exchanged contains sensitive information that needs to be
protected from privacy attacks. For instance location information is considered

© Springer Nature Switzerland AG 2018
G. Wang et al. (Eds.): SpaCCS 2018, LNCS 11342, pp. 146–155, 2018.
https://doi.org/10.1007/978-3-030-05345-1_12

sensitive. Thus privacy breaches may occur in different smart applications. Location based services and smart environments are vulnerable to privacy threats. In additional to location information, the other privacy concerns include privacy of queries and identification of users. Privacy concerns with respect to IoT applications where RFID authentication is used are investigated in [2]. In the literature it is found that RFID based authentication has privacy breaches. The privacy gaps around IoT projects are to be addressed. In this paper, a privacy preserving RFID based authentication scheme is proposed and evaluated by comparing with other state of the art techniques. Our contributions in this paper are as follows.

- We proposed a secure and privacy preserving RFID based access control (SPPRAC) scheme for smart buildings. The scheme supports mutual authentication, strong anonymity, availability, forward security, scalability, and secure localization. SHA-256 is simulated on mixed signal micro controller that MSP 430 family. The frequency considered is 8 MHz. The results are compared with state of the art authentication schemes.
- The SPPRAC is integrated with our baseline approach to evaluate it with RFID based privacy preserving approach coupled with biometric authentication. The performance of the integrated system is compared with baseline and other schemes.

The remainder of the paper is structured as follows. Section 2 reviews literature on RFID based secure authentication and privacy preserving RFID authentication. Section 3 presents our baseline approach with two-fold RFID based biometric authentication. It covers a system model that is used for illustrating smart building case study. Section 4 presents the proposed secure and privacy preserving RFID based access control scheme. Section 5 covers experimental results while the Sect. 6 concludes the work in this paper and gives directions for future work.

2   Related Works

This section reviews literature on privacy preserving RFID authentication. First, it covers RFID authentication schemes and then the current academic thinking on privacy preservation in RFID schemes.

2.1   RFID Authentication Schemes

Gope et al. [3] proposed and implemented a new RFID authentication scheme. The scheme is developed with privacy preservation to be adapted to Internet of Things (IoT) and suitable for smart cities. They explored mutual authentication, tag anonymity, availability, forward security, scalability, and secure localization. Their study found that RFID based authentication schemes should compute position information but it needs to be sent through legal RFID tag only. In the same fashion, the position computation messages should never be compromised.

The rationale behind this is that position information is considered sensitive. Arjunan et al. [4] explored RFID based access control for energy efficient smart buildings. Misplaced RFID enabled things without proper authentication can lead to theft of sensitive information Das et al. [5] proposed a multi-modal estimation approach to find the building occupancy in smart building applications. User location discovery methods for smart homes are reviewed in [6].

2.2   Privacy Preserving RFID authentication

Pervasing computing and pervasive inter-connection between divides with machine to machine (M2M) interactions prevail in IoT applications. In such applications RFID authentication is used. Ziegeldorf et al. [1] opined that RFID is behind the vision of Internet of Things (IoT) technology. The ubiquitous data collection and tracking supported in the IoT integrated applications cause privacy threats. Therefore privacy-aware handling of data pertaining to RFID is essential. Privacy implications and privacy threats are explored in Zhang et al. [7] foused on smart city applications in terms of privacy and security. Smart home is one of the applications of smart city. Privacy leakage in data sensing, privacy in data storage and availability, dependable control and trustworthiness, Celdran et al. [2] investigated user privacy in RFID based IoT applications that are context-aware. They proposed SeCoMan framework for achieving this. In the literature it is found that RFID based secure authentication needs privacy preserving approaches. Towards this end, in this paper a privacy preserving RFID based authentication scheme is proposed and evaluated by comparing with other state of the art techniques.

3   Baseline Approach for RFID Based Access Control

This section provides details of our baseline approach for RFID based access control. It is based on smart building case study. There are different components involved in the system. They include micro controller, GSM modem, camera, RFID reader, RFID tag, server, alarms and locks. Semi-passive RFID is used for experiments. This kind of RFID tag can make use of battery power and also power derived from radio waves. RFID reader is used to read tag information from RFID tag. Camera is used to capture live image of human as part of biometric authentication. When a person is willing to enter into smart home, camera gets human image and thus involved in authentication process. Server is a computer which has processing capability and storage facility. RFID tags are associated with legitimate persons who gain access to smart home. The microcontroller is meant for controlling execution flow. RFID tags and images of humans are registered with server for authentication process. Door locks are automatically operated based on result of authentication. Alarms are meant for providing notifications to stakeholders.

Camera and RFID reader can communicate with the server. RFID readers are associated with antenna. There are two scenarios in the system model. Scenario

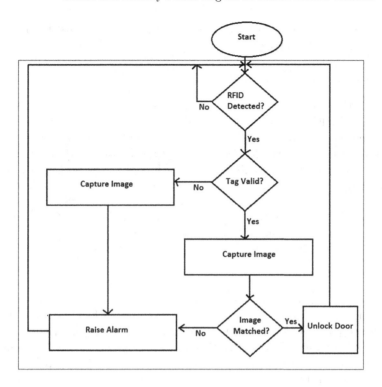

Fig. 1. RFID based biometric authentication process

(A) shows legitimate authentication process where an authorized person carries RFID tag. The RFID reader and camera capture corresponding information and send to server. The server performs authentication and based that door locks are controlled. The second scenario is unauthorized person carrying authorized RFID tag. In this case the tag information matches while the biometric authentication fails. The biometric authentication along with tag verification enhanced security. The operational procedure of the system is illustrated in Fig. 1.

As a human enters into the premise of the entrance of smart home, RFID tag information associated with the human is read by RFID reader. At the same time, the image of the person is captured and sent to server. RFID verification and image matching are performed by the server. If both are successful, the door is unlocked if not the door is not opened. When the authentication fails, an alarm is raised. In other words, security violations raise alarms so as to notify legitimate persons of smart building.

4 Privacy Preserving RFID Based Access Control to Smart Building

4.1 Problem Definition

Existing RFID based authentication schemes have certain limitations. An adversary may steal RFID-tag information leading to compromising privacy information. It can also result in forgery attacks. Location of RFID tag owner is sensitive information. The location information should not be disclosed. Another shortcoming is that RFID based authentication schemes are causing heavy computational complexity. Since RFID-tag has limited computing capability, it is a potential risk to smooth functioning of such schemes. Moreover many existing anonymous RFID-based authentication systems are not suitable for smart buildings. This is the motivation behind the work in this paper.

4.2 Proposed Scheme

We proposed a scheme known as Secure and Privacy Preserving RFID based Access Control (SPPRAC) for ensuring RFID based authentication that takes care of privacy preservation as well. The privacy of location information is preserved and its transit during authentication is protected from privacy breaches. Besides, the scheme ensures that the end-to-end security of the whole system is not jeopardized. Table 1 shows various notations used in the proposed scheme.

As part of security of the proposed system, RFID tags and RFID readers need to register with backend server denoted as S. They take security credentials from S. In the same fashion, every S needs to get registered with an Authenticate Cloud Server (ACS). The ACS is used to facilitate secure communications between two backend database servers. They can achieve mutual authentication with the help of ACS in other words. In the secure authentication process, besides ACS, three parties are involved. They are RFID tag, RFID reader and database server.

There are two phases in the proposed SPPRAC scheme. They are known as registration and verification. In the first phase, registration process is involved among the three parties. The RFID(T_j)wants to interact with reader. Before that it needs to register with S. Then S generates random number n_ss and tacking sequence number $T_{r_{seq}}$. After that it computes K_{ts} and prepare tuple representing pseudo identity. Each tuple contains unlinkable pseudo identities and emergency keys. After registration, the security credentials are given by S which helps in mutual authentication between S and T_j. After registering with backend server it generates random number N_t and computes location area identity LAI$_t$, AID$_T$,EL, N_x, V1. This whole information is put into $M_{A1}(AID_T, N_x, T_{r_{seq}}(if required), S_{id,EL,V1}$. Then it is sent to reader.

RFID Tag Side Operations
Generate:N_t, Compute:, $N_x = K_{ts} \oplus N_t$, $AID_T = h(ID_{Tj} \parallel K_{ts} \parallel N_t \parallel T_{r_{seq}})$, $\parallel operator for concatenation. AID_T is hashing function of ID_{Tj} \parallel K_{ts} \parallel N_t \parallel$

Table 1. Notations used in the paper

Notation	Description
T_j	jth RFID tag in a distributed environment
R_i	ith RFID tag reader in a distributed environment
S	Backend, database server in a distributed environment
ID_{Tj}	Identity of T_j
AID_T	One-time-alias identity of T_j
PID	Pseudo-identity of T_j
S_{id}	Identity of S
N_t	Random number generated by T_j
N_r	Random number generated by R_i
K_{ts}	Shared key between T_j and S
K_{em}	Shared emergency key between T_j and S
K_{rs}	Secret key shared between the R_i and S
$T_{r_{seq}}$	Track sequence number
LAI	Location area identifier
h(.)	One-way hash function
$\oplus$	XOR operator
$\parallel$	Concatenation operator

$T_{r_{seq}}, EL = LAI_t \oplus h(K_{ts} \parallel N_t)$, EL IS EX OR function of LAI_t and hashing function of $K_{ts} \parallel N_t$
$V1 = h(AID_T \parallel N_x \parallel K_{ts} \parallel R_i \parallel S_{id} \parallel EL)$,
   V1 hashing function of $AID_T \parallel N_x \parallel K_{ts} \parallel R_i \parallel S_{id} \parallel EL$, Or
$pid_j \in PID, K_{emj} \in K_{em}, AID_T = pid_j, K_{ts} = K_{emj}$
Reader gets information M_{A1} from RFID it generates random number N_r and computes N_y, K_{rs}, V_2, LAI_r. This information is put into the $M_{A2}(M_{A2} : [N_y, R_i, V_2, LAI_r, M_{A1})$. The total information M_{A2} sent to back-end server S for verification.

RFID Reader Side Operations
Generate N_r, Derive $N_y = K_{rs} \oplus N_r$
N_y is Ex OR operation of $K_{rs} \oplus N_r$, Compute $V_2 = h(M_{A1} \parallel N_r \parallel K_{rs} \parallel LAI_r)$
V_2 Hashing function of $M_{A1} \parallel N_r \parallel K_{rs} \parallel LAI_r$
After getting information from reader first it check with tracking number and simultaneously computes $AID_T, K_{ts}, N_x, R_i S_{id}$ and checks whether it is equal to V_1. If so, S computes $N_t = K_{ts} \oplus N_x$, and then verifies AID_T and LAI_t with LAI_r . Otherwise, S terminates the session. If verification is successful it generates random number m and update tracking sequence number. And then computes V_4, V_3 . This whole information is put into M_{A3} and send this M_{A3} to reader. After receiving M_{A3} computes $h(R_i \parallel N_r \parallel K_{rs})$ and verifies whether it

is equals to V_3. If it verifies so, R_i then sends M_{A4} to T_j

Compute and Check Operations at Reader
$V_3^* = h(R_i \mid N_r \mid K_{rs}) = V_3$, V_3^* is hashing function of $(R_i \mid N_r \mid K_{rs})$

Operations at Database Server
Check:? $T_{r_{seq}}$, Derive:$N_t = K_{ts} \oplus N_x, N_r = K_{rs} \oplus N_y$
Compute and verify:?V_2.?V_1.?$AID_T and LAI_t with LAI_r$

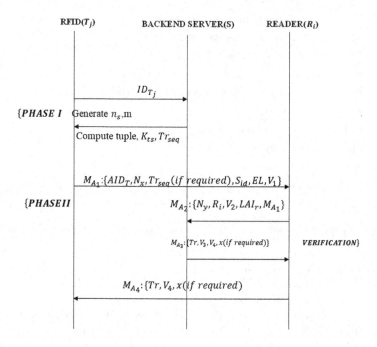

Fig. 2. Illustrates secure and privacy preserving RFID based authentication process

Generate m: , Compute: $T_{r_{seq_{new}}} = m$
$Tr = h(K_t s \| ID_{Tj} \| N_t) \oplus T_{r_{seq_{new}}}$, Tr is Ex OR operation of $T_{r_{seq_{new}}}$ and hashing function
$V_4 = h(Tr \| K_{ts} \| ID_{Tj} \| N_t)$, V_4 is hashing function of $Tr \| K_{ts} \| ID_{Tj} \| N_t$
$V_3 = h(R_i \| (\| N_r \|) \| K_{rs})$, V_3 is hashing function of $R_i \| N_r \| K_{rs}$ After getting M_{A4}, T_j computes and verifies whether it is equals toV_4
$V_4^* = h(Tr \| K_{ts} \| I_{Tj} \| N_t) = V_4$
Compute and update:
$T_{rseq_{new}} = h(K_{ts} \| ID_{Tj} \| N_t) \oplus Tr$, $T_{rseq_{new}}$ is Ex OR operation of Tr and hashing function.f ,$K_{ts_{new}} = h(K_{ts} \| ID_{Tj} \| Tr_{seq_{new}}) K_{ts_{new}}$ is hashing function of $K_{ts} \| ID_{Tj} \| Tr_{seq_{new}}$, $Tr_{seq} = Tr_{seq_{new}}$, $K_t s = K_{ts_{new}}$, Or

$K_{ts_{new}} = h(ID_{T_j}||k_{em_j}) \oplus x, K_{ts} = K_{ts_{new}}, K_{ts_{new}}$ is Ex OR operation of hashing function and x.

It is an anonymous authentication process which involves security and privacy preserving end to end communication among the three parties such as RFID tag, tag reader and database server. In the proposed scheme there is mutual authentication procedure, anonymity, availability of updated security information due to unlinkable emergency key and pseudo-identity, forward security as adversaries cannot obtain security information of old sessions, scalability due to usage of backend server which responds quickly, and secure localization as the location information is encoded. It can effectively prevent replay attack as old session information is not traceable. In the same fashion, and for the same reason forgery attack is not possible. Cloning attack can be prevente by the scheme as RFID-tags do not share a common secret key. The usage of emergency key and unlinkable pseudo-identity can prevent Denial of Service (DoS) attack as adversaries cannot take the advantage of synchronization problem (Fig. 2).

5 Experimental Results

Performance evaluation of the proposed scheme is made based on various security attributes required by RFID authentication. They are known as mutual authentication, strong anonymity, availability, forward security, scalability, an secure localization. These requirements and the performance of different schemes found in the literature including the proposed scheme are presented in Table 2.

Table 2. Performance comparison of RFID authentication schemes (Y: Support; N: Does not support)

Scheme	Mutual Authentication	Strong Anonymity	Availability	Forward security	Scalability	Secure localization	Execution time by msec
[8]	N	N	N	Y	N	N	0.45
[9]	Y	N	N	N	N	N	0.78
[10]	Y	N	N	Y	N	N	0.65
Proposed	Y	Y	Y	Y	Y	Y	0.92

As presented in Table 2, the proposed scheme is supporting all essential security attributes requird by RFID based authentication scheme. Only forward security is provided by the scheme in [8]. Mutual authentication is supported by the scheme in [9] while both mutual authentication and forward security are supported by the scheme in [10]. Our scheme outperforms all other schemes in terms of secure and privacy preserving RFID based authentication when these security attributes are considered. The execution time of the proposed scheme is compared with the existing schemes. The results are presented in Table 2. The results are obtained are from simulations study. SHA-256 is simulated on mixed signal micro controller that MSP 430 family. The frequency considered is 8 MHz.

The execution time of the proposed scheme is compared with the state-of-the-art schemes.

As shown in Table 2, it is evident that the execution time of the proposed scheme is 0.92 ms time which is higher than the other schemes. The least execution time is shown by the scheme in [8]. With respect to the execution time, the proposed scheme is taking more time comparatively but provide end-to-end security.

Comparison with Baseline Approach

The baseline approach [11] proposed by us is described in Sect. 3. It contains RFID based authentication with Image Matching Algorithm (IMA). In this paper the proposed scheme is tested with the case study scenario and application for smart buildings presented in [11]. Face images with 40 subject categories are obtained from Cambridge faces data-set. Each category has 10 images that are taken with different lighting conditions, times and facial expressions. The image size is 92×112 and it has 256 gray levels per pixel.

For biometric authentication these face images are used. Both tag information and images are registered with database server. When IMA is evaluated with other image processing algorithms such as SIFT and SURF, the average execution time of 100 experiments is presented in Table 3.

Table 3. Average execution time comparison

Algorithms	Average execution time (seconds)					
	S1	S2	S3	S4	S5	Average
SIFT	60.45	83.23	143.87	49.62	70.91	81.616
SURF	6.22	8.59	15.99	5.49	7.14	8.686
IMA	9.85	11.95	17.84	9.22	9.98	11.768
IMA with Proposed scheme	9.90	12.02	18.34	10.12	10.23	12.12

As presented in Table 3, the execution time of IMA with the proposed scheme is more than that of IMA. The reason behind this is that the proposed scheme has overhead of privacy preservation and compliance with several security attributes. Nevertheless IMA and IMA with the proposed scheme outperform SIFT and SURF algorithms. The rationale behind this is that the DAISY descriptor used in IMA algorithm reduces time complexity.

6   Conclusions and Recommendations

Of late, there is ever increasing usage of RFID authentication in smart applications including IoT applications. RFID based secure authentication is found to have severe privacy issues. Most of the privacy issues found in the literature are related to location information, disclosure of user identity and privacy of queries. To overcome privacy issues, this paper proposes a secure privacy preserving RFID based access control scheme. A smart building case study is considered. The scheme ensures that only authorized people can gain access to smart building. The proposed scheme provides end to end secure and privacy preserving communications among parties limitations in the proposed scheme. The database server is assumed to be honest. But it is not the case in the real world Another limitation is that physical security of RFID tags is not considered. Our future work focuses on overcoming these limitations.

References

1. Ziegeldorf, J.H., Morchon, O.G., Wehrle, K.: Privacy in the internet of things: threats and challenges. Secur. Commun. Netw. **7**(12), 2728–2742 (2014)
2. Celdrán, A.H., Clemente, F.J.G., Pérez, M.G., Pérez, G.M.: Secoman: a semantic-aware policy framework for developing privacy-preserving and context-aware smart applications. IEEE Syst. J. **10**(3), 1111–1124 (2016)
3. Gope, P., Amin, R., Islam, S.H., Kumar, N., Bhalla, V.K.: Lightweight and privacy-preserving RFID authentication scheme for distributed IOT infrastructure with secure localization services for smart city environment. Fut. Gener. Comput. Syst. **83**, 629–637 (2017)
4. Arjunan, P., et al.: Sensoract: a decentralized and scriptable middleware for smart energy buildings. In: 2015 IEEE 12th International Conference on Ubiquitous Intelligence And Computing and 2015 IEEE 12th International Conference on Autonomic and Trusted Computing and 2015 IEEE 15th International Conference on Scalable Computing and Communications and its Associated Workshops (UIC-ATC-ScalCom), pp. 11–19. IEEE (2015)
5. Das, A.K., Pathak, P.H., Jee, J., Chuah, C.-N., Mohapatra, P.: Non-intrusive multi-modal estimation of building occupancy (2017)
6. Ahvar, E., Daneshgar-Moghaddam, N., Ortiz, A.M., Lee, G.M., Crespi, N.: On analyzing user location discovery methods in smart homes: a taxonomy and survey. J. Netw. Comput. Appl. **76**, 75–86 (2016)
7. Zhang, K., Ni, J., Yang, K., Liang, X., Ren, J., Shen, X.S.: Security and privacy in smart city applications: challenges and solutions. IEEE Commun. Mag. **55**(1), 122–129 (2017)
8. Tan, C.C., Sheng, B., Li, Q.: Secure and serverless RFID authentication and search protocols. IEEE Trans. Wirel. Commun. **7**(4), 1400–1407 (2008)
9. Cai, S., Li, Y., Li, T., Deng, R.H.: Attacks and improvements to anrifd mutual authentication protocol and its extensions. In: Proceedings of the Second ACM Conference on Wireless Network Security, pp. 51–58. ACM (2009)
10. Cho, J.-S., Jeong, Y.-S., Park, S.O.: Consideration on the brute-force attack cost and retrieval cost: a hash-based radio-frequency identification (RFID) tag mutual authentication protocol. Comput. Math. Appl. **69**(1), 58–65 (2015)
11. Al-Sudania, A.R., Zhoub, W., Liuc, B., Almansoorid, A., Yange, M.: Detecting unauthorized RFID tag carrier for secure access control to a smart building. Int. J. Appl. Eng. Res. **13**(1), 749–760 (2018)

Answering the Min-Cost Quality-Aware Query on Multi-sources in Sensor-Cloud Systems

Mohan Li, Yu Jiang, Yanbin Sun, and Zhihong Tian[✉]

Cyberspace Institute of Advanced Technology, Guangzhou University,
Guangzhou 510006, China
tianzhihong@gzhu.edu.cn

Abstract. In sensor-cloud systems, a common scenario is that more than one sources can provide the data of the same object. Since the data quality of these sources might be different, when querying the observations, it is necessary to carefully select the sources to make sure that high quality data is accessed. A solution is to perform a quality evaluation in the cloud and select a set of high-quality, low-cost data sources (i.e. sensors or small sensor networks) that can answer queries. This paper studies the problem of min-cost quality-aware query which aims to find high quality results from multi-sources with the minimized cost. The measurement of the query results is provided, and two methods for answering min-cost quality-aware query are proposed. Experiments on real-life data verified that the proposed techniques are effective.

Keywords: Sensor-based systems · Sensor-cloud systems
Data quality · Quality-aware query · Source quality

1 Introduction

The quality of data can severely impact the data-driven applications. It is reported that data error rates of enterprises can be as high as 30% [11]. In some multi-sources applications, such as wireless sensor networks, internet of things or data fusion, data quality-aware sensing have been identified as one of the key concerns sensor-based data architecture [10]. A common fact is that although many sources provide the data of the same object, they vary in data quality, thus how to control and evaluate data quality is important.

In sensor-cloud systems which integrate sensor networks and cloud computing [2], a lot of historical data is accumulated in the cloud. The quality of data and sources can be evaluated in the cloud based on the classic data quality methods (which are not lightweight and therefore may be difficult to perform on the sensor). Then, a set of data sources that can provide relatively high quality data at low cost can be selected to provide the required data. In this way, we do not need to visit or wake up the rest of the data sources, and thus saving resources. Example 1 demonstrates a set of data sources with different data quality.

© Springer Nature Switzerland AG 2018
G. Wang et al. (Eds.): SpaCCS 2018, LNCS 11342, pp. 156–165, 2018.
https://doi.org/10.1007/978-3-030-05345-1_13

Example 1. Three sources in Fig. 1 provide weather conditions observed in same place at the same time. However, the sources provide different values of the same object. For instance, Source 1 claims that the temperature is 26 °C, but Source 2 and Source 3 claim that the temperature are 26.7 °C and 16 °C, respectively.

Some relative quality constraints can be used to infer the relative quality of the observations. For example, if we know that the temperature sensor used by Source 2 possibly be a newer model of the sensor of Source 1, we can infer that the value of temperature provided by Source 2 tends to be more accurate than Source 1. The arcs with probability can represent the existence of relative quality constraints. In Fig. 1, the arc from (*temperature*, 26 °C) to (*temperature*, 26.7 °C) indicates that there may exist a relative quality constraint that "the sensor of Source 2 provides higher quality temperature than the sensor of Source 1", and the probability of the existence of the constraint is 0.9.

According to relative quality constraints shown by Fig. 1, the value of temperature and wind speed of Source 3 might be less accurate than Source 1 and Source 2, thus if we only access the data from Source 3, we might get inaccurate values. In this case, if the user is willing to pay a higher cost, perhaps we can access the other two data sources to obtain higher quality data.

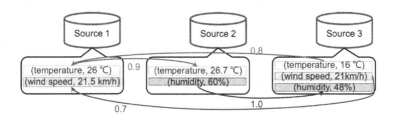

Fig. 1. Data sources with different data quality.

When selecting sources for answering query with relative quality constraints, both low cost and high data quality need to be guaranteed. In this paper, we study the min-cost quality-aware query (MQQ for short) answering problem which aims to get high quality results from multi-sources with the minimized cost. The contributions of this paper are as follows.

1. A general definition of MQQ answering problem is provided.
2. The data quality measurement of quality-aware query on multi-sources is defined based on relative data quality constraints.
3. Two methods for solving the min-cost quality-aware query answering problem are proposed.
4. The experiments on real-life data are conducted, which verifies the efficiency and effectiveness of the provided solutions.

The rest of this paper is organized as follows. Section 2 discusses the related work. Section 3 provides the problem definition. Section 4 gives the data quality measurement. Section 5 studies the solutions of MQQ answering problem. Section 6 shows the experimental results. Section 7 concludes the paper.

2   Related Work

There is currently a lot of work on constraint-based data quality [3,4,7,9,12]. The problem of data quality evaluation is studied in these work. The relative data quality constraints can be derived based on their methods. However, most of these methods focus on evaluating and repairing the entire data set rather than answering a query.

Data fusion and truth discovering study how to find high quality data from multi-sources [5,6,13]. These methods focus on estimating the quality of data sources based on the observations, but they do not consider how to evaluate and guarantee the data quality of query results.

Quality-aware query has been studied in some data-driven systems [14,15]. Yeganeh et al. provided a data quality-aware system architecture which supports data quality profiling and data quality aware SQL [15]. The sample conditional data profile generated by the system can be used as a type of quality constraints in our work, but the work does not focus on how to get a best query result with cost and quality requirements. Wu et al. studied the quality-aware query scheduling in wireless sensor networks. They provide a framework that can determine the target quality of each query. The work can be used as the basis for this study, but it does not consider optimization problems when there are multiple query results, and it also do not consider how to do quality-aware query in sensor-cloud systems.

3   A General Definition of MQQ Answering Problem

3.1   Preliminaries

First we provide some basic concepts which will be refered in the following sections.

Data Sources. Let $\mathbb{S} = \{S_1, \ldots, S_n\}$ be a set of data sources, where $S_i = \{\phi_1, \ldots, \phi_{m_i}\}$ is the ith data source consisting of m_i observations. An observation $\phi = (s, o, v)$ is a triple consisting of a source s, an object o and a corresponding value of the object v. For instance, $(S_2, humidity, 60\%)$ indicates that Source S_2 observes that the humidity is 60%. It is easy to observe that all the observations in a same source is with the same s.

Data Quality Constraints. Quality function hq is defined to represent data quality constraints. $hq(\phi, \phi') = p$ means that the quality of ϕ probably be *higher* than the quality of ϕ', and the existence probability of this constraint is p. For example, $hq(\phi, \phi') = 0.9$ means that the data quality of ϕ is higher than ϕ' with the probability 0.9. The quality constraints can be considered as the relative value of data accuracy or other data quality measurements [3,7].

Access Cost. Each data source S_i in $\mathbb{S}$ has a access cost $cost(S_i) \in R^+$, indicating the cost of querying S_i. High data quality sometimes means high access cost, thus how to balance the cost and quality is a key problem.

3.2   Definition of MQQ Answering Problem

Quality-Aware Query. The goal of a quality-aware query Q is a query with data quality requirements. Q is in the form of $Q = (O_Q, \theta)$, which is a pair of an object set O_Q and a quality lower bound θ. O_Q consists of the objects queried by Q. The quality lower bound θ means that the measurement of the returned observations must be no less than θ.

MQQ Answering Problem. A MQQ aims to find the observations of O_Q from sources in $\mathbb{S}$ which satisfying data quality lower bound and with minimized access cost. Formally, the MQQ answering problem can be defined as follows.

   Input: a quality-aware query $Q = (O_Q, \theta)$,
   Output: a observation set Φ which can satisfy the following conditions:
   1. For each $o \in O_Q$, $\exists \phi \in \Phi$ such that ϕ is the observation of o, that is, Φ contains the observations of all queried objects,
   2. Φ can satisfy the quality lower bound θ,
   3. $\nexists \Phi'$ returned by $\mathbb{S}_{\Phi'} \subseteq \mathbb{S}$ such that Φ' satisfies condition (1) and (2), and $\sum_{S \in \mathbb{S}_{\Phi'}} cost(S) < \sum_{S \in \mathbb{S}_\Phi} cost(S)$.
   As of now, we have not discussed how to calculate the data quality of query results. In the following sections we will first discuss how to calculate the data quality of a set of observations, and then present the analysis of MQQ answering problem.

4   Measuring Data Quality Based on Quality Constraints

Quality Graph. $hq(\phi, \phi') = p$ indicates the existence probability of quality constraints. Thus, uncertain graphs [16,17] can be used to model the constraints, that is, observations can be considered as nodes, and relative quality constraints can be considered as weighted arcs.

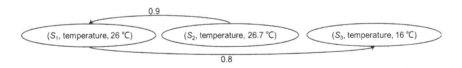

Fig. 2. The direct graph of the observations of temperature in Fig. 1.

Definition 1 (quality graph). *Given an object o, the observation set Φ_o containing all the observations corresponding to o, and the data quality function corresponding to Φ_o, the quality graph $G_o = (V, A)$ is defined as follows.*

1. Each node $v_\phi \in V$ corresponds to an observation in Φ_o.
2. For each pair (ϕ, ϕ'), if $hq(\phi, \phi') \neq null$, there exists an arc from ϕ to ϕ' in A, the weight of the arc (ϕ, ϕ') is $hq(\phi, \phi')$.

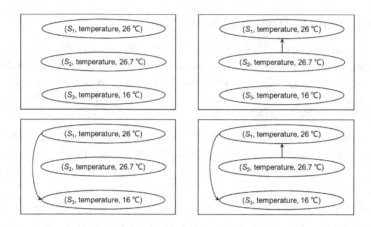

Fig. 3. The possible worlds of a quality graph.

In the definition, $hq(\phi, \phi') = null$ means that hq is not defined at (ϕ, ϕ'). Figure 2 is the quality graph of the object "temperature" in Fig. 1. For the arcs in G_o, the semantics of the weight of an arc is the probability of the arc's existence. For example, if the weight of an arc a is 0.9, the probability of a's existence is 0.9, and the probability of non-existence is $1 - 0.9 = 0.1$. Therefore, possible worlds [1] can be used to describe different situations of data quality. Figure 3 shows the possible worlds corresponding to Fig. 2, which consists of four possible worlds, and the probabilities are 0.02, 0.18, 0.08, and 0.72, respectively.

Data Quality Score. The data quality score of an observation ϕ of the object o_ϕ is defined as the probability that the quality of ϕ is NOT lower than any other observations of o_ϕ. Let G_{o_ϕ} be the quality graph of o_ϕ. In any possible world, the quality of ϕ is lower than ϕ' if there exists an arc from ϕ to ϕ'. Therefore, the quality score is the probability that v_ϕ's out-degree is 0, where v_ϕ is the node corresponding to ϕ.

Definition 2 (quality score of an observation). *Let W be the set of possible worlds corresponding to G_{o_ϕ}. $dq(\phi) = \sum_{w \in W} P_w \times f(w)$ is the quality score of Φ, where $f(w) = 1$ if node v_ϕ has an out-degree of 0 in w, otherwise $f(w) = 0$.*

According to the semantics of the arcs in the quality graph, a naive idea to calculate the quality score of a node is to enumerate all possible worlds and check in which possible worlds the node's out-degree is 0. However, if we assume that the existence of the arcs are independent of each other, calculating the quality score becomes calculating the probability that all out-arcs do not exist, that is, $dq(\phi) = \prod_{a \in out(v_\phi)} (1 - weight(a))$, where $out(v_\phi)$ is the outgoing arc set of v_ϕ, and $weight(a)$ is the weight of arc a in G_{o_ϕ}. Furthermore, the *quality of observation set Φ* can similarly be defined.

Definition 3 (quality score of observation set). *Given an observation set Φ, the quality of Φ is the probability that for each observation $\phi \in \Phi$, the quality of ϕ is not lower than any other observations, that is, $dq(\Phi) = \prod_{\phi \in \Phi} dq(\phi)$.*

Given a quality-aware query $Q = (O_Q, \theta)$, the query result of Q is a set of observations. Therefore, condition (2) in the definition of MQQ answering problem can be rewritten by "$dq(\Phi) \geq \theta$".

5 Methods for Solving MQQ Answering Problem

As is defined in Sect. 3.2, if Φ is a valid output of MQQ answering problem, Φ should satisfy three conditions, i.e., (1) Φ covers all the object in O_Q, (2) $dq(\Phi)$ is no less than θ, and (3) the access of returning Φ is minimized. Please note that if condition (2) is not considered, MQQ answering the problem is a equal problem of "weighted set cover" which is a NP-hard problem [8].

In this section, we first provide a search and prune method to accurately solve the MQQ answering problem, then provide an approximate method to try to get a feasible (but not necessarily optimal) solution quickly.

The Search and Prune Method. The main idea is that we first find the observation set with highest quality score, then we continually replace one observation in the current observation set by an unused observation with a lower or equal quality score, to see if we can get a new set that meets the quality threshold and with lower cost. The replacement step is repeated until the quality threshold can not be satisfied or there is no less-cost solution.

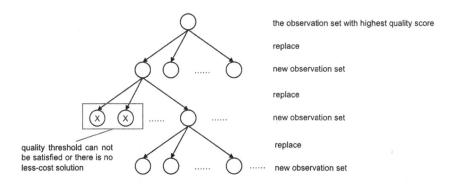

Fig. 4. The main idea of the search and prune method for MQQ answering.

Figure 4 shows the search tree of this process. Each node in the tree is an observation set, and a child corresponds to a substitution of its parent. Since we replace exactly one observation each time, for each node $\Phi = \{\phi_1, \dots, \phi_k\}$ in the search tree, if $\Phi' = \{\phi'_1, \dots, \phi'_k\}$ is the child of Φ, Φ' has exactly one observation different from Φ. That is, $\exists j$ s.t. $\phi_j \neq \phi'_j$ and for any $i \neq j$, ϕ_i is the same as ϕ'_i. Moreover, if $dq(\phi_j) \geq dq(\phi'_j)$.

To ensure that the search can finally enumerate all possible solutions, we sort all the observations associated with each object based on their quality scores. At the time of replacement, the current observation is replaced with the next observation in its sorted sequence. Please note that for each node Φ in the search tree, Φ may have 0 to $|O_Q|$ child nodes. The time complexity of the full search strategy is exponential, we need an effective pruning strategy to speed up the process. Since we always replace one observation by another observation with a equal or lower quality score, the quality score of a parent node is always not lower than its children. Theorem 1 formalizes this conclusion.

Theorem 1. *For any node Φ and its child Φ' in the search tree, $dq(\Phi) \geq dq(\Phi')$.*

Proof. Let $\Phi = \{\phi_1, \ldots, \phi_k\}$ and $\Phi' = \{\phi_1', \ldots, \phi_k'\}$. $\exists j$ s.t. $\phi_j \neq \phi_j'$, $dq(\phi_j) \geq dq(\phi_j')$, and for any $i \neq j$, ϕ_i is the same as ϕ_i'. Thus $dq(\Phi) = dq(\phi_j) \times \prod_{i \neq j}(dq(\phi_i))$, and $dq(\Phi') = dq(\phi_j') \times \prod_{i \neq j}(dq(\phi_i'))$. Therefore, $dq(\Phi) \geq dq(\Phi')$.

For any node Φ and its child Φ', $dq(\Phi') \leq \theta$ if $dq(\Phi) \leq \theta$. Thus, if the quality threshold θ can not be satisfied on node Φ, it also cannot be satisfied by any descendant node of Φ. Thus the subtree rooted at Φ can be pruned off.

Let O_Q be the object set queried by Q, the time complexity of the worst case is $O(|O_Q|^{|\mathbb{S}|})$. It is still unbearable in the condition of high efficiency requirement. Therefore, we propose an approximate search strategy which can quickly provide a feasible solution when the user is willing to relax the requirements for the cost.

Approximate Search. When we ask a specified data source to return one observation or multiple observations, the cost to pay is the same. For node Φ and its child Φ', let $\mathbb{S}_\Phi$ and $\mathbb{S}_{\Phi'}$ be the source set returning Φ and Φ' respectively, $cost(\Phi) = \sum_{s \in \mathbb{S}_\Phi} cost(s)$ to represent the cost of Φ. We have Theorem 2.

Theorem 2. $cost(\Phi) \leq cost(\Phi')$ *and* $dq(\Phi) \geq dq(\Phi')$ *if* $S \notin \mathbb{S}_\Phi$ *and* $\mathbb{S}_{\Phi'} = \mathbb{S}_\Phi \cup \{S\}$.

Proof. According to Theorem 1, $dq(\Phi) \geq dq(\Phi')$. Since $\mathbb{S}_{\Phi'} = \mathbb{S}_\Phi \cup \{S\}$, $cost(\Phi') = \sum_{S' \in \mathbb{S}} cost(S') + cost(S) = cost(\Phi) + cost(S)$, we have $cost(\Phi) \leq cost(\Phi')$.

According to Theorem 2, an idea to quickly get a feasible solution is to drop the substitution that add new data sources. That is, for any node Φ, only the observations returned by $\mathbb{S}_\Phi$ is used to do the replacement. More precisely, for any node Φ and its child Φ', we stipulate that a replacement should ensure either $\mathbb{S}_{\Phi'} = \mathbb{S}_\Phi$ or $\mathbb{S}_{\Phi'} = \mathbb{S}_\Phi \setminus \{S\}$, where $S \in \mathbb{S}_\Phi$. If the quality threshold can not be satisfied or there is no less-cost solution, the search is terminated.

It is easy to observe that this search strategy only considers the subset of the data sources which provide the observations with best quality score. The solution returned by this strategy necessarily satisfies the conditions (1) and (2) in the MQQ answering problem definition, but does not necessarily satisfy the condition (3) (i.e., the cost is not necessarily the lowest).

6   Experimental Results

We conduct the experiments on real-life data set. The codes are written in Python and run on a machine with i5 2.50 GHz Intel CPU and 8 GB of RAM. The dataset consists air quality data generated by network of 56 sources located in Krakow, Poland. The available object set is {temperature, humidity, pressure, pm1, pm25, pm10}. Since the data set does not provide the cost of data sources, we randomly assign each source a cost. In practical applications, the cost can be the bandwidth, power consumption, or the money of getting data, etc. We compared the accurate search and the approximate search.

6.1   Varying $|\mathbb{S}|$

Figure 5 shows the experimental results of runtime, cost and quality under different $|\mathbb{S}|$. Here we fixed $|O_Q|$ to 4 and the quality threshold to 0.95.

Runtime. The worst case of accurate search is $O(|O_Q|^{|\mathbb{S}|})$. This theoretical analysis is consistent with the experimental results. The efficiency of approximate search is significantly higher than that of accurate search. When the number of data sources is 10, the time cost of the two is similar, but as the number of data sources increases, the time cost of the accurate search increases exponentially, while the time cost of the approximate search is basically not change much because it controls the choice of the data sources.

Cost. We compared the cost of the result of query returned by the accurate search and the approximate search. As the number of available data sources increases, the costs of the results of the two methods are both declining. This is because that the more data sources we can access, the more likely we are to discover data sources with high-quality and low-cost. Overall, the cost of the accurate search results is significantly lower than that of the approximate search, because the accurate search returns the optimal solution.

Quality. The quality of the optimal solution returned by accurate search is usually closer to the quality threshold and therefore lower than the quality of the result of the approximate search. Please note that when the data source is 10, there is no result that satisfies the quality threshold. In order to comprehensively compare the two methods, when implementing the two methods, we require that both methods return the highest quality result in this case. At this time, the results of the two methods are the same, and the quality score is 0.945.

6.2   Varying $|O_Q|$

We fixed $|\mathbb{S}|$ to 56 (i.e. all the avaliable data sources) and the quality threshold to 0.95. We change $|O_Q|$ from 1 to 6. Figure 6 shows the experimental results.

Runtime. Since the runtime of the accurate search varies greatly, the vertical axis of Fig. 6(a) uses a logarithmic scale. As can be seen from the results that the time cost of accurate search is much higher than the approximate search. As

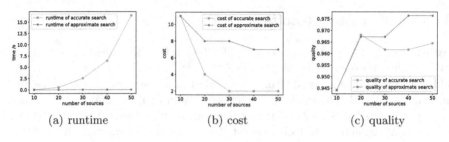

Fig. 5. Experimental results when varying $|\mathbb{S}|$.

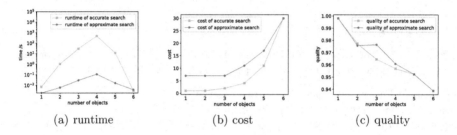

Fig. 6. Experimental results when varying $|O_Q|$.

$|O_Q|$ increases, the runtime increases first and then decreases. This is because when $|O_Q|$ is large enough, the result that satisfies the quality threshold is gradually reduced (the quality score is the probability multiplication, the more the observation, the smaller the value tends to be). Based on the pruning strategy of Theorem 1, the search space is also gradually reduced.

Cost. As $|O_Q|$ increases, the cost increases, because in order to find the records of all objects in O_Q, it is often necessary to access more data sources. Overall, the cost of accurate search is lower than the cost of approximate search, but when $|O_Q| = 6$, the two are the same, because no result meets the quality threshold at this time, both methods return the result with highest quality score.

Quallity. As $|O_Q|$ increases, the quality of results decreases. Accurate search sacrifices quality to reduce cost while ensuring that the quality threshold is met, so sometimes (in the case of $|O_Q| = 3$ or $|O_Q| = 4$ in this set of experiments) the resulting quality scores are lower than approximate search.

7   Conclusions and Future Work

This paper studies the problem of answering MQQ query on multi-sources in sensor-cloud systems. First, a general definition of MQQ answering problem in the multi-source environment are given. After that, the quality measurement is provided based on relative quality constraints, and two methods for solving the MQQ answering problem are proposed. In future work, we will study how to get more types of quality scores of different sources by the methods of data mining or machine learning, and will explore other forms of quality-preserving queries.

Acknowledgments. The work is supported by the National Natural Science Foundation of China (No. 61871140, 61702220, 61702223, 61572153) and the National Key Research and Development Plan (Grant No. 2018YFB0803504).

References

1. Abiteboul, S., Kanellakis, P., Grahne, G.: On the representation and querying of sets of possible worlds. Theoret. Comput. Sci. **78**(1), 159–187 (1991)
2. Alamri, A., Ansari, W.S., Hassan, M.M., Hossain, M.S., Alelaiwi, A., Hossain, M.A.: A survey on sensor-cloud: architecture, applications, and approaches. Int. J. Distrib. Sens. Netw. **9**(2), 917923 (2013)
3. Cao, Y., Fan, W., Yu, W.: Determining the relative accuracy of attributes. In: Proceedings of the 2013 ACM SIGMOD International Conference on Management of Data, pp. 565–576. ACM (2013)
4. Chu, X., Ilyas, I.F., Papotti, P.: Holistic data cleaning: putting violations into context. In: The IEEE 29th International Conference on Data Engineering (ICDE), pp. 458–469 (2013)
5. Dong, X.L., Berti-Equille, L., Srivastava, D.: Integrating conflicting data: the role of source dependence. PVLDB **2**(1), 550–561 (2009)
6. Dong, X.L., et al.: Knowledge-based trust: estimating the trustworthiness of web sources. Proc. VLDB Endow. **8**(9), 938–949 (2015)
7. Fan, W., Geerts, F.: Foundations of data quality management. Synth. Lect. Data Manag. **4**(5), 1–217 (2012)
8. Garey, M.R., Johnson, D.S.: Computers and Intractability: A Guide to the Theory of NP-Completeness. WH Freeman and Co., San Francisco (1979)
9. Ilyas, I.F., Chu, X., et al.: Trends in cleaning relational data: consistency and deduplication. Found. Trends® Databases **5**(4), 281–393 (2015)
10. Lazaridis, I., et al.: QUASAR: quality aware sensing architecture. ACM SIGMOD Rec. **33**(1), 26–31 (2004)
11. Rahm, E., Do, H.H.: Data cleaning: problems and current approaches. IEEE Data Eng. Bull. **23**, 3–13 (2000)
12. Rammelaere, J., Geerts, F., Goethals, B.: Cleaning data with forbidden itemsets. In: 2017 IEEE 33rd International Conference on Data Engineering (ICDE), pp. 897–908 (2017)
13. Rekatsinas, T., Joglekar, M., Garcia-Molina, H., Parameswaran, A., Ré, C.: SLiM-Fast: guaranteed results for data fusion and source reliability. In: Proceedings of the 2017 ACM International Conference on Management of Data, pp. 1399 –1414. ACM (2017)
14. Wu, H., Luo, Q., Li, J., Labrinidis, A.: Quality aware query scheduling in wireless sensor networks. In: Proceedings of the Sixth International Workshop on Data Management for Sensor Networks, p. 7. ACM (2009)
15. Yeganeh, N.K., Sadiq, S., Sharaf, M.A.: A framework for data quality aware query systems. Inf. Syst. **46**, 24–44 (2014)
16. Zou, Z., Gao, H., Li, J.: Discovering frequent subgraphs over uncertain graph databases under probabilistic semantics. In: Proceedings of the 16th ACM SIGKDD International Conference on Knowledge Discovery and Data Mining. KDD 2010, pp. 633–642 (2010)
17. Zou, Z., Li, J., Gao, H., Zhang, S.: Frequent subgraph pattern mining on uncertain graph data. In: Proceedings of the 18th ACM Conference on Information and Knowledge Management. CIKM 2009, pp. 583–592 (2009)

Balanced Iterative Reducing and Clustering Using Hierarchies with Principal Component Analysis (PBirch) for Intrusion Detection over Big Data in Mobile Cloud Environment

Kai Peng[1,2,3], Lixin Zheng[1,3(✉)], Xiaolong Xu[4], Tao Lin[5],
and Victor C. M. Leung[2]

[1] College of Engineering, Huaqiao University, Quanzhou 362021, Fujian, China
1275373176@qq.com
[2] Department of Electrical and Computer Engineering, The University of British
Columbia, Vancouver, BC V6T 1Z4, Canada
[3] Fujian Provincial Academic Engineering Research Centre in Industrial
Intellectual Techniques and Systems, Quanzhou 362021, Fujian, China
[4] School of Computer and Software, Nanjing University of Information Science
and Technology, Nanjing 210044, China
[5] State Key Laboratory of Networking and Switching Technology,
Beijing University of Posts and Telecommunications, Beijing 100876, China

Abstract. With the development of big data, mobile cloud computing, cyber security issues have become more and more critical. Thus, enabling an intrusion detection method over big data in mobile cloud environment is of paramount importance. In our previous research, we proposed an approach named Mini Batch Kmeans with Principal Component Analysis (PMBKM) for big data which can effectively solve the clustering problem for intrusion detection of big data, but it needs to preset the number of clusters. The best clustering number is selected by comparing the clustering results of different clustering values multiple times. To address the above issue, we propose a new clustering method named Balanced Iterative Reducing and Clustering Using Hierarchies with Principal Component Analysis (PBirch) in this paper. Compared to PMBKM, the experimental results show that PBirch can obtain a good clustering result without presetting clustering values, and the clustering result can be further improved by optimizing the relevant parameters. The clustering time of PBirch decreases linearly with the increasing of the cluster numbers. Thus, the larger the number of clusters, the smaller the PBirch time cost. All in all, our proposed method can be widely used for big data in mobile cloud environment.

Keywords: Mobile cloud environment · Big data · Intrusion detection
Birch · PCA

© Springer Nature Switzerland AG 2018
G. Wang et al. (Eds.): SpaCCS 2018, LNCS 11342, pp. 166–177, 2018.
https://doi.org/10.1007/978-3-030-05345-1_14

1 Introduction

Intrusion detection system (IDS) can discover the network malicious activities and provides an important basis for network defense [1–4]. Due to the development of the cloud computing, mobile cloud computing, wireless sensor network as well as big data, IDS is becoming more important than before [5–7].

Data mining is an intelligent data analysis technique [8, 9] which was firstly introduced to IDS in 1998 [10]. In general, IDS based on data mining mainly consists of two aspects, thus clustering [11] and classification [12]. Both issues are different but the indispensable parts of IDS. More specifically, each data record in the initial dataset of cluster problem is not labeled, and the goal of which is to put the data records with the same features into the same cluster. Differing from the former one, the main task of which is to operate on data that has been clustered. That is, for a new test sample, we determine which cluster it belongs to by comparing it to data records in each class. The clustering results is the input of the classification. In this study, we mainly focus on the former one.

In our previous research, we proposed an approach named Mini Batch Kmeans with Principal Component Analysis (PMBKM) for clustering of intrusion detection which can effectively solve the clustering problem of big data, but it needs to predetermine the number of clusters. The best clustering number is selected by comparing the clustering results of different clustering values in multiple times. To solve the above shortcomings, we propose a new clustering method named Balanced Iterative Reducing and Clustering Using Hierarchies with Principal Component Analysis (PBirch) in this paper.

Firstly, a preprocessing method is used to traverse the dataset and digitize the strings and then the data record is normalized. Secondly, principal component analysis (PCA) method [13–15] is used to reduce dimensionality on the processed dataset. Thirdly, Balanced Iterative Reducing and Clustering Using Hierarchies (Birch) [16] is used for the data clustering. In addition, the clustering time and Calinski Harabasz (*CH*) indicator is used for the experimental result evaluation [17]. Compared to PMBKM, the experimental results show that PBirch can achieve a good clustering result without presetting the clustering values, and *CH* can be further improved by optimizing the relevant parameters. Although the clustering time cost of PBirch is much longer than PMBKM, the clustering time decreases linearly with the increasing of the cluster numbers. Thus, the larger the number of clusters, the shorter the PBirch time cost. All in all, our proposed method can be widely used for big data environment.

The remaining parts of this paper are organized as follows. In Sect. 2, the preliminary is described. PBirch intrusion detection clustering method is introduced in Sect. 3. Section 4 presents the experimental result and discussion, followed by Sect. 5; we conclude the paper and show the future work.

2 Preliminary

In this section, we introduce algorithm theory in Sect. 2.1 and evaluation indicator in Sect. 2.2.

2.1 Algorithm Theory

In this section, we mainly introduce the relevant theory of Balanced Iterative Reducing and Clustering Using Hierarchies (Birch) in Sect. 2.1.1 and principal component analysis (PCA) in Sect. 2.1.2

2.1.1 Balanced Iterative Reducing and Clustering Using Hierarchies (Birch)

We firstly introduce basic definition. Suppose there are N data points in a cluster and denote as $\{\bar{X}_i, i = 1, 2, \ldots\ldots, N\}$. The metrics for a single cluster are shown as follows:

$$\text{Center point} \quad \bar{X}0 = \frac{\sum\limits_{i=1}^{N} \bar{X}_i}{N} \tag{1}$$

$$\text{Radius} \quad R = \left(\frac{\sum\limits_{i=1}^{N} (\bar{X}_i - \bar{X}0)^2}{N} \right)^{\frac{1}{2}} \tag{2}$$

$$\text{Diameter} \quad D = \left(\frac{\sum\limits_{i=1}^{N} \sum\limits_{j=1}^{N} (\bar{X}_i - \bar{X}_j)^2}{N(N-1)} \right)^{\frac{1}{2}} \tag{3}$$

In this paper, we mainly use the center point Euclidean Distance $D0 = ((\bar{X}0_1 - \bar{X}0_2)^2)^{\frac{1}{2}}$ for the metrics for the two clusters.

Birch is a clustering algorithm whose biggest feature is to use limited memory resources for high quality clustering of large-scale data dataset and only scan dataset once so as to minimize the overhead of I/O. Birch performs clustering using a similar B + tree structure, which is generally called a Clustering Feature Tree (CF Tree) [16]. As shown in Fig. 1, there are three types of nodes, such as root node, internal node, as well as leaf node. Each node is composed of several Clustering Features (CFs). Each node, including leaf nodes, has several CFs, and the CF of the internal node has a pointer to the child node, and all of the leaf nodes are linked by a doubly linked list.

Each CF is a triple, which can be represented by (N, LS, SS). Where N represents the number of sample points in a cluster, LS represents the sum of all data points in the cluster.

$$LS = \sum\limits_{i=1}^{N} \bar{X}_i \tag{4}$$

SS is the sum of the squares of all data points in a cluster.

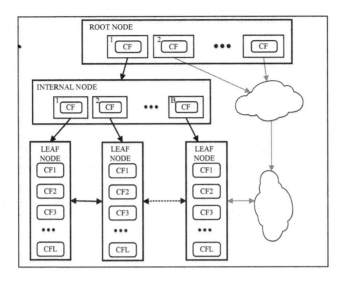

Fig. 1. CF Tree structure

$$SS = \sum_{i=1}^{N} \bar{X}_i^2 \tag{5}$$

There are three important parameters for CF Tree. The first one is the maximum CF number B of each internal node. And the second one is the maximum CF number L of each leaf node. The third one is for the sample point in a CF in the leaf node, which is the maximum sample radius threshold ts of each CF of the leaf node. That is, all sample points in this CF must be in the radius less than ts in a hypersphere.

2.1.2   Principal Component Analysis (PCA)

When a dataset has multiple features, many of which are related and some are even redundant. Consequently, we only use the most relevant features for clustering, which can improve the clustering efficiency without affecting the clustering results. In this study, we use Principal Component Analysis (PCA) [13–15] for the dimension reduction. For given dataset T with n features, the goal is reducing n features to d dimensions. The corresponding process and formulas are as follows.

(1) For each data record x in T_{m*n}, calculate the mean of each column in T_{m*n}. The first step is mean centering which subtracts the column mean from each record and the processed data is obtained and denoted as $TAdjust_{(m*n)}$.

(2) The covariance matrix of $TAdjust_{(m*n)}$ is calculated and denoted as C.
     Let

$$c_{ij} = Cov(x_i, x_j) = E\{[x_i - E(x_i)][x_j - E(x_j)]\} \tag{6}$$

Where $i, j = 1, 2, \ldots, n$

And then the covariance matrix can be expressed as follows.

$$C_{n*n} = \begin{bmatrix} c_{11} & c_{12} & \cdots & c_{1n} \\ c_{21} & c_{22} & \cdots & c_{2n} \\ \vdots & \vdots & \cdots & \vdots \\ c_{n1} & c_{n2} & \cdots & c_{nn} \end{bmatrix} \tag{7}$$

(3) The eigenvalues and eigenvectors of the covariance matrix C is calculated
(4) The eigenvalues are sorted in descending order, the largest d of them are selected, and then d eigenvectors corresponding to the eigenvalues are used as column vectors to form the eigenvector matrix, which is denoted as $EigenVectors_{n*d}$
(5) The sample point is projected onto the selected eigenvector and the processed dataset is obtained and denoted as $Finaldata_{m*d}$

$$FinalData_{m*d} = TAdjust_{m*n}*EigenVectors_{n*d} \tag{8}$$

2.2   Evaluation Indicator

(1) Clustering time

Clustering time represents the whole time of clustering process. The shorter the better.

(2) Calinski Harabasz (CH)

Differing from the classification of supervised learning, it is impossible to determine directly whether the clustering result is right by using precision or recall as there is no label for each data record in the given dataset. However, we can evaluate the clustering results based on the degree of in-cluster density and the degree of inter-cluster dis-cretization. Both Silhouette Coefficient (SC) and Calinski Harabasz (CH) [17] are the common evaluation indicators. In order to compare with PMBKM, we choose CH as the clustering evaluation indicator. In addition, the calculation process of CH is simple and the computation cost of CH is much lower than SC. Moreover, CH can be obtained by formula (9).

$$CH = \frac{SS_{Between}}{SS_{Within}} \times \frac{m - K}{K - 1} \tag{9}$$

Where K is the number of clusters, and m is the total number of data records, SS_{Within} represents the overall within-cluster variance and $SS_{Between}$ represents the overall between-cluster variance.

3   PBirch Intrusion Detection Method

As shown in Fig. 2, the PBirch intrusion detection system consists of four steps.

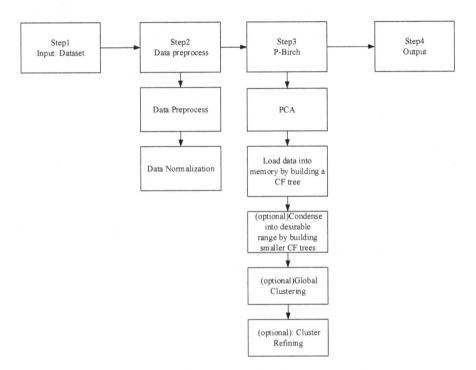

Fig. 2. PBirch intrusion detection clustering method

Thus, the data input, data preprocess, PBirch, as well as the output.

Step 1:   **Data input**

Input the initial dataset T. The data is usually captured online by some tools such as Wireshark, Snort, etc. Each record consists of several features. Note that the input data does not have any tag information. Our task is to divide these data records into different clusters, ensuring that the data record with the same feature is grouped into one category.

Step 2:   **Data preprocessing**

In clustering process of step3, we compare the similarities between two records using Euclidean distance, while Euclidean distance can only compare the similarity between numbers not the similarity between characters. Thus, we should make sure all the string in the dataset is the number. This step mainly contain two sub-step. The first one is the string preprocess. This process is mainly responsible for replacing non-numeric data record in dataset with random numeric data. The other one is data normalization. In addition, note that the range of numbers in the given dataset may not uniform. This means that a column with a large number of values may lead to the neglect of the roles of a column with relatively small values. And thus the normalization process should be performed before executing the clustering process, and the goal of normalization is make the feature data in the range of [0–1]. We use the pre-processing algorithm which we proposed in [12]. Algorithm 1 illustrates the process of PBirch. As shown in algorithm 1, for given dataset T, T is traversed and all the strings is found and the value S_n is returned (Line 2). Secondly, the Replacement function is called to replace S_n with random numbers n and the processed dataset T' is returned (Line 3). In addition, the normalization dataset T_1 is obtained by calling Normalization function (Line 4).

Step 3:   PBirch clustering

Birch is an effective clustering method, but it is not suitable for high-dimensional data sets. Therefore, PCA method is used to reduce dimensionality. PCA method consists of four steps and is implemented according to the formula (6) to (8) in Sect. 2.1. Firstly, the processed data TAdjust is obtained by Adjust function (Line 5). And then the covariance matrix C is obtained (Line 6). In addition, eigenvector matrix EigenVectors is obtained (Line 7). Finally, the dimension reduction data T_1' is obtained (Line 8).

Next, we discuss the process of Birch.

(1) Load data into memory and build a CF tree

The main process is shown in Sect. 2.1 and the corresponding function is CFTreeCreate (Line 9). There are two parameters, T_1' and threshold ts in CFTreeCreate. An initialized CF tree is created by scanning the data T_1', and then dense data is divided into several clusters and sparse data is treated as multiple isolated points. Note that the parameter threshold ts determines the size of the CF Tree. Generally speaking, the smaller the ts, the larger the size of the CF Tree. Different scales will affect the final clustering result. In the experiment phase, we will test different values of ts to get the best clustering result.

(2) Condense into desirable range by building smaller CF trees

The global or semi-global clustering algorithm of sub-step (4) has the requirements of the input range to achieve the speed and quality requirements. Therefore, based on sub-step (2), a smaller CF tree is established. The corresponding function is CFTreeSmaller (Line 10). This sub-step is optional.

(3) Global Clustering

Remedy the clustering of all leaf nodes using global/semi-global algorithms due to splitting due to input order and page size. The corresponding function is Global Clustering (Line 11). This sub-step is optional.

(4) Cluster Refining

The center point of sub-step (3) is used as a seed, and the data points are reassigned to the nearest seed to ensure that the duplicate data is divided into the same cluster, and the cluster label is added at the same time. The corresponding function is ClusterRefine (Line 12). This sub-step is also optional.

Step 4:   Output

Output the clustered data. We can further determine which is the normal behavior and which is the abnormal behavior based on the clustering result.

Algorithm 1. (PBirch)

Input: Given dataset T , Number of principal components d
Output: CH , K (number of clusters)
//Step 1
1.T← loading ( )
//Step 2
2. S_n ←Traverses (T)
3. T' ←Replacement (T , S (random (n)))
// n   is equal to the number of strings
4. T_1 ← Normalization (T')

//Step 3
5. T*Adjust* ←TAdjust (T)
6. C ←Covariancematrix (T*Adjust*)
7. *EigenVectors* ←EigenVectors (C, d)
8. $\dot{T}_1$ ← T*Adjust* * *EigenVectors*

9.CFTreeCreate (T_1' , *ts*)
10.CFTreeSmaller ( )
11.GlobalClustering ( )
12.ClusterRefine ( )
//Step 4
13. CH ←score ($\dot{T}_1$)
return CH ,K

---

4   Experimental Result and Discussion

4.1   Experimental Environment

In this section, our proposed IDS method PBirch is tested over NSL-KDD dataset [18], which is an improved dataset from KDDCUP99 dataset [19]. KDDCUP99 is a 9-week network connection data collected from a simulated LAN of US Air Force. NSL-KDD dataset removes redundant data from the KDDCUP99, which overcomes the problem that the classifier is biased towards recurring records, and the performance of the learning method is affected. The experiment is implemented by Python language on a Windows 10 OS, which the processor is Inter Core i7 2.7 GHz, the RAM is 16 GB, and the main software platform is Eclipse and Anaconda 2.7 SCIkit-learn [20].

4.2   Experimental Result Discussion

(1) Comparison of different scenarios of PBirch

First we test the clustering time and clustering score *CH* in both thread = 0.5 (Scenario 1) and thread = 0.35 (Scenario2). When thread = 0.5, the best clustering result is N = 4. Therefore, we mainly compare the clustering time and *CH* of scenario1 and scenario2 while N taking 2, 3, and 4.

As shown in Fig. 3, in the same clustering situation, the clustering time of scenario2 is longer than the clustering time of scenario1, but in general, in both scenarios, the clustering time decreases linearly with the increasing of the number of clusters; in both scenarios, the clustering scores *CH* increase as the number of clusters increases. In the same clustering situation, *CH* of scenario2 is higher than that of scenario1.

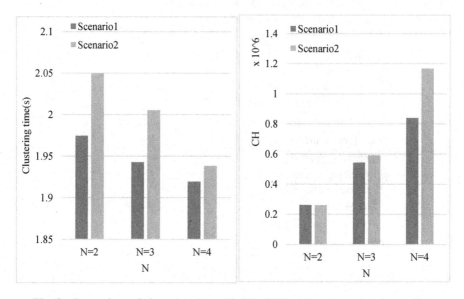

Fig. 3. Comparison of clustering time and *CH* of PBirch in scenario1 and scenario2

(2) Comparison of PBirch in scenario1 and scenario2 with PMBKM [11]

A. **Comparison of PBirch in Scenario1 with PMBKM**

When thread = 0.5, the best clustering result is N = 4. Therefore, we mainly compare the clustering time and *CH* of scenario1 and PMBKM and when *N* takes 2, 3, and 4. As shown in Fig. 4, in general, the clustering time of scenario1 is linearly decreased as the number of clustering increases, and the clustering time of PMBKM is relatively stable; in the same clustering, the clustering time of scenario1 is longer than clustering time of PMBKM. In general, in both scenarios, the cluster scores increase as the number of clusters increases. In the same cluster, *CH* of PMBKM is slightly higher than that of scenario1. In the best clustering situation, *CH* scores of these two methods are basically equal.

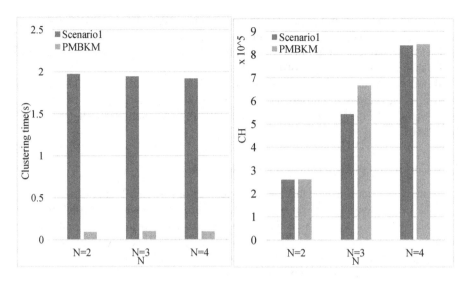

Fig. 4. Comparison of PBirch in scenario1 and PMBKM

B. Comparison of PBirch in Scenario2 with PMBKM

In scenario2, the best clustering result is $N = 6$. Therefore, we mainly compare the clustering time and clustering score CH of scenario2 and PMBKM when N takes 2, 3, 4, 5, 6

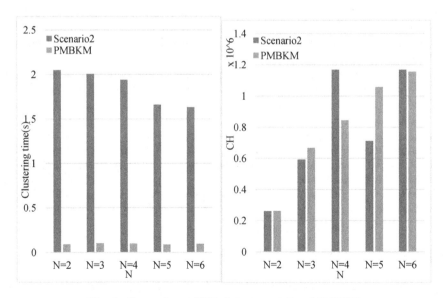

Fig. 5. Comparison of PBirch in scenario2 and PMBKM

As shown in Fig. 5, in general, the clustering time of PBirch in scenario2 decreases linearly with the increasing of the number of clusters, and the clustering time of PMBKM is relatively stable. In the same cluster, the time of scenario2 clustering is longer than the clustering time of PMBKM.

Based on the same number of clusters, in general, *CH* scores of both methods increase as the number of clusters increases. The PBirch in scenario2 has a higher *CH* than PMBKM. In the best clustering scenario, the PBirch algorithm is slightly higher than PMBKM.

4.3   Conclusion of Experimental Results

In summary, we can conclude that the time overhead of PBirch is higher than PMBKM from the perspective of clustering time, but the clustering time of the PBirch linearly decreases with the increasing of the number of clusters, so it is more suitable for clustering over big data. From the perspective of *CH*, PBirch does not need to specify clustering values in advance, it calculates an optimal clustering result, at the same time, and *CH* score can be improved by adjusting the parameters simply. Overall, PBirch is much better than PMBKM and can be widely used for big data.

5   Conclusion

In this study we implement a new clustering method named Balanced Iterative Reducing and Clustering Using Hierarchies with Principal Component Analysis (PBirch) for intrusion detection system over big data. Compared to PMBKM, the experimental results show that PBirch can obtain good clustering results without specifying clustering values, and the clustering result can be further improved by optimizing the relevant parameters simply. The clustering time is linearly decreasing with the increasing of the cluster numbers. All in all, our proposed method can be widely used for big data mobile cloud environment. In the future research, we will engaged in the parallel clustering algorithm to further reduce clustering time.

Acknowledgments. This work is supported by The Natural Science Foundation of Fujian Province (Grant No. 2018J05106), Quanzhou Science and Technology Project (No. 2015Z115), the Scientific Research Foundation of Huaqiao University (No. 14BS316). The Education Scientific Research Project for Middle-age and Young Teachers of Fujian Province (JZ160084). China Scholarship Council awards to Kai Peng for one year's research abroad at The University of British Columbia, Vancouver, Canada. The authors also wants to thank Jianping Liu, Zhiqiang Xu and etc. for sharing a lot of valuable information on his blog.

References

1. Anderson, J.P.: Computer security threat monitoring and surveillance. Technical Report, vol. 17. James P. Anderson Company, Pennsylvania (1980)
2. Denning, D.E.: An intrusion-detection model. IEEE Trans. Softw. Eng. **2**, 222–232 (1987)

3. Milenkoski, A., Vieira, M., Kounev, S., Avritzer, A., Payne, B.D.: Evaluating computer intrusion detection systems: a survey of common practices. ACM Comput. Surv. (CSUR) **48** (1), 1–41 (2015)
4. Wang, T., et al.: Fog-based storage technology to fight with cyber threat. Future Gener. Comput. Syst. **83**, 208–218 (2018)
5. Peng, K., Lin, R.H., Huang, B.B., Zou, H., Yang, F.C.: Link importance evaluation of data center network based on maximum flow. J. Internet Technol. **18**(1), 23–31 (2017)
6. Wang, T., et al.: Data collection from WSNs to the cloud based on mobile fog elements. Future Gener. Comput. Syst. (2017). https://doi.org/10.1016/j.future.2017.07.031
7. Wang, T., Zhang, G.X., Bhuiyan, M.Z.A., Liu, A.F., Jia, W., Xie, M.: A novel trust mechanism based on fog computing in sensor-cloud system. Future Gener. Comput. Syst. (2018). https://doi.org/10.1016/j.future.2018.05.049
8. Wu, X., Zhu, X., Wu, G.Q., Ding, W.: Data mining with big data. IEEE Trans. Knowl. Data Eng. **26**(1), 97–107 (2014)
9. Wang, T., Bhuiyan, M.Z.A., Wang, G.J., Rahman, A., Wu, J., Cao, J.N.: Big data reduction for smart city's critical infrastructure health monitoring. IEEE Commun. Mag. **56**(3), 128–133 (2018)
10. Lee, W., Stolfo, S.J.: Data mining approaches for intrusion detection. In: 7th USENIX. USENIX Security Symposium, pp. 79–93 (1998)
11. Peng, K., Leung, V.C.M., Huang, Q.J.: Clustering approach based on mini batch Kmeans for intrusion detection system over big data. IEEE Access **6**, 11897–11906 (2018)
12. Peng, K., Leung, V.C.M., Zheng, L.X., Wang, S.G., Huang, C., Lin, T.: Intrusion detection system based on decision tree over big data in fog environment. Wirel. Commun. Mob. Comput. (2018). https://doi.org/10.1155/2018/4680867
13. Halko, N., Martinsson, P.G., Tropp, J.A.: Finding Structure with Randomness: Stochastic Algorithms for Constructing Approximate Matrix Decompositions. http://resolver.caltech.edu/CaltechAUTHORS:20111012-111324407
14. Tipping, M.E., Bishop, C.M.: Mixtures of probabilistic principal component analyzers. Neural Comput. **11**(2), 443–482 (1999)
15. Martinsson, P.G., Rokhlin, V., Tygert, M.: A randomized algorithm for the decomposition of matrices. Appl. Comput. Harmonic Anal. **30**(1), 47–68 (2011)
16. Zhang, T., Ramakrishnan, R., Livny, M.: An efficient data clustering method for very large databases. In: Proceedings of the 1996 ACM SIGMOD International Conference on Management of Data (SIGMOD 1996), pp. 103–114. ACM, New York (1996)
17. Calinski, T., Harabasz, J.: A dendrite method for cluster analysis. Commun. Stat.-Theory Methods **3**(1), 1–27 (1974)
18. http://www.unb.ca/cic/datasets/nsl.html
19. KDDCUP99. http://kdd.ics.uci.edu/databases/kddcup99/kddcup99.html
20. Scikit-learn. http://scikit-learn.org/stable/index.html

A Four-Stage Hybrid Feature Subset Selection Approach for Network Traffic Classification Based on Full Coverage

Jingbo Xia[1(✉)], Jian Shen[2], and Yaoxiang Wu[1]

[1] Tan Kah College, Xiamen University, Zhangzhou 363000, China
jbxiad@sina.com
[2] Unit 95655 of PLA, Chengdu 610000, China
shenjian2018@126.com

Abstract. There is significant interest in network management and security to classify traffic flows. As the essential step for machine learning based traffic classification, feature subset selection is often used to realize dimension reduction and redundant information decrease. A four-stage hybrid feature subset selection method is proposed to improve the classification performance of hybrid methods at low evaluation consumption. The proposed algorithm is designed to dispose features in the level of block and evaluate every feature even the remaining ones which cannot provide much information by themselves to use the interactions among all of them. Additionally, a wrapper-based selection is designed in the last stage to further remove the redundant features. The performances are examined by two groups of experiments. Our theoretical analysis and experimental observations reveal that the proposed method selects feature subset with improved classification performance on every index while depleting fewer evaluations. Moreover, the evaluation consumption can keep at a low and stable level with different size of block.

Keywords: Full coverage · Machine learning · Hybrid feature subset selection
Network traffic classification · Network management

1 Introduction

Traffic classification is making a significant difference in network resource scheduling, safety analysis and future tendency prediction [1]. As the pre-processing step for machine learning based network traffic classification, Feature Subset Selection (FSS) is widely used [2–5]. This approach can not only point out critical features, but also decrease the noisy (unrelated) features from the original feature set.

The conventional filter-based and wrapper-based FSS methods have the intrinsic drawbacks. Recently the literatures contain numerous references to the use of hybrid FSS algorithms to combine the superiority of different methods. Xie & Wang [6] included a feature ranking in a sequential forward search method with the application of the F-score measure to rank the features, while Peng [7] added a random sampling method to choose features from the ranking. Zhang [8] and Bonillahuerta [9] proposed the similar methods including a Relieff estimation based ranking, which were also

© Springer Nature Switzerland AG 2018
G. Wang et al. (Eds.): SpaCCS 2018, LNCS 11342, pp. 178–191, 2018.
https://doi.org/10.1007/978-3-030-05345-1_15

applied to compress the searching space. These methods make much improvement on feature selection, but they are still stuck with the restriction of computational complexity and classification accuracy. It can be seen that ranking is widely embedded in the feature selection algorithms as the initial step to filter out the least promising features. Meanwhile, it is the principal and auxiliary selection mechanism with simplicity, scalability and good empirical success. The features ranking in the front are more likely to be selected into the subset, while the ones in the bottom are always neglected. As a result, the neglected features ranking in the bottom will never be taken into account in the following steps of selection. However, the variable that is completely useless by itself may provide a significant improvement on the classification performance when it is combined with the others [10]. The complex interaction among features plays an important role in representing the whole feature collection.

In this paper, a four-stage hybrid algorithm called full-covered feature selection (FCFS) is proposed to improve the efficiency and performance of network traffic classification. We still utilize the ranking strategy to take its advantages of simplicity and scalability. Then, features are disposed in the level of block to save the consumption of iteration. Meanwhile, all the features and their interactions are estimated, including the ones with less value by itself and ranking in the bottom. At last, we design a final wrapper-based selection to refine feature subset and further improve its classification ability.

The rest of the paper is organized as follows. The following section presents the related work of a set of typical FSS methods. In Sect. 3 we describe the proposed four-stage FSS algorithm in detail. The 4th section contains two groups of experiments and the corresponding analyses. We provide a summary of the paper and future work in Sect. 5.

2   Related Work

2.1   Filter-Based Feature Subset Selection

Filter-based feature ranking techniques use statistical measures to assign a score to each feature and rank the resulting features according to the value of the scores [11]. As common sense, the classification performance may be enhanced with the increasing of the selected features. However, the truth shows the opposite side. The termination criterion is always set at the certain threshold or percentage of the features that are on top of the rank, and the termination criterion is difficult to confirm according to different datasets. What is more, it is not guaranteed that the best performance can be got when the process of feature selection moves to the termination criterion.

Filter-based feature subset selection techniques use measurements to evaluate the quality of feature subsets. Filter-based FSS methods evaluate features as a preprocessing step, which is independent from the chosen predictor. As the most classical algorithm, correlation-based feature selection (CFS) was proposed to filter the features by defining a merit for each selected subset of features [12]. The merit is based on the hypothesis that a promising collection involves those features, which are uncorrelated or weakly correlated to each other but correlated to the class label. From the viewpoint of information theorem, the information of a set of features could be calculated by various statistical measures, and that is the core of the filter-based feature selection methods. Due to the fast speed of data processing, filters are often applied to feature selection in high-dimensional data [13]. However, the filters cannot guarantee the best result.

2.2 Wrapper-Based Feature Subselect

Wrapper-based feature subset selection method always pursues higher prediction accuracy through a machine learning method. It evaluates each feature subset with the specific indicator of classification performance, such as accuracy or F-measure. A machine learning algorithm is applied as a black-box to score subsets of features according to their predicted ability. They consider all the subsets and evaluate their merits by considering the built classification model only with the selected features. Sequential Forward Selection (SFS) method is one of the wrapper algorithms that are widely used [14]. It starts from an empty set and adds one feature at a time when the classification performance improves. The procedure would not stop until the test result starts to get worse or the number of features reaches a predefined threshold [13].

Conceptually, wrapper-based feature subset evaluation is very simple: the chosen feature subset is used as the basis for a classification model, and then the performance of this model is used as the score for that feature subset [15]. However, they are often criticized because they seem to be brute force methods which require massive amount of computation. The computational complexity is too high to be $O(n2)$ even with efficient search strategies like Bestfirst and Greedy.

2.3 Hybrid Feature Subset Selection

Hybrid method is a more recent and promising direction in the feature selection field [16–20]. Most of the hybrid FSS algorithms are based on double-stage model. They use the ranking information obtained from filter methods to guide the search in the optimization algorithms used by wrapper-based methods.

In the past few years, a set of typical literatures have contained numerous references to the use of hybrid FSS algorithms. Incremental Wrapper-based Subset Selection (IWSS) is a canonical method which was presented by Ruiz [21]. The features that satisfy the relevance criterion would be selected into the feature subset. The advantage of this method is the low computational complexity of $O(n)$. However, the problem is that the features are kept into the subset once they are selected, which may result in excessiveness of feature subset. The algorithm of IWSS with replacement (IWSSr) was proposed to alleviate this problem [22]. This method does not only add features to the subset, but also use them to replace the former ones. The selected subset is more representative, but it is also obvious that all the features are disposed once at a time. Therefore, the process is inefficient to deal with high-dimensional problems. Pablo Bermejo put forward the method of IWSS with re-ranking (IWSSrR) by the introduced concept of block [15]. The proposed algorithm can select features at the level of block and make much improvement on classification efficiency. The size of block is also required to be large enough to give some freedom to the wrapper algorithm, and that may increase extra evaluations.

3 Methodology

Our goal in this paper is to design an algorithm to select a feature subset with satis-factory classification performance and simultaneously at a reasonable computational cost. The FCFS is proposed to make use of all the features, including the ones of little value by itself but with available improvement when combined with the others. In the first stage, the features are ranked by the filter-based ranking method. Then, we divide the ranking features into blocks and iteratively select the features in the level of block in the second stage. Stage 3 evaluates the remaining features of stage 2 one by one and brings in the ones that make improvement on the base of the selected feature subset. Last stage, wrapper-based selection method is applied to delete the redundant infor-mation to improve the classification performance.

3.1 Filter-Based Ranking

Feature ranking is a filter-based method according to the classification performance [23]. The universally acknowledged benefits of feature ranking are computational simplicity and statistical scalability. Computationally, it is efficient because of the requirement of only n evaluations and sorting the scores, where n is the number of features. Statistically, it is robust against overfitting because of the introduction of bias but with considerable less variance [24]. We apply filter-based ranking method as the pre-processing method of the FSS algorithm. The process of feature selection starts from the top of the ranking. As a result, a provisional feature subset with relatively acceptable classification performance could be quickly obtained.

In this study, we use Information Gain (IG) which is one of the wildly used feature ranking methods to evaluate the predictive attributes [25]. It measures the difference between the entropy of the class label and the conditional entropy of class label when a feature is given. IG generalizes for nominal data but breaks down on continuous data. It is applicable to multi-class problems. If A is a feature and C is the class, (1) and (2) give the entropy of the class before and after observing the feature.

$$H(C) = -\sum_{c \in C} p(c) \log_2 p(c) \tag{1}$$

$$H(C|A) = -\sum_{a \in A} p(a) \sum_{c \in C} p(c|a) \log_2 p(c|a) \tag{2}$$

The amount by which the entropy of the class decreases reflects the additional infor-mation about the class provided by the feature [26]. Each feature is assigned a score based on the information gain between itself and the class as formula (3). The higher the IG value is, the more correlated the feature with the classes will be. Then, the features are sorted in descending order according to the score.

$$\begin{aligned} IG_i &= H(C) - H(C|A_i) \\ &= H(A_i) - H(A_i|C) \\ &= H(A_i) + H(C) - H(A_i, C) \end{aligned} \tag{3}$$

3.2   Iterative Feature Selection in the Level of Block

In the second stage, the features are separated into blocks according to the ranking order. The size of block should be large enough to supply sufficient combination of features to be evaluated by wrapper-based method, but not so large that the advantages of iteration process fade away. The size of 30 is thought to be suitable to keep the balance [14]. We start feature selection from the first block with wrapper-based method. In this stage, we apply SFS method which is one of the widely used wrapper algorithms. Let F_a be the subset of features selected from the block. The classification performance of F_a is evaluated by the same classifier that is embedded in SFS. Then, the same progress moves to the second block but taking into account the features that have already been selected into F_a. The newly selected features from the second block are also added into F_a. The process iterates until no new features are selected from the block or the classification performance of F_a stops increasing. The detailed process of stage 2 is shown in Algorithm 1.

Algorithm 1. Block based iterative feature selection.

Input: the whole collection of features F, the size of block B

Output: the selected feature subset F_a

1: divide the collection of features F by the size of block B, $\{F_1, F_2, ..., F_n\}$

2: $F_1' = SFS(F_1)$

3: set $F_a = F_1'$

4: **for** $F_i \square F$ do, $i = 2, ..., n$

5: $F_1' = SFS(F_a \cup F_i)$

6: evaluate F_1' with the specific classifier.

7: **if** $Acc(F_1') > Acc(F_{i-1}')$ **then** //Acc is the classification accuracy of the feature

collection

8:    $F_a = F_a \cup F_i'$

9:   **else break**

10: **end if**

11: **end for**

12: return F_a

It can be seen that all the features are disposed in the level of block, which can drastically reduce the number of evaluations to improve the efficiency of the algorithm. It should also be noticed that the features of F_a keep increasing but not being renewed. Once a feature has been selected into F_a, it stays in the subset but not interchange with the following selected ones. This strategy keeps all the promising features in the provisional feature collection until the last stage of the algorithm.

3.3   Selection from the Remaining Features

In stage 2, it can be seen that the selection process ceases at the termination criterion. The rest of the features ranking in the bottom have not been evaluated. Our purpose in this stage is to take the advantage of the remaining features. That is because the features with little value by themselves, which are usually abandoned, may make significant improvement when they are combined with the others.

In this stage, every remaining feature is evaluated with the combination of the features selected from stage 2. If the classification performance of F_a improves, the feature would be selected into the feature subset F_b, otherwise it is omitted. This stage can extract the potential value of the features that are usually ignored. As we know, the subset F_a selected from the features ranking in the top has strong classification ability. What's more, with the complement of the chosen remaining features in subset F_b, the classification performance can make a further improvement.

Algorithm 2. Selection from the remaining features

Input: the remaining collection features F_r, the feature subset selected from stage 2 F_a

Output: the selected feature subset F_c

1: set $F_b = \Phi$

2. **for** $f_i \square F_r$ **do**

3: evaluate the classification performance of $(F_a \cup f_i)$

4: **if** $Acc(F_a \cup f) > F_a$ **then** //Acc is the classification accuracy of the feature collection

5: $F_b = F_b \cup f_i$

6: **end if**

7: **end for**

8: $F_c = F_a \cup F_b$

9: return F_c

The evaluations cost in this stage is just the same as the number of the remaining features. However, many more promising features could be selected which can supply more deficient information. It can be seen that all the features in the subset F_c are either the ones with much meritorious information or the ones that can provide additional supplement.

3.4   Wrapper-Based Selection for Final Feature Subset

From the above three stages, we can get the feature subset of F_c containing all the promising features. However, there is still room for the reduction of features, and there is too much redundant information among the selected features which have repetitive or even negative effect on the classification performance. To overcome this problem and further reduce the dimensions of feature, another step of wrapper-based approach is added to refine the selected feature subset. In this stage, SFS method is applied to accomplish the final feature subset selection. So a more representative feature subset can be got with all the meritorious but less redundant information. Due to the feature subset of stage 3 is highly compressed comparing with the original collection, the evaluations cost by SFS method can be well controlled in a limited range. As a result, the exact final feature subset can make a further improvement both on dimension reduction and classification performance.

4   Experiments

4.1   Experimental Setup

This paper applies traffic flow dataset of Moore to the experiment [27]. The dataset contains 12 traffic categories, which are WWW, MAIL, FTP-CONTROL, FTP-PASV, ATTACK, P2P, DATABASE, FTP-DATA, MULTIMEDIA, SERVICES, INTER-ACTIVES and GAMES. There are 24863 flows with 248 features in the dataset. CFS, SFS and IWSSr^R are the three representative methods of filter-based, wrapper-based and hybrid FSS methods. They are presented as the comparisons of the proposed FCFS algorithm in this paper.

The experiment adopts Naivebayes as the classifier. The 10-fold cross-validation method is used to estimate the data. The result takes the average of the experiment which is conducted ten times.

4.2   Experiment 1: Comparing FCFS with Other Feature Selection Method

This experiment is designed to compare the classification performance of the feature subsets selected by different algorithms. In this part of experiment, the block size of FCFS and IWSSr^R is set to be 30. Therefore, the collection of 248 features is divided into 9 blocks.

From Table 1, we can observe the result of every step of FCFS algorithm. The features are targeted in bold when they are selected into the feature subset for the first time. It is obvious that there are new features being selected in the first three iterations.

The second stage of algorithm gets to the termination criterion when it selects the same feature subset on the fourth iteration. And then, 11 remaining features ranking in the second half of the rank are selected into the subset on stage 3. Stage 4 filters away the redundant features to simplify the subset to be smaller. From the analysis of the final feature subset, we can see that 9 out of the 11 selected remaining features are chosen into the final subset, which account for the half amount.

Table 1. Result of every step when the size of block is set to be 30.

Step	Feature subset
Iteration 1	**4, 99, 100, 101, 106, 107, 108, 183, 200, 205**
Iteration 2	4, **38, 57**, 99, 101, 106, 107, 108, **135**, 183, 200, **208**
Iteration 3	4, **8**, 38, 99, 107, 108, 183, 200, 208
Iteration 4	4, 8, 38, 99, 107, 108, 183, 200, 208
Stage 3	4, 8, 38, 57, **74, 76, 79, 83, 84, 85**, 99, 100, 101, 106, 107, 108, 135, **155, 181, 182**, 183, **195**, 200, 205, 208, **230**
Stage 4	4, 8, 38, 79, 83, 84, 85, 100, 107, 108, 155, 181, 182, 195, 200, 205, 208, 230

Figure 1 compares the performance of different algorithms on five indexes. The precision and recall represent for the ratio of correctly classified flows over all predicted flows and all flows respectively. The F-measure is the statistical technique to examine the classification performance of a system. It is defined to describe the comprehensive performance of precision and recall [28]. In this paper, F-measure is weighted equally to both precision rate and recall rate as shown in Eq. (4).

$$F - measure = \frac{2(Precision * Recall)}{Precision + Recall} \tag{4}$$

The indexes of precision, recall and F-measure stand for the classification ability of the FSS method. The area under the curve of ROC and PRC are the performances that

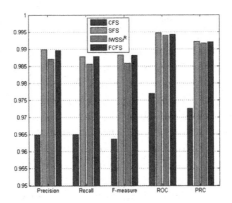

Fig. 1. Performance of different algorithms.

are frequently used to quantitatively assess the identification model. From the comparison, we can briefly come to the conclusion that the filter-based method CFS performs much worse than the other methods on all the aspects, while the wrapper-based method SFS always has the best performance. As to the hybrid methods, FCFS outperforms IWSSr^R on the classification indexes notably, and has similar performance as SFS. On the aspect of identification model, the three methods have similar scores. Without considering the computational cost, we can make a summary that SFS and FCFS have the similar best performance, filter-based method performs the worst and IWSSr^R scores in the middle. This experimental result corresponds to the former theoretical analysis.

Though SFS has the best performance on most of the aspects, its computational complexity of $O(n^2)$ is intolerable for the feature selection process. Table 2 shows the number of evaluations carried out by different algorithms. It can be seen that the two hybrid methods FCFS and IWSSr^R cost nearly the same quantity of evaluations, which is only the half consumption of SFS. The evaluations carried out by CFS are the least among all the methods, but considering its classification performance, it is still not an appropriate choice for accurate classification.

Table 2. Evaluations of different algorithms.

	CFS	SFS	IWSSr^R	FCFS
Evaluations	1479	6351	2797	2848

Concerning all the comparisons above, we can come to the conclusion that the proposed method FCFS succeeds the advantages of hybrid approaches on the overhead of evaluations. Moreover, its classification performance can reach the same level of the wrapper-based method SFS.

4.3   Experiment 2: Evaluating the Classification Performance with Different Size of Block

The block size is a key parameter in this approach. In this section of experiment, we test the effect of different initialized size of block on the performance of FCFS, IWSSr^R and SFS. Five experiments are conducted with the initialized size of block set from 10 to 50.

Figures 2, 3 and 4 show the classification performance of different algorithms. The performance of SFS is not influenced by the block, and it is applied as the baseline. It is obvious that IWSSr^R always performs worth than the other two methods. Meanwhile, FCFS and SFS have similar classification performance when the block size is set to be larger than 30. With the increase of the block size, the integrated performance of both FCFS and IWSSr^R shows a rising trend. The computational complexity of different algorithms can be compared from the result of evaluation consumption as shown in Fig. 5. FCFS has the similar evaluation consumption of IWSSr^R when the block size is set to be 10, 30 and 40, and it always keeps at the steady level of around 2000 with any block size. However, IWSSr^R shows a sudden rise of more than 4000 evaluations when the block size is set to be 20 and 50. It is because the termination criterion does not take effect to prevent the unnecessarily consuming of evaluations. IWSSr^R continues to iterate selection even when the classification performance is not improved, while FCFS stops at the proper threshold value to start the next stage of feature selection. The result shows that FCFS is able to realize accurate classification with stable and reasonable evaluation consumption with different block size.

We collect the result of all the five experiments with different block size to compare the relationships of evaluations consumption and classification performance as shown in Fig. 6. The classification accuracy of both methods, as a whole, improves with the increase of the evaluations. However, the jitter characteristic of FCFS is much inconspicuous than IWSSr^R, which means FCFS is more likely to perform better even with less cost. From the performance comparison of the two methods, it can be seen that FCFS always has better classification accuracy at the same evaluation consumption, and it only costs half evaluations of IWSSr^R when they get to the best classification performance respectively. So it can be concluded that FCFS can make full use of the consumed evaluations to get better classification performance.

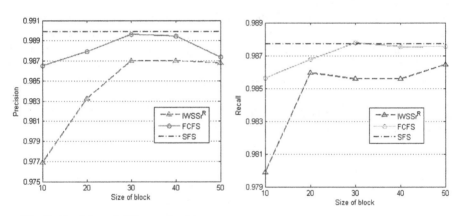

Fig. 2. Precision of different algorithms.   **Fig. 3.** Recall of different algorithms.

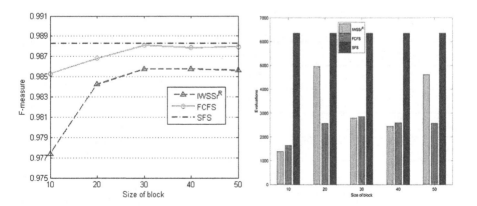

Fig. 4. F-measure of different algorithms.   **Fig. 5.** Evaluations of different algorithms.

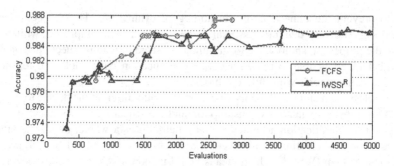

Fig. 6. Collection of classification performance at different evaluation consumption of the five experiments.

Figure 7 is the classification performance of FCFS method at each step with different size of block. The solid part is the target that the performance of FCFS can get. At each step, it can be seen that the larger the size of block is, the better performance it can get. That is because more evaluations are consumed when more features are taken into account at each iteration of selection. It can be seen that the classification performance improves with the increase of the steps. The last step corresponds to the third and fourth stage of FCFS. It is obvious that the last step of every experiment can always improve the classification accuracy to a great deal. That means some of the remaining features are of great value in the combination with the selected features and the strategy of final subset selection makes much contribution to the classification performance.

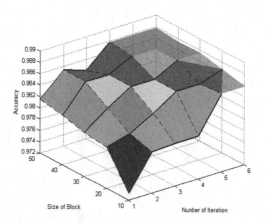

Fig. 7. Classification performance of FCFS method at each step.

5 Conclusion

A four-stage hybrid feature subset selection mechanism has been proposed and tested in this paper. The idea is based on full coverage of all the features. The novelty is that the remaining features of the selection in the level of blocks are reassessed by the interactions with the selected features one by one, and then the promising ones are brought into the feature subset. Moreover, wrapper-based selection method is applied to refine the final feature subset at the last stage. The advantage of this approach is that all the features are evaluated through the four stages, while the features filtered out by the termination criterion are reassessed to enrich the feature subset to enhance the classification performance and refined to restrict the size of final feature subset at the last stage. The disadvantage is that the approach is composed of several stages, the process of data processing is complex.

The result of our experiments shows that the proposed four-stage mechanism can combine the superior aspects of both wrapper-based and hybrid FSS methods. The selected feature subset of FCFS algorithm has similar classification performance as wrapper-based method on all the aspects, while the evaluation consumption is much less. Compared with hybrid methods, the classification of FCFS method is more accurate with the computational complexity at the same level. Meanwhile, the evaluation consumption of FCFS can keep in a stable standard and overcome the sensitiveness to the block size, which is a critical drawback of the other hybrid methods. From the description and analysis, it can be seen that the iterations of feature selection in blocks deplete most of the evaluation consumption. As future work, our research will be focused on decreasing the number of iterations to further improve the efficiency of FSS approach.

Acknowledgements. The authors gratefully acknowledge the financial support from Natural Science Foundation of Zhangzhou, Fujian (Project No. ZZ2018J22).

References

1. Khayari, R.E.A., Sadre, R,, Haverkort, B.R.: A validation of the pseudo self-similar traffic model. In: International Conference on Dependable Systems and Networks, pp. 727–734. IEEE Computer Society (2002)
2. Liu, Z., Wang, R., Tao, M., et al.: A class-oriented feature selection approach for multi-class imbalanced network traffic datasets based on local and global metrics fusion. Neurocomputing **168**(C), 365–381 (2015)
3. Nie, F., Huang, H., Cai, X., et al.: Efficient and robust feature selection via joint $\ell 2,1$-norms minimization. In: International Conference on Neural Information Processing Systems, pp. 1813–1821. Curran Associates Inc (2010)
4. Nie, F., Xu, D., Tsang, I.W., et al.: Flexible manifold embedding: a framework for semi-supervised and unsupervised dimension reduction. IEEE Trans. Image Process. **19**(7), 1921–1932 (2010)
5. Wang, R., Nie, F., Hong, R., et al.: Fast and orthogonal locality preserving projections for dimensionality reduction. IEEE Trans. Image Process. **PP**(99), 1-1 (2017)

6. Xie, J., Wang, C.: Using support vector machines with a novel hybrid feature selection method for diagnosis of erythemato-squamous diseases. Expert Syst. Appl. Int. J. **38**(5), 5809–5815 (2011)
7. Peng, Y., Wu, Z., Jiang, J.: A novel feature selection approach for biomedical data classification. J. Biomed. Inform. **43**(1), 15–23 (2010)
8. Zhang, L.X,, Wang, J.X., Zhao, Y.N., et al.: A novel hybrid feature selection algorithm: using ReliefF estimation for GA-wrapper search. In: International Conference on Machine Learning and Cybernetics, vol. 1, pp. 380–384. IEEE (2004)
9. Bonilla-Huerta, E., Duval, B., Hernández, J.C.H., Hao, J.-K., Morales-Caporal, R.: Hybrid filter-wrapper with a specialized random multi-parent crossover operator for gene selection and classification problems. In: Huang, D.-S., Gan, Y., Premaratne, P., Han, K. (eds.) ICIC 2011. LNCS, vol. 6840, pp. 453–461. Springer, Heidelberg (2012). https://doi.org/10.1007/978-3-642-24553-4_60
10. Guyon, I., Elisseeff, A., et al.: An introduction to variable and feature selection. J. Mach. Learn. Res. **3**(6), 1157–1182 (2003)
11. Vieira, S.M., Sousa, J.M.C., Kaymak, U.: Fuzzy criteria for feature selection. Fuzzy Sets Syst. **189**(1), 1–18 (2012)
12. Hall, M.A.: Correlation-based feature selection for discrete and numeric class machine learning. In: Proceedings of the Seventeenth International Conference on Machine Learning, pp. 359–366. Morgan Kaufmann Publishers Inc (2000)
13. Hsu, H.H., Hsieh, C.W., Lu, M.D.: Hybrid feature selection by combining filters and wrappers. Expert Syst. Appl. **38**(7), 8144–8150 (2011)
14. Bermejo, P., Ossa, L.D.L., Gámez, J.A., et al.: Fast wrapper feature subset selection in high-dimensional datasets by means of filter re-ranking. Knowl. Based Syst. **25**(1), 35–44 (2012)
15. Wald, R., Khoshgoftaar, T.M., Napolitano, A.: Stability of filter- and wrapper-based feature subset selection. In: IEEE International Conference on TOOLS with Artificial Intelligence, pp. 374–380. IEEE (2014)
16. Guyon, I., Gunn, S., Nikravesh, M., et al. (eds.): Feature Extraction: Foundations and Applications. Studies in Fuzziness and Soft Computing. Springer, New York (2005). https://doi.org/10.1007/978-3-540-35488-8
17. Shen, H., Wang, B.: An effective method for synthesizing multiple-pattern linear arrays with a reduced number of antenna elements. IEEE Trans. Antennas Propag. **PP**(99), 1 (2017)
18. Shen, J., Xia, J., Zhang, X., et al.: Sliding block based hybrid feature subset selection in network traffic. IEEE Access **5**(99), 18179–18186 (2017)
19. Shen, J., Xia, J., Dong, S., et al.: Universal feature extraction for traffic identification of the target category. PLoS ONE **11**(11), e0165993 (2016)
20. Fialho, A.S., et al.: Predicting outcomes of septic shock patients using feature selection based on soft computing techniques. In: Hüllermeier, E., Kruse, R., Hoffmann, F. (eds.) IPMU 2010. CCIS, vol. 81, pp. 65–74. Springer, Heidelberg (2010). https://doi.org/10.1007/978-3-642-14058-7_7
21. Ruiz, R., Riquelme, J.C., Aguilar-Ruiz, J.S.: Incremental wrapper-based gene selection from microarray data for cancer classification. Pattern Recogn. **39**(12), 2383–2392 (2006)
22. Bermejo, P., Gamez, J.A., Puerta, J.M.: Incremental Wrapper-based subset selection with replacement: an advantageous alternative to sequential forward selection. In: IEEE Symposium on Computational Intelligence and Data Mining, 2009 (CIDM 2009), pp. 367–374. IEEE (2009)
23. Kohavi, R., John, G.H.: Wrappers for Feature Subset Selection. Elsevier, Amsterdam (1997)
24. Friedman, J., Hastie, T., et al.: The Elements of Statistical Learning, vol. 27, no. 2, pp. 83–85. Springer, Heidelberg (2009)

25. Song, Q., Ni, J., Wang, G.: A fast clustering-based feature subset selection algorithm for high-dimensional data. IEEE Trans. Knowl. Data Eng. **25**(1), 1–14 (2012)
26. Quinlan, J.R.: C4. 5: Programs for Machine Learning. Morgan Kaufmann, Los Altos (1992)
27. Moore, A.W.: Dataset. http://www.cl.cam.ac.uk/research/srg/netos/nprobe/data/papers. Accessed Aug 2013
28. Croft, B., Metzler, D., Search, S.T.: Engines—information retrieval in practice. Comput. J. **54**(5), 831–832 (2011)

Application of Sensor-Cloud Systems: Smart Traffic Control

Chaogang Tang[1], Xianglin Wei[2(✉)], and Jin Liu[1]

[1] School of Computer Science and Technology, China University of Mining
and Technology, Xuzhou 22100, China
[2] Nanjing Telecommunication Technology Research Institute,
Nanjing 210007, China
wei_xianglin@163.com

Abstract. Smart transportation paradigm has been treated as a feasible solution to ease the pressures caused by the rapid growth of motor vehicles in the urban area. As a key building block, smart traffic signal control has motivated many efforts in both academia and industry due to its promised gains. State-of-the-art proposals rely heavily on a powerful centralized computation infrastructure to handle huge amount of heterogeneous traffic data gathered by diversified sensors and actuators. However, this process will typically incur very large response latency, which is also the main barrier for their real world deployment. To realize near real-time traffic signal control, traffic data need to be processed at the "edge" (i.e. the generated position). Hence, we in this paper propose a fog computing based traffic signal control architecture, in which the phase timing task for a single intersection will be handled by a local fog node in a timely fashion, and global or regional optimization task will be left for the centralized cloud. In this manner, a tradeoff between local optimization and global optimization can be achieved. Moreover, we address the challenges and open research problems of the proposed architecture in hope to provide insights and research directions for modern traffic control.

Keywords: Smart transportation · Traffic signal · Fog computing
Sensor-cloud

1 Introduction

Rapid increase of motor vehicles and rapid process of urbanization cause various traffic problems in cities. How to optimize Urban Traffic Control (UTC) to mitigate traffic flow has been a hot topic for both industry and academia in the past few decades. Traffic signal control, as a traditional and the most popular way to control the urban traffic flow, has been evolving in the past few years, e.g., from fixed-time control systems to more advanced control systems such as actuated and adaptive control systems, to cope with complicated traffic flow in real time.

Real-time adaptive traffic control systems require real-time traffic data collection and monitoring. Recent development of the Internet of Things (IoT), vehicles to vehicles (V2V) and vehicles to infrastructure (V2I) communication techniques enable

G. Wang et al. (Eds.): SpaCCS 2018, LNCS 11342, pp. 192–202, 2018.
https://doi.org/10.1007/978-3-030-05345-1_16

collection and monitoring of much richer real-time traffic information. With real-time traffic data and computation power, more sophisticated and efficient signal control strategies can be designed to alleviate traffic congestion.

With an explosive increase of real-time traffic flow data available, a new issue is on how to efficiently leverage the collected data for the phase timing optimization. We notice that a major shortcoming of existing control strategies is of the highly computational complexity and delay associated with the computation, i.e., the traffic flow may have already changed greatly by the time the optimization is completed. As a consequence, the decision making of the signal control strategies is based on the outdated traffic information rather than the current information.

To overcome the delay problem, we propose a fog computing based traffic signal control architecture in this paper. The fog computing paradigm, also known as the edge computing and considered as one of key enablers of IoT and big data applications [1–5], brings computation and storage resources to the edge of network, enabling highly computationally intensive applications to run while meeting strict delay requirements. The enormous amount of traffic information, including road situation (e.g., dry or wet, under construction, traffic accident), weather situation (e.g., sunny, rainy), vehicle states (location, speed, acceleration, etc.), and intersection information (e.g., the length of queue waiting at the intersection), can be collected and processed by fog nodes in real time, so that the traffic signal controller can make instant response (e.g., extending the green time or starting new phase timing) to alleviate the traffic congestion and further ensure the driving safety.

2 Related Works

Numbers of works aim to realize the real-time traffic signal control by optimizing the traffic signal light configuration such as the phase sequences and the phase timing plan, under assumption of a variety of conditions. Most metrics and optimization objectives focus on minimizing vehicle travel time, minimizing the total number of stops, reducing traffic delay, minimizing the queue length of vehicles waiting at the intersections. However, to design an efficient traffic controlling strategy is not straightforward, for the reason that numbers of issues need to be addressed, e.g., the unpredictability of traffic flow, the heterogeneity of vehicles and the communication via V2X techniques and fusion of traffic data under the backgrounds of Internet of Things (IoT).

Authors in [6] present an algorithm to improve the efficiency of the traffic control, based on the genetic algorithm merging with machine learning algorithm (ML). This algorithm schedules the phases of each traffic light according to realtime traffic flow based on the genetic algorithm, while taking into account the next phase of traffic flow at each intersection by ML. A traffic control algorithm which is integrated into SUMO [7] is presented in [8] to measure the queue length of vehicles at each intersection and further attempt to minimize the queue length of the vehicles at the intersection. In addition, many researchers leverage new communication techniques such as V2V and V2I to realize a better traffic control at the intersection under assumption of certain market penetration. For instance, authors in [9] reduce the waiting time and the queue length at the intersection via V2V communication. Authors in [10] utilize V2I communication techniques to collect the vehicle information such as speed, heading, and acceleration, with the purpose of improving the efficiency of the traffic control by minimizing the delay time of the waiting vehicles at the intersections. Authors [11] present a real-time adaptive signal phase allocation algorithm using V2I/V2V communication techniques, where two objective functions are taken into account (e.g., total delay minimization and queue length minimization).

Authors in [12] design an architecture called vehicular fog computing (VFC) to leverage a collaborative multitude of end-user clients or nearby edge devices to perform the communication and computation. Each vehicle (e.g., moving or stopped) can serve as a fog node to collect traffic information and share abundant computation resources with each other. Combined fog computing with Vehicular Ad-hoc Networks (VANETs), authors in [13, 14] discuss the characteristics of fog computing and services based on fog computing platform provided for VANETs. Some challenges and issues are posed, as well as some research directions of future works. However, these works focuses on resource sharing among vehicles rather than the traffic signal control via fog computing.

From the aforementioned works, we notice that the signal control strategies often suffer from a highly computational complexity of algorithms deployed for phase related optimization. The response latency sometimes makes the traffic control strategies not achieve the expected performance. Moreover, the existing works, which introduce the fog computing into the intelligent transportation system, mainly combine fog computing with VANETs to help improve the road safety and traffic efficiency. On another hand, it is necessary to introduce the fog computing for the phase related metric optimization, due to its low latency, location awareness, geographical distribution. To our best knowledge, it's the first attempt to construct an architecture for traffic signal optimization based on fog computing. As an application of sensor-cloud systems [15–17], combining fog computing with sensor-cloud systems can efficiently improve the efficiency of signal timing processing.

3 System Architecture

All the traffic flow data should be leveraged by intelligent signal control systems to help determine the optimal signal controlling strategies. In the fog computing based architecture proposed in this paper, it is the fog nodes' responsibility to gather traffic flow data via either infrastructure-based sensors (e.g., loop detectors, traffic monitoring cameras or radio) or vehicular networking technologies (e.g., V2V, V2I). Figure 1 depicts a scenario where the fog computing is introduced to aid make decision. While many smart devices with computational capabilities at the edge of network can serve as fog nodes, the special fog nodes with appropriate computational abilities are deployed in vicinity of the traffic signal controller in this scenario. This deployment is needed to process the on-site realtime traffic flow data efficiently in real time. Three common events are exemplified, e.g., car collision, emergency event and traffic jam. Different events should trigger different handling mechanisms. For instance, if a car collision occurs, the nearby traffic monitoring cameras or the connected vehicles report this situation to the fog nodes in vicinity once they capture this event. Then the fog nodes will start an emergency preplan to deal with this situation as follows. First, the fog nodes evaluate the extent to which the traffic is affected, and then decide whether or not to forward this collision as relay stations to other passing vehicles which may have a much wider communication range compared to the equipped vehicles themselves.

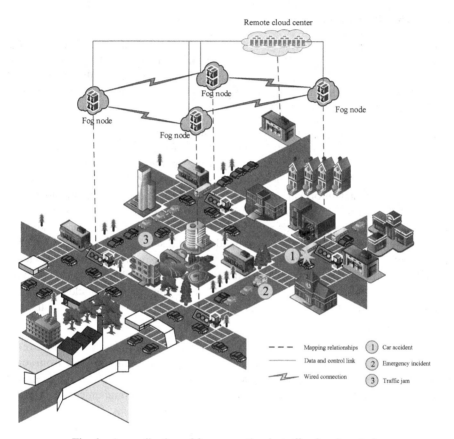

Fig. 1. An application of fog computing in traffic signal control.

In case of serious vehicle collisions, fog nodes can even directly communicate with the traffic management center for further help. In addition, if more and more vehicles are waiting at the intersections or even a traffic congestion occurs, the fog nodes should calculate the optimal phase timing plans to help traffic signal controller alleviate the traffic congestion. Note that we enhance abilities of the fog computing by adding a remote cloud, i.e., the cloud computing layer. Compared to the fog nodes, nodes in remote cloud usually have more powerful computing and storage abilities but at the cost of relatively longer transmission latency. The tasks can be further offloaded to the remote cloud if fog nodes are overwhelmed by workloads.

Based on the above descriptions, the fog computing based traffic signal control architecture actually consists of three layers, i.e., cyber physical layer, fog computing layer and cloud computing layer. The cyber physical layer is responsible for collecting traffic flow data, fog computing layer and cloud computing for determining the optimal traffic signal controlling strategies.

3.1   Cyber Physical Layer

This layer is composed of a densely distributed ecosystem which covers the connected vehicles and road side units (RSUs), such as infrastructure-based loop detectors and video surveillance systems. Thus, vehicles are able to communicate with each other and RSUs, and the traffic flow data captured by sensors and the equipped vehicles can be forwarded to the nearby fog nodes.

Data Structure: Note that enormous amount of information is continuously collected in the cyber physical layer and disseminated to the fog computing layer. In order to facilitate data extraction, storage and processing in the fog computing layer, the structure of the source data in the cyber physical layer should be carefully defined. Useless or redundant information should be excluded when the data stream is disseminated. Different data structures should be applied to the traffic flow data by different techniques (e.g., connected vehicles or traffic monitoring cameras), because the identical data structure can cause data redundancy and storage wasting even though it may facilitate data extraction and processing. For instance, in the data structure tailored for traffic information captured by monitoring cameras, an attribute called "Pedestrian volume", i.e., the number of pedestrians waiting at the intersections, should be included in the data structure to provide important references for decision making in the fog computing layer.

Communication: The communication is ubiquitous among all kinds of entities (e.g., the connected vehicles, fog nodes, sensors and the cloud data center). Aside from some common wireless communication technologies like 4G, WiFi, WLAN, ZigBee and Bluetooth, another technique named dedicated short-range communication (DSRC) [14] has been developed for both V2V and V2I communications. Without the preparation of association and authentication, DSRC (802.11p) supports fast data and information exchange when switch to the corresponding channels. DSRC also improves the flexibility of telecommunication service provisioning, via which the connected vehicles can communicate with each other and other infrastructures as long as the distance between them is within the designed communication range.

3.2   Fog Computing Layer

The fog computing layer consists of special fog nodes (servers) with computational and storage capabilities in the vicinity of the traffic signal controller. Fog nodes are responsible for data storage, analysis, traffic signal optimization and emergency call services.

The architecture is composed of multiple modules which perform different functions of intelligent traffic systems as denoted in Fig. 2. The traffic information database stores all the traffic flow data transmitted to the fog computing layer. The modules in the dashed line box are responsible for local optimization– – they decide the optimal phase timing for single intersection based on the traffic flow information retrieved from the traffic information database. The orchestrator module evaluates the extent to which the traffic is affected by analyzing and processing the data traffic flow. In case of vehicle collisions or emergency incident, it will directly communicate with the traffic management center for human services. During a normal operation, the fog nodes store and process the traffic flow data received from the traffic signal controllers as well as the connected vehicles, and feed back the resulting phase timing plans to the traffic signal controllers. The phase timing plans may extend the green time or re-set the phase accordingly in the next phase. When vehicles approach intersections with traffic signals, they disseminate the periodic beacon messages about the current traffic states to fog nodes as well as among those vehicles within the communication range. The message usually consists of current position, speed, as well as a timestamp when the information is sent. To obtain the waiting vehicle queue length, the V2I techniques can combine the loop detectors to provide more accurate services. The benefit of utilizing fog computing in the intelligent traffic signal control systems is the significant reduction of the response delay, compared to other existing controlling strategies.

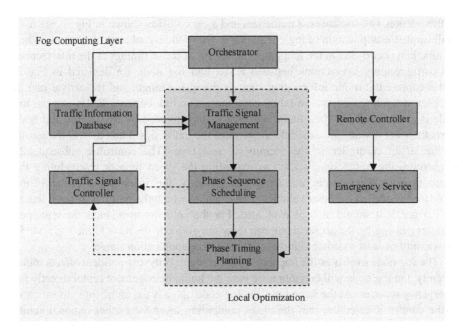

Fig. 2. The architecture of fog computing layer

3.3   Cloud Computing Layer

The cloud computing layer consists of multiple high performance servers, which provide more powerful computation and storage services than those provided by the fog computing layer. In the proposed traffic system architecture, the cloud computing layer differs from the fog computing layer mainly in that the cloud computing layer serves multiple intersections while the fog computing layer serves only one. The cloud computing layer focuses on coordinating regional traffic control based on the traffic flow information offloaded by fog computing layers. Each fog node determines the optimal phase timing plan for the corresponding intersection, without considering the traffic flows from upstream and downstream intersections. However, this kind of autonomous traffic signal control may not be globally optimal for multiple-intersection scenarios. For instance, the vehicles released at the current intersection according to the phase timing plan may result in the traffic congestion at the immediate downstream intersection. Intuitively, a tradeoff exists between local optimization and global optimization. Accordingly, it is the responsibility of the cloud computing layer to determine the globally optimal phase timing plans for multiple intersections. Thus, a multi-layer signal control system based on fog computing is proposed. It considers both signal and multiple intersections and aims to achieve local and global optimization of the traffic signal control while maintaining the real-time execution performance.

4   Use Case Study

In this section, two use cases, a traffic jam and a car collision shown in Fig. 1, are used to illustrate the application of fog computing in the traffic signal control systems. When a traffic jam occurs due to the inappropriate setting of phase timings at the intersection, the corresponding interactions between RSUs and fog node are depicted in Fig. 3. RSUs capture the traffic information such as the queue length and the arrival rate of vehicles at the intersection. An initial communication link between RSUs and the fog node is constructed and then traffic message is disseminated by RSUs. The fog node starts the local optimization module to optimize the traffic signal and deliver the results to the signal controller in the vicinity in real time. The controller subsequently reschedules the traffic signals such as extending the green time or rescheduling the phase timing. When a car accident takes place at the intersection, the collision avoidance is needed for other vehicles. The extent to which the traffic is affected due to the car accident should also be evaluated. For the collision avoidance, the equipped vehicles passing by the accident site can relay the accident situation to the fog node in the vicinity as well as other vehicles within the communication range.

   The fog node evaluates the impacts of the accident. If the car accident affects traffic severely, the fog node will communicate with the traffic management center directly for emergency services. At the same time, the fog node uploads the traffic flow information at the current intersection into the cloud computing layer for further regional signal control optimization. For instance, the fog node at the upstream intersection can forward the information about the car accident to the approaching vehicles so that they can choose to bypass the accident site. Besides, to prevent the possible traffic congestion, the fog node can reduce the traffic flow into the current intersection by extending the green time of the opposite direction at the upstream intersection. Note that the fog node can quickly make the decisions about the phase timing plans based on the information

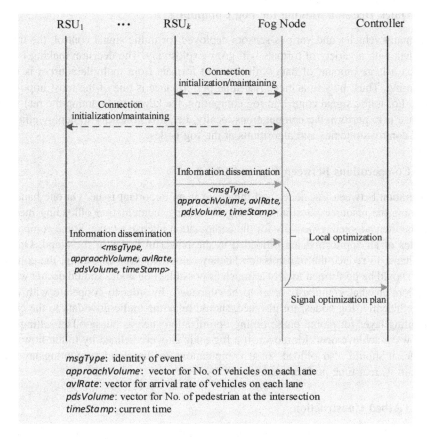

Fig. 3. Interactions between RSUs and fog node

from the cloud computing layer. The fog node at the downstream can also take similar countermeasures to avoid the traffic congestion.

5 Challenges and Open Research Issues

The fog computing based traffic signal control proposed in this paper involves several key techniques which are still in the early stages of development, such as V2V and V2I communications. While various vehicular services are not fully implemented, currently, we can envision the potentials and benefits these technologies can bring in the near future. Nonetheless, many challenges and open issues about the fog computing based architecture still exist and need solutions. In this section, we present and discuss these challenges and open issues in hope to provide inspiring guidance for the future research within this field.

5.1   Quick Decision Making for Fog Computing

With many vehicles and various sensors deployed for traffic signal control, the traffic flow data with a variety of formats will grow explosively. The decision making based on such a large amount of data with different formats from multiple sources is time consuming. Thus, how to achieve real-time performance is one of the most important issues. For traffic signal control in fog computing, the key to maintaining the real-time response is to perform the computations locally, i.e., it is necessary to deploy efficient signal control strategies and algorithms at the fog nodes.

5.2   Co-operations Between Fog and Cloud

Cooperation between fog nodes and the cloud is an important issue. On one hand, to overcome the resource constraints in fog computing, computation offloading mechanism is often adopted, especially for the computation intensive tasks. Some computing modules of an application are offloaded to the powerful nodes in the cloud. On the other hand, to reduce the transmission latency caused by task offloading, the computation should be performed locally as much as possible. Fog nodes should decide which behaviors at what granularity level to be offloaded. In order to cooperate with each other efficiently, fog nodes, for instance, should relay the traffic flow data to the cloud computing layer for global phase timing optimization such as phase offset setting and green wave achievement. Moreover, if a fog node is overwhelmed by traffic flow data volume, it should also offload some computations to the cloud computing layer to maintain its real-time performance.

5.3   Testbed Construction

To realize a practical fog computing based traffic signal control system, it requires the consideration of cost, deployment, operation and maintenance at both fog computing layer and cloud computing layer due to the large number of fog nodes to be deployed in a city. Therefore, a testbed should be designed based on these perspectives and with the flexibility to quickly deploy and investigate various algorithms and traffic signal control strategies.

5.4   Transportation-Oriented Software Design for Fog Nodes

To realize a fog-upgraded traffic light control, effective transportation specified software entities running at the fog nodes are very critical. The software entities include application software as well as a few middleware that could support dedicated software design with several APIs or functions. Besides the functions, these software entities must support flexible update and upgrade to adapt to new control policies.

5.5   Trace-Driven Evaluation

In the big data era, fog computing enables us to move the computation capability near the data source. In the smart signal control scenario, each fog node could ideally handle the heterogeneous data generated nearby and make control decision locally. To realize a data-driven traffic control system in this scenario, collecting a large amount of data with various types in different time period at different locations is important for designing and testing of effective architectures and fog nodes. A few traces collected in real transportation scenes could be used as the benchmark dataset for evaluating different proposals.

6 Conclusion

To cope with the highly computational complexity of existing traffic signal control strategies, we in this paper have presented a new traffic signal control paradigm. We proposed a fog computing based traffic control system where fog computing nodes are responsible for phase timing optimization for single intersections and cloud computing nodes for larger area traffic optimization. The architectures of both fog computing layer and cloud computing layer are presented in detail. While this paradigm presents tremendous potentials, many tough challenges exist. We addressed these technical challenges and open issues to provide guidance for future research within this field.

For the future work, we plan to implement, deploy, and evaluate efficient algorithms for the proposed architecture to solve the traffic signal control problems.

Acknowledgements. This research was supported in part by the Jiangsu Province Natural Science Foundation of China under Grant No. BK20150201.

References

1. Wang, T., Zeng, J., Lai, Y., Tian, H., Chen, Y.: Data collection from WSNs to the cloud based on mobile Fog elements. Fut. Gener. Comput. Syst. (2017). https://doi.org/10.1016/j.future.2017.07.031
2. Wang, T., Zhou, J., Huang, M., Bhuiyan, M., Liu, A.: Fog-based storage technology to fight with cyber threat. Future Generation Computer Systems **83**, 208–218 (2018)
3. Zhu, C., Rodrigues, J.J.P.C., Leung, V.C.M., Shu, L., Yang, L.T.: Trust-based communication for the industrial internet of things. IEEE Commun. Mag. **56**(2), 16–22 (2018)
4. Wang, T., Zhang, G., Bhuiyan, Z.A., Liu, A., Jia, W., Xie, M.: A novel trust mechanism based on fog computing in sensor-cloud system. Fut. Gener. Comput. Syst. (2018). https://doi.org/10.1016/j.future.2018.05.049
5. Zhu, C., Shu, L., Leung, V.C.M., Guo, S., Zhang, Y., Yang, L.T.: Secure multimedia big data in trust-assisted sensor-cloud for smart city. IEEE Commun. Mag. **55**(12), 24–30 (2017)
6. Zhao, B., Zhang, C., Zhang, L.: Real-Time Traffic Light Scheduling Algorithm Based on Genetic Algorithm and Machine Learning (2015)
7. Behrisch, M., Bieker, L., Erdmann, J., Krajzewicz, D.: Sumo-simulation of urban mobility: an overview. In: Simul (simul 2011), pp. 63–68 (2011)
8. Krajzewicz, D., et al.: Simulation of modern traffic lights control systems using the open source traffic simulation sumo. In: Industrial Simulation Conference, pp. 299–302 (2005)
9. Maslekar, N., Boussedjra, M., Mouzna, J., Labiod, H.: Vanet based adaptive traffic signal control. In: Vehicular Technology Conference, pp. 1–5 (2011)

10. Priemer, C., Friedrich, B.: A decentralized adaptive traffic signal control using v2i communication data. In: International IEEE Conference on Intelligent Transportation Systems, pp. 1–6 (2009)
11. Feng, Y., Head, K.L., Khoshmagham, S., Zamanipour, M.: A real-time adaptive signal control in a connected vehicle environment. Transp. Res. Part C **55**, 460–473 (2015)
12. Hou, X., Li, Y., Chen, M., Wu, D., Jin, D., Chen, S.: Vehicular fog computing: a viewpoint of vehicles as the infrastructures. IEEE Trans. Veh. Technol. **65**(6), 3860–3873 (2016)
13. Kang, K., Wang, C., Luo, T.: Fog computing for vehicular adhoc networks: paradigms, scenarios, and issues. J. China Univ. Posts Telecommun. **23**(2), 56–65 (2016)
14. Huang, C., Lu, R., Choo, K.K.R.: Vehicular fog computing: architecture, use case, and security and forensic challenges. IEEE Commun. Mag. **55**(11), 105–111 (2017)
15. Zhu, C., Li, X., Leung, V.C.M., Yang, L.T., Ngai, E.C.-H., Shu, L.: Towards pricing for sensor-cloud. IEEE Trans. Cloud Comput. (2017). https://doi.org/10.1109/tcc.2017.2649525
16. Zhu, C., Leung, V.C.M., Wang, K., Yang, L.T., Zhang, Y.: Multi-method data delivery for green sensor-cloud. IEEE Commun. Mag. **55**(5), 176–182 (2017)
17. Zhu, C., Zhou, H., Leung, V.C.M., Wang, K., Zhang, Y., Yang, L.T.: Toward big data in Green City. IEEE Commun. Mag. **55**(11), 14–18 (2017)

Strategy-Proof Mechanism for Provisioning Non-obedient Resources Without Payment

Wei Song[1(✉)], Min Li[1], and Shun You[2]

[1] School of Computers, Guangdong University of Technology,
Guangzhou 510006, China
color_unsw@126.com, songwei@gdut.edu.cn
[2] HSBC Software Development (GD) Limited, Guangzhou 510630, China

Abstract. Non-obedient nodes exist in some prevailing computing environments. They tend to pursue individual interests, provide resources strategically, and misreport private information. Strategy-proofness and group strategy-proofness mechanisms in social choice are stimulate nodes to report their true private information so as to enable cooperation and participation. But they are rarely applied in computer science. Our work has introduced concepts from social choice into computer science to solve the incentive issue of node's truth report about its private information, and get some meaningful results. First, we establish an environment of non-obedient resources, design a utility function without payment by considering nodes' internal resource costs and feelings, and define node preference scheme which is single-peaked. Second, we design a mechanism for provisioning non-obedient resources based on the median voter scheme with $(n - 1)$ phantom voters. This mechanism is strategy-proof and group strategy-proof when a node reports reduced value of its private information, while when it reports increased value, strategy-proofness and group strategy-proofness cannot be guaranteed but more resources are provided. Finally, experiments show the strategy-proofness and group strategy-proofness characteristics of this mechanism.

Keywords: Strategy-proof mechanism · Group strategy-proof mechanism
Provisioning non-obedient resources · Mechanism without payment
Median voter scheme

1 Introduction

With the strengthened function and the improved performance of desktop machines, handheld devices and wearable equipment, also with the popularity of mobile networks, resource providers have the non-obedient characteristic of tending to pursue individual interests and provide resources strategically. We say they are non-obedient nodes. They do not comply with central control. And they are more susceptible of interests driven to form malicious collusion group, destroy the reliability of the whole system.

Non-obedient nodes exist in some prevailing computing environments. Federated cloud [1] is to integrate resources from different providers whose sharing resources are self-interested parties with their own goals and objectives. Nodes in P2P system share

© Springer Nature Switzerland AG 2018
G. Wang et al. (Eds.): SpaCCS 2018, LNCS 11342, pp. 203–213, 2018.
https://doi.org/10.1007/978-3-030-05345-1_17

their resources such as compute cycles, files, and bandwidth. Their objectives are to maximize their own interests while participating in the system. In cloud computing [2–4], mechanisms are designed to make selfish cloud users do not have incentives to manipulate the system by lying about their requested bundles of VM and valuation. In Device-to-device load balancing [5], battery-limited devices must have incentives to contribute by sharing their resources. In ad hoc networks, if nodes are profit-oriented independent agents, some core functions of ad hoc will be affected, such as routing [6] and multicast [7]. In pervasive computing [8], selfish users may maximize their profits by falsely declaring their recommendations strategically. In cognitive radio networks [9], selfish secondary users expect to achieve a higher throughput with less extra energy cost. In vehicular ad-hoc network [10], on board unit and road side unit belong to different service providers, it is inevitable that noncooperation and collusive false data will happen. From above researches, resource users are always considered as non-obedient nodes, mechanisms economically motivate users to reveal their true valuation of resources. Resource or service providers are non-obedient nodes when the distributed application is to integrate different resources, make a decision from different information, such as [1, 5, 8, 10] mentioned.

To manage non-obedient nodes, economics and mechanism design offer approaches for cooperation. Mechanisms are designed especially for encouraging nodes to tell true information of their resources, so that cooperation and participation can be maintained. Strategy-proofness and group strategy-proofness are concepts in mechanism design. A mechanism is strategy-proof if no node has an incentive to any other information than his true private information, for nodes obtain maximum utility only when they show their true private information. A mechanism is group strategy-proof if no coalition of nodes has an incentive to collectively misreport their true private information. In computer science, the earliest study in this area began in 2001. Nisan and Ronen were the first to take algorithms and economics together into consideration, and called this Algorithmic Mechanism Design [11]. The VCG (Vickrey-Clarke-Groves) mechanism is a well-known strategy-proof mechanism [1, 3, 4, 13]. Its characteristic is that payment of each node has nothing to do with its reported private information, so a node's utility cannot be improved when lying. The study and design of group strategy-proof mechanisms were initiated by the seminal work of Moulin and Shenker [14] and focused on cost-sharing game $(A, c(S))$. In computer science, there are not many papers about applications of cost-sharing mechanism. Most researches focus on routing solution [15], multicast service [16], recommendation reporting [8]. These two mechanisms need payment to compensate nodes for their loss. Nevertheless, there are many important environments where monetary payment cannot be used as a medium of compensation, and monetary payment initialization, transfer, storage and management in discrete control are not easy to be solved, which affects the mechanism's deployment in practical environment [12].

In our paper, we solve the incentive issue of provisioning resources without payment in computer science by using the median voter scheme in the realm of social choice. Resource providers are non-obedient and resources is considered as compute cycle, storage capacity, the wifi time span, download or upload bandwidth, service time span limited by electric power and information about surrounding environment. The incentive issue mainly focuses on stimulating the node which owns resources to report the true value of its private information. The false value can destroy the cooperation of nodes. We use three terms to describe the node's behaviors, that is, true-reporting behavior, low-reporting behavior and high-reporting behavior. The main works we do is to design a mechanism for provisioning non-obedient resources based on the median voter scheme (*MPR*). This mechanism realizes strategy-proofness and group strategy-proofness when a node chooses low-reporting behavior, while when it chooses high-reporting behavior, strategy-proofness and group strategy-proofness cannot be reached but more resources are provided. The rest of this paper is organized as follows; In Sect. 2, we discuss related work. We introduce our environment of non-obedient resources as well as some notion in Sect. 3. In Sect. 4, we design a mechanism for provisioning non-obedient resources based on the median voter scheme (*MPR*) and analyze its strategy-proof and group strategy-proof characteristic. Section 5 presents the experiment results, and Sect. 6 concludes this paper.

2   Related Works

A very large body of work in strategy-proof mechanism and group strategy-proof mechanism without payment focuses on social choice in the realm of economy with ordinal preferences. It is rarely applied in computer science. In general, a social choice problem can be described by these parameters [17]: a set of agents N, a set of alternatives A, and for each agent $i \in N$ a set of preference relations R_i over the alternatives A, an allocation rule $f : \times R_i \rightarrow A$. It is strategy-proof if the rule makes it a weakly dominant strategy for agents to truthfully report their preferences. In work of [18], the preferences of the agents are single-peaked. The allocation rule is that adding $(n - 1)$ fixed ballots to the n agents ballots and then choosing the median of this larger set of ballots. The rule which is also called a generalized median voter scheme is proved to be anonymous, efficient and strategy-proof. In work of [19], the set of strategy-proof mechanism coincides with the set of generalized median voter schemes with n real voters and $(n - 1)$ phantom voters. The task of searching optimal mechanisms is reduced to finding the optimal position for the peaks of these $(n - 1)$ phantom voters. A distributed function of $(n - 1)$ phantom voters is given. In [20], a criterion was proposed to compare generalized median voter schemes according to their manipulability. In [21], a new facility game was studied, namely, an obnoxious facility game, on a network where the facility was undesirable and all agents tried to be as far away from the facility as possible. Mechanisms without money were designed to decide the facility location so that the obnoxious social welfare was maximized and all agents were enforced to report their true locations. They gave a first attempt at this game on different networks and design group strategy-proof deterministic and randomized mechanisms with approximate optimal social welfare. In [22], it was pointed that if agents' preference profile was a domain satisfying sequential inclusion, then any strategy-proof social choice rule on such domain was group strategy-proof. And then, they analyzed sequential inclusion for some preference profile domains such as single-peaked preferences, separable preferences, lexicographically separable preferences and the universal domain etc.

3 Preliminaries

Definition 1. *Environment of non-obedient resources.*

The whole environment is composed of non-obedient nodes which are rational and selfish. Let Ω be the set of nodes. Node can be a resource provider or a user. Complicated interaction is decomposed into several simple interactions. A simple interaction can be abstracted as 3-tuple (i, M, O). Let i be a resource user, $i \in \Omega$. Let M be the mechanism that user i executes to produce a mechanism outcome O. An outcome O is defined as 2-tuple (N, K), in which N denotes the resource providers set that mechanism M has chosen and $K = \{k_j\}_{j \in N}$. Each element k_j in K denotes the provision level that provider j has finally offered.

Definition 2. *Private information of resource provider.*

Let x_i be the private information known to node i only, $i \in \Omega$. x_i is continuously distributed on the interval $[1, |A|]$. The private information is a quantifiable value which is generated from provider's own usable resources, willingness and feelings.

Definition 3. *Provision level of resource provider.*

For each provider j, it will prefer a provision level k_j, which is related to its private information. Let A be the alternatives set of preferred provision level, which is composed of all the positive integers in $[1, |A|]$.

Definition 4. *Utility of resource provider.*

Provider i has utility $u_i(k, x_i)$, which shows the utility provider i has when its private information is x_i and the provision level is $k \in A$. In mechanism, the provision level k is finally determined by multiple providers' reported private information profile. In our paper, nodes are considered as entities with the same cognitive level, that is, they have the similar form of utility function. We assume that is $u_i(k, x_i) = k + (x_i - k)^2$.

Note 1. The utility shows the node's internal cost, and node is willing to minimize its utility. k presents the cost caused by node's final provision level. $(x_i - k)^2$ takes node's herd mentality into consideration, that is, the more deviation from other nodes, the worse it feels. Since k is formed among multiple providers, it is the common level and if node's private information deviates more from this level, its feeling is worse and its cost is higher.

Note 2. If $x_i < k$ exists for some reason (such as node i misreports its private information), it means node cannot provide enough resources. In such circumstance, we let the number of provided resources be x_i, utility is $u_i(k, x_i) = x_i + (x_i - k)^2$. Issues it brings will be discussed in Sect. 4.

Note 3. Given any two provision levels k and l with $l < k$, node i is indifferent between them if and only its private information x_i is satisfied as in Eq. (1).

$$u_i(k, x_i) = u_i(l, x_i) \Rightarrow k + (x_i - k)^2 = l + (x_i - l)^2 \Rightarrow x_i = (l + k + 1)/2 \quad (1)$$

Let

$$x^{1,k} \equiv x_i = (l+k+1)/2 \tag{2}$$

Denoted by

$$x^k \equiv x^{k-1,k} = (k-1+k+1)/2 = k \tag{3}$$

the private information x^k shows that node i is indifferent between two adjacent level $k-1$ and k. And then the inequality $x^1 < \ldots < x^k < \ldots < x^{|A|}$ exists.

Definition 5. *Node preference scheme of provision level.*
From Eqs. (1) and (2), we know if $x_i = x^{l,k}$, then node i is indifferent between level l and k. If $x_i > x^{l,k}$, then i prefers level k to l. If $x_i < x^{l,k}$, then i prefers level l to k. Similarly, if $x^k < x_i \leq x^{k+1}$, i prefers level k to all the other levels.

Lemma. *Node preference scheme is single-peaked.*
Proof is omitted here.

4 Mechanism for Provisioning of Non-obedient Resources Based on Median Voter Scheme

Definition 6. *Median voter scheme M.*

$$x_i \in [1, |A|], x^{ki} < x_i \leq x^{ki+1}, \; k_1, \ldots, k_n, \alpha_1, \ldots, \alpha_{n-1} \in A, M(x_1, \ldots, x_n)$$
$$= median(k_1, \ldots, k_n, \alpha_1, \ldots, \alpha_{n-1}) = a \tag{4}$$

In the basic median voter scheme M, there are n real voters. By [Definition 5] their private information profile $(x_1, \ldots, x_n)$ corresponds to a preferred level profile $(k_1, \ldots, k_n)$. Let $(\alpha_1, \ldots, \alpha_{n-1})$ denote the preferred level profile of $(n-1)$ phantom voters. Paper [19] points out that one can obtain a dominant strategy incentive compatible mechanism by adding $(n-1)$ fixed ballots to the n voters ballots and then choosing the median of this larger set of ballots. The task of searching optimal mechanisms is reduced to finding the optimal position for the peaks of these $(n-1)$ phantom voters. Let l_k denote the number of phantom voters with peak preference on level k in a median voter scheme with $(n-1)$ phantom voters. Let z denote the largest integer that is below z. Let $C(x) = E[X|X > x]$ be expectation of stochastic variable $X \in [1, |A|]$ when it is larger than x. Let $c(x) = E[X|X \leq x]$ be expectation of stochastic variable $X \in [1, |A|]$ when it is no larger than x. x^k is in Definition 4.
Distribution of l_k is given in [19].

$$l_k = \begin{cases} \left\lceil n \frac{x^2 - c(x^2)}{C(x^2) - c(x^2)} \right\rceil & k = 1 \\ \left\lceil n \frac{x^{k+1} - c(x^{k+1})}{C(x^{k+1}) - c(x^{k+1})} \right\rceil - \left\lceil n \frac{x^k - c(x^k)}{C(x^k) - c(x^k)} \right\rceil & 1 < k < |A| \\ n - 1 - \sum\limits_{m-1}^{A-1} l_m & k = |A| \end{cases} \tag{5}$$

The voter scheme will choose median number a among these $(2n - 1)$ voters' preferred level profile $(k_1, ..., k_n, \alpha_1, ..., \alpha_{n-1})$, that is the nth number in the ascending order.

Definition 7. *Mechanism for provisioning of non-obedient resources based on median voter scheme (MPR).*

$$\forall i \in N, x_i \in [1, |A|], x^{ki} < x_i \leq x^{ki+1} MPR(x_i, x_{-i}) = a_i \qquad (6)$$

Let $x_{-i} = (x_1, x_2, ..., x_{i-1}, x_{i+1}, ..., x_n)$ denote private information profile except node i. The form of *MPR* shows that the outcome of mechanism is the set of provision level $\{a_1, ..., a_n\}$, for node i, its provision level is a_i. Figure 1 describes the procedure of *MPR*.

Mechanism for Provisioning Non-obedient Resources Based on Median Voter Scheme(*MPR*)
Input: Resource user sends requests, and gets enough reported private information profile $(x_1,...,x_n)$ from resource providers set $N=\{1,...,n\}$, $x_i \in [1,|A|]$, $x^{ki} < x_i \leq x^{ki+1}$;

Procedure:
Resource user computes provision level profile $S=\{ k_1,...,k_n \}$ according to [definition 5];
WHILE N is not empty {
   compute distribution of $(|N|-1)$ phantom voters' preferred levels: $\{l_k\}_{k \in A}$;
   combine S and $\{l_k\}_{k \in A}$ into preference profile $(\{k_i\}_{i \in N}, \alpha_1, ..., \alpha_{|N|-1})$;
   order preference profile in ascend and rename the elements as $(y_1,... y_{2|N|-1})$;
   get the median number a of $(y_1,... y_{2|N|-1})$;
   FOR each node $i \in N$ {
       IF $k_i > a$ THEN {
           $a_i = a$,that is, node i provides level a;
           Delete k_i from S ;
           Delete i from N ; }
   Let $|A|=$max S , then adjust provision levels set A as positive integer in interval $[1,|A|]$; }

Output: resource providers set $N=\{1,...,n\}$ in the input phase; provision levels set $K=\{a_1,...,a_n\}$

Fig. 1. Mechanism for provisioning non-obedient resources based on median voter scheme.

Note 4. Mechanism executor is the resource user. The procedure of *MPR* can be regarded as a concrete description of a simple interaction mentioned in Definition 1.

Note 5. As a concern of a certain private information profile $(x_1, ..., x_n)$, suppose that node i loops r times to the end and provides level a_i; node j loops t times to the end and provides level a_j . There exists $a_i \geq a_j$ if and only if $r \leq t$; that is, the earlier node ends loop, the larger provision level it will provide.

Note 6. Figure 1 describes the main procedure. There are some branch cases that deserve to be mentioned. When levels set A is adjusted to only one level, that is, $A = 1$, the distribution of l_k does not need to be computed, and the medium number is 1. When only one node is left in N, the distribution of l_k does not need to be computed, and the medium number is its own preferred level.

Theorem 1. *MPR is a strategy-proof mechanism when a node chooses low-reporting behavior. While when it chooses high-reporting behavior, strategyproofness cannot be guaranteed but this node will provide more resources.*

Proof: Amechanism is strategy-proof if a node gets the minimum utility when it chooses true-reporting behavior. Suppose that when node i's true private information is $x^{ki} < x_i \leq x^{ki+1}$, node i prefers level k_i, and its final provision level is $MPR(x_i, x_{-i}) = a_i$; and under falsely reported value x_i', node i prefers level k_i', and its final provision level is $MPR(x_i', x_{-i}) = a_i'$. We need to prove that for $\forall i \in N$, $u_i(MPR(x_i, x_{-i}), x_i) \leq u_i(MPR(x_i', x_{-i}), x_i)$ is established, that is, $u_i(a_i, x_i) \leq u_i(a_i', x_i)$. There are two cases during the mechanism's execution when node i's reporting value is x_i.

Case 1. Node i ends up in one loop. Reorder $(k_i, k_{-i}, \alpha_1, ..., \alpha_{n-1})$ in ascend and rename it as $(y_1, ..., y_{2n-1})$. Then $MPR(x_i, x_{-i}) = median(y_1, ..., y_{2n-1}) = a_i$, and $k_i > a_i$. Let $Y = \{j | y_j \leq a_i\}$ denote node's subscript set in which the node's preferred level is not larger than a_i. Obviously, $|Y| \geq n$. Then, we reorder $(k_i', k_{-i}, \alpha_1, ..., \alpha_{n-1})$ in ascend, rename it as $(z_1, ..., z_{2n-1})$ and let $Z = \{j | z_j \leq a_i\}$. There are two behaviors that node i can choose. One is high-reporting behavior. Since k_i' cannot decrease the number of elements that is less than a_i, then $|Z| \geq n$ is still established. Note that for every β which satisfies $|\{j | z_j \leq \beta\}| \geq n$, we have $a_i' = median(z_1, ..., z_{2n-1}) \leq \beta$. Then, as for $|\{j | z_j \leq a_i\}| \geq n$, we have $a_i' \leq a_i \leq k_i$. From [Lemma], $u_i(k_i, x_i) \leq u_i(a_i, x_i) \leq u_i(a_i', x_i)$ is established. The other is low-reporting behavior. If node i still ends up in one loop, then k_i' increases the numbers of elements which is less than a_i at most, and $|Z| \geq n$ is still established. Similarly, we have that $a_i' \leq a_i \leq k_i$, that means $u_i(k_i, x_i) \leq u_i(a_i, x_i) \leq u_i(a_i', x_i)$. If node i ends up in multiple loops, then $a_i' \leq a_i \leq k_i$ is still established by [Note 5].

Case 2. Node i ends up in multiple loops. Consider two behaviors of node. One is low-reporting behavior. The lower value node reports the more loops it needs to end. Then $a_i' \leq a_i \leq k_i$ is still established. The other is high-reporting behavior, which makes the node end up in fewer loops. Then $a_i \leq k_i \leq a_i'$ and $a_i \leq a_i' \leq k_i$ will exist. From $x^{ki} < x_i \leq x^{ki+1}$, we have $k_i < x_i \leq k_i + 1$, then $a_i \leq k_i \leq a_i' \leq x_i$ or $a_i \leq a_i' \leq k_i < x_i$. It may exist $u_i(a_i, x_i) \geq u_i(a_i', x_i)$ that means utility of high-reporting behavior is less than utility of true-reporting behavior, and strategy-proofness cannot be guaranteed. But on the other hand, since a_i' is the final provision level node i will provide, it finally provides more resources. As for $a_i \leq k_i \leq x_i \leq a_i'$, node i's actual resource is not enough, and a rational node will not make such a decision. If this case happens, we let node i to provide all the resource it has, which also causes node i to provide more than in the case of true-reporting behavior.

Theorem 2. *MPR is a group strategy-proof mechanism when a node chooses low-reporting behavior. While when it chooses high-reporting behavior, group strategy-proofness cannot be guaranteed but this node will provide more resources.*

Since the proof is similar with Theorem 1, proof is omitted here.

5 Experiments

We implemented the experiments in Java. We did not choose the common network simulator for we only verified the strategyproofness and group strategy-proofness. Set 200 resource nodes, 100 provision levels $|A| = 100$, stochastic variable X in $C(x) = E$ $[X|X > x]$ and $c(x) = E[X|X \leq x]$ was uniformly distributed in $[1, |A|]$.

Experiment 1 and Experiment 2 were designed to prove strategy-proofness of *MPR*, we did multiple executions of *MPR*, and there was only one node misreport in one execution. Node selection was random and if a node was selected in an execution, it would not be selected any more.

Experiment 1. Two hundred executions of *MPR* were run. In every execution, only one of the 200 resource nodes chose low-reporting behavior and reported 60 levels lower than true-reporting behavior. Utility differences between the two behaviors were calculated. Figure 2 illustrated that the utility of low-reporting behavior was not less than the utility of true-reporting behavior, which meant strategy-proofness was guaranteed when the node chose low-reporting.

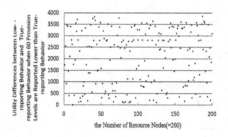

Fig. 2. Utility differences between low-reporting behavior and true-reporting behavior when 60 provision levels are reported lower than true-reporting behavior

Experiment 2. Nodes which end up in multiple loops were selected, and the provision level was reported 60 levels higher than true-reporting behavior. The utility differences and total number of final provided resources was calculated. Figure 3(a) illustrated that there existed nodes whose utility of high-reporting behavior were larger than utility of true-reporting behavior. Therefore, it was not strategyproofness when nodes chose high-reporting behavior. On the other hand, from Fig. 3(b), we saw that high-reporting behavior increased node's provision levels, and caused total number of final provided resources to increase.

Experiment 3 and Experiment 4 were designed to prove group strategy-proofness of *MPR*, we conducted one execution of *MPR*, selected a coalition from the 200 resource nodes, and let some nodes in the coalition misreport.

Experiment 3. In the nodes set which ended up in one loop, we randomly selected 30% nodes as a coalition, and let 80% nodes in the coalition choose high-reporting behavior or low-reporting behavior with the provision level was reported 60 levels

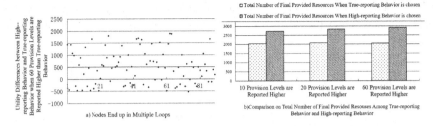

a) Nodes End up in Multiple Loops

b)Comparison on Total Number of Final Provided Resouses Among True-reporting Behavior and High-reporting Behavior

Fig. 3. Utility differences between high-reporting behavior and true-reporting behavior for nodes end up in multiple loops

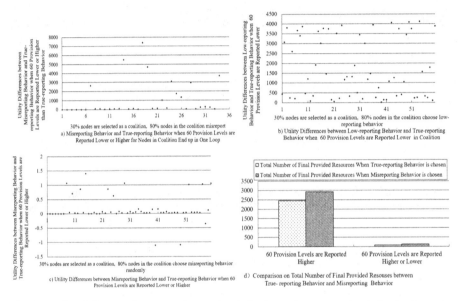

a) Misreporting Behavior and True-reporting Behavior when 60 Provision Levels are Reported Lower or Higher for Nodes in Coalition End up in One Loop

b) Utility Differences between Low-reporting Behavior and True-reporting Behavior when 60 Provision Levels are Reported Lower in Coalition

c) Utility Differences between Misreporting Behavior and True-reporting Behavior when 60 Provision Levels are Reported Lower or Higher

d) Comparison on Total Number of Final Provided Resouses between True- reporting Behavior and Misreporting Behavior

Fig. 4. Utility differences between misreporting behavior and true-reporting behavior for nodes in coalition

lower or higher randomly [Fig. 4(a)]. Experiments showed that utility of misreporting behaviour was not less than utility of true-reporting behaviour, it was group strategy-proofness for nodes which end up in one loop.

Experiment 4. In all the nodes, we randomly selected 30% nodes as a coalition, and let 80% nodes in the coalition choose (1) low-reporting behaviour with the provision level was reported 60 levels lower randomly [Fig. 4(b)], (2) low-reporting behaviour or high-reporting behaviour with the provision level was reported 60 levels lower or higher randomly. Since the negative utility difference from the original data was too small to show clearly in coordinates, we used log value of utility and get their differences [Fig. 4 (c)]. Experiments showed that it was group strategyproofness for any kind of nodes when they chose low-reporting behaviour. While, it was not group strategy-proofness when they chose high-reporting behaviour or randomly misreporting behaviour. From

Fig. 4(c), there were only 3 nodes that did not reach group strategy-proofness, but the total resources that they provided was larger than in true-reporting behaviour as shown in Fig. 4(d).

6 Conclusion

Our work has introduced concepts from social choice into computer science to get some meaningful results. Mechanism we designed is suitable for nodes with two characteristics. One is that rational nodes are trying to conceal their actual ability and provide fewer resources. Our work not only encourages nodes to show their true information but also makes nodes provide more resources when truth incentive fails. The other is nodes' utility can be described by their internal cost and feelings, so that payment is not important to effect nodes' choice. Our future work will focus on the utility function that can reflect nodes' cost and feeling in a suitable way.

Acknowledgments. This work was supported by the national natural science foundation of China (No. 41363003, No. 61502407), Study Abroad for Young Scholar Program sponsored by Guangdong University of Technology.

References

1. Mihailescu, M., Teo, Y.M.: Strategy-proof dynamic resource pricing of multiple resource types on federated clouds. In: Hsu, C.-H., Yang, Laurence T., Park, J.H., Yeo, S.-S. (eds.) ICA3PP 2010. LNCS, vol. 6081, pp. 337–350. Springer, Heidelberg (2010). https://doi.org/10.1007/978-3-642-13119-6_30
2. Liu, X., Li, W., Zhang, X.: Strategy-proof mechanism for provisioning and allocation virtual machines in heterogeneous clouds. IEEE Trans. Parallel Distrib. Syst. **29**(7), 1650–1663 (2017)
3. Nejad, M.M., Mashayekhy, L., Grosu, D.: Truthful greedy mechanisms for dynamic virtual machine provisioning and allocation in clouds. IEEE Trans. Parallel Distrib. Syst. **26**(2), 594–603 (2015)
4. Shi, W., Zhang, L., Wu, C., Li, Z., Lau, F.C.M.: An online auction framework for dynamic resource provisioning in cloud computing. IEEE/ACM Trans. Netw. **24**(4), 2060–2073 (2016)
5. Hajiesmaili, M.H., Deng, L., Chen, M., Li, Z.: Incentivizing device-to-device load balancing for cellular networks: an online auction design. IEEE J. Sel. Areas Commun. **35**(2), 265–279 (2017)
6. Anderegg, L., Eidenbenz, S.: Ad hoc-VCG: a truthful and cost efficient routing protocol for mobile ad-hoc networks with selfish agents. In: Proceedings of the 9th Annual International Conference on Mobile Computing and Networking, pp. 245–259. ACM (2003)
7. Gopinathan, A., Li, Z.P., Li, B.C.: Group strategyproof multicast in wireless networks. IEEE Trans. Parallel Distrib. Syst. **22**(5), 708–715 (2011)
8. Wei, Q., Zhou, W., Ren, X.J.: A strategy-proof trust based decision mechanism for pervasive computing environments. Comput. Sci. **35**(5), 871–882 (2012)

9. Wang, T., Song, L., Han, Z., Saad, W.: Distributed cooperative sensing in cognitive radio networks: an overlapping coalition formation approach. IEEE Trans. Commun. **62**(9), 3144–3160 (2014)
10. Liu, J., Wang, Q.: A false data detecting scheme based on coalition game for vehicular ad-hoc network. J. Xi'an Jiaotong Univ. **49**(2), 69–73 (2015)
11. Nisan, N., Ronen, A.: Algorithmic mechanism design. Games Econ. Behav. **35**(1), 166–196 (2001)
12. Xiao, Y., Han, Z., Chen, K.-C.: Bayesian hierarchical mechanism design for cognitive radio networks. IEEE J. Sel. Areas Commun. **33**(5), 986–1001 (2015)
13. Nejad, M. M., Mashayekhy, L., Grosu, D.: A family of truthful greedy mechanisms for dynamic virtual machine provisioning and allocation in clouds. In: Proceedings of the 6th IEEE International Conference on Cloud Computing, pp. 188–195. IEEE Computer Society, Santa Clara (2013)
14. Moulin, H., Shenker, S.: Strategyproof sharing of submodular costs: budget balance versus efficiency. Econ. Theor. **18**(3), 511–533 (2001)
15. Pal, M., Tardos, E.: Group strategyproof mechanisms via primal-dual algorithms. In: Proceedings 44th Annual IEEE Symposium on Foundations of Computer Science, pp. 584–593. IEEE, Cambridge (2003)
16. Li, Z.P., Chu, X.W.: On achieving group-strategyproof multicast. IEEE Trans. Parallel Distrib. Syst. **23**(5), 913–923 (2012)
17. Nisan, N., Roughgarden, T., Tardos, E., Vazirani, V.: Algorithmic Game Theory. Cambridge University Press, Cambridge (2007)
18. Moulin, H.: On strategy-proofness and single peakedness. Public Choice **35**(4), 437–455 (1980)
19. Gershkov, A., Moldovanu, B., Shi, X.W.: Optimal mechanism design without money. Technical Report, University of Toronto, 4 (2013)
20. Arribillagay, R.P., Massz, J.: Comparing generalized median voter schemes according to their manipulability. Technical Report, Universitat Autnoma de Barcelona and Barcelona GSE, 2 (2014)
21. Cheng, Y.K., Yu, W., Zhang, G.C.: Strategy-proof approximation mechanisms for an obnoxious facility game on networks. Theor. Comput. Sci. **497**, 154–163 (2013)
22. Barber, S., Berga, D., Moreno, B.: Individual versus group strategyproofness when do they coincide. J. Econ. Theory **145**(5), 1648–1674 (2010)

The 4th International Symposium on Dependability in Sensor, Cloud and Big Data Systems and Applications (DependSys 2018)

DependSys 2018 Organizing and Program Committees

Honorary Chairs

Rajkumar Buyya   University of Melbourne, Australia
Frank Hsu   Fordham University, USA

General Chairs

Lei Shu   Nanjing Agricultural University,
    China/University of Lincoln, UK
Md Zakirul Alam Bhuiyan   Fordham University, USA

Program Chairs

Jiankun Hu   University of New South Wales, Australia
Kim-Kwang Raymond Choo   University of Texas at San Antonio, USA
Mamoun Alazab   Charles Darwin University, Australia

Program Track Chairs

Track 1: Dependability Fundamentals and Technologies

Mahmuda Naznin   BUET, Bangladesh
Thaier Hayajneh   Fordham University, USA

Track 2: Dependable and Secure Systems

Akramul Azim   University of Ontario, Canada
Mohammad Mehedi Hassan   King Saud University, KSA

Track 3: Dependable and Secure Applications

Xuyun Zhang   The University of Auckland
A. Taufiq Asyhari   Cranfield University, UK

Track 4: Dependability and Security Measures and Assessments

Wenjia Li	NYIT, USA
Md. Arafatur Rahman	University Malaysia Pahang, Malaysia

Publicity Chairs

Joarder Kamruzzaman	Federation University Australia
Mohammad Shahriar	ULAB, Bangladesh
Fang Qi	Central South University, China
Sancheng Peng	Guangdong University of Foreign Studies, China
Yuan-Fang Chen	University of Paris VI, France

Program Committee

Alireza Jolfaei	Federation University, Australia
Amjad Anvari-Moghaddam	AALBORG University, Denmark
Angela Guercio	Kent State University at Stark, USA
Arcangelo Castiglione	University of Salerno, Italy
Bing Tang	Hunan University of Science and Technology
Carlos Juiz	Universitat de les Illes Balears, Spain
Christian Esposito	University of Naples "Federico II"
Constantinos Patsakis	University of Piraeus, Greece
Damien Hanyurwimfura	University of Rwanda, Rwanda
Farzana Rahman	Florida International University, USA
Franco Frattolillo	University of Sannio, Italy
Kiss Gabor	Obuda University, Hungary
Genaina Rodrigues	University of Brasilia, Brazil
Gerardo Pelosi	Politecnico di Milano, Italy
Gianluigi Me	University of Rome, Italy
Guoqi Xie	Hunan University, China
Hai Tao	Baoji University of Art and Science, China
Haider Abbas	NUST, Norway
Hossain Shahriar	Kennesaw State University, USA
Houbing Song	Embry-Riddle, Aeronautical University, USA
Jasni Mohamad Zain	Universiti Malaysia Pahang, Malaysia
Luis Javier Garcia Villalba	Complutense University of Madrid, Spain
Jianxun Liu	Hunan University of Science and Technology, China
Junggab Son	North Carolina Central University, USA
Kamal Zuhairi Bin Zamli	Universiti Malaysia Pahang, Malaysia
Georgios Kambourakis	University of the Aegean, Greece

Kenichi Kourai	Kyushu Institute of Technology, Japan
Kouichi Sakurai	Kyushu University, China
Lianyong Qi	Qufu Normal University, China
Lien-Wu Chen	Feng Chia University, Taiwan
M. Arifuzzaman Shaikh	University of New Orleans, USA
Mahmuda Naznin	BUET, Bangladesh
Manuel Mazzara	Innopolis University, Russia
Marco Guazzone	University of Piemonte Orientale, Italy
Md. Arafatur Rahman	University Malaysia Pahang, Malaysia
Mohamed Kheir	IMS Connector Systems GmbH, Germany
Mohammad Shojafar	University Sapienza of Rome, Italy
Mohammad Asad Rehman Chaudhry	University of Toronto, Canada
Mohammad Mehedi Hassan	King Saud University, KSA
Mubashir H. Rehmani	COMSATS Institute of Information Technology, Pakistan
Muhamed Turkanovic	University of Maribor, Slovenia
Nicola Zannone	Eindhoven University of Technology, Netherlands
Peng Hao	Beihang University, China
Prantosh Kumar Paul	Bengal Engineering and Science University, India
Qiong Huang	South China Agricultural University, China
Rukhsana Afroz Ruby	SIAT, China
Ryan K. L. Ko	The University of Waikato, New Zealand
Sajal Sarkar	National University of Singapore, Singapore
Salvatore Distefano	Politecnico di Milano, Italy
Selina Sharmin	Jagannath University, Bangladesh
Shigeng Zhang	Central South University, China
Philip Sumesh	Western Illinois University, USA
Syed Hassan Ahmed	Georgia Southern University, USA
Syropoulos Apostolos	Greek Molecular Computing Group, Greece
Toshihiro Yamauchi	Okayama University, Japan
Traian Truta	Northern Kentucky University, USA
Vladimir Podolskiy	Technical University of Munich, Russia
Xuyun Zhang	The University of Auckland, New Zealand
Yifan Zhang	Binghamton University, USA
Yu Wang	Guangzhou University, China
Yuan-Fang Chen	Hangzhou Dianzi University, China
Muhammad Z. Hasan	Texas A&M International University, USA
Zhitao Guan	North China Electric Power University, China
Yufeng Wang	Nanjing University of Posts and Telecommunications, China
Shahab Shmshir	NUST, Norway

Risk Identification-Based Association Rule Mining for Supply Chain Big Data

Abdullah Salamai$^{(\boxtimes)}$, Morteza Saberi, Omar Hussain, and Elizabeth Chang

School of Business, University of New South Wales, Canberra, Australia
a.salamai@student.unsw.edu.au, m.saberi@unsw.edu.au,
{o.hussain, e.chang}@adfa.edu.au

Abstract. Since most supply chain processes include operational risks, the effectiveness of a corporation's success depends mainly on identifying, analyzing and managing them. Currently, supply chain risk management (SCRM) is an active research field for enhancing a corporation's efficiency. Although several techniques have been proposed, they still face a big challenge as they analyze only internal risk events from big data collected from the logistics of supply chain systems. In this paper, we analyze features that can identify risk labels in a supply chain. We propose defining risk events based on the association rule mining (ARM) technique that can categorize those in a supply chain based on a company's historical data. The empirical results we obtained using data collected from an Aluminum company showed that this technique can efficiently generate and predict the optimal features of each risk label with a higher than 96.5% accuracy.

Keywords: Risk identification · Supply chain management
Association rule mining · Big data

1 Introduction

Due to the increasing varieties of uncertainties in supply chain management, the performance of a supply chain has become unreliable as it faces different risk events. A supply chain risk is defined as "the prospect and influence of surprising macro and/or micro level proceedings or conditions that poorly impact any portion of a supply chain yielding to irregularities, strategic level failures, or tactical or operational issues" [1]. Mitigating these risk events through SCRM approaches that inspect and control them as much as possible has become an ongoing interest of researchers [2].

Supply chain risks are categorized as either disruption or operation [1, 3]. The former occurs via natural disasters, such as earthquakes and floods, which are difficult to control or predict while the latter relates to supply-demand management and are a result of unsuccessful processes, people and systems, such as quality or delivery issues. As operational risk labels can be managed and predicted if their events are carefully analyzed [3], we focus on defining risk events based on the internal and/or external features of the relevant supply chain.

© Springer Nature Switzerland AG 2018
G. Wang et al. (Eds.): SpaCCS 2018, LNCS 11342, pp. 219–228, 2018.
https://doi.org/10.1007/978-3-030-05345-1_18

Operational risk events can emanate from either internal or external sources based on the features of the supply chain. Internal risk features include all the uncertainties originating from the flow of information between a customer and supplier while external ones involve issues regarding the environmental dynamics in various areas [4, 5]. The profitability of a supply chain depends mainly on identifying and managing all these events.

In this paper, we try to determine the important data features and their rules that can identify risk events from big data collected from supply chain systems. More specifically, we use the ARM technique that can estimate the highest correlation between features based on support and confidence measures [6, 7]. In order to validate the reliability of this method, we collected different internal and external data features associated with four risk labels (i.e., quality, delay, price and wrong products) identified by company experts. The experimental outcomes revealed that the ARM technique can reliably find the optimal rules and features of these labels.

The rest of this paper is organized as follows. Section 2 discusses the background and studies related to this research. Section 3 explains the proposed methodology and evaluation of its performance. Section 4 describes the experimental results. Finally, Sect. 5 presents the conclusion of the study.

2 Background and Related Studies

Over the last few years, the performance of a supply chain has been affected by operational risks [5]. Most recent research studies [1, 3–5] attempted to mitigate these risks by investigating the features in the historical data of a supply chain's process. Although a few studies considered the important features required to determine operational risk events [8], they did not clearly define the impacts of those that accurately indicate possible risk events.

Measuring and identifying the correlation and dependency between the internal and external features of a supply chain in order to recognize/mitigate risk events have become a big challenge. Some researchers tried to identify risk using variance-based, fuzzy logic and mining techniques [3, 9]. Heckmann et al. [11] developed a stochastic mathematical formulation for designing a network of multi-product supply chains comprising several capacitated production facilities, distribution centers and retailers in uncertain markets.

Rangel et al. [12] examined the external events which directly affect a supply chain, such as economic, governmental, social and technological risk operations. McGregor and Smit [13] investigated the roles of contractual completeness and complementary enforcement practices, such as monitoring and sanctioning under fluctuating risk scenarios, in identifying and minimizing risk. However, the authors stated that to undertake systematic rights with due diligence, there is still the issue of determining and mitigating the external features of risks in SCRM due to the shortage of supply chain information. Also, external risk labels are not sufficiently clear to evaluate the cycle of a supply chain.

Recently, many researchers applied data-mining algorithms to SCRM with enterprise resource planning (ERP) to mine and predict important patterns from the data collected. Haery et al. [10] implemented the ARM mechanism to determine and validate the criteria for selecting suppliers. Zhang et al. [14] qualitatively identified the delay risk labels of suppliers and quantitatively described the relationship between them and the degrees of delay of ARM algorithms. Ganguly et al. [15] assessed different supply chain risks linked to the agility of an organization using the ARM method to help decision-makers define risk events that could occur in the relevant organization in order to establish sustainability in the market.

3   ARM for Risk Identification

Since the ARM technique has several advantages in terms of accurately correlating all the information in a data collection [6, 7], we use it to define the important internal and external features that can recognize and mitigate risk events in the domain of a supply chain. It is a data-mining technique that calculates the degree of correlation between two (or more) variables in order to determine the greatest itemset of relationships between observations [6, 7]. For example, assuming a set of variables ($V = \{v_1, v_2, v_3, \ldots, v_N\}$) and a set of transactions ($T = t_1, t_2, t_3, \ldots, t_N$) from a data collection (D), for each transaction (t_j), each $1 \leq i \leq N$ is a set of features, where $t_i \subseteq r$, with the association rule $v_1(variable1) \Rightarrow v_2(variable1)$ subject to constraints (1) $\exists t_i, v_1, v_2 \in t_i$, (2) $v_1 \subseteq r, f v_2 \subseteq r$ and (3) $v_1 \cap v_2 = \emptyset$.

To create a rule, two functions in ARM, support and confidence, have to be estimated. Support defines the frequency ratio of each row's value to determine the association percentage using Eq. (1). Confidence is the frequency of a precedent if the antecedent has already occurred using Eq. (2).

$$support\ (v_1 \Rightarrow v_2) = \frac{|\#t_i|v_1, v_2 \in t_i|}{N} \tag{1}$$

$$confidence\ (v_1 \Rightarrow v_2) = \frac{|\#t_i|v_1, v_2 \in t_i|}{|\#t_i|v_1 \in t_i|} \tag{2}$$

The ARM technique discovers the existing itemsets that estimate the strongest rules by satisfying the conditions that: (i) *support* is equal to or greater than a user-specified minimum support (*support* $\geq$ minimum *support*); and (2) *confidence* is equal to or greater than the minimum confidence threshold (*confidence* $\geq$ minimum *confidence*).

The process of applying ARM to measure risk events in a supply chain is depicted in Fig. 1. In the training phase, we compute the strongest features and rules for each risk label and, in the testing phase, measure the accuracy in terms of correctly predicted rules based on the specified minimum support and confidence probabilities, as empirically explained in Sect. 4.

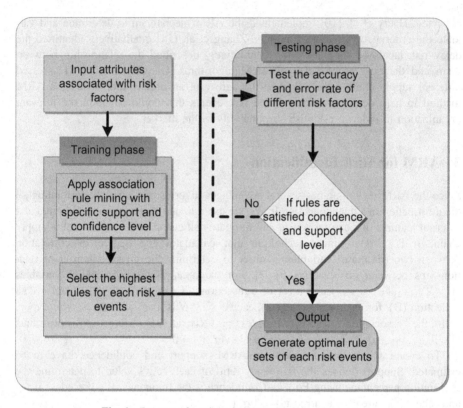

Fig. 1. Process of applying ARM to define risk events

4 Experimental Results and Explanation

This section discusses the data collection process, measures used to evaluate the ARM technique for defining risk events in a supply chain and experimental results obtained.

4.1 Big Data Collection Process and Evaluation Measures

The proposed technique is tested using a dataset collected from an Aluminum company, with the steps for pre-processing the data discussed in the following and depicted in Fig. 2. Firstly, big data from SLAs, including the data features and attributes of a supply chain, is collected. This requires a great deal of effort as it is in the XML format and involves a huge amount of data, known as big data [16]. Then, this data is recorded in a SQL format to make it easier for the proposed technique to define risk events and their likelihoods. The ARM technique is trained and tested using 5000 instances, where the training set includes 3500 instances and the testing set involves 1500 instances.

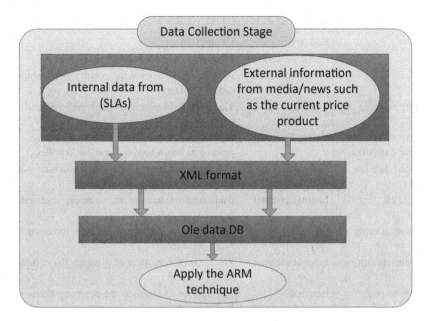

Fig. 2. Pre-processing steps for the dataset used

Secondly, the main label variables that can lead to defining supply chain risks, such as prices, and delay their effects on supply chain operations are identified by asking CEO/experts at the company how they are used. The experts assisted in defining accurate risk events that enable us to effectively train and validate the ARM technique. The dataset contains information about the components of the final products of Aluminum and their attributes, as shown in Table 1. According to the values of these attributes, the expert can manually specify the possible risks that face the company.

More specifically, this dataset comprises four risk labels, namely quality, delay, price, and wrong-product. For example, quality risks/issues have a great effect on manufacturers' businesses, which must have servers of the highest quality, with replacing their extremely expensive components related to high price risks (i.e., causing a considerable increase in a product's price). Finally, to automatically identify the likelihoods of risks at the company, the correlation between risk events and their attributes is determined using the ARM.

This technique is evaluated using accuracy and error rate measures which are the percentages of all items and rules correctly and incorrectly classified, respectively, where error = 100-accuracy.

4.2 Discussion Regarding Using ARM to Identify Risk Events in Supply Chain

The ARM technique is used to estimate the associations between the attributes of each product and their risk labels identified by experts in order to establish dynamic rules that can define any possible future risks, with the likelihood of each risk event occurring

Table 1. Attributes and corresponding risk labels of Aluminium dataset

Attribute	Risk type	Description
Products	Internal/external	Products manufactured and ready for sale
Location	Internal/external	A place inside/outside the country from which orders originate
Quantity on hand	Internal	The products available in the warehouse and ready to use
Quantity in the purchase requisition	Internal/external	A document used as part of the accounting process to begin buying goods or supplies
Estimated date for receipt	External	The expected date for receiving a purchase which could be in the long or short-term
Safety stock	Internal/external	Additional products in the inventory reserved to reduce shortages
Minimum quantity	Internal	The minimum number of products the company needs to order
Maximum quantity	Internal/external	The maximum number of products the company needs to order
Quantity to buy	External	The number of products the company needs to buy at one time
Price	External	The number of suppliers wanting to sell their products
Risk labels	Internal/external	Any attribute that may increase the likelihood of risk events developing

automatically estimated based on computing the average of the support and confidence measures (i.e., importance). As the importance level is specified by the probabilities 0.25, 0.50, 0.75 and 1, by determining which can achieve the best accuracy, we can decide which of the rules it generates can be best used to recognize risk events.

Table 2 presents an example taken from the Aluminum data collection that depends on the features of price and quantity to buy which indicates attributes and risk labels, with the same product and location possibly having different risk labels.

Table 2. Example is taken from Aluminum dataset with four risk events and their attributes

Products	Location	Initial Order	Quantity On hand	Quantity in PR	Estimate date to receive	Safety stock	MIN quantity	Max quantity	Quantity to buy	Price	Risk labels
Bottom block	Emc parts	4	1	4	48	6	116	383	91	30.9	Price
Bottom block	Emc parts	5	2	5	64	11	159	418	109	57.5	Quality
Distribution trough	Emc slab	1	0	1	15	5	134	345	550	350	Delay
Distribution trough	Emc slab	1	0	1	35	19	175	235	153	18.6	Price

Based on an expert's view, the first row is labeled 'price' because, although the price of the product was high at that time, to change the supplier would cost the company more. The second row, 'quality', indicates that the company bought a low-quality product at a relatively low price in order to survive in the market for some time. The third row is entitled 'delay' because the quantity to buy was so large and the supplier took too long to deliver the product to the company which meant that customers could not be provided with their orders on time. The fourth row is labeled 'price' as the price was high for that product and the estimated time for its delivery greater than that for the product in the first row at that time because the company had some of it in its safety stock.

Using the ARM technique, the important features are correlated with the risk events that might occur for the company; for example, although the price of a product increases considerably, the company has to buy it in order to retain its customers. In such a situation, the price, quantity to buy, quantity in stock and location affect the risk events in terms of a high price, delay or quality. Therefore, the values of these features should be associated with the events that differ from one company to another.

The ARM technique can generate a set of rules regarding the most repeated values of the features and then create the important ones, such as quantity on hand and quantity in PR, and correlate them with their risk labels, as shown in Fig. 3. It computes the best rules that can predict risk events related to both internal and external situations although the processes for identifying and managing them are different. Then, the feature values are estimated within particular ranges that automatically generate the best rules for each risk event based on the company's data.

Importance	Rule
0.356	Initial Order = 12 - 20, Estimate Date To Receive = 15 - 26 -> Label = price
0.342	Price < 1450.978458624, Estimate Date To Receive = 15 - 26 -> Label = price
0.327	Safety Stock = 9 - 12, MIN QTY = 42.9057079744 - 90.5481314816 -> Label = price
0.373	Estimate Date To Receive = 15 - 26, Max QTY >= 403.131288064 -> Label = quality
0.196	Initial Order >= 100, Safety Stock = 12 - 17 -> Label = price
0.587	Max QTY = 309.2839540224 - 355.5521475072, Safety Stock < 9 -> Label = delay
0.299	Initial Order < 2, MIN QTY = 133.7426973696 - 179.412877568 -> Label = wrong-product
0.240	Initial Order < 2, Quantity To Buy = 82.8077261568 - 118.841087808 -> Label = quality
0.035	Price = 1545.5727675392 - 1599.9948013568, Initial Order = 2 - 12 -> Label = price
0.299	Initial Order < 2, Quantity To Buy = 82.8077261568 - 118.841087808 -> Label = wrong-product
0.240	Initial Order < 2, Estimate Date To Receive < 15 -> Label = quality
0.299	Initial Order < 2, Estimate Date To Receive < 15 -> Label = wrong-product

Fig. 3. Some important features of four risk events and their rules

As shown in Fig. 4, the most important features of risk events are generated from the entire set of the ARM technique based on the highest importance that produces the best accuracy. In Fig. 5, it can be seen that the 0.75 importance level achieves the best

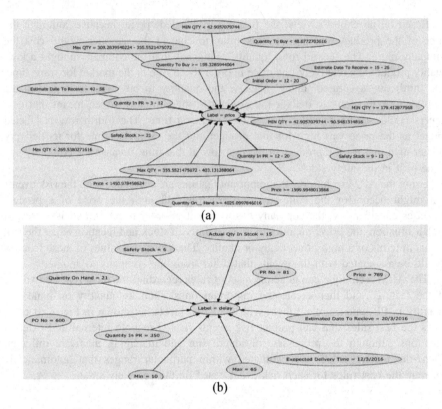

Fig. 4. Important features defining price and delay risk events

accuracy of 96.5% with a 3.5% error rate which means that this technique can define events based on the important features of Aluminum products by using the highest level of importance to build the best rules.

A company can benefit from this technique by feeding it different attributes of its products in order to assist in automating the way of defining and predicting risk events in supply chains. The technique depends on using historical data and small samples of each risk selected by experts in order to improve the performance of the technique.

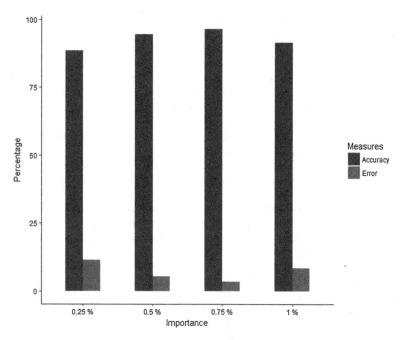

Fig. 5. Accuracy and error rates of importance probabilities determined by ARM

5   Conclusion

This paper discussed using the ARM technique to define risk labels in supply chain systems by training and validating it on data collected from an Aluminum company. It could select the strongest rules associated with the risk labels, and extract the most important features from them to clarify the significant features of each risk event. As the probability importance levels were adjusted to select those which could achieve/specify the best accuracy, this technique successfully defined the risk events in the data collection, with the experiments revealing that it could define risk labels with high accuracy. The aim of this proposal was to provide a company with the means to predict any risk issues in its supply chain by learning the technique using some samples of the products it deals within the market. In the future, we will extend this study to quantify these risks to decide which are very dangerous and how a company should mitigate them if they occur.

References

1. Ho, W., et al.: Supply chain risk management: a literature review. Int. J. Prod. Res. **53**(16), 5031–5069 (2015)
2. Giannakis, M., Papadopoulos, T.: Supply chain sustainability: a risk management approach. Int. J. Prod. Econ. **171**, 455–470 (2016)

3. Chen, J., Sohal, A.S., Prajogo, D.I.: Supply chain operational risk mitigation: a collaborative approach. Int. J. Prod. Res. **51**(7), 2186–2199 (2013)
4. Blome, C., Schoenherr, T., Eckstein, D.: The impact of knowledge transfer and complexity on supply chain flexibility: a knowledge-based view. Int. J. Prod. Econ. **147**, 307–316 (2014)
5. Wu, K.-J., et al.: Toward sustainability: using big data to explore the decisive attributes of supply chain risks and uncertainties. J. Clean. Prod. **142**, 663–676 (2017)
6. Agrawal, R., Imieliński, T., Swami, A.: Mining association rules between sets of items in large databases. In: ACM SIGMOD Record. ACM (1993)
7. Moustafa, N., Slay, J.: A hybrid feature selection for network intrusion detection systems: central points. arXiv preprint arXiv:1707.05505 (2017)
8. Duhamel, F., Carbone, V., Moatti, V.: The impact of internal and external collaboration on the performance of supply chain risk management. Int. J. Logist. Syst. Manag. **23**(4), 534–557 (2016)
9. Meulendijk, M.C., Spruit, M.R., Brinkkemper, S.: Risk Mediation in Association Rules: Application Examples. Utrecht University, UU-CS-2017-004 (2017)
10. Haery, A., et al.: Application of association rule mining in supplier selection criteria. World Acad. Sci. Eng. Technol. **40**(1), 358–362 (2008)
11. Heckmann, I., Comes, T., Nickel, S.: A critical review on supply chain risk—definition, measure and modeling. Omega **52**, 119–132 (2015)
12. Rangel, D.A., de Oliveira, T.K., Leite, M.S.A.: Supply chain risk classification: discussion and proposal. Int. J. Prod. Res. **53**(22), 6868–6887 (2015)
13. McGregor, A., Smit, J.: Risk management: human rights due diligence in corporate global supply chains. Gov. Dir. **69**(1), 16 (2017)
14. Zhang, F., Wei, F.-J., Tian, S.: Analysis of delay risk factors for the delivery of suppliers based on association rules. In: 2014 11th International Computer Conference on the Wavelet Active Media Technology and Information Processing (ICCWAMTIP) (2014)
15. Ganguly, A., Chatterjee, D., Rao, H.V.: Evaluating the risks associated with supply chain agility of an enterprise. Int. J. Bus. Anal. IJBAN **4**(3), 15–34 (2017)
16. Moustafa, N., Creech, G., Slay, J.: Big data analytics for intrusion detection system: statistical decision-making using finite Dirichlet mixture models. In: Palomares Carrascosa, I., Kalutarage, H.K., Huang, Y. (eds.) Data Analytics and Decision Support for Cybersecurity. DA, pp. 127–156. Springer, Cham (2017). https://doi.org/10.1007/978-3-319-59439-2_5

TrCMP: An App Usage Inference Method for Mobile Service Enhancement

Xuan Zhao[1], Md Zakirul Alam Bhuiyan[2], Lianyong Qi[3], Hongli Nie[1],
Wajid Rafique[1], and Wanchun Dou[1(✉)]

[1] State Key Laboratory for Novel Software Technology,
Department of Computer Science and Technology, Nanjing University,
Nanjing 210023, China
douwc@nju.edu.cn
[2] Department of Computer and Information Sciences,
Fordham University, New York 10458, USA
[3] School of Information Science and Engineering, Qufu Normal University,
Qufu 276826, China

Abstract. In order to improve the quality of life and the efficiency of work, users need timely and accurate services provided by mobile devices. However, for the same service, different users have various personalized use styles, such as usage time, invoking frequency, etc. As a result, the accuracy of real-time service recommendations often depends on effective user behavior analysis. Technically, user behaviors associated with a certain service could be reflected with traffic, CPU, memory and energy consumption during app running. In this paper, an app usage inference method, named **TrCMP**, is investigated. This method takes *Tr*affic, *C*PU, *M*emory and *P*ower into consideration in a comprehensive way for analyzing user behaviors. Extensive experiments are conducted to validate the efficiency and effectiveness of our method.

Keywords: App usage · Behavior · Service enhancement · Android

1 Introduction

Recently, the massive adoption of mobile devices has dramatically changed the life of people [1]. To satisfy different needs of mobile users, a large number of applications with various functions continue to emerge [2]. Meanwhile, mobile users are increasingly keen to use mobile applications to accomplish kinds of tasks. In fact, user running apps usually has a certain regularity [3]. For example, when a user is at leisure, he is accustomed to using mobile applications for shopping, watching videos, chatting or playing games. When a user is working, he is keen to use apps to view texts, view emails or edit documents. Therefore, through the analysis of the app usage, certain user behavior pattern can be obtained. It should be mentioned that behavior analysis has a positive effect on providing timely and accurate services for mobile users [4]. To obtain the regularity, the app usage information should be obtained properly.

© Springer Nature Switzerland AG 2018
G. Wang et al. (Eds.): SpaCCS 2018, LNCS 11342, pp. 229–239, 2018.
https://doi.org/10.1007/978-3-030-05345-1_19

How to get app usage information? Currently, there is a way through traffic analysis [1,5]. Another way is by analyzing public resources [3,6]. However, current methods usually take only one profile (e.g., traffic, power consumption) into consideration, which is suboptimal for inference result. Moreover, to the best of our knowledge, current methods cannot speculate apps running in offline state. In this paper, a method, named *TrCMP*, is investigated to infer app usage running on Android devices. This method takes *Tr*affic, *C*PU, *M*emory and *P*ower profiles into consideration for analyzing user behaviors.

The main contributions of this paper are three folds. Firstly, Android's public resources and mobile apps communication methods are introduced. Meanwhile, the communication packet structure to find app-related information are analyzed. Secondly, the similarity of CPU, memory and power profiles during different apps running, and the differences in online and offline states are studied. Lastly, we combine four profiles for overall analysis and demonstrate the performance of our method in both online and offline states through experiments.

The rest of this paper is organized as follows. In Sect. 2, preliminary knowledge about Android's public resources and network packets are introduced and problem of inferring app usage using single profile is analyzed. Subsequently, in Sect. 3, our method is described to infer app usage via traffic, CPU, memory and power analysis. Experimental results are presented in Sect. 4 to demonstrate the performance of our method. Section 5 summarizes the related work and Sect. 6 concludes the paper with some thoughts for future work.

2   Background and Motivation

2.1   Background

Public Resources. Public resources are a set of resources that apps can access and use freely. Most of the public resources in Android are located in two virtual file systems, i.e. `sys` and `proc`. The `sys` uses the Linux unified device model as a management function in addition to viewing and setting kernel parameters. The `proc` exists only in memory and does not occupy external memory space. It provides an interface for accessing system kernel data in the form of a file system. The voltage and current can be obtained from `sys`. The memory usage and CPU usage can be obtained from `proc`.

Mobile Telecommunication. Almost all mainstream applications use Internet Protocol (IP) in network layer, Transmission Control Protocol (TCP) or User Datagram Protocol (UDP) in transport layer and HyperText Transfer Protocol (HTTP) in application layer [5]. Since IP addresses of the remote server of mobile apps are fixed, it is possible to analyze the communication server from the IP address. The `Host`, recorded in the header of the HTTP packet that will be sent to the remote server, can be used to obtain the domain name of the server. Therefore, the server that the app communicate with can also be analyzed.

2.2 Motivation

In order to explore the profile features of different applications, we perform experiments on some apps and obtain the CPU, memory and power profiles during app running, as shown in Fig. 1. Figure 1(a) demonstrates the CPU usage profiles of QQ and iQIYI. Figure 1(b) demonstrates the memory usage profiles of Douyin and Weibo. Figure 1(c) demonstrates the power profiles of NetEase Cloud Music and WeChat. It is difficult to recognize different applications through single profile. Accordingly, it prompt us to take four profiles into consideration.

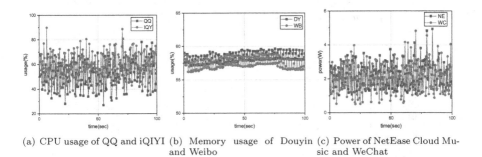

(a) CPU usage of QQ and iQIYI (b) Memory usage of Douyin (c) Power of NetEase Cloud Mu-
and Weibo   sic and WeChat

Fig. 1. Profiles comparison of several apps.

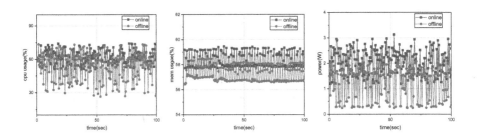

Fig. 2. NetEase Cloud Music running profiles in online and offline states.

We sample CPU, memory and power information of multiple applications in online and offline states and compare them. As shown in Fig. 2, the CPU usage, memory usage and power of NetEase Cloud Music in online and offline states are shown in Fig. 2(a), (b) and (c). In online state, due to the use of network, the usage of CPU and memory, as well as power are significantly higher than those in offline state. Therefore, it is necessary to separate the measurements and analyze them on the basis of different network conditions.

3 *TrCMP* Design

3.1 Method Overview

In this section, a general overview of our method is provided. As shown in Fig. 3, our method consists of the following four steps. (1) *Data Collection.* We introduce the data collection from Android device. Measurements of CPU, memory and power can be obtained from Android's public resources and traffic information can be obtained by collecting the network packets. (2) *Data Processing.* The data processing method is introduced. (3) *Classifier Training.* We use the processed data to train the classifier using machine learning technique. (4) *App Inference.* The app usage is inferred using our trained classifier.

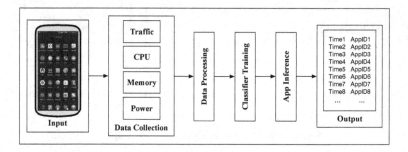

Fig. 3. Overview of TrCMP.

3.2 Data Collection

Traffic. The VPNservice interface in Android platform is used to establish a virtual VPN connection so that all traffic can pass through it. This allows us to collect all traffic packets. The specific implementation process is as follows.

According to the preliminary knowledge in Sect. 2.1, we know that most of the communication protocols used by mobile apps include IP, TCP, UDP and HTTP. Therefore, we mainly collect packets that send to the remote server using these four protocols. The prerequisite of collection is to obtain user authorization. When packets are collected, the timestamp, destination IP address, protocol type and host value of the HTTP packet header are extracted on the current device and will be sent to the server for analysis. The traffic data collected by the server should be multiple tuples (*timestamp, IP, protocol, host*).

CPU. The current CPU usage information can be checked by accessing file /proc/stat. The method for calculating CPU usage is as follows:

(1) Sample two CPU data of sufficiently short time intervals, denoted as t_1, t_2, respectively;

(2) Calculate CPU time at t_1 and t_2, denoted as $cpuTime_1$, $cpuTime_2$;

(3) Calculate CPU usage $cpuUsage$, where

$$cpuUsage = \frac{(cpuTime_2 - idle_2) - (cpuTime_1 - idle_1)}{cpuTime_2 - cpuTime_1} * 100\%.$$

After the CPU usage is obtained, it is needed to get the network state. As found in Sect. 2.2, an app in different network states has different CPU, memory and power profiles. The device network state (ON or OFF) can be checked by creating a `ConnectivityManager` object and calling a specific command. After getting the network state, there is a tuple $(timestamp, networkstate, cpuUsage)$. Multiple tuples should be collected on the device.

Memory. Since the memory used during the execution of each application has its own features, the memory usage is analyzed to infer the app used at a certain moment. By obtaining the data in `/proc/meminfo`, current memory information of the device can be got. Therefore, the memory usage $memoryUsage$ can be obtained by the formula,

$$memoryUsage = \frac{totalMemorySize - availableMemory}{totalMemorySize} * 100\%.$$

After memory usage and network states are obtained, the memory datasets on the device should be multiple tuples $(timestamp, networkstate, memoryUsage)$.

Power. Since the energy consumption in each application running has its own unique features, energy consumption will be analyzed to infer the app used at a certain moment. We can get the $Voltage$ and $Current$ measurements by checking `/sys/class/power_supply/battery` file, and calculate the $Power$ based on $Power = Voltage * Current$.

After the power and network states are obtained, the power profiles collected on the device should be multiple tuples $(timestamp, networkstate, Power)$.

3.3 Data Processing

When enough data is collected, it is transmitted to the server for analysis. The transmission method is using network in online state and data cable in offline state. The data of CPU, memory, power and traffic with same timestamp are combined into one measurement. Then the measurements are divided into online dataset and offline dataset by $networkstate$ and data processing are performed on dataset separately.

Firstly, we consider a dataset $D = (d_1, \ldots, d_n)$, where d_i is the i-th measurement for all $i \in [1, n]$ and n is the total number of measurements, $d_i = (timestamp, networkstate, cpuUsage, memoryUsage, Power, IP, protocol, host)$. Dataset D represents online or offline dataset.

Secondly, data cleaning techniques are used to separate noise data from normal data for measurements of CPU, memory and power, respectively. The recognition operation first calculate the population mean μ, the variance σ and the confidence interval $[\mu - \zeta\frac{\sigma}{\sqrt{n}}, \mu + \zeta\frac{\sigma}{\sqrt{n}}]$ using Chebyshev theorem. Then noise data is deleted based on the confidence interval. Next, the gap value is filled by neighboring data average method.

Thirdly, a sliding window of length W and offset factor r on D is applied to generate a sequence samples $S_1, \ldots, S_k$ of equal length, where

$$S_i = (D_{(i-1)rW+1}, \ldots, D_{(i-1)rW+W}),$$

for all $i = 1, \ldots, k$, and $k = \lfloor\frac{n-W}{rW}\rfloor$ [3]. In this paper, we empirically set r to 0.1 and choose W such that $rW \in \mathbb{Z}$.

Lastly, as for CPU data, the following features are extracted from sample S_i and CPU feature vector $cpuFeature$ is generated: the average, the 20th, 50th and 80th percentile, the standard deviation (SD), the maximum, and the minimum, denoted by C_{i_avg}, C_{i_20pctl}, C_{i_50pctl}, C_{i_80pctl}, C_{i_SD}, C_{i_max}, and C_{i_min}, respectively. In the same way, memory feature vector $memoryFeature = (M_{i\_avg}, M_{i\_20pctl}, M_{i\_50pctl}, M_{i\_80pctl}, M_{i\_SD}, M_{i\_max}, M_{i\_min})$ and power feature vector $powerFeature = (P_{i\_avg}, P_{i\_20pctl}, P_{i\_50pctl}, P_{i\_80pctl}, P_{i\_SD}, P_{i\_max}, P_{i\_min})$ can also be generated.

As for traffic data, the destination IP address and host value of the HTTP packet header are processed first. IP address intervals of known servers are collected as much as possible. Then the collected IP address are compared with the IP address intervals. When IP matches, the corresponding server id is used as our IP feature value. To process *host*, the key word that can represent a server or a company is extract as our host value. Then *IP*, *protocol* and *host* with the most occurrences are selected as traffic feature vector $trafficFeature = (IP, protocol, host)$ from sample S_i.

3.4   Classifier Training and App Inference

Initially, all the feature vectors extracted from samples are aggregated into a set. A feature vector include *cpuFeature*, *memoryFeature*, *powerFeature* and *trafficFeature*. Subsequently, the classifier is trained through lightweight machine learning techniques and a 10-fold cross validation is performed with the set on Random Forest (RF) [7] classifiers. We use Weka [8], an open source machine learning and data mining software based on JAVA environment for our experiment. Lastly, the trained classifier is used to infer app usage.

4   Performance Evaluation

In this section, we first introduce the experiment setup, and then give a detailed description and summary of the experimental results.

Table 1. Popular apps in different categories

Categories	Apps
Social	QQ, WeChat, Tantan, Weibo, Toutiao, QQ Postbox
Searching	Baidu, Zhihu
Video	Tik Tok, Kuaishou, iQIYI, Tencent Video
Music	NetEase Cloud Music, QQmusic
Reading	Anyview
Shopping	Taobao, JD, Pinduoduo, Alipay
Journey	Hellobike, Baidumap, Meituan
Game	PUBG Mobile, Glory of The King, Anipop

4.1 Experiment Setup

Target Apps. According to the rankings of the Android application markets like Wandoujia[1] and Google Play[2], the most popular 25 apps of various types are selected as target apps for our experiments. Most of these applications are required to be used normally in online state. In order to reflect the excellent performance in offline state of our method, some apps that can still be used offline such as NetEase Cloud Music, QQmusic, Baidumap, Tik Tok, Anyview, iQIYI have been chosen. The specific selected apps are shown in Table 1.

Data Collection. An Android app is developed whose main function is to obtain current, voltage, current networking states, memory usage, CPU usage, grab network traffic packets, and then transmit the data to the server for analysis.

In order to demonstrate that our method can perform well in different devices and different versions of the Android system, we use Motorola victara_retcn with Android 6.0 and Android 7.0 and Xiaomi with MIUI 6 and MIUI 7 to collect data. Fifteen volunteers are recruited for our experiment, i.e. five women and ten men. Volunteers are required to use 6 different apps within 60 min, and cannot run other apps in the background as one app is running. The collected datasets were divided into 80% for training and 20% for testing.

4.2 Experimental Results

A lot of experiments are finished to test the performance of our method and compare with the method via power, CPU, memory and traffic analysis, respectively. Our method also be tested in different devices with different system versions.

Offline Perfomance. Some experiments are finished to test the performance of using CPU, memory and power in offline state to infer app usage, and compare

---

[1] http://www.wandoujia.com/apps.
[2] https://play.google.com/store.

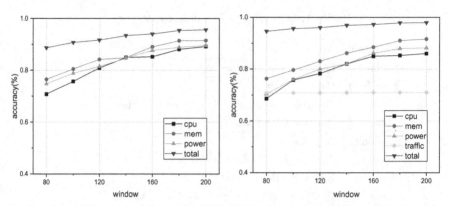

(a) Compare offline performance with CPU, (b) Compare online performance with traffic,
Memory and Power analysis separately.   CPU, Memory and Power analysis separately.

Fig. 4. TrCMP performance in online and offline states under different window size.

with the results obtained by considering individual profile. We test our method
using different algorithms and found that the best performance can be achieved
when using the RF algorithm. It can be seen from the Fig. 4(a), as the length
of the window increases, the number of measurements in one sample increases,
and the unique features of app from every sample become more precise, thereby
improve the accuracy of recognition. The recognition accuracy can be achieved
up to 88.09%, 86.94% 86.79% using RF algorithm when consider CPU, memory
and power profile, respectively. The accuracy of analyzing CPU, memory and
power comprehensively can be achieved up to 95.84%, is higher than that accuracy of analyzing a single profile. The relatively high accuracy indicates that our
method combining CPU, memory and power analysis in offline state is effective.

Online Performance. We experimentally test the performance of analyzing
traffic, CPU, memory and power profiles in online state to infer app usage, and
compare with the results obtained by analyzing individual profile. As can be seen
from the Fig. 4(b), under different window lengths, the recognition accuracy can
be achieved up to 89.71%, 87,53%, 85.79% and 70.86% using RF algorithm when
consider CPU, memory, power and traffic profile, respectively. The accuracy of
our method is obviously higher than the accuracy of analyzing a single profile
and can be achieved up to 97.75%. The relatively high accuracy indicates that
the method combining traffic, CPU, memory and power analysis in online state
is effective.

Performance in Different Devices and System Versions. A comparison
of **TrCMP** performance is made between online state and offline state using
RF in different devices, Motorola victara_retcn with Android 6.0 or Android
7.0 and Xiaomi with MIUI 6 or MIUI 7. As can be seen from the Fig. 5, our
method can achieve fine performance without being affected by different devices
or system versions. For Motorola, our method can achieve up to 94.77% and
95.84% in offline state and 97.29% and 97.75% in online state with Android 6.0

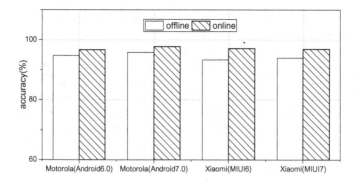

Fig. 5. Comparison of performance between online and offline states in different devices and system versions.

and Android 7.0, respectively. For Xiaomi, our method can achieve up to 93.31% and 93.92% in offline state and 97.15% and 96.95% in online state with MIUI 6 and MIUI 7, respectively.

5   Related Work and Comparison Analysis

In this section, we will introduce the current research progress on the app usage inference. Nowadays, app usage information has been attached importance by academia and industry and research on this topic has been increased during past some years.

The usage of mobile applications can be analyzed by many means. There is a way by traffic analysis [1,2,5,9]. In [5], Dai et al. proposed NetworkProfiler for automatically generating network profiles for identifying Android apps in the HTTP traffic. BIND [9] leveraged dependence in packet sequences on encrypted network traffic for end-node identification evaluated over app fingerprinting. In [2], Taylor et al. presented AppScanner for the automatic fingerprinting and real-time identification of Android apps from their encrypted network traffic. FLOWR [1] can automatically identify mobile apps by continually learning the apps' distinguishing features via key-value pairs in HTTP headers analysis.

There is another way to infer app usage by analyzing user states [10–12]. In [10], Liu et al. explored multiple aspects of such behavioral data and presented patterns of app usage. Shehu et al. in [11] proposed computing app fingerprints exploits invariants found among pairs of metrics, collected during app execution. In [12], Yang et al. characterized the usage pattern of mobile apps and exhibited how the mobility, geospatial properties and behaviors of subscribers affect their mobile app usage at a fine-grained level.

Another method is by public resources analysis [3,6]. In [3], Chen et al. presented the design and evaluation of POWERFUL, which can fingerprint sensitive mobile apps by analyzing the power consumption profiles on Android devices. In [6], Zhou et al. developed an app without any permission with three unexpected channels: per-app data-usage statistics, Address Resolution Protocol information, and speaker status to infer app usage.

In comparison with the above methods for app usage inference, our method integrates traffic, CPU, memory and energy consumption analysis to minimize the impact of many factors such as network states, environment, equipment and system versions on the accuracy of speculation. It can infer app usage whether the device is in both online or offline state. Inference accuracy for app usage can be achieved up to 95.84% in offline state and 97.75% in online state.

6   Conclusion

In this paper, we developed *TrCMP*, a method for app usage inference via *Tr*affic, *C*PU, *M*emory and *P*ower analysis. It can implement mobile app usage inference in both online and offline states on Android devices. A large number of experiments prove that our method can recognize the apps with up to 95.84% in offline state and 97.75% in online state. In the future, we plan to analyze more data to generate specific and accurate user behavior pattern and serve for providing precise service recommendation. At the same time, user privacy can be threatened in the process of speculating app usage. How to protect user data security without affecting apps functions is also a direction of our future work.

Acknowledgments. This work is supported in part by the National Science Foundation of China under Grant No. 61672276, the National Key Research and Development Program of China under Grant No. 2017YFB1400600, and the Collaborative Innovation Center of Novel Software Technology and Industrialization, Nanjing University.

References

1. Xu, Q., et al.: Automatic generation of mobile app signatures from traffic observations. In: 2015 IEEE Conference on Computer Communications (INFOCOM), pp. 1481–1489 (2015)
2. Taylor, V.F., Spolaor, R., Conti, M., Martinovic, I.: AppScanner: automatic fingerprinting of smartphone apps from encrypted network traffic. In: 2016 IEEE European Symposium on Security and Privacy (EuroS&P), pp. 439–454 (2016)
3. Chen, Y., Jin, X., Sun, J., Zhang, R., Zhang, Y.: POWERFUL: mobile app fingerprinting via power analysis. In: IEEE INFOCOM 2017, IEEE Conference on Computer Communications, pp. 1–9 (2017)
4. Taylor, V.F., Spolaor, R., Conti, M., Martinovic, I.: Robust smartphone app identification via encrypted network traffic analysis. IEEE Trans. Inf. Forensics Secur. **13**(1), 63–78 (2018)
5. Dai, S., Tongaonkar, A., Wang, X., Nucci, A., Song, D.: NetworkProfiler: towards automatic fingerprinting of android apps. In: 2013 Proceedings IEEE INFOCOM, pp. 809–817 (2013)
6. Zhou, X., et al.: Identity, location, disease and more: inferring your secrets from android public resources, pp. 1017–1028 (2013)

7. Ho, T.K.: The random subspace method for constructing decision forests. IEEE Trans. Pattern Anal. Mach. Intell. **20**(8), 832–844 (1998)
8. Hall, M., Frank, E., Holmes, G., Pfahringer, B., Reutemann, P., Witten, I.H.: The WEKA data mining software: an update. ACM SIGKDD Explor. Newslett. **11**(1), 10–18 (2009)
9. Khomh, F., Yuan, H., Zou, Y.: Adapting Linux for mobile platforms: an empirical study of Android. In: 2012 28th IEEE International Conference on Software Maintenance (ICSM), pp. 629–632 (2012)
10. Liu, X., Li, H., Lu, X., Xie, T., Mei, Q., Feng, F., Mei, H.: Understanding diverse usage patterns from large-scale appstore-service profiles. IEEE Trans. Softw. Eng. **44**(4), 384–411 (2018)
11. Shehu, Z., Ciccotelli, C., Ucci, D., Aniello, L., Baldoni, R.: Towards the usage of invariant-based app behavioral fingerprinting for the detection of obfuscated versions of known malware. In: International Conference on Next Generation Mobile Applications, Security and Technologies, pp. 121–126 (2016)
12. Yang, L., Yuan, M., Wang, W., Zhang, Q., Zeng, J.: Apps on the move: a fine-grained analysis of usage behavior of mobile apps. In: 35th Annual IEEE International Conference on Computer Communications, pp. 1–9 (2016)

A High-Performance Adaptive Strategy of Container Checkpoint Based on Pre-replication

Shuo Zhang, Ningjiang Chen$^{(\boxtimes)}$, Hanlin Zhang, Yijun Xue,
and Ruwei Huang

School of Computer and Electronic Information, Guangxi University,
Nanning 530004, China
chnj@gxu.edu.cn, 512318408@qq.com

Abstract. During the implementation of the container checkpoint strategy, checkpoint downtime is a pivotal performance indicator. Shorter downtime is especially important for systems that provide critical services. To reduce the checkpoint downtime, an adaptive pre-replication checkpoint strategy named APR-CKPOT is proposed in this paper. Through several rounds of pre-replication, the infrequently modified container memory pages are preferentially copied. The dirty pages generated in the previous round of Pre-Replication are saved in each round of pre-replication. The number of pre-replication checkpoints is adaptively determined by the workload of the user's operating system in the container. The coordination between fault-tolerance service capabilities and performance of the container can be achieved, and the downtime of the checkpoint can be reduced, which is verified by the given experimental results based on Docker container system.

Keywords: Docker · Container · Fault-tolerance · Pre-replication
Checkpoints

1 Introduction

As container [1] technology is being widely used in cloud computing systems, the reliability of containers has become a concern. Checkpoint technology is considered to be a highly efficient fault tolerant technology [2–4]. It makes the container running state of some specific time into a checkpoint and saves it to the storage medium. When the container crashes, the pre-stored status data are read from the checkpoint backup file [5] to ensure that the container continues to run from the checkpoint location [6, 7]. Checkpoint technology has been widely used because of its relatively small storage space and computing resources [8–11]. However, its performance depends on the frequency of checkpoints, the amount of data transferred, etc. Therefore, many works have studied a variety of checkpoint-oriented data memory migration and replication optimization strategies, such as stop-and-copy strategy and pre-copy strategy [12], post-copy strategy, lazy-copy strategy, etc. [13]. Downtime is a key performance indicator in the implementation of the container checkpoint strategy. Shorter downtime

© Springer Nature Switzerland AG 2018
G. Wang et al. (Eds.): SpaCCS 2018, LNCS 11342, pp. 240–250, 2018.
https://doi.org/10.1007/978-3-030-05345-1_20

is especially important for systems that provide critical services [14]. Around the indicator of downtime, the checkpoint implementation mechanism is mainly carried out in terms of time optimization and space optimization [15, 16]. In Google Kubernetes [9], there are corresponding container health check and recovery strategies [17–20]; Reference [21] designs a container checkpoint and restart method implemented in OpenVZ [2, 22]. Checkpoint technology is implemented through the migration of containers, and the proposed optimized migration algorithm reduces service latency.

In order to reduce the downtime of containers, this paper proposes a checkpoint fault-tolerant strategy based on pre-replication with Docker container system [23] as the research platform. Through multiple rounds of Pre-Replication, the container memory page that is not frequently modified will be replicated preferentially; the dirty pages generated in the previous round of Pre-Replication are then saved in each round of Pre-Replication by the freezer. There is a large difference in checkpoint downtime for different load state types of containers. The memory pages of memory-intensive workloads will be modified frequently, which will allow the Pre-Replication process to last longer and potentially increase the time overhead of checkpoints. Therefore, the strategy implemented in this paper, the number of Pre-Replication checkpoints is adaptively determined by the workload in the container. That is, when the number of dirty pages in the memory is too large or the number of pre-replicated rounds exceeds the threshold, the stop-replication phase is executed instead. As a result, downtime in the pre-replication phase is reduced, resulting in coordination between the container's fault-tolerant service capabilities and performance benefits.

The main contents of this paper are as follows: Sect. 2 designs the basic model of checkpoints, so that the container process maintains the consistency of the data; Sect. 3 elaborates on the proposed adaptive strategy of the container checkpoint, through pre-replication and stop-replication phase enables fewer checkpoint downtime, which increases the fault tolerance of the container. The fault-tolerant efficiency of the container checkpoint technology was verified by comparing the checkpoint downtime and the number of dirty pages under different load conditions in Sect. 4. The main contributions of this paper are explained in Sect. 5, the problems solved are summarized by the adaptive management strategy for container checkpoints and the challenges facing the future are proposed.

2 Basic Model of Container Checkpoint

The container's guest operating system can be thought of as a process tree with a series of processes, so the container's checkpoint is a system-level process group checkpoint. The resources of the container process and their previous relationships need to be saved to the checkpoint. For example, a checkpoint of Linux needs to save CPU registers, process files, address space, etc., while resources in the container are managed by Cgroups and are separated by Namespace [8]. The container's resources are stored in a checkpoint file (named CKP) through a specific data structure, which can later be rebuilt during the recovery process. Process related resources (TGID, PGID and other identifiers) and shared resources (IPC objects, sockets, etc.) are saved at the container checkpoint. Kernel objects and process trees are also saved in the container checkpoint. This data is stored in the checkpoint file (CKP) as a memory page.

The recovery of process hierarchies and process principals is key to container checkpoint recovery. Different process groups contain different Cgroups leaders, and processes in different Cgroups are linked through Cgroups leaders. The relationship between these Cgroups needs to be re-established in the checkpoint recovery of the container to ensure that the container process hierarchy is restored. The main steps to setup the container checkpoint include

(1) Process freeze: Migrating the container process to a known checkpoint state and disable the network.
(2) Container dump: Collecting the complete state of the faulty container process and the container itself to the dump file.
(3) Container Stop: Killing the container process and unload the container file system.

An important step in the checkpoint setup is the freezing of the container process to ensure that the process does not change its state and the process data is consistent. In addition, in the process of performing container recovery, it needs to rebuild the process tree and restore the relationship between processes. It also needs to restore shared resources (IPC objects, sockets, etc.) and dump files (memory map exact locations, threads, timers, etc.). During the startup of the container, all process dependencies and refactoring dependencies should be saved, including the process's related resources (TGID, PGID, and other identifiers) and shared resources.

3   The Adaptive Strategy of Docker Container Checkpoint Based on Pre-replication

This paper designs an adaptive pre-replication container checkpoint strategy (APR-CKPOT), taking Docker system as the research platform. Docker's memory page is saved by several rounds of pre-replication. During the checkpoint backup process, in the current process of pre-replication, compared with the result of the previous round of pre-replication, the memory and data will be changed to generate data memory dirty pages, and the dirty pages of memory are saved in the stop-replication phase. The principle of adaptive pre-replication is shown in Fig. 1.

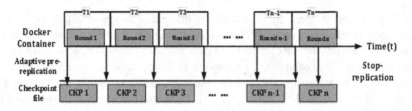

Fig. 1. Schematic of adaptive pre-replication

The process of APR-CKPOT includes the following sections: preparation of checkpoints; pre-replication; stop-replication; saving checkpoint data to files.

(1) At the checkpoint preparation stage, the main job is to obtain information of the target container (the maximum configuration of the container memory, the network adapter of the container process ID, etc.), and the memory file system will be installed.

(2) The pre-replication phase includes multiple rounds of the container checkpoint of pre-replication, it includes three phases. The memory page of Docker will be marked in pre-replication of the first round, and the marked memory pages will be saved to the checkpoint backup file (CKP). The dirty pages generated in the last round of Pre-replication and the resources of container are saved to the CKP files in phase 2 of stop replication. Docker will be frozen firstly, then the kernel object Cgroups and the process hierarchy will be exported in the phase 3.

(3) Stop-replication. All memory pages of the target container are copied at this stage. These memory pages mainly consist of two parts: one part is generated in the last round of pre-replication, and the other part is generated in the pre-replication phase without a modified CKP file, and the resources of the target container will be replicated, including CPU registers, IPC objects, and so on. The downtime in the stop-replication phase is the longest time in the adaptive pre-replication container checkpoint because the target container is frozen until all checkpoint data is obtained to obtain a consistent state of the container runtime.

(4) After the checkpoint pre-replication is completed, the checkpoint memory file system is emptied and the statistical data are collected (such as checkpoint delay time, checkpoint downtime, and checkpoint file size, etc.).

In the backup migration of container checkpoints, a certain container checkpoint overhead is generated. The performance overhead of the container checkpoint includes time overhead and space overhead. The time overhead is affected by space overhead. In the setting of the checkpoint, the factors that cause the increase in time overhead are mainly factors such as checkpoint downtime, checkpoint delay time, and checkpoint restart time.

- Downtime T of the checkpoint, which is the time of freezing containers due to the checkpoint.
- Delay time S of the checkpoint is the duration required to save the checkpoint, including the freeze time of the container and the time to save the checkpoint data.
- The checkpoint restart time is the duration from the checkpoint file read to the recovery container.

Assumed that the size of the container memory configuration is C, the maximum threshold of the number of pre-replication rounds is R_{max}, the maximum threshold value of the dirty page rate is D_{max}, and the minimum threshold of the number of dirty pages is L_{min}, Workload $LOAD_i$, i indicates the number of pre-replication rounds for the specified container checkpoint. The process of the APR-CKPOT strategy is shown in Fig. 2.

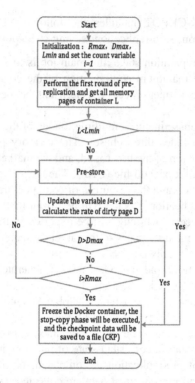

Fig. 2. Flowchart of the strategy

During the phase of pre-replication, when dirty pages are saved, the Docker container is frozen and the container stops running. Therefore, during the execution of pre-replication of the checkpoint, the alternate execution of the container freeze and resume operations has less impact on the service provided by the application in the container. Assume that the pre-replication number is $(R - 1)$, the number of dirty pages in the round i is L_i, the replication time delay of checkpoint is S_i in the round i, the speed of dirty pages is $D(t)$, and t is time, the size of each memory page is P_0, the write speed of the memory is D_{mem}, and the checkpoint downtime is T_i in the round i.

The calculation of L_i is as shown in Formula (1).

$$L_i = \begin{cases} L_0, & \text{if } i = 1 \\ D(t) \times S_{i=1}, & \text{if } i > 1 \end{cases} \tag{1}$$

where S_i involves two parts, one is checkpoint downtime, and the other is the time to write checkpoint data to the checkpoint file (CKP).

Equation (2) is a formula for calculation of S_i.

$$S_i = T_i + \frac{L_i \times P_0}{D_{mem}} \tag{2}$$

Checkpoint downtime T is calculated by Eq. (3):

$$T = \sum_{i=1}^{R} T_i \tag{3}$$

The checkpoint delay S is calculated by Eq. (4):

$$S = \sum_{i=1}^{R} S_i = \sum_{i=1}^{R} \left(T_i + \frac{L_i \times P_0}{D_{men}} \right) \tag{4}$$

Since the velocity produced by the dirty page $D(t)$ is instantaneous, the ratio of dirty pages is used in the formula instead of the rate of dirty pages. The ratio of the dirty page δ_i in the first round is defined as the absolute value of the difference between the dirty page of the previous round and the dirty page of the round, except for the dirty page of the previous round. δ_{min} is the minimum value of the dirty page ratio. There is a one-to-one relationship between δ_{min} and $D_{max}.\delta_i$, the formula is as follows.

$$\delta_i = \frac{|L_i - L_{i-1}|}{L_{i-1}} \tag{5}$$

Finally, the replication ratio of the dirty page of the round i is calculated by the number of dirty pages L_i.

According to the above process, the checkpoint copy time delay is S_i and the dirty page speed $D(t)$, the replicate number of dirty pages L_i of round i is calculated, and then the memory page is calculated according to the size of the memory page P_0 and the memory write speed D_{mem}. The replicate delay time checkpoint of the round i, then the total checkpoint downtime $\sum_{i=1}^{R} T_i$ is calculated by the number of dirty pages and the delay time in each round of pre-replication, and finally the replication ratio of the dirty page in round i is calculated by the number of dirty pages L_i. The number of dirty pages generated during pre-replication and the number of pre-replicated rounds are important factors for increasing the downtime of the checkpoint.

4   Experiment and Evaluation

Based on the Docker Swarm container cluster, the experiments are conducted for verifying the performance of checkpoint. In the design of the prototype system, there mainly include Docker client, Docker Zabbix, Swarm, DockerAPI, Consul Cluster, Mysql Database, Registry, Consul-Template, InfluxDatabase, etc. In the experiments, a Docker Swarm container cluster was built on four servers. The Docker Zabbix performance monitoring module is built in performance monitoring [24]. In the experimental environment, the host system of each node is Ubuntu14.04, and each node deploys Docker containers. Zabbix realizes the acquisition of performance index data such as CPU, memory, network import and export volume by calling python container monitoring script, and stores performance monitoring data in InfluxDatabase database to visualize performance monitoring data. In addition, by dividing the fault alarm level, the fault trigger threshold is set in the warning level. When the load reaches the threshold, the user wants to send the fault alarm email, thereby implementing a fault alarm mechanism based on the performance monitoring of the container cluster.

The checkpoint downtime comparison experiment under the high load and low load conditions of the container was designed, and the checkpoint downtime under different container configurations was compared. Finally, Idle was used as a control group, and Tomcat and Iozone were used as testing application to track and compare the number of dirty pages in memory (Table 1).

Table 1. Experimental environment

Name	CPU	Mem	Number
Physical server	Xeon E7-4820 2 GHz*32	126 G	1↑
Web server	QEMU Virtual CPU (CPU64-rhel6) 4.00 GHz	4 G	3↑
MySQL database server	QEMU Virtual CPU (CPU64-rhel6) 2.00 GHz	4 G	2↑
Message generator	Pentium(R) CPU G640 2.8 GHz	8 G	14↑
Web server Docker management	QEMU Virtual CPU (CPU64-rhel6) 2.00 GHz	4 G	1↑

(1) Evaluation of Checkpoint Downtime

By evaluating the performance of the checkpoint downtime of the APR-CKPOT strategy during checkpoint replication, this section compares the downtime of the different checkpoint methods and then the downtime of the other two checkpoints, SR-CKPOT (stop-replication Docker Container checkpoint), PR-CKPOT (pre-replication Docker container checkpoint) [12] and APR-CKPOT (adaptive pre-replication Docker container checkpoint) in the case of Docker container low load, comparisons of different checkpoint method downtime with APR-CKPOT strategy, they are shown in Fig. 3. The horizontal coordinate represents the memory allocation of the container is 512 MB, 1024 MB, 1536 MB, 2048 MB, 2560 MB, wherein the values of R_max, L_min, δ_min is 8, 2000, 0.1.

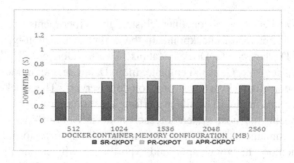

Fig. 3. Comparison of downtime for low load checkpoints

From Fig. 3, the APR-CKPOT checkpoint downtime is reduced by 0.96% to 7.6% compared to SR-CKPOT, and by 42.3% to 47.1% compared to PR-CKPOT, because of the low load Docker. When the container is idle, the load generates less dirty pages. The downtime reduction rate of APR-CKPOT is very low. PR-CKPOT checkpoints have the longest downtime due to several rounds of pre-replication.

In the case of high load of the Docker container, the difference between the three checkpoint methods in the downtime is compared. As can be seen from Fig. 4, the PR-CKPOT checkpoint downtime is the longest because the checkpoint in each round of pre-replication Downtime is a waste of time. The APR-CKPOT checkpoint downtime was reduced by 12.3% to 31.85% compared to SR-CKPOT, and by 20.2% to 77.2% compared to PR-CKPOT. Because Docker container operations under high load are IO-intensive tests, APR-CKPOT has a high reduction in container checkpoint downtime due to the large amount of memory dirty pages generated by Linux kernel compilation.

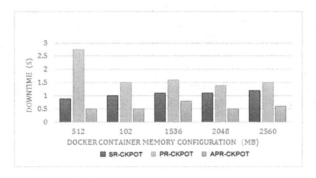

Fig. 4. Comparison of downtime for high load checkpoints

As can be seen from the above two comparison charts, the checkpoint delay of APR-CKPOT is medium compared to PR-CKPOT and SR-CKPOT, because some memory pages of the Docker container are copied multiple times, but, compared with the two checkpoint methods of PR-CKPOT and SR-CKPOT, the APR-CKPOT container checkpoint strategy downtime is relatively low as the container memory configuration increases with different Docker container loads.

(2) Evaluation of Dirty Page Number
Trace of dirty pages in container memory is a key issue in implementing adaptive pre-replication container checkpoints. This section verifies the effectiveness of reducing container checkpoint downtime by tracking the number of dirty pages generated by the container's pre-replication strategy. The results of the tracking of the number of dirty pages based on different test benchmarks are shown in Fig. 5.

As can be seen from Fig. 5, the difference in the number of dirty pages between Iozone and Tomcat is relatively large, followed by Idle. This is because the memory pages of Iozone and tomcat are often modified, so the number of dirty pages generated is relatively large. Although Iozone is an IO-intensive benchmark, its memory pages are always modified. Since memory pages are modified less frequently than Tomcat,

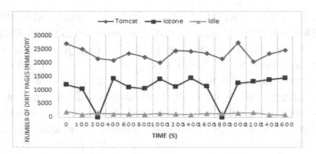

Fig. 5. Comparison of dirty page number

the number of dirty pages generated by Iozone is relatively small. Through the tracking comparison experiment on the number of dirty pages, the memory-intensive benchmark test generates a large number of dirty pages due to frequent modification of the memory page, which increases the downtime of the checkpoint, so It is necessary to stop the pre-replication and go to the execution of the stop-replication phase. This experiment mainly proves that when the number of dirty pages in the pre-replication phase is high or the rate of dirty page generation is high, in the APR-CKPOT strategy, the execution of the stop-replication phase improves the recovery efficiency of the container checkpoint.

5   Conclusions

This paper proposes an adaptive management strategy for container checkpoints. The main contributions of this paper includes: (1) Establishing a checkpoint process, stopping the restart model, implementing process freeze before checkpoint pre-replication, maintaining the consistency of the container running process; (2) Proposing an adaptive container checkpoint strategy based on pre-replication (APR-CKPOT), and triggering the checkpoint pre-replication mechanism to determine and copy the number of rounds adaptively based on the container load workload, thereby checkpoint downtime will be reduced and checkpoint recovery efficiency will be improved. In the future research, facing a larger and more complex load scenario, on the basis of reducing the checkpoint downtime, the real-time migration strategy in the event of a Docker container failure will be studied, so that the container failure recovery can be more rapid.

Acknowledgements. This work is supported by the Natural Science Foundation of China (No. 61762008), the Natural Science Foundation Project of Guangxi (No. 2017GXNSFAA 198141), the Key R&D project of Guangxi (No. AB17195014).

References

1. James, T.: The Docker Book: containerization is the new virtualization, pp. 10–20 (2014). http://www.dockerbook.com/. Accessed 22 Apr 2015
2. Siozios, K., Soudris, D., Hübner, M.: A framework for supporting adaptive fault-tolerant solutions. ACM Trans. Embed. Comput. Syst. **13**(5s), 1–22 (2014)
3. Bernstein, D.: Containers and cloud: from LXC to Docker to Kubernetes. Cloud Comput. **1** (3), 81–84 (2015)
4. Yang, C.T., Liu, J.C., Hsu, C.H., et al.: On improvement of cloud virtual machine availability with virtualization fault tolerance mechanism. In: IEEE Third International Conference on Cloud Computing Technology and Science, pp. 122–129. IEEE (2013)
5. Lillibridge, M., Kave, E., Deepavali, B.: Improving restore speed for backup systems that use inline chunk-based deduplication. In: Proceedings of the 11th USENIX Conference on File and Storage Technologies, pp. 183–197. USENIX Conference (2013)
6. Pradhan, S., Gokhale, A., Otte, W.R., et al.: Real-time fault tolerant deployment and configuration framework for cyber physical systems. ACM SIGBED Rev. **10**(2), 32 (2013)
7. LXC-checkpoint [EB/OL]. http://lxc.sourceforge.net/man/lxc-checkpoint.html
8. Burns, B., Grant, B., Oppenheimer, D., et al.: Borg, Omega, and Kubernetes. Queue **14**(1), 10–34 (2016)
9. LXC-checkpoint. http://lxc.sourceforge.net/man/lxc-checkpoint.html. Accessed 22 Apr 2015
10. Liu, Q., Jung, C., Lee, D., et al.: Compiler-directed lightweight checkpointing for fine-grained guaranteed soft error recovery. In: Proceedings of the International Conference for High Performance Computing, Networking, Storage and Analysis, pp. 228–239 (2017)
11. Lin, J.C., Leu, F.Y., Chen, Y.P.: Analyzing job completion reliability and job energy consumption for a heterogeneous MapReduce cluster under different intermediate-data replication policies. J. Supercomput. **71**(5), 1657–1677 (2015)
12. Dinh, T., Barkataki, S.: Distributed container: a design pattern for fault tolerance and high-speed data exchange. ACM SIGAda Ada Lett. **29**(3), 115–118 (2009)
13. Shao, Y., Zhu, X., Bao, W., et al.: CHIME: a checkpoint-based approach to improving the performance of shared clusters. In: International Conference on Parallel and Distributed Systems, pp. 1007–1014. IEEE (2017)
14. Xu, F., Liu, F.M., Liu, L.H., Jin, H., Li, B., Li, B.C.: iAware: making live migration of virtual machines interference-aware in the cloud. IEEE Trans. Comput. **63**(12), 3012–3025 (2014)
15. Piao, G.Y., Oh, Y.G., Sung, B., Park, C.: Efficient pre-replication live migration with memory compaction and adaptive vm downtime control. In: Proceedings of IEEE 4th International Conference on Big Data and Cloud Computing, pp. 85–90. IEEE (2014)
16. Louati, T., Abbes, H., Cérin, C., et al.: LXCloud-CR: towards LinuX containers distributed hash table based checkpoint-restart. J. Parallel Distrib. Comput. **12**(3), 12–16 (2017)
17. Beloglazov, A., Buyya, R.: OpenStack Neat: a framework for dynamic and energy-efficient consolidation of virtual machines in OpenStack clouds. Concurr. Comput. Pract. Exp. **27**(5), 1310–1333 (2015)
18. Yamato, Y., Katsuragi, S., Nagao, S., et al.: Software maintenance evaluation of agile software development method based on OpenStack. IEICE Trans. Inf. Syst. **E98.D**(7), 1377–1380 (2015)
19. Regola, N., Ducom, J.C.: Recommendations for virtualization technologies in high performance computing. In: Proceedings of 2010 IEEE Second International Conference on Cloud Computing Technology and Science, pp. 409–416. IEEE (2010)

20. Li, C., Xi, S., Lu, C., et al.: Prioritizing soft real-time network traffic in virtualized hosts based on Xen. In: IEEE Real-Time and Embedded Technology and Applications Symposium, pp. 145–156. IEEE (2015)
21. Chi, X., Liu, B., Niu, Q., et al.: Web load balance and cache optimization design based Nginx under high-concurrency environment. In: Third International Conference on Digital Manufacturing and Automation, pp. 1029–1032. IEEE (2012)

Cloud Enabled *e*-Glossary System: A Smart Campus Perspective

Musaddiq Majid Khan Al-Nadwi[1], Nadia Refat[1], Nafees Zaman[3],
Md Arafatur Rahman[1,2(✉)], Md Zakirul Alam Bhuiyan[4],
and Ramdan Bin Razali[1]

[1] University Malaysia Pahang, 26300 Kuantan, Malaysia
{musaddiq,arafatur,ramdan}@ump.edu.my,
atoshi.refat@gmail.com
[2] IBM, Center of Excellence, UMP, Gambang, Malaysia
[3] International Islamic University Malaysia, 53100 Selangor, Malaysia
zamannafees@gmail.com
[4] Department of Computer and Information Sciences, Fordham University,
New York, NY, USA
mbhuiyan3@fordham.edu

Abstract. Smart campus is a recent idea in the development of information and communication technology, being a combination of cloud computing, Internet of Things (IoT) and other emerging technologies. This paper demonstrates the result of our research efforts using IoT technology for the development of a smart campus, which also assures the improvement of vocabulary knowledge of the students. Our proposed system is mainly based on *e-learning* which provides definition of words and how to use that word in a sentence. However, students can take part in it and add more vocabularies in this glossary system under supervision through cloud computing. The quantitative research method is applied to validate the proposed system that provides the positive outcome. Therefore, it is an important research finding for vocabulary learning that can contribute to the building of smart campus exploiting the *e*-learning technologies.

Keywords: Cloud computing · IoT · e-Learning · Vocabulary learning

1 Introduction

Nowadays web-based learning system has winged a large paradigm in educational area which follows the revolutionary changes from instructional design to the implementation of the learning materials in exploiting different technologies. One of the most emerging and successful technologies applied in these days is e-learning Due to the expectation of learners to be made known to better learning technologies, many educational institutions are concentrating on the association of e-learning successfully [1]. This type of learning ultimately ends up with a good result and makes a campus from ordinary to a smart campus. However, there are few drawbacks of this learning system. One of the major problems is limitations of storage and accessibility. Moreover, many

© Springer Nature Switzerland AG 2018
G. Wang et al. (Eds.): SpaCCS 2018, LNCS 11342, pp. 251–260, 2018.
https://doi.org/10.1007/978-3-030-05345-1_21

educational institutions do not have enough funding to invest in this learning process to buy extra equipment. All these issues can be resolved through cloud computing. Cloud based learning process has lot of advantages because of its high scalability, high availability and less expensive. Our proposed system, E-glossary is the concept of collaborating cloud computing with e-learning in perspective of a smart campus.

This section further focuses on some aspects related to the present research such as cloud computing, e-learning and smart campus. Then it highlights the design of the proposed system, research method and findings of the research work. It finally draws discussion and conclusion in the end.

1.1 Cloud Computing

Various researchers have defined cloud computing differently. Some researchers believe cloud is an advancement of various computing resources and technologies at different times, combined to deliver new potentials through high speed internetworks. Other researchers think that cloud computing is a new standard with new technologies such as virtualisation [2]. Explanations have also been projected based on scalability and elasticity, ability to be carried and accessed in real time and cost reflections. The term cloud computing describes a type of parallel and distributed system consisting of a collection of inter-connected and virtualized computers that are vigorously provisioned and offered as one or more unified computing resource(s) based on facility level arrangements established through negotiations between the service provider and consumers [3].

1.2 E-Learning

e-Learning is learning to exploit electronic technologies to access educational curriculum outside of a traditional learning system. Most importantly, it denotes to a course, learning tools carried out entirely online. There are many terms used to describe learning that is delivered online, via the internet, ranging from distance education, to computerized electronic learning, online learning, internet learning and many others. e-learning has been authenticated to be a successful process of education system. It normally offers services in Intranet or Internet for a specified range of users. It is created by data centre and one or some servers [4].

1.3 Smart Campus

The word "smart" is used to describe the ability of an object in considering intelligence that has been implanted in it. For instance, a smart phone means that phone is capable of supporting many intellectual activities through various services provided. The concept of the word "smart" is not only limited to a single instance rather it contains many aspects of everyday life of human being. Smart campus is one of these aspects. This is the idea of being a combination of cloud computing, IoT (Internet of Things) and other emerging technologies. The modern definition of smart campus has not been conical to a mass understanding. Many researchers, who have built smart campus, convey the definition based on different approaches. If grouped, there are three approaches used to describe smart campus namely: technology driven, smart city concept adaption and based on the development of an organisation or business process [5].

The goal of the study is to make a smart campus through collaborating e-learning and cloud computing by our glossary system. It will not only increase the vocab knowledge of a learner but also ease the process of learning. One of the main benefits of cloud computing is collaboration efficiency. Collaboration in a cloud environment gives a business the ability to communicate and share more easily outside of the traditional methods. If someone is set up for a certain task across different or distant locations, he/she could use cloud computing to give third parties access to the same files. In our case, user can learn vocabularies from anywhere and can also help to update the library.

2   Design of the Proposed System

The blueprint shown in the Fig. 1, illustrates how cloud computing enabled environment can be implemented into e-learning system. This application is a glossary system made for vocabulary learning. In this learning system, students will not only know the meaning of the words but also know how to use a word in a sentence. However, one may ask what the difference between e-glossary and other existing relative applications is. To answer this question, we will discuss the concept of Cloud Computing.

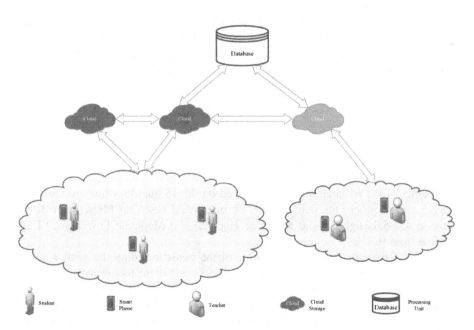

Fig. 1. Proposed system of the e-glossary system exploiting cloud computing

Cloud Computing, the practice of using a network of remote servers hosted on the Internet to store, manage, and process data, rather than a local server or a personal computer. One of the main benefits of cloud computing is self service provisioning. That means end users can spin up compute resources for almost any type of workload on demand. This is the unique thing of this e-Glossary system which differentiates it from others.

Suppose, a student wants to know a meaning of a word but he/she could not find the word into the glossary. At that moment he/she could contact with teachers through the system to know the meaning. Whoever amongst the teachers is online, could reply to the student. In another scenario, a student knows meaning of a certain word that is not included in the glossary system. Generally, glossary system has limitations of words and cannot be renovated by end users. But in this case, we will give end users this opportunity to add more vocabularies into this glossary. Student can send that word by his device which will go through cloud to the teacher. Each of words sent by students for adding must be supervised by any of the teachers. After supervision, teacher will add the vocab into the dictionary if that is legit. Unlikely to other applications, this learning technique will not only motivate learners but also will help to reduce the monotony and make things interesting. In this study, we consider Arabic language to improve Arabic vocabulary as a scope of the research.

3   Research Method

In this study, we used a quantitative research method by using a survey which was based on five criteria (attitude regarding the tool, benefit, motivational nature of the tool, importance technology for learning vocabulary and importance of e-learning technology for building the smart campus). To conduct the research, we randomly selected 50 participants from faculty of Islamic revealed knowledge, Islamic University Malaysia. There were 8 females and 42 males as the sample which is selected randomly.

4   Finding of the Research

The finding of the research questions is based on the 15 questions that are classified under 5 criteria where the outcome can be interpreted based on Mean Score Interpretation 4.1–5.0 High 3.1–4.0 Moderate High 2.1–3.0 Moderate Low 1.0-2.0 Low Adapted from [6, 7].

Table 1 represents the survey outcome of the items including the gender differences. It is illustrated that the attitude regarding the using of the tool (criteria 1) has got more likings of the students as the mean for both male (M = 4.09, SD = .90) and female (M = 4.25, SD = .25) are high than the other items under these criteria. In the benefit of the tool (criteria 2) females have scaled more in 2 items (exercises of the tool and knowledge acquisition) (M = 4.25, SD = .46; M = 4.37, SD = .70). In motivational nature of the tool there is also remarkable outcome of the females as they pointed in the 3 items higher than males (M = 4.62, SD = .51; M = 4.00, SD = .00; M = 4.25, SD = .75). It is significantly visible that in importance of e-learning vocabulary technology is highly demanding for building up smart campus as both males and females gave high consent to this item (male M = 4.15, SD = .93; female M = 4.25, SD = .74).

Table 1. Item based result of the Survey questions

Items	Criteria	Male		Female	
		Mean	SD	Mean	SD
1. Enjoy working with this tool	Attitude	3.95	.76	3.87	.83
2. Learning will be useful to me using the tool		4.09	.90	4.25	.46
4. The design of the tool is related to my expectations to enhance the vocabulary knowledge of any language		3.97	.84	3.75	.70
5. It is flexible in use	Benefit	3.88	.91	3.87	.83
6. The exercises included in the tool are good		3.78	.81	4.25	.46
7. I will benefit from the knowledge I acquired		3.85	.75	4.37	.70
8. I am not disappointed with this design of the tool	Motivational	3.88	.81	4.62	.51
9. I get enough feedback that makes me feel satisfied with the tool		3.78	.91	4.00	.00
10. The instructional design of the tool is motivational		3.75	.75	4.25	.70
3. The glossary tool is effective for the smart campus built up	Importance of vocabulary	3.88	.83	4.12	.64
12. It is highly important to learn vocabulary in order to communicate with others		3.69	.69	4.37	.74
14. As vocabulary gets strong, language skill is developed automatically		3.80	.80	4.00	.92
11. E-learning system is really needed to make the educational system more effective	*e*-learning technology	3.90	.95	3.87	.83
13. E-learning is important for every steps of classroom as well		3.97	.71	4.50	.53
15. Smart campus building is highly demanding issue in current era of technology-based learning		4.15	.93	4.25	.74

In the following, the total descriptive result of the survey is represented:

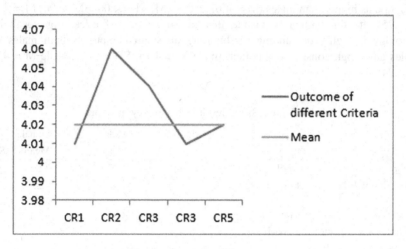

Fig. 2. Outcome of the survey

In the above Fig. 2, it is demonstrated that all students have liked the design of the tool as well as its importance for building smart campus. The figure illustrates that in attitude on the tool (criteria 1) has mean M = 4.01, SD = .17 (high); benefit of the tool (criteria 2) M = 4.06, SD = .31 (high); motivational nature of the tool (criteria 3) M = 4.04, SD = .33 (high); importance of the tool for learning vocabulary (criteria 4) M = 4.01, SD = .24 (high); importance of e- learning technology for building smart campus (criteria 5) M = 4.02, SD = .28 (high).

We can compare our results with few other reference studies that have also focused on e-vocabulary learning using web based technology. To compare, we only focused on the important criteria (attitude, benefit and motivational nature of the tool) and on those studies that have either or both focused the mentioned criteria. Therefore, the existing 1 [8], 2 [9], and 3 [10] have taken as concern to compare the outcome of the present study.

The first criteria we can focus on the attitude of the students on the usage of the e-vocabulary learning tool. In the present study, it is observed that the total outcome of the attitude is high. In the second and third important criteria (i.e., benefit and motivation) are also high compared to other studies.

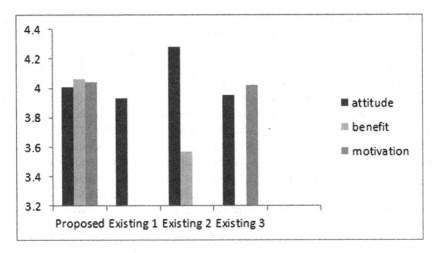

Fig. 3. Comparison of the criteria-based outcome to other studies

In the above Fig. 3, it is observed that the present study (attitude) is higher (M = 4.01) compared to other reference studies (i.e., existing study 1 and 3 got the outcome respectively M = 3.93 and M = 3.57) but lower than the existing 2 (M = 4.28). In the second criteria, benefit of the vocabulary learning system using web based technology the present research work gets higher scale (M = 4.06) than the existing work 2 (M = 3.57). Third criteria is based on the motivational nature of the technology used to learn vocabulary where the present work also received a higher scale of mean (M = 4.04) than the reference existing study 3 (M = 4.02).

5   Discussion

The section deals with the outcome of the present work and validity of the work in the light of the recent researcher's cloud system for smart campus building.

The findings of the survey are based on the 5 criteria but most important 3 criteria are focused where the first criterion is based on the attitude of the students on tool that demonstrates that positive outcome. All the students have a positive perception regarding the tool to learn vocabulary. Vocabulary learning using cloud computing technology is new and interesting to them and the design of the tool is also effective to enhance the knowledge of glossary. The individual gender based outcome is high on the two important item that focused on the usefulness of the tool to learn vocabulary received thus respectively male and female M = 4.09 and M = 4.25 while the mean is on this criterion M = 4.01. To consider this outcome based on the research validity, is high and even more the outcome of the present study is higher than one of the reference studies that also used web based technology to learn vocabulary [8]. Other researchers also suggested that educational institutions that works for the students enhancement of knowledge need to consider technology based language learning system in their curriculum [11].

The second criterion is focused on the benefit of the tool benefit of the tool that reveals the highly effective for knowledge enhancing tool for glossary system. Exploiting the modern cloud enabled technology, the tool helped to reach every student and facilitate the leaning process of vocabulary whenever they need to search new words. Therefore, the mean of survey regarding the question of benefit of the tool exposed M = 4.06 and in comparison with other tool it is though bit lower M = 4.28 [9]. It is being supported in different studies that technological resources are useful in improving ELLs reading ability, specifically vocabulary knowledge [12, 13].

The third criterion important in this present work is the motivational nature of the tool which also showed that the tool is helpful to attaining attentions and satisfaction of the learners which ultimately motivate towards the usage of the proposed system. The outcome of this motivational nature students remarked also satisfactory results i.e., M = 4.04 which is higher than the reference or existing technology based vocabulary system M = 4.02 [10] because of the innovative nature of the system. Researchers recently found that cloud system is helpful for learning as it motivates the students in a large scale which is found in few studies as well [14–16].

All these above three criteria is highlighted in the discussion is due to focus on the importance of cloud enabled system for building smart campus through helping the education as specifically in language learning system in modern era. Cloud enabled system is changing the performance of the actual e-learning tools or Medias like wireless connections, security (RFID authentication) and dimension of resources (cloud systems). Moreover, IoT smart campus can provide the adapted e-learning raised area that are adapted to the e-students' needs independently. Besides, IoT smart campus facilitates the integration of the e-citizens into the e-community as it increases the e-learner involvement in the process of the learning as well as other sectors [17–26]. As a consequent, introducing IoT on the proposed system will be direction of this research area.

6 Conclusion

Cloud enabled technology is an emerging sector that has brought revolutionary changes in the whole technology-based learning system. From the educational point of view, technology is not only helping to improve learning capacity of the students but also it reduced the effort to the process of learning. Smart campus is the one of the incarnations of blessing to this kind of technology that focuses on the flexible, motivational and effective learning system. The present work therefore, been attempted to influence on the learning particularly on vocabulary learning through designing a tool that has been planned under the frame work of cloud computing. The findings of the survey to know the effectiveness of the designed tool support the positive impact of the proposed system. Thus, it is helpful to increase the effectiveness on technology enhanced learning process.

Acknowledgments. This paper is partially supported by RDU grant "RDU1703232", funded by University Malaysia Pahang.

References

1. Masud, M.A.H., Huang, X.: An e-learning system architecture based on cloud computing. System **10**(11), 255–259 (2012)
2. Ewuzie, I., Usoro, A.: Exploration of cloud computing adoption for e-learning in higher education. Paper presented at the 2012 Second Symposium on Network Cloud Computing and Applications (2012)
3. Buyya, R., Yeo, C.S., Venugopal, S., Broberg, J., Brandic, I.: Cloud computing and emerging IT platforms: vision, hype, and reality for delivering computing as the 5th utility. Future Gener. Comput. Syst. **25**(6), 599–616 (2009)
4. He, Z., Yue, J.: Integrating e-learning system based on cloud computing. Paper presented at the 2012 IEEE International Conference on Granular Computing (GrC) (2012)
5. Muhamad, W., Kurniawan, N.B., Yazid, S.: Smart campus features, technologies, and applications: a systematic literature review. Paper presented at the 2017 International Conference on Information Technology Systems and Innovation (ICITSI) (2017)
6. Fabil, N.: Aplikasi teknik graph view dalam pemvisualan maklumat Sanad domain Ilmu Hadis (application of graph view techniques for visualizing information of Sanad in domain science of Hadith). Unpublished Ph.D. dissertation, Universiti Kebangsaan Malaysia, Bangi (2009)
7. Ismail, Z.: Penilaian kemahiran bertutur bahasa Arab dalam kurikulum bahasa Arab komunikasi di Sekolah Menengah Kebangsaan Agama. Unpublished Ph.D. Universiti Kebangsaan Malaysia, Bangi (2008)
8. Sahrir, M.S., Yusri, G.: Online vocabulary games for teaching and learning Arabic. GEMA Online® J. Lang. Stud. **12**(3), 249–263 (2012)
9. Suwantarathip, O., Orawiwatnakul, W.: Using mobile-assisted exercises to support students' vocabulary skill development. Turk. Online J. Educ. Technol. TOJET **14**(1), 163–171 (2015)
10. Ali, Z., Mukundan, J., Baki, R., Ayub, A.F.M.: Second language learners' attitudes towards the methods of learning vocabulary. Engl. Lang. Teach. **5**(4), 24–36 (2012)
11. Ghavifekr, S., Razak, A.Z.A., Ghani, M.F.A., Ran, N.Y., Meixi, Y., Tengyue, Z.: ICT integration in education: incorporation for teaching & learning improvement. Malays. Online J. Educ. Technol. **2**(2), 24–45 (2014)
12. Mays, L.: The cultural divide of discourse: Understanding how English-language learners' primary discourse influences acquisition of literacy. Read. Teach. **61**(5), 415–418 (2008)
13. Riasati, M.J., Allahyar, N., Tan, K.-E.: Technology in language education: benefits and barriers. J. Educ. Pract. **3**(5), 25–30 (2012)
14. Bayani, M., Leiton, K., Loaiza, M.: Internet of things (IoT) advantages on e-learning in the smart cities. Int. J. Dev. Res. **7**(12), 17747–17753 (2017)
15. Bululukova, D., Tabakovic, M., Wahl, H.: Smart cities education as mobility, energy & ICT hub. Paper presented at the 2016 5th International Conference on Smart Cities and Green ICT Systems (SMARTGREENS) (2016)
16. Soliman, M., Elsaadany, A.: Smart immersive education for smart cities: with support via intelligent pedagogical agents. Paper presented at the 2016 39th International Convention on Information and Communication Technology, Electronics and Microelectronics (MIPRO) (2016)
17. Bhuiyan, Z.A., Wang, G., Wang, T., Rahman, A., Wu, J.: Content-centric event-insensitive big data reduction in internet of things. In: 2017 IEEE Global Communications Conference GLOBECOM 2017—Proceedings, vol. 2018, pp. 1–6 (2018)

18. Rahman, M.A., Ali, J., Kabir, M.N., Azad, S.: A performance investigation on IoT enabled intra-vehicular wireless sensor networks. Int. J. Automot. Mech. Eng. **14**(1), 3970–3984 (2017)
19. Wang, M.Z.A., Bhuiyan, G., Wang, M.A., Rahman, J., Cao, J.: Big data reduction for a smart city's critical infrastructural health monitoring. IEEE Commun. Mag. **56**(3), 128–133 (2018)
20. Bhuiyan, Md.Z.A., Zaman, M., Wang, G., Wang, T., Rahman, Md.A., Tao, H.: Protected bidding against compromised information injection in IoT-based smart grid. In: The 2nd EAI International Conference on Smart Grid and Internet of Things (SGIoT 2018), Niagara Falls, Canada, July 11–13 (2018)
21. Rahman, Md.A., Kabir, M.N., Azad, S., Ali, J.: On mitigating hop-to-hop congestion problem in IoT enabled intra-vehicular communication. In: The IEEE International Conference on Software Engineering & Computer Systems, Kuantan, August 19–21 (2015)
22. Luo, M.Z.A., Bhuiyan, G., Wang, M.A., Rahman, J., Atiquzzaman, M.: PrivacyProtector: privacy-protected patient data collection in IoT-based healthcare systems. IEEE Commun. Mag. **56**(2), 163–168 (2018)
23. Cacciapuoti, A.S., Caleffi, M., Paura, L., Rahman, Md.A.: Link quality estimators for multi-hop mesh network. In: Euro Med Telco Conference (EMTC), Italy (2014)
24. Rahman, Md.A., Azad, Md.S., Anwar, F.: Integrating multiple metrics to improve the performance of a routing protocol over wireless mesh network. In: Proceedings of International Conference on Signal Processing Systems (ICSPS 2009), Singapore, pp. 784–787 (2009)
25. Rahman, Md.A: Design of wireless sensor network for intra-vehicular communications. In: Mellouk, A., Fowler, S., Hoceini, S., Daachi, B. (eds.) WWIC 2014. LNCS, vol. 8458, pp. 29–40. Springer, Cham (2014). https://doi.org/10.1007/978-3-319-13174-0_3
26. Rahman, Md.A, Mezhuyev, V., Bhuiyan, M.Z.A., Sadat, S.M.N., Zakaria, S.A.B., Refat, N.: Reliable decision making of accepting friend request on online social networks. IEEE Access. **6**, 9484–9491 (2018)

A Dynamic Integrity Transitivity Model for the Cloud

Rongyu He[1](✉), Haonan Sun[1], and Yong Zhang[2]

[1] Zhengzhou Information Science and Technology Institute,
Zhengzhou 450001, China
he_reongyu@hotmail.com
[2] ATR Key Laboratory of National Defense Technology, Shenzhen University,
Shenzhen 518000, China

Abstract. Utilizing Trusted computing technology to enhance the security of Cloud has become a hot research, and a large number of solutions have been proposed in recent years. However, all of these solutions are focused on separating one Virtual Machine (VM) from others, and it is too strict for practical scenario as it forbids the communication between VMs. In this paper we propose a trust transitive model, named Dynamic Integrity Measurement Model (DIMM), for two VMs communication, and then an implementation of DIMM prototype is given. When dataflow occurs between two VMs, the DIMM will keep the trustworthiness of a system by ensuring the integrity of VMs and the delivered message. We also demonstrate the effectiveness of the model by experiments.

Keywords: Cloud computing · Trust chain · Dynamic integrity
TPM · Virtualization

1 Introduction

Cloud computing, or Cloud, is seen as a trend in the IT service model, and it is widely penetrated into the IT domain, both in industrial and commercial areas. It delivers massively scalable computing resources as a service through the Internet, and allows its resources to be shared among a vast number of consumers. The basic unit of the delivered computing resource is Virtual Machine (VM) which runs user's dedicated operation system and applications. As Cloud adopted grows rapidly, security issues have attracted more attention in industry, and prevents organizations moving their datacenter to cloud. The resource shared architecture, inherent to Cloud, raises more threats in security and privacy. The Cloud user has no right to decide who shares the hardware with him, as well as no knowledge to know the information about the shared users. The user is possibly hosted on a cloud platform concurrently with some distrusted or even malicious users, so his/her data stored and processed in the Cloud will be exposed to the risk of being tampered or eavesdropped.

Therefore, VMs on the Cloud require a well-defined security mechanism to ensure its integrity and privacy. Utilizing the Trusted Computing technology, introduced and developed by the Trusted Computing Group (TCG) [1], to provide security solution for

© Springer Nature Switzerland AG 2018
G. Wang et al. (Eds.): SpaCCS 2018, LNCS 11342, pp. 261–271, 2018.
https://doi.org/10.1007/978-3-030-05345-1_22

cloud computing has become a hot research in cloud security domain, and many solutions were proposed by numerous of researchers [5–7, 16–18]. By virtualizing the TPM, a virtual TPM (vTPM) was built, which provides some hardware TPM functionalities in software. Each VM launched on Cloud associates with a unique vTPM and benefits from the vTPM by storing its launch measurements in vTPM.

However, most of these solutions were focused on enhance the isolation mechanism, and separating the VM from others on the host. But it is too strict for practical scenario as it doesn't consider communication between VMs. When an organization migrates its datacenter to cloud, it will rent multiple VMs to accommodate different applications, and chains or configures these applications to cooperation relation for a service. Then the communication between VMs appears. Sometimes a malicious user can attack the communication, and compromise the VM by injecting shellcode into communication.

In this paper we propose a Dynamic Integrity Measurement Model (DIMM) for VMs' communication. The DIMM can guarantee the integrity of VM at tuntime. The remainder of this paper is organized as follows. In Sect. 2 we give an overview of the DIMM firstly, then the trust transitive of the DIMM is described in detail in Sects. 3 and 4 evaluates our DIMM model in the usability and effectiveness. Section 5 covers related work on integrity model and Cloud platform security, and the conclusion is given in Sect. 6.

2 Dynamic Integrity Measurement Model (DIMM)

2.1 Overview

In a Cloud, the communication between the VMs is inevitable. For example, an enterprise migrates its IT resources to a public Cloud, it will deploy its Web server, Database server and Email server in different VMs on one or different hosts of a cloud provider, as Fig. 1 shown. So these servers need to work together to complete the enterprise service. For example, the Web server will access Database server to verifying the authenticity of a login user, the CRM system will send product information to the critical customer through Email server, etc. Therefore, VMs need communication each other. A malicious user can attack VMs by injecting spyware or Trojans into the traffics, and then the malware or viruses may be spread to all VMs through the communication, and the integrity of VMs, even the Cloud, will be compromised.

Trusted computing is one effective method for privacy and integrity protection, and many of cloud security schemes are employed the Trusted computing technology. However, most of them considered VMs as an independent component, and not considered the communication between VMs.

Literature [13] proposed a Tree-like Trust Chain for VM (TTCVM) model which builds the user's trust into cloud platform. In this paper, we will build trust into the VMs communication, and propose a Dynamic Integrity Measurement Model (DIMM) for virtual machines. The DIMM model is responsible for verifying all the messages interacted between the VMs, according to the integrity and confidentiality.

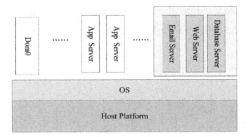

Fig. 1. An example for cloud service

2.2 The TTCVM Model and µTPM

The TTCVM model introduced in [13] is depicted in Fig. 2. The trust of a user VM is coming from two difference trust sources, one is the physical TPM on the host, and the other is the user.

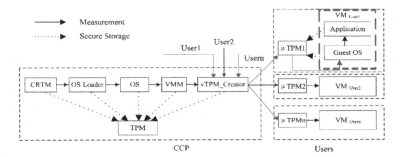

Fig. 2. The tree-like trust chain model

In the TTCVM model, a user-specific virtual TPM, labeled as µTPM, is created for the user. The µTPM is a user configurable security component which providing trust service for the associated VM. It stores the user's security policies for his VM, and provides the TPM service according to the user's security settings. So a user VM has two trust anchor, the Cloud provider (physical TPM on the host) and the user. When a user initiates his VM, the two trust are merged into the µTPM, and then forward the merged trust to the user's VM. This can be considered as that the user gets the right of control of his VM in term of security.

2.3 The Structure of DIMM

Building trust into the communication of two VMs is that, the message source is trusted and the message itself is verifiable for its integrity and confidentiality. So a Dynamic Integrity Measurement Model (DIMM) is designed. The overview of the DIMM is shown in Fig. 3. In the model, we introduce a secure module, named Input Authentication

Module for VMs (IAMV), into the cloud underlying infrastructure. The IAMV is responsible for verifying the integrity of the data flow between two VMs.

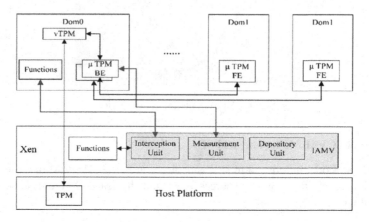

Fig. 3. The DIMM infrastructure

The Cloud platform will provide a virtual TPM for each guest VM by the TPM virtualization technology. The trustworthy of the Cloud platform is guaranteed by the trust chain defined in [13], the trust is transferred from the physical hardware TPM to the VMM according to the TCG specifications, then it is transferred to guest VM through the μTPM, where the user's security policies is loaded and stored. Because the μTPM is a user-specified component, the processes running in the VM as well as the VM itself are trusted. If the received data is coming from a trusted source and its integrity is intact, we say that the VM remain trust at runtime according to the Non-interference theory [4].

2.4   The Function of IAMV

The IAMV module is composed of three units logically, they are the Depository Unit (DU), the Interception Unit (IU) and the Measurement Unit (MU).

2.4.1   Depository Unit

The Depository Unit (DU) is a database storing the information about the virtual machines. It is created when the IAMV is initiated, and located in privilege ring0. When a virtual machine is mounted, the IU will intercept the provisioning information and register them in the DU. The provisioning information includes owner of the VM, the bound μTPM, the creation time and others. The DU is a protected unit which can only be accessed and modified by the IU. When the system is powered down, the information stored in the DU will be volatized.

2.4.2   Interception Unit

The Interception Unit (IU) is the interface of the IAMV. It monitors the communication between two VMs, and transparently intercepts the data flows. The communication is considered as some cross-border instructions, i.e., the instructions that access the memories outside the virtual machine. Only the two VMs is trusted and belong to the same owner, the communication between them can be permitted, and the others will be blocked immediately.

2.4.3   Measurement Unit

The Measurement Unit (MU) is the core component in the IAMV. It is responsible for validating the integrity of the source VM and measuring the integrity the exchanged data. The MU validates the integrity of the source VM through remote attestation, and measures the output data by the μTPM which is bound to the destination VM.

3   The Trust Chain and Security Analysis

In the TTCVM, a trust chain based on TPM is established from the physical TPM (tamper-resistant device) to the Xen Hypervisor. It provides trust service for all user, and is called as public trust chain. A μTPM is created in the Hypervisor before a guest VM is launched. The μTPM is a user-specific trust component where the physical TPM trust and user trust are merged. Then a trust chain is established from the μTPM to boot loader (kernel), to OS of the guest VM, to the user application. It provides trust service for a specified user, and is called as private trust chain. As Fig. 4 shown, the public trust chain concatenates one private trust chain forming a TPM-User trust chain, which stems from TPM, combines the user's policies by μTPM, to the user VM. Every VM has a TPM-User trust chain in the TTCVM, and it guarantees that a user VM compliance with the security policies of underlying host as well as user itself.

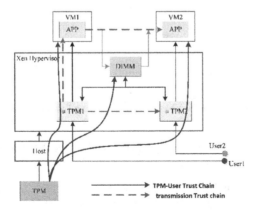

Fig. 4. The trust chain for cloud platform

However, a TPM-User trust chain is a static trust for the user or guest VM, since the malware can invade a VM while it interacts with outside. Therefore, it is necessary to measure the integrity of VMs and input data. So a transmission trust chain is established, shown in Fig. 4, which is extended from a trusted VM, controlled by the DIMM module, up to the destination VM alone the dataflow. A formal description of the transmission trust chain for Fig. 4 is

$$\mu TPM_2 \xleftarrow{\;PKI\;} \mu TPM_1 \xrightarrow{\;M/V\;} VM_1 \xrightarrow{\;Integrity\;} DIMM \xrightarrow[\mu TPM_2]{\;user-policy\;} VM_2$$

Assume VM_1 and VM_2 belong to one organization, each VM has been issued a certification by the organization, and the VM stores the certification in its μTPM when it is launched. When a dataflow from VM_1 to VM_2 is occurred, the μTPM_2 validates the authenticity of μTPM_1 firstly by the certification, then the μTPM_1 is considered as the anchor of trust for the dataflow. μTPM_1 transfers the trust to VM_1 by measurement and validation according to TCG specifications, VM_1 transfers the trust to DIMM by enforcing data-flow integrity, the DIMM transfers the trust to VM_2 by checking the user's security policy which stores in μTPM_2.

For example, the process of a transmission trust chain established, or a VM trust transferred, is shown in Fig. 5. We suppose a Web-Portals residing in virtual machine VM_1 will pass some data D_1 to the Database Server residing in virtual machine VM_2. The dotted arrow indicates the data flow logically, while the solid arrow indicates the data flow actually as well as the verification process.

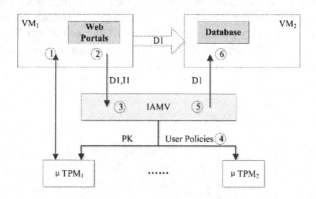

Fig. 5. The trust chain transitivity and verification

As Fig. 6 shown, to ensure the trustworthiness of the VM_1 and the data D_1, the following process is enforced.

(1) The process of VMs launched is as follows,

    (1.1) Before a VM is launched, a corresponding μTPM is created, the secure policies of organization and user are configured in the μTPM. The organization issues a certification to each VM, and the VM stores the certification and the public key in its μTPM.

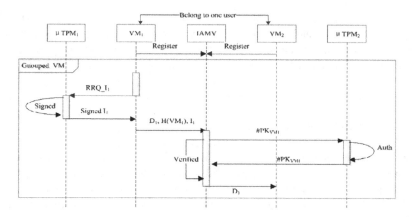

Fig. 6. Sequence for data transmission

(1.2) The VM is registered to IAMV. The IU intercepts the VM installing instructions, the MU measures the VM, and registers the measure value with the provisioning information to DU.

(1.3) All VMs of the organization are launched.

(2) The communication process between the VM_1 (Web-Portal) and VM_2 (Database Server) is as follows,

    (2.1) The Web-Portals residing virtual machine VM_1 generates data D_1, and wants pass the date D_1 to virtual machine VM_2. The μTPM_1, corresponding VM_1, signatures the data D_1 and VM_1 with its private key, forms I_1, $I_1 = \{\{H(D_1 \parallel VM)\}SK_{Auth}, \#PK_{VW_1}\}$, where the $\#PK_{VM_1}$ is the certification of VM_1.

    (2.2) The VM_1 then sends the output D_1 with the destination virtual machine VM_2 and the hash value I_1 to VM_2, i.e., $\{D_1, VM_2, I_1\}$.

    (2.3) The IAMV intercepts the dataflow including D_1, I_1, and destination VM_2, it firstly authenticates the $\#PK_{VM_1}$ by the μTPM_2, then authenticates the dataflow signature with public key of VM_1.

    (2.4) The IAMV validates the integrity of the VM_1 with the reference value stored in the DU, and check the security policies of the VM_2.

    (2.5) If all the result of the above is passed, the IAMV forward the D_1 to VM_2.

    (2.6) The VM_2 receives the dataflow D_1, and pass the data D_1 to Database server.

The integrity measurement can only guarantee the components being tamper-proofed, it is not enough for avoiding the interference between components at runtime [14]. The IAMV is used to prevent unexpected interference for the VMs, and ensures the integrity of the VMs at runtime. If the message and the VM which outputs the message have been verified to be trusted, IAMV is able to guarantee that the integrity of the VM which input the message in its runtime.

This verification method can also be applied to the communication between DomUs as well as the communications between DomU and Dom0. For the traditional communication between virtual machines, such as hyper-calls, interrupts, event channels, etc., IAMV can guarantee the trustworthiness of the input by verifying the integrity of the codes and the data source. For the data exchange model, such as memory-shared, authorization table or files shared, the trustworthiness of the shared memory need to be assured when it is created, and the details are out of the scope of this paper.

4   Experiment and Analyses

In this section we will test the usability of the DIMM model by experiment. The experiment environment is a ASUAK43SJ computer with Intel Corei5 2410M and 2.00 GB RAM. The underlying system is Fedora 10, the Linux kernel version is 2.6.32.26, and the virtual machine monitor is Xen 4.0. We realized a prototype of the DIMM model on the TTCVM infrastructure, and assume that the statics trust is guaranted by the TTCVM. So we focus on the implementation of IAMV module.

In order to test the performance of the DIMM system, we load two virtual machine, VM1 and VM2, on the original system and the DIMM system separately. We firstly make VM1 read a file from VM2 20 times, and take the average time, then we make VM1 write a file to VM2 20 times and take the average time too. The results are shown in Table 1.

Table 1. The performance comparison of the system

Operation	Original system	DIMM system	Performance degradation
Read	0.934 s	1.138 s	17%
Write	1.016 s	1.278 s	20%

According to the results of the above, we can find that the time of read operation is increased by an average of 17%, while the time of write operation is increased by an average of 20%. Because the write operation needs to check more user policies than that of read operation, its execution time is longer than that of read operation. The eventual experimental results shown that the DIMM model will bring more overhead to the system. However, the experiment is running on a single CPU environment with some poor performance hardware, such as 2.0G RAM. We estimate that it will be improved greatly on the cloud platform with high performance hardware.

5   Related Works

In the cloud platform, virtualization is one of the core technologies, and the security of the Cloud depends largely on the isolation mechanism of the virtual machines.

The Trusted Computing is widespread used to guarantee the security of the information system. It is also introduced in Cloud to enhance the isolation mechanism of VMs. Through the virtualization technology, each guest VM can be bound to a vTPM which offers the security functions similar physical TPM does. Berger [8],

Scarlata [9], England [10], Sadeghi [11] and Berlios et al. [12] propose some vTPM solutions. However, these solutions are only to ensure the integrity of virtual machines during its loading, and they cannot guarantee the integrity of the virtual machine at runtime.

The analysis of Zhang et al. [7] shows that the trust chain under the TCG specification is validation where there is no unexpected interference in the process of trust transitivity. Zhang et al. [5] present two conditions to determine whether a system is trusted based on the process level, and proved the correctness of the two conditions according to the definition of trustworthiness. SecureBus in Literature [6] provides strong isolation and transparent access control mechanism between processes. It verifies the integrity of input at the process level. However, it is designed only for ordinary platform, and cannot be applied in the cloud environment directly.

Virtual Machine Monitor (or Hypervisor) can also provide integrity protection for cloud platforms at virtual machine level. Terra [15] provides a flexible trusted computing architecture which uses virtual machine monitor as trusted base. However, Terra does not provide the ability to measure the virtual environment dynamically, nor does it guarantee the security for the installation of the virtual environment. Livewire [16], Antfarm [17] and XenAccess [18] also use this method to provide integrity protection for virtual machines. But this approach relies on the security services provided by Hypervisor, and studies in the literature [19, 20] show that the hypervisor suffers from malicious attacks and may be compromised.

Rongyu et al. [13] design a multi-source trust chain model for cloud computing, which presents a solution for extending trust from VMM to VM through the user-specific TPM, called μTPM. However, it is a static integrity measurement model which measures the integrity of all the components (including the virtual machine) before it is loaded, it cannot guarantee the virtual machine in a trust status when it is running. Furthermore, the model TTCVM did not consider the problem of the interference between virtual machines mutually.

6 Conclusion

Cloud computing could provide on-demand computing environments dynamically and allows companies turn their datacenter or other IT resources to the cloud platform for more flexibility and lower overhead. However, this new computing paradigm introduces a number of new security and privacy challenges, and several intrinsic features of Cloud amplify these challenges, such as multi-tenant host. Recently, many security solutions are proposed to protect the virtual machines from malware attacks. However, these solutions focus on providing a strong isolated environment for each VM, and ignored the input/out operations of VMs, such as database access, communication between two VMs for co-operation.

In this paper, based on the Tree-like Trust Chain for VM (TTCVM) model in literature [13], we propose a mechanism, named Dynamic Integrity Measurement Model, for trust transitive between two virtual machines at will. The mechanism will ensure the integrity of VMs when data or instructions are transmitted among them, as well as the integrity of the delivered message. However, the model suffers from performance problem, and the further work is to reduce the computing overhead and latency of the DIMM model by optimizing the security policy controls in the IAVM module.

Acknowledgments. This research was financially supported by National Natural Science Foundation of China (Project 61572517) and the Science and Technology Plan Projects of Shenzhen (JCY2017302145623566).

References

1. TCG Specfication Architecture Overview. https://www.trustedcomputinggroup.org
2. Khan, A.: Virtual machine security. Int. J. Inf. Comput. Secur. **9**(1–2), 49–84 (2017)
3. Roscoe, A.W., Goldsmith, M.H.: What is intransitive noninterference? In: Proceedings of the 12th IEEE Computer Security Foundations Workshop, pp. 228–238. IEEE (1999)
4. Fan, Z., Shu, C., Yongxuan, S.: Noninterference model for integrity. J. Commun. **32**(10), 78–85 (2011)
5. Zhang, X., et al.: A formal method based on noninterference for analyzing trust chain of trusted computing platform. Chin. J. Comput. **33**(1), 74–81 (2010)
6. Zhang, X., et al.: SecureBus: towards application-transparent trusted computing with mandatory access control. In: Proceedings of the 2nd ACM Symposium on Information, Computer and Communications Security, pp. 117–126. ACM (2007)
7. Zhang, X., Chen, Y.L., Shen, C.X.: Non-interference trusted model based on processes. J. Commun. **30**(3), 6–11 (2009)
8. Perez, R., et al.: vTPM: virtualizing the trusted platform module. In: Proceedings of the 15th Conference on USENIX Security Symposium, pp. 305–320 (2006)
9. Scarlata, V., et al.: TPM virtualization: building a general framework. In: Pohlmann, N., Reimer, H. (eds.) Trusted Computing, pp. 43–56. Vieweg+Teubner, Berlin (2008). https://doi.org/10.1007/978-3-8348-9452-6_4
10. England, P., Loeser, J.: Para-virtualized TPM sharing. In: Lipp, P., Sadeghi, A.-R., Koch, K.-M. (eds.) Trust 2008. LNCS, vol. 4968, pp. 119–132. Springer, Heidelberg (2008). https://doi.org/10.1007/978-3-540-68979-9_9
11. Sadeghi, A.-R., Stüble, C., Winandy, M.: Property-based TPM virtualization. In: Wu, T.-C., Lei, C.-L., Rijmen, V., Lee, D.-T. (eds.) ISC 2008. LNCS, vol. 5222, pp. 1–16. Springer, Heidelberg (2008). https://doi.org/10.1007/978-3-540-85886-7_1
12. Strasser, M.: A software-based TPM emulator for Linux. Department of Computer Science, Swiss Federal Institute of Technology, Zurich (2004)
13. Rongyu, H., Shaojie, W., Lu, I.: A user-specific trusted virtual environment for cloud computing. Inf. Technol. J. **12**(10), 1905–1913 (2013)
14. Rushby, J.: Noninterference, Transitivity, and Channel-Control Security Policies. SRI International, Computer Science Laboratory (1992)
15. Garfinkel, T., et al.: Terra: a virtual machine-based platform for trusted computing. In: ACM SIGOPS Operating Systems Review, pp. 193–206. ACM (2003)
16. Garfinkel, T., et al.: A virtual machine introspection based architecture for intrusion detection. In: Ndss, pp. 191–206 (2003)
17. Jones, S.T., Arpaci-Dusseau, A.C., Arpaci-Dusseau, R.H.: Antfarm: tracking processes in a virtual machine environment. In: ATEC 2006: Proceedings of the Annual Conference on USENIX 2006 Annual Technical Conference, p. 1 (2006)

18. Payne, B.D., Martim, D.P.A., Lee, W.: Secure and flexible monitoring of virtual machines. In: Twenty-Third Annual of Computer Security Applications Conference, ACSAC 2007, pp. 385–397. IEEE (2007)
19. Vulnerability in xenserver could result in privilege escalation and arbitrary code execution. http://support.citrix.com/article/CTX118766. Accessed Nov 2011
20. Garfinkel, T., Rosenblum, M., Boneh, D.: Flexible OS support and applications for trusted computing. In: HotOS, pp. 145–150 (2003)

Enhancing Dependability in Big Data Analytics Enterprise Pipelines

Hira Zahid[1], Tariq Mahmood[1(✉)], and Nassar Ikram[2]

[1] Department of Computer Science, Institute of Business Administration,
Karachi, Pakistan
{hzahid,tmahmood}@iba.edu.pk
[2] Department of Computer Science, National University of Science and Technology,
Islamabad, Pakistan
prorectorric@nust.edu.pk

Abstract. Big Data Analytics (BDA) brings extensive opportunities to enterprises to extract valuable information from high volume, velocity and variety data streams. However, the BDA dynamics can lead to significant project failures due to high-risk factors in terms of data availability, reliability, integrity, security and resilience which are the key components of a dependable system and are strongly linked to BDA process execution. Specifically, the heterogeneity of big data sources, diverse set of challenges related to big data integration and processing, along with a rapidly-expanding landscape warrant the need to make dependable big data systems capable of providing standard analytical solutions. In this paper, we propose the first dependable pipeline architecture for the BDA process which has a layered front-end and back-end implementation, employs the standard lambda architecture in a DataOps analytical cycle, incorporates state-of-the-art tools which are all open-source, and is coded entirely in the standard Python language to remove cross-platform implementation dependencies. We have implemented this architecture in five enterprise BDA projects but we are unable to present implementation details and results due to space limitations.

Keywords: Big Data Analytics · Dependability · DataOps · Pipeline
Enterprise

1 Introduction

Big data continues to increase in enterprises. Especially, the advent of IoT, sensor networks, smart phones, and social networks along with operational data lakes are resulting in a continuous stream of data to be stored, managed, analyzed and visualized by enterprises. Big Data Analytics (BDA) is a modification of the traditional KDD process to extract valuable data from these big data lakes. It has potential to bring significant benefits and improvements to KPIs of global enterprises [17,23]. It can provide useful insights about revenue opportunities,

© Springer Nature Switzerland AG 2018
G. Wang et al. (Eds.): SpaCCS 2018, LNCS 11342, pp. 272–281, 2018.
https://doi.org/10.1007/978-3-030-05345-1_23

cost reductions, marketing plans, better customer services, safety measures and other related trends by effective and real-time analytics. However, enterprise BDA initiatives are not dependable by nature [4,7,10,11,17,20,21,23,27,30]; according to Gartner, 85% of BDA projects in enterprises were failing in 2017 leading to significant losses [3].

The reasons are numerous. Enterprise big data is heterogeneous by nature; few examples include images, videos, tables, CSVs, documents, spreadsheets, PDFs, presentations, social network feeds, data formats and sensor data. These data types are structured, semi-structured and unstructured and lead to implementation of NoSQL technology of data stores for storage, processing and analytics. The heterogeneity of big data has lead to an exponential increase in NoSQL technology stack in the last decade [29], which is creating a serious problem in *selecting the right technology stack for enterprises interested in BDA*, particularly those who want to work open-source. NoSQL offers wide columnar stores (e.g., Hbase, Cassandra), key value stores (e.g., Redis, Memcached), document stores (e.g., MongoDB, CouchDB) and Graph Stores (e.g., Neo4j, Orient). There are tens of available solutions for each store type. BDA involves a large number of tasks to be executed in a pipeline, and *each task can be implemented through a variety of available solutions. Expertise is typically not available*, coupled with a *lack of mindset*, to experiment with different stores rigorously on a small scale before making a selection. These stores also vary in location, latency and product specifications. The data being used is in some cases historical and in other case is live streaming each requiring a unique set of tools and expertise to handle and process. *Financial constraints* may also restrict the forming of a big data/BDA/data science team within an enterprise to make such experiments and derive value later on. They may also restrict purchase of hardware or cloud computing for more complicated BDA tasks, e.g., machine learning and deep learning.

To put things in perspective, we show the enterprise BDA process at a generic level in Fig. 1. The heterogeneous input data sources (top-left) first need to be decrypted thoroughly by an analytical team manually and their relationship with the business requirements of BDA needs to be established clearly. This is a continuous activity taking input from other BDA activities later on to help define business goals clearly. Then, almost 90% time needs to be devoted to Stream ETL, i.e., data wrangling of big data lakes, involving application of data transformations, descriptive statistics, inferential statistics, attribute selection procedures and most importantly, effective integration of data sources. ETL is involves much effort and trial-and-error selections based on feedback from analytics. High expertise and effort is required here from the analytical team which is not available or executed readily. The clean data is then stored in NoSQL stores, either in-house or on the cloud, followed by analytical modeling of data. Both storage and modeling are plagued by the problem of selecting the relevant technology stack for ensuring and displaying optimized actionable insights to the enterprise users. Some other problems include *poor data management, failure to identify a clear business problem, expense involved in making scalable BDA pipelines, inef-*

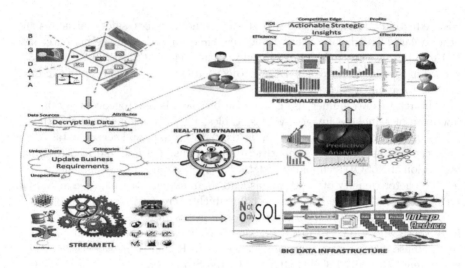

Fig. 1. Big Data Analytics Process Diagram

ficient analytical models, non-optimal hardware resource utilization, increase in hardware costs, and *failure to integrate different big data sources in an effective way.* Also, pipeline development is not a one-time activity; the pipeline needs to be continuously monitored, maintained and managed by a team and some of the tasks such as data cleaning could also need to be automated. All these problems make BDA an a non-dependable, expensive, resource-intensive and a complicated process. We believe that many of these problems can be addressed by selecting the right technology stack and defining a standard pipeline to apply this stack, in order to create a type of roadmap for BDA enterprise implementations. In this paper, we plan to address the aforementioned issues by answering the following research question: **RQ:** *Given the available technology and solution stack, what is the BDA pipeline infrastructure that can serve as a roadmap for solving the more crucial problems facing BDA implementations in enterprises, particularly leading to enhanced dependability in terms of performance, optimization, scalability and reliability?*

2   Related Work

We have found limited research work related to enhancing dependability in BDA infrastructures. In [33], the author proposed a data-driven analytical method to differentiate the workload and resource usage patterns to track performance bottlenecks, from development stages to online production systems for monitoring and debugging the operational behavior hence leading to optimized service engineering. In another paper [1] author propose Microservice-based architecture for autonomic computing in software intensive systems such as Electric power distribution (EDP) to foster scalability of such systems. Moreover, Pipeline61 framework has been proposed in [32] to reduce the effort for maintaining and managing big data pipelines across heterogeneous execution. It provides automated version control and dependency management for both data and components in each pipeline instance/context without major rewriting of the original jobs during its life cycle. Another author has discussed the hybrid technique in the form of an ensemble of replication and erasure coding in cloud storage system for big data applications to improve the performance with less storage overhead along with the conceptual architecture to further improve the reliability of data with the management perspective of application and data. In [22], the authors propose a novel hybrid technique based on dynamic replication in erasure coded storage systems is proposed. The proposed technique and the conceptual architecture can effectively handle the reconstruction issues of erasure code proactively with less storage overhead and improved reliability and energy consumption.

3   A Dependable Architecture for Enterprise BDA Pipelines

To answer our research question, in this section, we demonstrate and discuss a dependable architecture for enterprise BDA pipelines, shown in Fig. 2 which we propose to code entirely in the standard Python (version 3.0 or above) language which has facilitated BDA pipeline development in the last several years [4]. The technology stack of our architecture has been influenced by our experience on enterprise BDA projects along with several research papers targeting BDA implementations in enterprises [5, 6, 8, 9, 12, 14–16, 18, 19, 24, 26, 28]. We model our architecture on state-of-the-art *DevOps* methodology of software development, specifically *DataOps* which is an iterative life cycle for data flows including build, release and operate steps supported by data protection and is the only response to the fluidity of BDA implementations. We also propose use of cloud computing (through Amazon AWS and Microsoft Azure) as it has resolved doubts over privacy invasion of companies of diverse types [2,34]. Our architecture is state of the art and lambda in nature, allowing analytical processing of both static (batch) and real-time streaming data in parallel. It comprises seven layers: *connection, integration, static, dynamic, serving, interface* and *dashboard*, defined as follows:

Connection Layer: Connection layer provides an API gateway of data connectors to connect to diverse types of telecom data flowing in from different sources. Some of these connectors are readily available as separate installers (e.g., ODBC) while others are available as APIs in Python e.g., PyMongo for connecting to MongoDB. If a connector is not available, it can be easily programmed as a Python API.

Integration Layer: Integration layer collects the different telecom data streams and integrates them in a master database. For integration, we recommend storing different data types in relevant databases and then programming a *control*

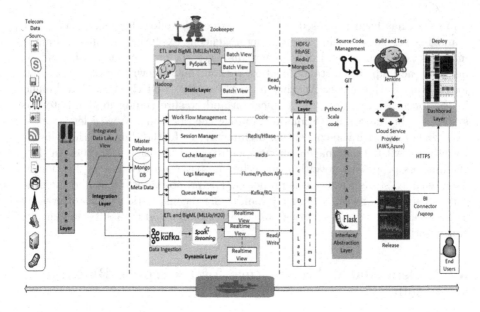

Fig. 2. Proposed Dependable Architecture for Enterprise BDA Pipelines

layer in Python as integrator. For instance, social network feeds are continuously stored in Neo4J and CDRs in MongoDB and control layer keeps meta-data of connections, data and storage actions to facilitate access. We recommend using Redis as a metadata store to facilitate faster retrieval and storage with lesser management overhead. We do not recommend usage of Talend and Pentaho tools for data integration; our recommendation is to program everything in Python for efficiency of BDA process.

Static Layer: Static layer takes static (less-velocity and stationary) data from master databases and processes it over a Hadoop cluster. Most Hadoop processing should be Spark-based and the more longer tasks can be programmed in MapReduce, e.g., computing average call time over a period of 5 years in 250 TB of data [31]. Static layer provides drilled-down (time-consuming) analyses to supplement analytics presented in dynamic layer.

Dynamic Layer: Dynamic layer processes real-time streaming data at a more superficial level to present basic analytics in real-time views. We recommend using Apache Kafka to ingest the stream and Spark Streaming for processing it. For ingestion in speed layer, Apache Flume can also be used but we use Kafka for its better feature set and more use cases. For the same reasons, we prefer Spark Streaming for processing (through PySpark API) over Apache Storm. Note that it could be inefficient to store high velocity streaming data in master databases; if the use case demands it, then we recommend storing in MongoDB or Redis.

Serving Layer: Serving layer facilitates querying and storage of results from static and dynamic layers. We store these results in an analytical data lake. We recommend MongoDB, Redis, HDFS or HBase for storage depending on require-ments and results data types. This lake can store results from static and dynamic layers separately or integrated after some NoSQL database management.

Interface Layer: Interface layer combines back-end layers (mentioned above) with front-end layers. We recommend implementing this layer using Python's Flask API as a standard RESTful API which effectively communicates user requests to back-end using stateless constraints and also enhances interoperability between different computer systems. Here DataOps team handle cluster provisioning, monitoring, autoscaling logs and metric aggregation and continuous delivery through these corresponding tools and API's. First engineers get an API of cluster operation through this abstraction layer then write analytical model/algorithm in python/Scala and store those in version control system such as GIT.

GIT: All of the above processing steps involves turning of raw data into useful information, i.e., source code. Code can control the entire data-analytics pipeline from end to end in an automated and reproducible fashion. In so many cases, the files associated with analytics are distributed in various places within an organization without any governing control. A revision control tool, such as Git, helps to store and manage all of the changes to code. It also keeps code organized, in a known repository and provides for disaster recovery. Revision control also helps software teams parallelize their efforts by allowing them to branch and merge.

Jenkins: It is CI/CD tool used by DataOps teams to deploy code from development into production. With the help of the Git plugin Jenkins can easily pull source code from any Git repository that the Jenkins build node can access. Now the build can be triggered for the purpose of unit testing. Builds can generate test reports in various formats supported by plugins (JUnit support is currently bundled) and Jenkins can display the reports and generate trends and render them in the GUI.

AutoScaling: In any project there can be one AWS server running Jenkins Master plus 1 Jenkins slave (2 executors) and might need more in future due to the build resource intensiveness. Jenkins has different autoscaling options on AWS depending on what is in the build queue and is a more stable and scalable approach.

Dashboard Layer: Dashboard layer comprises a series of dashboards to be viewed by different users across the telecom enterprise. Each dashboard connects to serving layer through interface layer by using different standard connectors, e.g., connectors provided by BI tools or Apache Sqoop in case we need to put dashboard data in some relational store backend. All standard BI tools, e.g., Tableau, SiSense, Microstrategy, or Oracle Business Intelligence can interface with serving layer. Dashboards can also be created on open-source Python APIs like plotly. Dashboards can be deployed on cloud instances of AWS or Azure which are configured over https protocol after configuration of standard SSL certificates over http. The front-end development should be done dynamically, e.g., through AngularJS, ReactJS (by Facebook) and Progressive Web Apps (by Google).

Dockerization: Reuse and containerization is a key step in DataOps since data analytics team members typically have a difficult time leveraging each others work. Code reuse is a vast topic, but the basic idea is to containarize functionalities in ways that can be shared. Complex functions, with lots of individual parts, can be containerized using a container technology like Docker. Containers are ideal for highly customized functions that require a skill set that isn't widely shared among the team. Here, we are proposing to dockerize the environment just to able to automate the workflow, while still keeping the necessary features in place (like performing tests and leveraging staging environments) to assure the quality of applications and configure the environment with autobuilds and auto-deployments.

Both static and dynamic layers can process data in parallel or exclusively. Also both should involve ETL (data cleaning) activities and (in most cases) machine learning and relevant statistical modeling, e.g., predictive analytics on big data which we label as BigML. In parallel, following data management modules need to be programmed in Python which implement background routines required for static and dynamic processing:

Workflow Management: Due to diversity of required analytics in telecommunication, a pipeline or *workflow* of Hadoop jobs may need to be executed in batch layer. We recommend using Apache Oozie Hadoop job scheduler for this purpose (which has no competitor). Oozie commands can be programmed as Python scripts; it allows creation of MapReduce, Hive, and Sqoop jobs (notably) as Directed Acyclic Graphs (DAGs). These jobs can also be triggered based on time and data availability as part of a bundle in the latest Oozie release.

Session Management: Session management stores each session of each telecom user in a stateless (self-contained) manner. Obviously, this can itself generate several hundred megabytes of data daily so BDA lead needs to decide the time for session analysis, session archiving and permanent removal (we cannot store sessions forever). We recommend using Redis for session storage and Python APIs for analysis along with a several hour analysis timeframe (so that data fits in main memory). If the timeframe is required to be more, then Apache Cassandra or HBase should be used for storage (making processing independent of main memory).

Cache Management: Caching speeds-up access by keeping mostly accessed data in main memory. We recommend Redis for managing a cache layer for BDA processing over other state of the art tools, due to its more robust data structures, a larger number of successful usecases, more data types which can be cached, and a larger number of policies for evicting (removing) data from memory [13, 25].

Log Management: We propose log management to log client, server processing and debugging data, according to standard practice. Administrator should ensure no overlap between user clickstream in sessions and logs. Logged data can be analyzed as a Hadoop (MapReduce) task. It can also assist in debugging the BDA pipeline in the DevOps and software testing scenario. We recommend Flume for log management, personalized Python scripts or Python APIs.

Queue Management: In the face of diverse analytical task requirements at different times, it is possible that tasks (e.g., in an Oozie instantiation) need to be queued. Kafka is an ideal data queueing framework for streaming data. For static data, we propose RQ (Redis Queue) software, which implements queues in Redis implemented in Python. RQ is also applicable for streaming data in case Kafka is not used.

Resource Management: In Hadoop 2.0, resource management for batch data processing is completely handled by YARN (Yet Another Resource Negotiator). Besides this, we recommend Zookeeper as a coordination service (on the base of a key-value store) to manage Hadoop or Spark clusters. It guarantees efficient execution of a host of services related to distributed computing and is a standard software for a Hadoop deployment.

4 Conclusions

BDA implementations in enterprises are currently plagued by many critical problems. The overall effect of these problems is to make BDA pipelines less dependable. In this paper, we have initially determined what needs to be done exactly in a BDA pipeline and then, on how it should be done. To this end, we proposed and discussed a BDA architecture which combines a set of state of the art data analytics activities in a layered model along with integrating them in a standard pipeline architecture. We focused on selecting the right technology stack for these activities. We have implemented this architecture in the following enterprise projects: (1) deep-learning based trade prediction system (currently under development but can be explored at codexnow.com), (2) an analytical business communication platform (darbi.io), (3) an analytical data collaboration platform (go-loop.us), (4) a data encryption platform (whose URL we cannot share due to legal binding) and (5) a big data integration and processing system (under development). In these projects, the architecture has largely helped to streamline all BDA activities and output results in a dependable manner without many of the problems outlined in Sect. 1. Of particular use in these projects was the rapid execution of DataOps and seamless integration with operational data stores on AWS cloud. We also found AWS's auto-scalability feature to be useful but the programming code also needs to be optimized through DataOps to facilitate scalability. We believe that this architecture presents a type of roadmap and can be extremely useful for a majority of global enterprises to solve their BDA problems. We are not able to provide experimental details in this paper due to space limitations.

References

1. Dimov, A., Davidovic, N., Stoimenov, L., Baylov, K.: Software dependability management in Big Data distributed stream computing systems (2017)
2. Anthony, A.: Mastering AWS Security: Create and Maintain a Secure Cloud Ecosystem, 1st edn. Packt Publishing - eBooks Account, Birmingham (2017)
3. Asay, M.: 85% of big data projects fail, but your developers can help yours succeed (2017). https://www.techrepublic.com/article/85-of-big-data-projects-fail-but-your-developers-can-help-yours-succeed/
4. Bahga, A., Madisetti, V.: Big Data Science & Analytics: A Hands-On Approach
5. Celebi, O.F., et al.: On use of big data for enhancing network coverage analysis. In: ICT 2013. IEEE, May 2013
6. Chang, B.R., Tsai, H.F., Lin, Z.Y., Chen, C.M.: Access-controlled video/voice over IP in hadoop system with BPNN intelligent adaptation. In: 2012 International Conference on Information Security and Intelligence Control (ISIC), pp. 325–328. IEEE (2012)
7. Chen, M., Mao, S., Liu, Y.: Big data: a survey. Mob. Netw. Appl. **19**(2), 171–209 (2014)
8. cloudera: apache-flume@ONLINE (2017). https://www.cloudera.com/products/open-source/apache-hadoop/apache-flume.html
9. Daki, H., El Hannani, A., Aqqal, A., Haidine, A., Dahbi, A., Ouahmane, H.: Towards adopting big data technologies by mobile networks operators: A moroccan case study. In: 2016 2nd International Conference on Cloud Computing Technologies and Applications (CloudTech), pp. 154–161. IEEE (2016)
10. Datafloq: Top reasons of Hadoop - big data project failures (2017). https://datafloq.com/read/top-reasons-of-hadoop-big-data-project-failures/2185
11. Demirkan, H., Dal, B.: The data economy: Why do so many analytics projects fail? (2014). http://analytics-magazine.org/the-data-economy-why-do-so-many-analytics-projects-fail/
12. George, J., Chen, C.A., Stoleru, R., Xie, G.: Hadoop MapReduce for mobile clouds. IEEE Trans. Cloud Comput., 1 (2016)
13. Haber, I.: Why redis beats memcached for caching (2017). https://www.infoworld.com/article/3063161/nosql/why-redis-beats-memcached-for-caching.html
14. He, Y., Yu, F.R., Zhao, N., Yin, H., Yao, H., Qiu, R.C.: Big data analytics in mobile cellular networks. IEEE Access **4**, 1985–1996 (2016)
15. Khan, N., et al.: Big data: survey, technologies, opportunities, and challenges. Sci. World J. **2014**, 1–18 (2014)
16. Khatib, E.J., Barco, R., Muñoz, P., De La Bandera, I., Serrano, I.: Self-healing in mobile networks with big data. IEEE Commun. Mag. **54**(1), 114–120 (2016)
17. Liebowitz, J.: Big Data and Business Analytics, 1st edn. CRC Press, Boca Raton (2013)
18. Liu, J., Liu, F., Ansari, N.: Monitoring and analyzing big traffic data of a large-scale cellular network with hadoop. IEEE Network **28**(4), 32–39 (2014)
19. Magnusson, J., Kvernvik, T.: Subscriber classification within telecom networks utilizing big data technologies and machine learning. In: Proceedings of the 1st International Workshop on Big Data, Streams and Heterogeneous Source Mining Algorithms, Systems, Programming Models and Applications-BigMine 2012. ACM Press (2012)
20. Manyika, J., et al.: Big Data: The Next Frontier for Innovation, Competition and Productivity (2011)

21. Marz, N., Warren, J.: Big Data: Principles and Best Practices of Scalable Realtime Data Systems. Manning Publications Co., Shelter Island (2015)
22. Nachiappan, R., Javadi, B., Calheiros, R.N., Matawie, K.M.: Cloud storage reliability for big data applications: a state of the art survey. J. Netw. Comput. Appl. **97**, 35–47 (2017)
23. Ohlhorst, F.J.: Big Data Analytics: Turning Big Data into Big Money, 1st edn. Wiley, Hoboken (2012)
24. Rathore, M., Paul, A., Ahmad, A., Imran, M., Guizani, M.: High-speed network traffic analysis: detecting VoIP calls in secure big data streaming. In: 2016 IEEE 41st Conference on Local Computer Networks (LCN). IEEE, November 2016
25. Redis: Using redis as an lru cache (2018). https://redis.io/topics/lru-cache
26. Senbalci, C., Altuntas, S., Bozkus, Z., Arsan, T.: Big data platform development with a domain specific language for telecom industries. In: 2013 High Capacity Optical Networks and Emerging/Enabling Technologies. IEEE, December 2013
27. Singh, P.: 10 reasons why big data and analytics projects fail (2017). https://analyticsindiamag.com/10-reasons-big-data-analytics-projects-fail/
28. Tseng, J.C., et al.: A successful application of big data storage techniques implemented to criminal investigation for telecom. In: Network Operations and Management Symposium, pp. 1–3. IEEE (2013)
29. Turck, M.: Firing on all cylinders: the 2017 big data landscape (2017). http://mattturck.com/bigdata2017/
30. Violino, B.: How to avoid big data analytics failures (2017). https://www.infoworld.com/article/3212945/big-data/how-to-avoid-big-data-analytics-failures.html
31. Weiss, G.: Data mining in the telecommunications industry. GI Global (2009)
32. Wu, D., Zhu, L., Xu, X., Sakr, S., Lu, Q., Sun, D.: A pipeline framework for heterogeneous execution environment of big data processing. IEEE Softw. 1 (2016)
33. Yang, R., Xu, J.: Computing at massive scale: scalability and dependability challenges. In: 2016 IEEE Symposium on Service-Oriented System Engineering (SOSE). IEEE, March 2016
34. Diogenes, Y., Shinder, T., Shinder, D.: Microsoft Azure Security Infrastructure (IT Best Practices - Microsoft Press), 1st edn. Microsoft Press, Redmond (2016)

Overview of Logistics Equilibrium Distribution Networks System: An Urban Perspective

Wang Wei[1], Md Arafatur Rahman[2,4(✉)], Md Jahan Ali[2],
Md Zakirul Alam Bhuiyan[3], Liu Yao[1], and Hai Tao[5]

[1] Faculty of Industrial Management, University Malaysia Pahang,
Gambang, Malaysia
kingweiwein@gmail.com, xiaoyao6554@gmail.com
[2] Faculty of Computer Systems and Software Engineering,
University Malaysia Pahang, Gambang, Malaysia
arafatur@ump.edu.my, jahancse@gmail.com
[3] Department of Computer and Information Sciences, Fordham University,
New York, NY, USA
mbhuiyan3@fordham.edu
[4] IBM, Center of Excellence, UMP, Gambang, Malaysia
[5] School of Computer Science, Baoji University of Art and Science,
Baoji, Shaanxi, China
haitao@bjwlxy.edu.cn

Abstract. Logistics Equilibrium Distribution Networks System is a design scheme which provides the logistics distribution mechanism effective and efficient in terms of several layering aspects: business layout layer, supervision and evaluation layer and planning control layer. It enhances the monitoring function of the information platforms and the design scheme of the planning by controlling the distribution layer moving forward to control the whole system macroscopically to ensure the effective operation. To develop such network toward Urban perspective is a challenging task because of the various distribution layouts control. To address such an issue, this paper proposes a hierarchical ranking urban logistics equilibrium system, which incorporates the functional structure, the distribution system structure, and the operation mechanism in order to realize the high-end and integration of distribution system. The outcome of this research will assist to design an urban distribution system which can improve the distribution efficiency of urban logistics, save transportation costs, reduce carbon emissions, protect the urban environment, and promote the development of urban economy.

Keywords: Logistics equilibrium · Distribution Networks System
Economic development · Urban logistics

1 Introduction

The development of regional economy is closely related to the development of urban logistics. For the urban logistics, because the end users of the logistics are concentrated in the city, the distribution of this logistics form and service mode is mainly concentrated

© Springer Nature Switzerland AG 2018
G. Wang et al. (Eds.): SpaCCS 2018, LNCS 11342, pp. 282–293, 2018.
https://doi.org/10.1007/978-3-030-05345-1_24

in the city, has become the support of urban operation of the logistics form. In recent years, China's urban trade volume has increased year by year, the importance of urban logistics and distribution system construction has become more prominent, to build a reasonable and efficient operation of the city logistics and distribution system for the good development of urban economy is of great significance [10].

There is a large number of published studies on City logistics and distribution is subject to many factors, the city logistics and distribution system is the flow of people, business flow and information flow is the need to integrate the logistics environment of human settlements [3–7]. Urban logistics and distribution system rely on the layout of urban industry and population distribution, high density of population distribution and industrial layout will greatly increase the amount of urban logistics and distribution [7]. In addition, the city's traffic conditions and ecological conditions affect the construction of urban logistics and distribution system, urban logistics and distribution need to focus on energy-saving emission reduction green direction. Additionally, the quality of distribution and delivery time factors more closely linked to the city logistics and distribution system to meet the needs of decentralized distribution needs, but also save the distribution of the distribution side of the distribution costs, the integration of common distribution, which requires the city logistics and distribution system planning [3].

A number of studies have investigated in the United States, Japan and other logistics and distribution management in the theoretical research and practice has six or seven decades of history, fruitful, and have established a more reasonable to promote economic development of the logistics and distribution system [11–23]. As Japan's land area is small, the trade volume is very large, Japan in the logistics infrastructure construction and distribution center distribution node construction into a lot of money [20]. To achieve the goods storage, acceptance, sorting, a library and other logistics operations throughout the process of computer management and control, improve efficiency and strengthen the management [15].

The contribution of this paper is to design the urban distribution system in order to provide urban logistics system by developing hierarchical ranking urban logistics equilibrium system. It improves the distribution efficiency of urban logistics by incorporating functional structure, distribution system structure, and different operational mechanisms with integration of distribution system.

The rest of this paper is organized as follows. In Sect. 2, we provide the theoretical background of urban logistics and distribution system that define the different equilibrium theory, relationship between logistics equilibrium and urban logistics and distributed system. In Sect. 3, we present urban logistics and distributed system that includes distribution system infrastructure, model, and center planning. Finally, we summarize the paper with conclusion with the way to future work.

2 Overview of Urban Logistics and Distribution System

2.1 Definition of Logistics Equilibrium Theory

Logistics for the economic services, according to the general equilibrium theory, the supply of production factors and demand through the production factor market and commodity markets and the supply of these two markets and the interaction between demand forces, so that each commodity and production factors and the demand will beat a price at the same time tend to equal, the socio-economic will reach a comprehensive equilibrium, this time the economic market can be the suitable development. Thus, the objective requirements of the logistics and distribution system design also need to pursue the equilibrium of supply and demand, and further, is to achieve in the number, time and structure of the equilibrium [1].

Logistics time equilibrium is defined as the logistics demand and logistics supply in time accurate and timely convergence of the state in the distribution of the timeliness, accuracy and distribution efficiency. Logistics equilibrium is an idealized state, in practice, mostly difficult to achieve, therefore, the Logistics equilibrium can be understood as to meet the logistics needs under the premise of the logistics supply and logistics demand in the amount of the smallest difference in the structure Proportion of roughly the same time in the convergence of time as timely, accurate and efficient, in order to achieve the logistics of the equilibrium state. Logistics equilibrium is a relative process, the logistics of the above three-dimensional structure is mainly for the logistics of static equilibrium analysis, in addition to the logistics should be fully aware of the equilibrium is a dynamic equilibrium process, is constantly evolving to high-level equilibrium. And logistics technology has become a decisive factor affecting the level of logistics equilibrium, which together with the role of demand and supply constitutes the impact of Logistics equilibrium level of internal factors, to influence the evolution of equilibrium. In the construction of urban distribution system, we can find the equilibrium point of the distribution system based on the logistics equilibrium theory, so that the distribution in the supply and demand to achieve an equilibrium, in order to save logistics costs and improve distribution efficiency [2].

2.2   The Relationship Between Logistics Equilibrium Theory and Urban Logistics and Distribution System

City logistics and distribution system, including urban logistics infrastructure, logistics equipment, logistics network, logistics management, logistics information systems and other modules. This choice needs to be based on a certain theoretical basis, that is, what we call the theory of logistics equilibrium. Logistics equilibrium theory is the theory of equilibrium theory in the logistics industry extension theory, logistics equilibrium pursuit of logistics supply and demand in the total to achieve equal, including time equilibrium, spatial equilibrium and quantitative equilibrium [9]. For the design of the information input and output of the distribution system, the choice of distribution center needs to use the Logistics equilibrium theory, the pursuit of the whole city to maximize the distribution of income, cost minimization, and to achieve low-carbon environmental protection and short-term efficient distribution.

Urban Logistics and Distribution System Equilibrium Adjustment Mechanism

The good operation of urban logistics and distribution system not only needs the support of logistics equilibrium theory, but also need the effective adjustment mechanism to escort the system. The urban logistics and distribution system introduced in the previous paper is based on the time equilibrium, quantitative equilibrium and structural equilibrium construction of logistics equilibrium theory [14]. The present value of the various indicators of equilibrium, time equilibrium and structural equilibrium is always uploaded to the information flow platform of the city logistics and distribution system. The data processor is used to decompose and analyze various data and output the equilibrium report. Through the analysis, Time equilibrium and structural equilibrium of the completion of the indicators, if there is an un-equilibrium situation, the use of relevant methods to adjust the data, re-export distribution program, so the cycle, repeated integration, feedback and regulation, from a simple static equilibrium to the system within the dynamic equilibrium Conversion.

To achieve a high degree of integration of urban logistics and distribution platform information, the need for government, enterprises, industry associations and other strong support. The state introduced the relevant policy to build information platform, enterprises and other policies with the country to complete the information into the system. The operation of the information platform requires the entire platform to have a consistent standard, all the data conform to the same standard, so that the data can be better analyzed and maximized use. The adjustment model of the information platform is shown in Fig. 1.

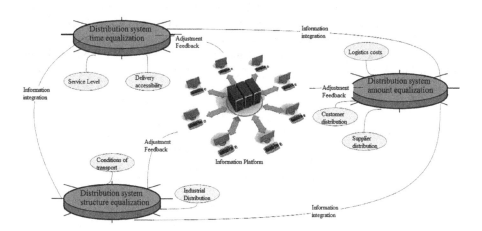

Fig. 1. Urban logistics distribution system equilibrium adjustment mode

2.3 Urban Logistics and Distribution Model Planning

After the study concluded that the existing urban logistics and distribution model after several decades of development can be divided into self-distribution, third-party distribution and common distribution of three models [22]. Self-service distribution is a self-sufficient distribution model, by the supply of goods (generally refers to the production enterprises) will be sent to the needs of customers in the hands of the goods. This approach appears to be simple and straightforward, but does not take into account the fact that multiple suppliers and multiple demand customers often have the same distribution needs, virtually increasing the cost of distribution and increasing the delivery of transport vehicles, adversely affecting the environment The The third party distribution is defined as the fact that the goods are not delivered directly from the supplier to the demand side, but by the supplier to the third party logistics company to help them deliver the goods to the customer. The rise of e-commerce led to the development of third-party distribution, a large number of third-party logistics enterprises: such as ShunFeng, ShenTong, Yunda, etc. These enterprises run gradually into the people's attention. Third-party distribution to a certain extent while saving the supplier's delivery costs also increased the demand for customer satisfaction with the distribution service, while the community to create more output value.

Common distribution model is a relatively intelligent distribution model, is the supply of goods to a number of goods to the needs of multiple customers demand delivery mode. There is no doubt that the common distribution model has been greatly improved in terms of shortening delivery time, saving delivery costs and improving delivery quality. In this paper, combined with the characteristics of the other two distribution models to give a common distribution and self-distribution, third-party distribution combined with the new common distribution model. (1) to self-oriented common distribution model for supplier-oriented distribution requirements, to entrust a unified distribution, centralized distribution of the distribution model. For retailer-led distribution requirements, take self-built network distribution, enterprise alliance distribution model. (2) to the third party-based common distribution model monopoly business type, a total of collectively with the type of enterprises to transport enterprises as the leading distribution, for the market-led, information platform-oriented co-distribution, to choose government-led Third party common distribution mode, as shown in Fig. 2.

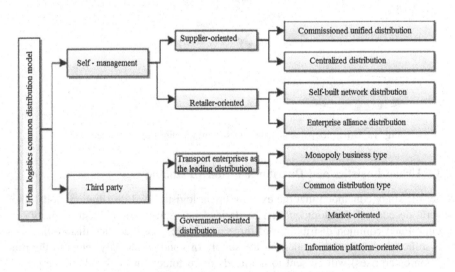

Fig. 2. Urban logistics joint distribution pattern classification

2.4 Urban Logistics Distribution Center Planning

The location and construction of the city logistics distribution center can be used in many ways. 0–1 integer programming method, fuzzy evaluation method, analytic hierarchy process and ant colony algorithm can help to select the address of the distribution center. This paper, from the unique perspective of logistics equilibrium, uses the combination of analytic hierarchy process and fuzzy evaluation method, the pursuit of logistics and distribution time, space and structural equilibrium, select the evaluation index. This paper constructs urban distribution from 7 second-level indicators such as structural equilibrium, quantity equilibrium and time equilibrium, three primary indicators and industrial structure, transportation conditions, supplier distribution, customer demand distribution, logistics cost, accessibility, service level Center location evaluation index system [8].

1. Structural equilibrium: The impact of industrial structure factors on urban logistics and distribution system includes three kinds of distribution of agricultural products, distribution of industrial products and distribution of consumer goods. The selection of the distribution center is related to the situation of the three industries in the city and the location of the industry center. The condition of transportation is an important factor influencing the structural equilibrium of urban logistics and distribution system. The rationality of urban road network structure directly affects the equilibrium of distribution structure. For this structural indicator, it can be simplified for the evaluation of road grade and road smoothness.

2. The number of equilibrium: The secondary indicators under the quantitative equilibrium index can be divided into three indicators: supplier quantity distribution, customer demand distribution and logistics cost. The distribution of suppliers and customers directly affects the location of the distribution center. Logistics costs include distribution costs, storage costs, and new distribution center costs. The three secondary indicators of the equilibrium can be measured according to the cost of the supplier, the distance from the main consumer group, and the land price, as shown in Fig. 3 and Table 1.

3. Time equilibrium: The accessibility of the delivery time is an important indicator of whether the delivery item can arrive in time from the supply side to the demand side. Customer satisfaction can be used as the observation variable. The level of service delivery can be used as a measure of policy support.

4. Analytic Hierarchy Process: In this paper, we use the analytic hierarchy process to select the three first-level indicators and seven secondary indicators that affect the location of urban logistics distribution centers. Combining with the matrix analysis and the index data given by the expert scoring method, we first find the weight of the first and then use the judgment matrix to calculate the weight value of the secondary index, and obtain the general ranking of the importance of the index. Judgment matrix construction method is to ask the decision-makers on the same layer of the elements of the two comparisons, and the relative importance between the two to quantify the final formation of the judgment matrix. The general level analysis method uses the 1–5 scale to convert the qualitative comparison result into the quantitative judgment data matrix. The scale meaning is shown in Table 2. The

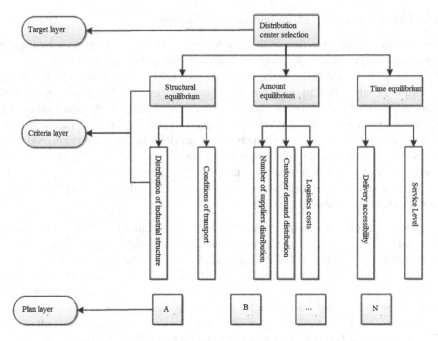

Fig. 3. Urban logistics distribution center selection model

Table 1. Urban distribution center selection evaluation index Level indicators

	Secondary indicators	Observation variables
Structural equilibrium	Distribution of industrial structure	Distance from the industry center
	Conditions of transport	Road grade and smoothness
	Number of suppliers' distribution	Supplier cost
Quantity equalization	Customer demand distribution	Main consumer group distance
	Logistics costs	Land price
Time equilibrium	Delivery accessibility	Customer satisfaction
	Service level	Policy support

judgment process and the knowledge diversity need to be consistent with the judgment matrix.

The single order of the hierarchy is based on the judgment matrix to calculate the relative importance of the low-level factors to the corresponding upper-level factors. The feature vector and the eigenvalue of the judgment matrix are the key steps of hierarchical single ordering. According to the matrix theory, we can get the following relation:

Table 2. Judgment matrix scale table scale

Value	Scale meaning
1	Is as important as
2	Is slightly more important than
3	Is more important than
4	Is strongly more important than
5	Is extremely more important than

If $\lambda_1, \lambda_2 \ldots, \lambda_n$ is the number satisfying $\lambda_x = A_x$, that is the eigenvalue of matrix A, and for all $a_{ii} = 1$, as shown in Eq. (1)

$$\sum_{i=1}^{n} \lambda_i = n \tag{1}$$

It can be seen that when the matrix is completely consistent, $\lambda_1 = \lambda_{max} = n$ the other characteristic roots are zero; and when the matrix is not completely consistent $\lambda_1 = \lambda_{max} > n$

the other characteristic roots $\lambda_2, \lambda_3 \ldots, \lambda_n$ relationship as shown in Eq. (2)

$$\sum_{i=2}^{n} \lambda_i = n - \lambda_{max} \tag{2}$$

On the basis of this, the negative average of the other characteristic roots other than the largest eigenvalue of the judgment matrix is used as the index of the degree of consistency deviation of the judgment matrix, and the consistency of the index judgment is checked by the formula (3).

$$CI = \frac{\lambda_{max} - n}{n - 1} \tag{3}$$

The larger the CI is, the greater the degree of consistency deviation of the judgment matrix. The smaller the CI is, the better the consistency of the judgment matrix. And it is easy to conclude that the judgment matrix is the exact consistency with CI = 0, and the judgment criterion is CI = 0, $\lambda_1 = \lambda_{max} = n$.

For the total order of the hierarchy, the single ordering results of the level factor $(B_1, B_2, \ldots, B_n)$ corresponding to a_i is $(b_{1i}, b_{2i}, \ldots, b_{ni})$. Assuming that the total ranking of all the factors $(A_1, A_2, \ldots, A_m)$ has been completed, the weight values are $(a_1, a_2, \ldots, a_m)$, and if A_i and B_j are not related, so, $b_{ji} = 0$. The overall ranking of the hierarchy is shown in Table 3.

This part combined with expert scoring method combined with analytic hierarchy process to calculate the weight of each index. The root of the maximum eigenvalue and its eigenvector of the matrix is as follows:

Table 3. Hierarchy total sorting table

Index	A_1	A_2	......	A_m	B hierarchy total sorting
B_1	b_{11}	b_{12}	....	b_{1m}	$\sum_{i=1}^{m} a_i b_{1i}$
B_2	b_{21}	b_{22}	....	b_{2m}	$\sum_{i=1}^{m} a_i b_{2i}$
....	....	....	....	....	....
B_n	b_{n1}	b_{n2}	....	b_{nm}	$\sum_{i=1}^{m} a_i b_{ni}$

(1) Calculate the product M_i of each row element of the matrix;

(2) Calculate the nth power root of M_i

(3) Normalize the vector $\vec{w} = \left(\overrightarrow{w_1}, \overrightarrow{w_2}, \ldots, \overrightarrow{w_N} \right)^T$ as shown in Eq. (4):

$$W_i = \frac{\overrightarrow{w_1}}{\sum_{j=1}^{n} \overrightarrow{w_j}} \tag{4}$$

(4) Calculate the largest eigenvalue of the matrix as shown in Eq. (5). Where $(AW)_i$ represents the i-th element of the vector AW

$$\lambda_{max} = \sum_{j=1}^{n} \frac{(AW)_i}{nW_i} \tag{5}$$

5. Fuzzy comprehensive evaluation: For the problem of unclear boundaries of urban logistics and distribution, fuzzy comprehensive evaluation method is the most suitable, it can establish a mathematical model to simplify the complex problem, abstract the problem of specific. Combined with the hierarchical analysis method for the secondary index ranking can determine the weight of the secondary index corresponding to the vector, and then normalized, it will be fuzzy evaluation results. The application of the fuzzy comprehensive evaluation method in the distribution center location is shown in the formula (6):

(1) to determine the fuzzy comprehensive evaluation factor set U.

(2) to determine the fuzzy comprehensive evaluation set V.

(3) to obtain the evaluation matrix R.

$$R = \begin{pmatrix} r_{11} \cdots r_{1m} \\ \cdots \ddots \cdots \\ r_{n1} \cdots r_{nm} \end{pmatrix} \tag{6}$$

(4) Establish a judgment model, using fuzzy synthesis matrix for comprehensive evaluation, as shown in Eqs. (7) and (8).

$$B = \alpha^* R = (\alpha_1, \alpha_2, \ldots, \alpha_n)^* \begin{pmatrix} r_{11} \cdots r_{1m} \\ \cdots \ddots \cdots \\ r_{n1} \cdots r_{nm} \end{pmatrix} = (b_1, b_2, \ldots, b_m) \tag{7}$$

$$B_j = \frac{b_j}{\sum_{j=1}^{n} b_j}, \ b_j = \max_{i=1}\left(\max_{i=1}\left(\alpha_i, r_{ji}\right)\right) \tag{8}$$

In the future direction of this work will be incorporation emerging technology with this network, such as IoT, Software Design Network, Crowd Associated Network and so on [24–34].

3   Conclusion

The importance of urban logistics and distribution system construction is prominent to build a reasonable and efficient operation of the city logistics and distribution system for the good development of the city economy. Based on the industrial resources and advantages, this paper presents the rational distribution of the urban logistics and distribution system by considering the distribution time, quantity and structure of the distribution system, and optimizes the basic physical layout of the city logistics and distribution system. Additionally, the supply and demand of urban logistics and distribution in the quantity, time and structure are difficult to achieve an equilibrium. The existing urban logistics and distribution system has been difficult to fulfill the needs of urban logistics and distribution requirements. Therefore, a reasonable design of urban logistics and distribution system is improved with the help of city logistics and distribution system with the quantity, time and structure of the equilibrium. It enhances system efficiency, distribution cycle, supply chain link, and reduces logistics costs by creating an equilibrium supply and demand of high-end urban logistics and distribution system. Moreover, the developed system increases the economy of the urban, improve the transport and storage capacity both for city and urban, promote the green development of urban logistics and distribution system.

Acknowledgments. This work is partially supported by Grants (PGRS170330) and (RDU180341) funded by University Malaysia Pahang.

References

1. Taniguchi, E., Thompson, R.G. (eds.): City Logistics: Mapping the Future. CRC Press, Boca Raton (2014)
2. Anderson, S., Allen, J., Browne, M.: Urban logistics—how can it meet policy makers' sustainability objectives? J. Transp. Geogr. 13(1), 71–81 (2005)
3. Bodnar, T., Okhrin, O., Parolya, N.: Optimal shrinkage estimator for high-dimensional mean vector (2016)
4. Chen, Y., Jiang, Y., Wahab, M.I.M., Long, X.: The facility layout problem in non-rectangular logistics parks with split lines. Expert Syst. Appl. 42(21), 7768–7780 (2015)
5. Cheng, Z., Zhang, P.: Notice of retraction study on logistics equilibrium early warning control of steel corporation industrial port, vol. 3, July 2010
6. dell'Olio, L., Moura, J.L., Ibeas, A., Cordera, R., Holguin-Veras, J.: Receivers' willingnessto-adopt novel urban goods distribution practices. Transp. Res. Part A: Policy Pract. 102, 130–141 (2016)

7. Devi, K., Yadav, S.P.: A multicriteria intuitionistic fuzzy group decision making for plant location selection with ELECTRE method. Int. J. Adv. Manuf. Technol. **66**, 1–11 (2013)

8. Engel, T., Sadovskyi, O., Boehm, M., Heininger, R.: A conceptual approach for optimizing distribution logistics using big data (2014)

9. Gonzalez-Feliu, J., Semet, F., Routhier, J.L.: Sustainable Urban Logistics: Concepts, Methods and Information Systems. Springer, Heidelberg (2014). https://doi.org/10.1007/978-3-642-31788-0

10. Gutjahr, W.J., Dzubur, N.: Bi-objective bilevel optimization of distribution center locations considering user equilibria. Transp. Res. Part E: Logist. Transp. Rev. **85**, 1–22 (2016)

11. Hu, J.S., Zhao, G.L.: Supply chain network equilibrium with loss-averse retailers under fuzzy demand. Control Decis. **29**, 1899–1906 (2014)

12. Kova´cs, G.: Possible methods of application of electronic freight and warehouse exchanges in solving the city logistics problems. Period. Polytech. Transp. Eng. **38**(1), 25 (2010)

13. Lan, B., Peng, J., Chen, L.: An uncertain programming model for competitive logistics distribution center location problem. Am. J. Oper. Res. **5**(6), 536 (2015)

14. Li, L., Liu, Y.: Nonlinear regression prediction of the social logistics demand forecast in our country. J. Jiangnan Univ. (Nat. Sci. Ed.) **3**(13), 375–377 (2014)

15. Liu, W., Ge, M., Yang, D.: An order allocation model in a two-echelon logistics service supply chain based on the rational expectations equilibrium. Int. J. Prod. Res. **51**(13), 3963–3976 (2013)

16. Ma, Y., Yan, F., Kang, K., Wei, X.: A novel integrated production-distribution planning model with conflict and coordination in a supply chain network. Knowl. Based Syst. **105**, 119–133 (2016)

17. Mancini, S., Gonzalez-Feliu, J., Crainic, T.G.: Planning and optimization methods for advanced urban logistics systems at tactical level. In: Gonzalez-Feliu, J., Semet, F., Routhier, J.L. (eds.) Sustainable Urban Logistics: Concepts, Methods and Information Systems. EcoProduction (Environmental Issues in Logistics and Manufacturing). ECOPROD, pp. 145–164. Springer, Heidelberg (2014). https://doi.org/10.1007/978-3-642-31788-0_8

18. Quak, H.: Sustainability of urban freight transport: retail distribution and local regulations in cities (2008)

19. Rodrigue, J.P., Comtois, C., Slack, B.: The Geography of Transport Systems. Taylor & Franci, Milton Park (2016)

20. van Schagen Lindawati, J., Goh, M., Souza, R.: Collaboration in urban logistics: motivations and barriers. Int. J. Urban Sci. **18**(2), 278–290 (2014)

21. Sheriff, K.M.M., Nachiappan, S., Min, H.: Combined location and routing problems for designing the quality-dependent and multi-product reverse logistics network. J. Oper. Res. Soc. **65**(6), 873–887 (2014)

22. Wang, G., Gunasekaran, A., Ngai, E.W., Papadopoulos, T.: Big data analytics in logistics and supply chain management: certain investigations for research and applications. Int. J. Prod. Econ. **176**, 98–110 (2016)

23. Yamada, T.: Cooperative freight transport systems. In: City Logistics: Mapping The Future (2014)

24. Bhuiyan, Z.A., Wang, G., Wang, T., Rahman, A., Wu, J.: Content-centric event-insensitive big data reduction in internet of things. In: 2017 IEEE Global Communications Conference GLOBECOM 2017—Proceedings, vol. 2018, pp. 1–6, January 2018

25. Rahman, M.A., Ali, J., Kabir, M.N., Azad, S.: A performance investigation on IoT enabled intra-vehicular wireless sensor networks. Int. J. Automot. Mech. Eng. **14**(1), 3970–3984 (2017)

26. Wang, T., Bhuiyan, M.Z.A., Wang, G., Rahman, M.A., Wu, J., Cao, J.: Big data reduction for a smart city's critical infrastructural health monitoring. IEEE Commun. Mag. **56**(3), 128–133 (2018)

27. Bhuiyan, Md.Z.A., Zaman, M., Wang, G., Wang, T., Rahman, Md.A., Tao, H.: Protected bidding against compromised information injection in IoT-based smart grid. In: The 2nd EAI International Conference on Smart Grid and Internet of Things (SGIoT 2018), Niagara Falls, Canada, 11–13 July 2018

28. Rahman, Md.A., Kabir, M.N., Azad, S., Ali, J.: On mitigating hop-to-hop congestion problem in IoT enabled intra-vehicular communication. In: The IEEE International Conference on Software Engineering and Computer Systems, Kuantan, 19–21 August 2015

29. Luo, M.Z.A., Bhuiyan, G., Wang, M.A., Rahman, J., Atiquzzaman, M.: PrivacyProtector: privacy-protected patient data collection in IoT-based healthcare systems. IEEE Commun. Mag. **56**(2), 163–168 (2018)

30. Abbas, A.M., Ali, J., Rahman, M.A., Azad, S.: Comparative investigation on CSMA/CA-based MAC protocols for scalable networks. In: 2016 International Conference on Computer and Communication Engineering (ICCCE), pp. 428–433. IEEE (2016)

31. Rahman, M.A., Mezhuyev, V., Bhuiyan, M.Z.A., Sadat, S.N., Zakaria, S.A.B., Refat, N.: Reliable decision making of accepting friend request on online social networks. IEEE Access **6**, 9484–9491 (2018)

32. Kabir, M.N., Rahman, M.A., Azad, S., Azim, M.M.A., Bhuiyan, M.Z.A.: A connection probability model for communications networks under regional failures. Int. J. Crit. Infrastruct. Prot. **20**, 16–25 (2018)

33. Abbas, A., Rahman, M.A., Kabir, M.N., Zamli, K.Z.B.: Scalable MAC strategy for emergency communication networks. Adv. Sci. Lett. **24**(10), 7407–7417 (2018)

34. Rahman, M.A., Asyhari, A.T., Bhuiyan, M.Z.A., Salih, Q.M., Zamli, K.Z.B.: L-CAQ: joint link-oriented channel-availability and channel-quality based channel selection for mobile cognitive radio networks. J. Netw. Comput. Appl. **113**, 26–35 (2018)

CRAB: Blockchain Based Criminal Record Management System

Maisha Afrida Tasnim[1], Abdullah Al Omar[1(✉)],
Mohammad Shahriar Rahman[2], and Md. Zakirul Alam Bhuiyan[3]

[1] Department of Computer Science and Engineering, University of Asia Pacific,
Dhaka 1215, Bangladesh
maishaafrida@hotmail.com, omar.cs@uap-bd.edu
[2] Department of Computer Science and Engineering,
University of Liberal Arts Bangladesh, Dhaka 1209, Bangladesh
shahriar.rahman@ulab.edu.bd
[3] Department of Computer and Information Sciences, Fordham University,
New York, NY 10458, USA
mbhuiyan3@fordham.edu

Abstract. Criminal records are highly sensitive public records. By incorporating criminal records in a blockchain, authenticity and rigidity of records can be maintained; which also helps to keep the data safe from adversaries. A peer to peer cloud network enables the decentralization of data. It helps prevent unlawful changes in the data. This paper introduces a criminal record storage system by implementing blockchain technology to store the data, which helps to attain integrity and security. Our system presents ways in which the authority can maintain the records of criminals efficiently. Authorities (e.g., Law enforcement agencies and courts) will be able to add and access criminal data. General users (e.g., selected organizations and/or individuals, airports, visa application centers etc.) will have access to the data so that they can look up criminal records. Proper and timely access to authentic criminal records is essential to enforce the law. The effect of corruption on the law enforcement forces will also decrease, as this will cut off an entire scope of corruption by removing any possibility of tampering with criminal records data by thorough accountability.

Keywords: Criminal records · Blockchain · Authenticity
Cloud network · Decentralization · Law enforcement

1 Introduction

A chief function of the government is to preserve data about individuals. Administering and utilizing these data can prove to be cumbersome, even for advanced governments. Different government law enforcement agencies have separate databases, which creates a barrier in the fluidity of data flow between different government agencies. The existence of such multiple databases also

© Springer Nature Switzerland AG 2018
G. Wang et al. (Eds.): SpaCCS 2018, LNCS 11342, pp. 294–303, 2018.
https://doi.org/10.1007/978-3-030-05345-1_25

increases the cost of their security and thus, the probability of unlawful changes are increasing gradually [1].

With the growing size of records, a good record keeping and information sharing system has become necessary in todays global environment. Law enforcement agencies have to communicate between themselves and across countries in order to keep national security intact. Having accurate and time stamped records makes it easier to accomplish the mission [2].

This is where blockchain comes into the picture. The blockchain ledger ensures no single party can control the peer to peer network so the risk of data tampering is abating. In addition, the dispersed characteristic of the blockchain ledger means that it is extremely difficult to break and also the risk of information being meddled with is greatly reduced compared to current systems that use traditional digital databases [3]. One of the aims of our system is to ensure that evidence information is not tampered during court proceedings by storing the data in cloud and keeping the transaction log and provenance data in blockchain.

A central database can be subjected to many types of hacks, most of which may severely damage the integrity and validity of the data. The security of the system depends on the database system itself. SQL injection attacks have become more common in recent days [4]. SQL injection is a highly destructive attack in which hackers try to access information stored in a database. The decentralized nature of blockchain guarantees that inherent problems of the system, like hardware and software malfunctions, have no effect on integrity of the data, as the data has multiple copies stored on each node of the network. Data in blockchain is immutable, implying that any and all changes are clearly visible on the entire network. Data updated by a node is verified by multiple nodes, and thus falsified data can seldom find its way into the blockchain [5]. Any attempt to destabilize the system will have to include simultaneous attacks on at least 51% of nodes of a certain blockchain to affect a single block. This decreases the chance of attacks exponentially with the increasing number of nodes [6].

Our system uses a decentralized data management process. The users of the system are pre-registered. Data senders must sign in to the system first. Then they digitally sign the data. The digital signature is verified by the system to make sure the data is authentic. The verified data is encrypted with a randomly generated encryption key and is sent to the cloud data storage. The metadata of this transaction is sent to the blockchain. The location of this data on the blockchain is retrieved by the system. The system then stores essential searching parameters, like case number, name of offender, passport number and national identification number in a local database. The encryption key and location of the data on the blockchain is also stored on the local database. Data receivers also have to login to the system. Then they can search for data using the aforementioned parameters. The system fetches the data and decrypts it. The system then adds this data retrieval event to the blockchain as a transaction and forwards the decrypted data to the data receiver. Even if any adversary gains access to the encryption key, they can possibly just view the data. They cannot modify data since data upload requires a valid digital signature from a pre-registered user. Also, any change to the data will be recorded on the blockchain as a transaction.

Our Contribution. Our proposed system stores an individual's criminal records. The purpose of our system is to ensure that the stored information is secure and cannot be accessed or altered by attackers. Currently large amounts of data is stored in databases which makes it highly vulnerable to attacks. Databases might as well crash, resulting in loss of data. In our system such problems will not arise since we use blockchain to store the data transaction logs alongside encrypting the data so it cannot be altered. Each node will have a copy of the transaction logs [7]. The data itself will be stored in a decentralized cloud system. Decentralization increases redundancy of the data. Elliptic Curve Cryptography (ECC) [8] encryption scheme is used in our platform to encrypt the criminal data. We generate the digital signature according to Schnorr digital signature scheme [9].

Our system uses a data provenance architecture. Information regarding upload, access or changes in Cloud data is stored in the blockchain which ensures security, privacy and integrity [10]. These security parameters are crucial while dealing with such sensitive data. CRAB makes the stored information accessible to courts, selective government organizations and individuals, all police stations, visa application centers, airports etc.

Organization of the Paper: The remainder of the paper is organized as follows: Sect. 3 outlines the protocol and details the steps, Sect. 4 briefly analyses the features of the protocol, and Sect. 5 includes some concluding statements on the probable outcome of the implementation of such a system.

2 Related Work

Various data sharing systems using blockchain have been developed [11]. Research work has been done on cloud data provenance architecture. Two such platforms are ProvChain [10] and SmartProvenance [12]. ProvChain is a decentralized cloud data provenance architecture that uses blockchain technology. When a user accesses data from the cloud, records are kept in the blockchain as transactions. It ensures that the records cannot be tampered. In ProvChain, the provenance auditor endorses provenance data by fetching transactions from the blockchain network by using blockchain-receipt which contains data in block and transactional information [10]. Here the Provenance Auditor (PA) cannot be fully trusted. Since PA has access to both user and provenance data; it can cause devastating damage to the system. To avoid this, the data is encrypted before uploading to the cloud. As such, the PA cannot directly access the data without the decryption key [10]. The SmartProvenance system is built on the existing Ethereum system, which uses smart contracts. These are used to store metadata of a file and include an event log. The event log is an immutable record consisting of the changes made to the file or data. This system can only guarantee honest behavior if at least half of the users able to access the data and provenance are honest. There also must exist a secure platform for exchanging external keys among the users, so a user can provide access to other users [12].

Work based on the Etheruem system is efficient, as mentioned in Forensic-Chain [13], where the smart contracts help to do most of the transaction verification work [13]. Similar to SmartProvenance and Forensic-Chain, MedRec [14] is a system which is also based on Ethereum. However, it uses Ethereum smart contracts to allocate each block to a single file's access permission data and state transition records. This system primarily focuses on securing access permissions to medical records through the blockchain [14].

The UK Ministry of Defence (MoD) agency is considering the use of blockchain to improve the reliability of a network that uses sensors to track national concerns. HoustonKemp, a Singapore based tech firm is working in Australia to develop a blockchain based, reliable and feasible system that will be used to keep records of all investigative intelligence [3].

Controllability and traceability are key features of a privacy preserving system [15]. Our system rules out any human intervention from data storage, integrity, privacy and traceability aspects. Ethereum based smart contracts facilitate our systems functionality, making the process of designing and implementing the blockchain simple. This also allocates the mining tasks to an existing market, generating less cost. Blockchain in government [7] talks about how the government can benefit from various applications of blockchain technology.

3   CRAB-Protocol

In this section we demonstrate the design and architecture of our system. Table 1 shows the notations that are used in this section.

Table 1. Terminology table

Notation	Description
ID	Data sender's ID
PWD	Data sender's password
U_D	Criminal data uploaded by sender
V_D	Verified criminal data
T_D	Transaction data
B_{id}	Block number where meta data of transaction is saved
CID	Criminal identification data
UAD'	Consists of CID, B_{id}, and Enc(Key)
ID_X	Sender X's ID
PWD_X	Sender X's password
U_{DX}	Criminal data uploaded by sender X
V_{DX}	Verified data of sender X
T_{DX}	Transaction data of sender X
B_{idX}	Block number where transaction data of user X is saved

3.1 Protocol Entities

Figure 1 shows the high-level view of our system. The entities and their roles in the system is described below.

Data sender is the authorized personnel from Police station, court, law enforcement agencies and armed forces, who will have to store criminal record and information into the system. The data will be verified using the sender's digital signature, and then encrypted and stored in Data Storage along with CID.

Data Receiver. Data senders, airports, visa application centers and selected organizations will play the role of data receiver in our system, they will have to sign in to the system and request for accessing data from the system using CID.

Functional Unit (FU) is the most important part of our system. This module authenticates users, verifies and encrypts data. It sends the data to the Data Storage after encrypting it. This unit also retrieves the B_{id} corresponding to a transaction. When a user has to retrieve data from the cloud, it accesses the FU and requests for data using CID. FU interacts with Local server, blockchain and Data Storage to fetch the data and it sends decrypted data to the user.

Data Storage is a part of the global cloud. It receives encrypted data from FU. Data storage stores encrypted criminal data and CID.

Blockchain stores the meta data of transactions(T_D). It is present on the cloud. It can only be accessed directly by the FU. We are using Ethereum based permissioned blockchain, which ensures data security since only FU will have the permission to access the blockchain.

Local Server stores UAD' which comprises of CID, B_{id}, and Enc(key). It sends UAD' to FU upon request.

3.2 Steps Involved

- **Step-1.** The sender accesses the system using their ID and PWD.
- **Step-2.** The sender digitally signs the U_D and sends it to the FU.
- **Step-3.** V_D is encrypted and sent to **Data Storage** along with CID.
- **Step-4.** T_D is sent to **blockchain**.
- **Step-5.** B_{id} is sent to the FU from **blockchain**.
- **Step-6.** UAD' is sent to the **Local Server**.
- **Step-7.** The receiver accesses the system with ID and PWD
- **Step-8.** FU requests Local Server for data with CID.
- **Step-9.** UAD' is returned to FU.
- **Step-10.** FU requests for data from **Data Storage** with CID.
- **Step-11.** **Data Storage** sends encrypted data to FU.
- **Step-12.** T_D is sent to **blockchain**.
- **Step-13.** B_{id} is returned to FU.
- **Step-14.** FU sends updated UAD' to **Local Server**.
- **Step-15.** Decrypted data is sent to the receiver.

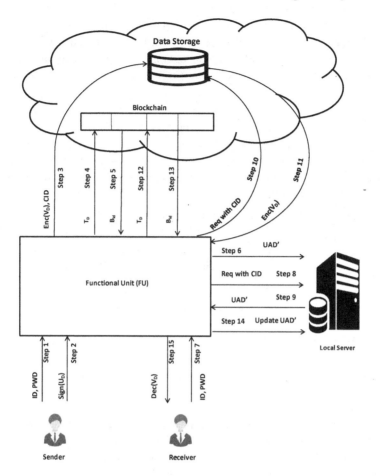

Fig. 1. Overview of the CRAB protocol

3.3   Formal Description of Protocol

In this section we describe how Data Sender, Data Receiver, and our system interact with each other while sending and receiving data. For any transaction in our system, parties need to be pre-registered. Any data transmission from parties who are not registered will be ignored by the system.

Protocol Between Data Sender and System

Police station, court, law enforcement agencies and armed forces will play the role of data sender in this protocol. Digitally signed data will be verified; the data will then be encrypted and sent to the Data Storage. The equation for key generation can be written as:

$$KeyGen(Random) = Enc(Key) \tag{1}$$

Suppose a Data Sender X wants to upload a file to the Data Storage. X signs in to the system with ID_X, and PWD_X. X digitally sign the data (U_{DX}) and send it to FU. FU verifies the digital signature against the data. A random encryption key is generated, V_{DX} is encrypted according to the following equation:

$$Enc(V_{DX}, Key) = Enc(V_{DX}) \qquad (2)$$

V_{DX} and UAD is sent to Data storage. The meta data of X's transaction, T_{DX} is sent to the blockchain. The location of the transaction data on the blockchain, B_{idX} is sent to FU. UAD' is sent to Local Server to be used for accessing data. Upon receiving B_{idX} the sender can be assured that the data has been uploaded successfully to the Data Storage.

Protocol Between System and Data Receiver
Suppose X is a Data Receiver. X uses ID_X PWD_X to sign in to the system, FU requests for data using CID, the Local Server returns UAD' to FU. FU requests for data from Data Storage. Data Storage returns encrypted V_D to FU. FU decrypts U_D according to the following equation:

$$Dec(Enc(V_D), Key) = V_D \qquad (3)$$

The decrypted data is then sent to the receiver.

4   Protocol Analysis

- **Integrity:**
  - **Authentication data integrity:** Only pre-registered users will be able to enter or retrieve data. Data sender X and receiver Y first need to authenticate themselves. They will·have to use ID and PWD provided by the authority, which are stored in the **Local server**. When X or Y provides ID and PWD, the system retrieves the actual ID and PWD from the **Local server**; if the user provided ID and PWD matches with the retrieved ID and PWD, the user is granted access to the system. Therefore authentication data is only know to X, Y and the system.
  - **User data integrity:** Using the encryption function below the criminal data is encrypted.

$$Enc(V_{DX}, Key) = Enc(V_{DX}) \qquad (4)$$

This ensures data integrity since the data stored in the **Data Storage** will not make any sense to anyone except for the data sender X. If X or Y requests for the data, the **FU** retrieves the data from the **Data Storage** and decrypts it using the following equation:-

$$Dec(Enc(V_D), Key) = V_D \qquad (5)$$

To break this integrity level adversaries need to break the ECC encryption scheme.

– **Accountability:** Transactions in blockchain help to monitor data changes. When the data sender X with ID_X sends V_D, the metadata T_{DX} is recorded in the blockchain.

$$Transact(ID_X, V_D, Current\_time, Set) = T_{DX} \tag{6}$$

When a data receiver Y with ID_Y attempts to retrieve V_D, this access T_{DY} is also recorded as in the blockchain.

$$Transact(ID_Y, V_D, Current\_time, Get) = T_D \tag{7}$$

Due to the blockchain transactions, all data senders and receivers are accountable for any interaction with the data on the cloud.
– **Security:** Data is stored in an encrypted form and cannot be accessed without the encryption key which is stored separately.
When X sends U_D, the **Functional Unit(FU)** verifies and encrypts it. V_{DX} and $Enc(V_{DX})$ are not visible to X and is completely handled by the **FU**.
When Y requests to retrieve V_{DY}, the **FU** decrypts $Enc(V_{DY})$ and forwards it to Y. Y is privy to any access in the system except its initial request. So the data is completely secure and void of direct access by sending receiving entities.
– **Automation:** The system is totally automated and requires no human intervention, which reduces risk of error.
– **Sustainability:** Since the system is automated; there is a very low risk of errors occurring. Our platform uses tried and tested methods of encryption. Thus, the system is sustainable.

Table 2. Summary table

Feature	Blockchain	Traditional database
Storage	Decentralized	Centralized
Mutability	Immutable	Mutable
Redundancy	Redundant	Non-redundant
Cost	Decreasing cost for increasing amount of data	Cost increases with increasing data size
Transparency	All nodes attest to validity of data	Validity of data may only be checked by database administrator
Point of failure	Fails only if all nodes simultaneously fail	Failure may result from any hardware or software failure of the server machine
Interoperability	Good interoperability	Hard to achieve interoperability

Table 2 shows the comparisons of features using blockchain and traditional databases. Storage refers to the manner in which the data is stored. Mutability is the ability of data to be changed. Redundancy refers to whether the data can be easily recovered if lost. Cost refers to the financial cost of implementing and maintaining these systems. Transparency means whether the data activity in the systems is visible or not. Point of failure indicates the weakest attribute of the system that can be used to destabilize or destroy it. Interoperability refers to communication between multiple similar systems.

5   Conclusion

Public records often are tampered with, and their effects are adverse. Our system lets us remove all such problems by means of decentralized data storage. Digital signatures confirm the authenticity of uploaded data. Each data sender bears the complete responsibility of the data contents. Encryption furthers the security objective of this system. The randomly generated encryption keys ensure that no two files have the same key, which exponentially reduces the risk of attacks. The cloud components, which are data storage and blockchain, are not directly accessible by any user. All these together ensure maximum security of data and precise provenance recording, and also helps overcome other possible software/hardware failure issues. Further research on this topic can bring a whole scale implementation in a city, region, state or even country.

References

1. Cheng, S., Duab, M., Domeyer, A., Lnudqvis, M.: Using blockchain to improve data management in the public sector. https://www.mckinsey.com/business-functions/digital-mckinsey/our-insights/using-blockchain-to-improve-data-management-in-the-public-sector
2. Ariq, M., Shakeel, S., Ali, Z.: Report on criminal record management system. https://www.slideshare.net/hashimabbasi786/criminal-recordmanagementsystem-report
3. Open Trading Network: UK police - blockchain solutions on the horizon. https://medium.com/@otncoin/uk-police-blockchain-solutions-on-the-horizon-60e3e1932ef3
4. Thoms, N.: SQL injection: still around, still a threat. https://www.fasthosts.co.uk/blog/digital/sql-injection-still-around-still-threat
5. Anh, D.T.T., Zhang, M., Ooi, B.C., Chen, G.: Untangling blockchain: a data processing view of blockchain systems. IEEE Trans. Knowl. Data Eng. **30**(7), 1366–1385 (2018)
6. Miles, C.: Blockchain security: what keeps your transaction data safe? https://www.ibm.com/blogs/blockchain/2017/12/blockchain-security-what-keeps-your-transaction-data-safe/
7. Ølnes, S., Ubacht, J., Janssen, M.: Blockchain in government: benefits and implications of distributed ledger technology for information sharing (2017)
8. Setiadi, I., Kistijantoro, A.I., Miyaji, A.: Elliptic curve cryptography: algorithms and implementation analysis over coordinate systems. In: 2015 2nd International Conference on Advanced Informatics: Concepts, Theory and Applications (ICAICTA), pp. 1–6. IEEE (2015)

9. Boneh, D.: Schnorr digital signature scheme. In: van Tilborg, H.C.A., Jajodia, S. (eds.) Encyclopedia of Cryptography and Security, pp. 1082–1083. Springer, Boston (2011). https://doi.org/10.1007/978-1-4419-5906-5

10. Liang, X., Shetty, S., Tosh, D., Kamhoua, C., Kwiat, K., Njilla, L.: Provchain: a blockchain-based data provenance architecture in cloud environment with enhanced privacy and availability. In: Proceedings of the 17th IEEE/ACM International Symposium on Cluster, Cloud and Grid Computing, pp. 468–477. IEEE Press (2017)

11. Crosby, M., Pattanayak, P., Verma, S., Kalyanaraman, V.: Blockchain technology: beyond bitcoin. Appl. Innov. **2**, 6–10 (2016)

12. Ramachandran, A., Kantarcioglu, M.: Smartprovenance: a distributed, blockchain based dataprovenance system. In: Proceedings of the Eighth ACM Conference on Data and Application Security and Privacy, pp. 35–42. ACM (2018)

13. Lone, A.H., Mir, R.N.: Forensic-chain: ethereum blockchain based digital forensics chain of custody. Sci. Pract. Cyber Secur. J. (2018). ISSN 2587-4667. https://journal.scsa.ge/issues/2017/12/783

14. Azaria, A., Ekblaw, A., Vieira, T., Lippman, A.: MedRec: using blockchain for medical data access and permission management. In: International Conference on Open and Big Data (OBD), pp. 25–30. IEEE (2016)

15. Al Omar, A., Rahman, M.S., Basu, A., Kiyomoto, S.: MediBchain: a blockchain based privacy preserving platform for healthcare data. In: Wang, G., Atiquzzaman, M., Yan, Z., Choo, K.-K.R. (eds.) SpaCCS 2017. LNCS, vol. 10658, pp. 534–543. Springer, Cham (2017). https://doi.org/10.1007/978-3-319-72395-2_49

Secure Passive Keyless Entry and Start System Using Machine Learning

Usman Ahmad[1](✉), Hong Song[1], Awais Bilal[2], Mamoun Alazab[3], and Alireza Jolfaei[4]

[1] School of Software, Beijing Institute of Technology, Beijing 100081, China
{usmanahmad,anniesun}@bit.edu.cn
[2] National University of Sciences and Technology, Islamabad 44000, Pakistan
13msccsabilal@seecs.edu.pk
[3] Charles Darwin University, Darwin, NT 0800, Australia
alazab.m@ieee.org
[4] Federation University Australia, Mt Helen, VIC 3350, Australia
a.jolfaei@federation.edu.au

Abstract. Despite the benefits of the passive keyless entry and start (PKES) system in improving the locking and starting capabilities, it is vulnerable to relay attacks even though the communication is protected using strong cryptographic techniques. In this paper, we propose a data-intensive solution based on machine learning to mitigate relay attacks on PKES Systems. The main contribution of the paper, beyond the novelty of the solution in using machine learning, is in (1) the use of a set of security features that accurately profiles the PKES system, (2) identifying abnormalities in PKES regular behavior, and (3) proposing a counter-measure that guarantees a desired probability of detection with a fixed false alarm rate by trading off the training time and accuracy. We evaluated our method using the last three months log of a PKES system using the Decision Tree, SVM, KNN and ANN and provide the comparative analysis of the relay attack detection results. Our proposed framework leverages the accuracy of supervised learning on known classes with the adaptability of k-fold cross-validation technique for identifying malicious and suspicious activities. Our test results confirm the effectiveness of the proposed solution in distinguishing relayed messages from legitimate transactions.

Keywords: Internet of Things · Machine learning
Passive keyless entry and start · Relay attack · Vehicle security

1 Introduction

Over the past decade, the automotive industry has advanced the traditional ways of accessing and starting the vehicles by making use of embedded processors and wireless communications. Now, there is no need to insert a physical key to open or start the vehicle. Instead, vehicles can be opened remotely with a push of a

© Springer Nature Switzerland AG 2018
G. Wang et al. (Eds.): SpaCCS 2018, LNCS 11342, pp. 304–313, 2018.
https://doi.org/10.1007/978-3-030-05345-1_26

button on the key fob or even without it. Car manufacturers have introduced modern passive keyless (PK) systems, including passive keyless entry (PKE), passive keyless start (PKS), and passive keyless entry and start (PKES) systems. PKES systems enable drivers to unlock and start their vehicles by just possessing the key fob in their pockets. The PKES communication model involves two parties: a vehicle with a receiver and a transmitter, and a portable key fob that is used to passively authorize a user to carry out a vehicle function (for example, door unlock). Generally, PKES uses a challenge-response based security protocol between the vehicle and the key fob, where the vehicle periodically scans the key fob to determine its proximity. When the key fob acknowledges its proximity, the vehicle sends a challenge along with its ID and waits for the response of the key fob. Upon the true response from the key fob, the vehicle unlocks itself.

The concept of PKES was first introduced by Waraksa et al. [1] and it was firstly implemented by Mercedes-Benz in 1998 [2]. Since then, many car manufacturers have implemented similar PK systems. Despite the convenience of PKES, it is vulnerable to man-in-the-middle attacks [3,4]. This is mainly because PKES technology communicates between the car and the key fob over an insecure channel, and hence, the communication could be eavesdropped, snooped, intercepted and re-transmitted (for example, replay attacks [5]). A group of researchers from the University of Washington and the University of California San Diego have demonstrated some remote attacks capable of braking, speeding and turning off the engine [6,7]. In addition, the authors of [2] and [8] examined the security of PKES protocol against relay attacks. They have demonstrated practical relay attacks that can unlock and start the vehicle even if the key fob is out of the vehicle's communication range.

In relay attacks, the adversary does not need to physically tamper the key fob or even decrypt the communications between the vehicle and key fob. The adversary would only requires two inexpensive power amplifiers to carry out the attack; one amplifier in the proximity of the vehicle and second one in the proximity of the key fob. The power amplifiers establish an ultra-high frequency relay line between themselves in both directions. The attacker would then relay the messages between the vehicle and the key fob. The attacking device at the vehicle side receives signals from the vehicle and replays them to the second attacking device that is in the proximity of the key fob. The key fob assumes these signals as if from the vehicle and responds accordingly. This response is then replayed back to the vehicle through both of amplifiers. The vehicle could not distinguish between the relayed signals and the real key fob signals and assumes as if the key fob is in its proximity and open the locks.

The study of the literature on the security of PKES shows a number of physical, cryptographic and anomaly detection solutions to mitigate adversarial threats, as mentioned in Sect. 2. However, the PKES protocol is still vulnerable to relay attacks, which is due to the impracticality of physical solutions and that the vehicle would only verify the proximity of the key fob rather than the verification of the physical location of the key fob.

In this paper, we propose a security layer for protecting the PKES system against well-known relay attacks. Firstly, we propose the use of a set of seven security features, including key fob acceleration, signal strength, location, time, date, type of day, and elapsed time. Then, our security layer uses machine learning techniques to identify whether a key fob signal conforms to the pattern of relayed signals. We use a 10-fold cross-validation in order to enhance the detection accuracy rate. We compare various algorithms, including the Decision Tree, Support Vector Machine (SVM), K-Nearest Neighbors (KNN) and Artificial Neural Network (ANN), with respect to accuracy rate, confusion matrix, training time and prediction time. We demonstrate the results of relay attack detection after testing our method using the last three months log of PKES system as it is sufficient to train our model and observe the system if there is a significant change in the driving routine. To the best of our knowledge, this is the first work which provides a detection strategy for PKES relay attacks using machine learning algorithms.

The rest of the paper is organized as follows: Sect. 2 reviews the related work. Section 3 proposes a machine learning based relay attack detection mechanism. Section 4 evaluates the proposed solution and demonstrates a comparative analysis of different machine learning models. Finally, Sect. 5 concludes the paper.

2   Related Work

In [9], Miller and Valasek demonstrated various remote attacks against the 2014 Jeep Cherokee. In [10], Benadjila et al. exposed a cryptographic weakness and opened the door of a target vehicle without retrieving the cryptographic key. In [2], Francillon et al. demonstrated a relay attack on PKES system by amplifying the low-frequency radio signals between the vehicle and key fob. They amplified the signal so that the vehicle could sense the key fob signal is in its proximity range and would unlock itself. In [11], Garfinkel and Rosenberg suggested to place the key fob inside a protective metallic shield, and thus, create a Faraday cage around the key. This would in theory disable the PKES system until the driver is within a very short distance to the car in order to unlock the car. However, the adversary is still able to eavesdrop the fob signal when it is unshielded.

In [12] and [13], the implementation of cryptographic solutions, including electronic control unit (ECU) authentication, integrity checks and encryption of the emitted frames, were suggested to prevent man-in-the-middle attacks. However, the computation required to perform strong enough encryption or decryption of the messages can be very time and resource consuming, which is an important concern in a real-time system such as a vehicle. This problem can be addressed by using a hardware module entirely dedicated to cryptographic operations in order to free the ECUs computational capacities. [14] and [15] give examples of a secure key exchange protocol and a message encryption using a hardware security module and an ECU dedicated to key management. However, the complete deployment of hardware security modules will take a long time because of the compatibility issues of the standard as well as the hardware issues. For example, there are still many cars in operation that have no cryptographic acceleration. In addition, the key fob can not process computationally expensive cryptographic operations because of its tiny battery power.

Another famous cryptography technique is the solution given by the Microchip Technology [16]. The proposed solution encrypts the communication between the vehicle and key fob using the KeeLoq block cipher. Microchip Technology also introduced several authentication protocols. Similarly, RSA, the Security Division of EMC, developed RSA SecurID authentication mechanism for the key fob [17]. However, despite the use of strong cryptographic and authentication techniques, the PKES system is still vulnerable to relay attacks.

In [18], Ranganathan and Capkun proposed a proximity verification method using distance bounding protocols to repel relay attacks. The proposed method determines how close the key fob and vehicle is from each other in terms of physical distance. Similarly, in [8], Choi et al. proposed a sound-based proximity detection method to prevent the relay attacks on PKES systems. Despite the novelty of this method, it has implementation constraints. The sound wave refracts when it passes through a medium with a gradually varying property. For example, the sound wave bends away from the ground during the day, while it bends towards the ground during the night.

Over the past decade, machine learning has extensively been used in automotive industry. For example, in [19], a machine learning based system was proposed to identify the faulty engine behavior of the vehicle, and in [20], a framework using conventional supervised learning was proposed to recognize and track vehicles on the road. In addition to pattern recognition and tracking, machine learning has been widely used as a powerful tool to provide security solutions in the vehicular industry, especially to detect anomalies [21]. For example, in [22], Weber et al. introduced a machine learning based anomaly detection method to identify anomalous communications using the ECU of the vehicle. The authors extracted some features from the data exchanged between ECUs and applied an unsupervised anomaly detection algorithm. In [23] and [24], the authors proposed the use of a rich set of features to profile normal and malicious packets. In [25], the author proposed a machine learning method to avoid the theft attacks on vehicles. This model continuously profiles the driver behavior by analyzing data retrieved by controller area network (CAN) bus and identify the person on driving seat as a driver or thief. In [26], the authors showed the usability of a statistical anomaly detection method in classifying malicious CAN messages in in-vehicle networks. To detect the intrusion, the proposed method checks the frequency of the exchanged messages in a fixed time slot. In [27], Kang and Kang proposed an intrusion detection system using deep neural networks to secure the in-vehicle network. The authors used CAN packet features to identify anomalous behaviors.

3   Proposed Relay Detection

This section outlines the proposed detection method for securing PKES system from relay attacks. Figure 1 demonstrates the block diagram of a relay attack and the proposed method, which is based on a supervised machine learning

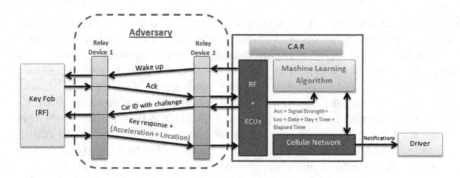

Fig. 1. Block diagram of the proposed method

algorithm that uses seven security features (listed in Table 1) including key fob acceleration, signal strength, location, time, date, type of day, and elapsed time, to detect abnormal/irregular key fob behavior. Key fob acceleration and location are embedded in the command and control data CMD, and are transmitted along with the unlock code. The rest of the features are obtained by vehicle's ECU. A greedy algorithm uses these features to train a Classification and Regression Trees (CART) algorithm [28]. The CART algorithm is a powerful and popular machine learning model that is used for both classification and regression. We have used an optimized version of the CART algorithm for classification. CART constructed a binary decision tree by splitting a node into two child nodes repeatedly, beginning with the root node that contains the whole learning sample.

The branches of the tree represent results of observed security features, while the leaf nodes denote the outcome of classification: normal (legitimate key fob signal) or malicious (relayed key fob signal). To figure a regular behavior profile, the vehicle monitors the security features for a period of three months. As the model learns the behavior of the PKES system, it modifies and updates the profile. Vehicle's ECU would use the learned decision tree to differentiate between normal and malicious key fob behaviors. When the vehicle detects a deviation from the normal behavior, it initiates a passive response and will not unlock. In addition, the vehicle would also send a warning to owner's mobile phone or other personal devices.

Table 1. PKES features

Feature	Description
Key fob acceleration	To make sure that driver is moving while unlock signal is transmitted
Signal strength	Strength of the key fob signal
Location	Current location of the key fob while transmitting the unlock signal
Time	Time at which unlock signal is transmitted from the key fob
Date	Date at which unlock signal is transmitted from the key fob
Type of day	Weekend or working day
Elapsed time	Elapsed time since the occurrence of last unlock action

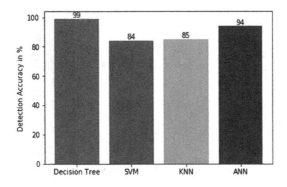

Fig. 2. Comparison of the detection accuracy rate using train/test split learning

4   Experimental Validation and Evaluation

This section illustrates the experiments conducted to validate and evaluate the performance of the proposed relay attack detection. This section also compares the proposed detection method with SVM, KNN, and ANN learning algorithms with respect to accuracy rate, confusion matrix, training time and prediction time. We used the Python programming language for our implementations. These classification algorithms require training data to train the models, and testing data to test those models using the PKES system data. We used a dataset with a total sample size of 500 that is derived from a three-month log of PKES system. We used 80% of the dataset for training and used the remaining 20% for testing. We used a k-fold cross-validation for generating an independent datasets to evaluate the results of our statistical analyses.

Figure 2 compares the rate of accuracy. The experimental results show that the decision tree has the best performance as compared to SVM, KNN, and ANN algorithms. Compared to SVM and KNN, ANN achieves a good accuracy, that is, 94%, and includes 82% true positive and 12% true negative rate. KNN has 85% accuracy, and includes 82% true positive and 3% true negative rate. SVM has achieved 84% accuracy, contains 82% true positive and 2% true negative rate. Finally, the decision tree has the best performance, that is, 99% accuracy, 82% true positive and 17% true negative rate. Our results show that SVM has a weaker performance with a higher false positive rate. SVM and KNN achieve the false positive rate of 16% and 15%, respectively. ANN performs slightly better with 6%. The decision tree has an extremely low false positive rate that is 1% only. Figure 3 illustrates the training and prediction speed of the decision tree, SVM, KNN and ANN. The decision tree and KNN have same and comparatively fast training speed among all. SVM involves some data transformations to generate the support vectors, so it demonstrates a slower training speed, that is, 9 ms. ANN takes about 160 ms to get trained. Figure 4 compares the prediction speeds. The results show that SVM has the fastest prediction speed among the algorithms under study. From Fig. 4, both decision tree and ANN have a slow prediction speed, but they are faster than KNN.

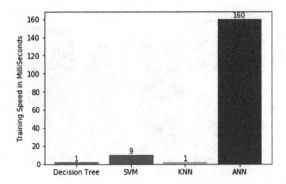

Fig. 3. Comparison of the training speed with train/test split learning

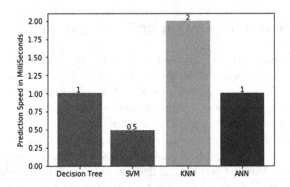

Fig. 4. Comparison of the prediction speed using train/test split learning

4.1 K-fold Cross-validation

To overcome the limitations of the train/test split procedure, we used a 10-fold cross-validation. The dataset is partitioned into 10 sized equal folds or partitions. Then, 10 repetitions of training are performed such that within each repetition a different fold of the dataset is held-out for validation, while the remaining 9 folds are used for learning. The benefit of a 10-fold cross-validation is that all the observations in the dataset are eventually used for both training and testing. Having 10 folds means 90% of the full dataset that is 400 records in our dataset is used for training and 10% (100 records) for testing in each fold test. We evaluated decision tree, SVM, KNN and ANN algorithms with respect to *True Positive (TP)*, *True Negative (TN)*, *False Positive (FP)*, *False Negative (FN)*, *True detection rate (TP rate)*, *False alarm rate (FP rate)*, *F-Measure*, and *Overall Accuracy*.

The 10-fold cross-validation has eventually used all 500 observations in our dataset for both training and testing. The result of our analysis shows an improvement in performance compared to a train/test split method. Figures 5 and 6 compare the detection accuracy and training speed of all four algorithms using 10-fold cross-validation. As shown in figures, the decision tree has the highest accuracy, and decision tree and KNN have probably the same and comparatively fast training speed among all. The comprehensive analysis of supervised learning of decision tree, SVM, KNN, and ANN is summarized in Table 2.

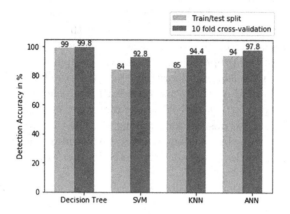

Fig. 5. Comparison of detection accuracy against relay attack using train/test split and 10 Fold cross-validation learning

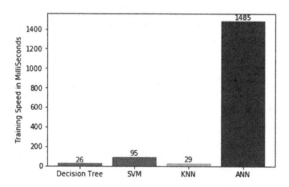

Fig. 6. Comparison of training speed using 10 fold cross-validation learning

Table 2. Learning comparison results

		Decision tree	SVM	KNN	ANN
Train/test split	Detection accuracy %	99	84	85	94
	Training time (ms)	1	9	1	160
	Prediction time (ms)	1	0.5	2	1
	True positive	82	82	82	82
	True negative	17	2	3	12
	False positive	1	16	15	6
	False negative	0	0	0	0
10 fold cross-validation	Detection accuracy %	99.8	92.8	94.4	97.8
	Training time (ms)	26	95	29	1485

5 Conclusion

In this paper, we proposed a detection method for relay attacks, making use of a CART algorithm that uses six security features for profiling normal key fob messages. Moreover, we used a k-fold cross-validation to overcome the limitations of train/test split procedure and to improve the accuracy rate. We used a three-month log of a PKES system and demonstrated an experiment to test the performance of the proposed algorithm. We compared our algorithm with SVM, KNN, and ANN leaning algorithms, and the result of our tests demonstrated that our method outperforms other learning techniques. Our algorithm achieves the best relay attack detection accuracy rate, fast training and prediction speed, and low false positive rate among all. For the future work, we plan to conduct experiments by making use of deep learning algorithms including recurrent neural networks to enhance the detection performance.

References

1. Waraksa, T.J., Fraley, K.D., Kiefer, R.E., Douglas, D.G., Gilbert, L.H.: Passive keyless entry system. Google Patents, US Patent 4,942,393 (1990)
2. Francillon, A., Danev, B., Capkun, S.: Relay attacks on passive keyless entry and start systems in modern cars. In: Proceedings of the Network and Distributed System Security Symposium (NDSS) (2011)
3. Fu, K., Xu, W.: Risks of trusting the physics of sensors. Commun. ACM **61**(2), 20–23 (2018)
4. Bacchus, M., Coronado, A., Gutierrez, M.A.: The insights into car hacking (2017)
5. Jolfaei, A., Kant, K.: A lightweight integrity protection scheme for fast communications in smart grid. In: International Conference on Security and Cryptography, pp. 31–42 (2017)
6. Koscher, K., et al.: Experimental security analysis of a modern automobile. In: 2010 IEEE Symposium on Security and Privacy (SP), pp. 447–462 (2010)
7. Checkoway, S., et al.: Comprehensive experimental analyses of automotive attack surfaces. In: USENIX Security Symposium (2011)
8. Choi, W., Seo, M., Lee, D.H.: Sound-proximity: 2-factor authentication against relay attack on passive keyless entry and start system. J. Adv. Transp. (2018)
9. Miller, C., Valasek, C.: Remote exploitation of an unaltered passenger vehicle. Black Hat USA, vol. 2015 (2015)
10. Benadjila, R., Renard, M., Lopes-Esteves, J., Kasmi, C.: One car, two frames: attacks on hitag-2 remote keyless entry systems revisited. In: USENIX Workshop on Offensive Technologies (2017)
11. Garfinkel, S., Rosenberg, B.: RFID: Applications, Security, and Privacy. Pearson Education India, Chennai (2006)
12. Van Herrewege, A., Singelee, D., Verbauwhede, I.: CANAuth - a simple, backward compatible broadcast authentication protocol for CAN Bus. In: ECRYPT Workshop on Lightweight Cryptography, vol. 2011 (2011)
13. Groza, B., Murvay, S., Van Herrewege, A., Verbauwhede, I.: LiBrA-CAN: a lightweight broadcast authentication protocol for controller area networks, pp. 185–200(2012)

14. Schweppe, H., Roudier, Y., Weyl, B., Apvrille, L., Scheuermann, D.: Car2X communication: securing the last meter-a cost-effective approach for ensuring trust in Car2X applications using in-vehicle symmetric cryptography. In: IEEE Vehicular Technology Conference, pp. 1–5 (2011)

15. Guan, L., Lin, J., Luo, B., Jing, J., Wang, J.: Protecting private keys against memory disclosure attacks using hardware transactional memory. In: IEEE Symposium on Security and Privacy, pp. 3–19 (2015)

16. Bruwer, F.: Microchips and remote control devices comprising same. Google Patents, US Patent 6,108,326 (2000)

17. Brainard, J., Juels, A., Rivest, R.L., Szydlo, M., Yung, M.: Fourth-factor authentication: somebody you know. In: ACM Conference on Computer and Communications Security, pp. 168–178 (2006)

18. Ranganathan, A., Capkun, S.: Are we really close? Verifying proximity in wireless systems. IEEE Secur. Priv. (2017)

19. Park, J., et al.: Intelligent vehicle power control based on machine learning of optimal control parameters and prediction of road type and traffic congestion. IEEE Trans. Veh. Technol. **58**(9), 4741–4756 (2009)

20. Sivaraman, S., Trivedi, M.M.: A general active-learning framework for on-road vehicle recognition and tracking. IEEE Trans. Intell. Transp. Syst. **11**(2), 267–276 (2010)

21. Avatefipour, O., Malik, H.: State-of-the-art survey on in-vehicle network communication (CAN-Bus) security and vulnerabilities. arXiv preprint arXiv:1802.01725 (2018)

22. Weber, M., Klug, S., Sax, E., Zimmer, B.: Embedded hybrid anomaly detection for automotive CAN communication. In: 9th European Congress on Embedded Real Time Software and Systems (2018)

23. Alazab, A., Hobbs, M., Abawajy, J., Alazab, M.: Using feature selection for intrusion detection system. In: International Symposium on Communications and Information Technologies (ISCIT), pp. 296–301. IEEE (2012)

24. Tran, K.-N., Alazab, M., Broadhurst, R., et al.: Towards a feature rich model for predicting spam emails containing malicious attachments and URLs. In: 11th Australasian Data Mining Conference, Canberra (2013)

25. Martinelli, F., Mercaldo, F., Nardone, V., Orlando, A., Santone, A.: Who's driving my car? A machine learning based approach to driver identification (2018)

26. Kuwahara, T., et al.: Supervised and unsupervised intrusion detection based on CAN message frequencies for in-vehicle network. J. Inf. Process. **26**, 306–313 (2018)

27. Kang, M.-J., Kang, J.-W.: Intrusion detection system using deep neural network for in-vehicle network security. PloS ONE **11**(6), e0155781 (2016)

28. Breiman, L.: Bagging predictors. Mach. Learn. **24**(2), 123–140 (1996)

The 10th International Symposium on UbiSafe Computing (UbiSafe 2018)

UbiSafe 2018 Organizing and Program Committees

Steering Committee

Vipin Chaudhary	University at Buffalo, SUNY, USA
Jingde Cheng	Saitama University, Japan
Yuanshun Dai	University of Tennessee, USA
Thomas Grill	Johannes Kepler Univ. Linz, Austria
Runhe Huang	Hosei University, Japan
Qun Jin	Waseda University, Japan
Ismail Khalil	Johannes Kepler Univ. Linz, Austria
Xiaolin (Andy) Li	University of Florida, USA
Jianhua Ma	Hosei University, Japan
Guojun Wang	Guangzhou University, China
Laurence T. Yang	St. Francis Xavier University, Canada
Qiangfu Zhao	The University of Aizu, Japan

General Chairs

Shuhong Chen	Guangzhou University, China
Xiaoyong Li	Beijing University of Posts and Telecommunications, China

Program Chairs

Fuhua (Oscar) Lin	Athabasca University, Canada
Xiaojiang (James) Du	Temple University, USA
Zhangbin Zhou	China University of Geosciences, China and TELECOM SudParis, France

Program Committee

Ali Dewan	Athabasca University, Canada
Joshua Ellul	University of Malta, Republic of Malta
Vasilis Friderikos	King's College London, UK
Honghao Gao	Shanghai University, China
Abdelmajid Khelil	Landshut University of Applied Sciences, Germany
Xiangyong Liu	Central South University, China
Entao Luo	Hunan University of Science and Engineering
Amjad Mehmood	Kohat University of Science & Technology, Pakistan

Albena Mihovska	Aarhus University, Denmark
Danda B. Rawat	Howard University, USA
Qin Tan	Athabasca University, Canada
Wenjuan Tang	University of Waterloo, Canada
Wei Wang	University of Waterloo, Canada
Fan Wu	University of Waterloo, Canada
Yang Xu	Central South University, China
Ming Yan	Georgia State University, USA
Jianhua Yin	Shandong University, China
Sherali Zeadally	University of Kentucky, USA
Wei Zhou	Victoria University, Australia

Publicity Chairs

Sheng Wen	Swinburne University of Technology, Australia
Jianqi Li	Hunan University of Arts and Science, China
Xilong Qu	Hunan University of Finance and Economics, China

Webmaster

| Yao Li | Guangzhou University, China |

Towards New Privacy Regulations in Europe: Users' Privacy Perception in Recommender Systems

Itishree Mohallick[1], Katrien De Moor[2], Özlem Özgöbek[1(✉)],
and Jon Atle Gulla[1]

[1] Department of Computer Science, NTNU, Trondheim, Norway
itishrem@stud.ntnu.no, {ozlem.ozgobek,jon.atle.gulla}@ntnu.no
[2] Department of Information Security and Communication Technology, NTNU,
Trondheim, Norway
katrien.demoor@ntnu.no

Abstract. Despite the fact that recommender systems are becoming increasingly popular in every aspect of the web, users might hesitate to use these personalization-based services in return of their personal information if they believe their privacy is compromised in any possible way. While new privacy regulations in Europe bring more transparency and control over data collection to users, this study aims to provide a better understanding of the users' perception over privacy in recommender systems domain over several aspects such as behavioral preferences, privacy preferences, trust, data ownership and control over own data through an on-line survey. The results indicate that the majority of the respondents consider that recommender systems violate user privacy in different ways. Further, the results indicate that increased control and perceived sense of ownership over one's own data may help to decrease the negative attitudes towards recommender systems and providers and to re-instate and increase users' trust. However, the findings also indicate that users' trust may be hard to re-establish in cases where the thought of "apparently"/in theory go hand in hand with more transparency and user control will in reality/in practice not lead to drastic changes.

Keywords: Privacy · Recommender systems · Privacy perception
EU GDPR · User study

1 Introduction

The presence of personalization-based systems in every corner of the World Wide Web has marked itself as a powerful tool. However, this optimistic outlook of such technologies possess a severe threat to user privacy due to their need of collection, processing and transfer of personal data [14]. The growing concern about the violation of privacy with the rise of ubiquitous recommendation technologies, is a potential research area for many researchers.

© Springer Nature Switzerland AG 2018
G. Wang et al. (Eds.): SpaCCS 2018, LNCS 11342, pp. 319–330, 2018.
https://doi.org/10.1007/978-3-030-05345-1_27

Recommender systems need to collect, store and process user's personal information in order to provide tailored services for individual users. This indeed is the primary source of user's privacy invasion in recommendation domain. Users are concerned about their online privacy which is found from various earlier researches [1–3,11,14]. Most of these research indicate that the privacy breach of user data is a result of directly accessing user data and indirectly, inferring from user's preference data or unauthorized usage by the external entities. A detailed research consisting of numerous survey results performed in the past decades concerning user's privacy perception supports the aforesaid user concern about privacy [10,19,20].

On the other hand, the protection of users' private data is a similarly important research topic in the modern information society. However the users' privacy behavior varies in practice as compared to the theoretical preferences. This is a privacy paradox [4,5,21] in the personalization-based systems and it is well studied through user-centric research. Generally, surveys on user privacy focus on information disclosure to on-line service providers. However, the sharing of user profiles across services, trust to the service provider, and control and ownership over personal data are less studied areas of user-centric research related to privacy and/in the recommender systems domain.

The primary purpose of this study is not only to gain better insights into the privacy preferences, perception, and behavior of users in the context of recommender systems but also to explore the ways of increasing the trust on the service provider and user control over personal data. With the current enforcement of the EU GDPR (European Union General Data Protection Regulation), this research can shed light on the promises of the GDPR and remaining challenges in this respect. The new set of GDPR rules aim to bring two primary changes over the existing regulation. This sets a higher bar for the collection of personal data by the various service providers. In addition, the informed and explicit consent of the user is made mandatory while obtaining the user data. Secondly, the penalties for the non-followers (service providers who will not adhere to the new GDPR) are made severe enough. This study is based on an on-line survey on user's privacy perception in a season of rising privacy concerns in personalized systems, in which 200 participants of 28 different nationalities participated. The research was conducted at the Norwegian University of Science and Technology in Trondheim, Norway.

This paper is structured as follows. A brief background study related to user perception on privacy in recommender systems is given in Sect. 2. Section 3 explains the methodological approach and study set-up. Section 4 reports on the main findings from the study. Finally, Sect. 5 further discusses and summarizes the results and suggests a number of potential directions for future research on user perception in recommender systems.

2   Related Work

The concept of privacy is an explicit human perception which is inherently associated with data collection, data distribution (sharing) and re-use of the disclosed data. In general, users prefer to share a fair amount of personal data for personalized recommendation purposes [4,7,13,23]. But at the same time, users express their concern for invasion of their information privacy through excessive data collection, incorrect inference and inappropriate after usage by these recommender systems.

Periodically, multiple surveys are performed in the past to understand user's online attitude with ubiquitous computing [1,15,19]. The largest survey conducted till date by the European Commission to find out European citizens attitude towards data protection, user privacy and identity management reveals the awareness, views and wish regarding the European user's data protection [8]. Given the three primary privacy threats in the recommender systems, namely: the recommender systems itself, other users of the systems and external entities, several privacy solutions have been adopted [13,16] over the last years. These measures and solutions range from technical solutions, algorithmic solutions, and more recently also legislative approaches such as EU GDPR. The recent commencement of EU GDPR is an approach to address the concerns expressed in the aforesaid survey and to protect the European user's personal data. The various key concerns to protect the fundamental rights and freedom of individual users added in GDPR [9] includes the following set of rules: (a) The right to be forgotten, (b) better control over who holds ones private data, (c) the right to switch ones personal data to another service provider, (d) the right to be informed in clear and plain language, (e) the right to know if your data has been hacked, (f) clear limits on the use of profiling, (g) special protection for children. This legislature also works towards the free movement of European data across all the member states.

As user's attitude towards privacy differs in different situations, it is important to study user perception on privacy within diverse cultural backgrounds and with different demographic aspects to explore the changes on user's privacy concern and behavior. In one such prior research [17], we have studied the privacy perspective of Norwegian users as compared to the other non-Norwegian users in a recommendation environment. As a continuation of the aforesaid approach, we have continued the data collection for the similar survey on diverse set of people. With an objective of understanding user's privacy attitude and information sharing behavior against different demographic setting, the user-centric survey is conducted after the GDPR is implemented.

3   User Study: Methodology

The primary objective of a survey strategy is to gather similar data from a group of people in an organized manner. Then the found statistical patterns are utilized to establish a general trend for a larger population [18]. In this study, data has been collected by using the on-line survey method in order to further investigate the users' broader perceptions of (violation of) user privacy, and attitudes towards recommender systems and service providers. In the following section we briefly present the included topics, before describing a number of key characteristics of the respondents.

3.1 Survey Design and Distribution

The survey was designed to include the privacy perception in recommender systems in general and in relation to specific recommender systems domains. Moreover, we also aimed to explore potential preferences in cross-domain recommendations and willingness of users to let their profile be shared across domains.

The survey consisted of 25 (both closed and open-ended) questions in English. From previous experience we know that users are not always aware of the fact that they are using recommender systems, as they often look like a natural part of the web page. This means that a regular Internet user may be exposed to several recommendations in a day, yet she or he may not be aware of it. Therefore, a brief description of recommender systems with a number of screen-shots of frequently used services was provided at the beginning of the survey, before any questions related to the use of and attitudes towards recommender systems were asked.

This short description was followed by a number of basic socio-demographical and general use-related questions. Next, the survey contained a number of questions related to perceived privacy issues and violation of privacy by and related to the use of recommender systems. Further, preferences in terms of recommender systems and cross-domain recommendations, as well as willingness to share one's user profile in a cross-domain environment were queried. Finally, questions concerned with trust and trustworthiness of recommender systems/providers and with data control and ownership were included.

The data have been collected in three phases in a total time span of 6 weeks. The first two phases were held in 2017 (May and July 2017) and the last phase was held in February 2018. The total number of participants to the user survey was 200 (52 participants in the first phase, 48 participants in the second and 100 participants in the third phase). A convenience sampling approach was used: the link to the survey was distributed via the involved researchers' own networks and existing channels. This approach has the advantage that it is more affordable as it draws on the recruitment of easily accessible subjects to the study. It has however also disadvantages as it may introduce a certain bias and does not allow for generalizations towards the entire population [12]. Yet, as the main goal with the study was not to generalize, but to further explore and gain better insights into users' perceptions and attitudes towards privacy issues with recommender systems, we consider the use of this sampling approach is justified here.

3.2 Sample Description

As mentioned above, in total 200 respondents filled out the entire survey. While they stem from 28 different countries, the majority are Norwegian (which is due to the fact that the survey was distributed through channels at the Norwegian University of Science and Technology). The top 4 nationalities participated to the user survey is as follows: Norwegian (39%), Indian (22.5%), Turkish (8.5 %) and Chinese (7%). In terms of gender, the sample consists of 68.5% male participants, whereas 31.5% are female. In terms of age, it should be noted that most of the participants (52%) are between 25 and 34 years old. This is followed by the age group 35–44 which includes 22.5% of all the participants. Even though no formal question on the educational level of the participants was included, we assume that the sample primarily consists of participants with a relatively high education level, as the survey invitation was primarily distributed via networks and channels linked to the university.

4   Results

Before addressing attitudes related to (violation of) user privacy, trust, and data ownership and control, we briefly present a number of general usage-related aspects.

The majority of the participants (78.7%) can be considered as frequent users of recommender systems. Around 8 out of 10 frequent users report that they use recommender systems and personalized services on a daily basis (up to several times a day). We found no significant differences between male and female participants and the different age groups in this respect. Even though we did not collect fine-grained data on which specific services participants use (and how), data were collected on the importance of recommendations/personalized services in different domains (on a scale from 1 to 10). Overall, recommendations are considered more important in the domains of books, movies, and music compared to the domains of news and tourism. We found no gender differences in this respect, but for frequent users, analyses using the Mann-Whitney U test indicated that getting recommendations for books ($U = 2855, p < .05$, Median $= 6$), movies ($U = 2691, p < .01$, Median $= 7$) and music ($U = 2153, p = .000$, Median $= 7$) is significantly more important than it is for sporadic users.

As part of the further analysis, we systematically checked for potential differences in attitudes linked to usage frequency, basic demographical variables such as gender, age group, and where relevant, attitude-related variables. Finally, one more behavior-related variable was systematically included in this respect, and where relevant, we compare participants that already have requested to see their user profile or other information the provider has about them (32%) with those that have never done so (68%).

4.1   Violation of User Privacy

First we present the results related with the violation of user privacy. As it is shown in Fig. 1, less than 1 out of 10 respondents think that recommender systems that they use/have used respect laws and regulations on privacy and security. While around 1 out of 3 respondents clearly disagree here, it is interesting to note that more than half is in a grey zone: they do not know or are not sure.

When asked to which extent they think that existing recommender systems violate user privacy (on a scale from 1 to 10, where the lowest rating is 1 and the highest is 10), this uncertainty is also reflected. The average rating is 5.96, but the variance and spread of the values is rather large, indicating that the opinions are

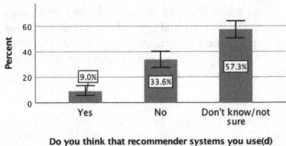

Do you think that recommender systems you use(d)
respect laws/regulations on privacy and security?

Error Bars: 95% CI

Fig. 1. Users' perception towards respect/violation of privacy laws and regulations

rather mixed. Even though no differences could be observed between the different age groups and frequent versus sporadic users, the data show a tendency that men are more skeptical in this respect and think to a significantly higher extent that recommender systems do violate user privacy ($U = 3781, p < .01$). This can be observed in Fig. 2, which also indicates that the opinions overall are rather mixed, also among men and women.

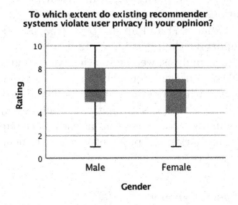

Fig. 2. Extent to which recommender systems are perceived to violate user privacy, by gender

As can be observed in Fig. 3, main concerns of users are the sharing of data with third parties (66%), collection of more data than what has been approved (49%) and the use of data for other purposes than what was approved (44%). Respondents also had the possibility to further elaborate on this issue in an open question. Here several participants noted that privacy terms and conditions represent a challenge in itself, as consent is often implicitly hidden in terms and conditions. As one respondent puts it: *"Often it can be difficult to know what is approved. You may not read all the terms before accepting because of long text and it being hard to understand".*

4.2   Trust and How to Increase It

The findings presented above where only a minority of respondents think that privacy-related laws and regulations are respected by service providers and a majority perceives that privacy is violated in several ways, imply that trust in recommender systems/providers and their practices in terms of e.g., data sharing and usage, is rather low. This raises the important question of how trust to service providers could be improved and what recommender system users consider as essential elements that could contribute to the trustworthiness of recommender system providers. As shown in Fig. 4, the top 3 elements in this respect are: asking permission before using/sharing the users' data (77%), respecting the applicable laws and regulations (70%) and having the option to change and/or delete one's user profile (66%). Entries to the follow-up open question however also indicate that there is a user segment who will never really trust providers, as *"they are dependent on collecting and selling users' data"*. In addition, as some respondents point out, even if providers respect the laws and regulations, there is a risk of *surveillance* by governmental bodies. Finally, some respondents fear that even with some of the above options (e.g., being able to change and/or delete one's user profile), there will still not be real transparency and control over own data. As one respondent puts it: *"I don't trust 'delete' to be a true delete. Data is still kept"*. Another respondent even coins that some well-intended measures may *"give the appearance of transparency and control"*, while they in practice essentially may not change much.

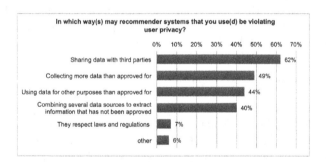

Fig. 3. Violation of user privacy by recommender systems, as perceived by the survey participants

While follow-up analyses did not yield any statistical differences between men and women or depending on the usage frequency or users' age in terms of the potentially trust-enhancing characteristics, we can observe a significant difference between respondents that already have at some point asked to see their user profile and information that the provider has about them and those who never did so: the former consider the option to modify and delete one's user profile to a larger extent as a characteristic associated with a trusted provider $(\chi^2(1) = 4.602, p < .05)$.

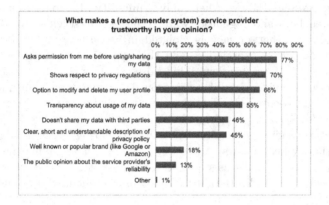

Fig. 4. Characteristics of trusted and trustworthy providers

The extent to which a service provider is trusted also seems to be relevant in the context of cross-domain recommendations. When asked whether they would be willing to let their user profile be shared across applications, 61% of the respondents reply negatively and they indicate that even if they would be able to choose the applications themselves, they do not want their profile to be shared. However, when asked to which extent this would be the case if the service provider is one that they trust, the number of respondents that says no drops to 41% and the willingness to let the user profile be shared under certain conditions increases considerably.

4.3 Control over Personal Data

Ownership and control over user's own personal data plays a crucial role in empowering users in the recommendation domain. As has been shown in previous studies, a minimal level of control and ownership increases the trust on the service provider and decreases the privacy concerns of users [22].

In the study presented here, it is also clear that a lack of trust is implicitly linked to lack of control over own data (sharing data with other parties, using data for other purposes than approved etc.). Providing users with real possibilities to control their own data (e.g., possibility to inspect, modify and delete their user profile) could increase both users' agency and empowerment, but could also result in more positive attitudes. As shown in Fig. 5, this possibility would make most respondents less worried about privacy risks when using recommender systems (63%) and would also increase their trust to service providers (52%). No

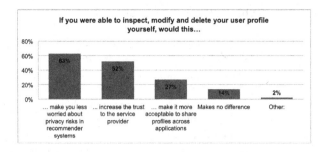

Fig. 5. Anticipated implications of being able to inspect, modify, delete own data and user profile

significant differences between groups (in terms of gender, usage frequency, age) could be observed here.

When it comes to data ownership and the use of recommender systems, the findings indicate that overall, respondents consider it as rather important to own their own data (average: 7.23, standard deviation: 2.31). For respondents who think that the applicable laws and regulations are not respected, data ownership is significantly more important than for those who do not know or are not sure ($H = 7.14(2), p < .05$).

However, what does "owning your own data" in the recommender systems domain actually mean for users? The results indicate that only a limited number of respondents (14%) associate this with storing data on one's own device. For the majority, ownership in this respect means being able to decide how one's data is shared (72%) and being able to modify and delete one's data (77%). Still, as mentioned in the beginning of this section, only slightly under 1 out 3 has already requested to see their online user profile or other information that the provider has about them, which indicates a potential discrepancy between the attitudes towards control and ownership over own data and respondents' actual behavior. In this respect, one respondent also underlined the importance of *"educating users"* by making them more aware of *"the value and amount of data that is collected about them on a daily basis"* and by making them more aware of their rights and possibilities when it comes to data control and ownership.

5   Discussion and Conclusions

In this paper, we have presented the results from an online survey on privacy perception of users in the recommender systems domain within three main categories: violation of user privacy, trust and data ownership. The main findings of the study can be summarized as it is shown in Table 1.

According to the results, there is no significant age group of usage frequency difference that affects the findings. However, gender seems to have an effect on the perception of privacy violation of recommender systems, where men are found to be more skeptical about their personal data than women.

Table 1. Summary of main findings.

Violation of user privacy	Only 10% of the users think that the recommender systems respect existing laws and regulations
	There is no significant perception difference between age groups and frequent versus sporadic users, however men are more skeptical than women about recommender systems violating user privacy
	Main concerns of the users are that the recommender systems share personal data with third parties, collect more data and use the personal data for other purposes than what has been approved
Trust	Trust to the recommender system service providers is found to be low
	Incorporating the users more by asking permission for sharing their data and giving the option for users to modify/delete their user profiles can increase trust
	Trust affects the common data usage for cross domain recommendations
Data ownership	For most of the users, ownership of personal data is important
	According to the users, ownership means deciding how the personal data is used/shared and being able to modify/delete it
	Ownership can increase the level of trust to the service provider by reducing user's privacy concern

With the new privacy regulations in Europe, EU GDPR seems to be the answer for some of these privacy concerns. As mentioned in Sect. 2, GDPR gives a better control to users over their own data which can decrease the privacy concerns of users in recommender systems domain. However, the concern about the recommender systems (or service providers) not respecting the laws and regulations may not be affected by the change of regulations. As some of the survey participants noted that a delete of a user profile by its owner may not be a true delete and it can still be available somewhere in the service provider's database implies that the service provider may not follow the regulations. Similarly, as noted by some participants, giving the appearance of transparency and control may not be a real solution to the privacy violations. Even though the GDPR is a big step towards the protection of privacy and fundamental rights of the users in Europe, the control of the service providers' respect to the regulations is important. EU GDPR strengthens the conditions of consent where the service providers have to provide an intelligent and easily accessible form for the users which must be written in simple language. The users no longer have to go through the hassle of long illegible terms and conditions full of legalese anymore while giving their consent. Similarly, withdrawal of the user consent is made easier with the new regulation.

Recommender systems should primarily focus on privacy-driven user-centric approaches to accomplish the milestones of EU GDPR. In addition to this, recommender systems might have to change or adjust many of the currently used algorithms for individual decision making including profiling in order to comply with "the right to be forgotten". The practice of "privacy by design" [6] concept has the potential to attain the privacy regulation (GDPR) in recommender systems and the various service providers as well. However, the limitations of the aforesaid concept might restrain to gain complete privacy protection for the recommender systems. Sensible user engagement is thus required by these service providers, depending on the context. Also the privacy compatibility of worldwide online services remains several questions in the minds of users. The multicultural background of participants in this study shows that the users from all over the world share similar privacy concerns and requirements.

Acknowledgments. This work is a part of the master thesis which is supported by the NTNU SmartMedia program on news recommendation.

References

1. Ackerman, M.S., Cranor, L.F., Reagle, J.: Privacy in e-commerce: examining user scenarios and privacy preferences. In: Proceedings of the 1st ACM Conference on Electronic Commerce, pp. 1–8. ACM (1999)
2. Adams, A.: Users' perception of privacy in multimedia communication. In: Extended Abstracts on Human Factors in Computing Systems, CHI 1999, pp. 53–54. ACM (1999)
3. Antón, A.I., Earp, J.B., Young, J.D.: How internet users' privacy concerns have evolved since 2002. IEEE Secur. Priv. **8**(1), 21–27 (2010). https://doi.org/10.1109/MSP.2010.38. ISSN: 1540-7993
4. Awad, N.F., Krishnan, M.S.: The personalization privacy paradox: an empirical evaluation of information transparency and the willingness to be profiled online for personalization. MIS Q. **30**(1), 13–28 (2006). http://www.jstor.org/stable/25148715
5. Barnes, S.B.: A privacy paradox: social networking in the United States. First Monday **11**(9) (2006). http://journals.uic.edu/ojs/index.php/fm/article/view/1394
6. Cavoukian, A., Fisher, A., Killen, S., Hoffman, D.A.: Remote home health care technologies: how to ensure privacy? Build it in: privacy by design. Identity Inf. Soc. **3**(2), 363–378 (2010)
7. Chellappa, R.K., Sin, R.G.: Personalization versus privacy: an empirical examination of the online consumers dilemma. Inf. Tech. Manag. **6**(2–3), 181–202 (2005)
8. European Commission: Attitudes on data protection and electronic identity in the European Union, June 2011. http://ec.europa.eu/commfrontoffice/publicopinion/archives/ebs/ebs_359_en.pdf
9. European Commission: 2018 reform EU data protection rules, May 2018. https://ec.europa.eu/commission/priorities/justice-and-fundamental-rights/data-protection/2018-reform-eu-data-protection-rules_en

10. Cranor, L.F., Reagle, J., Ackerman, M.S.: Beyond concern: understanding net users attitudes about online privacy. In: The Internet Upheaval: Raising Questions, Seeking Answers in Communications Policy, pp. 47–70 (2000)
11. Fox, S., Rainie, L., Horrigan, J., Lenhart, A., Spooner, T., Carter, C.: Trust and privacy online: why Americans want to rewrite the rules. The Pew Internet and American Life Project, pp. 1–29 (2000)
12. Henry, G.T.: Practical Sampling, vol. 21. Sage, Thousand Oaks (1990)
13. Knijnenburg, B.P., Berkovsky, S.: Privacy for recommender systems: tutorial abstract. In: Proceedings of the Eleventh ACM Conference on Recommender Systems, pp. 394–395. ACM (2017)
14. Kobsa, A.: Tailoring privacy to users' needs[1]. In: Bauer, M., Gmytrasiewicz, P.J., Vassileva, J. (eds.) UM 2001. LNCS (LNAI), vol. 2109, pp. 301–313. Springer, Heidelberg (2001). https://doi.org/10.1007/3-540-44566-8_52
15. Lederer, S., Mankoff, J., Dey, A.K.: Who wants to know what when? Privacy preference determinants in ubiquitous computing. In: Extended Abstracts on Human Factors in Computing Systems, CHI 2003, pp. 724–725. ACM (2003)
16. Mohallick, I., Özgöbek, Ö.: Exploring privacy concerns in news recommender systems. In: Proceedings of the International Conference on Web Intelligence, pp. 1054–1061. ACM (2017)
17. Mohallick, I., Özgöbek, Ö.: A survey on Norwegian user perspective on privacy in recommender systems. In: Proceedings of the 3rd Norwegian Big Data Symposium (NOBIDS 2017) in Conjunction with NxtMedia Conference 2017. CEUR Workshop Proceedings (2017)
18. Oates, B.J.: Researching Information Systems and Computing. Sage Publications Ltd., Thousand Oaks (2006)
19. Olson, J., Grudin, J., Horvitz, E.: Toward understanding preferences for sharing and privacy. In: Proceedings of the CHI (2004)
20. Olson, J.S., Grudin, J., Horvitz, E.: A study of preferences for sharing and privacy. In: Extended Abstracts on Human Factors in Computing Systems, CHI 2005, pp. 1985–1988. ACM (2005)
21. Pötzsch, S.: Privacy awareness: a means to solve the privacy paradox? In: Matyáš, V., Fischer-Hübner, S., Cvrček, D., Švenda, P. (eds.) Privacy and Identity 2008. IAICT, vol. 298, pp. 226–236. Springer, Heidelberg (2009). https://doi.org/10.1007/978-3-642-03315-5_17
22. Taylor, D.G., Davis, D.F., Jillapalli, R.: Privacy concern and online personalization: the moderating effects of information control and compensation. Electron. Commer. Res. 9(3), 203–223 (2009)
23. Toch, E., Wang, Y., Cranor, L.F.: Personalization and privacy: a survey of privacy risks and remedies in personalization-based systems. User Model. User-Adap. Interact. 22(1–2), 203–220 (2012)

SafeTECKS: Protect Data Safety in Things-Edge-Cloud Architecture with Knowledge Sharing

Shangfo Huang[1], Weifeng Lv[1], Zhipu Xie[1], Bo Huang[2], and Bowen Du[1(✉)]

[1] Key State Laboratory, Beihang University, Beijing 100083, China
{huangshangfo,lvf,xiezhipu,bohuangb2017,bowendu}@buaa.edu.cn
[2] Network and Digital Media Laboratory, Beihang University, Beijing 100083, China

Abstract. With the rapid development of Internet of Things (IoT) technology, massive data are generated by IoT terminals. Cloud computing is the current mainstream method to process these massive data effectively. However, the centralized cloud computing has the risk of data leakage during data transmission. To address the issue of data safety, we propose a novel edge computing architecture, called SafeTECKS. It consists of three-layer functional structure: IoT Devices, Edge Nodes, Cloud Center. Each edge node converts private data to knowledge by Agent component, and keeps them in Knowledge Store. Edge node shares knowledge with each other, instead of raw data, which can prevent data leakage caused by data transmission. An algorithm named MKF (Multi-Knowledge Fusion) is presented to integrate all knowledge learned from edge nodes. We use taxi demand prediction as a case to verify the effectiveness of our SafeTECKS on a real-world large scale data generated by taxis in Beijing. Results show that our method not only outperforms the baselines, but also can ensure data security.

Keywords: Massive data · Data safety · Cloud computing
Edge computing · Share knowledge

1 Introduction

With the rapid development of Internet of Things (IoT) technology, new service modes and businesses such as intelligent transportation and smart city keep emerging, followed by massive data generated by IoT terminals. Cloud computing [1] is the current mainstream method to maintain and process these massive data effectively. However, the centralized cloud computing cannot guarantee real-time responsiveness, and the network bandwidth and transmission speed have come to a bottleneck. Furthermore, private data and enterprise data asset are likely to leak during the communicating process between IoT devices and cloud servers. Such dilemma urges us to focus on a new architecture, called edge computing.

© Springer Nature Switzerland AG 2018
G. Wang et al. (Eds.): SpaCCS 2018, LNCS 11342, pp. 331–340, 2018.
https://doi.org/10.1007/978-3-030-05345-1_28

Edge computing [2] is a method of optimizing cloud computing systems by performing data processing at the edge of the network, near the source of the data. Edge computing brings three major improvements to the cloud computing: (1) Real-time data processing. As data is analyzed at edge nodes, it can reduce the transmission latency and improve the response speed of the application. (2) Sending data to remote clouds is not necessary, which can reduce the amount of data transmitted and mitigate the network bandwidth pressure. (3) Private data is analyzed directly at the edge without worrying about data leakage.

In recent years, researchers from both academia and industry have investigated a wide-range of issues to edge computing, including systems, architectures and applications [3]. Change et al. [5] described edge-cloud federation, of which edge apps were used to deliver services at the edge as well as in distant cloud centers. Du et al. [6] proposed a knowledge-information-data (KID [23])-driven TDaaS edge computing (TEC) paradigm for TDaaS. However, the architecture of edge computing makes nodes independent with each other, preventing nodes sharing data safely. Recently, some researchers use encryption technology to protect data. The identity-based encryption was proposed by Shamir et al. [7] as a simplification scheme of certificate management in e-mail systems. Louk et al. [8] constructed a homomorphic encryption algorithm in a mobile cloud computing environment to provide data security protection for mobile users. Whereas, these encryption algorithms may also be cracked.

Cloud computing can't satisfy the demand of high response speed and data security, thereby, in this paper, we study the problem of protecting data safety in edge computing architecture. However, it is very challenging because of the following three reasons: (1) It is nontrivial to ensure data security during data transmission. No matter what encryption algorithm you use, they can be cracked anyway. (2) Due to high latency and expensive bandwidth caused by large scale of data, it is intractable to share information among edge nodes. (3) The data of each edge node is different, maybe the domain is different too. It is challenging to transfer and integrate the information in different domains. To tackle the above challenges, we propose a SafeTECKS (Data **Saf**ety in **T**hings-**E**dge-**C**loud Architecture with **K**nowledge **S**haring) framework to ensure the data security. Inspired by transfer learning [9], we convert data into knowledge (viz. model, parameters, features) with machine learning algorithms. Data safety is guaranteed by sharing knowledge, instead of raw private data. The main contributions of this article are summarized as follows:

- We proposed a novel edge computing architecture, called SafeTECKS, which can ensure data security and privacy protection. Edge node shares knowledge with each other, instead of raw data, which can prevent data leakage caused by data transmission.
- An algorithm named MKF (**M**ulti-**K**nowledge **F**usion) is presented to integrate all knowledge learned from edge nodes. MKF can not only learn knowledge from local data, but also adapt knowledge from other nodes and domains to target domain.

- Using taxi demand prediction as a case, we conduct extensive experiments on a real-world large scale data generated by taxis in Beijing. Results show that our method not only outperforms the baselines, but also can ensure data security.

The remainder of this article can be outlined as follows. Section 2 reviews the related work. The details of our SafeTECKS framework are presented in Sect. 3. Experiments and case study are given in Sect. 4, followed by conclusions in Sect. 5.

2   Related Work

Edge computing plays an essential role in the field of IoT. In [4], Satyanarayanan et al. applied edge computing to a video based monitoring system. When vehicles enter and exit an area, an edge node near the camera can capture and analyze the video, then send the recognized plate number to a cloud. The size of data to the cloud is far smaller compared to the original video. Change et al. [5] described edge-cloud federation, of which edge apps were used to deliver services at the edge as well as in distant cloud centers. Deep learning was first exploited in edge computing environment by Liu et al. [10]. They proposed a deep-learning-based food recognition application by employing edge-computing-based service infrastructure. Li et al. [11] also introduced deep learning for IoT into the edge computing environment to optimize network performance. In their study, AlexNet [20] was used to identify the object in the collected video data.

No matter whether it is cloud computing or edge computing, data security and privacy protection are the most crucial problem to concern about. In recent years, many researchers focus on data security of cloud computing and edge computing. Most of them exploited encryption algorithms to implement data security. Pasupuleti et al. [12] proposed an Efficient and Secure Privacy-Preserving Approach (ESPPA) for mobile devices, which uses probability public key encryption (PPKE) and ranking-keyword-search (RKS) algorithm to implement privacy protection on resource-constrained mobile terminals. Bahrami et al. [13] proposed a light-weight method for mobile clients to store data on one or multiple clouds by using pseudo-random permutation based on chaos systems. The replacement operation is performed on the mobile device, not in the cloud, thereby protecting data privacy. Khan et al. [14] proposed Cloud-Manager-based Re-encryption Scheme (CMReS) that combines the characteristics of manager-based re-encryption and cloud-based re-encryption for providing better security services with minimum processing burden on the mobile device.

3   SafeTECKS

3.1   Overview

In this section, we describe the architecture of our proposed SafeTECKS, as shown in Fig. 1. SafeTECKS comprises three-layer functional structure: Things-Edge-Cloud (IoT Devices, Edge Nodes, Cloud Center). Firstly, IoT devices include all types of devices (e.g. vehicles, mobile terminals, video monitors) connected to the Edge Nodes, which play a role as data producers to participate in the distributed infrastructure for all three layers. Secondly, edge nodes are the most essential component of the proposed framework, which have the functions of data collecting, processing (computing and learning), and service provision. In addition, edge nodes realize the connection between edge devices and the cloud center with wireless network, Bluetooth and the Internet. Each node has a Knowledge Store to keep the knowledge learned from raw data. Its internal structure will be detailed in Sect. 3.2. Finally, cloud center provides the core network access (e.g. Internet) and centralized cloud computing services. Besides, cloud center has a Global Knowledge Store to collect, store and distribute the knowledge from each edge node, achieving the purpose of sharing knowledge among nodes.

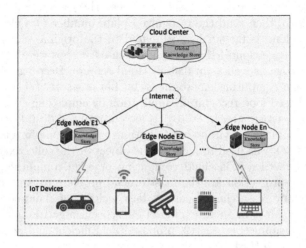

Fig. 1. Architecture of our proposed SafeTECKS

3.2   Edge Node

Here we give a detailed description of the edge node, the structure of which is shown in Fig. 2. In brief, the edge node consists of three parts: Data Access, Agent, Knowledge Store. We introduce them respectively.

A. Data Access

This part mainly collects data from the IoT devices, such as vehicles, video cameras, mobile phones etc. Due to the diverse types of data (text, photos, video, GPS), these data should be preprocessed before analyzing and learning. Obviously, a fair amount of these data involves privacy of users. For sake of data security, private data is not supposed to be transmitted to cloud center directly. Therefore, we convert data to knowledge by Agent part.

B. Agent

Agent is a processor or a learner, which have the ability to process data from local IoT devices and knowledge from other edge nodes. We proposed an algorithm called MKF (Multi-Knowledge Fusion) to integrate all the models learned from edge nodes. The details of MKF are shown in Algorithm 1.

Firstly, the local data X is split into training data and testing data. Then, we train the **local learning** model LM by X_{train} and Y_{train}. It can be any learning method, including traditional machine learning algorithms (KNN, SVM, RF etc.) and deep learning algorithms (DNN, CNN, RNN etc.). Lines 3–5 represent the **knowledge adaptation** part according to Fig. 2. Inspired by transfer learning [9], we transfer knowledge among different nodes and domains. While the knowledge maybe not adaptive to the target domain, which brings the challenge of domain adaptation [15]. Common methods of domain adaptation include Finetune [16], DDC [17] and DAN [18]. The core of these methods is fixing some parameters of model and adjusting other parameters to adapt to the target scenario. Here we use the DDC method, which is easy and effective.

Lines 7–12 outline the model fusion and training process. W is the weight vector of LM and M, which is trained via Adam [19] to minimize the mean absolute error (MAE) between predictions and ground values. Finally we can get the fusion model MKF.

C. Knowledge Store

Just as its name implies, knowledge store is a container to store the knowledge learned from Agent and got from other nodes. As we mentioned before, knowledge is diverse, which can be a model, features, even parameters. The cloud center also has a global knowledge store, like a transfer station. Edge nodes upload their knowledge to the cloud center with a regular interval. In the meantime, they can download knowledge from the cloud center to keep updated.

4 Experiments

In the experiment, we use taxi demand prediction as a case to verify the effectiveness of our SafeTECKS on a large scale data generated by taxis in Beijing. Four servers are deployed as three edge nodes and a cloud center according to SafeTECKS architecture. Three edge nodes represent Haidian District, Dongcheng District and Xicheng District respectively. Each server has one GeForce 1050 GPU (8 GB DDR5) and 8 CPU cores (3.6 GHz). Firstly, we describe the details of our dataset and the parameters setting, and then introduce several baseline methods. The results of our model, including prediction accuracy and the effectiveness of protecting data safety, are presented in Sect. 4.3.

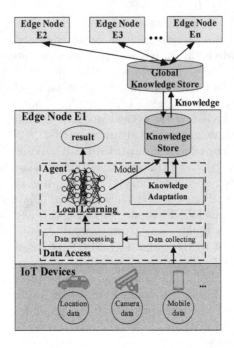

Fig. 2. Structure of edge node

Algorithm 1. MKF: Multi-Knowledge Fusion.

Input:

  Local time series data $X = \{x_1, x_2, ..., x_T\}$;

  Number of edge nodes n;

  Models from other edge nodes $M = \{m_1, m_2, ..., m_{n-1}\}$

Output: Learned MKF model

1: $X_{train}, Y_{train}, X_{test}, Y_{test} = split(X)$

2: LM $\Leftarrow$ train the local model by X_{train} and Y_{train}

3: **for** i=1,2,...,n-1 **do**

4:     $m_i = \mathrm{DDC}(m_i, X_{train}, Y_{train})$

5: **end for**

6: Set $W = \{w_i = \frac{1}{n}\}$, epochs=100

7: **for** $k = 1, 2, ..., epochs$ **do**

8:     $Y_{pre} = w_1 \cdot LM.predict(X_{test}) + \sum_{i=2}^{n} w_i \cdot m_i.predict(X_{test})$

9:     $loss = \mathrm{MAE}(Y_{test}, Y_{pre})$

10:    optimizer=AdamOptimizer.minmize(loss)

11:    Update W

12: **end for**

13: MKF = $W \cdot (LM, M)$

14: **return** MKF

4.1 Experiment Setting

Data Description. The dataset contains taxi orders from 06/01/2017 to 08/31/2017 in Haidian District (1,027,055 orders), Dongcheng District (201,394 orders), Xicheng District (177,214 orders). The orders in dataset consist of number plate, origin GPS, destination GPS, start time, end time, mileage and price. Each district is split into several areas (each area is 3 km × 3 km large), namely Haidian District has 20 areas, Dongcheng District and Xicheng District has 3 areas respectively. Each day from 6 am to 23 pm is divided into 34 slots, like $[T_0, T_1, \ldots, T_{33}]$. 30 min is set as the length of the time interval. The training data is from 06/01/2017 to 08/24/2017 (55 days in total), and the test data is from 08/25/2017 to 08/31/2017 (7 days in total).

Parameters Setting. When testing the prediction result, we use the previous three days, which are the same day of week with current day, to predict the taxi demand of the current day (for example, if we want to predict the taxi demand of 08/25/2017, we use the data of 08/04/2017, 08/11/2017 and 08/18/2017). In our model MKF, the local learning method is LSTM [21], which is well known to handle the problem of time series prediction. EarlyStopping mechanism is exploited to stop the training when the error on the validation set is higher than it was the last time checked.

Metric. The evaluation metrics are mean absolute error (**MAE**) and mean square error (**MSE**). The MAE and MSE are calculated by the following two equations,

$$MAE = \frac{1}{n} \sum_{i=1}^{n} |y_{pre}^i - y_{true}^i|$$

$$MSE = \frac{1}{n} \sum_{i=1}^{n} (y_{pre}^i - y_{true}^i)^2$$

where y_{pre} represents the prediction value, and y_{true} represents the truth value.

4.2 Baselines

Our model MKF is compared with the following methods:

- **Historical average (HA):** Historical average predicts the demand using average values of previous demands at the area given in the same relative time slot.
- **Autoregressive integrated moving average (ARIMA):** ARIMA [22] is a widely-used time series prediction method in statistics.
- **Multiple layer perceptron (MLP):** In our experiment, the neural network has four fully connected layers, and the number of hidden units are 128, 128, 64, and 34 respectively.

- **LSTM:** LSTM is a well-known and useful for predicting future values in a time series. The setting of LSTM is same as our model, but it does not have the part of knowledge sharing.

4.3   Results

Performance of prediction

We present the comparison results with baselines in Table 1. From this table, we can see our model MKF outperforms the others in two districts with two metrics. Among all the baselines, HA and ARIMA simply use the historical data, which leads them to performing poorly. LSTM can model the temporal dependency during deep learning, so it achieves the best prediction accuracy among all baselines. However, all these baselines do not utilize the knowledge learned from other nodes. Consequently, our proposed method significantly outperforms those methods. MKF achieves 2.27 (MAE) and 23.26 (MSE) when predicting the taxi demand of Dongcheng District. The reason of why all methods perform worse in Xicheng District, we guess, is the data volume in Xicheng District less than that in Dongcheng District.

We also give the performance of MKF model by the form of chart in Fig. 3. Figure 3(a) and (b) show the taxi demand prediction of Dongcheng District and

Table 1. Comparison with different baselines

Model name	Dongcheng district		Xicheng district	
	MAE	MSE	MAE	MSE
HA	5.43	87.39	5.96	93.64
ARIMA	4.25	69.14	4.37	71.83
MLP	2.76	33.47	2.79	35.26
LSTM	2.39	29.4	2.48	30.51
MKF	**2.27**	**23.26**	**2.30**	**25.34**

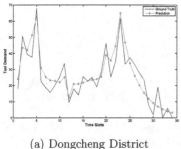

(a) Dongcheng District   (b) Xicheng District

Fig. 3. Performance of MKF (Color figure online)

Xicheng District respectively. The X-coordinate represents 34 time slots of target day, and the Y-coordinate is the average taxi orders of areas in each district. The blue lines and the orange lines show the ground truth and prediction values. From the chart, we can tell that prediction values are very close to actual value, which illustrates our model is effective for taxi demand prediction.

Performance of data security
In SafeTECKS architecture, it is not necessary to transmit the data to cloud center, which mitigates the risk of data leakage. In the phase of knowledge sharing, we convert raw private data to model (viz. knowledge), which will be transferred to the knowledge store of other edge nodes. Our learning model are MKF, which only contains the weight vector W and LSTM parameters. That means edge nodes only share parameters with each other, instead of private data. Even if data leakage occurs during transmission, data thieves cannot obtain the raw private data from the model parameters. In other words, our architecture SafeTECKS can protect the data security by knowledge sharing.

5 Conclusion

In this paper, we propose a SafeTECKS (Data **Safe**ty in **T**hings-**E**dge-**C**loud Architecture with **K**nowledge **S**haring) framework to ensure the data security. It consists of three-layer functional structure: IoT Devices, Edge Nodes, Cloud Center. Edge node can not only compute and analyze the local data, but also share knowledge with other nodes. An algorithm named MKF (**M**ulti-**K**nowledge **F**usion) is presented to integrate all knowledge learned from edge nodes. We use taxi demand prediction as an experiment case, and the results show that our method outperforms the baselines. In the meantime, our framework can ensure data security too. As for future works, we will study new edge computing frameworks and research some other methods to protect the data safety.

Acknowledgments. This paper is supported by science and technology project of Beijing Municipal Commission of Transport and project of Beijing Municipal Science & Technology Commission (No. Z171100005117001).

References

1. Lu, G., Zeng, W.: Cloud computing survey. Appl. Mech. Mater. **530–531**, 650–661 (2014)
2. Yu, W., Liang, F., He, X., et al.: A survey on the edge computing for the Internet of Things. IEEE Access **6**, 6900–6919 (2018)
3. Mao, Y., You, C., Zhang, J., et al.: Mobile edge computing: survey and research outlook. arXiv preprint arXiv:1701.01090 (2017)
4. Satyanarayanan, M., Simoens, P., Xiao, Y., et al.: Edge analytics in the internet of things. IEEE Perv. Comput. **2**, 24–31 (2015)
5. Chang, H., Hari, A., Mukherjee, S., et al.: Bringing the cloud to the edge. In: 2014 IEEE Conference on Computer Communications Workshops (INFOCOM WKSHPS), pp. 346–351. IEEE (2014)

6. Du, B., Huang, R., Xie, Z., et al.: KID model-driven things-edge-cloud computing paradigm for traffic data as a service. IEEE Netw. **32**(1), 34–41 (2018)
7. Shamir, A.: Identity-based cryptosystems and signature schemes. In: Blakley, G.R., Chaum, D. (eds.) CRYPTO 1984. LNCS, vol. 196, pp. 47–53. Springer, Heidelberg (1985). https://doi.org/10.1007/3-540-39568-7_5
8. Louk, M., Lim, H.: Homomorphic encryption in mobile multi cloud computing. In: 2015 International Conference on Information Networking (ICOIN), pp. 493–497. IEEE (2015)
9. Pan, S.J., Yang, Q.: A survey on transfer learning. IEEE Trans. Knowl. Data Eng. **22**(10), 1345–1359 (2010)
10. Liu, C., Cao, Y., Luo, Y., et al.: A new deep learning-based food recognition system for dietary assessment on an edge computing service infrastructure. IEEE Trans. Serv. Comput. **11**(2), 249–261 (2018)
11. Li, H., Ota, K., Dong, M.: Learning IoT in edge: deep learning for the internet of things with edge computing. IEEE Netw. **32**(1), 96–101 (2018)
12. Pasupuleti, S.K., Ramalingam, S., Buyya, R.: An efficient and secure privacy-preserving approach for outsourced data of resource constrained mobile devices in cloud computing. J. Netw. Comput. Appl. **64**, 12–22 (2016)
13. Bahrami, M., Singhal, M.: A light-weight permutation based method for data privacy in mobile cloud computing. In: 2015 3rd IEEE International Conference on Mobile Cloud Computing, Services, and Engineering (MobileCloud), pp. 189–198. IEEE (2015)
14. Khan, A.N., Kiah, M.L.M., Ali, M., et al.: A cloud-manager-based re-encryption scheme for mobile users in cloud environment: a hybrid approach. J. Grid Comput. **13**(4), 651–675 (2015)
15. Weiss, K., Khoshgoftaar, T.M., Wang, D.D.: A survey of transfer learning. J. Big Data **3**(1), 9 (2016)
16. Schmidhuber, J.: Deep learning in neural networks: an overview. Neural Netw. **61**, 85–117 (2015)
17. Tzeng, E., Hoffman, J., Zhang, N., et al.: Deep domain confusion: maximizing for domain invariance. arXiv preprint arXiv:1412.3474 (2014)
18. Long, M., Cao, Y., Wang, J., et al.: Learning transferable features with deep adaptation networks. arXiv preprint arXiv:1502.02791 (2015)
19. Kingma, D.P., Ba, J.: Adam: a method for stochastic optimization. arXiv preprint arXiv:1412.6980 (2014)
20. Krizhevsky, A., Sutskever, I., Hinton, G.E.: Imagenet classification with deep convolutional neural networks. In: Advances in Neural Information Processing systems, pp. 1097–1105 (2012)
21. Gers, F.A., Schmidhuber, J., Cummins, F.: Learning to forget: continual prediction with LSTM (1999)
22. Pai, P.F., Lin, C.S.: A hybrid ARIMA and support vector machines model in stock price forecasting. Omega **33**(6), 497–505 (2005)
23. Xie, Z., Lv, W., Qin, L., et al.: An evolvable and transparent data as a service framework for multisource data integration and fusion. Peer-to-Peer Netw. Appl. **11**(4), 697–710 (2018)

NTRDM: A New Bus Line Network Optimization Method Based on Taxi Passenger Flow Conversion

Bo Huang[✉], Guixi Xiong, Zhipu Xie, Shangfo Huang, and Bowen Du

School of Computer Science, Beihang University, Beijing 100000, China
bohuang2017@buaa.edu.com

Abstract. The large amount of traffic data collected by urban traffic mobile terminals and sensing equipments provides us the opportunity to study group travel patterns and laws. In this paper, we built a New Transit Require Design Module (NTRDM) from the perspective of passenger flow conversion based on multi-source traffic data, which realized the adjustment and optimization of the current bus network. Specifically, CTDaaS was used for data fusion and processing to protect the passengers' privacy. Then we established the NTRDM with minimum transfer time as the optimization goal, and proposed the Three-Step site adjustment method, which was solved with ant colony algorithm. Finally, we verified the calculating results with real data. Experimental results demonstrated the effectiveness of our method.

Keywords: CTDaaS service · Passenger flow conversion
Intelligent transportation · Heuristic search · Ant colony algorithm

1 Introduction

With the rapid development of intelligent transportation, the amount of data generated daily from video surveillance, bayonet alarm, GPS positioning information, RFID identification information etc., even reaches PB level. Combining these data with related big data technologies can provide better services for people, such as travel path planning, passenger flow forecasting, network optimization, and operation control.

As an important part of diversified public transportation, ground bus system has a direct impact on the living standards of residents and development speed of society. The number of passengers has decreased year by year, from 5,150 million in 2012 to 3,430 million in 2017 [1]. However, taxi, as a supplement to large-capacity public transportation, has become a more common travel mode gradually [2]. Figure 1 shows the distribution of hot boarding sites of two modes of transportation. For the area in black box, taxi travel is heavy but bus coverage is insufficient. We choose these areas as our main research objects. This paper first accomplishes the bus route optimization, through integrating

© Springer Nature Switzerland AG 2018
G. Wang et al. (Eds.): SpaCCS 2018, LNCS 11342, pp. 341–350, 2018.
https://doi.org/10.1007/978-3-030-05345-1_29

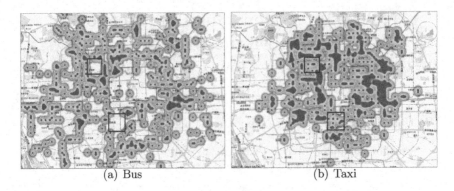

(a) Bus   (b) Taxi

Fig. 1. The choropleth map of bus and taxi boarding sites

the data collected from taxi and bus, transforming the taxi passenger flow into the bus passenger flow through the big data correlation algorithm [3]. Above all, in order to protect user privacy, the CTDaaS model is applied to fuse taxi GPS data, taximeter data, AFC data and geographic data [4]. Then we identify hot taxis boarding sites through grid matching, passenger flow calculation and OD clustering [5]. Next, turn the passenger flow conversion problem into DTRDM; that is, regard the hot taxi OD as the new traffic requirements, and optimize the target with the minimum total transfer time. Finally, propose the Three-Step adjustment method, and solve the model with the ant colony algorithm. The above method aims to reduce the difference between the travel mode of bus and taxi, through adjusting the bus route and transforming taxi passenger flow into bus passenger flow as much as possible.

The structure of this paper is organized as follows:

- Section 2 carries out the related work.
- Section 3 introduces the methods and models proposed in this study.
- Section 4 gives and verifies the experimental results.
- Section 5 is the summary of this paper.

2   Related Work

With the booming of urban sensor data (GPS, AFC data and meter data), much research work has been done to analyze them in recent years. In this section, we will briefly introduce the related research work.

Due to the rapid development of advanced technology, the transportation infrastructure generates a large amount of urban traffic data, such as user card data, network car data and taxi data. We can get effective information with the help of these data. Meanwhile, it also contains users' personal privacy information, which can lead to user privacy disclosure easily if it's used improperly. Therefore, we use CTDaaS (City Traffic Data-as-a-Service) framework for data processing, which fuses data from distributed providers. In the framework, the data in traffic domain requested by the developer or researcher is implemented as a data request through the CTDaaS proxy, which acts as a broker building a relationship between TC and a data service provider that distributes information users request. The CTDaaS Agent coordinates data services by breaking them into four consolidated stages: request and response, discovering and composition, consumption, and feedback. Through this framework, we could not only fully integrate multi-source data and mine data information, but also protect users' personal privacy.

In addition, there are many researches on bus line network optimization design in theory and method. Pattnaik studied the application of standard genetic algorithm (SGA) [6]; Agrawal used parallel genetic algorithm (PGA) for improving bus routes [7]. In general, there are three main problems in the existing research results: First, a lot of researchers only simplify the actual complex road network optimization into mathematical problems, ignoring the effect of the actual geographical environment. Secondly, their work mainly tends to be on the overall "planning" of the bus network, rather than "optimization". Finally, under the trend of parallel development of various modes of transportation, the simple optimization of public transport buses has exposed various limitations. Therefore, how to integrate multiple traffic data effectively is of great importance.

3   Passenger Flow Conversion

This section presents the key components of our passenger flow conversion system. Firstly, the related process of data fusion and processing is introduced. Then the NTRDM and the Three-Step adjustment method are proposed. Finally, the ant colony algorithm is used to solve the model and the experimental results are verified.

3.1   The Framework

There are five main models involved in this paper, namely CTDaaS module, NTRDPM module, OD Filter Module, Three-Step Adjustment module and Ant-colony Algorithm module. The overall framework is shown in Fig. 2. In the first step, input the dataset into CTDaaS model for data fusion and data processing, including map division, grid matching, OD extraction, passenger flow analysis and Abnormal data filtering. After the data is processed, the result is input into OD Filter module for the hot taxi OD mining, and the extracted hot taxi OD is transmitted into the NTRDM. NTRDM consists of four main parts: Determine optimization goals and constraints, select adjustment method, adjustment plan evaluation and make adjustment plan. Among them, in the second step, we propose the Three-Step site adjustment method. In the third step, we use the ant colony algorithm to solve the model, and finally get the optimization plan of the bus line network in the fourth part.

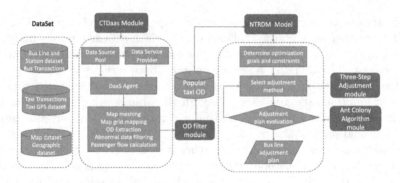

Fig. 2. The framework of passenger flow conversion

3.2 NTRDM

To understand the problem more clearly, we can summarize the problem into the New Transit Require Design Module(NTRDM) [8], and consider the taxi hot OD as the new bus travel demands. The basic framework is to give a newly added traffic demands distribution, that is, how to make adjustments and optimizations of the current network based on a newly added OD distribution. It consists of four steps, namely, determining optimization objectives and constraints, selecting adjustment methods, adjusting program evaluation, and generating optimization plans [9]. In this paper, we consider the minimum differences on travel service level between the two transportation modes on hot taxi OD as our optimization goal, and further transfer it into the minimum total time spent by bus on hot OD:

$$\min T_{OD} = \sum_{i \in F} (T_{wo}^i + T_{drive}^i + T_{tran}^i + T_{wd}^i) \tag{1}$$

T_{total} indicates the total time spent on all hot ODs, F indicates all OD sets, T_{wo}^i is the walking time to the stop from departure point, T_{drive}^i is the driving time, T_{tran}^i is the transfer time, and T_{wd}^i is walking time from the stop to the destination.

Next, we discuss the constraints of the NTRDM [10], including: (1) Line length: $l_{\min} \leq l \leq l_{\max}$, $l_{\min}$ and $l_{\max}$ are the maximum and minimum line lengths respectively, and take 5 km and 15 km respectively according to the operation requirements [11]. (2) Line non-linear coefficient: Generally, $l/d \leq 1.4$, l is the length of the line, and d is the linear distance of the line from the beginning and end of the line. (3) Adjacent site length: The research scope of this paper is within the four rings, so it needs to meet $500 \leq l_a \leq 800$, where l_a is the distance of adjacent sites. Line overlap factor: In general, $e \leq 3$, e is the overlap factor. (4) Impact of the original bus line: If the passenger flow after one line adjustment is greater than the passenger flow before the adjustment, that is $P_{old} < P_{new}$, then adjust the line, otherwise no adjustment will be made [12].

In summary, we get the NTRDM as follows:

$$\min T_{OD} = \sum_{i \in F} (T_{wo}^i + T_{drive}^i + T_{tran}^i + T_{wd}^i) \tag{2}$$

$$T_{wo} = L_o \times V_w, T_{wd} = L_d \times V_w, T_{drive} = L_r \times V_{drive} \tag{3}$$

$$s.t. \begin{cases} l_{\min} \leq l \leq l_{\max} \\ l/d \leq 1.4 \\ 500 \leq l_a \leq 800 \\ e \leq 3 \\ P_{old} < P_{new} \\ O, D \in F \end{cases} \tag{4}$$

V_w is average speed; V_{drive} is average driving speed; L_o is the distance from the departure point to the stop; L_d is the distance from the destination to the stop; L_r is driving distance; l is the length of the bus line; l_a is the distance between two adjacent stops; e is the overlap coefficient; P_{old}, P_{new} are the passenger flow before and after the line adjustment, respectively; F is hot taxi OD collection.

3.3   A Three-Step Adjustment Method

For hot taxi ODs, the ideal adjustment result is that the walking distance is shortest with no transfer. Therefore, we adopt three adjustment methods to approach it: First, gradually adjust the two site positions on the same line, so that the time spent is minimal and direct. Secondly, if two stations on any line are adjusted, the transfer may occur. Finally, establish a new bus station at the destination or departure point and join the adjacent line. When adjusting and optimizing each OD pair, we compare the total time spent by these three methods under the constraint conditions, and select the shortest time as the final adjustment plan. The main idea of bus route adjustment is to find the optimal sites to adjust according to travel needs. This feature is very similar to ant colony algorithm [13]. Assume that the passenger flow is an ant colony, the O point is the ant nest, and D is the food source. Considering NTRDM as the ant colony foraging from the ant nest according to the pheromone [14], it can be described as taking the total time from O to D. Point to search for the optimal bus route, and then adjust the site according to the optimal bus route. Figure 3 shows the main process of this method.

Here are some details for key steps: (1) Initialization: including network initialization, ant colony initialization and pheromone matrix initialization. (2) Search lines and sites: first, according to the position of the O point, find all the site collections within the radius of the center and the radius of 2000 m, and search for the first site in the collection according to the transfer rule. The transfer rule includes the pheromone density and the visible value of the link of the link, wherein the pheromone density is derived by iteratively updating the pheromone matrix, and the visible value is calculated by the greedy principle, then the probability of selecting the site to the site is:

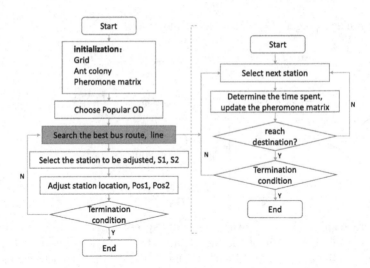

Fig. 3. Ant colony algorithm flow for solving NTRD

$$p_{ij}(k) = \begin{cases} \dfrac{\tau_{ij}^{\alpha} \times \eta_{ij}^{\beta}}{\sum\limits_{h \in T_{sta}} \tau_{ih}^{\beta} \times \eta_{ij}^{\beta}} & j \in T_{sta} \\ 0 & Others \end{cases} \tag{5}$$

where $p_{ij}(k)$ is the probability for number k of OD to select i and j; τ_{ij}^{α} and η_{ij}^{β} are pheromone density and visible value, respectively; T_{sta} is the set of feasible stations of this OD.

4   Experimental Results

Our experimental data comes from the real traffic data in November 2017, provided by the Beijing Municipal Transportation Commission.

4.1   Data Preparation

In order to fuse and correlate the ODs of the two transportation modes, we adopt the method of map grid division. Since 300 m toward the bus stop is the maximum walking distance that passengers could accept, we choose 300 m * 300 m as the grid size. We know that the service scope of the bus is mainly within five rings, so we choose a total of 7433 grids in this range as the main research objects. Figure 4 gives the results of grid mapping in Beijing. Then, by combining the taxi GPS and the meter data, the travel route and OD position information of taxi can be obtained, and the position information is converted into the grid number by calculating which grid the position belongs to. Figure 5 illustrates the OD distribution of some taxis.

Not all taxi OD data is available, "Hot" reflects the strong taxi travel demands on the OD that the current bus service system can not satisfy [15].

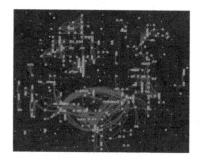

Fig. 4. Map meshing results.   **Fig. 5.** The OD distribution of taxis.

First, filter out the OD of the small passenger flow, and then filter out the OD with higher bus service level. Ultimately, we found that most of the OD distributions in Fig. 5 are similar. We choose 500 m as the combination condition and use the density-based clustering method (DBSCAN) [16] for OD merging. As a result, we got 200 taxi hot OD.Its distribution and specific information are shown in Table 1.

Table 1. Some taxi hot OD information

OD num	Map grid number	OD name	Average passenger/day
1	154713→154712	Silutong No.17 Court-yard →Taoranting Park	303.6
2	164287→164289	Sun Palace Park→Jinyu Nanhu Park	294.63
3	176307→177508	PingGuoYuan→ Binhe Century Square Park	261.51

Table 2. Results

Item	Result
Number of adjusted sites	214
Number of new sites	37
Total time spent before adjustment/min	6215
Total time spent after adjustment/min	4309
Time reduction rate	30.67%
Number of lines affected	85
Expected number of converted passengers/day	37980

4.2 Results Summary

The 200 hot taxi ODs will be input the NTRDM, and the results in Fig. 5 will be calculated. It can be seen that the total time spent on these ODs under the

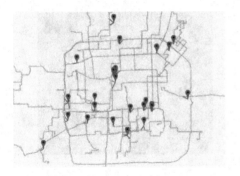

Fig. 6. Map meshing results.   **Fig. 7.** The OD distribution of taxis.

current bus network is 6215 min [17], and the adjusted total time is 4309 min, which is reduced by 30.67%. It is expected that 37800 taxi passengers can be converted into bus passengers every day (see Table 2).

The specific situation of site adjustment is shown in Figs. 6 and 7, where the red icon refers to the location of the added or adjusted sites, and the green icon refers to the site coordinates. Table 3 provides some specific data for bus station adjustments.

Table 3. Result summary

Station number	Coordinate change	Bus line	Station name	Expected conversion passenger flow
1	(116.3883419, 39.8727228) ↑ (116.3807773, 39.8725724)	14	Kaiyang Bridge	650/day
2	(116.4084953, 39.8285324) ↑ (116.3890146, 39.8295385)	501	Jiujingzhuang	742/day
3	(116.3958852, 39.9284817) ↑ (116.3919426, 39.9174886)	109	Beihai	589/day

In addition, we compare the results of ant colony algorithm, genetic algorithm and artificial neural network to solve this model. The results show that the ant colony algorithm performs best, and the time reduction rate is about 30%.

4.3   Sample Verification

In order to verify the precision of the test results, we analyze $No.151$ OD as an example. The coordinates of the starting point were (116.381893, 39.86651279) and the coordinates of the end point were (116.3760274, 39.89380228). Figure 8 suggests the comparison of travel paths before and after adjustment [18], where the blue is driving path and the red is walking path. Before the optimization, we obtain the walking distance of 2.1 km by calling Baidu map API, and the total time spent is 1 h. After the adjustment, the walking distance is shortened to 300 m due to the adjustment of the departure sites and the destination sites respectively. The total time spent is 37 min, saving 23 min of travel time for the traveler. It can be seen that the method proposed in this paper is feasible.

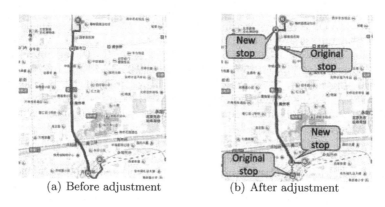

(a) Before adjustment   (b) After adjustment

Fig. 8. An sample travel path comparison

5   Conclusion

In this paper, we propose a bus line network optimization method that uses a large amount of traffic data to convert taxi passenger flow into bus passenger flow. First, we use the CTDaas method to process a large amount of user data, which guarantees the users' privacy security, and makes full use of the data information. Then we propose the NTRDP model to abstract the passenger flow conversion problem into the new bus route optimization based on travel demand. The problem is solved by the ant colony algorithm. Finally, we use the real data to test and verify the experimental results, which proves the precision and effectiveness of our method.

Acknowledgments. This research is supported by Beijing Municipal Transportation Commission, Beijing Science and Technology Commission (No. Z171100005117001) and partially supported by the Beijing Transportation Development Research Institute.

References

1. Beijing Municipal Bureau of Statistics Homepage. http://www.bjstats.gov.cn. Accessed 20 Aug 2018
2. Zhang, Y.: Analyzing Chinese consumers' perception for biofuels implementation: the private vehicles owners investigatingin Nanjing. Renew. Sustain. Energy Rev. **15**(5), 2299–2309 (2011)
3. Kuan, S.N.: Solving the feeder bus network design problem by genetic algorithms and ant colony optimization. Adv. Eng. Softw. **37**(6), 351–359 (2005)
4. Du, B., Huang, R.: Active CTDaaS: a data service framework based on transparent IoD in city traffic. IEEE Trans. Comput. **65**(12), 3524–3536 (2016)
5. Rand, W.M.: Objective criteria for the evaluation of clustering methods. J. Am. Stat. Assoc. **66**(336), 846–850 (1971)
6. Ngamchai, S., Lovell, D.J.: Optimal time transfer in bus transit route network design using a genetic algorithm. J. Transp. Eng. **129**(5), 510–521 (2003)
7. Agrawal, J., Mathew, T.V.: Transit route network design using parallel genetic algorithm. J. Comput. Civil Eng. **18**(3), 248–256 (2004)
8. Mandl, C.E.: Evaluation and optimization of urban public transportation networks. Eur. J. Oper. Res. **5**(6), 396–404 (1980)
9. Bielli, M., Caramia, M., Carotenuto, P.: Genetic algorithms in bus network optimization. Transp. Res. Part C **10**(1), 19–34 (2002)
10. Jing, C.: Model and solution algorithm of bus network design problem under clusters urban structure. In: Proceedings of the 3rd International Conference on Vehicle, Mechanical and Elec-trical Engineering (ICVMEE 2016), p. 5. Wuhan Zhicheng Times Cultural Development Co. (2016)
11. Gleason, J.M.: A set covering approach to bus stop location. Omega **3**(5), 605–608 (1975)
12. Bielli, M., Caramia, M., Carotenuto, P.: Genetic algorithms in bus network optimization. Transp. Res. Part C: Emerg. Technol. **10**(1), 19–34 (2002)
13. Zheng, J.: Research on logistic distribution routing based on improved ant colony algorithm. In: Proceedings of 2015 4th International Conference on Mechatronics, Materials, Chemistry and Computer Engineering (ICMMCCE 2015), p. 7. International Informatization and Engineering Associations Atlantis Press (2015)
14. Mazzeo, S., Loiseau, I.: An ant colony algorithm for the capacitated vehicle routing. Electron. Notes Discrete Math. **18**, 181–186 (2004)
15. Zhan, X., Hasan, S., Ukkusuri, S.V., et al.: Urban link travel time estimation using large-scale taxi data with partial information. Transp. Res. Part C: Emerg. Technol. **33**, 37–49 (2013)
16. Birant, D., Kut, A.: ST-DBSCAN: an algorithm for clustering spatial temporal data. Data Knowl. Eng. **60**(1), 208–221 (2007)
17. Liu, L.: Research & development of e-map service system based on Baidu map API for regional seismic network. In: Proceedings of 2012 3rd International Conference on Information Technology for Manufacturing Systems (ITMS 2012), p. 4. Hong Kong Education Society (2012)
18. Omi, M., Ito, T.: Navigation system having travel path replacing function. U.S. Patent 6,418,373, 9 July 2002

BDCP: A Framework for Big Data Copyright Protection Based on Digital Watermarking

Jingyue Yang[1], Haiquan Wang[1,2], Zhaoyi Wang[1], Jieyi Long[1],
and Bowen Du[3(✉)]

[1] College of Software, Beihang University, Beijing 100044, China
{yang_jingyue,whq,wangzhaoyi,longjy}@buaa.edu.cn
[2] State Key Laboratory of Software Development Environment,
Beihang University, Beijing 100044, China
[3] School of Computer Science and Engineering, Beihang University,
Beijing 100044, China
Dubowen@buaa.edu.cn

Abstract. In this study, we propose a general framework to protect big data copyright when processing data sharing. The framework consists of two parts: one is the storage of the copyright watermarks and data sharing records, and the other is watermark extraction and comparison. In order to achieve the purpose of data copyright protection, we embed copyright information into the data when data sharing using digital watermarking technology and adopt blockchain to store the data sharing record and watermarking. For the digital watermarking technology, we provide a algorithm suitable for big data, and our experiments demonstrate that the algorithm is robust to attacks.

Keywords: Big data · Blockchain · Digital watermarking algorithm

1 Introduction

The emergence and development of big data related-technologies have led to the promotion of many novel works. These studies cover various fields, such as medicine, astronomy, transportation, finance, and sociology. The development of mobile Internet has eased the publication and collection of data. Such convenience not only promotes the growth of big data technology but also reduces the crime cost for data breaches, illegal transactions, and other improper behaviors. While the entire society gives much attention to privacy security, big data copyright protection has become the top priority to curb data leakage and illegal transactions.

However, it is very difficult to protect data copyright during data transaction, since a data set can be easily copied indefinitely after it is transmitted. In [7], data ownership determination is defined as determining the right holder of the data, which implies finding out who owns the ownership, tenure, and use and beneficiary rights of the data and who is responsible for protecting the privacy of the individual involved in the data. Beijing Software and Information Services Exchange defined data ownership confirmation from the perspective of data transaction. From this perspective, data ownership confirmation refers to clarifying the rights and responsibilities during data transactions

G. Wang et al. (Eds.): SpaCCS 2018, LNCS 11342, pp. 351–360, 2018.
https://doi.org/10.1007/978-3-030-05345-1_30

and guiding transaction parties to complete data transactions scientifically, uniformly, and securely by giving terms such as data rights holders, rights, data sources, time of acquisition, age of use, data usage, data volume, data format, data granularity, nature of the data industry, and data transaction methods [6].

For relational databases, digital watermarking technology developed from multimedia digital watermarking technology is widely used to protect data copyright. By embedding a unique digital watermark into the data, one can trace the path of the data propagation and provide solid evidence for the rightful owner when dispute occurs. At present, the relational database robust watermarking algorithm is mature, and it is feasible and robust to insert information such as meaningless watermark information or image fingerprint.

In this paper, we improve and extend the data watermarking technology considering the characteristics of big data. Furthermore, we combined it with the blockchain technology by storing the digital watermark on the blockchain. Since the data on the blockchain is non-tamperable and unforgeable, the security of the data copyright is guaranteed.

2   Related Works

2.1   Digital Watermarking Technology

Digital watermarking technology refers to the use of signal processing methods to embed inconspicuous and difficult-to-remove tags in the host data. This technology can protect data security without destroying the original data content and object availability. In digital communication, watermark embedding is a narrowband signal (watermark) transmitted over a wideband channel (carrier data) by using spread spectrum communication techniques.

In 2002, Agrawal and Kiernan proposed the first database watermarking algorithm [8]. The main idea of the algorithm is to first use the one-way hash function and then use the given watermark to embed the key code and the required value of the tuple in the relational database. The watermark embedding ratio is used to determine the tuple of the relational database that needs to be embedded in the watermark. The attribute of the embedded watermark and its bit position are determined using the numbers of attributes and bits of the watermark that can be embedded in the relational database. The qualified database is selected in the relational database. The bit value of some numeric attribute values of some tuples is set to 0 or 1 to complete the embedding of the relational database watermark information. In the entire algorithm process, only the owner of the relational database knows the watermark key, and the watermark key must be known when detecting the watermark in the relational database. Later in 2003, Li extended this algorithm, proposed a database data fingerprint embedding mode, and quantitatively analyzed its robustness [11].

Zhang proposed a database watermarking algorithm based on content features [9]. This algorithm first selects the local features of a certain attribute of a tuple as a watermark. Then, the watermark is embedded into another attribute of the tuple. The choice of watermark embedding tuples of the algorithm is independent of the primary key.

In [10], Franco-Contreras implemented a lossless watermarking scheme based on integer wavelet transform and singular value decomposition in database watermarking as an improvement of the quantized index modulation algorithm commonly used in digital watermarking.

Some watermarking algorithms do not rely on numerical attributes or partial distortion method. In [13], Khanduja used the K-means clustering algorithm to divide each attribute value in a certain attribute column into multiple subsets to embed the watermark. In [12], database watermarking based on cryptographic sorting and grouping is proposed. On the basis of a one-way, secretly keyed cryptographic hash method, the numerical data set S is sorted lexicographically first and then divided into subsets and embedded with 1-bit watermark information.

2.2 Blockchain Technology

The earliest application of blockchain technology appeared in the Bitcoin project. At present, no uniform definition of blockchain technology exists. The "Chinese Blockchain Technology and Application Development White Paper 2016" defined blockchain technology in a narrow and broad sense. In a narrow sense, a blockchain is a chained data structure that combines data blocks in a sequential manner in chronological order and cryptographically guarantees non-tamperable and unforgeable distributed ledgers [4, 5].

At present, blockchain technology has become a major breakthrough technology known as a revolutionary change in the way businesses and organizations operate. Unlike the new generation of information technology such as cloud computing, big data, and the Internet of Things, blockchain technology is a combination of unique technologies and innovations based on existing technologies.

2.3 Data Copyright Protection

The traditional data copyright protection system usually only focus on the data itself, no matter with what kinds of encryption algorithm or watermarking algorithm and the application of getting origin from the data being encrypted [1]. This make it passive to protect data copyright for it is impossible to found who leak out the data when it was being unlawfully using [2]. However, BDCP uses blockchain to store data sharing records and watermarking copyright information. On the one hand, compared with the preservation ability of traditional databases, blockchain has the feature that it can't be changed easily which can ensure the validity of watermarking information and evidence sharing information [3]. On the other hand, the framework also uses digital watermarking technology to embed the sharing information into big data. When leaving the blockchain network, the watermarking embedded in the data can be extracted and it can pursue legal liability for illegal infringers.

3 Methodology

We propose a framework for big data copyright protection based on blockchain and digital watermarking technology. The blockchain is used to store embedded watermarks and their sharing information. The digital watermark is used for copyright authentication and traitor tracking.

3.1 Framework Overview

Our framework for big data copyright protection consists of two parts: one is the storage of the watermark and record of data transaction, and the other is the watermarking extraction and comparison with the record stored in blockchain when illegal suspicious data are found.

Figure 1 shows that, when performing data sharing, a watermark with the shared information of both parties is first embedded into the data to be shared. Then, the watermark and the data sharing record are stored in the blockchain to ensure the reliability of data sharing in the entire blockchain network.

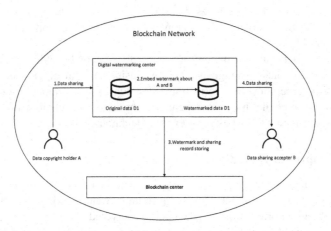

Fig. 1. Data sharing part

However, if the party accepting the data sharing copies the data and leaves the blockchain network for violent trafficking and other infringements (Fig. 2), then the data rights holder can extract the watermark information in the suspicious data, compare it with the watermark stored in the blockchain, and investigate legal liability for the infringing party to protect the copyright of data.

In general, the framework uses blockchain to store data sharing records and watermarking copyright information.

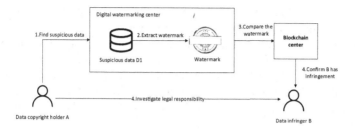

Fig. 2. Copyright protection part

3.2 Digital Watermarking Algorithm

We propose a watermarking algorithm to embed copyright information into big data. The embedded watermarks can be extracted completely after suffering a certain damage. However, the proposed algorithm is used only for numerical data and presupposes that the distortion of data within certain error range is acceptable. The digital watermarking algorithm comprises two parts: embedding and detecting watermarks. The embedding algorithm is used to insert the information of watermark W into the data D, whereas the detecting algorithm is used to extract watermark information W from the suspicious data D1. The notations related to the algorithm are defined as shown in Table 1.

Table 1. Notations

Notation	Meaning
P	Unique identifier
N	Number of tuples
V	Number of the candidate attributes to be marked
K	The owner's secret key
1/y	Fraction of tuples used in watermark
H	Hash function
L	Length of watermark
G	Constraint set of data

The constraint set G is defined as the error range in which the attribute can be changed. It contains the changeable attribute name and the changeable range to ensure data availability after embedding the watermark. We apply the hash function H to the unique identifier P and the secret key K of the data. Then, we select the data row with the same probability, in which the watermark is embedded.

Watermark Insertion

As shown in Fig. 3, the first step of the watermarking embedding algorithm is to select the embedded tuples. Then, we use the unique identifier P, the key K, and the embedding ratio y to determine the tuple. Lines 3 and 4 use the same method to select the embedded attributes and watermark bits. Line 5 selects the least significant bit

(LSB) of the attribute. For example, the LSB of 321 is 1, whereas the LSB of 321.142 is 2. The algorithm compares the embedded watermark bit with the LBS of the attribute. If the parity is the same, then the attribute value is not changed; otherwise, the LSB is incremented by 1 (Line 7), thereby modifying the attribute value (Line 8). After modifying the attribute to embed the watermarking, the algorithm checks whether the attribute value is within the scope of the constraint set G; otherwise, the attribute is not modified (Line 10). The algorithm finally returns the data D embedded with the watermark.

Algorithm of Watermarking Insertion

1.foreach $P \in D$ do
2. if($H(P+K)$ mod $y == 0$)
3. $i = H(P+K)$ mod V // mark this attribute A_i
4. $j = H(P+K)$ mod L // select this watermark bit j
5. $k = findLBS(A_i)$ // find the attribute's least significant bit k
6.   if($W[j]$ mod $k == 1$)
7. $k = k+1$
8.   modify(A_i)
9.   if($!(A_i \in G)$)
10.   set A_i to original A_i
11.return D

Fig. 3. Algorithm of watermarking insertion

In the watermarking embedding algorithm, the selected tuples are relatively independent and evenly distributed. On average, N/Y tuples are used to embed a watermark, and each watermark bit $W[i]$ is embedded in N/yL times.

Watermark Extraction

The watermark extraction algorithm is the inverse of the embedded algorithm. The private key and embedding ratio are the same as the embedding algorithm. The main purpose of the algorithm is to extract the watermark from the suspicious data. The recovery of the watermark adopts the voting mechanism.

As shown in Fig. 4, in the extraction algorithm, two array variables $count_0$, $count_1$ are used to ensure that the number of watermark information of a certain bit is 0 and 1 for the subsequent watermark recovery. The selection of tuples, attributes, and watermark bits is consistent with the embedding algorithm (Lines 3–6). If the LSB of the embedded attributes is even, then the bit is embedded with watermark 0, and $count_0[j]$ is incremented by 1; otherwise, watermark 1 is embedded, and $count_1[j]$ is incremented by 1 (Lines 8–11). Watermark recovery is performed until all tuples have been traversed. The watermark recovery uses the voting rule (Lines 12–19). If the number of watermark 0 divided by the total number of 0 and 1 is greater than the threshold t, which represents the ranges from 0.5 to 1, then the watermark is considered to be 0. This method is used to restore each bit of watermark information for obtaining a complete watermark.

Algorithm of Watermarking Extraction

1.foreach k=0 to L-1 do

2. $count_0[k] = 0, count_1[k] = 0, W[k] = ?$ // initiate watermark and count

3.foreach $P \in D$ do

4. if(H(P+K) mod y ==0) // this line has been marked

5. i = H(P+K) mod V // this attribute A_i has been marked

6. j = H(P+K) mod L // this watermark bit j has been chosen

7. m = findLBS(A_i) // find attribute's least siginificant bit k

8. if(m mod 2 == 0)

9. $count_0[j]$ ++

10. else

11. $count_1[j]$ ++

// Watermark Recovery

12.foreach k=0 to L-1 do

13. if($count_0[k] + count_1[k]$ == 0)

14.   W[k] = ?

15.   return none suspected

16. if($count_0[k]$ / $count_0[k]+count_1[k]$ > t) // t is a threshold, $t \in [0.5,1)$

17.   W[k] = 0

18. if($count_1[k]$ / $count_0[k]+count_1[k]$ > t)

19.   W[k] = 1

20.return W

Fig. 4. Watermark extraction

4   Experiment

We use the blockchain named fabric to store watermarks and data sharing records. We randomly generate data of 10,000 tuples that contain a unique identifier and 20 attributes. The embedded watermark is "0110010110100100." The embedding ratio is 1/50, which is equivalent to 200 lines of data used to embed the watermark. In the terms of robustness, we compared our algorithm with the algorithms of [14]. And we demonstrated experimental analyses from three aspects: subset selection, subset modification and mix-and-match attacks.

4.1   Subset Selection Attack

Subset selection attack refers to an attacker attempting to delete parts of the data to destroy the watermark. We use data of 10,000 tuples for watermark embedding experiments. Figure 5 shows that, although the data are deleted by 30%, the watermark information can still be extracted by 100%. Therefore, the extracted watermark can match the blockchain watermark. When the data are deleted by 40%, the watermark information can only be extracted by approximately 85%, and the extracted watermark is similar to "0010011100?011?". When the data are deleted on a large scale, such as 70%–90%, the watermark extraction capacity can only be 60% to 40%. Nonetheless, large-scale deletion of data will damage the availability of data, and the watermarking cannot be erased completely when deleting the data in a small part. Compared with the algorithm of paper [14], the proposed algorithm of this paper has better robustness in the face of large-scale subset selection attacks.

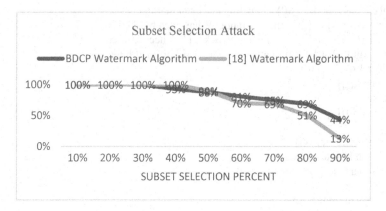

Fig. 5. Result of subset selection attack

4.2   Subset Alteration Attack

Subset alteration attack refers to an attacker attempting to modify a portion of a data value to erase the watermark. The experiment randomly selects the tuples and changes all attributes in a small scope. Figure 6 shows that, when 20% of the data rows are changed, the watermark can be extracted by 100%. When 50% of the data are changed, the watermark can only be extracted by 50%. Similarly, large-scale modification of data will result in decreased data availability. Watermarks cannot be completely erased when a small amount of data are modified. And compared with the [14], no matter how much the modification ratio is, the algorithm of this paper has obvious advantages in the face of subset modification attacks.

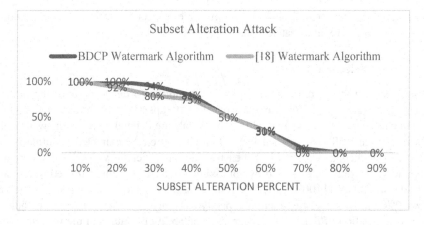

Fig. 6. Result of subset alteration attack

4.3   Mix-and-Match Attack

Mix-and-match attack indicates that an attacker attempts to extract some data and combine them with other similar data to erase the watermark. The experiment extracted 10%–20% of embedded watermark data and mixed them with similar data. Figure 7 shows that, when 20% of the watermark data are mixed with new data, the watermark can be extracted by 100%. When 60% of the data are extracted and mixed with new data, the watermark can be detected by approximately 80%. The results of this experiment show that our algorithm performs well in mix-and-match attacks. We Compared the algorithm with the paper [14], the performance is not as good as x after 30% hybrid attack, however, while the attack strength getting stronger, the algorithm of this paper perform obviously excellent.

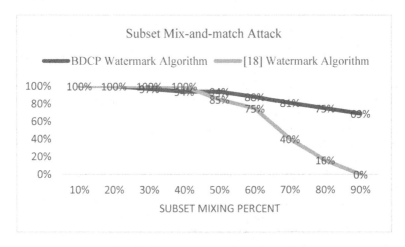

Fig. 7.   Result of mix-and-match attack

5   Conclusion

In this study, we propose a general framework for big data copyright protection using blockchain and digital watermarking technology. We store the copyright watermarks together with data sharing records in the blockchain and compare the extracted watermarks with the stored records. The results show that our framework is robust to attacks and allows easy determination of ownership of a certain copy of data.

Acknowledgment. This research was supported by the Technology Project of Beijing Municipal Transportation Committee and the National Key R&D program under Grant No. 2016YF C0801700, Beijing Municipal Science and Technology Project No. Z171100000917016, the National Natural Science Foundation Project under Grant No. U1636208.

References

1. Chen, X.: The geospatial data copyright protection research based on rubust watermarking. North China Institute of Aerospace Engineering (2018)
2. Sk, A., Masilamani, V.: A novel digital watermarking scheme for data authentication and copyright protection in 5G networks. Comput. Electr. Eng. (2018)
3. He, P., Yu, G., Zhang, Y., et al.: The prospective review of blockchain technologies and applications. Comput. Sci. **44**(4), 1–7 (2017)
4. Pu, H.E., Ge, Y.U., Zhang, Y.F., et al.: Survey on blockchain technology and its application prospect. Comput. Sci. (2017)
5. Porru, S., Pinna, A., Marchesi, M., et al.: Blockchain-oriented software engineering: challenges and new directions. In: IEEE/ACM, International Conference on Software Engineering Companion, pp. 169–171. IEEE (2017)
6. Yun, P.: Research on data confirmation in big data environment. Mod. Telecommun. Technol. **46**(05), 17–20 (2016)
7. Zhen-Hua, D.U.: Research on data confirmation right in big data application. Mob. Commun. (2015)
8. Agrawal, R., Kiernan, J.: Watermarking relational databases. In: International Conference on Very Large Databases, pp. 155–166 (2002)
9. Zhang, Y., Niu, X., Zhao, D., et al.: Relational databases watermark technique based on content characteristic. In: International Conference on Innovative Computing, Information and Control, pp. 677–680. IEEE (2006)
10. Franco-Contreras, J., Coatrieux, G.: Robust watermarking of relational databases with ontology-guided distortion control. IEEE Trans. Inf. Forensics Secur. **10**(9), 1939–1952 (2015)
11. Li, Y., Swarup, V., Jajodia, S.: Fingerprinting relational databases: schemes and specialties. IEEE Trans. Dependable Secure Comput. **2**(1), 34–45 (2005)
12. Sion, R., Atallah, M., Prabhakar, S.: Rights protection for relational data. In: ACM SIGMOD International Conference on Management of Data, pp. 98–109. IEEE (2003)
13. Khanduja, V., Chakraverty, S., Verma, O.P., et al.: A robust multiple watermarking technique for information recovery. In: Advance Computing Conference, pp. 250–255. IEEE (2014)
14. Guo, F., Wang, J., Li, D.: Fingerprinting relational databases. In: ACM Symposium on Applied Computing, pp. 487–492. ACM (2006)

A Privacy-Preserving Attribute-Based Access Control Scheme

Yang Xu[1(✉)], Quanrun Zeng[1], Guojun Wang[2], Cheng Zhang[1], Ju Ren[1], and Yaoxue Zhang[1]

[1] School of Information Science and Engineering, Central South University, Changsha 410083, China
{xuyangcsu,zengqquanrun,zhangcheng_sy,renju,zyx}@csu.edu.cn
[2] School of Computer Science and Technology, Guangzhou University, Guangzhou 510006, China
csgjwang@gmail.com

Abstract. The emerging attribute-based access control (ABAC) mechanism is an expressive, flexible, and manageable authorization technique that is particularly suitable for current distributed, inconstant and complex service-oriented scenarios. Unfortunately, the inevitable disclosure of attributes that carry sensitive information bring significant risks to users' privacy, which obstructs the further development and popularization of the ABAC severely. In this paper, we propose an effective privacy-preserving ABAC (P-ABAC) scheme to defend against privacy leakage risks of users' attributes. In the P-ABAC approach, the necessary sensitive attributes are securely handled on the service requester side by using the homomorphic encryption method for privacy protection. And meanwhile, the service provider is still able to make accurate access decisions according to the received attribute ciphertext and pre-set policies with the help of the homomorphic encryption-based secure multi-party computation techniques, while learning no privacy information. The theoretical analysis proves that our model contributes to making an efficient and effective ABAC model with the enhanced privacy-protection feature.

Keywords: Attribute-based access control · Privacy
Security · Secure multi-party computation · Homomorphic encryption

1 Introduction

The emergences of novel network computing and communication technologies enable more convenient and flexible service provisioning schemes that benefit billions of end users. With the supports of mobile cloud computing [1], edge computing [2], transparent computing [3] and underlying 4G/5G networks, current users can easily acquire numerous service resources via various types of devices any time, any where. Meanwhile, such innovations bring about very complicated resource access scenarios with distributed, dynamic, and changeable features, which presents difficulties in access control.

© Springer Nature Switzerland AG 2018
G. Wang et al. (Eds.): SpaCCS 2018, LNCS 11342, pp. 361–370, 2018.
https://doi.org/10.1007/978-3-030-05345-1_31

Traditional access control techniques like the mandatory access control (MAC) [4], the discretionary access control (DAC) [5], and the more typical role-based access control (RBAC) [6] become ineffective and unmaintainable in these complex access scenarios due to their simple and unitary decision-making methods without adequate granularity, flexibility, and diversification for dynamic authorizations.

With progresses in access control, diverse security factors such as real-time states of subjects, objects, and environments are considered, which leads to the emergence of an advanced attribute-based access control (ABAC) mechanism [7]. By enforcing expressive access policies consisting of different attributes on requests, the ABAC achieves fine-grained control, high flexibility, scalability and manageability, which is well adaptable to complex and inconstant authorization scenarios [8–11]. Currently, the ABAC approach has been applied in many IT hot fields including cloud computing [12,13], big data [14,15], and Internet of things (IoT) [16,17] scenarios, and has also evolved into impressive mature commercial solutions [18,19].

Unfortunately, such a promising technique is born with potential risks. Since the disclosure of relevant attributes is essential and indispensable for making final access decisions in the ABAC model, consequently, these unprotected attributes carrying users' sensitive information can be exposed to service providers which brings significant risks to users' privacy. This drawback has naturally sparked public concerns [20] and thereby influenced the further development and popularization of the ABAC technique.

To defend against the privacy disclosure threats incurred by the primary ABAC model, several tentative and exploratory approaches have already been proposed [21–26]. However, some solutions that block normal attribute deliveries only protect the limited privacy at the unacceptable expense of service usability, while the others suffer from significant limitations due to the introductions of online third parties that are not always available and may cause performance bottlenecks.

Motivated by the challenges above, in this paper, we propose an effective and sophisticated privacy-preserving ABAC model (P-ABAC) without a trusted third party (TTP) for protecting the attribute privacy. In our P-ABAC scheme, the necessary sensitive attributes undergo security processing on the service requester side by the mean of homomorphic encryption, so as to avoid privacy leakage. And meanwhile, the service provider is equipped with the ability to make access decisions accurately according to the attribute ciphertext and pre-set policies by using the homomorphic encryption-based secure multi-party computation techniques without learning any sensitive information. A concrete example is given to illustrate the details of its working process. And the theoretical analysis reveals that the P-ABAC model is effective in protecting the privacy of users' attributes with reasonable costs and no interferences of normal decision-making processes.

The rest of this paper is organized as follows. In Sect. 2, we discuss several relevant work about ABAC, especially the ones focusing on its privacy issues.

Section 3 introduces some background knowledge of secure multi-party computation based on homomorphic encryption which is used in this paper. Section 4 proposes the P-ABAC model together with a case study. In Sect. 5, we discuss our model in terms of security and efficiency. At last, we conclude our work and outline some possible enhancements in Sect. 6.

2   Related Work

Access control is one of the most direct and effective security protection mechanisms to defend resources against illegal accesses. The past decades have witnessed the emergences and successes of several typical schemes such as MAC [4], DAC [5], and RBAC [6]. Unfortunately, when it comes to current dynamic, distributed and complex scenarios, these famous models are gradually underpowered for meeting dynamic and changeable authorization demands due to their simple and unitary decision-making methods without enough flexibility, expressibility, and scalability.

Therefore, more security factors such as real-time states of subjects, objects, and contexts are comprehensively considered, which leads to the emergence of the novel attribute-based access control (ABAC) mechanism [7] where access decisions are determined based on a group of policies consisting of different types of attributes such as age, department, location, etc. With the outstanding features of powerful expression ability, fine granularity, high flexibility, scalability, and manageability, ABAC has been becoming the dominating access control mechanism for the next generation. Researches about the ABAC and its applications have sprung up [8–11] and have already achieved substantive progresses in some IT hot areas such as cloud computing [12,13], big data [14,15], and IoT [16,17] environments. Further, more practical efforts have been made by other forces such as standards organizations [7] and enterprises [18,19], which further drives the development and popularization of the ABAC technique.

Although the ABAC has enticing benefits, this model lacks provisions for privacy issues. Its inevitable disclosure of user's attributes that contain sensitive information causes clear privacy risks, which has gradually eroded public confidences in ABAC, thereby affecting its development and popularization [20].

For mitigating the privacy threats in original ABAC model, some tentative and exploratory researches have already been studied. Wu et al. [21] presented an extended ABAC model with attribute release control in which service requesters can choose to submit the sensitive attributes to only trusted service providers. Similarly, Sang et al. [22] designed and implemented an attribute disclosure control mechanism for ABAC. In this approach, a user only submits a reduced attribute set that is necessary for accessing corresponding resources, to ensure the minimal disclosure of sensitive attribute information. Moreover, Zhang et al. [23] proposed a trust-based sensitive attributes protection mechanism. In their solution, the release of users' attributes was determined by the comparison results of attribute sensitivity and service provider's trust level. However, these schemes obstruct the normal submission processes of attributes to provide partial protections for users' privacy, which unreasonably interferes with proper availability of normal services.

Besides, Esmaeeli et al. [24] proposed a distributed ABAC model in which user attributes were inspected by the user's home organization, so as to protect users' privacy from being accessed by service providers. More general, Kolter et al. [25] developed an ABAC system with privacy preserving mechanism in which the decision-making points were decoupled from the service provider sides, and a user could choose one trusted third-party authorization server to make access decisions. Put et al. [26] presented a privacy-friendly ABAC mechanism for online services. They developed a suite of privacy-friendly protocols for obtaining users' attributes from third-party platforms, so as to prevent service providers from obtaining precise attribute values and eliminate the information linkabilities. Unfortunately, these approaches suffer from significant limitations as they highly rely on trusted online third parties that are not always available in dynamic and distributed environments, and may cause performance bottlenecks.

Therefore, more efficient, independent and sophisticated privacy enhancement mechanisms are urgently required for making the ABAC a more secured and reliable model so that users can feel comfortable to use it.

3   Preliminary

This section goes through the secure multi-party computation and the homomorphic encryption-based solution applied in our model.

3.1   Yao's Millionaires' Problem

The Yao's Millionaires' (i.e., "greater than" or "GT") problem is a secure multi-party computation problem of data comparison. The involved parties compare their own data without revealing the actual value [27]. In P-ABAC model, we use the solution of GT problem to help to make access decisions without privacy leakage.

3.2   Homomorphic Encryption

Homomorphic encryption is a kind of encrypted form that allows computation on ciphertexts without accessing the plaintexts [28]. Given an encryption operation E and a decryption operation D, $\odot$ is the operation in the plaintext key space, $\oplus$ is the operation in the ciphertext key space. For any two plaintexts a and b, if $D(E(a) \odot E(b)) = a \oplus b$, then this cryptosystem is a homomorphic encryption.

Secure Multi-party Computation with Homomorphic Encryption. As a tool to solve the secure multi-party computation problem, the homomorphic encryption is widely used in various GT solutions. The comparison scheme raised by Lin [29] is an effective solution of secure multi-party computation based on homomorphic encryption as follows:

Assuming that $x = (x_1 x_2 \ldots x_n)_2, y = (y_1 y_2 \ldots y_n)_2$ are the binary form private inputs of two parties respectively. One party with the input x will first generates the corresponding encryption matrix M as follows, in which $E(1)$ is the ElGamal encrypting function:

$$M_{x_i, j} = E(1), \ M_{\overline{x_i}, j} = random()$$

Then, for all $y_i = 0$, the other party will calculate the corresponding result $c_i = M_{y_1, 1} \odot M_{y_2, 2} \odot \ldots M_{y_{i-1}, i-1} \odot M_{1, i}$, and for $y_i = 1$ we have $c_i = random()$. Then, the reshuffled result will be sent to the first party. According to the following theorem, $x > y$ if and only if there exists an c_i satisfied that $D(c_i) = 1$:

Theorem 1. *For two binary numbers $x = x_1 x_2 \ldots x_n, y = y_1 y_2 \ldots y_n, x > y$ if and only if there exists an $i \in n$ which satisfies*

$$\begin{cases} y_i = 0 \\ \overline{x_1 x_2 \ldots x_i} = \overline{y_1 y_2 \ldots y_{i-1}, 1} \end{cases} \tag{1}$$

4 P-ABAC Scheme

In this section, we define the necessary notations and introduce the architecture of P-ABAC and describe its workflow step by step. And then, we study a detailed case to help readers understand the P-ABAC better.

4.1 Architecture and Workflow

Generally, the P-ABAC model modifies the verification process of the standard ABAC model. In the P-ABAC model, the public attributes are treated in the same way in the standard ABAC model. And as for the attributes that involve users' sensitive information, we employ the solution to GT problem for making the access decision. As shown in Fig. 1, the P-ABAC is an extension of the standard ABAC model in which a privacy-preserving policy matching component is added for making access decisions without disclosure of privacy.

When a request arrives, the service provider firstly collects the related states of the non-privacy attributes, such as the attributes of object, environment and operation, as well as some non-privacy attributes of user. Then the standard policy matching component will perform the policy matching process for the non privacy attributes in the same way in the standard ABAC (step 1). And the privacy-preserving policy matching will be performed by the privacy-preserving polices matching component (step 2). Subsequently, the P-ABAC system synthesizes the results of the two components and obtains the final access decision (step 3). The final result is delivered to the enforcement facility which will mediate the corresponding access to the object accordingly (step 4–5).

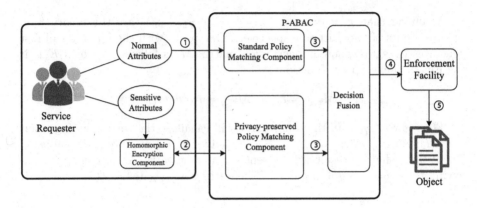

Fig. 1. Architecture and workflow of P-ABAC

4.2   Privacy-Preserving Policy Matching Process

Each policy involving a privacy attribute x will be divided into several restriction clauses containing only one comparison operator by the service provider, e.g., $(a > x.value)$. Then, for each boundary number a, the service provider will transform it into the corresponding binary string $SP = sp_1, sp_2, \ldots, sp_n$, then a $2 \times n$ ciphertext matrix M will be generated accordingly as follows.

$$
M_{ij} = \begin{cases} E(1), & sp_i = j \\ random(), & \text{otherwise} \end{cases} \tag{2}
$$

After receiving the ensemble of ciphertext matrices of all M from the service provider, for any ciphertext matrices M, the service requester will firstly figure out the binary string $SR = sr_1, sr_2, \ldots, sr_n$ according to the value of corresponding attribute x. Then for each $sr_i = 0$, the service requester will figure out the ensemble of $c_1, c_2, \ldots, c_n$ as follows:

$$
c_i = \begin{cases} M_{sr_1,1} \odot M_{sr_2,2} \odot \cdots \odot M_{sr_{i-1},i-1} \odot M_{1,i-1}, & sr_i = 0 \\ random(), & sr_i = 1 \end{cases} \tag{3}
$$

Then the service requester will reshuffle the $c_1, c_2, \ldots, c_n$ and send the shuffled ensemble $c'_1, c'_2, \ldots, c'_n$ to the service provider. When receiving the ensemble $c_1, c_2, \ldots, c_n$, the service provider will try to decrypt $c'_1, c'_2, \ldots, c'_n$. According to Theorem 1, $a > x$ only when there exists a i satisfied that $\overline{sp_1, sp_2, \ldots, sp_i} = sr_1, sr_2, \ldots, sr_{i-1}, 1$ and $sr_i = 0$, i.e. the service requester will be considered satisfying the restriction clause if and only if there exists i so that $D(c'_i) = 1$.

4.3   Case Study

To help readers understand the P-ABAC better, a case study is described in this subsection. Assuming there exists a P-ABAC system with one privacy-related policy as follows:

$$\text{IF } (age \text{ is less than } 30) \text{ THEN granted}$$

Then, the policy will be converted into the following restriction clause:

$$(age < 30) \rightarrow \text{true}$$

Then, we derive the corresponding boundary number $a = 30$. We assume that a service requester SR who has an attribute $age = 25$ initiates an access request. When receiving the request, the service provider will firstly generate the corresponding binary string S_a of a and the ciphertext matrix M. Assuming that the sizes of the boundary number a and the corresponding attribute are both 5 bits, then we get that $S_a = 11110_2$ and the ciphertext matrix M as follows:

$$M = \begin{Bmatrix} random() & E(1) \\ random() & E(1) \\ random() & E(1) \\ random() & E(1) \\ E(1) & random() \end{Bmatrix}$$

Then the service provider will send M to the service requester. As the service requester has the attribute $age = 25$, it will figure out the corresponding binary string $S_{age} = 11001_2$. Then, according to M, the corresponding $\{c_i\}$ will be generated as follows:

$$C = \begin{Bmatrix} c_1 = random() \\ c_2 = random() \\ c_3 = M_{1,1} \odot M_{1,2} \odot M_{1,3} \\ c_4 = M_{1,1} \odot M_{1,2} \odot M_{0,3} \odot M_{0,4} \\ c_5 = random() \end{Bmatrix}$$

According to the properties of ElGamal solution, the service requester can obtain the $C = \{random(), random(), E(1), random(), random()\}$ and then reshuffles it. Then, the requester submits the reshuffled result $C' = \{random(), E(1), random(), random(), random()\}$ to the service provider. After decryption, the service provider finds out $D(E(1)) = 1$ from the ensemble C'. Therefore, the request will be granted accordingly.

5 Discussion

5.1 Effectiveness

We suppose that there is a policy $(a > v) \rightarrow$ granted in the P-ABAC system, in which a is the boundary number defined above and v is the corresponding value of user's attribute. For any v which satisfies $a > v$, there exists a c_i in the reshuffled calculating results $\{c_1, c_2, \ldots, c_n\}$ which satisfied that $D(c_i) = 1$. Let v, v' be two values which satisfy $a > v$ and $a > v'$, and $D(c_i) = 1, D(c'_j) = 1$,

There exist no polynomial algorithms for the service provider to distinguish the reshuffled calculating results c_1, c_2, ..., c_{i-1}, c_{i+1}, ..., c_n from c'_1, c'_2, ..., c'_{j-1}, c'_{j+1}, ..., c'_n due to the computational intractability of the ElGamal homomorphic encryption, which means that the service provider can not learn extra information except the comparison result[1].

5.2   Efficiency

We firstly analyze the computing complexity of the P-ABAC decision-making process on the service provider side. Suppose that the sizes of private attributes involved in P-ABAC are n-bits and p is the modulus used in the encryption. For any involved attribute, the generation of the corresponding $2 \times n$ ciphertext matrix needs n times encryption operations, which runs in $O(n \log p)$ as the encryption operation of ElGamal runs in $O(\log p)$. Then, when the service provider received the calculation result $\{c'_1, c'_2, \ldots, c'_n\}$ from the service requester, n decryption operations will be executed to calculating all $D(c'_i)$ and find out weather there exists an i so that $D(c'_i) = 1$. Therefore, the whole computing complexity of the P-ABAC decision-making process for a single restriction clause on the service provider side is $O(n \log p)$.

When it comes to the service requester side, for any involved attribute, n corresponding results of ciphertext matrix will be calculated, and each calculation of c_i runs in $O(n)$, i.e., the computing complexity on the service requester side is $O(n^2)$.

6   Conclusion

In this paper, a non-TTP-based P-ABAC model is proposed to defend against the privacy leakage threats existing in the basic ABAC model. In the P-ABAC model, all sensitive attributes are secured through the homomorphic encryption technique, which eliminates privacy leakage risks. Besides, the service provider can still make correct access decisions properly based on the ciphertext of attributes and pre-defined policies with the aid of homomorphic encryption-based secure multi-party computation techniques, while learning no additional privacy information. A case study illustrates the working process of our P-ABAC scheme concretely, and the theoretical analysis further demonstrates its effectiveness and efficiency.

In the future, we would like to equip our approach with the ability to automatically identify sensitive attributes for protections with the aid of artificial intelligence techniques, so as to achieve a more efficient access control scheme with adequate privacy protections. Besides, we plan to implement a prototype of our P-ABAC for further experimental evaluations.

---

[1] Note that the authenticity and accuracy of the submitted attributes can be guaranteed with the supports of digital signature and terminal-oriented trusted computing techniques, which are orthogonal to our work and out of the scope of this paper.

Acknowledgments. This work was supported by the National Natural Science Foundation of China under Grants 61702561, 61702562, and 61632009, the Hunan Provincial Innovation Foundation for Postgraduate under Grant CX2015B047, and the Guangdong Provincial Natural Science Foundation under Grant 2017A030308006.

References

1. Fernando, N., Loke, S.W., Rahayu, W.: Mobile cloud computing: a survey. Future Gener. Comput. Syst. **29**(1), 84–106 (2013)
2. Mao, Y., You, C., Zhang, J., Huang, K., Letaief, K.B.: A survey on mobile edge computing: the communication perspective. IEEE Commun. Surv. Tutor. **19**(4), 2322–2358 (2017)
3. Zhang, Y., Guo, K., Ren, J., Wang, J., Chen, J.: Transparent computing: a promising network computing paradigm. Comput. Sci. Eng. **19**(1), 7–20 (2017)
4. Lindqvist, H.: Mandatory access control. Master's thesis, Umea University, Sweden (2006)
5. Li, N.: Discretionary access control. In: IEEE Symposium on Security & Privacy, vol. 13, pp. 96–109. IEEE (2011)
6. Sandhu, R.S., Ferraiolo, D., Kuhn, R.: The NIST model for role-based access control: towards a unified standard. In: ACM Workshop on Role-Based Access Control, pp. 47–63. ACM (2000)
7. Hu, C., Ferraiolo, D., Kuhn, R., Schnitzer, A., Sandlin, K., Scarfone, K.: Guide to attribute based access control (ABAC) definition and considerations (draft). NIST Special Publication (2014)
8. Servos, D., Osborn, S.: Current research and open problems in attribute-based access control. ACM Comput. Surv. **49**(4), 65–107 (2017)
9. Ni, D., Shi, H., Chen, Y., Guo, J.: Attribute based access control (ABAC)-based cross-domain access control in service-oriented architecture (SOA). In: IEEE International Conference on Computer Science & Service System (CSSS 2012), pp. 1405–1408. IEEE (2012)
10. Xu, Y., Gao, W., Zeng, Q., Wang, G., Ren, J., Zhang, Y.: FABAC: a flexible fuzzy attribute-based access control mechanism. In: Wang, G., Atiquzzaman, M., Yan, Z., Choo, K.-K.R. (eds.) SpaCCS 2017. LNCS, vol. 10656, pp. 332–343. Springer, Cham (2017). https://doi.org/10.1007/978-3-319-72389-1_27
11. Xu, Y., Gao, W., Zeng, Q., Wang, G., Ren, J., Zhang, Y.: A feasible fuzzy-extended attribute-based access control technique. Secur. Commun. Netw. **2018**, 1–11 (2018)
12. Jin, X.: Attribute-based access control models and implementation in cloud infrastructure as a service. Doctoral thesis. The University of Texas at San. Antonio, USA (2014)
13. Qiu, M., Gai, K., Thuraisingham, B., Tao, L., Zhao, H.: Proactive user-centric secure data scheme using attribute-based semantic access controls for mobile clouds in financial industry. Future Gener. Comput. Syst. **80**, 421–429 (2018)
14. Gupta, M., Patwa, F., Sandhu, R.: An Attribute-based access control model for secure big data processing in Hadoop ecosystem. In: ACM Workshop, pp. 13–24. ACM (2018)
15. Cavoukian, A., Chibba, M., Williamson, G., Ferguson, A.: The importance of ABAC: attribute-based access control to big data: privacy and context. Research report. Ryerson University, Canada (2015)

16. Sciancalepore, S., et al.: Attribute-based access control scheme in federated IoT platforms. In: Podnar Žarko, I., Broering, A., Soursos, S., Serrano, M. (eds.) InterOSS-IoT 2016. LNCS, vol. 10218, pp. 123–138. Springer, Cham (2017). https://doi.org/10.1007/978-3-319-56877-5_8
17. Monir, S.: A lightweight attribute-based access control system for IoT. Master's thesis. University of Saskatchewan, Saskatoon (2017)
18. Axiomatics. https://www.axiomatics.com. Accessed 5 Sept 2018
19. NextLabs. https://www.nextlabs.com. Accessed 17 June 2018
20. Irwin, K., Yu, T.: Preventing attribute information leakage in automated trust negotiation. In: 12th ACM Conference on Computer and Communications Security, pp. 36–45. ACM (2005)
21. Wu, K., Gao, H.: Attribute-based access control for web service with requester's attribute privacy protected. In: International Conference on Informational Technology and Environmental, pp. 932–936 (2008)
22. Sang, P., Chung, S.: Privacy-preserving attribute-based access control for grid computing. Int. J. Grid Util. Comput. 5(4), 286–296 (2014)
23. Zhang, G., Liu, J., Liu, J.: Protecting sensitive attributes in attribute based access control. In: Ghose, A., et al. (eds.) ICSOC 2012. LNCS, vol. 7759, pp. 294–305. Springer, Heidelberg (2013). https://doi.org/10.1007/978-3-642-37804-1_30
24. Esmaeeli, A., Shahriari, H.R.: Privacy protection of grid service requesters through distributed attribute based access control model. In: Bellavista, P., Chang, R.-S., Chao, H.-C., Lin, S.-F., Sloot, P.M.A. (eds.) GPC 2010. LNCS, vol. 6104, pp. 573–582. Springer, Heidelberg (2010). https://doi.org/10.1007/978-3-642-13067-0_59
25. Kolter, J., Schillinger, R., Pernul, G.: A privacy-enhanced attribute-based access control system. In: Barker, S., Ahn, G.-J. (eds.) DBSec 2007. LNCS, vol. 4602, pp. 129–143. Springer, Heidelberg (2007). https://doi.org/10.1007/978-3-540-73538-0_11
26. Put, A., De Decker, B.: Attribute-based privacy-friendly access control with context. In: Obaidat, M.S. (ed.) ICETE 2016. CCIS, vol. 764, pp. 291–315. Springer, Cham (2017). https://doi.org/10.1007/978-3-319-67876-4_14
27. Yao, A.: Protocols for secure computations. In: 23rd Annual Symposium on Foundations of Computer Science (SFCS 1982), pp. 160–164. IEEE (1982)
28. Rivest, R., Adleman, L., Dertouzos, M.: On data banks and privacy homomorphisms. Found. Secure Comput. 4(11), 169–180 (1978)
29. Lin, H.-Y., Tzeng, W.-G.: An efficient solution to the Millionaires' problem based on homomorphic encryption. In: Ioannidis, J., Keromytis, A., Yung, M. (eds.) ACNS 2005. LNCS, vol. 3531, pp. 456–466. Springer, Heidelberg (2005). https://doi.org/10.1007/11496137_31

Checking an Authentication of Person Depends on RFID with Thermal Image

Ahmed Raad Al-Sudani[1]([✉])[iD], Shang Gao[1], Sheng Wen[2],
and Muhmmad Al-Khiza'ay[1]

[1] School of Information Technology, Faculty of Science, Engineering and Built
Environment, Deakin University, Geelong, Australia
{aralsuda,shang.gao,malkhiza}@deakin.edu.au
[2] School of Information Technology, Swinburne University,
Hawthorn, Australia
swen@swin.edu.au

Abstract. The developed cameras help researchers attempting to imitate the human brain by distinguishing between people by many techniques were mentioned in the literature. Distinguishing between the human beings is being done by the image picked up by the visible light cameras in a classical method, because of this cameras do not provide enough amount of information. Therefore, the Kinect camera is distinguished assists researchers in obtaining tangible results from cameras development which presented the normal of integrative of the depth information and RGB information. This paper presents a model for face detection and recognition by the Kinect technique to some fundamental problems in the computer vision. This model is suggested in the environment of the company: firstly, to prove the reliability of the Kinect outputs. Secondly, detection about the depth of the human face by using maps drawing to distinguish the real human face, and get rid of the fraud processes, from which technique of face detection and recognition suffer. Finally, the suggested model has used the tracking algorithm that represents one of the system stages to provide the most significant amount of security. And in the end, tests are done by using our database obtained from the RGB camera in Kinect.

Keywords: RFID authentication · Smart building · Kinect
Thermal image · IOT

1 Introduction

The digital image consists of a limited number of numeric representations; each of these has a specific location and value. This representation refers to a finite set of digital values, called pixels. This type of image contains a fixed number of rows and columns of pixels. The processing of the digital image that defines to execute image processing on digital images by utilising computer algorithms.

© Springer Nature Switzerland AG 2018
G. Wang et al. (Eds.): SpaCCS 2018, LNCS 11342, pp. 371–380, 2018.
https://doi.org/10.1007/978-3-030-05345-1_32

It includes some critical steps like image acquisition, image enhancement, pre-processing, edge detection, segmentation, representation, description, matching, and recognition to produce an image or an image attributes [1,2]. Digital images have many uses. One of the most important methods is the recognition of the people because it provides information about the person and personality, in addition to, its easy accessibility, usage and the ability of better acceptance by person [1,3]. Many researchers are seeking to develop a computer system to accomplish the same functions of the human mind in recognising human faces through computer algorithms in digital image processing. The human face recognising is prepared in two procedures: face detection procedure and face recognition procedure. Face recognition is a biological system that used in many applications. 3D facial recognition is used to achieve high recognition because it is exceptionally safe [4–6]. Despite its many uses and excellent benefits, face recognition requires great effort in processing and uses many very complicated and expensive tools [7–9]. In this paper, we will explain to use the Kinect camera to achieve more efficiency in the authentication process with increased reliability in RFID.

1.1 Problem Statement

Recently, the Kinect camera has been deployed in many applications, especially in the field of games. The propagation based on the many advantages of the Kinect camera offer such as reducing the cost and ability to provide RGB-D data and depth data. It has been used in real applications, away from games, especially security applications, and it applied with RFID to identify the user is authorised or not. In this paper, some questions were asked about this position, which is as follows:

- How is user identification?
- How to apply the system mechanism?
- How can I make use of the proposed idea?

1.2 Objectives

With the development of technology, the Kinect device has become famous for its availability and low cost. The latest version of this device known as Kinect for windows and is characterized by providing the depth of information from a close distance from 500 mm to 3000 mm. Thus, the Kinect device suited for many applications. In this paper:

- The Kinect device used to identify the human is considered as real filed because it is providing RGB-D data as well as the depth data.
- The Kinect device has been utilized in the security field.
- The database used shall be suitable to detect and recognize the face from 2D and 3D images.
- Achieving the valid identification results by reducing mistakes rate.
- Results will be discussed based on a number of experiments on different users.

1.3 Motivation

This paper focuses on the use of the Kinect camera in a context other than gaming and at a much lower cost from traditional 3-D cameras with RFID system for purposing authentication of the legal person. Additionally, the Kinect camera has a complementary nature of the depth, and visual (RGB) information provided by it bootstraps potential new solutions for classical problems in computer vision especially in the short-term environments. This makes these devices might be a better choice over the other cameras for many applications including 2d and 3d facial analysis systems.

1.4 Contribution

The face recognition and detection are the methods of verifying or identifying a face from its image where these methods assisted various systems to provide appropriate security. Therefore, the proposed system presents an approach to the identification of the human face to be the goal of this proposal to address the following points:

- Applying the Kinect device in face detection, face recognition and animation.
- The user identification system using the Kinect device.
- Using the proposed identification system with RFID.

2 Literature Review

In the recent time, human face recognition has been based on computer vision and video-based techniques. In which the execution of recognition depends fundamentally on light conditions, shadow, camera angles, and head position. So, the system performance may suffer in these circumstances using a 2D camera. There are many researchers presented in this area, each of which employed different methods to solve the mentioned problems:

[10] present an algorithm that uses a low-resolution 3D sensor for robust face recognition under challenging conditions. A preprocessing algorithm proposed which exploits the facial symmetry at the 3D point cloud level to acquire a canonical frontal view, shape, and texture, of the faces irrespective of their initial pose. This algorithm also fills holes and smoothes the noisy depth data produced by the low-resolution sensor. The canonical depth map and texture of a query face are then sparse approximated from separate dictionaries learned from training data. The texture is changed from the RGB to Discriminant Color Space before meager coding, and the reconstruction errors from the two sparse coding steps are added for individual identities in the lexicon. The query face is assigned the identity of the smallest reconstruction error. Experiments are performed using a publicly available database containing over 5000 facial images (RGB-D) with varying poses, expressions, illumination and disguise, acquired using the Kinect sensor. Recognition rates are 96.7% for the RGB-D data and

88.7% for the noisy depth data alone. Our results justify the feasibility of low-resolution 3D sensors for robust face recognition [10].

Goswami et al. [11]: In this paper, we have proposed a novel algorithm that utilizes the depth information along with RGB images which obtained from Kinect, to improve the recognition performance. The proposed algorithm computes a descriptor based on the entropy of RGB-D faces along with the saliency feature derived from a 2D face. The probe RGB-D descriptor is used as input to a random decision forest classifier to establish the identity. This research also presents a novel RGB-D face database consisting of RGB-D images about 106 subjects captured exclusively using Kinect is prepared. The experiments, performed on Kinect face databases, indicate that the RGB-D information obtained by Kinect can be used to achieve improved face recognition performance compared to existing 2D and 3D approaches [11].

Ghiass et al. present a comprehensive and timely review of the literature on this subject [12]. Their key commitments are the first a synopsis of the inherent properties of infrared imaging which makes this methodology promising in the context of face recognition. The second a deliberate audit of the most influential approached, with a focus on emerging common trends and additionally critical differences between alternative methodologies. The third a description of the fundamental databases of infrared facial images accessible to the scientist. The lastly forth exchange of the most promising avenues for future examination. Additionally, it was reviewed a range of data sets currently available to researchers. Considering the results distributed to date, in the conclusion of these authors two particularly promising ideas stand out. The first thought which the improvement of identity descriptors in light of constant physiological features such as vascular networks. The second thought which the utilization of methods for multi-modal fusion of complementary data types, most notably those based on visible and infrared images. Both are still in their initial stages, with a potential for substantial further improvement [12].

There is much research presented in a detection and recognition field through face and gait, some of these researches use the Kinect camera to provide aim of the major from each study. The proposed model will be expanding the Kinect work outside the boundaries of the Games for using in the human identification field through face detection and recognition.

3   Proposed Framework

Recently, focus on the interest has been devoted to detect and recognize the human face, especially in the field of security. The presentation of new sensor devices in this field, for example, the Kinect originally designed for the Microsoft Xbox, has permitted to defeat the limitations of computer-vision classical 2D vision algorithms, The most dependable approach to address the 2D vision problem is with 3D face models, in another hand, it is hard to acquire 3D data with high speed and low cost. By the Kinect sensor that can provide these properties and can be connected with a personal computer that makes it more appealing for face recognition applications. The proposed model will use the Kinect camera in the company environment, and it fully deployed will reduce the rate of fraudulent activities on the RFID such that only the registered owner of card access to the company ID. Security approaches in the company environment can be the effective role in preventing attacks on customers. These approaches considered the most important companies must meet specific standards to ensure a safe and secure company environment for their customers. The proposed model provides security to the company through the techniques of face detection and recognition with RFID, which is by using depth and RGB data, obtained from the Kinect Camera. This Model provides security by making sure if the user is allowed to enter or not by recognizing the face as illustrated in Figs. 1 and 2.

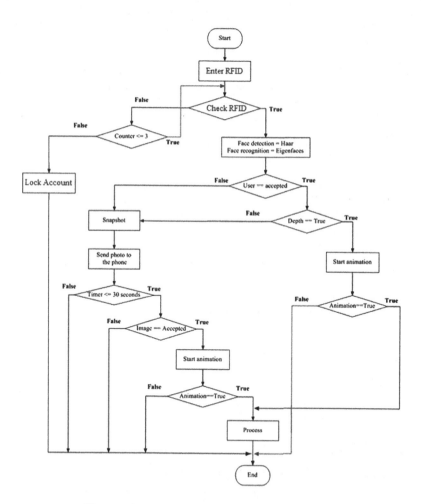

Fig. 1. The methodology of the proposed system

3.1   Scenario for the Proposed System

This algorithm is implemented in several steps to reduce Kinect problems in operating outside the gaming field. All these steps attempt to find a suitable solution to client identification problem as declared below:

Step1: Enter the RFID code
Step2: Check if the RFID Code is true
then Go To step3
Else GoTo step 6
Step3: Applying Haar and Eigenfaces algorithms to identify the user of system
Step4: Check if the user is authorized
then Go To step 5
Else Go To step9
Step5: Check if depth image is true
then Go To step7
Else Go To step12
Step6: Check if the RFID counter is less than (3) then Go To step1
Else Go To step16
Step7: Start animation
Step8: Check if the animation is true
then Go To step15
Else Go To Step 16
Step9: Taking a Snapshot to user
Step10: Send the Snapshot to system
Step11: Check if response timer is less than (30)
then Go To step12
Else Go To step 16
Step12: Check if response system is accepted then Go To step 13
Else Go To step16
Step13: Start animation
Step14: Check if the animation is true
then Go To step15
Else Go To Step 16
Step15: Process
Step16: Finish.

3.2   Depth Detection

Scenario for Depth Detection

This algorithm represents the Depth Detection approach; it is differentiating between deception operation as photographic form, and correct process of entry (true user) through several steps as declared below:

Step1: Take Snapshot to user.
* Taking Kinect Snapshot of the user.

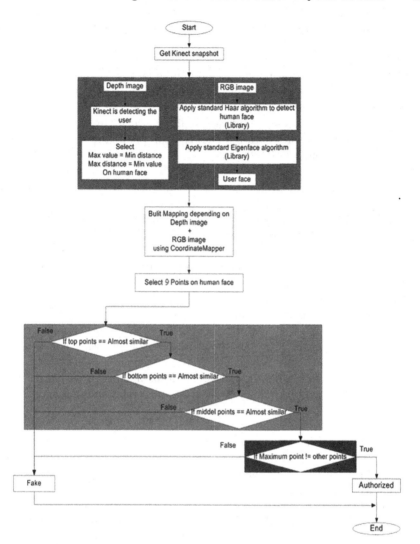

Fig. 2. The depth detection algorithm

Step 2: Applying Haar and Eigenfaces algorithms to detect and recognize human face.

* Applying the algorithms to determine the user's facial area on RGB frame
Step 3: Calculate the minimum and maximum reliable depth for the current frame (on the user's face).

* Calculated the minimum distance (maximum value) and maximum distance (minimum value) of the user image

Step4: Building mapping between locations on the depth image and RGB image.
* Build mapping using Coordinate Mapper tool
Step5: Determined seven points on the human face
* Identified points depending on the distance from the boundary 20 pixels upon rectangle of Haar algorithm
Step 6: Checking if the top points are similarity then Go to step 7
* Check if differences in depth between two top points are a similarity and it does not exceed the rate (0–2) mm
Else Go To step11
Step 7: Checking if the bottom points are similarity
then Go to step 8
* Check if differences in depth between two bottom points are a similarity and it does not exceed the rate (0–2) mm
Else Go To step11
Step 8: Checking if the middle point is similarity
then Go to step 9
* Check if differences in depth between two middle points are a similarity and it does not exceed the rate (0–2) mm
Else Go To step11
Step 9: Checking if the Maximum point is not equal the other points then Go to step 10
* Check if differences in depth between the Maximum point with other points (The other 9 points on the human face) are not equal and it is greater than (10) mm.
Else Go To step11
Step 10: The user is authorized
then Go to step 12
* The user is reliable to complete the requested operation, go to the animation process as shown in Fig. 4
Step 11: The user is fake
* Depth information not detected, it is considered cheating process through displaying a photo of a registered user, the camera reports for the owner of the account about the cheating process as shown in Fig. 4
Step 12: Finish.

Finally, the method divides into three stages program. The first stage to detect human face used Haar algorithm. The second stage is to recognize the human face used Eigenfaces algorithm, the third stage is to detect depth information to a human face, and the last stage detects human animation. The proposed model is implemented to handle company system through the Kinect camera, and focused on the suitable security method for the company, by dealing with the face detection and recognition. Good results are shown previously in this section. The results show the ability of Kinect camera to handle problems of human identification in the different fields. The following section explains the conclusion of this paper works and demonstrates some views of future work remarks, which could be done in researches related to the field of this thesis. The main contribution of this work is the use of Kinect device for human identification in the real world. This system enhanced the reliability of previous methods, such as (using the Kinect camera for human activity recognition, and for face detection and recognition) in a context other than gaming. The proposed system presented an approach to the human identification for increased reliability Kinect camera in the security field, through using many methods in one system, while in the previously mentioned systems used one approach only.

4   Conclusion

Face detection and recognition in the field of biometrics issues used widely in many applications such as: (surveillance systems, attendance, and left applications) but not used in determining a person's identity to provide security in hazardous environments. There are many gaps, such as the possibility of deception using the photo of the person registered, as well as there is a high probability of suspicion among people. The proposed model presented approach uses RGB images and depth information obtained through the Kinect camera to improve the performance of detection and recognition techniques with RFID. A system was organized to provide security to the most dangerous environments (company system), where people approved by detection and facial recognition techniques. Also, the influence of suspected cases of the over-mover advantage provided by Kinect camera had got rid of, as well as a proposal depth approach uses pictures to get rid of fraud in photos and advantages of this approach:

- The absence of an excessive load on the database because it does not contain pictures of the depth. Therefore the comparison takes place among points within the depths of memory.
- In this model does not need training all algorithms for recognition of faces on the proposed database, for it contains RGB images only. They are axioms of facial recognition technology.
- The proposed approach does not affect the processing time of an algorithm, because it is completely separated.
- Using any RGB camera to collect image in the database.

References

1. Mohammed, T.S., Al-Azzo, W.F., Al Mashani K.M.: Image processing development and implementation: a software simulation using Matlab®. In: Proceedings of the 6th International Conference on Information Technology (2013)
2. Bougrine, A., Harba, R., Canals, R., Ledee, R., Jabloun, M.: A joint snake and atlas-based segmentation of plantar foot thermal images. In: 2017 Seventh International Conference on Image Processing Theory, Tools and Applications, IPTA, pp. 1–6. IEEE (2017)

3. Lakshmi, K.D., Muthaiah, R., Kannan, K., Tapas, A.M.: Evaluation of local feature detectors for the comparison of thermal and visual low altitude aerial images. Defence Sci. J. **68**(5) (2018)
4. Zhang, L., Xie, X., Feng, S., Luo, M.: Heuristic dual-tree wavelet thresholding for infrared thermal image denoising of underground visual surveillance system. Opt. Eng. **57**(8), 083102 (2018)
5. Zhu, Y.: Research on the architecture and behavior model of high-speed channel for thermal image processing. Wirel. Pers. Commun. **102**(4), 3869–3877 (2018)
6. Si, L., Wang, Z., Liu, Y., Tan, C.: Online identification of shearer cutting state using infrared thermal images of cutting unit. Appl. Sci. **8**(10), 1772 (2018)
7. Kähm, O., Damer, N.: 2D face liveness detection: an overview. In: 2012 BIOSIG-Proceedings of the International Conference of the Bio-Metrics Special Interest Group, BIOSIG, pp. 1–12. IEEE (2012)
8. Fornaser, A., Tomasin, P., De Cecco, M., Tavernini, M., Zanetti, M.: Automatic graph based spatiotemporal extrinsic calibration of multiple Kinect V2 ToF cameras. Robot. Auton. Syst. **98**, 105–125 (2017)
9. Al-Sudania, A.R., Zhoub, W., Liuc, B., Almansoorid, A., Yange, M.: Detecting unauthorized RFID tag carrier for secure access control to a smart building. Int. J. Appl. Eng. Res. **13**(1), 749–760 (2018)
10. Li, B.Y., Mian, A.S., Liu, W., Krishna, A.: Using Kinect for face recognition under varying poses, expressions, illumination and disguise. In: 2013 IEEE Workshop on Applications of Computer Vision, WACV, pp. 186–192. IEEE (2013)
11. Goswami, G., Bharadwaj, S., Vatsa, M., Singh, R.: On RGB-D face recognition using Kinect. In: 2013 IEEE Sixth International Conference on Biometrics: Theory, Applications and Systems, BTAS, pp. 1–6. IEEE (2013)
12. Ghiass, R.S., Arandjelović, O., Bendada, A., Maldague, X.: Infrared face recognition: a comprehensive review of methodologies and databases. Pattern Recogn. **47**(9), 2807–2824 (2014)

Integrating Ant Colony Algorithm and Node Centrality to Improve Prediction of Information Diffusion in Social Networks

Kasra Majbouri Yazdi[1]([✉]), Adel Majbouri Yazdi[2], Saeid Khodayi[3], Jingyu Hou[4], Wanlei Zhou[5], and Saeed Saedy[6]

[1] School of Information Technology, Deakin University, Melbourne 3125, Australia
kmajbour@deakin.edu.au
[2] Department of Computing, Kharazmi University, Tehran, Iran
majbourii.adel@gmail.com
[3] Faculty of Computer and Electrical Engineering, Qazvin Islamic Azad University, Qazvin, Iran
s.khodayi20@gmail.com
[4] School of Information Technology, Deakin University, Melbourne 3125, Australia
jingyu.hou@deakin.edu.au
[5] School of Software, The University of Sydney, Sydney 2006, Australia
wanlei.zhou@uts.edu.au
[6] Faculty of Engineering, Khavaran Higher Education Institute, Mashhad, Razavi Khorasan, Iran
s.saedy@hotmail.com

Abstract. One of the latest and most important research topics in the field of information diffusion, which has attracted many social network analyst experts in recent years, is how information is disseminated on social networks. In this paper, a new method is proposed by integration of ant colony algorithm and node centrality to increase the prediction accuracy of information diffusion paths on social networks. In the first stage of our approach, centrality of all nodes in the network is calculated. Then, based on the distances of nodes in the network and also ant colony algorithm, the optimal path of propagation is detected. After implementation of the proposed method, 4 real social network data sets were used to evaluate its performance. The evaluation results of all methods showed a better outcome for our method.

Keywords: Information diffusion prediction
Information diffusion patterns · Ant colony algorithm
Node centrality · Community detection

1 Introduction

One of the latest and most important research topics in the field of information diffusion, which has attracted many social network analyst experts in recent

© Springer Nature Switzerland AG 2018
G. Wang et al. (Eds.): SpaCCS 2018, LNCS 11342, pp. 381–391, 2018.
https://doi.org/10.1007/978-3-030-05345-1_33

years, is how information is disseminated on social networks. Indeed, the focus of this topic is on finding an efficient method to predict and model information dissemination in the network. This issue has many applications in different fields, such as e-shopping, distributing viruses and computer contaminants, posting blogs in social networks and so on [1]. To find the diffusion pattern, nodes that have been affected by a news story in the past, are considered and based on a series of parameters, nodes that will be influenced in future will be predicted as a function of time. One of the parameters used in this model is the popularity of the news, which the affection to other nodes in the future is based on that. Various approaches have been proposed so far to solve the problem of information diffusion. One of the problems with previous solutions is that they have high computational and complexity in high-dimensional networks. This paper presents a new approach using combination of the ant colony algorithm and node centrality criterion to predict optimal information diffusion paths in the network. In our proposed method, at the initial stage, the node centrality is calculated for all nodes in the network. Then, based on the distances of nodes, the optimal path of propagation is determined by using ant colony algorithm and then based on that, the information diffusion is predicted. In the remainder of this paper, Sect. 2 reviews the previous work, Sect. 3 states the details of the proposed method, Sect. 4 evaluates the proposed method and compares it with previous works, and finally, this paper is concluded in Sect. 5.

2   Related Work

Social networks improve the accuracy of the traditional advisory system by using social trusts and interests which exists among users. Popular social networks rank users and items based on the extent of information diffusion that created by users. So one of the important issues and challenges in social networks is predicting information diffusion routes [2]. The more accurate prediction, can provide users more optimal results. For example, in [3], for each pair of friends (u, v), the similarity of their rank is measured using a set of conditional probabilities $P(u|v)$ and $P(v|u)$, and the distribution of a user's rating is obtained from another user. $P(u|v)$ is calculated by commonly ranked items between user u and v. Then, the value of the user v ranking is obtained and then, the distribution of user u ranking is calculated from shared ranked items. When a user wants to perform a rating action for a particular user, first creates a diffusion tree based on other users, and then sends a rating query to its direct friends on the social network. As soon as a query is received for a rating of a user, the user who received the query returns the rating (if it has already been ranked), otherwise sends the query to its friends.

The centrality of a node represents the importance and influence of that node in the network. The nodes in the center of the network are scientifically more influential [4]. More centrality means more communication and a better position for the node, which ultimately makes it more powerful. In order to evaluate the centrality of the nodes, degree, proximity, betweenness, and special vector are the most common criteria to rank nodes in social network [4,5].

The centrality rating criterion [6] is one of the indicators which is useful in analysing the structure of networks and people positions on the network. It emphasizes that those who have more connections are likely to be stronger and more influential because they can directly affect others in the network [7]. The proximity centrality criterion is evaluated by the calculating proximity of one node to others. People who are able to reach other members with shorter track lengths, are in a privileged position and generally have more power and influence in the network [6]. The betweenness centrality criterion [8] is an indicator that offers a more precise pathway to measure the node centrality. This criterion shows that to what extent a particular node is among other people on the network.

3   Proposed Method

In this paper, a new method is proposed by integrating ant colony algorithm and node centrality criterion to increase the accuracy of information diffusion routes prediction in social networks. Figure 1 illustrates our proposed method for predicting information diffusion in social networks. The details of this algorithm is described in the following sections.

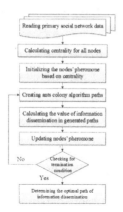

Fig. 1. The proposed method flowchart

3.1   Calculation of the Node Centrality

After reading the network data and forming the neighbouring matrix, the second step of the proposed method is to calculate the centrality for all nodes as shown in Fig. 1. Laplaceyn's centrality, is a criterion that calculates the centrality on weighted networks [5]. It uses local structure of nodes and also global structure of networks to calculate centrality.

If $G(V, E, W)$ is a weighted graph with a set of vertices $V(G) = \{v_1, v_2, .., v_n\}$, and a set of edges E connecting $e(v_i, v_j)$ by the weight of w_{ij}, then two matrices of W and X are calculated as Eqs. (1) and (2).

$$W(G) = \begin{bmatrix} 0 & w_{1,2} & .. & w_{1,n} \\ w_{2,1} & 0 & .. & w_{2,n} \\ .. & .. & .. & .. \\ w_{n,1} & w_{n,2} & .. & 0 \end{bmatrix} \tag{1}$$

$$X(G) = \begin{bmatrix} X_1 & 0, & .. & 0 \\ 0 & X_2 & .. & 0 \\ .. & .. & .. & .. \\ 0 & 0 & .. & X_n \end{bmatrix} \tag{2}$$

Here $X_i = \sum_{j=1}^{n} W_{i,j} = \sum_{u \in N(v_i)} W_{v_i, u}$ indicates the total weight of the node v_i, and $N(v_i)$ represents the set of neighbours of the node v_i. If there are no edges between v_i and v_j, then $W_{i,j} = 0$. Laplacian energy is also calculated for the graph G by Eq. (3).

$$E_L(G) = \sum_{i=1}^{n} X_i + 2 \sum_{i<j} w_{i,j}^2 \tag{3}$$

Also, Laplacein centrality criterion for node v_i is calculates in Eq. (4).

$$C_L(v_i, G) = \frac{(\Delta E)_i}{E_L(G)} = \frac{E_L(G) - E_L(G_i)}{E_L(G)} \tag{4}$$

G_i represents G graph after deleting node v_i.

3.2   Initializing the Pheromone of Nodes Based on the Centrality Criterion

In this paper we use a graph to represent the problem. In this graph, nodes represent the problem states, and the edges presents the transition between states. The information collected by the ants during the search process is pheromone on the edges (for example, $\tau(i, j)$ represents pheromone between node i and j). Also on each edge, an exploratory value is presented as representational of initial information in the problem (for example, $\eta(i, j)$ represents the value of the edge between the two node(i and j). In our method, the value of the initial pheromone on each edge is set equal to the sum of centrality of the two nodes of that edge.

$$\eta(i, j) = Centrality(i) + Centrality(j) \tag{5}$$

3.3   Creating Ant Colony Algorithm Paths

In this step, we try to identify the optimal routes of information dissemination according to the ant colony algorithm. For this purpose, each node in the social network is considered as a node in the ant colony algorithm. In general, the colony optimization algorithm acts as follows. First, some ants are randomly assigned to the nodes of the graph. Each ant produces a possible solution to the problem by applying a continuous state transfer rule (Eqs. 6 and 7). Ants prefer to move into nodes that are connected by shorter edges with high pheromones. When the motion of all ants is terminated and their solution achieved, a general pheromone update rule is used. In this rule, some of pheromones evaporate on all edges, and then each ant puts a pheromone on the edges for its own solution. Indeed, the edges that belong to a better solution will receive more pheromones. This process continues until a predetermined stop condition is met. The rule of transfer mode is determined by ant colony optimization algorithm, which combines exploratory information and pheromone values. When an ant is in node r, the node s is selected by applying the rule shown in Eq. (6).

$$s = max_{u \in J_k^r} \left[\tau(r, u)^\alpha . \eta(r, u)^\beta \right], \text{if q } \leq q_0 \tag{6}$$

Where J_k^r is the collection of unrecognized nodes by ant k in the node r. Also, α and β are parameters to show the importance of pheromone and exploratory information. When $\beta = 0$, no heuristic information on nodes is used, and when $\alpha = 0$, pheromones on the edges are not used. Also q represents a random number in range of zero to one, and q_0 is a parameter in $0 \leq q_0 \leq 1$. In fact, $q0$ determines how much the next node will be chosen based on the best choice. In probability mode ($q > q_0$), the next node s is chosen based on the probability $P_k(r, s)$ using Eq. (7).

$$P_k(r, s) = \begin{cases} \frac{\tau(r,s)^\alpha . \eta(r,s)^\beta}{\sum_{u \in J_r^k} \tau(r,u)^\alpha . \eta(r,u)^\beta} & , \text{if } s \in J_r^k \\ 0, otherwise \end{cases} \tag{7}$$

Equation (8) shows the pheromone update rule:

$$\tau(r, s) = (1 - \rho) . \tau(r, s) + \sum_{s \in S_{upd}} g(s) \tag{8}$$

Where $\rho \in (0, 1)$ is the pheromone evaporation parameter and $g(s)$ is a function for determining the quality of the solution which is called evaluation function. $g(i)$ is calculated by dividing the pheromone value of the node i, on sum of all nodes pheromones (S_{upd} is the sum of all nodes in the network).

The first step of the ant colony optimization algorithm is to calculate the probability of selecting the next node to continue the path. The transfer rule (Eqs. 6 and 7) determines the next node. In this rule, both suitability and similarity of the node to the previously selected nodes are influenced by the ant. So, at each step, the nodes that are more suitable and have less redundancy with the nodes previously selected by the same ant, are more likely to be selected. Before starting the process of moving ants in the routing process we act in such a way that the nodes are grouped into a number of clusters based on a community detection algorithm. One of the most active and challenging research areas in social networks is the issue of community detection. The main purpose of recognizing communities is to put the nodes in the same cluster together. Therefore, nodes in a cluster share common characteristics and the connections between nodes within each cluster are denser than the nodes' connections with other clusters. In this paper, Louvain algorithm is used for clustering nodes which is one of the fastest and efficient algorithms for community detection [9]. After identifying the clusters, the routes are selected by ants. At this point, the proposed algorithm will be used to construct the path by ants so that each ant randomly selects a node to start motion. Through applying the transfer rule (Eqs. 6 and 7) on the nodes of that cluster, ant selects a node. The next node F_j can be selected in two ways of greedy or probabilistic algorithms by the ant k. In greedy method, the next node is obtained according to Eq. (9).

$$F_j = arg_{F_u \in UF_i^k} \max \left\{ [\tau_u]^\alpha [\eta(F_u, VF_k)]^\beta \right\}, \text{ if } q \le q_0 \qquad (9)$$

UF_i^k is the collection of nodes not selected by ant k in cluster i, τ_u represents the corresponding pheromone to the node F_u, VF_k represents collection of the nodes chosen up to this moment by ant k and $\eta(F_u, VF_k)$ is an exploratory function that shows the suitability of the node F_u. Also, α and β are two parameters for controlling the importance of the value of the pheromone and the exploratory function. When $\alpha = 0$, the value of the pheromone on nodes will have no effect on the choice of the next node, and the next node will only be selected based on the exploratory information. Also, when $\beta = 0$, the next node is selected only based on the amount of pheromone on the nodes. Also, q_0 is a predefined parameter, and q is a random number in the range of zero to one. In probability mode, the node F_j is selected with the probability $P_k(F_j, VF_k)$ obtained using Eq. (10).

$$P_k(F_j, VF_k) = \begin{cases} \frac{[\tau_j]^\alpha [\eta(F_j, VF_k)]^\beta}{\sum_{u \in UF_i^k} [\tau_u]^\alpha [\eta(F_u, VF_k)]^\beta}, \text{if } j \in UF_i^k \text{ , if } q > q_0 \\ 0, \text{ otherwise} \end{cases} \qquad (10)$$

The rule of transfer mode depends on two parameters of q and q_0. This rule creates a balance between the existing information and the new discovered solutions. If $q < q_0$ then, the ant chooses the next node in a greedy manner based on the information, otherwise, the next node is selected based on the probability calculated in Eq. (10). Indeed, the next node is selected based on the new discovered solutions. Furthermore, using the new discovered solutions prevent the algorithm to stuck in the local optimization.

3.4   Calculating the Value of Information Dissemination in Generated Paths

In our method, a specific exploratory function is proposed to calculate the usefulness of the next node. In this function, the suitability of the node and its redundancy with the previously selected nodes have been involved. Therefore, unrelated and redundant nodes will have less chance to be selected. The exploratory function is calculated as follows in Eq. (11).

$$\eta(F_i, VF_k) = \left[FS(F_i) - \frac{1}{|VF_k|} \sum_{F_x \in VF_k} sim(F_i, F_x) \right] \qquad (11)$$

$FS(F_i)$ represents the centrality of F_i node, $Sim(F_i, F_x)$ represents the similarity between the F_i and F_x nodes and $|VF_k|$ is the number of nodes selected by the ant k up to this moment. To calculate the similarity between two nodes, the cosine similarity criterion is used.

In the first part of the proposed exploratory function, the suitability of the node, and in the second part, the redundancy with previously selected nodes is considered. So, combination of these two parts will provide selection of the most relevant nodes to the target node with minimum redundancy.

3.5   The Rule of Updating Pheromone

At the end of each iteration of the ant colony algorithm, when all ants finish their paths, the amount of pheromone on each node is updated. The rule of updating pheromone, forms an important aspect of the ant colony optimization algorithm. In fact, according to this rule, there are nodes that have come up with better solutions with more pheromones being allocated. These nodes will have more chances to be selected in subsequent iterations. This rule is used to update the node's corresponding pheromone after each iteration of the algorithm. The pheromone updating rule is calculated as follows in Eq. (12).

$$\tau_i(t+1) = (1-\rho)\tau_i(t) + \sum_{k=1}^{A} \Delta_i^k(t) \tag{12}$$

$\tau_i(t)$ and $\tau_i(t+1)$ respectively indicate the value of the pheromone on the F_i node in the iteration of t and $t+1$, ρ is the pheromone evaporation parameter, A denotes the number of ants, and Δ_i^k shows the amount of pheromone deposited by the ant k on the F_i node. Δ_i^k is calculated as follows:

$$\Delta_i^k(t) \begin{cases} J(FS^k(t)) \text{ if } F_i \in FS^k(t) \\ 0, \text{ Otherwise} \end{cases} \tag{13}$$

$FS^k(t)$ denotes the set of nodes selected by ant k in the iteration of t, also, $J(FS^k(t))$ is the evaluation function for calculating the usefulness of the subset of the $FS^k(t)$ node, which is used to calculate the distance between the source and destination node. The shorter the distance, the more useful diffusion of information from that path. In fact, the usefulness of a route is considered as the reverse distance of the source to destination node of that route.

4   Performance Evaluation of the Proposed Method

In this section, the performance of our proposed method is evaluated in 2 parts. In the first part, the accuracy of the community detection algorithm used in our approach is considered and compared with Bayesian [10] and Genetic [11] community detection algorithms. Then in the second part, the performance of our method in predicting optimal information dissemination paths using; centrality and ant colony algorithm; is compared with other 2 approaches of predicting optimal diffusion paths which are based on Bayesian [12] and Genetic [13] algorithms.

Details of the 4 real data sets of karate clubs [14], dolphin [15], political books [16] and American Football College [17] networks are shown in Table 1.

Table 1. Details of the data sets

Network	Nodes	Edges	Network description
Karate	34	78	Zachary's karate club
Dolphin	62	159	Dolphin social network
Political books	105	441	Books on US politics
Football	115	613	American Football College

We believe detecting more accurate communities in the network can improve predicting optimal information diffusion paths. Therefore, the performance of the community detection algorithm used in our method is evaluated in the first step. For this purpose, we use Modularity [18] and Normalized Mutual Information (NMI) [19] metrics. Tables 2 and 3 show, the performance of community detection algorithm for all methods respectively based on Modularity and NMI.

According to the results obtained by all methods, the genetic algorithm has the lowest accuracy in comparison to others. This is because the genetic algorithm tries to model the network graph based on matrix which is less accurate for big networks. Bayesian applies mathematics approaches to optimize the community detection process which is also not appropriate for big networks. In the other hand, the Louvain algorithm improves the evaluation criterion of the community detection step by step and evolutionary which results detecting more accurate communities.

Table 2. The Modularity accuracy results obtained by each algorithm

Network	Bayesian [12]	Genetic algorithm [11]	Proposed method (Louvain [9])
Karate	0.64	0.61	0.75
Dolphin	0.76	0.73	0.81
Political books	0.84	0.78	0.88
Football	0.81	0.75	0.89

After evaluation of the community detection algorithms, the performance of our approach in detecting optimal information diffusion paths was evaluated along with other methods. The results show a better outcome for our work. This is because both penetration and centrality criteria of the nodes are considered to

Table 3. NMI criteria obtained by each algorithm for community detection accuracy

Network	Bayesian [12]	Genetic algorithm [11]	Proposed method (Louvain [9])
Karate	0.72	0.069	0.77
Dolphin	0.79	0.78	0.82
Political books	0.86	0.81	0.88
Football	0.85	0.82	0.91

identify the optimal paths of information diffusion based on ant colony algorithm. Also, in each iteration, before the stop condition is checked, all conditions of combining communities are investigated to detect the most optimal communities for the next step, then future iterations will be based on that. Therefore, in each iteration there will be the most optimal communities that will result finding the optimal paths for information diffusion.

To consider and compare the performance of the aforementioned methods, we used Mean Absolute Error (MAE) and Mean Absolute User Error (MAUE) criteria [20]. MAE calculate the difference between the predicted values and the actual values. Therefore, whatever the information diffusion errors of the case study are smaller, the estimated rates are closer to actual rates and the performance will increase. The $MAUE$ is the mean absolute user error which is calculated for each node.

According to the results, our method has less MAE and $MAUE$ in comparison to other methods which means it has less error in predicting the optimal information diffusion paths. Figure 2 shows the results of the proposed method for different data sets based on MAE and $MAUE$ criteria.

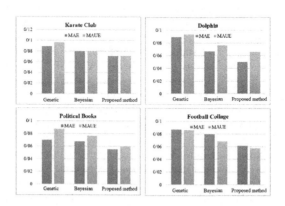

Fig. 2. Comparable evaluation results of all method based on MAE and $MAUE$ metrics

5   Conclusion

In this paper, we proposed a new method for prediction optimal information diffusion paths using integration of ant colony algorithm and node centrality criterion. At the first stage of our algorithm, the node centrality of all nodes in the network was calculated. Then, based on the distances of nodes and also according to ant colony algorithm, the optimal routes of information dissemination were predicted. After evaluation and comparison of all methods, the results showed that our method has a better outcome than others in terms of NMI and MAE metrics.

References

1. Yu, J., Gao, M., Rong, W., Li, W., Xiong, Q., Wen, J.: Hybrid attacks on model-based social recommender systems. Phys. A: Stat. Mech. Appl. **483**, 171–181 (2017)
2. Zhao, Y., Cai, S., Tang, M., Shang, M.: Coarse cluster enhancing collaborative recommendation for social network systems. Phys. A: Stat. Mech. Appl. **483**, 209–218 (2017)
3. Yang, X., Guo, Y., Liu, Y.: Bayesian-inference-based recommendation in online social networks. IEEE Trans. Parallel Distrib. Syst. **24**, 642–651 (2013)
4. Yan, X., Zhai, L., Fan, W.: C-index: a weighted network node centrality measure for collaboration competence. J. Inf. **7**, 223–239 (2013)
5. Qi, X., Fuller, E., Wu, Q., Wu, Y., Zhang, C.: Laplacian centrality: a new centrality measure for weighted networks. Inf. Sci. **194**, 240–253 (2012)
6. Jiang, Y., Jia, C., Yu, J.: An efficient community detection method based on rank centrality. Phys. A: Stat. Mech. Appl. **392**, 2182–2194 (2013)
7. Moradi, P., Rostami, M.: A graph theoretic approach for unsupervised feature selection. Eng. Appl. Artif. Intell. **44**, 33–45 (2015)
8. Li, Y., Jia, C., Yu, J.: A parameter-free community detection method based on centrality and dispersion of nodes in complex networks. Phys. A: Stat. Mech. Appl. **438**, 321–334 (2015)
9. Blondel, V., Guillaume, J., Lambiotte, R., Lefebvre, E.: Fast unfolding of communities in large networks. J. Stat. Mech: Theory Exp. **2008**, P10008 (2008)
10. Chen, Y., et al.: Overlapping community detection in weighted networks via a Bayesian approach. Phys. A: Stat. Mech. Appl. **468**, 790–801 (2017)
11. Guerrero, M., Montoya, F.G., Baños, R., Alcayde, A., Gil, C.: Adaptive community detection in complex networks using genetic algorithms. Neurocomputing **266**, 101–113 (2017)
12. Varshney, D., Kumar, S., Gupta, V.: Predicting information diffusion probabilities in social networks: a Bayesian networks based approach. Knowl.-Based Syst. **133**, 66–76 (2017)
13. Bai, C., Hong, M., Wang, D., Zhang, R., Qian, L.: Evolving an information diffusion model using a genetic algorithm for monthly river discharge time series interpolation and forecasting. J. Hydrometeorol. **15**, 2236–2249 (2014)
14. Zachary, W.W.: An information flow model for conflict and fission in small groups. J. Anthropol. Res. **33**, 452–473 (1977)

15. Lusseau, D., Schneider, K., Boisseau, O.J., Haase, P., Slooten, E., Dawson, S.M.: The bottlenose dolphin community of Doubtful Sound features a large proportion of long-lasting associations - Can geographic isolation explain this unique trait? Behav. Ecol. Sociobiol. **54**, 396–405 (2003)

16. Krebs, V.: Books about U.S.A. politics (2004). http://www.orgnet.com/divided2.html

17. Girvan, M., Newman, M.E.J.: Community structure in social and biological networks. Proc. Natl. Acad. Sci. **99**, 7821–7826 (2002)

18. Newman, M.E.J.: Modularity and community structure in networks. Proc. Natl. Acad. Sci. **103**, 8577–8582 (2006)

19. Danon, L., Díaz-Guilera, A., Duch, J., Arenas, A.: Comparing community structure identification. J. Stat. Mech: Theory Exp. **2005**, P09008 (2005)

20. Massa, P., Avesani, P.: Trust-aware recommender systems (2007)

An Efficient Provable Multi-copy Data Possession Scheme with Data Dynamics

Zuojie Deng[1], Shuhong Chen[2(✉)], Xiaolan Tan[1], Dan Song[1], and Fan Wu[1]

[1] School of Computer and Communication, Hunan Institute of Engineering,
Xiangtan 411104, China
[2] School of Computer Science and Technology, Guangzhou University,
Guangzhou 510006, China
shuhongchen@gzhu.edu.cn

Abstract. A user can use a provable multi-copy data possession schemes (PMDP) to ascertain whether its copies in cloud storage are kept securely. Unfortunately, all existing PMDP are not secure and efficient. To address this problem, we propose an efficient provable multi-copy data possession scheme with data dynamics (EPMDP). We design a kind of authenticated 2-3 tree with arrays in ordered leaves (A2-3AOL) and use the A2-3AOL and a kind of RSA tag to construct EPMDP. The analysis results of the security and performance show that EPMDP has strong security and good performance.

Keywords: Cloud storage · Data dynamics · Multi-copy
Provable data possession

1 Introduction

Some IT enterprises have deployed cloud storage. Outsourcing files to the cloud storage will bring some benefits [1]. However, after outsourcing a file to the cloud storage, the user cannot determine whether the file is securely stored in the cloud. In 2008 Amazon S3 experienced server outage and many S3 users were unable to access their own files stored in S3. The outage of Amazon S3 server has demonstrated that if S3 stores multiple copies of a file in its different servers, when some servers occur outage, the user can retrieve its file from the undowntime S3 servers. However, after outsourcing its copies to the cloud storage, the user cannot determine whether its copies are securely stored in the cloud storage, we refer to it as the provable multi-copy data possession problem.

To resolve the provable multi-copy data possession problem, Curtmola et al. proposed a multiple-replica provable data possession scheme (MR-PDP) [2]. Subsequently, Barsoum et al. proposed a probabilistic efficient multi-copy provable data possession scheme (PEMC-PDP) [3]. However, there are two shortcomings in both schemes. To overcome these shortcomings, in 2015 Barsoum et al. proposed a map based provable multiple-copy dynamic data possession scheme (MB-PMDDP) [4]. However, MB-PMDDP requires the user and the public data

© Springer Nature Switzerland AG 2018
G. Wang et al. (Eds.): SpaCCS 2018, LNCS 11342, pp. 392–402, 2018.
https://doi.org/10.1007/978-3-030-05345-1_34

auditor to store the states of the copies. If there exists an error of the states of the copies in the user local storage system due to disk corruption, etc., it will make the MB-PMDDP failure.

In this work, we have studied the provable multi-copy data possession problem and proposed an efficient provable multi-copy data possession scheme with data dynamics (EPMDP), which can overcome the shortcomings of MB-PMDDP.

The paper is organized as follows: In Sect. 2, we describe the problem and introduce the efficient provable multi-copy data possession scheme with data dynamics. The authenticated 2-3 tree with arrays in ordered leaves (A2-3AOL) is presented in Sect. 3. In Sect. 4, we construct EPMDP by using the A2-3AOL and a kind of RSA tag. In Sect. 5, we give some theorems about the security and the performance of the construction. In Sect. 6, we do some experiments for EPMDP and experiment results are presented here. Finally, conclusions are given in Sect. 7.

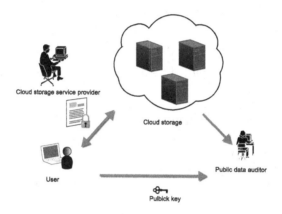

Fig. 1. A cloud storage system model.

2   The Problem and the EPMDP Scheme

2.1   The Problem

The cloud storage system model is described in Fig. 1, which is composed of three different entities. Each entity performs a different function. The user stores its files to the remote cloud storage server by a PC or a smartphone. After uploading its files to the cloud storage server, the user will delete its files from its local storage system. The cloud storage service provider owns the cloud storage server. It manages and maintains the files that the user stored in the cloud storage server. When the user initiates a challenge to the cloud storage server to check the integrity of a file that it stored in the cloud storage server, the server will give the user a proof that the file is kept intact. The user can give its own public key to a PDA and entrust the PDA to check the integrity of its files on its behalf.

There are three kinds of threats in the cloud storage system model. Firstly, the cloud storage service provider will delete some copy blocks or only keep a copy instead of preserving m copies of a file to save its storage space. Secondly, the cloud storage service provider tries to obtain some useful information from the files. Thirdly, The PDA will perform the audit protocol faithfully, but it will do everything possible to get some useful knowledge from the audit process, so we can regard the PDA as an honest and curious adversary. Therefore, there are three security requirements in EPMDP. We refer to them as security against the cloud storage service provider, privacy against the cloud storage service provider and privacy against the PDA.

2.2 The EPMDP Scheme

In order to resolve the above problem, we design an efficient provable multi-copy data possession scheme with data dynamics.

Definition 1. (EPMDP). An efficient provable multi-copy data possession scheme with data dynamics is a tuple of algorithms as follows:

- Setup(v) $\rightarrow$ $\{p_k, s_k, k, sgk, vk\}$: It is a probability algorithm which run by u. It takes the parameter v as input and outputs a block encryption key k, a key pair(p_k, s_k), a signature key sgk and a public key for signature vk. s_k represents the private key and p_k represents the public key. u stores k, s_k and sgk secretly and publishes vk and p_k publicly.
- Gencopy(F, m, k) $\rightarrow$ $\{F_i(i = 1, 2, \ldots, m)\}$: This algorithm is run by u, it takes F, m and k as input and outputs a copy set $F_i(i = 1, 2, \ldots, m)$. Without the block encryption private key k, no adversary can use F_j to generate F_k, where $j \neq k$.
- GenTag($F_i(i = 1, 2, \ldots, m), s_k, sgk$) $\rightarrow$ $\{\varphi_i(i = 1, 2, \ldots, m), sig_{sgk}(H(R))\}$. This algorithm is run by u, it takes the copies $F_i(i = 1, 2, \ldots, m)$, the s_k of u and the signed private key sgk of u as input and outputs $\varphi_i(i = 1, 2, \ldots, m)$ and $sig_{sgk}(H(R))$. $\varphi_i(i = 1, 2, \ldots, m)$ is the copy block tag set of $F_i(i = 1, 2, \ldots, m)$. $F_i = \{B_{i1}, B_{i2}, \ldots, B_{in}\}$, $sig_{sgk}(H(R))$ is the signature of the root R, where R is the root of the tree used to organize the copy block tag set $\varphi_i(i = 1, 2, \ldots, m)$.
- Challenge(p_k) $\rightarrow$ $\{chal\}$. This algorithm is run by u or PDA. It takes the user's public key p_k as input and outputs a challenge $chal$ for all the copies of F.
- GenProof($F_i(i = 1, 2, \ldots, m), chal, \varphi_i(i = 1, 2, \ldots, m)$) $\rightarrow$ $\{\gamma\}$. This algorithm is run by the server. It inputs the challenge $chal$, $F_i(i = 1, 2, \ldots, m)$ and the file block tag set φ and outputs γ, where γ is the integrity proof of the file block for all the copies of F described by $chal$.
- CheckProof($p_k, vk, chal, \gamma$) $\rightarrow$ $\{success, failure\}$: This algorithm is run by u or PDA. It inputs a public key p_k, the public key of the signature vk, the challenge $chal$, and the file block integrity proof γ that is returned by the

server. If γ passes the integrity check, it outputs *success*, otherwise it outputs *failure*.

- Update$(F_i, B_{ij}(i = 1, 2, \ldots, m), \varsigma, \varphi_i) \rightarrow \{F_i', \varphi_i', sign_{sgk}(H(R'))\}$: This algorithm is run by the cloud storage server. ς represents the type of dynamic operation. If ς equals to I, it represents the insertion operation; if ς is equal to M, it represents the modification operation; if ς is equal to D, it represents the delete operation. R' is the root of the new tree used to organize the copy block tag sets $\varphi_i'(i = 1, 2, \ldots, m)$. It inputs F_i, B_{ij}, T and φ_i and outputs F_i' and φ_i' and gets $sign_{sgk}(H(R'))$ signed by u.

3   An Authenticated 2-3 Tree with Arrays in Ordered Leaves

To improve the efficiency of EPMDP and to prevent the server from tampering the copy blocks of F in the cloud storage, we have design a kind of tree authentication structure, we refer to this tree structure as the authenticated 2-3 tree with arrays in ordered leaves.

Definition 2. An authenticated 2-3 tree with arrays in ordered leaves is a 2-3 tree with the difference that each leaf preserves the cryptographic hash value(e.g. SHA-1) of the array which is organized by the hash values of the blocks that have the same sequence number in all copies that are generated from the same file. All leaves are labeled with a sequence number from left to right, which corresponds to the block sequence number in the file. Its internal nodes keep the hash values of their children nodes. Each leaf node stores a pointer to the array of the block hash values in addition to a block number BN and the cryptographic hash value of the array.

An A2-3AOL has the following properties:

- All leaf nodes in the tree have a sequence number.
- Each internal node has 2 or 3 child nodes.
- The length of each path from the root to the leaves are equal and the root node of the tree authenticates the whole tree.

An example of an A2-3AOL tree is shown in Fig. 2 and the node structure of the A2-3AOL tree is shown in Fig. 3.

4   The Construction of EPMDP

We have defined EPMDP in Sect. 2.2. In this section we use the A2-3AOL and a kind of RSA tag to construct the EPMDP.

- Setup$(v) \rightarrow \{(g, N, e), d, k, \hat{x}, (\hat{p}, \hat{q}, \hat{g}, \hat{y})\}$: It takes the security parameter v as input and outputs a block encryption key k, a public key $p_k = (N, g, e)$, a private key $k_s = d$, a signature private key $sgk = \hat{x}$ and a signature verification public key $vk = (\hat{p}, \hat{q}, \hat{g}, \hat{y})$, where $ed = 1 \bmod (p-1)(q-1)$. N is

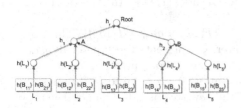

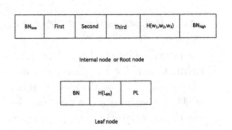

Fig. 2. A example of the A2-3AOL tree.

Fig. 3. The node structure of the A2-3AOL.

an RSA modulus, which is the product of two primes p and q. QR_N is the square residual multiplicative cyclic group of modulo N and g is a generator of QR_N. In order to make the scheme secure, it requires p and q to be two large prime numbers. According to the large prime number generation rule, we can make $p = 2p' + 1, q = 2q' + 1$, where p' and q' are also two large prime numbers. We use the DSS [10] to sign the root of the A2-3AOL in the EPMDP construction.

– GenCopy$(F, m, k) \rightarrow \{F_i(i = 1, 2, \ldots, m)\}$: It takes F, m and k as input and outputs $F_i(i = 1, 2, \ldots, m)$. The copy F_i is obtained by connecting the copy number i to each file block and using AES to encrypt it with k. $B_{ij}(1 \leq i \leq m, 1 \leq j \leq n)$ is generated according to (1). The user u stores k secretly for later to recover F. Since k is kept in secret, no one can recover F except the user. Since modern block cryptography has an avalanche feature [5], changing a bit of a plaintext will result in a tremendous change in its output of the ciphertext. Therefore F_i is completely different from F_j, where $i \neq j$.

$$B_{ij} = E_k(B_j \| i) \tag{1}$$

– GenTag$(F_i, d, \hat{x}, g) \rightarrow \{\{T_{i1}, T_{i2}, \ldots, T_{in}\}, Sig_{\hat{x}}(H(R))\}$: It takes $F_i, d, \hat{x}$ and g as input and outputs $\{T_{i1}, T_{i2}, \ldots, T_{in}\}$ and $Sig_{\hat{x}}(H(R))$, where $T_{ij}(1 \leq j \leq n)$ is the copy block tag which is generated according to (2) and $Sig_{\hat{x}}(H(R))$ is the root signature of the A2-3AOL used to organize all copies blocks of F. For the sake of simplicity, we use φ_i to denote $\{T_{i1}, T_{i2}, \ldots, T_{in}\}$. It sends φ_i and $Sig_{\hat{x}}(H(R))$ to the cloud storage server.

$$T_{ij} = (H(B_{ij})g^{B_{ij}})^d \bmod N \tag{2}$$

– Challenge$(g, N, e) \rightarrow \{k_1, k_2, g_s, c\}$: In order to check whether all copies of F is stored in the cloud storage server intactly, u or PDA initiates a challenge to the cloud storage server to check a subset blocks of all the copies of F randomly. The challenge consists of four parts: k_1, k_2, g_s and c. k_1, k_2 and s are randomly selected in each challenge. c is the number of copy blocks that need to be checked. k_1 is the key of the pseudorandom permutation Π_1 used to determine the copy block subscript that need be checked. k_2 is the key of the pseudorandom function Π_2 used to determine some pseudorandom coefficients. $g_s = g^s \bmod N$.

– GenProof($\{F_1, F_2, \ldots, F_m\}, (k_1, K_2, g_s, c), \{\varphi_1, \varphi_2, \ldots, \varphi_m\}$) $\rightarrow$ $\{P, T, \{H(L_j), L_j, w_j\}_{j \in J}, Sig_{\hat{x}}(H(R))\}$: When the server receives the challenge, it generates the copy block subscript j_t according to (3) and generates the pseudorandom number a_{it} according to (4). Finally, it generates the proof $\gamma = (P, T, \{H(L_j), L_j, w_j\}_{j \in J}, Sig_{\hat{x}}(H(R)))$ for the copy blocks that need to be checked. J is the set of the subscript of the blocks P is generated according to (5) and T is generated according to (6). $\{w_j\}_{j \in J}$ are all siblings of the A2-3AOL tree from the leaf $\{H(L_j), L_j\}_{j \in J}$ to the root R. L_{j_t} is an array of hash values of the copy blocks that need to be checked on the A2-3AOL tree. L_{j_t} and B_{ij_t} satisfy (7).

$$j_t = \Pi_{1,k_1}(t)(1 \le t \le c) \tag{3}$$

$$a_{it} = \Pi_{2,k_2}(i,t)(1 \le i \le m, 1 \le t \le c) \tag{4}$$

$$P = g_s^{(\sum_{i=1}^m a_{i1}B_{ij_1} + \sum_{i=1}^m a_{i2}B_{ij_2} + \cdots + \sum_{i=1}^m a_{ic}B_{ij_c})} \bmod N \tag{5}$$

$$T = \prod_{i=1}^m (T_{ij_1})^{a_{i1}} \times \prod_{i=1}^m (T_{ij_2})^{a_{i2}} \cdots \times \prod_{i=1}^m (T_{ij_c})^{a_{ic}} \bmod N \tag{6}$$

$$L_{j_t}(i) = H(B_{ij_t}) \tag{7}$$

– CheckProof($(g, N, e), (k_1, k_2, g_s, c), (P, T, \{H(L_j), L_j, w_j\}_{j \in J}, Sig_{\hat{x}}(H(R)), H(R)), s, vk$) $\rightarrow \{success, failure\}$: u or PDA uses vk to check $Sig_{\hat{x}}(H(R))$. If the check fails, it stops and outputs $failure$, otherwise it uses $\{H(L_j), L_j, w_j\}_{j \in J}$ to generate R' and checks $H(R)$ whether is equal to $H(R')$. If the check fails, it stops and outputs $failure$, otherwise it checks whether $(T^e)^s / (\prod_{i=1}^m \prod_{t=1}^c (H(B_{ij_t})^{a_{it}}))^s$ is equal to P, if it is equal then it outputs $success$, otherwise it outputs $failure$.

– Update($\{F_1, F_2, \ldots, F_m\}, \{B_{1j}, B_{2j}, \ldots, B_{mj}\}, \varsigma, \{\varphi_1, \varphi_2, \ldots, \varphi_m\}$) $\rightarrow \{\{F_1', F_2', \ldots, F_m'\}, \{\varphi_1', \varphi_2', \ldots, \varphi_m'\}, sign_{\hat{x}}(H(R'))\}$: ς represents the type of dynamic operation. If ς equals to I, it represents the insertion operation; if ς is equal to M, it represents the modification operation; if ς is equal to D, it represents the delete operation. R' is the root of the new A2-3AOL that organizes all the block hash values of the copies. It takes $\{F_1, F_2, \ldots, F_m\}, \{B_{1j}, B_{2j}, \ldots, B_{mj}\}, T$ and $\{\varphi_1, \varphi_2, \ldots, \varphi_m\}$ as input and outputs $\{F_1', F_2', \ldots, F_m'\}, \{\varphi_1', \varphi_2', \ldots, \varphi_m'\}$. it also outputs $Sig_{\hat{x}}(H(R'))$ which is gotten from the user.

5   The Security and Performance of EPMDP

Theorem 1. *Under KEA1-r assumption, integer factorization assumption and the signature is secure, the construction of EPMDP achieves security against the cloud storage service provider*

Theorem 2. *If AES is secure, the construction of EPMDP achieves privacy against the cloud storage service provider.*

Theorem 3. *If AES is secure, the construction of EPMDP achieves privacy against the PDA.*

Theorem 4. *Assume m be the copy number of F and n be the block number of F, checking all copies of F, the computational time complexity of the server is $O(\log n)$, the computational time complexity of the user or the PDA is $O(\log n)$, the network communication space complexity of the server is $O(\log n)$, the space complexity of the user or the PDA is $O(1)$ which is independent of the copy number m.*

6   Experiments

To evaluate the performance of EPMDP we have realized the construction of EPMDP using C and conduct performance comparison experiment between EPMDP, TB-PMDDP [4] and MB-PMDDP [4]. The experiment system is made up of two PCs, which simulate the client and the cloud storage server respectively. The configuration of the experiment system is shown in Table 1. We use OpenSSL (0.98g version) to implement the cipher operation of EPMDP and use the pairing-based cryptography (PBC) library to implement the cipher operation of MB-PMDDP and TB-PMDDP. All experiment data represents the mean of 10 executions. In our experiments, we choose linux-2.6.24.tar.bz2 as the experimental file. The size of the file block is 4 KB and all data represents the mean of 10 executions.

Table 1. The system configure of the experiment system.

	Hardware configure	OS configure
Client	CPU: Pentium E2160 1.8 GHz RAM: 4 GB Disk:WD 320 GB/7200rpm/4MB	Linux Fedora Kernel 2.6.23.1
Server	CPU: Xeon E3-1225 3.1 GHz RAM:4 GB Disk:WD 500 GB/7200 rpm/8 MB	Linux Fedora Kernel 2.6.23.1

We first evaluated the performance of EPMDP in the provable data possession checking. The number of the file blocks of each challenge in our experiments is set to 460. The experiment results are shown in Figs. 4 and 5. From these figures, we can see that the computation time of TB-PMDDP increases with the increasing of copy number in the server, while the computation time of EPMDP and MB-PMDDP are independent of the copy number in the server. This is because each challenge of TB-PMDDP can only check a copy of a file, while MB-PMDDP and EPMDP can check all copies of a file in each challenge. From these figures, we can find that the performance of TB-PMDDP is worst and the performances of EPMDP and MB-PMDDP outperform that of TB-PMDDP. Since MB-PMDDP uses PBC library to implement the cipher operation and EPMDP uses OpenSSL cryptography library to implement that, the time of EPMDP is about 11% less than that of MB-PMDDP. In the data dynamics experiments, the copy number of the experiments is 4. Since TB-PMDDP can operate a copy in one round, and MB-PMDDP and EPMDP can operate all copies of a file in one round, therefore, in the data dynamics experiment, TB-PMDDP must perform multiple round operations, in each round, it only operates a copy. The results of the data dynamics experiment are shown in Figs. 6, 7 and 8. Figure 6 shows that though the server block insertion time of all the schemes increases with the increasing block number, the time of the EPMDP and MB-PMDDP increases very slowly, while the time of TB-PMDDP increases very fast. From Figs. 7 and 8, we can see that the block deletion time and the block modification time also increases with the increasing block number.

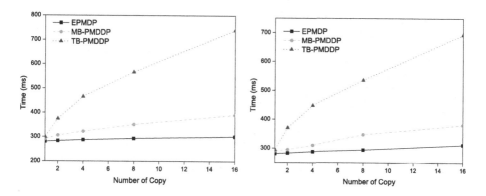

Fig. 4. Server computation time.   **Fig. 5.** Verifier computation time.

However, Figs. 6, 7 and 8 show that since EPMDP and MB-PMDDP operate all copies in one round which is unrelated to the number of copy and their performances are better than that of TB-PMDDP. MB-PMDDP requires the user or the public data auditor to store the states of all copies in their local storage system, but EPMDP only wants the user or the public data auditor to keep the public key of the signature of the A2-3AOL and the public key of the user.

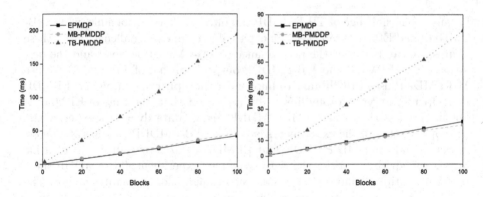

Fig. 6. Server insertion block time.   **Fig. 7.** Server deletion block time.

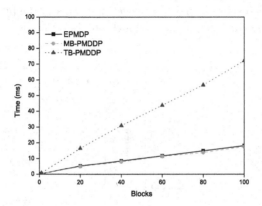

Fig. 8. Server modification block time.

7 Conclusions

Storing multiple copies of a file to the cloud storage system can improve the reliability of the file. But, to make sure that all the copies are intact, the user needs to audit the cloud storage system. To resolve this problem, we have designed an efficient provable multi-copy data possession scheme with data dynamics (EPMDP). We design an authenticated 2-3 tree with arrays in ordered leaves (A2-3AOL), and use the A2-3AOL and a kind of RSA tag to construct EPMDP. Checking all copies of F, the computational time complexity of the server is $O(\log n)$, the computational time complexity of the user or PDA is $O(\log n)$, the network communication space complexity is $O(\log n)$, the space complexity of the user or PDA is $O(1)$ which is independent of the copy number m. EPMDP can audit the copies in cloud storage system securely and efficiently.

Acknowledgement. The research was partially funded by the Doctoral Program of Hunan Institute of Engineering (Grant No. 17RC028), the Scientific Research Fund of Hunan Provincial education Department (Grant No. 16A049), the Natural Science Foundation of Hunan Province (Grant No. 2016JJ3051, 2016JJ6031) and the National Natural Science Foundation of China (Grant No. 61502163).

References

1. Armbrust, M., Fox, A., Griffith, R., Joseph, A.D., et al.: Above the clouds: a berkeley view of cloud computing. Technical report UCB/EECS-2009-28, EECS Department, University of California, Berkeley (2009)
2. Curtmola, R., Khan, O., Burns, R., Ateniese, G.: MR-PDP: Multiple-replica provable data possession. In: Proceedings of the 28th International Conference on Distributed Computing Systems. ICDCS 2008, pp. 411–420. IEEE Press, New York (2008)
3. Barsoum, A.F., Hasan, M.A.: Provable possession and replication of data over cloud servers. Report, vol. 32, Centre For Applied Cryptographic Research (CACR), University of Waterloo (2012)
4. Barsoum, A.F., Hasan, M.A.: Provable multicopy dynamic data possession in cloud computing systems. IEEE Trans. Inf. Forensics Secur. **10**(3), 485–497 (2017)
5. Agrawal, H., Sharma, M.: Implementation and analysis of various symmetric cryptosystems. Indian J. Sci. Technol. **3**(12), 1173–1176 (2010)
6. Ateniese, G., et al.: Provable data possession at untrusted stores. In: Proceedings of the 14th ACM Conference on Computer and Communications Security. CCS 2007, pp. 598–609. ACM Press, New York (2007)
7. Ateniese, G., et al.: Remote data checking using provable data possession. ACM Trans. Inf. Syst. Secur. (TISSEC) **14**(1), 1–34 (2011)
8. Bowers, K.D., Juels, A., Oprea, A.: Proofs of retrievability: theory and implementation. In: Proceedings of the 2009 ACM Workshop on Cloud Computing Security. CCSW 2009, pp. 43–54. ACM, New York (2009)
9. Erway, C., Kupcu, A., Papamanthou, C., Tamassia, R.: Dynamic provable data possession. In: Proceedings of the 16th ACM Conference on Computer and Communications Security. CCS 2009, pp. 213–222. ACM Press, New York (2009)
10. Gallagher, P., Kerry, C.: FIPS pub 186-4: digital signature standard (DSS), National Institute of Standards and Technology (NIST) (2013)
11. Goldreich, O.: Foundations of Cryptography: Basic Applications. Cambridge University Press, Cambridge (2004)
12. He, D., Kumar, N., Zeadally, S., et al.: Certificateless provable data possession scheme for cloud-based smart grid data management systems. IEEE Trans. Ind. Inf. **14**(3), 1232–1241 (2018)
13. Juels, A., Kaliski, B.: PORs: proofs of retrievability for large files. In: Proceedings of the 14th ACM Conference on Computer and Communications Security. CCS 2007, pp. 584–597. ACM Press, New York (2007)
14. Manasa, A., Saritha, S.J.: An evidence multi-copy dynamic data possession in multi cloud computing system. In: International Conference on Communication and Electronics Systems, pp. 1–4. IEEE Press, New York (2017)
15. Needham, R.M.: Denial of service. In: Proceedings of the 1st ACM Conference on Computer and Communications Security. CCS 1993, pp. 151–153. ACM Press (1993)

16. Shacham, H., Waters, B.: Compact proofs of retrievability. J. Cryptol. **26**(3), 442–483 (2013)
17. Shen, S.-T., Tzeng, W.-G.: Delegable provable data possession for remote data in the clouds. In: Qing, S., Susilo, W., Wang, G., Liu, D. (eds.) ICICS 2011. LNCS, vol. 7043, pp. 93–111. Springer, Heidelberg (2011). https://doi.org/10.1007/978-3-642-25243-3_8
18. Wang, C., Chow, S.M., Wang, Q., Ren, K., Lou, W.J.: Privacy-preserving public auditing for secure cloud storage. IEEE Trans. Comput. **62**(2), 362–375 (2013)
19. Wang, C., Wang, Q., Ren, K., Lou, W.J.: Privacy-preserving public auditing for data storage security in cloud computing. In: Proceedings of the 29th Conference on Information Communications. INFOCOM 2010, pp. 525–533. IEEE Press, Piscataway (2010)
20. Wang, F., Xu, L., Wang, H., et al.: Identity-based non-repudiable dynamic provable data possession in cloud storage. Comput. Electr. Eng. **69**, 521–533 (2018)
21. Wang, H., Zhang, Y.: On the knowledge soundness of a cooperative provable data possession scheme in multicloud storage. IEEE Trans. Parallel Distrib. Syst. **25**(1), 264–267 (2014)
22. Wang, Q., Wang, C., Li, J., Ren, K., Lou, W.: Enabling public verifiability and data dynamics for storage security in cloud computing. In: Backes, M., Ning, P. (eds.) ESORICS 2009. LNCS, vol. 5789, pp. 355–370. Springer, Heidelberg (2009). https://doi.org/10.1007/978-3-642-04444-1_22
23. Wang, Q., Wang, C., Ren, K., Lou, W.J., Li, J.: Enabling public auditability and data dynamics for storage security in cloud computing. IEEE Trans. Parallel Distrib. Syst. **22**(5), 847–859 (2011)

The 7th International Symposium on Security and Privacy on Internet of Things (SPIoT 2018)

SPIoT 2018 Organizing and Program Committees

Steering Chairs

Guojun Wang   Guangzhou University, China
Gregorio Martinez   University of Murcia, Spain

Program Chairs

Marios Anagnostopoulos   Singapore University of Technology and Design, Singapore
Georgios Kambourakis   University of the Aegean, Greece
Constantinos Kolias   George Mason University, USA

Program Committee

Afrand Agah   West Chester University of Pennsylvania, USA
Mohamad Badra   Zayed University, UAE
Cataldo Basile   Politecnico di Torino, Italy
Vittoria Cozza   University of Padua, Italy
Dimitrios Damopoulos   Stevens Institute of Technology, USA
Fernando Pereniguez Garcia   University Centre of Defence, Spanish Air
Dan Garcia-Carrillo   University of Murcia, Spain
Dimitris Geneiatakis   Joint Research Centre, European Commission
Vinh Hoa La   Telecom SudParis, France
Hsiang-Cheh Huang   National University of Kaohsiung, Taiwan
Youssef Iraqi   Khalifa University of Science, Technology, and Research

Roger Piqueras Jover   Bloomberg Lp - Security Research Lab
Georgios Karopoulos   University of Athens, Greece
Riccardo Lazzeretti   Sapienza University of Rome, Italy
Wissam Mallouli   Montimage, France
Daisuke Mashima   Advanced Digital Sciences Center, Singapore
Sofia Anna Menesidou   Democritus University of Thrace, Greece
Weizhi Meng   Technical University of Denmark, Denmark
Edmundo Monteiro   University of Coimbra, Portugal
Juan Pedro Munoz-Gea   Universidad Politecnica de Cartagena, Spain
Renita Murimi   Oklahoma Baptist University, USA
Christoforos Ntantogian   University of Piraeus, Greece
Zeeshan Pervez   University of the West of Scotland, UK
Rodrigo Roman   University of Malaga, Spain

Corinna Schmitt	University of Zurich, Switzerland
Asaf Shabtai	Ben-Gurion University, Israel
Angelo Spognardi	Sapienza Univ. of Rome, Italy
Corrado Aaron Visaggio	University of Sannio, Italy
Lanier A. Watkins	The Johns Hopkins University, USA
Peng Zhou	Shanghai University, China

Steering Committee

Mauro Conti	University of Padua, Italy
Hua Wang	Victoria University, Australia
Vasilis Katos	Bournemouth University, UK
Jaime Lloret Mauri	Polytechnic University of Valencia, Spain
Yongdong Wu	Institute for Infocomm Research, Singapore
Zhoujun Li	Beihang University, China

An Enhanced Key Management Scheme for LoRaWAN

Jialuo Han$^{(\boxtimes)}$ and Jidong Wang$^{(\boxtimes)}$

School of Engineering, RMIT University, Melbourne 3000, Australia
jialuo.han@student.rmit.edu.au,
jidong.wang@rmit.edu.au

Abstract. LoRaWAN appears as one of the new Low Power Wide Area Network (LPWAN) standards in recent IoT market. The outstanding features of LPWAN are the low power consumption and long-range coverage. The LoRaWAN 1.1 specification has a basic security scheme defined. However, the scheme can be further improved in the aspect of the key management. In this paper, the overall LoRaWAN 1.1 security is reviewed and an enhanced LoRaWAN security with a root key update scheme is proposed. The root key update will make the cryptanalysis on security keys in LoRaWAN more difficult. The analysis and simulation have shown that the proposed root key update scheme has the lowest requirement on computing resources compared with other key derivation schemes including the one used in LoRaWAN session key update. The results have also shown the key generated in the proposed scheme has high randomness which is a basic requirement for a security key.

Keywords: LoRaWAN · IoT security · Key derivation · Stream cipher
Randomness

1 Introduction

In recent years, the Internet of Things (IoT) technology has been emerging as a trend in wireless communication applications. The IoT could enable billions of physical entities and sensors deployed in the context of smart homes, smart cities, and smart industries. These entities are connected to the Internet for monitoring and control type of applications [1]. The current wireless communication protocols, such as Bluetooth, WIFI, and 3G/4G, support high data rate but cannot meet both the requirement of low power consumption and wide area coverage. Low-Power Wide-Area Network (LoRaWAN) is one of Low Power Wide Area Network (LPWAN) protocols, which eliminates the complexity of deployment, while supports both the features of power efficiency and long-range transmission. The LoRaWAN 1.1, a MAC layer protocol, is implemented as a star of star topology to regulate the LoRa devices. A LoRaWAN is made of End-Devices (ED), Radio Gateways (GW), Network Servers (NS) and Application Servers. The ED is responsible for transmitting the collected data from the sensor; GW is a middle bridge forwards packets between ED and NS. NS is the center of the star topology, linking with all the nodes based on Lora MAC. An AS handles the application layer payloads with data encryption/decryption applied [2]. There are two ways

© Springer Nature Switzerland AG 2018
G. Wang et al. (Eds.): SpaCCS 2018, LNCS 11342, pp. 407–416, 2018.
https://doi.org/10.1007/978-3-030-05345-1_35

to enable ED to join LoRaWAN network. They are Over the Air (OTA) procedure and Activation by Personalization (ABP) procedure. OTA performs exchange of two MAC messages between ED and NS (Join-Request and Join-Accept) for the activation. A group of session parameters will be generated and exchanged in LoRa devices for securing the session.

Original LoRaWAN Specification 1.0 has a basic security mechanism. LoRaWAN Specification 1.1 [3], released at the end of 2017, has a big improvement on the aspects of key management and data confidentiality. Two 128-bit pre-shared root keys (NwkKey, AppKey) are stored in both ED and Join Server (JS). They are used to derive network and application session keys respectively, which are used to ensure the payload integrity in MAC layer and the confidentiality in the application layer. The network session keys include Forwarding Network session integrity key (FNwkSIntKey), Serving Network session integrity key (SNwkSIntKey), and Network session encryption key (NwkSEncKey). The first two are used for calculating Message Integrity Code (MIC) of up/downlink messages by using AES-CMAC. NwkSEncKey is responsible for the encryption/decryption of MAC commands. The application session key, AppSKey is used to encrypt application payload with AES in counter mode. Thus, the network session key and the application session key are only known and handled in NS and AS respectively to prevent malicious access to the application payload in the transmission. However, the LoRaWAN 1.1 still has some weakness in root key management. The symmetric encryption implementation means that root keys should be stored at two places, i.e. in ED and JS. The EDs are most vulnerable to various attacks, such as the side channel analysis as they are remotely allocated in most applications. The hackers can detect the fluctuation of power consumption from the LoRa transceiver during AES encryption, and that can help to derive the key used [4]. Once the root keys were stolen by the adversary, the ED will be compromised for its lifetime as the root keys are fixed. To overcome the problem, a root key update procedure can be adopted to enhance the security of root key handling.

The rest of the paper is organized as follows. Firstly, the review of LoRaWAN 1.1 security scheme is presented focusing more on key management. The discussion followed has revealed the flaws in that scheme. Then, a new key management solution is proposed. Analysis and discussion of the new scheme are presented with some comparison with the existing scheme. The conclusion has summarized the improvements of the new scheme.

2 LoRaWAN Security Review

LoRaWAN 1.1 security scheme provides the packet confidentiality by symmetric encryption between ED and NS, and also ED and AS. Root keys are stored in the entities that are responsible for the derivation of session keys [4]. In LoRaWAN 1.1, two AES-128 pre-shared keys which are stored in non-volatile memory of ED and JS before activation are NwkKey and AppKey. Compared with the LoRaWAN 1.0, NwkKey eliminates the risk of payload unauthorized accessing and stealing before application server because NS could be a third-party device that is neither necessary to know AppSKey, nor desirable [4, 5]. Meanwhile, the detailed network session keys are introduced in the latest LoRaWAN, which are responsible for message integrity check and MAC payload encryption respectively. In the rest of this section, these LoRaWAN 1.1 features are briefly introduced, i.e. key generation in join-procedure, the key distribution, and payload encryption methods.

2.1   Key Derivation and Distribution

The derivation of session keys is closely related to the join procedure which is carried out by the entities of ED, NS, and JS. The unencrypted Join-Request message is signed with NwkKey, which will be initialized from ED that forwards to NS and handled by JS. The packet structure of Join-Request contains 8-byte JoinEUI and DevEUI, and 2-byte DevNonce. JoinEUI is a global application ID and DevEUI is a global end device ID. The DevNonce has been changed to a counter value instead of a pseudo-random value, and it cannot be reused with the same JoinEUI to prevent the replay attack [6, 7]. The NS will reply a Join-Accept message to ED once the Join-Request is accepted. In the Join-Accept message, the JoinNonce value is a crucial parameter which is involved in key derivation, the Join-Accept is encrypted by the AES in ECB mode using NwkKey. The MIC is produced for the whole encrypted content using NwkKey. JoinNonce is also modified to a counter value to prevent the replay attack. In the join procedure, the symmetric keys are not transmitted over the air, but the Join Nonce is used to generate session keys on both sides.

In the latest LoRaWAN, three network session keys are defined, and they are FNwkSIntKey, SNwkSIntKey, and NwkSEncKey. These session keys are responsible for the up/downlink data message integrity check and encryption of MAC payload separately. Application session key the application payload encryption between ED and AS. The session key derivation has adopted AES-128 in ECB mode and requires the parameters included in the Join-Accept message with root keys NwkKey and AppKey which are stored in an ED and the JS through their life time. The three parameters used for session key derivation are JoinEUI, DevNonce, and JoinNonce. Both nonce values are counter values generated in each join procedure, which are unencrypted. Totally four session keys are defined. The derivation and the use of each session key is explained in the following:

1. Forwarding Network session integrity key (FNwkSIntKey): It is one of the three network session keys of 128-bit length. It is used to calculate partial MIC (The second two bytes) of uplink data messages. NS would verify the MIC when it receives the message from ED. The key derivation can be represented as follows:

$$FNwkSIntKey = aes128\_encrypt(NwkKey, 0x01|JoinNonce|JoinEUI|DevNonce|pad_{16})$$
$$(1)$$

2. Serving Network session integrity key (SNwkSIntKey): It is also a 128-bit long network session key which is used to calculate the first two bytes of the MIC of the uplink data messages. It is also used to calculates the totally 32-bit MIC of downlink data message. The MIC of downlink data message would be verified in ED to secure the message integrity. Its key derivation can be represented as follows:

$$SNwkSIntKey = aes128\_encrypt(NwkKey, 0x03|JoinNonce|JoinEUI|DevNonce|pad_{16}) \tag{2}$$

3. Network session encryption key (NwkSEncKey): It is the third network session key which is for encryption/decryption of MAC commands of uplink and down link. ED and NS are the only LoRa devices hold the knowledge of it. Its derivation is as follows:

$$NwkSEncKey = aes128\_encrypt(NwkKey, 0x04|JoinNonce|JoinEUI|DevNonce|pad_{16}) \tag{3}$$

4. Application session key (AppSKey): It is a 128-bit application session key as defined in LoRaWAN 1.0, i.e. it is used for the application payloads encryption/decryption between ED and AS. It derives as follows:

$$AppSKey = aes128\_encrypt(AppKey, 0x02|JoinNonce|JoinEUI|DevNonce|pad_{16}) \tag{4}$$

2.2   Data Confidentiality

LoRa devices are generally deployed in remote locations. Data confidentiality is often an important consideration as the radio transmission can be intercepted. With the new keys defined in LoRaWAN 1.1, the data encryption and authentication have been enhanced. The following section describes the operations of the data encryption and message authentication in the new release.

The MAC frame payload is encrypted using AES-128 in Counter mode (CTR), and the MIC is calculated after the encryption. The keystream () generation and payload encryption/decryption are described as follows:

$$
\begin{aligned}
&i = 1..k \, where \\
&k = ceil(len(FRMPayload)/16) \\
&Ai = (0x01|0x00 * 4|Dir|DevAddr|FCntUp \, or \, NFCntDown \, or \\
&AFCntDown|0x00|i)
\end{aligned} \tag{5}
$$

$$
\begin{aligned}
&Si = aes128\_encry(K, Ai), K \in \{AppSKey, NwkSEncKey\} \\
&S = S1|S2..|Sk \\
&[FRMPayload] = (S1|S2..|Sk) \oplus (FRMPayload|pad_{16})
\end{aligned}
$$

'Dir' indicates to the direction of uplink/downlink message (uplink = 0x00, downlink = 0x01). 'Cnt' is a 32-bit counter that can be either uplink or downlink counter in the calculation. The downlink counter in v1.0 has been replaced with two counters in LoRaWAN 1.1. They are NFCntDown and AFCntDown for differentiating the counter applied in NS (Port 0) and AS (Port 1-233). Both counters will be initialized to 0 at session start and increment in each transmission in the synchronized manner. 'DevAddr' is a static value presented as device address obtained from the NS and delivered in the Join-Accept message. The encryption/decryption method is AES in counter mode and the ciphertext is formed as the result of XOR operation on the keystream [8] and the padded payload.

To provide the integrity of the ciphertext, 4-byte MIC is used as the authentication tag between ED and Servers, which is computed with AES-CMAC. In LoRaWAN 1.1, SNwkSIntKey and FNwkSIntKey have been introduced to calculate the MIC of uplink/downlink data separately, and that is different from LoRaWAN 1.0 in which only one session key is for both uplink and downlink MIC. MIC calculation contains one network session key that indicates different types of message, an encrypted payload, and a 16-prefix block represented as B_0 and B_1. After the calculation, the result will be truncated to a 4-byte MIC and appended to the corresponding message, then it will be checked once arrived at NS/ED. If the check fails, the message will be discarded. This is an efficient method to detect the bit-flipping attack and the replay attack. The MIC for data message is computed with msg = $MHDR|FHDR|FPort|$ $FRMPayload$ as follows:

2.3 Security Key Management

The LoRaWAN 1.1 key derivation, distribution and data confidentiality have been presented. The security scheme is on confidentiality and integrity of messages in the IoT scenario. In this section, the discussion is on the possible attack on the network with OTA activation. The security assets to be protected are most important parameters in LoRaWAN network, and they are the core of the security of network.

In the OTA procedure, all the session keys are generated from two static root keys, NwkKey and AppKey, that are pre-shared between ED and JS. Some of the contents are not protected in the transmission. For example, the Join-Request message is not encrypted. Its contents including JoinEUI and DevNonce can be sniffed by the adversary. But JoinNonce is a confidential parameter transmitted with the Join-Accept message. These are common values applied to derive session keys with one of the root keys. As described that the session keys and root keys are the most important assets, the LoRaWAN network will be compromised once the knowledge of these keys obtained by the adversary. Thus, according to William Stallings that frequent key exchanges are usually desirable to limit the amount of data compromised if an attacker learns the key, it is necessary to consider a mechanism that updating session contents and root keys over time. The update can lower the risk of node capture attacks and side-channel attacks, such as the EM emission, power consumption, because the LoRa device is generally remotely located [9–11]. A session key update scheme has been introduced in LoRaWAN 1.1, which is enabled and configured by the MAC commands, static root keys cannot be updated for a lifetime, which are used to derive all session keys. In this scenario, static root keys can cause a serious issue with the key leakage because the rest of the parameters of session key derivation can be easily obtained as described. The root key update scheme with the low power consumption should be introduced to enhance the LoRaWAN security based on various studies of the key management and NIST that has given the key must be updated periodically [12, 13].

3 Lightweight Root Key Update Scheme

Based on the analysis of current LoRaWAN key management, LoRa ED is the most vulnerable part of the LoRaWAN network because it is remotely located, and it stores all pre-shared root keys which are used for session keys derivation. The root key is static through its lifetime, and the adversary has sufficient time to obtain the knowledge of session key derivation. This risk can be reduced by periodically update root keys. The current session key derivation method, AES-ECB mode, is not suitable for the root key derivation because AES-ECB is vulnerable for pattern analysis with sufficient knowledge and has higher power consumption. Rabbit is a high efficiency synchronous stream cipher based on simple arithmetic and other basic operations. The output from its keystream generator is a 128-bit string in each round, and it has good randomness. In the following section, the process of a Rabbit-based two-step Key Derivation Function (KDF) is presented for the LoRaWAN root key update scheme.

3.1 Key Derivation Function

The two-step KDF involves two phases that are the extractor and the expander. Both phases are based on the Pseudo-random Number Generator (PNG) of Rabbit Stream Cipher to obtain keystreams. The randomness extractor is used to take a root key K_a and a series of shared contexts c, which are assumed as the non-uniformly random value. Session keys can be considered as a part of contexts because they will be immediately renewed once the root key updated. Both K_a and c are used to generate a pseudo-random value [14]. The key expander takes the output of the extractor and another root key as the input. The output of the expander, a sequence of 128 bits will be the new root key, and it is a pseudo-random number whose randomness is close to a uniform distribution as shown in later section. The operation block diagram and model of two-step KDF proposed in the LoRaWAN root key update scheme is:

$$KDF(k_a, k_b, c) = Expander\{Extractor(k_a, c), k_b\} \tag{6}$$

Randomness Extractor
As described above the Randomness Extractor is based on the PNG of Rabbit stream cipher. As shown in Table 1, it has two steps which are initialization process and keystream generation. In the first step, the keying material contains a root key and a series of contexts. The root key is divided into v-bit long blocks and the contexts are divided to w-bit bit long blocks (where $v + w = 128$) for the Rabbit Stream Cipher. If the length of the block is less than $v + w$ bits, it will be padded with '0's. In the second step, the number of iterations in the state function has an impact on the randomness of the stream generated. Its selection should balance the resulting randomness and computing requirement. The 128 bits pseudo-random keystream from the PNG will be XORed with the next block of the keying material and the result will be fed back to the next loop of the PNG. The pseudo-random keystream is '0's in the initial loop. When it reaches the last block of keying material, a 128-bit keystream k_{kdk} will be extracted and that will be the input of the Key Expander.

Table 1. Rabbit based KDF algorithm

$for\ i = 0 : L, do$ $if\ i == 0$ 　$k_a = B_i[0:v];$ 　$c = B_i[v:v+w] = 0x00;$ 　$[k_a, c] = keystream[v+w]$ 　　　$\oplus B_{i+1}$ $else\ if\ 0 < i < L$ 　$k_a = B_i[0:v];$ 　$c = B_i[v:v+w];$ 　$keystream[v+w];$ 　$keystream[v+w] \oplus B_{i+1}$ 　$i = i+1;$ $else\ i = L$ 　　$k_a = B_i[0:v];$ 　$c = B_i[v:v+w];$	$for\ i = 0 : L, do$ $if\ i == 0$ 　$k_{kdk} = B_i[0:v];$ 　$k_b = B_i[v:v+w];$ 　$keystream[v+w];$ 　$[k_{kdk}, k_b] = keystream[v+w]$ 　　　$i = i+1;$ 　$Output\ a\ 128\ bits\ strings\ as\ k_a{}'$ $else\ if\ i == 1$ 　　$k_{kdk} = B_i[0:v];$ 　$k_b = B_i[v:v+w];$ 　$keystream[v+w];$ 　$Output\ a\ 128\ bits\ strings\ as\ k_b{}'$ $else$ 　end

$Output\ a\ 128\ bits\ string, k_{kdk}[0:s];$

Where:

$[v+w] = 128\ bits$

$B_i: the\ i^{th}\ v+w\ bits\ block\ of\ keying\ material$

$k_{kdk}: Key\ derivation\ key$

$k_a, k_b: old\ root\ keys$

$k_a', k_b': new\ root\ keys$

　　　　$v, w, s: root\ key\ block\ size, contexts\ block\ size, k_{kdk}\ size$

$c: Contexts$

$$L = \frac{pl}{v+w} - 1 : the\ total\ number\ of\ blocks$$

Key Expander. In the second phase of the KDF, the Key Expander has also used PNG of Rabbit stream Cipher. The keying material in this step includes a 128-bit k_{kdk} and root key k_b Another root key is divided to blocks each with the length of v and the k_{kdk} is divided to blocks each with the length of w where $v + w = 128$ bits. The total length of keying material is 256-bit in this scenario and two loops of Rabbit Stream Cipher will be executed. Two 128-bit new root keys will be generated in the first and second loop respectively, each loop takes $B_i = v + w$ as the input. If the keying material length is greater than 256-bit, more loops can be carried out to generate more keys in the future if needed.

4 Analysis of Root Key Update Scheme

In this proposed scheme, the Rabbit Stream Cipher based KDF is the core of LoRaWAN root key update. Compared with the current KDFs, such as HKDF [15] and AES-CMAC based KDF [16, 17], it has lower computing-weight of the key derivation and does not have cryptographical weaknesses revealed with Rabbit stream cipher [18]. The two-step KDF [16] includes Randomness Extractor phase and Key Expansion phase. It is used to obtain the key derivation key from shared secrets and derives updated keys. Hence, Rabbit Stream Cipher is used in two-step KDF for the LoRaWAN root key update scheme. For the scheme evaluation, a PC with the following specification is used: Intel (R) Core (TM) i7-7700 K CPU 4.2 GHz 4.2 GHz, 8 GB RAM and running a 64-bit Windows 10. The performance of three key derivation methods, Rabbit-based KDF, HKDF (SHA1), and LoRaWAN 1.1 Session Key derivation (AES128-ECB) are analyzed in separate experiments.

The key derivation computing times are compared in Table 2 for the three methods. The computing time is for 10,000 repeats for each method. It is obtained by using a built-in Windows C++ function *QueryPerformanceCounter()*. As shown in the Table 2, it is obvious that the Rabbit-based KDF is the fastest one, and the AES-ECB mode used in LoRaWAN 1.1 session key derivation is the slowest method among the three. Furthermore, the LoRaWAN 1.1 session key derivation generates only one 128-bit key each time, and it takes the longest time in generating a 128-bit key.

Table 2. Performance of key derivation methods.

Algorithm	pl	kl	ul	t
Rabbit based KDF	80	16	32	0.0092
Hash based KDF	80	80	32	0.1215
AES-ECB mode	16	16	16	0.1313

*pl: size of keying material, kl: size of input key
*ul: size of updated key, t average execution time (ms)

Compared with the LoRaWAN 1.1 session key update period, the root key update period should be longer to make the root update meaningful. The session key update period should depend on the amount of message transferred. If enough messages have been transferred in one session, a new session key is necessary to count attack cryptoanalysis. LoRaWAN 1.1 recommends the following the range of session key update period: $period_{session} = 2^{T+10}$. Thus, the root key update period should be longer than session key update period, and it will be at least 2^{11} seconds.

Apparently, frequent root key update will make the LoRaWAN security stronger. However, the more frequent the update, the higher computing resource required. As Rabbit KDF has dramatically reduced the key derivation time, this has made the frequent root key more affordable for LoRa EDs with constrained power [19].

The key randomness is a basic and essential factor to measure the performance of a KDF. Rabbit KDF key randomness is evaluated on 1,000 key samples, which are used to calculate the standard deviation σ and Probability Density Function PDF for checking the randomness of the updated key. The 128-bit updated key is split into sixteen 8-bit blocks. The analysis is based on the randomness of blocks. Figure 1 shows the PDF of updated keys in each block. The PDF is close to a uniform distribution that leads to the less correlation among the blocks to ensure the key randomness.

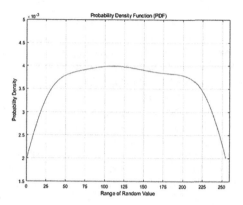

Fig. 1. Probability density function of updated key

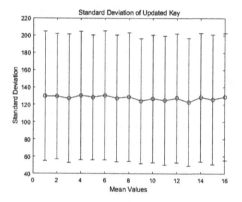

Fig. 2. Standard deviation of updated key

The standard deviation of 16-octet is shown in Fig. 2 with the average value (mean). It has shown that the block values spread evenly over a wider range and the root key randomness is guaranteed in the proposed Rabbit KDF.

5   Conclusion

In this paper, the LoRaWAN security is reviewed, and some vulnerabilities on the key update are identified. A root key update scheme is proposed to strengthen the security of session key derivation. The proposed scheme applies Rabbit Stream Cipher based KDF to update the root key. The full root key update procedure is provided, and its evaluation is carried out on a Window PC. Compared with LoRaWAN session key derivation method and Hash-based KDF, the proposed scheme has the highest computing efficiency and offers good randomness of the updated key generated. As the root key update will make the overall LoRaWAN security stronger, the proposed KDF can be a candidate for the introduction of root key update in the future LoRaWAN release.

References

1. Naoui, S., Elhdhili, M.E., Saidane, L.A.: Enhancing the security of the IoT LoraWAN architecture. In: 2016 International Conference on Performance Evaluation and Modeling in Wired and Wireless Networks (PEMWN), pp. 1–7 (2016)
2. Sornin, N., Yegin, A.: LoRaWAN backend interfaces 1.0 specification. Lora Alliance Standard Specification, 11 October 2017. www.lora-alliance.org. Accessed 20 Mar 2018
3. Sornin, N., Yegin, A.: LoRa specification 1.1. Lora Alliance Standard Specification, 11 October 2017. www.lora-alliance.org. Accessed 20 Mar 2018
4. Miller, R.: LoRa security: building a secure LoRa solution, 1st edn. MWR LABS (2016)
5. Roman, R., Alcaraz, C., Lopez, J., Sklavos, N.: Key management systems for sensor networks in the context of the Internet of Things. Comput. Electr. Eng. **37**, 147–159 (2011)
6. SeungJae, N., DongYeop, H., WoonSeob, S., Ki-Hyung, K.: Scenario and countermeasure for replay attack using join request messages in LoRaWAN. In: 2017 International Conference on Information Networking (ICOIN), pp. 718–720 (2017)
7. Kim, J., Song, J.: A simple and efficient replay attack prevention scheme for LoRaWAN. In: ACM International Conference Proceeding Series, pp. 32–36 (2017)
8. Gildas Avoine, L.F.: Rescuing LoRaWAN 1.0. INSA Rennes, CNRS, France (2016)
9. Zhang, Z.-K., Cho, M.C.Y., Shieh, S.: Emerging security threats and countermeasures in IoT. In: Proceedings of the 10th ACM Symposium on Information, Computer and Communications Security (ASIA CCS 2015), pp. 1–6. ACM (2015)
10. Hossain, M.M., Fotouhi, M., Hasan, R.: Towards an analysis of security issues, challenges, and open problems in the internet of tings. In: Proceedings of the IEEE World Congress on Services, SERVICES, pp. 21–28 (2015)
11. Zhao, K., Ge, L.: A survey on the internet of things security. In: Proceedings of the 9th International Conference on Computational Intelligence and Security, CIS, pp. 663–667 (2013)
12. He, J., Zhang, X., Wei, Q.: EDDK: energy-efficient distributed deterministic key management for wireless sensor networks. EURASIP J. Wirel. Commun. Netw. **2011**, 765143 (2011)
13. Barker, E., Barker, W., Burr, W., Polk, W., Smid, M.: Recommendation for Key Management Part 1: General (Revision 4). NIST Special Publication (2016)
14. Krawczyk, H.: Cryptographic extraction and key derivation: the HKDF scheme. In: Rabin, T. (ed.) CRYPTO 2010. LNCS, vol. 6223, pp. 631–648. Springer, Heidelberg (2010). https://doi.org/10.1007/978-3-642-14623-7_34
15. National Institute of Standards and Technology, FIPS 198-1, The Keyed-Hash Message Authentication Code, Federal Information Processing Standard (FIPS), Publication 198-1 (2008)
16. Chen, L.: SP 800-56C. Recommendation for key derivation through extraction-then-expansion. National Institute of Standards & Technology (2011)
17. Dworkin, M.J.: SP 800-38B. Recommendation for block cipher modes of operation: the CMAC mode for authentication. National Institute of Standards & Technology (2005)
18. Boesgaard, M., Vesterager, M., Zenner, E.: The rabbit stream cipher. In: Matthew, R., Olivier, B. (eds.) New Stream Cipher Designs, pp. 69–83. Springer, Berlin (2008). https://doi.org/10.1007/978-3-540-68351-3_7
19. Suárez-Albela, M., Fernández-Caramés, T.M., Fraga-Lamas, P., Castedo, L.: A practical evaluation of a high-security energy-efficient gateway for IoT fog computing applications. Sensors **17**(9), 1978 (2017)

Identifying Devices of the Internet of Things Using Machine Learning on Clock Characteristics

Pascal Oser[1,2](✉) (iD), Frank Kargl[2] (iD), and Stefan Lüders[1] (iD)

[1] European Organization for Nuclear Research CERN, 1211 Geneva, Switzerland
{p.oser,stefan.lueders}@cern.ch
[2] Ulm University, 89081 Ulm, Germany
frank.kargl@uni-ulm.de

Abstract. The number of devices of the so-called Internet of Things (IoT) is heavily increasing. One of the main challenges for operators of large networks is to autonomously and automatically identify any IoT device within the network for the sake of computer security and, subsequently, being able to better protect and secure those.

In this paper, we propose a novel approach to identify IoT devices based on the unchangeable IoT hardware setup through device specific clock behavior. One feature we use is the unavoidable fact that clocks experience "clock skew", which results in running faster or slower than an exact clock. Clock skew along with twelve other clock related features are suitable for our approach, because we can measure these features remotely through TCP timestamps which many devices can add to their packets. We show that we are able to distinguish device models by Machine Learning only using these clock characteristics. We ensure that measurements of our approach do not stress a device or causes fault states at any time.

We evaluated our approach in a large-scale real-world installation at the European Organization for Nuclear Research (CERN) and show that the above-mentioned methods let us identify IoT device models within the network.

Keywords: Internet of Things · Identification · Security
Clock characteristics · Machine Learning

1 Introduction

A problem we face today is that the number of embedded devices is exploding and therefore introduces vulnerabilities on an uncountable number of networks. Gartner, Inc. published a report that the world will face 20.4 billion connected things by 2020 [1]. This indicates the breakthrough of integrating these devices into open enterprise networks. In large heterogeneous computer networks like at CERN, we find tens of thousands of registered general purpose devices.

© Springer Nature Switzerland AG 2018
G. Wang et al. (Eds.): SpaCCS 2018, LNCS 11342, pp. 417–427, 2018.
https://doi.org/10.1007/978-3-030-05345-1_36

The specialty of an organization like CERN is that it pursues an open network policy where staff can register a network device of any type needed for their work. This results in an immense growth of various smart interconnected devices, like closed-circuit television (CCTV) cameras, IP-phones, printers, network attached storages, oscilloscopes, industrial control systems etc. and increases the complexity of protecting this network against cyber-threats. IoT manufacturers approach a short time-to-market and do not provide firmware updates for a longer time, as PC operating system providers do. Furthermore, IoT manufacturers design hardware, but they often re-use source code and libraries that are outdated at the time of releasing a new IoT device. Due to this, IoT devices are generally and intrinsically insecure and it becomes easier to compromise them. This is why using them in home or open enterprise networks is so dangerous that it becomes a serious threat, especially when the devices have security, safety or operational implications.

A first step towards securing an open network is to know which IoT devices exist within the network, which becomes most important if a new security vulnerability comes up. The operator then needs to know which device models are affected and endanger the overall network. Making an inventory of thousands of different IoT devices by hand is not feasible, since there is no way to gather model related information from devices easily. Moreover, getting this information for different IoT device manufacturers over the network was not yet done in large scale.

To address this problem, we propose and evaluate a novel approach based only on thirteen clock characteristics to remotely identify different IoT device models of various manufacturers in a more reliable and non-invasive way compared to related work. The approach will not harm the device or attached equipment and works without any preconditions. The approach does not need a reference device that is present all the time either. The widely used and simple TCP timestamp feature allows us to identify multiple devices under test in parallel and a device does not even need to be in the same subnet than the fingerprinter. These facts point out the benefit of using our approach within a complex network environment.

1.1   Contributions

In this paper, we present a novel approach to identify IoT device models based only on clock characteristics and evaluate it on a large heterogeneous network with Machine Learning. We focus on interference-free network packets, the ability to scan large networks, being adaptable for heterogeneous devices and not causing faults on remote devices. Installing or modifying anything on the device under test (DUT) is not needed. In the following,

- we show a new approach to IoT device fingerprinting by measuring clock behaviors of embedded devices;
- we fingerprint 562 physical IoT devices in a highly heterogeneous, large-scale network at CERN;

- we validate our approach by distinguishing 51 different device models of our network;
- our evaluation shows that we are able to detect IoT devices with 97.03% precision, 94.64% recall and 99.76% accuracy on a validation-set using Machine Learning.

Section 2 introduces related work and background on computer clocks in general. It shows clock characteristics and why these clock characteristics occur. After that, it shows how one can measure them. Section 3 identifies clock characteristics in TCP timestamps and how we can use them to identify devices. After that, the section introduces our dataset and the features we use for Machine Learning. Finally, we show our evaluation results before we conclude.

2   Background and Related Work

This section introduces related work and the origin of the features we use for our approach. It begins with the definition of a timestamp clock that generates the timestamp values we measure. Afterwards, the section points out how we measure the clock characteristics and how clock skew is defined. The section then shows timestamp overflows we recognized on several devices and how we define this behavior.

2.1   Related Work

Most of the related work to identify network devices require preconditions on the infrastructure. Passive fingerprinting approaches need a software-defined-network [2] to interact with IoT devices or to mirror [3] the network traffic of multiple routers. Thus, they distinguish by the generated network traffic of the IoT device when it is in a setup process [2] or operation [3]. Active fingerprinting approaches like port scanners are too inaccurate and bring up operational and safety implications for IoT devices. Other approaches need to take over control on the equipped auxiliary, e.g. measuring opening times [4] of a valve when connected to a programmable logic controller to identify the IoT device. Another active approach is to send malformed packets to an IoT device and detect the device on the replied error message [5]. Other work focuses only on clock skew approaches and calculate the clock skew based on a reference device that always needs to be present [6,7]. Researchers [8] also use clock skew to fingerprint the users of a cloud environment via asynchronous JavaScript and XML (AJAX) that is not adaptable for IoT environments, since IoT devices can not be forced to open and process a JavaScript web-page. In addition, all before-mentioned approaches were tested only on a few devices and therefore miss a large and heterogeneous dataset for verification.

2.2 TCP's Timestamp Clock

A clock is a continuous counter triggered by an oscillator. The oscillator for the majority of devices with a real-time clock is a quartz that oscillates with a fixed frequency. We use the characteristic feature of how monotonic timestamp clocks generate TCP [9] timestamp values to detect model specific characteristics. A monotonic clock avoids clock corrections that would change the timestamp value periodically, which leads to a systematic clock drift that one can measure over time. The resolution [10] of the timestamp clock is defined to be in the range between 1 ms up to 1 s per tick [11] that describes the step-size of the counter. A timestamp clock is designed to generate incrementing values which a system can use for different measurements. In case of our usage, the timestamp values are stored in the option field [11] of TCP packets that let the communication partner measure the round trip time.

2.3 Defining Clock Skew

Every clock experiences clock skew that one can measure as clock drift over time. In comparison to an exact clock, the quartz crystal, integrated in most IoT devices, can have a typical error of ± 100 parts per million which results in a clock drift of ± 8.64 sec per day. The clock drift rate at a point in time is the clock skew and can be positive or negative, if the clock is faster or slower than an exact clock. This positive or negative skew remains constant over time as Kohno et al. [12] showed. The clock skew becomes measurable by periodically sending TCP packets to the DUT and processing the included TCP timestamps. The clock skew $\alpha(t)$ is a derivation over time and is defined as follows:

$$\theta(t) = C_B(t) - C_A(t) \tag{1}$$

$$\alpha(t) = \frac{d\theta(t)}{dt} = \delta_B(t) - \delta_A(t) \tag{2}$$

C_A and C_B in Eq. 1 are the current clock values of a computer and the DUT in absolute time t. We calculate the relative clock offset between these clocks for our approach. Equation 2 specifies $\delta_B(t)$ and $\delta_A(t)$ that is the frequency error of a clock at an absolute point in time t. Moreover, Eq. 2 shows that clock skew is calculated by the frequency error of an oscillator. We use these equations to calculate the clock skew of every device model and add it as a feature for Machine Learning in Sect. 3.2.

2.4 Timestamp Overflows

A conspicuous feature we detected on longer scans is an overflow of the TCP timestamp values that happened on several IoT devices during our tests. This overflow of the timestamp values is caused, because the monotonic timestamp clock does not synchronize the time periodically. Thus, the timestamp values will not be corrected if the clock drifts and timestamp overflows will happen more often. In the following, we show how we detect timestamp overflows and how we take advantage of this behavior. Figure 1 shows timestamp overflows of a printer and a telepresence device. The Hewlett-Packard Laserjet P3010 printer drops from the maximum timestamp value d_m of 114,221,300 to a lower value d_b with 34,731 at packet number 25. The Matrox Monarch HD telepresence device drops from the maximum of 8,598,140 to the lower value 18,775 at packet number 144. We detect these overflows by multiple Machine Learning features and use this behavior to identify devices more accurate.

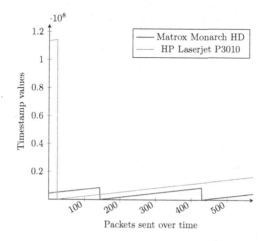

Fig. 1. Overflows of timestamp clocks

We specify the observed clock characteristics in the following formula:

$$clock_d(n) = d_b + n * d_r \bmod d_m \qquad (3)$$

$$d_b = \begin{cases} d_b = 0, & \text{initially} \\ d_b = \varphi \text{ and } n = 0, & \geq d_m \end{cases} \qquad (4)$$

We define Eq. 3 that calculates the timestamp clock value $clock_d$ in relation to n ticks that happened during start. This equation is device model specific and starts on boot with d_b set to zero. When an overflow occurred, it is set to an implementation specific value φ. The device specific constant d_r is the resolution of the timestamp clock. Every iteration n adds this constant d_r, where n zeroes after an overflow has occurred. The upper limit of d_m is defined by RFC1323 [11] to the upper limit for unsigned 32 bit integers, but implementations sometimes differ and set a smaller value where they wrap. We observed that the drops in Fig. 1 occur in a device-model-specific periodicity. This shows us that d_m in Eq. 3 corresponds not always to the highest value defined by RFC1323. An additional implementation specific behavior occurs, when a timestamp clock begins to increment after an overflow greater than zero as $0 < d_b < d_m$. It is obvious that the closer d_m is to the upper limit for unsigned 32 bit integers, the longer the scans need to be to detect an overflow. Using this information about overflows and lower value characteristics increases the preciseness for distinguishing specific models.

3   Clock-Characteristic-Based Device Identification Using Random Forest Classifier

This section introduces the different device classes of our approach along with the amount of scans in the different data sets. After that, the section lists which Machine Learning features we define to detect the different clock characteristics. The section then shows the comparison of different Machine Learning algorithms for our approach and points out the results we achieved with the Random Forest classifier.

3.1   Dataset of Devices at CERN

CERN has a large-scale infrastructure with tens of thousands of devices, where 1000 of them are IoT devices. For our evaluation, we use a subset of these devices and limit our dataset to 562 devices. We encountered that 100 of the devices are only sporadically online. Hence, we are currently not able to gather enough scans for the training phase of Machine Learning. We also found four device models of different manufacturers that do not support TCP timestamps or reply with zero continuously. The remaining amount of 300 IoT devices are within a restricted network for accelerator purposes only. Therefore, one is not able to get access to this network due to security and safety restrictions. The device classes and physical quantities of our dataset are listed in Table 1. This table represents 51 device models categorized by their device class. Summing all quantities together results in 562 physical devices for our dataset. All network devices at CERN are registered at a database, where we extracted hostnames, device manufacturer and model information of all IoT devices. Since device manufacturer and model information are not mandatory fields, we investigated manually for certain devices to identify them correctly. Correct labeled information is mandatory for the training and validation phase of Machine Learning.

Due to the high quantity of *Printers* one can find at CERN, our dataset contains a comparatively larger amount of scans for this device class. On the one hand, more devices help us to generate our dataset faster. On the other hand, we mention in Sect. 3.3 that the classification algorithm is not biased by this fact. Table 1 also shows scans of the training and test set that we use in Sect. 3.3 for the Machine Learning algorithm. We hereby point out that a single scan consists of 576 values taken over time from the TCP timestamps. Our evaluation showed that the first timestamp overflows happen within this range for different devices. Before we can start with Machine Learning in Sect. 3.3, we split the dataset into a training and test set first as we show in Table 1. We train the Machine Learning algorithm after this split on the training set and use the test set to put the classifier to the proof. After that, we use the validation set shown in Table 1 to verify our approach on never processed scans, point out the features for Machine Learning in Sect. 3.2 and show the results in Sect. 3.3.

Table 1. Device overview with physical quantity and scans per data-set

Device class	Models	Quantity	Training set	Test set	Validation set
Arduino	1	4	225	49	14
IP to serial converter	1	4	787	224	58
IP phone	1	2	68	9	7
Light management	1	11	63	22	3
Network attached storage	16	35	4021	1054	294
Oscilloscope	1	2	70	21	9
Printer	11	390	78903	21006	5231
Projector	3	12	384	111	28
Telepresence system	4	37	2934	795	195
Video streaming system	1	25	12177	3263	810
Webcam	11	40	2416	658	155

3.2 Defining Features for Random Forest Classifier

We first used clock skew as a single feature to identify devices of our dataset, which was not giving us the intended results for our large dataset. One can see in Fig. 2 of Sect. 3.3 that clock skew is the fourth most important feature for the Machine Learning algorithm to identify devices. This makes clear that by using clock skew as the only feature, one would not be able to identify the majority of devices within our dataset. Thus, we use 12 additional features besides clock skew to better identify devices, which are specified in Table 2. We defined these features to detect the changes of consecutive timestamps and the properties of the overall scan. Timestamp overflows are also detected with the combination of several features. All features are based on two types of sets. First, we define the set $A = a_0, ..., a_{n-1}, a_n$ as the set of all timestamp values of one scan period from a device model. One scan period is represented by 576 timestamp values; hence a is one single timestamp value of A. Secondly, we define the set $O = \{a_{i+1} - a_i\}_{i=1}^{N-1}$ that represents the offset of two consecutive timestamps of the set A.

3.3 Detection of Devices

We take the dataset that we introduced in Sect. 3.1 and the features of Sect. 3.2 as input and evaluated our approach with different Machine Learning algorithms.

Table 2. Features used for Random Forest classifier

ID	Features	Definition
0	Clock skew	See Sect. 2.3
1	Increase over all consecutive timestamp values	$a_n - a_1$, where $n = |A|$
2	Largest increase of two consecutive timestamp values	$max(O)$
3	Mean increase over all consecutive timestamp offsets	$mean(O)$
4	Smallest increase of two consecutive timestamp values	$min(O)$
5	Timestamp overflow occurred	if $a_{i+1} < a_i$, where $a \in A$
6	Sum over all consecutive timestamp offsets	$\sum_{i=1}^{N} o_i$
7	Last timestamp in A	a_n, where $n = |A|$
8	Largest timestamp in A	$max(a)$
9	Median over all timestamps	$median(A)$
10	Smallest timestamp in A	$min(a)$
11	Cardinality of timestamp values	$|A|$
12	Sum over all timestamp values	$\sum_{i=1}^{N} a_i$

We compared algorithms designed for classification problems, as in multilayer perceptron [13], support vector machine [14] and Random Forest [15] on the test set shown in Table 1. With the multilayer perceptron algorithm, we get a precision [16] of 91.65%, a recall [16] of 92.47% and an accuracy [16] of 99.22%. Support vector machine results in a precision of 92.05%, a recall of 83.27% and an accuracy of 99.14%. The Random Forest algorithm shows a precision of 93.61%, a recall of 93.44% and an accuracy of 99.67%.

Our approach makes use of the uniqueness of device models in the TCP timestamp changes and makes them detectable. Distinguishing between different classes is a typical classification problem [17], because the Machine Learning algorithm needs to detect unique timestamp characteristics and assign it to a device model. Thus, we chose features that clearly separate the devices what one can see in the results above. The results for precision, recall and accuracy of Random Forest reached in average higher values in comparison to other algorithms that we show in the beginning. In the following, we continue with Random Forest.

Random Forest creates one decision tree classifier [18] for each device model during the training phase. In the test phase, the algorithm takes new scans as inputs. Each tree outputs the probability of every scan belonging to a certain device model. Finally the predicted device model is the tree with the highest mean probability estimate of all trees. Since our results are very distinct, we already mentioned in Sect. 3.1 that the Machine Learning algorithm is not biased. We examined this by splitting the training set into a test and validation set. First, we trained the Machine Learning algorithm with the training and test set. After that, the algorithm classified the scans of the validation set that were never processed before. We even used our classifier to identify scans of never seen devices and identified them successfully. The Random Forest results of predicting the device models of the validation set reach a precision of 97.03%, a recall of 94.64% and an accuracy of 99.76%.

As mentioned in related work, other researchers as Bratus et al. [5] or Kohno et al. [12] rely only on clock skew as a feature to identify devices. We applied our features related to TCP timestamp changes and the Random Forest algorithm to the initial clock skew feature, which resulted in better results that we present in this work. These additional features help us to identify different devices more clearly on a large-scale network with a bigger dataset compared to related work [2,4,19]. To increase our results, we performed several iterations of feature selection on our dataset. Removing features by method [20] with low information gain resulted in choosing the features in Table 2. Furthermore, we show in Fig. 2 the importance [21] of every single feature, where 100% importance would be 1.0 on the y-axis. Our evaluation showed that even the feature with the lowest importance correlates with other features; hence removing it would worsen our results significantly. For reasons of clarity, we use the Feature-IDs of Table 2 to match the numbers shown in Fig. 2.

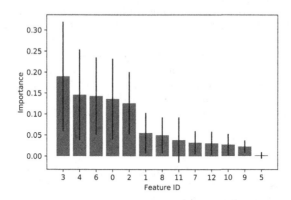

Fig. 2. Feature importance of the Random Forest classifier

4   Conclusion

We presented a novel approach to reliably identify various IoT device models in a real-world environment. Preconditions on the infrastructure, like software-defined-networks, network mirroring or reference devices are not needed. We showed that the approach is working on a large-scale network with a larger dataset compared to related work. Moreover, no other work was able to classify this amount of heterogeneous IoT device models by using just a single and easy accessible information source like TCP timestamps.

Due to the fact that our classification approach is non-intrusive, one can also use this approach for other infrastructures as in industrial IoT environments. For future work, we want to identify new types of IoT devices that come up together with industrial IoT devices on our accelerator complex test bed.

Acknowledgment. This work has been sponsored by the Wolfgang Gentner Programme of the German Federal Ministry of Education and Research.

References

1. GARTNER. https://www.gartner.com/newsroom/id/3598917. Accessed 05 Feb 2018
2. Miettinen, M., et al.: IoT sentinel: automated device-type identification for security enforcement in IoT. In: 2017 IEEE 37th International Conference on Distributed Computing Systems (ICDCS), pp. 2177–2184. IEEE (2017)
3. Meidan, Y., et al.: ProfilIoT: a machine learning approach for IoT device identification based on network traffic analysis. In: Proceedings of the Symposium on Applied Computing, pp. 506–509. ACM (2017)
4. Jaafar, F.: An integrated architecture for IoT fingerprinting. In: 2017 IEEE International Conference on Software Quality, Reliability and Security Companion (QRS-C), pp. 601–602. IEEE (2017)
5. Bratus, S., et al.: Active behavioral fingerprinting of wireless devices. In: Proceedings of the first ACM Conference on Wireless Network Security, pp. 56–61. ACM (2008)
6. Kassem, M.M., et al.: A clock skew addressing scheme for Internet of Things. In: 2014 IEEE 25th Annual International Symposium on Personal, Indoor, and Mobile Radio Communication (PIMRC), pp. 1553–1557. IEEE (2014)
7. Huang, D.-J., et al.: Clock skew based node identification in wireless sensor networks. In: Global Telecommunications Conference 2008. IEEE GLOBECOM 2008, pp. 1–5. IEEE (2008)
8. Huang, D.-J., et al.: Clock skew based client device identification in cloud environments. In: 2012 IEEE 26th International Conference on Advanced Information Networking and Applications (AINA), pp. 526–533. IEEE (2012)
9. Internet Engineering Task Force, Transmission Control Protocol. https://tools.ietf.org/html/rfc793. Accessed 05 July 2018
10. Kamp, P.-H.: Timecounters: efficient and precise timekeeping in SMP kernels. In: Proceedings of the BSDCon Europe (2002)
11. Internet Engineering Task Force, TCP Extensions for High Performance. https://tools.ietf.org/html/rfc1323/. Accessed 05 July 2018
12. Kohno, T., et al.: Remote physical device fingerprinting. IEEE Trans. Dependable Secur. Comput. **2**(2), 93–108 (2005)
13. Hornik, K.: Approximation capabilities of multilayer feedforward networks. Neural Netw. **4**(2), 251–257 (1991)
14. Vapnik, V.: Estimation of Dependences Based on Empirical Data. Springer, New York (2006). https://doi.org/10.1007/0-387-34239-7

15. Breiman, L.: Random forests. Mach. Learn. **45**(1), 5–32 (2001)
16. Davis, J., Goadrich, M.: The relationship between precision-recall and ROC curves. In: Proceedings of the 23rd International Conference on Machine Learning, pp. 233–240. ACM (2006)
17. Liaw, A., et al.: Classification and regression by randomForest. R News **2**(3), 18–22 (2002)
18. Safavian, S.R., Landgrebe, D.: A survey of decision tree classifier methodology. IEEE Trans. Syst. Man Cybern. **21**(3), 660–674 (1991)
19. Radhakrishnan, S.V., et al.: GTID: a technique for physical device and device type fingerprinting. IEEE Trans. Dependable Secur. Comput. **12**(5), 519–532 (2015)
20. Kraskov, A., et al.: Estimating mutual information. Phys. Rev. E **69**(6), 066138 (2004)
21. Breiman, L.: Classification and Regression Trees. Routledge, Abingdon (2017)

A Systematic Mapping Study on Security Requirements Engineering Frameworks for Cyber-Physical Systems

Shafiq Rehman[1](✉), Volker Gruhn[1], Saad Shafiq[2], and Irum Inayat[2]

[1] Institute of Software Technology, University of Duisburg-Essen,
45127 Essen, Germany
shafiq.rehman@uni-due.de
[2] National University of Computer and Emerging Sciences,
Islamabad 44000, Pakistan

Abstract. Since the world is moving towards secure systems which makes security a primary concern and not an afterthought in software development. Secure software development involves security at each step of development lifecycle from requirements phase to testing. With surging focus on security requirements, we can see an increase in frameworks/methods/techniques proposed to deal with security requirements for variable applications. However, to summarise the literature findings till date and to propose further ways to handle security requirements a systematic and comprehensive review is needed. Our objective is to conduct a systematic mapping study for cyber-physical systems: (i) to explore and analyse security requirements engineering frameworks/ methods/techniques proposed till date, (ii) to investigate on their strengths and weaknesses, and (iii) to determine the security threats and requirements reported in literature. We conducted a systematic mapping study for which we defined our goals and determined research questions, defined inclusion/exclusion criteria, and designed the map systematically based on the research questions. The search yielded 337 articles after deploying the query on multiple databases and refining the search iteratively through a multistep process. The mapping study identified and categorised the existing security requirements engineering frameworks/methods/techniques focused on their implementation and evaluation mechanisms. Second, we identified and categorised the proposed to deal with security requirements for multiple domains, determined their strengths/weaknesses, and also security requirements and threats reports in the selected studies. The study provides an overall view of the state-of-the-art frameworks/methods/techniques proposed till date to deal with security requirements. The results of this study provide insights to researchers to focus more on developing frameworks to deal with security requirements for particular kinds of systems like cyber-physical systems. Also, it motivates future work to devise methods to cater domain specific security risks and requirements.

Keywords: Security requirements · Security requirements engineering
Security requirements engineering frameworks · Threat · Security goal
Cyber-physical systems

© Springer Nature Switzerland AG 2018
G. Wang et al. (Eds.): SpaCCS 2018, LNCS 11342, pp. 428–442, 2018.
https://doi.org/10.1007/978-3-030-05345-1_37

1 Introduction

In today's world, the software development industry is striving hard to increase productivity. Yet this goal cannot divert software development team's attention from important aspects like security and risk assessment. Software industry has faced loss of billions of dollars due to major security attacks worldwide. One of the major reasons behind these attacks are incomplete and vague security requirement elicitation and analysis [1]. The professionals seem to have developed an interest in security requirements engineering (SRE) and have started considering it as a preliminary step towards secure and efficient software development.

In present day software development industry, cyber-physical systems (CPS) are gaining much attention of the researchers and practitioners due to their high impact on the world's economy. These systems are considered as a modern age of computing power with support for physical systems. With rising use and important of CPS, the developers have come to terms with the importance of security in these systems, as any error if left unhandled can be fatal. For instance, any disturbance in the communication protocols of self-driving cars with minimal human intervention can be disastrous.

To summarise, the important of security is established in modern day systems including CPS. Software development teams need to know that security is not an afterthought but a very important aspect of the lifecycle. This proves that if not considered in the preliminary phases of development, security issues can become hazardous for systems for instance safety critical systems used in health or combat industry. Little attention has been given to sensor, hardware, network, and third party elements in security requirements engineering for cyber-physical systems [30, 31]. Therefore, the main aim of the study is to identify the security requirements engineering solutions that help in ensuring maximum security and also facilitate to understand the threats, vulnerabilities, and security requirements of these systems. The study provides an overview of the current techniques on SRE available in literature and motivates the practitioners and researchers to strengthen this area of research by providing implications.

The rest of the paper is organized as follows: Sect. 2 describes the background and related work in the area. Section 3 describes the research methodology and articles selection process. Section 4 explains the construction of systematic map of the study. Article evaluation is described in Sect. 5. Discussion on the results is available in Sect. 6. Threats to validity of the study are mentioned in Sect. 7 and conclusion of the study is described in Sect. 8.

2 Background and Related Work

There are several studies available in literature till date that focused on reviewing security requirements engineering from various perspectives as discussed below:

Mellado et al. studied the software requirement engineering techniques proposed in the literature of information systems (IS) [2]. The study revealed interesting insights regarding the techniques, model and their integration of standards. The paper summarized the existing techniques to provide the researchers with an overview of which techniques are suitable in particular implementation.

In order to understand the relationship between the security requirement engineering (SRE) and the Model driven engineering (MDE), Munante et al. carried out a study in which he explained that the transformation of security requirement elicited in early phase into security policies is complicated and difficult [3]. For this purpose, the study explained how Model driven engineering (MDE) can be integrated with the existing SRE techniques in order to better define the security policies. As the MDE provides a better way to model the system and validate the model formally using domain specific modelling languages.

A review has been conducted on tool supports for security requirement engineering [4]. The study has evaluated seven tools developed to deal with security requirements engineering and identified the problems and gaps existing. The study concluded that a considerable amount of research has been conducted on formalizing model to capture the security requirements. However, capturing requirement from textual representations still needs attention. Therefore, the authors plan to explore Essential Use Case (EUC) approach in order to deal with the problem.

Smart grids are one of the prime examples of cyber-physical systems. A study was conducted to explore on the potential security issues of the complex smart grid systems [5]. The study also discussed the vulnerabilities and security threats and explained the research interests in dealing with the cyber-attacks on smart grid systems.

It can be inferred from the review of existing literature that there is a need of a comprehensive review of security requirements for software systems especially for cyber-physical systems, techniques/frameworks/tools/techniques in use to handle security requirements, and to identify the threats and vulnerabilities listed in the literature. This extensive study would also reveal the demographic details in the area to have a broader view of the research perspective.

3   Research Method

3.1   Goals

Following are the goals of this systematic mapping study:

Goal-1: To identify the existing security requirements engineering solutions proposed for software and cyber-physical systems in literature.

Goal-2: To understand the security goals, threats, and vulnerabilities that are essential for a requirement analyst to follow in order to identify the security requirements for CPS.

Goal-3: To investigate the process of validation for the proposed security requirements engineering solutions?

Goal-4: To identify the relevant trends in the area of security requirements engineering in terms of demographics and bibliography.

3.2   Research Questions

The goals of the study are then refined into the formulated research questions.

RQ 1.1: Which security requirements engineering solutions for software and cyber-physical systems exist in literature?

RQ 1.2: How to implement these security requirements engineering solutions?

RQ 1.3: What are the strengths and weaknesses of each framework/model/technique?

RQ 2.1: Which security goals are considered important particularly for CPS?

RQ 2.2: What are the main security threats and vulnerabilities for CPS?

RQ 3.1: What contribution and research facets are identified in security requirement engineering?

RQ 3.2: What empirical methods are used to evaluate the proposed security requirements engineering solutions?

RQ 4.1: Which continent and country participated the most in security requirements engineering research?

RQ 4.2: Who are active researchers in the area of security requirements engineering?

RQ 4.3: Which conferences/journals/workshops having highest number of published articles in the area?

3.3   Articles Selection Process

3.3.1   Search String

The search strategy is designed to obtain maximum articles relevant to the area and scope of the study. For this purpose, the query string is formulated based on the guidelines of Petersen et al. [6]. The query string shown below is applied on four well known database repositories which include IEEE Xplore, ACM Digital Library, Springer and Elsevier. "((Security requirements) OR (Security requirements engineering) OR (Security requirements engineering methodology) OR (Security requirements engineering process) OR (Security requirements engineering framework) OR (Security requirements engineering for cyber-physical systems) OR (cyber-physical systems))". The query yielded the highly relevant articles making the initial pool of 337 articles in total. The obtained articles were assessed based on our quality assessment process as shown in Table 1. We assessed each articles accordingly and ranked it with "Yes" and "No" where "Yes" means "Accepted" and "No" means "Rejected".

The articles then underwent the scrutiny process through our defined exclusion and inclusion criteria. A detailed process of article selection from each individual repository and the final pool is shown in Table 2 which turned out to be of 322 articles after the successful assessment of the highly relevant articles.

3.4   Research Protocol

In order to make the study meaningful and systematic, we employed a research protocol. The research protocol is followed based on the guidelines of Petersen et al. [6]. The protocol establishes the criteria to be followed while study is being carried out. The protocol that we have followed in the study is shown in Fig. 1.

Table 1. Quality assessment process

Phase	Method	Assessment criteria	Count
1st Phase	Identify articles using search string	Keywords/Query string execution	337
2nd Phase	Remove duplicate articles	Duplicate removal	336
3rd Phase	Exclude articles based on titles	Search strings in titles Yes = Accepted No = Rejected	322
4th Phase	Exclude articles based on abstracts	Search strings in abstracts Yes = Accepted No = Rejected	322
5th Phase	Obtain selected articles that meet the goals of the study	Addressing security requirement engineering and cyber physical systems, empirical studies Yes = Accepted No = Rejected	322

Table 2. Number of articles obtained

Repositories	Relevant articles obtained	After exclusion/inclusion (full text review)	Final Pool
IEEE	215	204	204
ACM DL	54	51	51
Springer	24	24	24
Elsevier	44	43	43
Total	337	322	322

4 Mapping Design

4.1 Research Map

Initially, we constructed a research map based on the above research protocol. The map establishes the baseline of the study on which the evaluation of the papers is done. The identified articles were then categorized based on their evaluation results. Formulated research questions and the identified attributes along with their description is shown in Table 3.

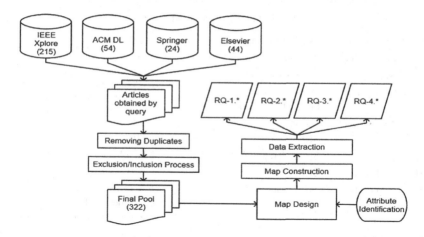

Fig. 1. Research protocol

5   Evaluation of Articles

In this section, we discuss the study's evaluation of articles. We address each posed research question in detail and report the results accordingly. We have also made the analysed data regarding the articles available to public in the form of a repository [29]. To address RQ-1.1 and RQ-1.2, we identified solutions proposed in the articles. Some of them are shown in Table 4 along with their implementation tool support.

Table 3. Research map

Research questions	Attributes	Description
RQ-1.*	Security requirement solutions, Strengths and weaknesses	To identify security requirement engineering frameworks, tools and techniques proposed in the articles
RQ-2.*	Security goals, Security threats, vulnerabilities	To identify security risks, threats and vulnerabilities mentioned explicitly in the articles
RQ-3.*	Evaluation method, how to implement	To identify whether the articles evaluated empirically and what empirical methods are employed to do so
RQ-4.*	Demographics and bibliography	To identify the demographics and bibliography in the area

To address RQ-1.3, we identified the strengths and weaknesses of some solutions with respect to their compatibility with standards. Table 5 shows the strengths and weakness of some of the proposed solutions.

Table 4. Solutions proposed in articles

Ref.	Contribution	Contribution name	Implementation tool
[7]	Framework	STS-ml extension	STS-tool
[8]	Approach	Autofocus extension	AUTOFOCUS tool
[9]	Framework	UML based business process-driven framework	UML
[10]	Technique	Hazop	UML Use case model
[10]	Technique	SRL	UML
[11]	Framework	Secure Tropos framework	ST-tool
[12]	Approach	SREP	CARE tool
[13]	Approach	Trust assumptions	Use of trust assumptions embedded in the solution
[14]	Approach	Secure Tropos extension	Off-the-Shelf LPG-td planner
[15]	Method	MOQARE	Misuse tree
[16]	Process	Agent oriented process	Meta agents
[17]	Approach	Scenario driven	Conceptual model
[18]	Framework	Three layer security analysis framework	Goal modeling
[19]	Process	Security ontology	SQWRL
[20]	Method	Conceptual framework	Reference implementation
[21]	Framework	Parmenides	NFL
[22]	Method	UMLsec	UMLsec
[23]	Approach	Modular approach	SecureUML
[24]	Framework	Extended previous framework	CONCHITA tool
[25]	Approach	SURE	ASSURE
[26]	Method	i* framework extension	si* Tool
[27]	Method	STPA	Rodin toolset

Table 5. Strengths and weaknesses [3]

Solution	Strength	Weakness
SQUARE	-	Not Compatible with ISO 27005
GBRAM	ISO 27005 compatible	-
ISSRM	ISO 27005 compatible	-
SREF	Almost compatible with ISO 27005	-
SREP	Almost compatible with ISO 27005	No own model
KAOS	Almost compatible with ISO 27005	Absence of risk
Secure Tropos	Almost compatible with ISO 27005	Absence of assets
Secure i*	Almost compatible with ISO 27005	Absence of risk

To address RQ-2.1 and RQ-2.2, we identified security goals, threats and vulnerabilities mentioned by the researchers in their articles. Table 6 describes the security goals, threats and vulnerabilities in cyber-physical systems.

Table 6. Security goals, threats, and vulnerabilities in CPS [2, 28]

Security goal	Layer	Threat	Vulnerability
Security goals aim is to protect the system from threats and vulnerabilities and reduce risk factor. Some of the Goals include Confidentiality, Integrity, Availability, Authenticity	Physical layer	Hardware failure, DoS attack, Sybil attack, Node intruder/capture, electromagnetic interference	Platform configuration, Platform hardware, Platform malware
	Network layer	Routing attack, Flooding, Blackhole, Spoofing	Network hardware, Network parameter, Network communication, connectivity
	Application layer	Virus, Trojan horse, SQL injection, Loophole, Malicious code	XSS exploit

To address RQ-3, we identified the articles that were evaluated empirically as shown in Figs. 2 and 3. We found that 44% (140/313) articles were not empirically evaluated. Furthermore, we found that for empirical evaluation researchers used case study as the most used empirical method in articles 42% (132/313) followed by controlled experiment 9% (29/313), and survey 2% (8/313) respectively.

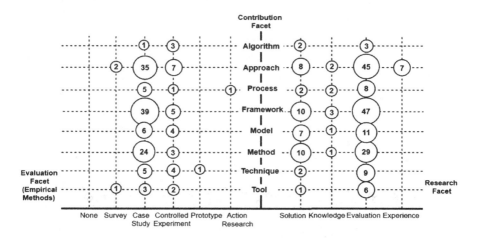

Fig. 2. Research vs contribution vs evaluation facet

To address RQ-4, we identified comprehensive demographics and bibliography in the area. We found that Europe (141 articles) was the most active continent in this particular area of research followed by USA (90 articles) and Asia (67 articles) respectively. Figure 4 shows the continent-wise distribution and articles' frequency.

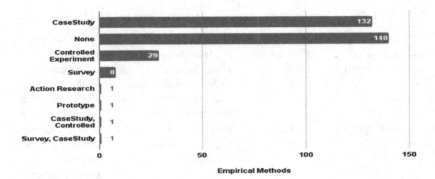

Fig. 3. Empirical methods used for evaluation in selected studies

Fig. 4. Continent-wise article distribution

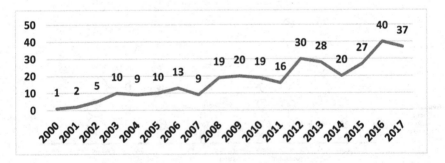

Fig. 5. Year-wise articles frequency

The results showed that the highest number of articles were published in year 2016 (40 articles) followed by 2017 (37 articles), and 2012 (30 articles) respectively. The result showed an overall increase in interest among the researchers worldwide. Figure 5 shows the year-wise distribution of articles.

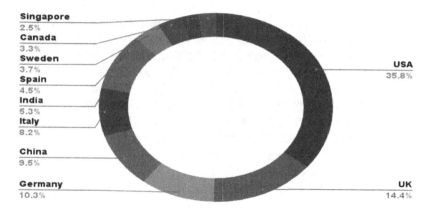

Fig. 6. Country-wise articles distribution

We also identified the highly participating countries in this particular area of research. We found that the most of the authors were from the US (35.8%), followed by UK (14.4%), and Germany (10.3%) respectively. Figure 6 shows the country-wise distribution of articles.

Further analysis showed that most of the articles were published as Conference proceedings (69%), and workshops (60%) turned out to be the second most frequently published at venue, followed by Symposiums (20%), and Journals (16%) respectively. Figure 7 shows the venue type-wise distribution of articles in the area.

Fig. 7. Venue type-wise articles distribution

Moving towards to most active researchers in the area. Giorgini, Paolo and Mouratidis, Haralambos (10 articles) are the most active researchers in the area followed by Fernandez-Medina, Eduardo and Mellado, Daniel (9 articles) and Nuseibeh, Bashar and Piattini, Mario (8 articles) respectively. Figure 8 shows the top ten authors with highest number of articles.

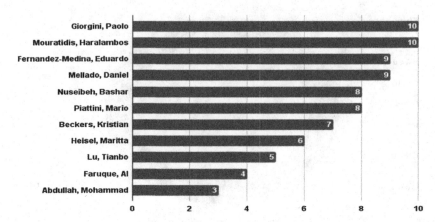

Fig. 8. Top 10 authors with highest number of articles

Figure 9 shows the top seven venues with highest number of published articles. International IEEE Conference on Requirement Engineering (23 articles) was the leading venue with highest number of articles followed by Computers and Security Journal (7 articles), and Workshop on Evolving Security and Privacy Requirements (6 articles) respectively.

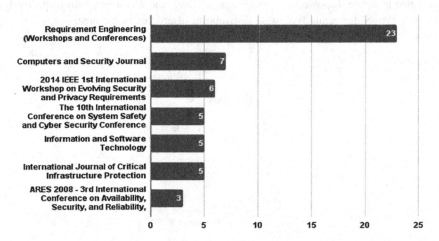

Fig. 9. Top 7 venues with highest number of articles

We also identified highest article citations with respect to year. Year 2002 (4993 citations) seems to be leading with highest citations followed by year 2012 (2064 citations) and 2006 (1188 citations) respectively. Figure 10 shows the years with highest citations.

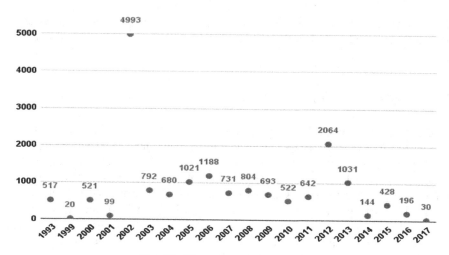

Fig. 10. Year-wise articles citations

6 Discussion

We addressed all the posed research questions and reported the results accordingly. Looking at the results of the review study, we can say that the trend of research in security requirement engineering is evolving with time. Researchers are paying attention to this field from various perspectives including identification of security requirements and devising ways to deal with them. Also, the trend shows that due attention is being given to cyber physical systems' security requirements. However, we can say that this field still needs more empirical evidence to back the ideas. As the results report that most of the authors proposed frameworks and methods to deal with security requirements for variable applications. Also, we can see that most of the articles were proposed in conferences, workshops, and symposiums putting the evaluation of those ideas in question. This diverts our attention towards the fact that despite the pragmatic solutions proposed by various researchers regarding security in CPS, the lack of empirical evidence still persists. Therefore, more empirical investigations should be conducted to back the proposed ideas in terms of frameworks, models, etc. This provides a practical implication for the researchers and tool vendors to empirically take up the evaluation task and develop the tools based on the proposed ideas, respectively.

As reported, most of the studies were tossed by authors from Europe. Thus Europe seems to be prominent in this area with slightly less but close interest of authors from the US. This shows that insights from significant software industry in Asia (including China, Malaysia, India) and North America (including Brazil) significant in software engineering research and practice are missing. Considering the differences of software development patterns in Asia and Europe interesting results can be gathered from such studies. Moreover, uneven distribution of authors across the globe puts the generalisability of the proposed studies in question. The results reported in the study are generic and meaningful insights that would help researchers in gaining an overview and in depth knowledge the proposed pragmatic solutions. Furthermore, the demographics and bibliography identified in the area gives a broader view of the overall trends to build research on.

7 Threats to Validity

Despite the reviews conducted in the area, the term systematic mapping study is still new to the software engineering domain and its guidelines need to be defined properly. The bias in systematic mapping is still prominent as there are no defined or established standards on evaluation of articles in software engineering. The evidence regarding software engineering techniques is dispersed and not easily available. Apart from this, the study is also prone to external validity regarding obtaining articles from few repositories. To overcome this threat, we are confident that the repositories selected in the study are the most prominent and well known it their domain. The research method is also posed to internal threat which we overcame through refining the query iteratively and employing goal, question and metrics approach thus obtaining the most relevant articles.

8 Conclusion

This systematic mapping study provided fruitful insights regarding security requirements engineering pragmatic solutions and their implementation tool support proposed by the researchers. The study illustrated that not all software security frameworks perform all the basic and important activities in the development of secure software systems, which may lead to the development of an unsecure cyber-physical systems. We determined various security requirements frameworks for software but there are no comprehensive security requirements engineering framework for CPS that can provide a complete guideline for practitioners and researchers that help to build a secure CPS. Furthermore, the study helps us to identify the short-comings in SRE frameworks. Moreover, the results reported in the study revealed that the trend of research interest is increasing in the domain of SRE especially for cyber-physical systems. The analysed data regarding the articles have also been available to public in the form of a repository which is also a contribution of the study. The study would help its readers to better understand the techniques being employed to ensure security and what are the threats and vulnerabilities that might affect the cyber-physical systems operations.

Acknowledgments. This work has been supported by the European Community through project CPS.HUB NRW, EFRE Nr. 0-4000-17.

References

1. Anderson, R.J.: Security Engineering: A Guide to Building Dependable Distributed Systems. Wiley, Hoboken (2010)
2. Mellado, D., Blanco, C., Sánchez, L.E., Fernández-Medina, E.: A systematic review of security requirements engineering. Comput. Stand. Interfaces **32**(4), 153–165 (2010)
3. Muñante, D., Chiprianov, V., Gallon, L., Aniorté, P.: A review of security requirements engineering methods with respect to risk analysis and model-driven engineering. In: Teufel, S., Min, T.A., You, I., Weippl, E. (eds.) CD-ARES 2014. LNCS, vol. 8708, pp. 79–93. Springer, Cham (2014). https://doi.org/10.1007/978-3-319-10975-6_6
4. Yahya, S., Kamalrudin, M., Sidek, S.: A review on tool supports for security requirements engineering. In: IEEE Conference on Open Systems, ICOS 2013, pp. 190–194 (2013)
5. Yadav, S.A., Kumar, S.R., Sharma, S., Singh, A.: A review of possibilities and solutions of cyber attacks in smart grids. In: 1st International Conference on Innovation and Challenges in Cyber Security, ICICCS 2016, pp. 60–63 (2016)
6. Petersen, K., Feldt, R., Mujtaba, S., Mattsson, M.: Systematic mapping studies in software engineering. In: EASE, vol. 8, pp. 68–77 (2008)
7. Paja, E., Dalpiaz, F., Giorgini, P.: Managing security requirements conflicts in socio-technical systems. In: Ng, W., Storey, V.C., Trujillo, J.C. (eds.) ER 2013. LNCS, vol. 8217, pp. 270–283. Springer, Heidelberg (2013). https://doi.org/10.1007/978-3-642-41924-9_23
8. Wimmel, G., Wisspeintner, A.: Extended description techniques for security engineering. In: Dupuy, M., Paradinas, P. (eds.) SEC 2001. IIFIP, vol. 65, pp. 469–485. Springer, Boston, MA (2002). https://doi.org/10.1007/0-306-46998-7_32
9. Vivas, J.L., Montenegro, J.A., López, J.: Towards a business process-driven framework for security engineering with the UML. In: Boyd, C., Mao, W. (eds.) ISC 2003. LNCS, vol. 2851, pp. 381–395. Springer, Heidelberg (2003). https://doi.org/10.1007/10958513_29
10. Srivatanakul, T., Clark, J.A., Polack, F.: Effective security requirements analysis: HAZOP and use cases. In: Zhang, K., Zheng, Y. (eds.) ISC 2004. LNCS, vol. 3225, pp. 416–427. Springer, Heidelberg (2004). https://doi.org/10.1007/978-3-540-30144-8_35
11. Giorgini, P., Massacci, F., Zannone, N.: Security and trust requirements engineering. In: Aldini, A., Gorrieri, R., Martinelli, F. (eds.) FOSAD 2004-2005. LNCS, vol. 3655, pp. 237–272. Springer, Heidelberg (2005). https://doi.org/10.1007/11554578_8
12. Mellado, D., Fernández-Medina, E., Piattini, M.: Applying a security requirements engineering process. In: Gollmann, D., Meier, J., Sabelfeld, A. (eds.) ESORICS 2006. LNCS, vol. 4189, pp. 192–206. Springer, Heidelberg (2006). https://doi.org/10.1007/11863908_13
13. Haley, C.B., Laney, R.C., Moffett, J.D., Nuseibeh, B.: Using trust assumptions with security requirements. Requir. Eng. **11**(2), 138–151 (2006)
14. Bryl, V., Massacci, F., Mylopoulos, J., Zannone, N.: Designing security requirements models through planning. In: Dubois, E., Pohl, K. (eds.) CAiSE 2006. LNCS, vol. 4001, pp. 33–47. Springer, Heidelberg (2006). https://doi.org/10.1007/11767138_4
15. Herrmann, A., Paech, B.: MOQARE: misuse-oriented quality requirements engineering. Requir. Eng. **13**(1), 73–86 (2008)
16. Moradian, E., Håkansson, A.: Controlling security of software development with multi-agent system. In: Setchi, R., Jordanov, I., Howlett, R.J., Jain, L.C. (eds.) KES 2010. LNCS (LNAI), vol. 6279, pp. 98–107. Springer, Heidelberg (2010). https://doi.org/10.1007/978-3-642-15384-6_11

17. Rieke, R., Coppolino, L., Hutchison, A., Prieto, E., Gaber, C.: Security and reliability requirements for advanced security event management. In: Kotenko, I., Skormin, V. (eds.) MMM-ACNS 2012. LNCS, vol. 7531, pp. 171–180. Springer, Heidelberg (2012). https://doi.org/10.1007/978-3-642-33704-8_15

18. Li, T., Horkoff, J.: Dealing with security requirements for socio-technical systems: a holistic approach. In: Jarke, M., et al. (eds.) CAiSE 2014. LNCS, vol. 8484, pp. 285–300. Springer, Cham (2014). https://doi.org/10.1007/978-3-319-07881-6_20

19. Souag, A., Salinesi, C., Mazo, R., Comyn-Wattiau, I.: A security ontology for security requirements elicitation. In: Piessens, F., Caballero, J., Bielova, N. (eds.) ESSoS 2015. LNCS, vol. 8978, pp. 157–177. Springer, Cham (2015). https://doi.org/10.1007/978-3-319-15618-7_13

20. Neureiter, C., Eibl, G., Engel, D., Schlegel, S., Uslar, M.: A concept for engineering smart grid security requirements based on SGAM models. Comput. Sci.-Res. Dev. **31**(1–2), 65–71 (2016)

21. Rosa, N.S., Justo, G.R.R., Cunha, P.R.F.: A framework for building non-functional software architectures. In: Proceedings of the 2001 ACM Symposium on Applied Computing, pp. 141–147 (2001)

22. Jürjens, J.: Using UMLsec and goal trees for secure systems development. In: Proceedings of the 2002 ACM Symposium on Applied Computing, pp. 1026–1030 (2002)

23. Basin, D., Doser, J., Lodderstedt, T.: Model driven security for process-oriented systems. In: Proceedings of the Eighth ACM Symposium on Access Control Models and Technologies, pp. 100–109 (2003)

24. De Landtsheer, R., Van Lamsweerde, A.: Reasoning about confidentiality at requirements engineering time. In: Proceedings of the 10th European Software Engineering Conference Held Jointly with 13th ACM SIGSOFT International Symposium on Foundations of Software Engineering, pp. 41–49 (2005)

25. Romero-Mariona, J.: Secure and usable requirements engineering. In: Proceedings of the 2009 IEEE/ACM International Conference on Automated Software Engineering, pp. 703–706 (2009)

26. Cui, J.-S., Zhang, D.: The research and application of security requirements analysis methodology of information systems. In: 2nd International Conference on Anti-counterfeiting, Security and Identification, ASID, pp. 30–36 (2008)

27. Howard, G., Butler, M., Colley, J., Sassone, V.: Formal analysis of safety and security requirements of critical systems supported by an extended STPA methodology. In: 2017 IEEE European Symposium on Security and Privacy Workshops (EuroS&PW), pp. 174–180 (2017)

28. Gao, Y., et al.: Analysis of security threats and vulnerability for cyber-physical systems. In: 2013 3rd International Conference on Computer Science and Network Technology (ICCSNT), pp. 50–55. IEEE (2013)

29. Repository link. http://sysmapsecre.azurewebsites.net

30. Rehman, S., Gruhn, V.: Security requirements engineering (SRE) framework for cyber-physical systems (CPS): SRE for CPS. In: Proceedings of the 16th International Conference on New Trends in Intelligent Software Methodologies, Tools and Techniques, SoMeT_17, vol. 297, p. 153 (2017)

31. Rehman, S., Gruhn, V.: An effective security requirements engineering framework for cyber-physical systems. Technologies **6**(3), 65 (2018)

Interacting with the Internet of Things Using Smart Contracts and Blockchain Technologies

Nikos Fotiou$^{(\boxtimes)}$, Vasilios A. Siris, and George C. Polyzos

Mobile Multimedia Laboratory,
Department of Informatics School of Information Sciences and Technology,
Athens University of Economics and Business, 76 Patision, 10434 Athens, Greece
{fotiou,vsiris,polyzos}@aueb.gr

Abstract. Despite technological advances, most smart objects in the Internet of Things (IoT) cannot be accessed using technologies designed and developed for interacting with powerful Internet servers. IoT use cases involve devices that not only have limited resources, but also they are not always connected to the Internet and are physically exposed to tampering. In this paper, we describe the design, development, and evaluation of a smart contract-based solution that allows end-users to securely interact with smart devices. Our approach enables access control, Thing authentication, and payments in a fully decentralized setting, taking at the same time into consideration the limitations and constraints imposed by both blockchain technologies and the IoT paradigm. Our prototype implementation is based on existing technologies, i.e., Ethereum smart contracts, which makes it realistic and fundamentally secure.

Keywords: IoT · Distributed Ledger Technologies · Ethereum
Interoperability · Access control · Authentication · Payments

1 Introduction

The Internet of Things (IoT) is an emerging paradigm that has already attracted the attention of both academia and industry. The IoT is expected to penetrate various aspects of our life, allowing the creation of cyber-physical applications that will improve our living conditions by enabling healthier and cheaper agricultural products, smarter energy production and consumption, safer transportation, better entertainment and wellness activities, and innovative services. The IoT will be composed of smart devices and protocols that will allow human-to-device and device-to-device interactions. Nevertheless, these devices–henceforth simply referred to as Things–as well as the mainstream IoT use cases, present some limitations and particularities that create the need for new, innovative interaction protocols. In particular, Things will be far less powerful than traditional Internet clients and servers. Furthermore, Things will not always be

© Springer Nature Switzerland AG 2018
G. Wang et al. (Eds.): SpaCCS 2018, LNCS 11342, pp. 443–452, 2018.
https://doi.org/10.1007/978-3-030-05345-1_38

connected to the Internet, e.g., in order to preserve energy or because they will be physically located in places where Internet access is not possible (at times). Finally, it should be easier for a malicious user to tamper with a Thing, hence Things should not be used for storing "important" secrets or for processing very sensitive information. To this end, in this paper we design, implement and evaluate a solution that enables secure interaction with the IoT by leveraging blockchain technologies and smart contracts.

A blockchain is an append-only ledger of transactions distributed throughout a network. Transactions are validated by a number of network nodes and are added in the ledger upon consensus, assuring this way that no single entity has control over the ledger. A smart contract is a distributed application that lives in the blockchain. Users can interact with a smart contract by sending transactions to its "address" in the blockchain. For any interaction with a smart contract, all operations are executed by the blockchain, in a deterministic and reliable way. Smart contracts can verify blockchain user identities and digital signatures and they can perform a number of operations. The code of a smart contract is immutable and it cannot be modified even by its owner/creator. Moreover, all transactions sent to a contract are recorded in the blockchain.

Although, blockchains and smart contracts–henceforth simply referred to as Distributed Ledger Technologies (DLTs)–are considered a "democratic" way for maintaining transactions [2] and are envisioned to provide novel security mechanisms [7], they have some properties that limit their (direct) applicability in the context of the IoT. Firstly, interacting with a DLT involves some computationally intensive security operations (e.g., the creation of a digital signature). Secondly, DLTs require users to maintain a private key: this key is an important secret that protects the assets of the users stored in the blockchain. Thirdly, information stored in smart contracts is public, hence smart contracts cannot be used for storing, e.g., user credentials, access control policies, etc. Similarly, information stored in smart contracts is immutable and all interactions with a smart contract are recorded in the blockchain, hence it is trivial for a third party to deduce, for example, all modifications to an access control policy. Finally, smart contracts cannot directly interact with the physical world: the execution of a smart contract relies solely on information stored in the blockchain.

In this paper, we design and build a solution that allows users to securely interact with the IoT using DLTs even if Things are not connected to the Internet continuously or directly. Our solution, which is built using the Ethereum transaction ledger [10], takes into consideration the limitations and particularities of the IoT and the DLTs, is secure and realistic. With our approach we make the following contributions:

- We enable access control, Thing authentication, and payments in a decentralized, secure, and efficient way.
- We build on existing technologies and do not propose a new blockchain, neither yet another specification for smart contracts.
- We preserve end-user privacy (to the degree that it is preserved by the specific blockchain used).

– We assure that Things are oblivious to the existence of the blockchain, do not
store any blockchain-specific secret and the underlay blockchain technology
is completely transparent to the Things.

2   System Overview

Our solution leverages our previous work, published in [5], that allows a Thing
and an authorized user to establish a shared, session specific secret key; this key
can be used for securing (using symmetric encryption) all message exchanges.
This operation is achieved with the help of a third party, referred to as the
Access Control Provider. From a very high perspective, the solution described
in [5] operates as follows. ACPs maintain a user management system, as well
as access control policies, associated with a (Thing provided) resource. Furthermore, each Thing shares a unique key with each ACP that handles access to
its resources. Whenever a user requests a protected resource, the Thing generates a *token* and sends it back to the user. The token is sent in plaintext over
an unsecured communication channel: mechanisms (not detailed in this paper)
make sure that any message modification, replay and man in the middle attack
can be detected. ACPs and Things can calculate a new secret key, referred to as
the *session key* using a secure keyed-hash message authentication code (HMAC)
with inputs the shared secret key and the generated token. ACPs are responsible for authenticating users and for securely transmitting the session keys to the
authorized ones.

The solution described in [5] assures that the session keys calculated by
an ACP and a Thing are the same if (a) the user is interacting with the real
Thing, (b) the user is authorized to access the resource, (c) the user has not
lied about his identity, and (d) no messages have been modified. Otherwise, the
calculated session keys will be different, hence it will not be possible for the
user to communicate with the Thing. In other words, this solution offers Thing
and user authentication, user authorization, message integrity protection, and
session key agreement. Furthermore, this solution has two notable properties:
(a) the Thing does not have to be able to communicate with the ACP (as a
matter of fact the Thing can be completely disconnected from the rest of the
world) and (b) the ACP does not have to be aware of the services provided by
the Things, i.e., an ACP and the *service provider* can be two distinct entities.

In this work we consider a similar setup with the addition that users have to
make some form of payment (not necessarily monetary) to the service providers–
henceforth they will be simply referred to as providers–every time they interact
with a protected resource. In order to give a better overview of our system
we present the use case of a "smart coffee machine". In this use case, a smart
coffee machine is installed in a shared kitchen of a building where the offices of
many companies are located. Users interact with the coffee machine using their
mobile phones and Wi-Fi direct. The coffee machine operator has come to an
agreement with one of the companies located in that building, Company A, and
each employee of that company is offered 300 free cups of coffee per year. Every

time an employee of Company A wishes to order a coffee the following process is followed. The employee sends a request to the coffee machine, the coffee machine sends a token, the employee authenticates with the ACP of Company A[1] and receives the session key, the employee pays the coffee machine operator (the first 300 times 0.00 EUR and then with the value of the coffee), the employee sends a coffee request encrypted with the session key, and finally the coffee machine sends a receipt encrypted with the session key and disposes the coffee. All interactions among the user, the ACP, and the coffee operator (but not between the user and the coffee machine) utilize a smart contract, stored in a blockchain. Our system achieves the following:

- **Low complexity**. Coffee machines are oblivious about the existence of the blockchain and perform only some very lightweight operations. ACPs are not aware of the services the coffee machine operator offers, neither do they have to handle payments. The coffee machine operator does not have to be aware of the user management system of Company A.
- **Support for payments**. A smart contract makes sure that users have the necessary amount of money required for an order. Furthermore, the same contract makes sure that all payments are made prior to placing the order.
- **User privacy protection**. No user personal information is stored in the blockchain. Similarly, coffee machines learn nothing about users.
- **Endpoint authentication**. A smart contract makes sure that a user is authenticated and that the ACP and the coffee machine indeed share a secret key *before the user places the order*, by utilizing the session key.

Our system does not provide any guarantees for the interactions that take place in the physical world, e.g., in our use case, our system does not guarantee that the coffee machine does deliver the requested coffee. However, the interaction and payment is recorded in the blockchain (in an immutable way), which can be used as proof in court, if it comes to that.

3   System Design

3.1   Preliminaries and Notation

In our system, service providers and users own a blockchain specific public/private key pair. We refer to the public key of a user as P_{user}, and to the encryption of a message m using (the private key corresponding to) P_{user} as $E_{user}(m)$. For simplicity, we assume that an ACP knows all P_{user} of its users and all access control policies are based on these keys. ACPs, access control policies, smart contracts, and resources are identified by a URI. We refer to a URI of an entity as URI_{entity}. Smart contracts implement functions, which can

---

[1] For simple access control policies, e.g., lists of blockchain specific public keys, this authentication process can take place over the blockchain, otherwise, further information has to be exchanged using an off-chain communication channel.

be invoked using transactions, and generate events; $f(x, y, z)$ denotes the invocation of a function f with arguments x, y, z, and $E(x, y, z)$ denotes an event E with arguments x, y, z. Our system uses a keyed-hash message authentication code (HMAC), as well as a simple hash function. We refer to the digest of a message m using an HMAC function H and a key k as $H_k(m)$ and to the hash of a message m as $H(m)$. As already discussed, an ACP and a Thing end up generating a session key. We refer to this key as sk and to the encryption of a message m, using sk and a symmetric encryption algorithm as $C_{sk}(m)$. For each user P_{user} there is a cost for accessing a resource $URI_{resource}$. This cost is known to the smart contract. Similarly to users, each ACP owns a blockchain specific public/private key pair denoted by P_{ACP}.

3.2   Protocols

Set Up. The protocols described in the following assume a setup phase. During this phase, the smart contract is configured with the available $URI_{resource}$ and the corresponding URI_{policy} and P_{ACP}. For simplicity of presentation it is assumed that each $URI_{resource}$ is protected by a single URI_{policy} provided by a single P_{ACP}.

Straw Man Approach. Firstly, we present a simple protocol that implements our solution. This protocol is illustrated in Fig. 1. This protocol is based on a smart contract that provides the following methods:

- **request** (deposit, token, $URI_{resource}$): Examines if the deposit of the user suffices for accessing the resource $URI_{resource}$. If this is true, it creates a DEPOSIT event with arguments, P_{user}, token, URI_{policy}, and $URI_{resource}$.
- **authorize** (P_{user}, token, $URI_{resource}$, $E_{user}(sk)$): Transfers the deposit that the user P_{user} made (when she invoked the request method) to the service provider. Then it creates a KEY event using the method input parameters as arguments.

With this protocol, initially, a user P_{user} requests a protected resource from a Thing and the Thing responds with a token (generated using the process described in [5]) and the URI of a smart contract that protects the requested resource. Then, the user invokes the *request* method of the smart contract. The DEPOSIT event is broadcast and received by the appropriate ACP which examines if P_{user} can be authorized to access $URI_{resource}$. If this is true, the ACP generates the session key sk (using the process described in [5]), encrypts it using P_{user}, and invokes the *authorize* method of the smart contract. The smart contract examines if the ACP that invoked the *authorize* method is allowed to do so. This check is simply implemented by examining if the public key of the entity that invoked that method is equal to the P_{ACP} of the legitimate ACP.

The drawback of the straw man approach is that the payment to the provider takes place without any check. Note that with the solution described in [5], the user is able to perform certain verifications *after* trying to use the received sk.

However, with the straw man approach, these verifications can only be used for a dispute resolution.

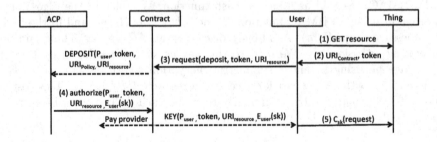

Fig. 1. The straw man protocol.

A First Construction. We now present an improvement to the straw man approach by allowing an ACP to verify that a user is communicating with a legitimate Thing (Fig. 2). In order to achieve this goal, we extend the *request* method of the smart contract to include an additional field, i.e., $H_{sk}(token)$. The value for this field is provided by the Thing, in its response to a user request. Furthermore, we extend the DEPOSIT event to include this field. Now an ACP, after generating the sk, calculates $H_{sk}(token)$, and checks if the value of the latter calculation is equal to the value provided by the Thing. If this is true, then the Thing is considered legitimate.

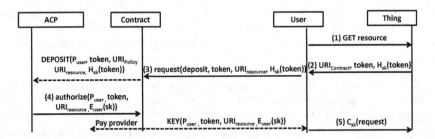

Fig. 2. Our first construction.

A Second Construction. We now extend our previous construction to enable smart contracts to verify the relationship between a Thing and an ACP, i.e., the contract can verify that the Thing and the ACP indeed share a secret key. This functionality is achieved by having the user "challenging" the Thing during her request. The *challenge* used is a random number, which the Thing should obfuscate in a way that only an ACP that shares a secret key with the Thing could read. The smart contract should therefore learn the challenge from the user and should expect it from the ACP. In order to "hide" the challenge we leverage a hash function using the process described below.

The Thing responds to a challenge with $H(H_{sk}(challenge))$. Given a challenge, only an entity that can generate the session key sk can calculate $H_{sk}(challenge)$. Note that, in addition to the Thing, this key can be calculated by the ACP that protects the resources stored in that Thing. Furthermore, given $H_{sk}(challenge)$ any entity, including the smart contract, can easily calculate $H(H_{sk}(challenge))$ (but the reverse process is not possible due to the properties of the hash functions). Hence, the *request* method is extended to include $H(H_{sk}(challenge))$ and the *authorize* method is extended to include $H_{sk}(challenge)$. Then, the smart contract can calculate the hash $H_{sk}(challenge)$, received by the ACP, and compare the output to the hash value it received from the user. If both hash outputs are the same, the contract sends the KEY event (Fig. 3).

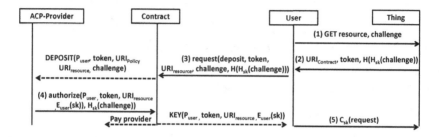

Fig. 3. Our second construction.

4   Implementation and Evaluation

We have implemented the presented solution using Ethereum smart contracts.[2] This technology has some limitations that have led us to certain design choices. In particular, although each user in Ethereum owns a public/private key pair, a smart contract has access only to each user's "address", i.e., the last 20 bytes of the hash of her public key. This means that users have to explicitly include their public keys with every smart contract function invocation; in our implementation we have added an additional field in each function which is used for storing callee's public key. Furthermore, Ethereum keys are constructed using the secp256k1 elliptic curve; encrypting content using this curve can be cumbersome since specialized constructions, such as the elliptic curve integrated

---

[2] Source code of our implementation can be found at: https://github.com/SOFIE-project/spiot.

encryption scheme [9], are required. For these reasons we have selected to not use Ethereum's keys in our constructions, but instead we are using keys based on the Curve25519 elliptic curve [1]. Curve25519 is a well supported, fast curve which is ideal for key establishment, as it allows a user A to generate a symmetric encryption key that can be used for communicating with a user B, using only $B's$ public key.

The main constructions of our smart contract, which is deployed in a local testbed, are implemented in five functions: $requestS()$, $request1()$, $request2()$, each implementing the $request()$ method for our three protocols (straw man, first construction, and second construction), and $authorize1()$ and $authorize2()$, that implement the $authorize()$ method for the first two protocols and for the last protocol respectively. The table below illustrates the cost, measured in Ethereum "gas", for invoking each function (Table 1).

Table 1. Cost for invoking smart contract functions

Function	Cost measured in gas
requestS()	123.186
request1()	128.218
request2()	253.488
authorize1()	57.950
authorize2()	63.746

Endpoints are implemented using JavaScript. Interactions with the Ethereum blockchain are implemented using the Ethereum JavaScript API,[3] whereas cryptographic operations are implemented using the TweetNaCl library.[4]

5   Related Work

Prior work on blockchain-assisted access control has proposed schemes that store access control policies in the blockchain. For example, Maesa et al. [3] use the Bitcoin blockchain to store "Right Transfer Transactions", i.e., a transaction that indicates that a user is allowed to access a particular resource. These transactions are then used by "Policy Enforcement Points". Zyskind et al. [11] use the Bitcoin blockchain to store access control polices to protect personal data. Similarly, Shafagh et al. [8] store access control policies in the Bitcoin blockchain for controlling access to data produced by IoT devices. However, storing so sensitive information in the blockchain clearly constitutes a privacy and security threat. Even if we ignore the fact that blockchain should not be used for storing "secrets", the immutability of the blockchain may allow 3rd parties to deduce

---

[3] https://github.com/ethereum/web3.js/.
[4] https://tweetnacl.js.or.

information about the access patterns of a particular user, or even about the security policies of a content owner.

A growing body of work propose the use of custom blockchains in order to overcome similar challenges. For example, Dorri et al. [4] implement a custom made blockchain for a smart home application and consider per-home miners, which also act as trusted proxies for the home devices. Similarly, Ouaddah et al. [6] propose a blockchain solution that can be used for providing access control for IoT applications. Such approaches however, provided they are secure, require a critical mass of users that will adopt the proposed technology.

6   Conclusions and Future Work

In this paper we presented a solution that allows end-users to interact with IoT devices. The proposed design, which is based on DLTs, enables access control, Thing authentication, and payments, protecting at the same time end-user?? privacy. These properties are achieved without requiring Things to be capable of interacting with DLTs; instead end-users seamlessly and transparently bridge smart contracts with Things and the physical world. Our construction protects end-users from malicious Things, since it withholds payments until the relationship between a Thing and its owner is verified. Furthermore, by recording all critical information in the blockchain, our solution facilitates dispute resolution. Finally, our Ethereum-based implementation proves that our solution can be realized with existing technologies.

In our implementation, each user is using two pairs of public/private keys, one for the blockchain operations and one for encrypting the secret information of our protocol. Furthermore, these pairs are decoupled. The use of multiple, decoupled key pairs enable some interesting extensions to our system. For example, a user may use different blockchain-specific keys in each transaction avoiding this way tracking by 3rd parties. Furthermore, a user may include in a request() transaction the pubic key of another user or back-end service, e.g., an additional access control service that will forward the session key to the user only if certain conditions are met.

The use of the blockchain technology adds a layer of protection to our system against (D)DoS attacks. With our solution attackers would require to pay a fiscal cost in order to attack an ACP. Furthermore, smart contracts are replicated to multiple nodes (miners) which execute them simultaneously, providing this way redundancy to our system. Finally, since all events are broadcasted, an ACP can be easily moved (or replicated) to a new network location. It is in our future work plans to further analyze and measure this feature of the blockchain technology.

Compared to traditional Internet applications, IoT applications have a unique property: they involve interactions with the physical world. The outcomes of these interactions cannot be easily verified by the cyber world. This can be easily understood when our solution is considered: it is not easy to verify that the key provided by the Thing owner is the correct one and, even more obvious, it is not easy to verify that Things respond with a correct answer to user requests. Although blockchain technologies are a useful tool that can be used by humans to verify that all physical activities took place correctly, the interweaving of the physical and the cyber world creates challenges that cannot yet be overcome in a guaranteed secure manner using only technological means.

Acknowledgments. The research reported here has been undertaken in the context of project SOFIE (Secure Open Federation for Internet Everywhere), which has received funding from EU's Horizon 2020 programme, under grant agreement No. 779984 (and at AUEB it is managed through AUEB-RC). The authors thank Dmitrij Lagutin for his valuable comments.

References

1. Bernstein, D.J.: Curve25519: new diffie-hellman speed records. In: Yung, M., Dodis, Y., Kiayias, A., Malkin, T. (eds.) PKC 2006. LNCS, vol. 3958, pp. 207–228. Springer, Heidelberg (2006). https://doi.org/10.1007/11745853_14
2. Cohn, J., Finn, P., Nair, S., Sanjai, P.: Device democracy: saving the future of the Internet of Things. IBM Institute for Business Value (2014). http://www-01.ibm.com/common/ssi/cgi-bin/ssialias?htmlfid=GBE03620USEN. Accessed 30 Aug 2018
3. Di Francesco Maesa, D., Mori, P., Ricci, L.: Blockchain based access control. In: Chen, L.Y., Reiser, H.P. (eds.) DAIS 2017. LNCS, vol. 10320, pp. 206–220. Springer, Cham (2017). https://doi.org/10.1007/978-3-319-59665-5_15
4. Dorri, A., Kanhere, S.S., Jurdak, R., Gauravaram, P.: Blockchain for IoT security and privacy: the case study of a smart home. In: 2017 IEEE International Conference on Pervasive Computing and Communications Workshops (PerCom Workshops), pp. 618–623 (2017)
5. Fotiou, N., Kotsonis, T., Marias, G.F., Polyzos, G.C.: Access control for the Internet of Things. In: 2016 ESORICS International Workshop on Secure Internet of Things (SIoT), pp. 29–38 (2016)
6. Ouaddah, A., Abou Elkalam, A., Ait Ouahman, A.: FairAccess: a new blockchain-based access control framework for the Internet of Things. Secur. Commun. Netw. **9**(18), 5943–5964 (2015)
7. Polyzos, G.C., Fotiou, N.: Blockchain-assisted information distribution for the Internet of Things. In: Proceedings of the 2017 IEEE International Conference on Information Reuse and Integration, pp. 75–78 (2017)
8. Shafagh, H., Burkhalter, L., Hithnawi, A., Duquennoy, S.: Towards blockchain-based auditable storage and sharing of IoT data. In: Proceedings of the 2017 on Cloud Computing Security Workshop, CCSW 2017, pp. 45–50. ACM, New York (2017)
9. Shoup, V.: A proposal for an ISO standard for public key encryption. Cryptology ePrint Archive, Report 2001/112 (2001). https://eprint.iacr.org/2001/112
10. Wood, G.: Ethereum: a secure decentralised generalised transaction ledger. Ethereum Project Yellow Paper 151 (2014)
11. Zyskind, G., Nathan, O., Pentland, A.: Decentralizing privacy: using blockchain to protect personal data. In: 2015 IEEE Security and Privacy Workshops, pp. 180–184 (2015)

The 9th International Workshop on Trust, Security and Privacy for Big Data (TrustData 2018)

TrustData 2018 Organizing and Program Committees

Steering Committee

Jemal H. Abawajy	Deakin University, Australia
Isaac Agudo	University of Malaga, Spain
Jose M. Alcaraz Calero	University of the West of Scotland, UK
Jiannong Cao	Hong Kong Polytechnic University, Hong Kong
Raymond Choo	The University of Texas at San Antonio, USA
Minyi Guo	Shanghai Jiao Tong University, China
Jiankun Hu	University of New South Wales at the Australian, Australia
Konstantinos Lambrinoudakis	University of Piraeus, Greek
Jianhua Ma	Hosei University, Japan
Peter Mueller	IBM Zurich Research Laboratory, Switzerland
Indrakshi Ray	Colorado State University, USA
Bhavani Thuraisingham	The University of Texas at Dallas, USA
Guojun Wang	Guangzhou University, China
Jie Wu	Temple University, USA
Yang Xiang	Deakin University, Australia
Laurence T. Yang	Francis Xavier University, Canada
Kun Yang	University of Essex, UK
Wanlei Zhou	Deakin University, Australia

General Chairs

Qin Liu	Hunan University, China
Arun Kumar Sangaiah	VIT University, India
Wei Chang	Saint Joseph's University, USA

Program Chairs

Jiankun Hu	University of New South Wales at the Australian, Australia
Isaac Agudo	University of Malaga, Spain

Program Committee

Publicity Chairs

Weiwei Chen   Hunan University, China
Bo Ou   Hunan University, China

Webmaster

Baishuang Hu   Hunan University, China

Research on Multi-focus Image Fusion Algorithm Based on Quadtree

Senlin Wang, Junhai Zhou[✉], Qin Liu, Zheng Qin, and Panlin Hou

Hunan University, Chagnsha 410082, China
rj_zjh@hnu.edu.cn

Abstract. Most of the multi-focus fusion algorithms currently are prone to image blur and loss of detail information. This paper proposes a multi-focus fusion algorithm based on quadtree decomposition which can almost overcome the above shortcomings. The research on multi-focus fusion algorithm based on quadtree decomposition is to divide the original image into several image sub-blocks and check regional consistency for each block to obtain the optimal block of the source image, and then detect the focus area for each block to obtain the initial fused decision image. Finally, the fused decision image is subjected to perform morphological processing to obtain a final fused image. Through extensive experiments on different source images, we show that the proposed method has better adaptability.

Keywords: Quadtree · Optimal block · Regional consistency

1 Introduction

Multi-focus image fusion is to merge the images of the same scene and different focused regions into a single image with complete information. The goal is to make the merged image look sharper and improve resolution and reduce blurriness for easy recognition, and it greatly reduces the redundant information of the image [1]. At present, multi-focus image fusion has been applied in many fields, such as computer vision, remote sensing, medicine, military and so on.

The spatial domain-based fusion algorithm can fully retain the pixel information in the original image, which is easy to implement, and it has low time complexity. The simplest spatial domain fusion algorithm weights the pixels of the source image directly. The fusion image obtained by this method has low contrast. In order to improve the quality of the fusion image, a region-based fusion algorithm is proposed. However, the key to the quality of the region-based fusion algorithm is the size of the block. If the block size is too small, the accuracy of the focus area detection will be reduced. If the block is too large, some areas will contain both the focus area and the non-focus area. This will cause the merged image to not contain the complete information.

In this paper, the multi-focus image fusion in the spatial domain is studied. For the problem that the fused image of multi-focus image is not clear and easy to lose detailed information, we propose a novel idea and solution based on the quadtree decomposition algorithm which are listed as follows:

G. Wang et al. (Eds.): SpaCCS 2018, LNCS 11342, pp. 457–464, 2018.
https://doi.org/10.1007/978-3-030-05345-1_39

1. An image fusion algorithm based on quadtree is proposed. The quadruple tree decomposition of the two source images is performed to obtain the optimal block.
2. A regional consistency check is performed on the focus region for each block to obtain the final fused image.

The remaining of the paper is organized as follows. Related work is presented in Sect. 2. Section 3 introduces the model algorithm and evaluation indicators. In Sect. 4, we present our experimental results and analysis. We conclude and give some perspectives in Sect. 5.

2   Related Work

In the field of multi-focus image fusion, many people have done a lot of work. Zhang proposed a principal component analysis (PCA) algorithm [2]. The PCA fusion algorithm simply replaces the first principal component of the low-resolution image with a high-resolution image, which leads to lose some information reflecting the spectral characteristics of the first principal component of the low-resolution image. Zhang proposed an image fusion algorithm based on non-sampling discrete wavelet transform (WT) algorithm [3]. The WT algorithm decomposes the image into low-frequency and high-frequency parts. It lacks the ability to dilute the image. A fusion algorithm based on singular value decomposition (SVD) is proposed by Kurian [4]. SVD is an algorithm for feature extraction, which is easy to bring redundant information. Cai used pulse coupled neural network (PCNN) and proposed an effective fusion algorithm of multi-focus image [5]. The fused image based on LP-PCNN has uncertainties and instability in the reconstruction process. Ding proposed the improved pulse-coupled neural network (NSCT-PCNN) model [6]. Based on NSCT-PCNN image fusion, the image can be restored very well. But its time is relatively large. The model algorithm proposed in this paper can almost overcome the above shortcomings.

3   Model Algorithm

At present, the quadtree is a very important tree structure with only one root node and four child nodes for each intermediate node. Quadtrees are widely used in the field of image processing. The quadtree has a unique advantage in two-dimensional pixel positioning.

The quadtree can be used to implement the region segmentation and merging algorithm. The two-dimensional space is divided into four quadrants or regions by recursive splitting to realize the square or rectangular region division of the two-dimensional space. Quadtree decomposition is an image analysis method. The original image is divided into several image sub-blocks by recursive splitting. The pixel consistency in these sub-blocks is greater than the consistency of the image itself. Quadtree decomposition requires that the length and width of the image be an integer power of two. The decomposition model of the quadtree is shown in Fig. 1.

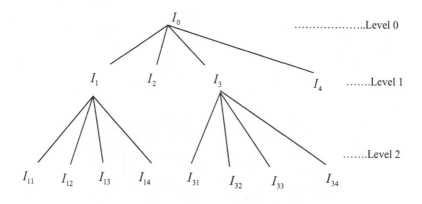

Fig. 1. The decomposition model of the quadtree.

3.1 Fusion Algorithm

Firstly, the source image is divided into four sub-blocks. If the image sub-blocks do not meet regional conformance criteria, they will continue to be partitioned until regional conformance criteria are met. And then, detect the focus area for each block to obtain the initial fused decision image and the fused decision image is subjected to perform morphological processing to obtain a final fused image. The detailed steps are as follows:

Step1: Decompose the two source images of A and B through a quadtree.
Step2: Detect the focus area for each block to obtain the initial fused decision matrix by using pixel-based focus metrics. And perform morphological processing of the initial decision matrix to obtain the final decision matrix.
Step3: Fuse images of A and B through the final decision matrix.

3.2 Regional Conformance Standards

Regional consistency standards is a key element in image region segmentation [9] and it directly affect the effect of image region segmentation. Common regional conformance standards which includes using the maximum grayscale difference in the region to measure the similarity of pixels in the image region, and if the consistency of the region is not satisfied, the decomposition is continued until the consistency check is satisfied.

In this paper, the image gradient energy (EOG) [10] is used to measure the similarity of the pixels in the image region. If the difference between the gradient energy in the region is less than T, the decomposition is no longer performed. In this paper, the threshold T is equal to 0.5. In order to prevent infinite decomposition, the area of the divided block is not decomposed when it is less than 1/m*n. The image of flower and quadtree decomposition image is shown in Fig. 2.

$$\begin{cases} EOG(i,j) = \displaystyle\sum_{m=-(M-1)/2}^{(M-1)/2} \sum_{n=-(N-1)/2}^{(N-1)/2} (I_{i+m}^2 + I_{j+n}^2) \\ I_{i+m} = I(i+m+1,j) - I(i+m,j) \\ I_{j+n} = I(i,j+n+1) - I(i,j+n) \end{cases} \tag{1}$$

Fig. 2. The image of flower and quadtree decomposition image.

3.3 Fusion Rules

There are two source images of A and B. Firstly, we construct an initial decision matrix H. The method of detecting the focus of an image using NSML is as follows:

$$H^U(i,j) = \begin{cases} 1, & EOG_{(i,j)}^{U_A} \geq EOG_{(i,j)}^{U_B} \\ 0, & otherwise \end{cases} \tag{2}$$

$EOG_{(i,j)}^{U_A}$ and $EOG_{(i,j)}^{U_B}$ respectively represent the EOG value of the current pixel (x, y) obtained by the source images of A and B after being decomposed by the quadtree. When H(x, y) equals to one, the current position (x, y) of the source image of A is the focus point. Otherwise, the current position (x, y) of the source image of A is the focus point.

Through the EOG measurement method, it is impossible to detect all the focus points. In order to solve the problem that there may be small isolated areas with small area in the focus area, we use a small area filter to fill a small area in the focus area. Assuming that the size of the image is M × N, then we define a region smaller than (M × N)/50 as a small region. Finally, the final decision diagram H′(x, y) is obtained.

In order to verify the effectiveness of the method, experiments has been carried out on four pairs of focused images. The images selected in this paper have been pre-processed. The computer used in the experiment is equipped with Intel i7-6500U processor and 4G memory, and the experiment tool is Matlab2015a.

3.4 Evaluation Indicators

We compare our method with existing methods, which including wavelet transform, principal component analysis, NSCT-PCNN, singular value decomposition, and LP-PCNN. We have selected average gradient (AG), spatial frequency (SF), mutual information (MI), and running time are our evaluation criteria.

- Average gradient (AG)
  The larger the average gradient, the fused image clearer it is.
- Spatial frequency (SF)
  The larger the spatial frequency, the better quality of the fused image is.
- Mutual Information (MI)
  The larger the mutual information, the better quality of the fused image is.

4   Experimental Results and Analysis

From the Figs. 3, 4, 5 and 6 we can see that the singular value decomposition [7], wavelet transform [8], PCA fused image will appear obvious blur and artifacts. From the Fig. 7, we can see that using singular value decomposition, wavelet transform, PCA, LP-PCNN and NSCT-PCNN will have some residual in the local area. The method of this paper can extract more of the focus area of the image without introducing artifacts.

Fig. 3. The fused image of clock obtained by the method of PCA (a), WT (b), SVD (c), LP-PCNN (d), NSCT-PCNN (e) and proposed (f).

Fig. 4. The fused image of flower obtained by the method of PCA (a), WT (b), SVD (c), LP-PCNN (d), NSCT-PCNN (e) and proposed (f).

Fig. 5. The fused image of book obtained by the method of PCA (a), WT (b), SVD (c), LP-PCNN (d), NSCT-PCNN (e) and proposed (f).

Fig. 6. The fused image of lab obtained by the method of PCA (a), WT (b), SVD (c), LP-PCNN (d), NSCT-PCNN (e) and proposed (f).

Fig. 7. The difference between the merged image of lab and the left focus source image of lab by the method of PCA (a), WT (b), SVD (c), LP-PCNN (d), NSCT-PCNN (e) and proposed (f).

Tables 1, 2, 3 and 4 and Fig. 8 show the evaluation indexes and running times of the fused images obtained by each method. In the experiment of flower image, our algorithm is 17% to 46% higher than that of the PCA, WT and SVD algorithm in the AG index, 52% to 62% higher than that of the PCA SVD, WT and SVD algorithm in the MI index, and 20% to 57% higher than that of the PCA, WT and algorithm in the SF index, although our run time is longer than these algorithms. We can see that the methods using LP-PCNN and NSCT-PCNN are not much different with our method. But their algorithms run far longer than we do.

Table 1. The performance comparison of clock image.

Method	AG	MI	SF	Time
PCA	2.6125	4.7367	5.9771	0.220213
WT	2.8065	4.5813	6.3942	0.255930
SVD	3.3934	5.1189	7.7270	0.6630
LP-PCNN	3.6029	6.3677	9.3077	59.677473
NSCT-PCNN	3.8995	5.1862	9.3352	201.560634
Proposed	3.779	6.7750	9.3150	1.469910

Table 2. The performance comparison of flower image.

Method	AG	MI	SF	Time
PCA	5.0770	4.1204	11.2137	0.172834
WT	5.6687	4.1883	12.5547	0.381235
SVD	6.2181	4.4219	13.9275	1.2273
LP-PCNN	7.7720	6.4846	17.7349	69.173710
NSCT-PCNN	7.3646	6.4681	16.72419	350.531832
Proposed	7.3509	6.7593	16.8495	2.576908

Table 3. The performance comparison of book image.

Method	AG	MI	SF	Time
PCA	5.2595	4.2962	14.8833	0.153810
WT	5.6862	4.3075	15.9476	2.068909
SVD	7.2176	5.0513	20.3372	1.1888
LP-PCNN	8.2578	6.6316	25.4773	62.973563
NSCT-PCNN	8.5049	5.3992	25.7212	353.427193
Proposed	8.3828	6.8888	25.7804	2.553315

Table 4. The performance comparison of lab image.

Method	AG	MI	SF	Time
PCA	2.7380	4.9369	7.7416	0.220213
WT	3.0218	4.7913	8.4042	0.369846
SVD	3.5969	5.5469	10.485	0.8310
LP-PCNN	4.6771	6.3172	12.9685	60.791892
NSCT-PCNN	4.4967	5.1938	12.9384	251.709319
Proposed	4.4016	6.4429	12.9839	1.445249

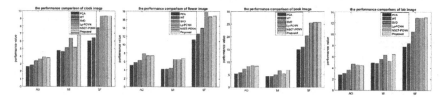

Fig. 8. The performance comparison of clock image, flower image, book image, and lab image

The image fusion algorithm based on PCA simply replaces the first principal component of the low-resolution image with a high-resolution image, thus losing some information reflecting the spectral characteristics of the first principal component of the low-resolution image and blurring the image in some areas. The insufficiency of image fusion based on wavelet transform is that wavelet transform has three high-frequency sub-bands of horizontal, vertical and diagonal. But it is difficult to reflect the singular lines of lines and faces, and it lacks the ability to dilute natural images. Therefore, it is difficult to restore all the information of the image by using the wavelet transform. The image fusion based on SVD is an image adaptive transform, it transforms the matrix of the given image into product USVT, which allows to refactor a digital image into three matrices called tensors. So it is easy to bring redundant information. The image fusion based on LP-PCNN transform has uncertainties and instability in the reconstruction process, which may lead to the blurring of the fusion result, and the time expenditure of PCNN is large. Based on NSCT-PCNN transform image fusion, NSCT uses a non-downsampled pyramid and a non-downsampled direction filter bank to perform multi-scale, multi-directional decomposition of the image. Although it can restore images very well, its time overhead is relatively large.

5   Conclusions

In this paper, based on the quadtree decomposition algorithm, multi-focus image fusion is performed. And a new detection standard is proposed in the detection of focus area, which is based on image gradient energy detection. Experiments have been carried out with "clock", "flower", "book" and "lab" source images. The proposed method has a clear advantage in quality compared to PCA, WT and SVD, although the running time is longer than the three methods. The proposed method achieves a slight advantage in quality compared to LP-PCNN and NSCT-PCNN, but the running time is much smaller than the two methods. The effectiveness of the proposed method in obtaining multi-focus images is illustrated. Experiments show that the method has better adaptability. The main disadvantage of this paper is that the algorithm has higher time complexity, resulting in longer running time. In the future, our main job is to optimize the algorithm, so that it can reduce the time complexity of the algorithm and get a better fusion effect.

Acknowledgements. This work is partially supported by the National Science Foundation of China under Grant Nos. 61872133, 61472131, 61772191.

References

1. Liu, Y., Chen, X., Ward, R.K.: Image fusion with convolutional sparse representation. IEEE Signal Process. Lett. **23**(12), 1882–1886 (2016)
2. Zhang, Y., Chen, L., Zhao, Z.: Multi-focus image fusion based on robust principal component analysis and pulse-coupled neural network. Int. J. Light Electron Opt. **125**(17), 5002–5006 (2014)
3. Zhang, X., Li, X., Feng, Y.: Image fusion based on simultaneous empirical wavelet transform. Multimed. Tools Appl. **76**(6), 1–19 (2017)
4. Kurian, A.P., Bijitha, S.R., Mohan, L.: Performance evaluation of modified SVD based image fusion. Int. J. Comput. Appl. **58**(12), 38 (2012)
5. Cai, M., Yang, J., Cai, G.: Multi-focus image fusion algorithm using LP transformation and PCNN. In: 6th IEEE International Conference on Software Engineering and Service Science, pp. 237–241. IEEE, Beijing (2015)
6. Ding, S., Zhao, X., Xu, H.: NSCT-PCNN image fusion based on image gradient motivation. IET Comput. Vis. **12**(4), 377–383 (2018)
7. Bai, B., Li, F., Shen, Q.: Image fusion via nonlocal sparse K-SVD dictionary learning. Appl. Opt. **55**(7), 1814 (2016)
8. Xu, X., Wang, Y., Chen, S.: Medical image fusion using discrete fractional wavelet transform. Biomed. Signal Process. Control **27**(3), 103–111 (2016)
9. Liu, Z., Li, X., Luo, P.: Semantic image segmentation via deep parsing network. In: 2015 IEEE International Conference on Computer Vision, pp. 1377–1385. IEEE, Santiago (2015)
10. Lee, K., Ji, S.: Multi-focus image fusion using energy of image gradient and gradual boundary smoothing. In: TENCON 2015–2015 IEEE Region 10 Conference, pp. 1–4. IEEE, Macao (2016)

Uncertainty Evaluation for Big Data of Mass Standards in a Key Comparison

Xiaoping Ren[1,2(✉)], Fang Nan[1], and Jian Wang[2]

[1] National Center for Science and Technology Evaluation, Beijing 100081, People's Republic of China
renxiaoping@ncste.org
[2] National Institute of Metrology, Beijing 100029, People's Republic of China

Abstract. This paper describes a key comparison of mass standards APMP.M.M-K5, conducted between nineteen participating members of the Asia-Pacific Metrology Programme (APMP). The application of the Monte Carlo method is used in the processing of the measurement result of APMP.M.M-K5, which is a kind of big data set. Monte Carlo method can get over the limitations that apply in certain cases to the method described in GUM.

Keywords: Big data · Monte Carlo method · Key comparison
Reference value · Degree of equivalence

1 Introduction

The APMP.M.M-K5 comparison was launched during the 13th meeting of the Technical Committee for Mass and Related Quantities APMP-TCM (2012). Two sets of stainless steel weights with five nominal mass values: 2 kg, 200 g, 50 g, 1 g, and 200 mg were used as travelling standards. Due to that nineteen participants have been divided into five petals and the corresponding five sets of transfer standards have been circulated within the groups simultaneously. The final measurement results are a big data set. We need to find a possible solving method to process the data and establish a RV and the degrees of equivalences for all the participants.

Many reports and papers have been written on methods for establishing the KCRV for a CIPM key comparison, like: CCM.M.K1 [1], CCM.M.K2 [2], CCM.M.K3 [3], CCM.M.K4 [4], CCM.M.K5 [5], CCM.M.K6 [6], CCM.M.K7 [7].

However, the key comparison may occur [8]: some or all of the measurements are mutually dependent, or the travelling standard is not stable enough. We can know that many CIPM key comparisons are not simple; reference [9] does not apply to CIPM key comparisons at some situations. That's why researchers intend to develop further guidelines to cover these complications, and the Monte Carlo method (MCM) is used to overcome these limitations.

Among all the key comparisons [10], only CCM.M.K6 and CCM.M.K7 was evaluated based on Monte Carlo method (MCM). Xiaoping Ren used Monte Carlo method to re-analyze the measurement result of CCM.M-K1 [8], CCM.M-K5 [11], comparison and APMP.M.M-K1 [10]. Risk software and LabVIEW software were

G. Wang et al. (Eds.): SpaCCS 2018, LNCS 11342, pp. 465–471, 2018.
https://doi.org/10.1007/978-3-030-05345-1_40

used respectively. Besides, there are software applications that have been specifically developed for calculating uncertainties based on MCM method, like @RISK [12] and toolbox in MATLAB [13]. This kind of method and software has been proved effective.

In this paper, a Monte Carlo method was adopted to evaluate the uncertainty of big data of Mass Standards measurement in APMP.M.M-K5 comparison.

2 Numerical Simulation by Monte Carlo Method

2.1 Basic Principle

In order to estimate the RV for this comparison (m_{RV}), the mass differences (D_i) between participants and RV, and the mass differences ($d_{i,j}$) between any pair of participating laboratories, numerical simulation based on MCM was adopted.

The differences between mass reported by the participant laboratories and the RV were calculated as follows,

$$D_i = diffm_{i,PL} - m_{RV} \tag{1}$$

In order to calculate the DoE for any pair of participant laboratories, the mass differences between two laboratories, were calculated as follows,

$$d_{i,j} = diffm_{i,PL} - diffm_{j,PL} \tag{2}$$

Due to the inconsistencies found in the reported data and in order to consider relevant correlations, the RV was determined by using the median in combination with the Monte Carlo method as recommended by Cox [9]. The method to compute the value of $m_{RV}, diffm_{i,PL}, \varepsilon_{drift}$ and ε_{reprod} can be find in [14].

2.2 Input Quantities for Monte Carlo Method

The input quantities for the numerical simulation are listed in Table 1, where $N(\mu, \sigma^2)$ means normal distribution and $U(a,b)$ means uniform distribution, besides, a and b are lower limit and upper limit respectively.

The pilot laboratory measured two sets of travelling standards. The correlation coefficient between mass measurements done by the same laboratory was considered as $r(m_{NIM,i}, m_{NIM,j}) = 0.3$ for any pair of them. The correlation coefficient indicated above, was estimated as 0.3 due to the fact that the variance contribution of the type B uncertainty is around 30% with regard to the variance of the travelling standard estimated by the pilot laboratory [7].

The results $m_{NIM-i}(i = 1, 2, \ldots, 10)$ are correlated with the correlation matrix:

Table 1. Input quantities for the numerical simulation (200 g)

Xi	Distribution	Expectation	Stand. dev.	Expectation	Semi-width
		μ	σ	$(a + b)/2$	$(a - b)/2$
$m_{\text{NIM-1}}$	$N(\mu,\sigma^2)$	0.1842	0.0059	/	/
$m_{\text{NML-Phil}}$	$N(\mu,\sigma^2)$	0.1350	0.0353	/	/
m_{MSL}	$N(\mu,\sigma^2)$	0.1768	0.0040	/	/
m_{MASM}	$N(\mu,\sigma^2)$	0.1745	0.0099	/	/
$m_{\text{NIM-2}}$	$N(\mu,\sigma^2)$	0.0738	0.0059	/	/
$m_{\text{NIM-3}}$	$N(\mu,\sigma^2)$	0.2004	0.0059	/	/
m_{VMI}	$N(\mu,\sigma^2)$	0.1935	0.0156	/	/
m_{SCL}	$N(\mu,\sigma^2)$	0.1900	0.0212	/	/
m_{ITRI}	$N(\mu,\sigma^2)$	0.1583	0.0044	/	/
m_{KRISS}	$N(\mu,\sigma^2)$	0.1925	0.0031	/	/
$m_{\text{NIM-4}}$	$N(\mu,\sigma^2)$	0.1915	0.0059	/	/
$m_{\text{NIM-5}}$	$N(\mu,\sigma^2)$	0.2020	0.0059	/	/
$m_{\text{RCM LIPI}}$	$N(\mu,\sigma^2)$	0.1600	0.0064	/	/
m_{NMIA}	$N(\mu,\sigma^2)$	0.2060	0.0078	/	/
m_{NISIT}	$N(\mu,\sigma^2)$	0.0100	0.0708	/	/
m_{NMIM}	$N(\mu,\sigma^2)$	0.2015	0.0219	/	/
$m_{\text{NIM-6}}$	$N(\mu,\sigma^2)$	0.1958	0.0059	/	/
$m_{\text{NIM-7}}$	$N(\mu,\sigma^2)$	0.1972	0.0059	/	/
$m_{\text{NMC/A-STAR}}$	$N(\mu,\sigma^2)$	0.1900	0.0071	/	/
m_{MUSSD}	$N(\mu,\sigma^2)$	0.2270	0.0236	/	/
m_{NPLi}	$N(\mu,\sigma^2)$	0.2070	0.0141	/	/
m_{NIS}	$N(\mu,\sigma^2)$	0.1535	0.0038	/	/
$m_{\text{NIM-8}}$	$N(\mu,\sigma^2)$	0.1868	0.0059	/	/
$m_{\text{NIM-9}}$	$N(\mu,\sigma^2)$	0.2052	0.0059	/	/
$m_{\text{NML-BSTI}}$	$N(\mu,\sigma^2)$	0.1880	0.0332	/	/
m_{NIMT}	$N(\mu,\sigma^2)$	0.1850	0.0141	/	/
m_{NMIJ}	$N(\mu,\sigma^2)$	0.1915	0.0035	/	/
$m_{\text{NIM-10}}$	$N(\mu,\sigma^2)$	0.1956	0.0059	/	/
ε_{drift1}	$U(a,b)$	/	/	0	0.0030
ε_{drift2}	$U(a,b)$	/	/	0	0.0026
ε_{drift3}	$U(a,b)$	/	/	0	0.0018
ε_{drift4}	$U(a,b)$	/	/	0	0.0030
ε_{drift5}	$U(a,b)$	/	/	0	0.0028
$\varepsilon_{reprod1}$	$U(a,b)$	/	/	0	0.0018

$$r(m_{\text{NIM},i}, m_{\text{NIM},i}) = \begin{pmatrix} 1 & 0.3 & 0.3 & 0.3 & 0.3 & 0.3 & 0.3 & 0.3 & 0.3 & 0.3 \\ 0.3 & 1 & 0.3 & 0.3 & 0.3 & 0.3 & 0.3 & 0.3 & 0.3 & 0.3 \\ 0.3 & 0.3 & 1 & 0.3 & 0.3 & 0.3 & 0.3 & 0.3 & 0.3 & 0.3 \\ 0.3 & 0.3 & 0.3 & 1 & 0.3 & 0.3 & 0.3 & 0.3 & 0.3 & 0.3 \\ 0.3 & 0.3 & 0.3 & 0.3 & 1 & 0.3 & 0.3 & 0.3 & 0.3 & 0.3 \\ 0.3 & 0.3 & 0.3 & 0.3 & 0.3 & 1 & 0.3 & 0.3 & 0.3 & 0.3 \\ 0.3 & 0.3 & 0.3 & 0.3 & 0.3 & 0.3 & 1 & 0.3 & 0.3 & 0.3 \\ 0.3 & 0.3 & 0.3 & 0.3 & 0.3 & 0.3 & 0.3 & 1 & 0.3 & 0.3 \\ 0.3 & 0.3 & 0.3 & 0.3 & 0.3 & 0.3 & 0.3 & 0.3 & 1 & 0.3 \\ 0.3 & 0.3 & 0.3 & 0.3 & 0.3 & 0.3 & 0.3 & 0.3 & 0.3 & 1 \end{pmatrix} \tag{3}$$

All the other input quantities are considered to be uncorrelated.

The DoE (Degree of Equivalence) is the degree to which the measured value of a participant is consistent with the RV. This is expressed by the deviation D_i from the RV and the expanded uncertainty of this deviation compared at the 95% level of confidence. The criteria for the equivalence is: if DoE < 1, then the measurement result is equivalent; if DoE $\geq$ 1, then the result is not equivalent.

DoE were estimated in each step of MCM by the following equation, which can give a normalized value for the DoE.

$$D_i = mean\{\Delta m_i - \Delta m_{RV}\} \tag{4}$$

$$DoE_i = \frac{|D_i|}{2 \cdot u_{D_i}} \tag{5}$$

where, i is index of participants, u_{D_i} denotes the standard uncertainty of D_i.

3 Simulation Result

Table 2 shows the mean of RV, its standard uncertainty, and the shortest 95% coverage interval obtained from 1×10^5 iterations. Figure 1 give out histogram resulting from simulation corresponding to the RV.

Table 2. Data of the median resulting of numerical simulation for 200 mg weight

Measurement results	Values
m_{RV} (mg)	−0.0019
$u(m_{RV})$ (mg)	0.0031
$U(m_{RV})$, $k = 2$ (mg)	0.0062
$P[x_1, x_2]$ (mg)	[−0.0086, 0.0038]

Figure 2 shows the results of numerical simulations for DoE, the mass difference between RV. Besides, from the histogram, the probability density function for each physical quantity can be derived.

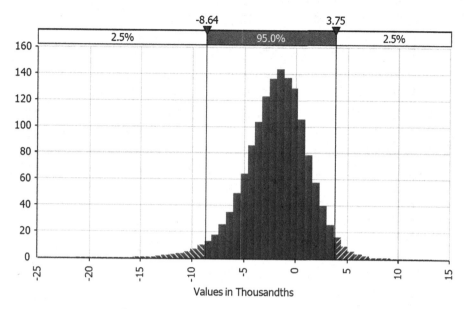

Fig. 1. The histograms of RV for 200 g standard

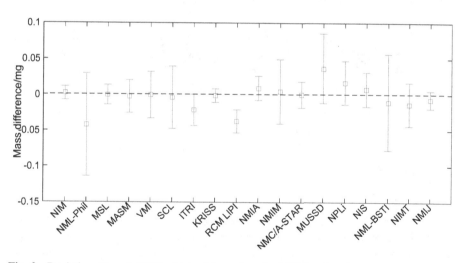

Fig. 2. Deviation D_i and $U(D_i)$ obtained by using the MCM estimation with the travelling standards as the RV.

Histograms resulting from numerical simulation for DoE between NMIs and RV, are shown in Fig. 3.

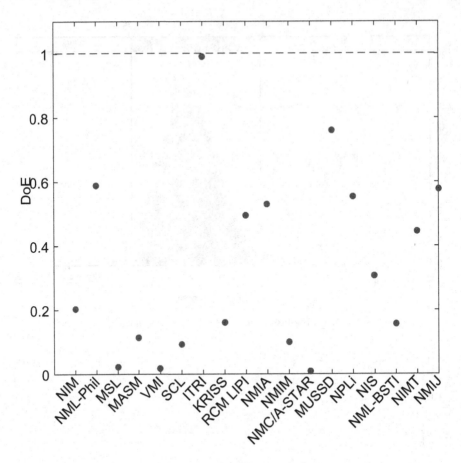

Fig. 3. DoE for 200 g standards

4 Conclusion

The paper presented the analysis procedure and results of APMP.M.M-K5, a RMO comparison of 2 kg, 200 g, 50 g, 1 g and 200 mg stainless steel mass standards, based on Monte Carlo method. This method was adopt to evaluate the measurement uncertainty for big data of mass standards in a APMP.M.M-K5 key comparison. This method was developed to overcome some of the limitations of the GUM, especially when an interval of confidence with a stipulated coverage probability is needed.

Acknowledgments. The grants that have been received from the National Key R&D Program of China (2016YFF0200102).

References

1. Aupetit, C., Becerra, L.O., Bignell, N., et al.: Final report on CIPM key comparison of 1 kg standards in stainless steel. Metrol. Tech. Suppl. **41**, 1–31 (2004)
2. Becerra, L.O., Bich, W., et al.: Final report on CIPM key comparison of multiples and submultiples of the kilogram (CCM.M-K2). Metrologia **40**(1A), 1–27 (2003)
3. Gosset, A., Madec, T.: Final report: CCM.M-K3 comparison/50 kg mass. Metrologia **42**, 1–19 (2005)
4. Becerra, L.O., Borys, M., et al.: Key comparison of 1 kg stainless steel mass standards CCM.M-K4. Metrologia **51**, 1–22 (2014)
5. Andel, I.V., Becerra, L.O., et al.: Report on CIPM key comparison of the second phase of multiples and submultiples of the kilogram (CCM.M-K5). Metrologia **48**, 1–40 (2011)
6. Abbott, P.J., Becerra, L.O., et al.: Final report of CCM key comparison of mass standards CCM.M-K6, 50 kg. Metrologia **52**, 1–24 (2015)
7. Lee, S.J., Borys, M., et al.: The final report for CCM.M-K7: key comparison of 5 kg, 100 g, 10 g, 5 g and 500 mg stainless steel mass standards. Metrologia **54**, 1–23 (2017)
8. Cai, C., Ren, X., Hao, G., Wang, J., Huang, T.: Statistical analysis of CCM.M-K1 international comparison based on Monte Carlo method. In: Carretero, J., et al. (eds.) ICA3PP 2016. LNCS, vol. 10049, pp. 146–155. Springer, Cham (2016). https://doi.org/10.1007/978-3-319-49956-7_12
9. Cox, M.G.: The evaluation of key comparison data. Metrologia **39**, 589–595 (2002)
10. Ren, X.P., Wang, J., Wang, X.L., Dong, Y., Yang F.: Evaluation of APMP.M.M-K1 inter-comparisons by monte carlo method. In: 36th Chinese Control Conference Proceeding, pp. 9879–9882. IEEE Press, Dalian (2017)
11. Ren, X.P., Wang, J., Wang X.L., et al.: Evaluation of measurement inter-comparison (CCM.M-K5) by Monte Carlo method. In: IMEKO International Seminar on Measurement Proceeding, pp. 160–162. IMEKO, Hangzhou (2017)
12. Sugiyama, S.: Monte carlo simulation/risk analysis on a spreadsheet: review of three software packages. Foresight **9**, 36–42 (2008)
13. Beascoa, M., et al.: Implementation in MATLAB of the adaptive monte carlo method for the evaluation of measurement uncertainties. Accred. Qual. Assur. **14**, 95–106 (2009)
14. Ren, X.P., Wang, J., Hu, M.H., et al.: APMP.M.M-K5 mass comparison based on monte carlo method. In: APMF2017, pp. 1–3. APMF, Krabi (2017)

Research on Wireless Spectrum Sensing Technology Based on Machine Learning

Heng Xiao[1(⊠)], Xianchun Zhou[1], and Yue Tian[2]

[1] Sanya University, Sanya 572022, Hainan, China
4383642@qq.com
[2] School of Information Science and Electronic Engineer, Hunan University,
Changsha 410082, Hunan, China

Abstract. In this paper, based on the spectrum sensing problem of the primary user signal in low SNR environment, an improved random forest spectrum sensing algorithm is proposed by using the advantage of strong forest classifier. The algorithm uses the mean and variance of the signal cycle spectrum with the largest extraction energy at each cycle frequency as the characteristic parameter to generate the samples in the sample set; On the basis of this, some samples in the presence of the primary user are selected as positive samples, and some samples in the absence of the primary user are used as negative samples to realize the construction of random forests; Finally, the trained random forests are used to classify the detected signals to achieve effective perception of the primary user signals. Thereby improving the perceptual performance of the main user signal in the case of low signal to noise ratio. Thereby improving the perceptual performance of the main user signal in the case of low signal to noise ratio. The experimental results show that the proposed algorithm has strong classification detection effect, can achieve spectrum sensing of the main user signal better under low SNR, and is generally suitable for solving the spectrum sensing problem of primary user signal in low SNR environment.

Keywords: Spectrum sensing · Primary user · Random forest
Decision tree

1 Introduction

With the rapid development of wireless communication technology, the demand for high transmission rate data communication is increasing, which makes the limited spectrum resources become more and more tense, which seriously restricts the further development of wireless communication technology. However, existing spectrum resources have not been fully utilized due to unreasonable distribution systems. The current resource allocation method divides the spectrum into two parts: the licensed band and the unlicensed band. Authorized frequency bands such as mobile communications and broadcast television occupy most of the spectrum resources. Compared with unlicensed bands, the licensed band can only be used by specific authorized users in a specific area. This exclusive strategy leads to a low level of utilization of spectrum resources in time and space. The fixed allocation method is the main reason for the low

© Springer Nature Switzerland AG 2018
G. Wang et al. (Eds.): SpaCCS 2018, LNCS 11342, pp. 472–479, 2018.
https://doi.org/10.1007/978-3-030-05345-1_41

utilization of spectrum resources. In order to solve this problem, cognitive radio technology based on dynamic spectrum resource allocation has become the main direction of future development of wireless communication.

In recent years, with the continuous development and maturity of machine learning theory, the application of machine learning to spectrum sensing technology has become a hot topic in spectrum sensing technology research. In wireless cognitive networks, secondary users need to perceive the surrounding wireless communication environment, and adjust their transmission parameters in time according the changes of the spectrum environment and network topology, so that they can effectively sense the primary user signal. This requires secondary users to have more intelligent sensing and adaptive capabilities, which is precisely the advantage of machine learning methods. Therefore, the use of machine learning methods to solve the cognitive network spectrum sensing problem has become a hot topic in the research of experts and scholars at home and abroad, and it has important theoretical significance.

Machine learning can be divided into supervised learning and unsupervised learning. The autonomous unsupervised learning algorithm can explore the environmental characteristics without a priori information and perform corresponding adaptive operations. It is mainly used to solve the mechanism design problems in cognitive networks, such as decision making and rule formulation. The main methods include game theory, threshold learning, and reinforcement of learning. Compared with unsupervised learning, supervised learning can be considered that secondary users need prior knowledge of knowledge when they are perceiving, and learn by using supervised learning techniques. For example, if the characteristics of the target signal waveform are known to the secondary user before sensing, the training algorithm can help the secondary user better detect signals with these characteristics. Therefore, spectrum sensing problems for primary users are often performed using supervised learning methods. At present, the machine learning methods applied to the cognitive network spectrum sensing technology mainly include artificial neural networks and support vector machines. This paper mainly uses the random forest algorithm in machine learning to solve the spectrum sensing problem of wireless network.

2 Description of the Problem

The essence of spectrum sensing technology is signal detection, which is to judge the use status of the licensed frequency band by the main user signal detection. At present, the research on spectrum sensing technology mainly involves hiding the main user problem, sensing time and reliability [8], decision fusion in collaborative sensing [4], and main user signal modulation type identification [1].

Similar to the hidden node problem in carrier sense multiple access, the hidden primary user problem is mainly caused by factors such as multipath fading and shadow fading that the secondary user has in the process of sensing the primary user signal. An interference signal is generated to the primary user receiver due to the secondary user location, which prevents the primary user signal from being detected and received by the receiver [3]. In order to overcome the problem of hidden primary users and make the cognitive network system more flexible in the design process, it is necessary for the secondary users to more effectively detect the signals of the primary users in a low SNR environment [2]. Considering that the primary user can occupy its authorized frequency band for communication at any time without having to consider the use of the frequency band by the secondary user [6], this requires the secondary user to have the ability to quickly and accurately identify the presence of the primary user in the frequency band over a certain time range. At the same time, the secondary user withdraws from the use of the frequency band, thereby avoiding interference to the primary user [5]. Therefore, how to quickly and reliably detect the main user signal in a low SNR environment to overcome the hidden main user problem is the focus of this paper.

Suppose there is one primary user and N secondary users in a wireless cognitive network. For any secondary user, the presence or absence of the primary user can be summarized into two states: the primary user signal does not exist as H_0, and the primary user signal exists as H_1. In the detection sampling time, s(t) is the primary user signal, which is the cyclostationary signal, and n(t) is the additive Gaussian white noise, the mean value is 0, and the variance is σ_n^2.

$$H_0: y(t) = n(t)$$

$$H_1: y(t) = s(t) + n(t)$$

When detecting the channel, the secondary user first receives the signal, and pre-processes the received signal to extract the characteristic parameter s(k) of the primary user signal of different modulation types, that is, the mathematical expectation E(s) and variance D(s) of the maximum energy, then generate a feature vector C as the training samples and the test samples. Next, random forest training is performed on the training samples to obtain K decision trees [7], then generate random forests, and use the trained random forest to classify and test the test samples to identify the main user signal modulation type. Finally, the result is output, and the spectrum of the main user signal is successfully perceived [9].

3   Primary User Signal Recognition Algorithm

In order to better perceive the spectrum of the primary user signals of different modulation types, this paper improves the random forest algorithm in machine learning, and uses the random forest algorithm to combine multiple weak classifiers to enhance the overall classification effect, then to improve the accuracy of spectrum sensing.

The algorithm extracts the cyclic spectrum characteristic parameters $v_1, v_2, \ldots v_n$ of the signal of the absence of the primary user multiple times, then each feature vector is $c_i = (v_1, v_2, \ldots v_n)^T$, $(i = 1, 2, \ldots n$, T is the detection sampling time of the received signal), and those feature vectors constitute a training sample G of the random forest, and then a random forest is generated. Each decision tree function in a random forest can be expressed as $y = g_k(c_i)$, k is the number of decision trees contained in the random forest, and $g_k(c)$ is the decision function of the decision tree. Through the decision tree function, the decision result of each tree can be obtained, and then the final judgment result is obtained, and the classification of the signal to be detected is completed.

In the process of spectrum sensing, there are two steps: one is the extraction of characteristic parameters from the spectrum, and the other is the construction and classification of random forests. In the process of feature extraction, considering the characteristics of the received signal, when each cycle frequency is not 0, the feature parameter data $(E(s), D(s))$ in the signal cycle spectrum with the largest energy is selected for extraction. $E(s)$ and $D(s)$ are the mean and variance of $s(t)$ obtained by discrete Fourier transform in the received signal. Then, several eigenvalues in the presence of the primary user are selected as positive samples, and several eigenvalues in the absence of the primary user are used as negative samples. This can more effectively reflect the important characteristics of the signal cycle spectrum, which is conducive to the construction of random forests and accurate perception of the primary user signals.

The algorithm is designed as follows:

(1) Each primary user signal adopts multipath transmission mode, which are independent of each other, each path has different delays, and respectively enter the subsequent modulation recognition system.

(2) Feature parameter extraction is performed on the received main user signal, a feature vector $c = (v_1, v_2, \dots vn)^t$ is generated, and then, a training sample set U is constructed.

(3) Design a training mechanism based on dynamic sample selection, filter the difference samples by multiple iterative sampling, so as to obtain samples that are beneficial to improve classification performance, and train random forest classifiers. Then construct a random forest classifier with more significant classification effect.

(4) In the node splitting of random forest decision tree, it is different from the traditional random forest splitting mode, it adopts the unbiased splitting method based on conditional probability to improve the classification performance of the classifier.

For example, in the H_1 state, it is assumed that the number of sampling points for the signal of the secondary user received is n, and $E(S)$ and $D(S)$ are calculated by every m sampling points. Supposes $c_s^i(c_s^i = (E_s^i(S), D_s^i(S))^T, s = 0,1)$ is any feature vector for this signal, then the number of feature vectors is n/m. Substitutes all the feature vectors into the trained random forest can obtain the judgment result: in this, 1 means that there is a primary user, and 0 means that there is no primary user. As a result of the statistical judgment, p1 indicates the number of judged to be 1, and p0 indicates the number of judged to be 0, and the detection rate Pd = p1/(p1 + p0) can be obtained, where p1 + p0 = n/m. Also in the H0 state, the false alarm rate is Pf = p1/(p1 + p0), where p1 + p0 = n/m.

As a result of the judgment, p1 is the number of judged to be 1, and p0 is the number of judged to be 0, and the detection rate Pd can be obtained: Pd = p1/(p1 + p0), where p1 + p0 = n/m.

Similarly, in the H_0 state, the false alarm rate Pf can be obtained: Pf = p1/(p1 + p0), where p1 + p0 = n/m.

4 Algorithm Implementation

The algorithm is designed in the case where the presence of the primary user as H_1 and the absence of the primary user as H_0. The process is as follows:

(1) The mean and variance of the signal cycle spectrum with the largest energy in each cycle frequency are extracted separately in the case of H0 and H1, respectively, and the corresponding feature vectors are generated. In the H0 state, the extracted mean and variance are $E_0(S)$, $D_0(S)$, and the feature vector is $c0 = (E_0(S), D_0(S))^T$. In the H_1 state, the extracted mean and variance are $E_1(S)$, $D_1(S)$, and the feature vector is $c1 = (E_1(S), D_1(S))^T$.

(2) For the signals received by the secondary users, N feature vectors with the presence of the primary user are collected as positive samples for the training random forest, and any one of the feature vectors can be expressed as $c_1^i = (E_1^i(S), D_1^i(S))^T$, $i = 1, 2, \ldots N$

(3) M feature vectors with the absence of the primary user are collected as negative samples for the training random forest, and any one of the feature vectors can be expressed as $c_0^i = (E_0^i(S), D_0^i(S))^T$, $i = 1, 2, \ldots M$

(4) Nc as positive samples and Mc as negative samples are randomly selected in the N positive samples and M negative samples as a training sample and use them to generate a single decision tree. In this way, a spectrum sensing decision tree of a random forest is established.

(5) Repeat step (4) to establish a random forest of K decision tree.

(6) Repeat steps (1)–(3) to generate test samples of random forests. And use the trained random forest to classify the test samples.

(7) The spectrum sensing result of the primary user signal is realized by the output result of the random forest.

Through these 7 steps, it is possible to achieve effective detection and perception of the presence of the primary user, and its perceived performance can be verified by the detection rate and the false alarm rate.

5 Experimental Analysis

Through MATLAB experiments, OFDM and 2FSK signals are selected as the primary user signals. It is assumed that there are two paths in the channel to transmit these two signals. The carrier frequency is 1 MHz, which is evenly distributed between 3.1 and 4.8 GHz. The signal-to-noise ratio is 0, −5, −10, −15, −20, −25. The sampling frequency is 500 MHz, there are 4000 sampling points, and the mean E(s) and variance D(s) of the two signals are calculated every 512 points. The OFDM signal data rate is 5 Mbps, its signal bandwidth is 5.5 MHz. The data rate of the 2FSK signal is 0.8 Mbps, and its signal bandwidth is 12.5 MHz. The experiment compares the spectrum sensing algorithm based on random forest with SVM-based and ANN-based. The number of random forest decision trees is K = 100, the number of sample categories is J = 2, the average number of single experimental training samples is 2000, the number of test samples is 200, and the number of statistical times of each experiment is 10^6 orders of magnitude.

It is found in the experiments that spectrum sensing based on random forest has a good effect on detection rate in different SNR environments. When the signal-to-noise ratio is −5 dB, the detection rate of the SVM algorithm is 0.88, the detection rate of the ANN algorithm is 0.77, and the detection rate of the random forest algorithm is 0.96, which is 8% and 19% higher than the SVM and ANN respectively. When the signal-to-noise ratio is reduced to −25 dB, the detection rate of SVM algorithm is 0.43, the detection rate of ANN algorithm is 0.31, and the detection rate of random forest algorithm is 0.72, which is 29% and 41% higher than SVM and ANN respectively. The advantage is very obvious. From the test data, as the signal-to-noise ratio decreases, the detection algorithms of each analysis algorithm are reduced. However, the detection rate based on the random forest algorithm is still significantly higher than the other two algorithms, which fully demonstrates the superiority of the algorithm in low SNR environment (Figs. 1, 2).

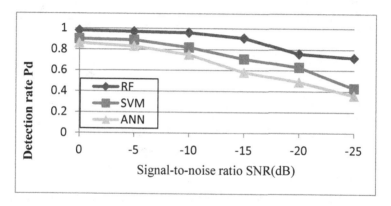

Fig. 1. The detection rate of the different algorithms for OFDM

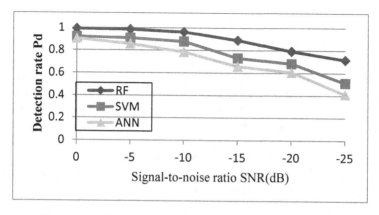

Fig. 2. The detection rate of the different algorithms for 2FSK

In terms of false alarm rate, the false alarm rate based on the random forest algorithm is significantly lower than other algorithms when there is no primary user signal. It can be seen from the data that for different noise powers, the false alarm rate of the ANN algorithm and the SVM algorithm is on the order of 10^{-4}, and the false alarm rate of the random forest algorithm is also on the order of 10^{-4}. As the noise power decreases, the false alarm rate of the random forest algorithm increases, but compares with the other two algorithms, the false alarm rate of the random forest algorithm proposed in this chapter is still significantly lower than other algorithms. This is because the random forest algorithm can extract the feature parameters more effectively under different noise powers, and use the random forest with strong classification performance to classify the generated samples, which greatly reduces the false alarm rate and obtains better results (Fig. 3).

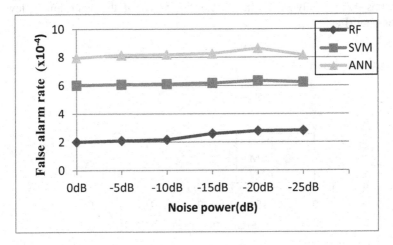

Fig. 3. The false alarm rate of different algorithms in the different nosie powers

6   Conclusion

The above results show that the spectrum sensing algorithm based on random forest has good detection performance. This is because the algorithm extracts the characteristics of the signal cycle spectrum parameters and selects the mean and variance which better reflect the characteristics of the signal cycle spectrum as the sample parameters. It effectively overcomes the shortcomings of the low detection rate of the energy detection method in the case of low signal to noise ratio. In addition, the algorithm uses a random forest with strong classification performance to classify and detect the presence or absence of the primary user, avoiding over-fitting. However, the SVM algorithm is prone to over-fitting, and the ANN algorithm is prone to the optimal solution, which will affect the detection performance. Therefore, the detection effect based on the random forest algorithm is more accurate.

Acknowledgments. This paper is funded by the following project funds: The Natural Science Foundation of Hainan Province (No. 617182, 618MS083), Sanya City Institute of Science and Technology Cooperation Project (No. 2015YD11, No. 2015YD57).

References

1. Xiao, H., Lv, S.: Efficient spectrum sensing mechanism with interference cancellation in cognitive radio network. J. Comput. Appl. **34**(5), 1243–1246 (2014)
2. Sun, S., Kadoch, M., Gong, L., et al.: Integrating network function virtualization with SDR and SDN for 4G/5G networks. IEEE Netw. **29**(3), 54–59 (2015)
3. Pourgharehkhan, Z., Taherpour, A., Sala-Alvarez, J., et al.: Correlated multiple antennas spectrum sensing under calibration uncertainty. IEEE Trans. Wirel. Commun. **14**(12), 6777–6791 (2015)
4. Xiong, G., Kishore, S., Yener, A.: Spectrum sensing in cognitive radio networks: performance evaluation and optimization. Phys. Commun. **9**, 171–183 (2013)
5. Xiao, H., Lv, S.: Parallel channel competition mechanism in wireless network based on frequency domain. Comput. Eng. **41**(8), 89–94 (2015)
6. Wang, X., Wang, J., et al.: Primary user signal recognition algorithm based on random forest in cognitive network. J. Northeast. Univ. (Nat. Sci.) **12**, 1706–1709 (2015)
7. Wang, X., Wang, J.-k., et al.: Spectrum sensing algorithm based on random forest in cognitive network. Chin. J. Sci. Instrum. **34**(11), 2471–2477 (2013)
8. Xue, M., Li, Y.: An activity recognition algorithm on smart environment based on improved random Forest algorithm. Comput. Eng. **44**(4), 1–8 (2018)
9. Wen, B., Dong, W., Xie, W., et al.: Parameter optimization method for random forest based on improved grid search algorithm. Comput. Eng. Appl. **54**(10), 154–157 (2018)

The 10th International Workshop on Security in e-Science and e-Research (ISSR 2018)

ISSR 2018 Organizing and Program Committees

Steering Committee

Guojun Wang (Chair)	Guangzhou University, China
Wei Jie (Chair)	University of West London, UK
Aniello Castiglione	University of Salerno, Italy
Liang Chen	University of West London, UK
Kim-Kwang Raymond Choo	University of Texas at San Antonio, USA
Scott Fowler	Linkoping University, Sweden
Jiankun Hu	UNSW Canberra (Australian Defence Force Academy), Australia
Georgios Kambourakis	University of the Aegean, Samos, Greece
Peter Komisarczuk	Royal Holloway, University of London, UK
Gregorio Martinez	University of Murcia, Spain
Kouichi Sakurai	Kyushu University, Japan
Sabu M. Thampi	Indian Institute of Information Technology and Management, India
Lizhe Wang	China University of Geosciences, China
Carlos Becker Westphall	Federal University of Santa Catarina, Brazil
Jeff Yan	Lancaster University, UK
Deqing Zou	Huazhong University of Science and Technology, China

General Chairs

Shaobo Zhang	Hunan University of Science and Technology, China
Entao Luo	Hunan University of Science and Engineering, China

Program Chairs

Wanlei Zhou	Deakin University, Australia
Indrakshi Ray	Colorado State University, USA

Program Committee

Marios Anagnostopoulos	Singapore University of Technology and Design, Singapore
Elena Apostol	University 'Politehnica' Bucharest, Romania
Junaid Arshad	University of West London, UK
Bruce Beckles	University of Cambridge Information Services, UK
Nik Bessis	Edge Hill University, UK
Andrea Bruno	University of Salerno, Italy
Pinial Khan Butt	Sindh Agriculture University, Pakistan
Arcangelo Castiglione	University of Salerno, Italy
Dan Chen	China Wuhan University, China
Xu Chen	Sun Yat-Sen University, China
Zesheng Chen	Indiana University - Purdue University Fort Wayne, USA
Chang Choi	Chosun University, Korea
Chao Gong	University of Mary Hardin-Baylor, USA
Ying Guo	Central South University, China
Guangjie Han	Hohai University, China
Su Xin	Hohai University, China
Wolfgang Hommel	University der Bundeswehr, Germany
Frank Jiang	University of Technology Sydney, Australia
Wenjun Jiang	Hunan University, China
Pankoo Kim	Chosun University, Korea
Hoon Ko	Sungkyunkwan University, Korea
Saru Kumari	Ch. Charan Singh University, India
Juan Li	North Dakota State University, USA
Xiong Li	Hunan University of Science and Technology, China
Jing Liao	Hunan University of Science and Technology, China
Chi Lin	Dalian University of Technology, China
Qin Liu	Hunan University, China
Sofia Anna Menesidou	Democritus University of Thrace, Greece
Francesco Palmieri	University of Salerno, Italy
Dimitrios Papamartzivanos	University of the Aegean, Greece
Raffaele Pizzolante	University of Salerno, Italy
Yizhi Ren	Hangzhou Dianzi University, China
Yupeng Wang	Shenyang Aerospace University, China
Sheng Wen	Deakin University, Australia
Sheng Wen	Swinburne University of Technology, Australia
Chao Wu	Tsinghua University, China
Ming Xu	Hangzhou Dianzi University, China

Wencheng Yang	Edith Cowan University, Australia
Congxu Zhu	Central South University, China

Publicity Chairs

Thomas Tan	Edinburgh Napier University, UK
Yang Xu	Central South University, China

Webmaster

Jiating Huang	Hunan University of Science and Technology, China

A Novel Method for Bearing Safety Detection in Urban Rail Transit Based on Deep Learning

Jie Tao[1,2(✉)], Shaobo Zhang[1], and Dalian Yang[2]

[1] School of Computer Science and Engineering,
Hunan University of Science and Technology, Xiangtan 411201, China
caroltaojie@126.com
[2] Hunan Provincial Key Laboratory of Health Maintenance for Mechanical
Equipment, Hunan University of Science and Technology,
Xiangtan 411201, China

Abstract. The double tapered roller bearing is widely used in urban rail transit, due to its complex structure, the traditional safety detection is difficult to recognize the early weak fault. In order to solve this problem, a deep learning method for safety detection of roller bearing is put forward. In the experiment, vibration signals of bearing are firstly separated into a series of intrinsic mode functions by empirical mode decomposition, then we extracted the transient energy to construct the eigenvectors. In the pattern recognition, deep learning method is used to generate the safety detector by unsupervised study. There are three states of rolling bearings in experiments, as normal, inner fault and outer fault. The results show that the proposed method is more stable and accurately to identify bearing faults, and the classification accuracy is above 98%.

Keywords: Deep learning · Roller bearing · Empirical mode decomposition
Safety detection

Double tapered roller bearing is widely used in urban rail transit, which itself has a certain axial clearance and preload, so it can support combined loads from radial and axial directions [1]. While the train is in motion, since the centrifugal force, inertia force, abnormal axial and radial forces, the components of the bearing engender collision and friction between each other, which are easily made into pitting, stripping and crack of the bearing, that would cause bearing abnormal work [2]. According to statistics, over the past two years, more than 80% of railway train accidents in China are related to bearing damage [3, 4]. Once the bearing fails, it will affect the safety of the train operation and cause the loss of properties even casualties. Therefore, the research on safety detection of double tapered roller bearing has important theoretical and practical significance.

Among all kinds of bearing safety detection methods, vibration analysis is one of the foremost and effective techniques [5]. At present, the safety detection of rolling bearing in urban rail transit is mainly based on the generalized resonance demodulation technology to judge the working state of the bearing [6]. However, when the bearing of the train is damaged, the noise in train motion is large and the working environment is complex. So the fault information is often mixed with working frequency of other parts

G. Wang et al. (Eds.): SpaCCS 2018, LNCS 11342, pp. 485–496, 2018.
https://doi.org/10.1007/978-3-030-05345-1_42

or equipment. Therefore, the generalized resonance demodulation technology is not good for the early weak safety detection of the bearing. It easily appear to misstatement and false report.

In the intelligent diagnosis, current technology mainly combine signal processing and pattern recognition [7], such as fast Fourier transform (FFT), Wavelet transforms (WT), empirical mode decomposition (EMD), time-frequency analysis and so on. However, the vibration signals are usually non-stationary and noisy, so people study many kinds methods for signal processing and feature extraction to deal with the signals. He et al. [8] proposed fault diagnosis method of urban rail train bearing based on empirical mode decomposition and support vector machine, which has achieved good diagnosis results in experiments. Liu et al. [9] put forward the intelligent diagnosis method of bearing fault based on the wavelet packet analysis of vibration signal, which proves that the method can get rid of human participation and automatically identify the bearing fault in the train. Based on the train bearing dynamics modeling, Wang et al. [10] analysis vibration signal frequency band and complete wheelset bearing fault diagnosis. Yang et al. [11] uses Laplace wavelet analysis method to effectively extract fault characteristics of locomotive bearing from impact response and identify train bearing fault. These studies have achieved some results in the fault diagnosis of the bearing of the train, but the pattern recognition method is based on the "shallow learning" algorithm. It needs to complete function fitting or data mapping [12, 13] in the model structure of one to two layers, the expression of complex functions is limited in pattern recognition, especially in the case of limited samples.

Nowadays, deep learning has become popular in the artificial intelligence and data mining [14]. As a major framework of deep learning, deep belief network (DBN) simulates the human's brain learning process and builds a hierarchical structure, which can effectively deal with high dimension data and extract the data characteristics through a successive learning process [15, 16]. Recently, deep belief network gets the preliminary application in mechanical fault diagnosis. Tamilselvan et al. [17] originally presented a novel multi-sensor diagnosis methodology which used the DBN in system health diagnosis such as aircraft engine and electric power transformer. Tran [18] presented the Teager-Kaiser energy operation to estimate the amplitude envelopes of vibration and applied the DBN to classify the faults of compressor valves. Shao et al. [19, 20] extracted some time domain features from vibrations and developed particle swarm to optimize the structure of the DBN to recognize the bearing faults. Gan et al. [21] introduced the feature extraction based on wavelet packet transform and constructed a two-layer DBN of rolling-element bearing safety detection. Li, Chen et al. [22, 23] adopt deep learning to identify the bearing fault and detect the machine operation safe. Unfortunately, these studies still need the sophistic signal processing and manual feature extraction, therefore some meaningful information about machine condition may be removed or lost.

In this study, a novel fault diagnosis is proposed by instantaneous energy of IMF and DBN for bearing safety detection. Since the instantaneous energy of IMF contain abundant information about bearing conditions, we apply the DBN to automatically learn the features from the IMF and classify the bearing faults. The remainder of this paper is organized as follows. In Sect. 1, the basic theory of deep belief network is introduced. In Sect. 2, it descript the procedure for bearing fault diagnosis based on instantaneous energy vector of IMF and DBN. In Sect. 3, a bearing test rig is explained and experiments are conducted for the proposed method. In Sect. 4, the obtained results and their evaluation are described. And conclusions and future work are given in Sect. 5.

1 Deep Learning

In 2006, Hinton etc. proposed the deep belief network (DBN), which is a generation model based on probability statistics. The core idea is to maximize the generation probability of the whole model by adjusting the weights between each node [20]. As shown in Fig. 1, DBN consists of several Restricted Boltzmann Machines (RBM), in which the output layer of one RBM is used as the next input layer of the next RBM, and is continuously stacked to form a deep network structure of the DBN.

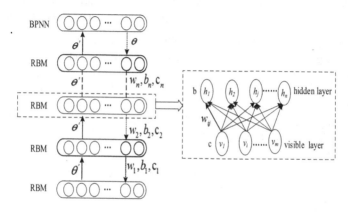

Fig. 1. The basic structure of deep belief network

In deep belief network, v_i is visible node, h_i is hidden node, v_i and h_i have full directed connection, c is bias of input layer, b is bias of output layer. w is the weight from v_i to h_i. The parameter set θ is consist of c, b and w. The energy function of RBM is defined as:

$$E(v, h, \theta) = -\sum_{i=1}^{n} c_i v_i - \sum_{j=1}^{m} b_j h_j - \sum_{i=1}^{n} \sum_{j=1}^{m} v_i w_{ij} h_j \tag{1}$$

The joint probability of hidden node and visible node:

$$p(v, h; \theta) = \frac{1}{Z(\theta)} e^{-E(v, h; \theta)} \tag{2}$$

$$Z(\theta) = \sum_{v} \sum_{h} e^{-E(v, v; \theta)} \tag{3}$$

Because there is no connection between hidden nodes and visible nodes, given the input vectors, the activation probability of hidden nodes is:

$$P(h_i=1|v; \theta) = \frac{1}{1 + \exp\left(-b_j - \sum_i v_i w_{ij}\right)} \tag{4}$$

Given the output vector, the activation probability of the visible node is:

$$P(v_i=1|h; \theta) = \frac{1}{1 + \exp\left(-c_i - \sum_j v_j w_{ji}\right)} \tag{5}$$

Through "layer by layer training" and "fine adjustment", deep belief network develop training process of the model. Above all, the first RBM is fully trained, then the bias and weight of the RBM is fixed, the output result of the RBM is used as the input of the next RBM, and the next RBM is trained in turn. The training of RBM mainly adopts Contrastive divergence (CD) algorithm to train parameter set θ.

(1) The visible layer is initialized: $v^0 = x_0$, $\theta_0 = (b_0, c_0, w_0)$, $k = step$, where x_0 is the input sample, θ_0 is a random initialization parameter set, step is the iteration number;
(2) The visible and hidden layer vectors h^0, v^1, h^1 of RBM are calculated by formula (4) and (5).
(3) The joint probability distribution of RBM initial state and update state is obtained by formula (3), and the modified parameter set θ is obtained.

$$\begin{cases} w_{t+1} \leftarrow w_t + \eta\left(\langle v_i h_i \rangle^0 - \langle v_i h_i \rangle^1\right) \\ c_{t+1} \leftarrow c_t + \eta\left(\langle v_i \rangle^0 - \langle v_i \rangle^1\right) \\ b_{t+1} \leftarrow b_t + \eta\left(\langle h_i \rangle^0 - \langle h_i \rangle^1\right) \end{cases} \tag{6}$$

(4) Repeat the process of 2–3 and iterate k times;
(5) Take another group training sample and repeat the process of 2–4.

In DBN training, the bottom-up progress make the parameters of each hidden layer achieve the best, but the error of each layer will also be transmitted layer by layer. Therefore, BPNN is set at the top of the model, and the back propagation algorithm is used to transfer the error back to the hidden layers, and the weights of each hidden layer are finely tuned to make the parameters of the whole model optimal.

(1) Random initialization of the top parameters in BPNN;
(2) Forward error calculation: Given original input d_j, layer by layer transfer, computing network output value $y_j^k(n) = \sum w_{ji}(n) y_i^{k-1}(n)$ get the error $e_j(n) = y_j(n) - d_j(n)$, hereinto y_j^k represent the first j-th node of the k-th layer;
(3) Back Propagation: Calculation of each layer error: calculate each layer error δ
(4) update weight: $w_{ji}^k(n+1) = w_{ji}^k(n) + \eta \delta_j^k y_i^{k-1}(n)$

2 Instantaneous Energy Feature Extraction Based on Empirical Mode Decomposition

2.1 Empirical Mode Decomposition

In 1988, Huang et al. proposed the Empirical mode decomposition (EMD) method, and pointed out that the signal can be decomposed into a set of data sequences with different characteristic scales. The frequency components contained in each sequence are related to the characteristic frequency. EMD is not only suitable for non-stationary nonlinear vibration signals, after EMD decomposition, the instantaneous frequency of signals has physical meaning [6]. Therefore, this paper uses EMD to obtain the instantaneous energy sequence of bearing operation, which is used to describe the fault status of bearing and to complete the sate detections of bearing.

For the vibration signal sequence $x(t)$, it is assumed that the signal has at least two extreme points, one is the maximum value and one is a minimum. The local time domain characteristic of the data sequence is uniquely determined by the time scale between the extremum points; if there is no extreme point but an inflection point in the data sequence, the extreme value can be obtained by the differential or multiple values of the data. The decomposition results are obtained by the integral. The EMD process of vibration signal $x(t)$ is shown in Table 1.

Table 1. The procedure of EMD

(1)	Initialization: $r_0 = x(t), i = 1$
(2)	Extracting the i-th intrinsic mode function
	(a) Initialization: $h_i(k-1) = r_i$, $k = 1$
	(b) Extracting $h_i(k-1)$ Local maximum and minimum
	(c) Cubic spline function are used to fit the upper envelope and the lower envelope of the data series respectively
	(d) Calculate average value of upper envelopes and the lower envelopes: $c_i(k-1)$
	(e) Subtracting the average value from the original data sequence, get a new sequence: h_{ik}: $h_{ik} = h_i(k-1) - c_i(k-1)$
	(f) If h_{ik} is a IMF, then $m_i = h_{ik}$, else $k = k + 1$, turn to (b), and repeat (b) – (h)
(3)	Calculate $r_{i+1} = r_i - m_i$
(4)	If extremal points of r_{i+1} are not less than two, then $i = i + 1$, and turn to (2); else the decomposition end, r_{i+1} is residual component

2.2 Instantaneous Energy Feature Extraction

If the rolling bearing has local damage, when the damage point passes through other components, the vibration energy will become confused. Since various fault damage, energy mutation caused is different energy mutation. The EMD is used to process the vibration signals, and obtained a series of different characteristic intrinsic mode function. Correlation coefficient is calculated with IMF and original vibration signal, then we select the IMF with the greatest correlation, and extract instantaneous energy sequence value with the greatest correlation IMF.

(1) k data samples constitute data set $X = \{X_1, X_2, ...X_k\}$, each data sample is composed of j vibration signals $X_i = [x_1, x_2, ...x_j]$;

(2) Empirical mode decomposition for X_i, get t IMFs;

(3) Calculated the correlation coefficient between M_i and X_i

$$\delta_i = \frac{\text{cov}(m_i, X_i)}{\sqrt{\text{cov}(m_i, m_i) \times \text{cov}(X_i, X_i)}} \tag{7}$$

(4) Select the M_p with the largest correlation coefficient to perform the Hilbert transformation.

$$\tilde{m}_p(t) = H[m_p(t)] = \frac{1}{\pi} \int_{-\infty}^{+\infty} \frac{m_p(\tau)}{t - \tau} d\tau \tag{8}$$

(5) Corresponding analytic signal is obtained by the formula:

$$M(t) = m_p(t) + j\tilde{m}_p(t) \tag{9}$$

(6) Calculating the instantaneous amplitude of an analytical signal:

$$A_i = |M_i(t)| = \sqrt{m_1^2(t) + \tilde{m}c_1^2(t)} \tag{10}$$

(7) Calculating the instantaneous amplitude of A_i:

$$E_i(t) = \frac{1}{2}A_i^2(t) \tag{11}$$

(8) Eigenvectors is get by normalization of instantaneous energy sequence $E_i = [e_1, e_2, ...e_m]$, $e_k = \frac{E_k}{\max(E_i) - \min(E_i)}$.

3   Experimental Explanation

To illustrate the effectiveness of the proposed method, experiments are carried out on the normal bearing and defective bearings. The experiment platform is QPZ-II which is produced by the Chinese company of Qian Peng. The experimental apparatus is mainly constituted with motor, belt coupling, bearing pedestal. And the bearing is installed in the pedestal. The accelerometer sensor is vertically installed at the top of the pedestal (labeled by S1). During the experiments, a variable velocity motor directly drives the shaft. The belt on the right of the shaft brings along the coupling which runs with the same speed of motor.

In order to verify the feasibility and effectiveness of the proposed method, a fault diagnosis experimental platform for double tapered roller bearings is built. The HRB352005 double tapered roller bearing is used in the experiment to classify and identify the faults of the normal, inner and outer parts of the specimen respectively. As shown in Fig. 2, the specimen bearing is processed by fault, the width of wire cutting is 0.8 mm, and the depth is 0.5 mm.

Fig. 2. Figures of experiment bearings: (a) normal; (b) inner race fault; (c) outer race fault

In the experimental platform, the motor power is 0.55 kw and the maximum speed is 1450 rpm. The specimen bearing is installed in the bearing base, and fitting fits with the spindle. The motor drives the main shaft to rotate synchronously, and the spindle drives the inner ring of the bearing to rotate. A spring pressure device is installed above the spindle, and the radial pressure is applied to the bearing seat through the spring deformation. The PCB608A11 accelerometer is used to transform the vibration signal into analog voltage signal to the computer through the Austria DEWE-16 signal acquisition instrument. Because the bearing vibrates and transfers to the bearing base, the sensor is installed on the bearing seat to extract the radial vibration signal of the bearing rotation.

In the experiment, the bearing speed is 1200 rpm, the load is 500 N, the sampling frequency is 10000 Hz, and the sampling time is 10 s. In safety detection, the length of vibration signal has a certain effect on the result of fault diagnosis. If the vibration signal is too long, the feature information is redundant; if the vibration signal is too short, the feature information contained may not be complete. Therefore, this article intercepts the vibration signal of 1 week rotation to form a data sample $Xi = [x1, x2, \ldots\ldots xm]$, where $m = \frac{f \times 60}{h}$, The f is the sampling frequency (Hz) and the h as the speed (RPM).

In each state, 1000000 vibration signals are collected continuously to intercept the vibration signals of the bearing rotation for one week (500 signal sampling points) as a data sample, and each state bearing has 200 data samples. The bearing vibration data of three states constitute a 500 * 600 training data set. 100 data samples are randomly selected to form a test set to judge the accuracy of classification. The experimental sample is shown in Table 2.

Table 2. Experiment dataset

Bearing state	Sample dimension	Number of training samples	Test sample number
Normal	500	200	100
Inner-race fault	500	200	
Outer-race faults	500	200	

The original vibration signal of double tapered roller bearing is shown in Fig. 3. The vibration waveform of the three samples is similar in time domain, and the fault characteristics are not obvious.

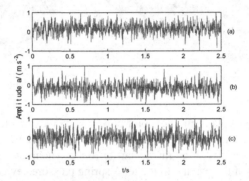

Fig. 3. Time-domain graphics of bearings' vibration signals: (a) normal; (b) inner fault; (c) outer fault

Therefore, empirical mode decomposition is performed on the original vibration signal, and a series of intrinsic mode functions are obtained. In this paper only gives the intrinsic mode functions of the vibration signals of outer ring fault after empirical mode decomposition, as shown in Fig. 4.

As shown in Fig. 4, EMD separates the original vibration signals from time to scale according to "screening". In the same way, the EMD of normal bearing vibration signal and inner ring fault bearing vibration signal is carried out, and the correlation coefficient between the epigenome function and the original signal is calculated, as shown in Table 3.

It is known from Table 3 that the correlation coefficient between imf_1 and the original vibration signal is the largest, including the main energy change in the original signal, which reduces the noise interference to the signal, and can more clearly reflect the bearing fault characteristics. Therefore, we choose the imf_1 and calculate the instantaneous energy by steps in 2.2 to construct the eigenvector.

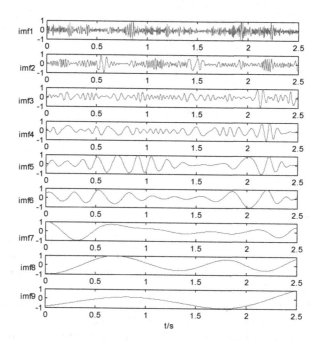

Fig. 4. Empirical mode decomposition of outer fault signal

Table 3. The correlation coefficient between the intrinsic mode function and the original signal

IMF	Original vibration signal		
	Normal	Inner-race fault	Outer-race fault
imf_1	0.6047	0.5889	0.6291
imf_2	0.4577	0.4999	0.4904
imf_3	0.3845	0.5505	0.5521
imf_4	0.3038	0.2058	0.2149
imf_5	0.1712	0.1031	0.1317
imf_6	0.0219	0.0169	0.0181
imf_7	0.0193	0.0128	0.0073
imf_8	0.0227	0.0097	0.0013

4   Experimental Results and Analysis

In the experiment, the training sample set includes 600 samples, which belong to 3 categories respectively, each sample dimension is 500, so the number of input layer nodes of the DBN model is 500 and the number of output layer nodes is 3. The main parameters of the DBN model are shown in Table 4.

Table 4. The parameters of DBN

Parameter	Value
Input	500
Output	3
Iteration	50
Batchsize	10
l	2
n_1	140
n_2	50
a	0.1
m	0.1

In order to verify the performance of the proposed method, support vector machine (SVM), nearest neighbor distance classifier (KNN) and artificial neural network (BPNN) were used to conduct comparative experiments. In SVM, the radial basis function is used, the penalty factor and the kernel parameter are 2.618 and 1.832 respectively; the KNN uses the Euclidean distance as the discriminant standard; the BPNN uses the network structure of 500-28-3. After empirical mode decomposition of experimental data, eigenvectors are constructed according to formula (10) and (11), and eigenvectors are identified by DBN, SVM, KNN and BPNN. In the experiment, each data set is run 10 times repeatedly, and the accuracy of fault classification is shown in Fig. 5.

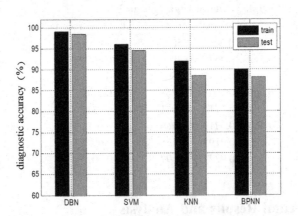

Fig. 5. The accuracies of four methods

As shown in Fig. 5, the accuracy of DBN for the training set (train) is 99%, and the classification accuracy for the test set (test) is 98.5%; the accuracy of the SVM for the training set is 96%, but the accuracy of the test set is reduced to 94%. The classification accuracy of KNN and BPNN for training set and test set is about 90%, which is obviously lower than DBN.

DBN, SVM, KNN and BPNN classify the test set after learning the training set, but the stability and generalization ability of the classification are different. KNN and BPNN as shallow structure algorithms have limited expressive power for complex functions. In the experiment, the data sample dimension is relatively high. KNN and BPNN cannot fully excavate the fault characteristics in the data sample. SVM extracts data features through the mapping of training samples by the kernel function, but the generalization ability of the model is not strong and the accuracy of the test sample is not high, which shows that the mapping of the data features is incomplete. DBN is a production model based on probability. Through the connection between the hidden elements in the network layer, the information statistics between all the variables are realized. Therefore, the data structure and feature information can be extracted well. Deep belief network has higher classification accuracy for training set and test set, and shows good generalization ability.

5   Conclusion

This paper mainly research bearing safety detection in urban rail transit. EMD is used to extract the instantaneous energy sequence of bearing to construct the eigenvector. DBN is carried out for bearing fault diagnosis. The results show that the accuracy rate of fault diagnosis based on deep learning is 98%.

Compared with the traditional fault diagnosis method, deep learning can extract the characteristic information of the data more completely through the multi-layer structure, and improve the fault accuracy of the double row conical rolling bearing. After decomposing the vibration signal by EMD, a series of adaptive functions are obtained, which can reflect the fault characteristics of the bearing from different frequency bands. Therefore, the instantaneous energy sequence based on EMD decomposition can more accurately characterize the bearing fault information. Deep learning can extract the feature information of the data, but the difficulty lies in the setting of multi-layer structure, so how to optimize the number of network layers in depth learning and the number of nodes in each layer should be further studied.

Acknowledgments. This paper was supported by the National Natural Science Foundation of China (Grant No. 11702091), and the Natural Science Foundation of Hunan Province of China (Grant No. 2018JJ3140).

References

1. Hu, L., Wang, W., Zhao, Z., et al.: Lubricated contact analysis of roller large end-flange in double-row tapered roller bearing. Tribology **33**(1), 22–28 (2013)
2. Zhiliang, L., Deng, P., Ming, Z., et al.: A review on fault diagnosis for rail vehicles. J. Mech. Eng. **52**(14) (2016)
3. Yingying, L.I.A.O., Yongqiang, L.I.U., Shaopu, Y.A.N.G., et al.: Numerical simultion and experimental study of a railway vehicle roller bearing with outer ring fault. J. Vib. Meas. Diagn. **34**(3), 539–594 (2014)

4. Deyao, T.A.N.G.: Fault Diagnosis and Safety Engineering for Generalized Resonance Demodulation (Urban Rail Transit). China Railway Publishing House, Beijing (2013)
5. El-Thalji, I., Jantunen, E.: A summary of fault modelling and predictive health monitoring of rolling element bearings. Mech. Syst. Signal Process. **60**, 252–272 (2015)
6. Yao, Y., Zhang, X.: Fault diagnosis approach for roller bearing based on EMD momentary energy entropy and SVM. J. Electron. Meas. Instrum. **27**(10), 957–962 (2013)
7. Lei, Y., Jia, F., Lin, J., et al.: An intelligent fault diagnosis method using unsupervised feature learning towards mechanical big data. IEEE Trans. Ind. Electron. **63**(5), 3137–3147 (2016)
8. Guangjian, H.E., Zongyi, X.I.N., Cheng, Z.U.O., et al.: Fault diagnosis method for rolling bearing of metro vehicle based on EMD and SVM. Railw. Comput. Appl. **24**(8), 1–5 (2015)
9. Liu, J., Zhao, Z., Zhang, G., et al.: Research on fault diagnosis method for bogie bearings of metro vehicle. J. China Railw. Soc. **37**(1), 30–36 (2015)
10. Jing, W.A.N.G.: Research of the Key Technologies for the Train's Wheel set Fault Vibration Characteristics and Diagnosis Method. Central South University, Changsha (2012)
11. Jiangtian, Y.A.N.G., Mingyuan, Z.H.A.O.: Fault diagnosis system for locomotive bearings based on vehicle bus and laplace wavelet. J. China Railw. Soc. **33**(8), 23–27 (2011)
12. Chenglin, W.E.N., Feiya, L.V., Zhejing, B.A.O., MeiQin, L.I.U.: A review of data driven-based incipient fault diagnosis. Acta Autom. Sin. **42**(9), 1285–1299 (2016)
13. Licheng, J.I.A.O., Shuyuan, Y.A.N.G., Fang, L.I.U., et al.: Sevety years beyond neural networks: retrospect and prospec. Chin. J. Comput. **39**(8), 1697–1716 (2016)
14. Hinton, G.E., Osindero, S., Teh, Y.W.: A fast learning algorithm for deep belief nets. Neural Comput. **18**(7), 1527–1554 (2006)
15. Hinton, G.E., Salakhutdinov, R.: Reducion the dimensionality of data with neural networks. Science **313**, 504–507 (2006)
16. Schmidhuber, J.: Deep learning in neural networks: an overview. Neural Netw. **61**(9), 85–117 (2015)
17. Tamilselvan, P., Wang, Y., Wang, P.: Deep belief network based state classification for structural health diagnosis. Reliab. Eng. Syst. Saf. **115**(3), 124–135 (2013)
18. Tran, V.T., Althobiani, F., Ball, A.: Anapproach to fault diagnosis of reciprocating compressor valves using Teager-Kaeser energy operator and deep belief networks. Expert Syst. Appl. **41**(9), 4113–4122 (2014)
19. Shao, H., Jiang, H., Zhang, X., et al.: Rolling bearing fault diagnosis using an optimization deep belief network. Meas. Sci. Technol. **26**(11), 1–17 (2015)
20. Shao, H., Jiang, H., Zhang, H., et al.: Rolling bearing fault feature learning using improved convolutional deep belief network with compressed sensing. Mech. Syst. Signal Process. **100**, 743–765 (2018)
21. Gan, M., Wang, C.: Construction of hierarchical diagnosis network based on deep learning and its application in the fault pattern recognition of rolling element bearings. Mech. Syst. Signal Process. **72**, 92–104 (2016)
22. Weihua, L.I., Waiping, S.H.A.N., Xueqiong, Z.E.N.G.: Bearing fault identification based on deep belief network. J. Vib. Eng. **29**(2), 340–347 (2016)
23. Chen, Z., Li, W.: Multisensor feature fusion for bearing fault diagnosis using sparse autoencoder and deep belief network. IEEE Trans. Instrum. Meas. **66**(7), 1693–1702 (2017)

Malicious Domain Name Recognition Based on Deep Neural Networks

Xiaodan Yan[1], Baojiang Cui[1], and Jianbin Li[2(✉)]

[1] Beijing University of Posts and Telecommunications, Beijing 100876, China
[2] North China Electric Power University, Beijing 102206, China
lijb87@ncepu.edu.cn

Abstract. Malware steals private information by randomly generating a large number of malicious domain names every day using domain generation algorithms (DGAs), which pose a great threat to our daily Internet activity. To improve recognition accuracy for these malicious domain names, this paper proposes a malicious domain name detection algorithm based on deep neural networks to capture the characteristics of malicious domain names. The resulting model is called a Discriminator based on Hierarchical Bidirectional Recurrent Neural Networks (D-HBiRNN).

Keywords: Security · Domain name · Neural networks · BiRNN
LSTM

1 Introduction

With the popularity of the Internet of Things (IoT), a large number of devices are now linked to the Internet, and many security issues have been exposed. One of the most serious types of security threats is distributed denial-of-service (DDoS) attacks using domain generation algorithms (DGAs) [1, 2, 12]. Attackers often use DGAs to generate domain names instead of using hard-coded domain names because the latter are vulnerable to blacklist detection. With a DGA, an attacker can generate a pseudorandom string to be used as a domain name, which can effectively avoid blacklist detection. Such a pseudorandom domain name is similar to a string that has been successfully encoded in chronological order. Therefore, a deep neural network based on time series can help us to better discover the characteristics of malicious domain names and improve the accuracy of their identification [3]. The goal of [4] is to provide a complete framework for classifying and transcribing sequential data with RNNs only.

To extract information on malicious activity from massive amounts of traffic, [5] exploited the association between packet and traffic information through a machine learning approach that correlates packet-level alerts with feature vectors derived from traffic records for the same traffic. The authors described a system framework that can be used for network-traffic alarms and the steps required to create a proof of concept.

Bidirectional recurrent neural networks (Bi-RNNs) are trained to predict in both the positive and negative time directions simultaneously. In this paper, we study the effect of a hierarchy of Bi-RNNs on time series processing. This architecture allows us to perform hierarchical processing on difficult temporal tasks and to more naturally

© Springer Nature Switzerland AG 2018
G. Wang et al. (Eds.): SpaCCS 2018, LNCS 11342, pp. 497–505, 2018.
https://doi.org/10.1007/978-3-030-05345-1_43

capture the structure of time series. We show that this architecture can achieve state-of-the-art performance for recurrent networks in the modeling and detection of malicious domain names when trained with a simple stochastic gradient descent approach.

Our main contribution is to propose and train Bi-RNNs to predict in both the positive and negative time directions simultaneously. We devise a new algorithm based on hierarchical bidirectional recurrent neural networks to improve the recognition accuracy for malicious domain names.

2 Related Works

Since the 1990s, the ways in which people can access information have changed dramatically. The Internet has become a bridge for people and information, enabling us to obtain information faster. Especially in recent years, with the spread of the mobile Internet, we have entered the era of big data. These security problems include malicious websites, which continue to threaten our online behavior through phishing, DDoS attacks and other means, resulting in many instances of network fraud, network paralysis and a series of other problems [14].

For network security, malicious URLs are a common and serious threat. Malicious URLs host unsolicited content (spam, phishing, drive-by exploits, etc.) and lure unsuspecting users to become victims of scams (monetary loss, theft of private information, and malware installation), causing billions of dollars in losses each year. Unfortunately, blacklist detection is not perfect, and its ability to detect newly generated malicious URLs requires improvement [6, 7]. Unfortunately, blacklist detection is not perfect, and its ability to detect newly generated malicious URLs requires improvement [15].

Hidden Markov models (HMMs) for describing host security states have been established to evaluate the real-time security risks to networks, using intrusion detection system alerts as inputs. The probability for a host to be attacked can be calculated with such a model. With a focus on attack alerts, a new method of calculating attack success probability was presented in [6, 13], which used attack threat levels to calculate the risk index of each host node. In [7], a large deep convolutional neural network was trained to classify 1.3 million high-resolution images in the LSVRC-2010 ImageNet training set into 1000 different categories.

The deeper a neural network is, the harder it is to train. In [8], a residual learning framework was proposed to allow deeper networks to be more feasibly trained. The layers were redefined explicitly as the learning of residual functions referenced to the layer input rather than functions with no reference. Moreover, [16] discussed practical issues in system design as well as open research challenges and pointed out some important directions for future research.

The traditional RNN considers only the forward-to-backward construction of time series features, but does not consider backward-to-forward feature construction. [9] presented the extension of a conventional RNN to a bidirectional recurrent neural network (BRNN).

An important benefit of RNNs is their ability to use contextual information when mapping between the input and output sequences. [10] proposed a new architecture called long short-term memory (LSTM) to solve the problems with traditional RNNs. LSTM can lead to more successful executions and, more importantly, enable faster learning. In addition, LSTM can be used to solve problems that previous recurrent network algorithms have never solved, namely, complex tasks with artificial long time delays.

3   The Hierarchy of Bidirectional Recurrent Neural Networks

Although gradient clipping can cope with gradient explosion, the problem of gradient dispersion cannot be solved for traditional RNN units. Therefore, given a domain name that has been abstracted into a time series, it is actually difficult for an RNN to capture the dependencies between pairs of text elements whose separation distances are relatively large. We therefore use bidirectional LSTM (Bi-LSTM) networks units as the basic abstraction units and stack multiple Bi-LSTM units to obtain the final result. The diagram of the final framework is given in Fig. 1.

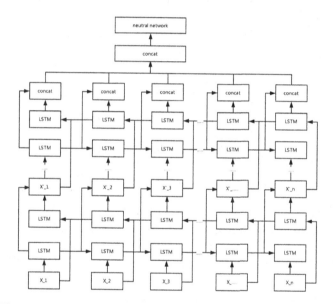

Fig. 1. Hierarchy of Bi-LSTM units for detecting DGA characteristics.

Just as Bi-LSTM units are the basic building blocks of this hierarchical Bi-LSTM structure, individual LSTM cells are the basic building blocks of each Bi-LSTM unit. The LSTM structure represents an improvement over the RNN structure in that it includes an additional control gate, as shown in Fig. 2.

Suppose that the length of the implicit state is h, the number of samples is m, and the dimensionality of the eigenvector is n. We specify the batch data $X_t \in R^{m \times n}$ at time t and the implied state $H_{t-1} \in R^{m \times h}$ at the previous time. Since an LSTM unit is used as the control unit, this unit includes an input gate $I_t \in R^{m \times h}$, a forget gate $F_t \in R^{m \times h}$, and an output gate $O_t \in R^{m \times h}$. The detailed definitions are as follows:

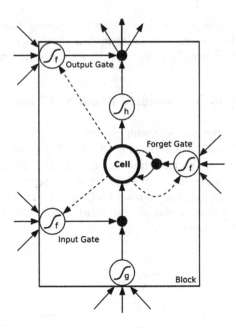

Fig. 2. The LSTM framework.

$$I_t = \sigma(X_t \cdot W_{ni} + H_{t-1} \cdot W_{hi} + b_i)$$

$$F_t = \sigma(X_t \cdot W_{nf} + H_{t-1} \cdot W_{hf} + b_f)$$

$$O_t = \sigma(X_t \cdot W_{no} + H_{t-1} \cdot W_{ho} + b_o)$$

Here, the parameters W_{ni}, W_{nf}, and W_{no} belong to $R^{n \times h}$; W_{hi}, W_{hf}, and W_{ho} belong to $R^{h \times h}$; and b_i, b_f, and b_o belong to $R^{1 \times h}$. All of them are parameters of the whole model.

The LSTM unit contains an important candidate cell $\tilde{C} \in R^{m \times h}$, where $\tilde{C} = \sigma(X_t \cdot W_{xc} + H_{t-1} \cdot W_{hc} + b_c)$. The three control gates are used to modify the candidate cell $\tilde{C}$, and finally, the cell C_t associated with the current time is obtained. The calculation of C_t combines the information of the cell at the previous moment with the information of the candidate cell at the current moment by controlling the flow of information through the forget gate and the input gate:

$$C_t = F_t \cdot C_{t-1} + I_t \cdot \tilde{C}$$

This design can address the gradient attenuation problem in RNNs and better capture more widely spaced dependencies in sequential data. In this cell design, the flow of information from the cell to the hidden layer variable is controlled by the output gate:

$$H_t = O_t \cdot \sigma(C_t)$$

By arranging multiple cells of the type described above in chronological order, a one-way LSTM network is obtained. To incorporate information from both sides of the sequence, we use Bi-LSTM networks, which operate in both the forward and backward directions. The update of each Bi-LSTM unit can be precisely written as follows:

$$h_t = \overrightarrow{h_t} + \overleftarrow{h_t}$$

In the above formula, $\overrightarrow{h_t}$ and $\overleftarrow{h_t}$ both denote hidden layers arranged in chronological order. $\overrightarrow{h_t}$ represents the hidden layer arranged in forward time order, while $\overleftarrow{h_t}$ represents the hidden layer arranged in reverse time order.

Algorithm 1 The iterative updating algorithm for LJGNMF

Input: $\overrightarrow{x}$, $\overrightarrow{y}$, Δw, Δb, η.

/* L represents the total number of layers */

/* n_l represents the number of nodes in the lth layer */

Output: w and b.

Process:

1) $\overrightarrow{a} = sigmod(w\overrightarrow{x})$

2) $\overrightarrow{\delta} = \overrightarrow{y} \cdot (1 - \overrightarrow{y}) \cdot (\overrightarrow{t} - \overrightarrow{y})$ /* the last layer */

3) $\overrightarrow{\delta^l} = \overrightarrow{a^l} \cdot (1 - \overrightarrow{a^l}) \cdot w^T \cdot \delta^{l+1}$ /* $l = 2 \cdots L - 1$*/

4) **for** $j \leftarrow 1, n_{l+1}$

5) **for** $i \leftarrow 1, n_l$

6) $w_{ji} = w_{ji} + \eta \cdot \delta_j \cdot x_{ji}$

7) $w = w + \eta \cdot \overrightarrow{\delta} \cdot \overrightarrow{x}^T$

8) $\overrightarrow{b} = \overrightarrow{b} + \eta \cdot \overrightarrow{\delta}$

9) **end**

From Algorithm 1, it can be seen that X here is actually h because the output of the hierarchical bidirectional neural network structure is taken as the input to the neural network. Since the neural network can have multiple hidden layers, W represents the weight matrix between two adjacent hidden layers. If it is the weight matrix between the Lth layer and the L + 1th layer, this indicates that the Lth layer contains a certain number of nodes.

4   The Performance of the Hierarchy of Bidirectional Recurrent Neural Networks

In this article, the top1w domain names collected from the Alexa website are used as positive samples, and the malicious domain names published by 360 Netlab [11] are used as negative samples. Regarding the latter, 360 Netlab has published malicious domain names in multiple categories (including Conficker, Necurs, and Bamital); detailed examples are given in Table 1.

Table 1. Comparison of domain name information

Positive samples	Negative samples
Baidu.com	josmxvlp.net
qq.com	utctskeza.biz
Taobao.com	ylowidijfq.info
Tmall.com	nyyybibdi.tv
Sohu.com	spdnktwhkfeheweffyw.xxx
Jd.com	gviiqqwyjdvxck.cc
Weibo.com	hbxxkfbujp.net
360.cn	odajwpyfcl2z.com
Alipay.com	8hiv4tif0pmz.org
Hao123.com	01e381afc9yr.com

4.1 Model Training and Evaluation Indicators

In the embedding process, character segmentation is performed on the domain name data (for example, baidu.com is divided into b a i d u . c o m), and then the corresponding segmented domain name sequence is created via character-based (char) embedding. Since the embedding of the character sequence of each domain name depends on a large amount of data, the character embedding of the training data is performed only after the preprocessing of 1 million normal domain names and 1 million malicious domain names.

To obtain a better hierarchical Bi-RNN model, this paper separately evaluates the model in terms of its loss score and prediction accuracy. The loss score of the model is the loss value of the entire model. Over time, the model loss should become increasingly smaller and should tend to converge.

4.2 Results

4.2.1 Suitable Parameters

To present the results obtained throughout our experiments, we have plotted the training epochs on the horizontal axis and the loss values of the model on the vertical axis. Each epoch contains multiple batches. The details are shown in Fig. 3.

As shown in this figure, the value of the loss function drops rapidly at the first epoch, and as the number of epochs increases, the model gradually converges.

In addition to the convergence speed and the loss value, we also need to evaluate the accuracy of the model. The details of this evaluation are shown in Fig. 4.

In the first epoch, the accuracy of the model is approximately 88%. In the third epoch, the accuracy of the model is equal to 96%. Subsequently, with a further increase in the number of epochs, the accuracy remains basically stable; thus, the accuracy of the final model is 96%.

Since we adopt a hierarchy of Bi-RNNs for feature extraction, we must explore the effect of the number of layers on the accuracy of the model to find the optimal number of layers. To this end, we consider the accuracies achieved with n layers, where n ranges from 1 to 10. The details are shown in Fig. 5. As shown in Fig. 5, the accuracy

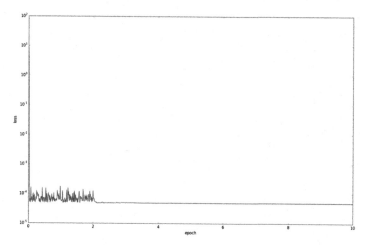

Fig. 3. Model loss map

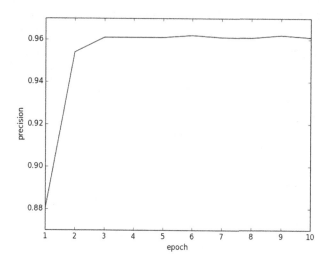

Fig. 4. Model accuracy rate

of the model initially increases as the number of layers increases. However, when the number of layers exceeds 5, the model accuracy begins to decline; with 3 and 4 layers, the model accuracy is located at its highest point of 96.1%, and when the number of layers is equal to 3, less time is required for training the model and for generating predictions than is required in the case of 4 layers. Therefore, the final number of layers is chosen to be 3.

4.2.2 Performance Comparison Among Different Algorithms

We also evaluate the performance of decision tree, neural network, support vector machine (SVM), and logistic regression algorithms to obtain the corresponding relationships between accuracy and epoch. The details are shown in Fig. 6. As shown in

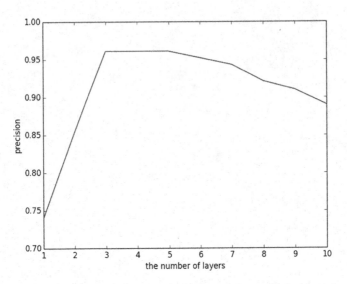

Fig. 5. Model accuracy with different numbers of layers in the hierarchy

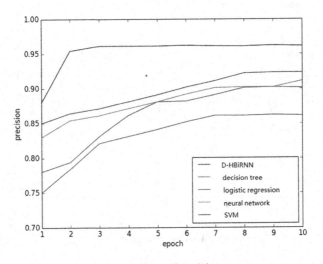

Fig. 6. Comparison of model accuracy

this figure, the other classifiers are far less accurate than the proposed model is in the identification of malicious domain names.

5   Conclusion

In this paper, we propose a malicious domain name detection algorithm based on deep neural networks to capture characteristic information of malicious domain names. We use hierarchical Bi-RNNs to model the domain name data, which is used to extract more semantic features to more accurately describe the domain names. Through experiments, we find that the accuracy of the proposed algorithm is much higher than that of conventional algorithms based on feature engineering, including decision tree, logistic regression, neural network and SVM algorithms. We introduce D-HBiRNN to improve the recognition accuracy for malicious domain names. In the future, we will systematically evaluate the performance of D-HBiRNN in terms of detection quality.

References

1. Hoque, N., Bhattacharyya, D.K., Kalita, J.K.: Botnet in DDoS attacks: trends and challenges. IEEE Commun. Surv. Tutor. **17**(4), 2242–2270 (2015)
2. Rossow, C.: Amplification hell: revisiting network protocols for DDoS abuse. In: Proceedings 2014 Network and Distributed System Security Symposium. Internet Society, Reston, VA (2014). https://doi.org/10.14722/ndss.2014.23233
3. Thatte, G., Mitra, U., Heidemann, J.: Parametric methods for anomaly detection in aggregate traffic. IEEE/ACM Trans. Netw. **19**(2), 512–525 (2011)
4. Graves, A.: Supervised Sequence Labelling with Recurrent Neural Networks, vol. 385. Springer, Berlin (2012). https://doi.org/10.1007/978-3-642-24797-2
5. Duffield, N., Haffner, P., Krishnamurthy, B., et al.: Rule-based anomaly detection on IP flows. In: INFOCOM, pp. 424–432. IEEE (2009)
6. Chen, T., Xu, S., Zhang, C.: Risk assessment method for network security based on intrusion detection system. Comput. Sci. **37**(9), 94–96 (2010)
7. Krizhevsky, A., Sutskever, I., Hinton, G.E.: ImageNet classification with deep convolutional neural networks. In: International Conference on Neural Information Processing Systems, pp. 1097–1105. Curran Associates Inc. (2012)
8. He, K., Zhang, X., Ren, S., et al.: Deep residual learning for image recognition. In: Computer Vision and Pattern Recognition, pp. 770–778. IEEE (2016)
9. Schuster, M., Paliwal, K.K.: Bidirectional recurrent neural networks. IEEE Trans. Signal Process **45**(11), 2673–2681 (1997)
10. Hochreiter, S., Schmidhuber, J.: Long short-term memory. Neural Comput. **9**(8), 1735–1780 (1997)
11. Netlab 360 Homepage. https://data.netlab.360.com/dga. Accessed 21 Sept 2018
12. Haddadi, F., Kayacik, H.G., Zincir-Heywood, A.N., Heywood, M.I.: Malicious automatically generated domain name detection using stateful-SBB. In: Esparcia-Alcázar, A.I. (ed.) EvoApplications 2013. LNCS, vol. 7835, pp. 529–539. Springer, Heidelberg (2013). https://doi.org/10.1007/978-3-642-37192-9_53
13. Xiong, C., Li, P., Zhang, P., Liu, Q., Tan, J.: MIRD: trigram-based Malicious URL detection Implanted with Random Domain name recognition. In: Niu, W., et al. (eds.) ATIS 2015. CCIS, vol. 557, pp. 303–314. Springer, Heidelberg (2015). https://doi.org/10.1007/978-3-662-48683-2_27
14. Jamdagni, A., Jamdagni, A., He, X., et al.: A system for denial-of-service attack detection based on multivariate correlation analysis. IEEE Trans. Parallel Distrib. Syst. **25**(2), 447–456 (2014)
15. Buczak, A.L., Guven, E.: A survey of data mining and machine learning methods for cyber security intrusion detection. IEEE Commun. Surv. Tutor. **18**(2), 1153–1176 (2017)
16. Thomas, K., Grier, C., Ma, J., et al.: Design and evaluation of a real-time URL spam filtering service. In: Security and Privacy, pp. 447–462. IEEE (2011)

The 8th International Symposium on Trust, Security and Privacy for Emerging Applications (TSP 2018)

TSP 2018 Organizing and Program Committees

General Chairs

Xiaodong Lin   University of Ontario Institute of Technology, Canada
Khalid Alharbi   Northern Border University, Saudi Arabia

Program Chairs

Imad Jawhar   United Arab Emirates University, UAE
Deqing Zou   Huazhong University of Science of Technology, China
Xiaohui Liang   University of Massachusetts at Boston, USA

Program Committee

Ying Dai   Temple University, USA
Toon De   Pessemier Ghent University, Belgium
Xiaofeng Ding   Huazhong University of Science and Technology, China
Ed Fernandez   Florida Atlantic University, USA
Xiaojun Hei   Huazhong University of Science and Technology, China
Abdessamad Imine   Lorraine University, France
Ricky J. Sethi   Fitchburg State University, USA
Haitao Lang   Dept. Physics & Electronics, China
Xin Li   Nanjing University of Aeronautics and Astronautics, China
Chi Lin   Dalian University of Technology, China
Pouya Ostovari   Temple University, USA
Filipa Peleja   Yahoo Research Barcelona, Spain
Chao Song   University of Electronic Science and Technology of China, China
Guangzhong Sun   University of Science and Technology of China, China
Yunsheng Wang   Kettering University, USA
Yanghua Xiao   Fudan University, China
Xuanxia Yao   University of Science and Technology Beijing, China
Lin Ye   Harbin Institute of Technology, China
Mingwu Zhang   Hubei University of Technology, China
Yaxiong Zhao   Google Inc., USA
Huan Zhou   China Three Gorges University, China
Youwen Zhu   Nanjing University of Aeronautics and Astronautics, China

Web Chair

Mingmin Shao	Hunan University, China

Steering Chairs

Wenjun Jiang	Hunan University, China
Guojun Wang	Guangzhou University, China

Steering Committee

Laurence T. Yang	St. Francis Xavier University, Canada
Minyi Guo	Shanghai Jiao Tong University, China
Jie Li	University of Tsukuba, Japan
Jianhua Ma	Hosei University, Japan
Peter Mueller	IBM Zurich Research Laboratory, Switzerland
Indrakshi Ray	Colorado State University, USA
Kouichi Sakurai	Kyushu University, Japan
Bhavani Thuraisingham	The University of Texas at Dallas, USA
Jie Wu	Temple University, USA
Yang Xiang	Deakin University, Australia
Kun Yang	University of Essex, UK
Wanlei Zhou	Deakin University, Australia

Investigation on Unauthorized Human Activity Watching Through Leveraging Wi-Fi Signals

Md Zakirul Alam Bhuiyan[1,2] (ID), Md. Monirul Islam[1], Guojun Wang[2](✉) (ID), and Tian Wang[3](✉)

[1] Department of Computer and Information Sciences, Fordham University, New York 10458, USA
{mbhuiyan3,mmonirulislam}@fordham.edu
[2] School of Computer Science and Technology, Guangzhou University, Guangzhou 510006, China
csgjwang@gzhu.edu.cn
[3] Department of Computer and Information Sciences, Huaqiao University, Quanzhou 362000, China
wangtian@hqu.edu.cn

Abstract. Wireless signals, including Wi-Fi signals have become ubiquitous. Recent advancement shows that such signals can be leveraged for many applications including healthcare and people motion monitoring. An interesting question would be what if Wi-Fi signals can also be used in monitoring human activities in unauthorized and unauthenticated manner. In this paper, we study of watching human activities through leveraging Wi-Fi signals and discuss a few application prototypes. These prototypes are used to detect, track, and identify any moving objects, including those behind obstacles using multiple-input Multiple-output (MIMO) technology to calculate the change in frequency reception. We attempt to learn whether or not our Wi-Fi router is not watching our Internet activity as well as physical activities. With all new technologies, one must be aware that unauthorized use of these technology can be used by criminals to their advantage, and we discuss some of the countermeasures to mitigate this risks.

Keywords: Wi-Fi signals · Signal compromise
Unauthorized human activity monitoring
Wi-Fi based security attack · Risk

1 Introduction

Current research efforts have thrust the limit of ISM (Industrial Scientific and Medical) band radiometric detection to a new level, including motion detection, gesture recognition, localization, and even classification. It is now possible to detect motions and recognize human gestures, or even detect and locate tumors

© Springer Nature Switzerland AG 2018
G. Wang et al. (Eds.): SpaCCS 2018, LNCS 11342, pp. 511–521, 2018.
https://doi.org/10.1007/978-3-030-05345-1_44

inside human. A few years earlier, the question was unknown whether or not it is possible to leverage Wi-Fi signals to track heartbeat and chest movement, or human motions or gestures? Wi-Fi signals are ubiquitous, particular in home or office environments. Wi-Fi signals are typically information carriers between a wireless transmitter and a receiver. Various prototypes and schemes have been developed, including Wi-Vi, FreeSense, Wi-Hear, Wi-key [1–5,10,11]. However, this Wi-Fi based technology is still not mature. A lot of research still need to be done to make it practical.

In this paper, we discuss various Wi-Fi signal application prototypes developed by various universities leveraging Wi-Fi signals and multiple-input Multiple-output (MIMO) technology to calculate the change in frequency reception. These prototypes are used to detect, track, and identify any moving objects or human, including those behind obstacles. Imagine the scene in Batman the Dark Knight trilogy, where Batman searches for the Joker. He uses Sound Navigation and Ranging technology, also known as SONAR. By emitting a tone from a cellphone, he is able to produce a real-time image of the surrounding environment. It is the same premise but the tone generated isn't a tone; it is the radio frequency already widely available and surrounding us, Wi-Fi. However, the prototypes do not share the same technology as SONAR; these prototypes signals' characteristics are similar to the SONAR system that could be found in submarines, although instead of tone they use radio frequency to get image of the surrounding environment.

At an enterprise level, wireless networking requires certain types of equipment to connect people within the organization. These include servers, switches, access points, routers etc. At this point in time where the world is becoming increasingly connected, networking is no longer considered a luxury but a necessity. Wi-Fi is not a new concept in the world of technology; it operates on the electromagnetic spectrum, it falls between radio and microwave frequencies. These waves are used to transmit data using MHz, and a router transmits data wirelessly through a frequency of 2.412 GHz–2.472 GHz although some routers have started using a frequency of 5 GHz to broadcast Wi-Fi [6,12–14]. The reason behind routers providing these different frequencies is that with so many devices using the 2.4 GHz frequency the channels available have become saturated with devices, causing interference within signals. Today, Wi-Fi signals can be used to perform as surveillance system. Cognitive System Corp, a home monitoring company, developed a home detection using Wi-Fi signals inside a home.

Aura "is a beacon based system that monitors motion in the home" by identifying the disturbance of Wi-Fi Signal. It pairs with the existing home Wi-Fi router and utilizes the signal from the router to detect disturbance. Users interact with Aura via their smartphone when the user is home, Aura can detect the phone and disengage alerts. When the registered device is away from home, Aura will automatic arm and detect movement within the house. This is just one example of how Wi-Fi technology can be leveraged. Wi-Fi has increased efficiency for our lifestyle. With the luxury of Wi-Fi, how can we make sure our router is not watching our activity both in physical and digital spectrum? For example, there is a cyberattack in a Wi-Fi router, which is compromised to leak its physical signal collection. An attacker (may be within the communicating rage or from remote place) collected the Wi-Fi signals and utilize them what is being done around the router working area, what is done in office or at a home. This might not still be a serious issue now, but it can be a serious issue in 10 years or later when cyberattackers will be more intelligent and they can directly compromise Wi-Fi device and collected.

In this paper, we attempt to learn whether or not our Wi-Fi router is not watching our Internet activity as well as physical activities. We focus on a few combat methods. We will also assess the security issues involving Wi-Fi connectivity. With all new Wi-Fi technologies, one must be aware that unauthorized use of these technology can be used by criminals to their advantage, and we discuss some of the countermeasures to mitigate this risks.

The rest of the paper is organized as follows. Section 2 discusses potential abuse of Wi-Fi router by cyberattackers, while Sect. 3 gives examples of attacking situations of the Wi-Fi routers. Wi-Fi security measures and some potential solutions are discussed in Sects. 4 and 5, respectively. Finally, we conclude the paper with future work.

2   Potential Abuse of Wi-Fi Router by Cyberattackers

In this section, we identify risks as a result of new technologies introduced in the society. Also, We briefly identify the exploitation of various advanced technologies and their vulnerabilities.

The Wi-Fi can be used to save lives, fight crime, and even spy on you. Yes, we can read this it correctly. This technology can be used to spy on people's physical and digital activities by cyberattackers. With every new technology introduced in society, a new type of risk is raised. Computer science researchers, and engineers and security researchers around the world would want to get their hands on this newly developed product. They usually perform static code analysis on the software the product to try to exploit any unknown vulnerability. This is known as a Zero-day vulnerability. Should any Zero vulnerabilities be discovered, those researchers will disclose the findings to product developers privately. At this stage, researchers will notify the product developer their intent to publish the Zero vulnerability to public. This method ensures the product developers fix these Zero day vulnerabilities before anyone else uses them. Going back to the malicious use of Wi-Fi tracking technology, researchers are not the only ones looking for Zero day vulnerabilities within the product. Malicious hackers and nation state sponsored spies are looking to exploit this technology. Leveraging the research of Wi-Vi, FreeSense, WiKey, and WiHear, and with large amount of financial resources and technical talent provided by Nation state, a similar technology can be developed with the sole purpose of invading one's privacy.

3 Attacking on the Wi-Fi Routers

In this section, we identify the possible attacks on the WI-Fi routers. Routers can also be severely compromised to cause retrieval of private information of individuals sharing a network. With respect to packet transmission, it is possible to use various software applications to decrypt WPA encryptions and later on to cause packet interference. The end result of interference could be message interception or even stealing information for illegal use. Home routers are designed to do both switching and routing, where the home router requires the user to enter a password in order to allow an endpoint to become part of the network. The recommended level of encryption is WPA2, and WPA2 enterprise if you are in an enterprise network.

For this section, we would like to look at server theoretical ideas that will allow the user, and the network be more secure. There are many websites that give you tools, methods, and detailed instructions on how to hack a Wi-Fi network, in order to defend against an attack there are many steps an individual would have to take to make it as difficult as possible to breach the network. Using a router forensic analysis system to recognize when and where the Wi-Fi signal data originating from and when the signals are going outside from the router may allow homes or office to be more secure (Fig. 1).

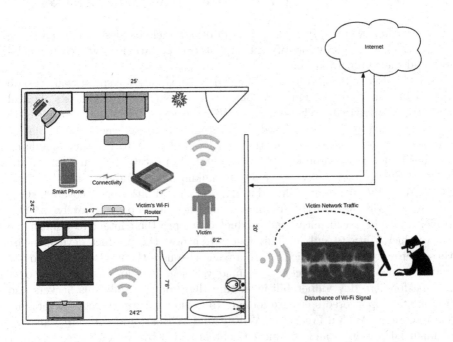

Fig. 1. Cyberattacker receiving Wi-Fi signals from outside the user's home.

To simplify our terminology and focus on Wi-Fi, we replace term computer researchers, malicious hacker and state sponsor threat actors with "cyberattacker". We assume they have developed a technology with two surveillance capabilities:

Promiscuously Monitoring Victim's Wi-Fi Channel for Network Packets. There are tools with the capability of monitoring victim's Wi-Fi channel for network packets is available in Wireshark [9], Aircrackng, more recent development, Krack [8]. Next stage of attack following this method can be vary. In Aircrackng, attacker can either monitor a particular Wi-Fi source to collect Initial Vector (IV) and generate a key or perform dictionary attack to gain access into the Wi-Fi network. Under Krack approach and we assume the victim setup WPA2 as their Wi-Fi security protocol, attacker can monitor victim's Wi-Fi source and inject false information during the 4 ways handshake. Next, attacker can join victim's Wi-Fi network. Readers are encouraged to read [8–11] for more detailed approaches on compromising Wi-Fi security.

Monitoring Physical Activities. Cyberattacker monitors and studies victim physical movement, keyboard key stroke, and successfully distinguish different victims in close proximity. Attacker's technology leverages victim's Wi-Fi signal to accomplish their surveillance [7, 10, 11].

4 Security Measures

In this section, we discuss a set of Wi-Fi security situations and measures. Today's technology allows the ability for someone to track another person and find out if they are in their house using RF and the victim's Wi-Fi router. An attacker can also use Auro-like technology against the occupants of the house if they are able to gain access to the network. This can be utilized against the victim for plotting a home invasion. A potential Wi-Fi forensic system can sense if a person has entered a room by the change in movement of the received wireless signal. Each movement disrupts the broadcast signal of the Wi-Fi router. Home security appliances such as Aura register with the user's Wi-Fi router to detect object movement. Once Aura detects movement, it sends an alert to the owner's device. To make this technology safer, our goal is to demonstrate the security concern. Wi-Fi router can be compromised with a few terminal commands. Once the Wi-Fi router is compromised, the attacker can register with the victim's router using their own radio frequency device like Aura to monitor victim' home. Attackers can develop RF capture devices to capture and record Wi-Fi signal disruption. This disruption of Wi-Fi signals can be gathered for analytic purposes by attackers. Over a period of time, attackers can create algorithms and a schedule that will identify what type of movements was produced by the victim. The privacy of the victim is being abused without their knowledge.

4.1 Securing Radio Frequency

It is important to understand that attackers can use a Wi-Fi router just as the Aura to track down innocent people and harm them. Preventing hackers from accessing the router is the surest way of safeguarding the privacy of the users and from being surveyed, but we cannot always rely on software and hardware upgrade thanks to Zero Day vulnerabilities. We extend our research to develop a "Wi-Fi Hasher", a device that emits a silence white noise using radio frequency to further disrupt Wi-Fi signal reflection. Wi-Fi Hasher hashes the reflection of radio frequency by giving immeasurable baseline for the attacker, while home users can still utilize their Wi-Fi router to surf the web and detect home invasion. To make Wi-Fi Hasher safer to use, we need to make this easy to use. Hence, Wi-Fi Hasher is designed to be a plug and go device. It has no Random-Access Memory (RAM), Read Only Memory (ROM), internal storage, and cannot be programmable. It can only be turned on and off as a fan from 1970s. Turning Wi-Fi Hasher into a dumb device makes it difficult to compromise wirelessly. Radio frequencies released by Wi-Fi Hasher are safe for all human and animals but not insects. As shown in Fig. 2, using the Wi-Fi Hasher, it might be possible to scramble the router signals to keep the attackers in the dark.

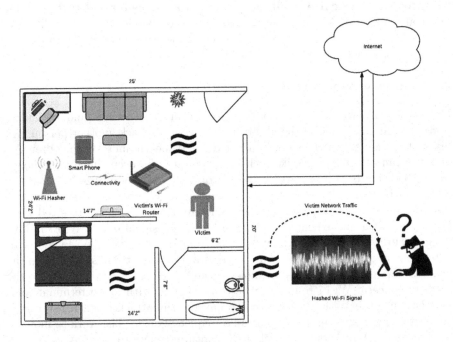

Fig. 2. Scrambling the router signal to keep the attacker in the dark

4.2   Securing Wireless Signal

Technologies that use Wi-Fi signals in order to track a person's movement as well as implementations for the key logging abilities in the disturbance of Wi-Fi signals draws a very large concern when implementing a wireless network.

Not only does one have to secure the data being transmitted in the signals but also how the signals are travelling. In order to secure the signals from bouncing and setting off patterns that attackers can use, signal redirection or signal noise can be used to disrupt the way these signals travel. Signal redirecting in the sense that the signals would bounce around sporadically producing false positives and random data, this would make it hard to distinguish what is moving, if anything at all. Another way to stop the weaponization of these signals would be to create extra noise heading outward from the area. Internally signals will function as normal but at the outskirts of the perimeter the signals will radiate straight out of the routers flooding the outside of the house, this would cause anyone trying to track the movement to receive undisturbed signals not being able to detect anything useful. These security implementations will be used to prevent an attacker from using the signals to track the users. Implementing these preventative measures alongside the software side of security this will add layers to the defensive measures on the network. Making all information that can be gathered by attackers useless is the best step towards securing the network, as it is harder to remediate the breach after it has occurred.

4.3   Securing Wi-Fi Traffic

Wi-Fi traffic on the other hand can be secured by creating simple authentication layers like passwords and other identification methods. Often times users create simple passwords because they wouldn't be able to remember a complex one or even leave the default password for the router, giving attackers an easier chance to compromise and take control over the router. By changing the password to something complex it makes the attacker have to work harder in trying to crack the password and reduces the chance of a brute force entry. Another preventative step would be hiding the SSID broadcast for the access points, hiding the name of the available networks may not seem like much but a quick scan done by a potential attacker would yield other targets that they may potentially go after rather than resorting to other tools to find the hidden signals. Securing the router is essential because a user's computer sends the data to the NIC and this is turned into radio waves, which is send out to the router which receives this signal and converts it into usable data, forwarding the packets of information to where it needs to go.

Securing the network is not a one-time activity, it takes many distinct resources and forces a user to use a layered defense method. It is vital that firewalls are put in place to sift manage traffic coming in and out of the router. As well as IDS systems placed on the router and at each endpoint. This allows a user to monitor activities happening on the network and raises red flags if something seems out of the ordinary. Having an antivirus allows the user to have an extra layer of defense by blocking known attack signatures that may be employed to compromise the network. A network may be compromised many different ways, either through an endpoint tricked into clicking a suspicious link or through a backdoor in the router that was left by the manufacturer which can allow a person to sniff traffic which will compromise the network. When determining whether or not a router is being compromised, some inherent variables are first considered: the number of users, basic capacity of a network's bandwidth and the times in which the network experiences a lot of use. The overall intention is to achieve Confidentiality, Integrity and Availability.

5   Potential Solutions

For this portion of the research, we have come up with some theory on how to try and help the user determine if someone is hacking the router's signal. Using a two-step authentication scheme would allow us to focus on a hardening security on the devices within the user's person. Allowing the user to enter in something they know, and then authenticating with something they have will be key to securing the devices.

5.1   Two-Step Solution

First, we need to establish a baseline for the number of users and devices in the network. The amount of data being used throughout any given day [15], and the times that the bandwidth normally used by known users/devices on the network. This brings other issues into question like what if one of the devices were compromised, how would we know and how to prevent data from breaking Confidentiality, Integrity, Availability (C.I.A)? One of the ideas that can be implemented is dual authentication and encryption of the data. By implementing dual login, we can prevent attacks resulting in authorized users being recognized as legitimate users ensuring that the system integrity is secure, and if this is compromised the encryption will render the captured data unusable. This would be a multi factor sign in process where the user enters in the username and password and authenticates with something that the user has like a mobile phone. The "two step" program would be installed into only one device to limit the number a potential compromised devices.

Encrypting the data would make any compromised signals to be useless to the attacker because they would not be able to decrypt it back to plaintext. The encryption type that we could use is asymmetric to allow for the router and the PC to create their own keys. Another preventative step is pairing your smartphone to authenticate you into your own system. This method would allow only trusted devices onto the network, and would help determine, if a device was compromised, which device it was and how. The idea could be designed around software or coding that collects user input information that resides on the hardware portion of the router/server. This user input would be but not limited to number of devices connected to the network. This input would be to establish a trusted devices IP and MAC addresses allowing the software to monitor each devices in/output. Another input would be type of device, for example some appliances like LG refrigerators with the cameras have vulnerabilities that hackers are able to hijack the camera and look inside the user's home. Another issue with the LG devices is that the oven can be put on pre-heat, which leads to safety concerns. In creating this, the software will create a baseline where it averages the times that each device is used within the network, the statistics of data that is leaving and entering the network and what ports are being used on a weekly basis. This information will be able to be viewed by the router administrator.

5.2   Two-Factor Solution

Reinforcing the encryption will be Multi Factor Authentication, using Two Factor Authentication for Wi-Fi security. Two Factor Authentication Wi-Fi security adds a layer of defense. First is the password protected encrypted signal. Second is time sync/duo push authentication to authenticate device and receive internet traffic. First layer of defense is primary use to let Wi-Fi router establish a recognition to the device logged in to router. At the first layer of defense, user can only navigate to Wi-Fi duo authentication page. No internet traffic or Wi-Fi router configuration page are available at this layer. During the password authentication process at the first layer, Mac address of the device will be matched with router's mac filtering list. Below shows the algorithm of how router mac filtering list works:

if PASSWD == wifi_router and MAC in router-mac-list:
allow to enter to second layer Auth page;
else
device not allow to connect;

Mac filtering list can be configured during initial installation. At the first layer of defense, Wi-Fi router authenticate and recognize the connected device Mac address should the password is valid using the Mac Filtering list. Once user enters the correct Wi-Fi password, user can navigate to second layer authentication process in the browser. At the second layer of defense, the device is connected to Wi-Fi but no internet access. User will need to enter a six digits pin given by Google Authenticator/Duo application in their smartphone or physical token. The six digits randomly generated pin is in sync with router's pin. Router is in-sync with Google authenticator/duo application server to receive the same pin as user via Time-based One Time Password (TOTP) algorithm [1]. Should user and router be out of sync, multiple entries of pin will require in order to re-establish synchronization between router and connected device.

When the user enters a pin that is parallel with router's pin, the router will only target the mac address of the connected device and allow internet traffic to be forwarded to connected device. Should the Wi-Fi router detect multiple identical mac addresses (mac spoofer is in used in one of the device) in the Local Area Network (LAN), user will need to enter a newly generated pin again to validate itself as a legitimate device. Only the device with the correct pin entered is allowed to receive internet traffic.

6   Conclusion

In conclusion, technology has advanced to such a degree that a sense of locking our door is not enough to secure a room. Going back to the scene from Batman the Dark Knight, this type of technology is great in the right hands but dangerous in the wrong ones. Routers are able to identify movements, calibrate temperature and depending on the situation, look at your password. This theoretical research allows us to look for different countermeasures to the problems that advancing technology might present. The focus was on deterring someone from looking at your data and securing the customer/user's router. The ability to allow the customer/user to have flexibility within their own home while hardening the router to deny or render the compromised data unusable is a difficult balance. The research shows that we have mitigated many issues and newer ideals can be built upon our research. As part of the future work, extensive research and experiment on hashing Wi-Fi signals will be conducted to see full results. Another issue will be addressed is the Mac Filtering, whose lists is not effective when dealing with a device listening for Wi-Fi traffic in promiscuous mode.

References

1. Adib, F., Katabi, D.: See through walls with Wi-Fi. In: Proceedings of ACM SIGCOMM 2013, pp. 75–86 (2013)
2. Xin, T., Guo, B., Wang, Z., Li, M., Yu, Z., Zhou, X.: FreeSense: indoor human identification with Wi-Fi signals. In: Proceedings of IEEE GLOBECOM 2016, pp. 1–6 (2016)
3. Wang, G., Zou, Y., Zhou, Z., Wu, K., Ni, L.: We can hear you with Wi-Fi. In: Proceedings of ACM MobiCom, pp. 2907–2920 (2014)
4. Ali, K., Liu, A., Wang, W., Shahzad, M.: Keystroke recognition using Wi-Fi signals. In: Proceedings ACM of MOBICOM, pp. 90–102 (2015)
5. Bennett, J.: Researchers use Wi-Fi to invent real X-ray vision. Popular Mechanics, pp. 1–8 (2017)
6. Atkinson, J., Mitchell, J., Rio, M., Matich, G.: Your WiFi is leaking: what do your mobile apps gossip about you? Future Gener. Comput. Syst. **80**, 546–557 (2018)
7. Jessey, B.: Decrypting TLS, capturing USB, keyloggers, and network graphing. In: Shimonski, R. (ed.) Wireshark® for Security Professionals. LNCS, vol. 9999, pp. 199–219. Springer, Heidelberg (2016)
8. Henry, A.: How to Tap Your Network and See Everything that Happens on it. http://lifehacker.com/how-to-tap-your-network-and-see-everything-that-happens-1649292940. Accessed 22 Oct 2017
9. Vanhoef, M., Piessens, F.: Key reinstallation attacks. In: Proceedings of ACM, CCS 2017, pp. 1313–1328 (2017)
10. How to Hack Wi-Fi: Getting Started with the Aircrack-Ng Suite of Wi-Fi Hacking Tools. null-byte.wonderhowto.com/how-to/hack-wi-fi-getting-started-with-aircrack-ng-suite-wi-fi-hacking-tools-0147893/. Accessed 22 Oct 2017
11. M'Raihi, D., Machani, S., Pei, M., Rydell, J.: TOTP: time-based one-time password algorithm. IETF Tools. https://tools.ietf.org/html/rfc6238. Accessed 27 Nov 2017
12. Khang, M.F., Wang, G., Bhuiyan, M., Li, X.: Wi-Fi signal coverage distance estimation in collapsed structures. In: Proceedings of IEEE ISPA 2017, pp. 1–8 (2017)

13. Khang, M.F., Wang, G., Bhuiyan, M., Xing, X.: Towards Wi-Fi radar in collapsed structures. In: Proceedings of IEEE UIC 2018, pp. 1–8 (2018)
14. Khang, M.F., Wang, G., Bhuiyan, M., Xing, X., Tao, P.: Wi-Fi halow signal coverage estimation in collapsed structures. In: Proceedings of IEEE DASC 2018, pp. 1–8 (2018)
15. Wang, T., Bhuiyan, M., Wang, G., Rahman, A., Wu, J., Cao, J.: Big data reduction for smart city's critical infrastructural health monitoring. IEEE Commun. Mag. **56**(3), 128–133 (2018)

E²STA: An Energy-Efficient Spatio-Temporal Query Algorithm for Wireless Sensor Networks

Liang Liu, Zhe Xu[✉], Yi-Ting Wang, and Xiao-Lin Qin

College of Computer Science and Technology,
Nanjing University of Aeronautics and Astronautics,
Nanjing Yudao Street 29, Mailbox 274, Nanjing 210016, China
{liangliu,xuzhe,eda,qinxcs}@nuaa.edu.cn

Abstract. After wireless sensor networks are deployed, spatio-temporal query is frequently submitted by users to obtain all the sensor readings of an area of interest in a period of time. Most of existing spatio-temporal query processing algorithms organized all the nodes in the whole network or the nodes in the query area into a single routing tree guided by which the sensor readings of the nodes in the query area are sent back to the sink. This study attempts to answer the following two questions: first, is it feasible to processing spatio-temporal query by multiple routing trees? Second, for the single tree based algorithms and the multiple trees based algorithms, which one outperforms the other? We pointed out that the path along which the query results are sent back to the sink is fairly long when a single routing tree is adopted, which leads to a large amount of energy consumption. Organizing the nodes in the query area into multiple routing trees can avoid this problem. Based on the above findings, we designed a protocol of constructing multiple routing trees for the nodes in the query area, and proposed an energy-efficient spatio-temporal query processing algorithm called E²STA. Theoretical and experimental results show that the proposed algorithm based on multiple routing trees outperforms the existing algorithms based on one single routing tree in terms of energy consumption.

Keywords: Wireless sensor networks · Query processing Spatio-temporal query · Energy-efficiency

1 Introduction

Wireless Sensor Network (WSN) is composed of a large number of sensor motes deployed in a specific area to monitor and process the relevant information of interested objects. WSN has greatly extended human ability and scope of obtaining information, which has very broad application prospects in the military defense, industrial control, environmental monitoring and so on.

WSN is a data-centric network deployed to obtain its sensory readings by users, there is a philosophy to see WSN as a distributed database [1], so many

© Springer Nature Switzerland AG 2018
G. Wang et al. (Eds.): SpaCCS 2018, LNCS 11342, pp. 522–531, 2018.
https://doi.org/10.1007/978-3-030-05345-1_45

studies have been focusing on designing in-network processing algorithms for different queries that are suitable for WSN to extract sensory readings for users, such as aggregation query [26], top k [2], skyline [24,27], knn [22], join [19] and etc. Spatio-temporal query is somewhat overlooked since there's less research on it compared with above ones.

Actually, spatio-temporal query is frequently used in many WSN applications. For example, in the scene of wildlife monitoring, when a rare animal is found dead somewhere, a spatio-temporal query may be submitted to inquire the sensor readings of surrounding area a period before the death to infer the cause. In forest monitoring, when a fire happens, we can submit a spatio-temporal query to retrieve the sensor readings of the surrounding area for evaluating the fire situation and predicting its spreading trend.

In [5,6,8,13,18,25] in-network processing technique is adopted to take advantage of computing and storage resources of the motes themselves to reduce the data communication through distributed collaborative computing. However, the algorithm proposed in [5] needs to send a large amount of query messages to the nodes out the scope of the query area, while the algorithms proposed in [6,8,13,25] consume a considerable amount of unnecessary energy during collecting sensor readings to the sink.

In order to tackle the problems of existing algorithms, this paper proposes an energy-efficient spatio-temporal query processing algorithm called E²STA for wireless sensor networks. It first divides the entire query area into m subareas and the sink sends a query message to a node within each subarea using geographic routing protocol [15]. These nodes receiving the query messages are defined as coordinator nodes which flood the query messages to other nodes within the query area. Sensor nodes within the query area will be organized into m routing trees, one per subarea rooted at the corresponding coordinator node. Then leaf nodes in these trees send their readings to their parent respectively, non-leaf nodes, after collecting readings of all their children, send them together with their own readings to their parent. This process continues until all the readings reach that m coordinator nodes of subareas. Finally, these coordinator nodes return their collected dataset to the sink using geographic routing protocol.

E²STA only transmits query message to the nodes in query area, and optimizes the path length of forwarding sensor readings of nodes in query area to the sink, hence reducing the energy of distributing query message and collecting sensor readings. Theoretical analysis and experimental results show that in most cases, E²STA consumes less energy than existing SWIF algorithm that is currently optimal.

The rest of this paper is organized as follows: related algorithms and their shortcomings are discussed in Sect. 2; Sect. 3 describes E²STA proposed in this paper systematically; a theoretical comparison of energy consumption between E²STA and SWIF [6] is carried out in Sect. 3.1 and experimental comparison in Sect. 4. Section 5 concludes the paper and gives the vista of potential future work.

2 Related Work

Suppose node can get its own location through localization algorithms [1,2,20, 23] or through the GPS module and all the nodes maintain the locations of their one-hop neighbors. Sensor nodes are homogeneous and energy constrained. Sensor nodes and the sink are stationary. The optimization of spatio-temporal query processing algorithm mainly focuses on reducing the data transmission because it consumes much more energy than computing. Currently the existing spatio-temporal query processing algorithms in WSN can be divided into the following categories:

In FullFlood [5], after the sink receives a spatio-temporal query, it broadcasts the query to all its neighbors. For a node n in the network, node n takes the source node of the first query message received as its parent node, and broadcasts the query message to all its neighbors. When receiving other query messages, node n just discard them without any processing. After the above process is finished, the query message is flooded to all nodes in the network and these nodes are organized into a routing tree rooted at the sink. After the routing tree is formed, there is a shortest path to the sink for each node.

The R-tree based algorithms proposed in [8,11,13] improved FullFlood by organizing the nodes in the network into a distributed R-tree. Non-leaf nodes in the R-tree are in charge of maintaining their children's MBR (minimum bounding rectangle). After receiving a query message, they only forward it to their children which locate in the intersection of query area and their MBRs. This improvement reduces energy consumption by reduction of unnecessary access of sub-trees which do not fall in the range of query area.

SWIF [6] divides the query processing into three stages:

1. The sink sends a query message to the query coordinator node in the query area through geographic routing protocol [16].
2. The query coordinator node floods the query message to all the nodes in query area, and then uses the same method as FullFlood to organize the nodes in query area into a routing tree. The nodes in the query area send their sensory data to the query coordinator node through the routing tree.
3. The query coordinator node sends its own data and the sensory readings received from the nodes in query area to the sink through the reverse path which is formed in the first stage.

The energy consumption of SWIF algorithm is related to the location of the query coordinator node. Due to space limitation, how to choose the query coordinator node is discarded, which is described in detail in [6].

In mobile sensor networks, the network topology is instable due to nodes moving, thus maintaining routing tree will consume a large amount of energy. An itinerary-based algorithm called IWQE [25] which do not rely on routing tree is proposed.

3 Energy-Efficient Spatio-Temporal Query Processing Algorithm for Wireless Sensor Network E²STA

In order to avoid the problems of existing algorithms, this paper proposes an energy-efficient spatio-temporal query processing algorithm for wireless sensor networks. E²STA has the following four steps:

1. Divide query area. It divides the query area ABCD into a number of subareas $qa_i(1 \leq i \leq m)$ by several lines through the sink;
2. Send query messages. In this step the sink sends query messages to its closest nodes in each subarea. We define these nodes as coordinator nodes denoted as $cn_i(1 \leq i \leq m)$.
3. Construct multiple routing trees. After the coordinator node $cn_i(1 \leq i \leq m)$ receiving the query message from the sink, it floods the query message to the nodes in the query area to organize the nodes within the query area into m routing trees rooted at $cn_i(1 \leq i \leq m)$ (as shown in Fig. 1). Specifically, for a node n in query area, node n takes the source node of the first query message received as its parent, and broadcasts the query message to all its neighbors. When receiving other query messages, node n just discard them without any processing. We denote these routing trees by $rt_i(1 \leq i \leq m)$.
4. Collect sensor readings. Leaf nodes of the routing trees $rt_i(1 \leq i \leq m)$ send their readings to their respective parent. As the non-leaf nodes in $rt_i(1 \leq i \leq m)$ receive sensor readings of its all children, they send them with their own readings to their parent. This process continues until all readings reach the roots $cn_i(1 \leq i \leq m)$ to be returned to sink using geographic routing protocol. Next every step of E²STA will be discussed in detail.

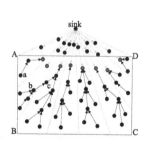

Fig. 1. E²STA algorithm

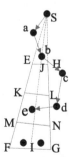

Fig. 2. Send a query message to the coordinator node.

3.1 Send Query Messages to Coordinator Nodes

As shown in Fig. 2, node S is the sink, region EFGH is a subarea of the query area ABCD after being divided, and line SI is the bisector of FSG. Those lines perpendicular to SI like KL, MN combine to divide EFGH into a number of sub regions $ra_j (1 \leq i \leq k)$, where the center of ra_{j+1} is further than the center of ra_j from the sink. Line SI intersects each sub region $ra_j (1 \leq i \leq k-1)$ at two points, the distances between them which is the height of sub region $ra_j (1 \leq i \leq k-1)$ are the same. These subdivided regions are referred to routing regions in this paper and we assume that subarea $qa_i (1 \leq i \leq m)$ is divided into n_i routing regions $ra(i, j_i)(1 \leq j_i \leq n_i)$ according to the above strategy (as shown in Fig. 3).

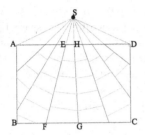 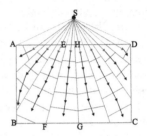

Fig. 3. Divide query area into some routing regions.

Fig. 4. The itinerary of sending query message to coordinator nodes.

Since node only maintains locations of its one-hop neighbors, the topology and distribution of the nodes within query area are unknown to the sink. In order to disseminate the query messages from the sink to the nearest nodes in each subarea namely coordinator nodes, this paper proposes a **g**eographic **r**outing protocol for sending **q**uery messages from the sink to coordinator nodes (GRPQ). GRPQ identifies the coordinator nodes of each subarea along the itinerary shown in Fig. 4 and sends query message to these nodes.

The whole process of sending query message to the coordinator node of subarea $qa_i (1 \leq j_i \leq m)$ using GRPQ is given as below:

1. Set the current node $curN$ as the sink, the index of the current routing region j_i is set to 1 and the current routing region $curRa$ is set to $ra(i, j_i)$.
2. Node $curN$ sends a query message to the node that is closest to the center of $curRa$ by geographic routing protocol. Suppose the specified node is ln, node ln determines whether or not it is in $curRa$.
   (a) If so, node ln becomes the coordinator node of subarea qa_i, and the protocol is finished.
   (b) If not, turn to step 3
3. Set $curN$ as ln, determines whether $j_i < n_i$.
   (a) If so, $j_i = j_i + 1$, $curRa$ is set to $ra(i, j_i)$, turn to step 2
   (b) If not, the subarea qa_i is an empty area, there's no coordinator node in this subarea and the protocol is finished.

Algorithm 1. Construct routing trees

Input: NULL
Output: NULL
1: **while** true **do**
2:    Waiting for the query message fp from its neighbors
3:    **if** Node n do not resides in $fp.sw$ **then**
4:      drop this message without processing
5:    **else**
6:      **if** $n.hop$ equals $+\infty$ **then**
7:        $n.hop := fp.hop + 1$
8:        $n.parent := fp.sid$
9:        $fp.sid := n.id$
10:       $fp.hop := fp.hop + 1$
11:       node n broadcasts fp to its neighbors
12:     **else**
13:       drop this message without processing
14:     **end if**
15:   **end if**
16: **end while**

3.2 Construct Routing Trees Within Query Area

The coordinator nodes $cn_i(1 \leq i \leq m)$, after receiving the query message from the sink, floods query messages into the whole query area to organize the nodes within query area into a number of routing trees rooted at $cn_i(1 \leq i \leq m)$ in the same way as SWIF does. The coordinator node $cn_i(1 \leq i \leq m)$, once receiving a query message sent from the sink, initiates the flooding packet fp whose field list is shown in Table 1: $fp.sp$ is set to the location of the sink, $fp.sid = cn_i.id$ $fp.hop = 0$ $fp.sw = sw$ $fp.tw = tw$, $fp.m = m$. Then packet fp is broadcasted to its neighbors. For a node n within the network, its depth in the routing tree $n.hop$ is set to $+\infty$ at first and its parent node $n.parent$ is initialized as NULL. Node n uses Algorithm 1 to find its parent.

Table 1. Field list of query message

Field name	Description
sp	Location of the sink
sid	Id of source node sending this packet
hop	Depth in routing tree
tw	Time window of the query
sw	Query area
m	Number of subareas

It should be noted that in this phase the coordinator nodes should broadcast flooding packets immediately after receiving the query message from the sink.

Next, for a node n within the query area, node n chooses the source node of the first query message received as its parent node. Figure 1 shows an example, the first query message received by node b is sent by node c so node b set its parent to node c and its depth in the routing tree namely $n.hop$ to 3. Then node b receives the query message from node a, it will drop this query message without any processing since node b has been added to a routing tree.

4   Performance Evaluation

In this section we evaluate our algorithm experimentally. We implement E^2STA and SWIF upon the simulator in [5] and make a comparison of the energy consumption of these two algorithms under different node density, size of query area, size of query message and size of sensor readings. The network topology is generated in the same way as in [5]. The sensors' placement follows a uniform distribution over a two dimensional region. The data compression and approximation algorithms proposed in [3,4,7,9,10,12,14,17,21] are vertical to our algorithms, they can be adopted in our algorithm to make a further reduction of energy consumption, so we do not compare E^2STA with these algorithms.

The experiments are conducted on a PC with a P4 3.0 GHz CPU and 512 MB memory running Ubuntu operating system. According to [6], the energy used to transmit and receive 1 bit of information in wireless communication are $E_t = \alpha + \gamma \times d^n$ and $E_r = \beta$ resp. Parameters in [6] are adopted here: $\gamma = 10pJ/bit/m^2$, $\alpha = 45nJ/bit$, $\beta = 135nJ/bit$, $n = 2$. The following Table 2 summarizes the default parameters used in our simulations.

Table 2. Default parameter settings

Parameter	Default value
Area covered	$100 \times 100\,m^2$
Wireless range	10 m
Number of sensors	480
Sensed data size	150 bytes
Query message size	50 bytes
The ratio of query area to area covered	50%
The height of route region	5 m

Figure 5 shows the energy consumption of the two algorithms under different network topologies. The ten different network topologies are generated synthetically. It can be seen from the experimental result that in the most case E^2STA consumes less energy than SWIF does. The reason is: although the energy consumed by E^2STA to distribute query messages is a little greater than that of SWIF, E^2STA optimizes the path length of forwarding sensor readings of nodes in query area to the sink, reducing the energy of collection sensor readings greatly, which results in its less energy consumption.

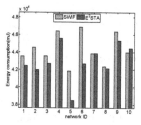

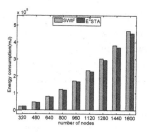

Fig. 5. Energy consumption under different network topologies.

Fig. 6. Influence of node density on energy consumption.

Figures 6 and 7 shows the energy consumption of the two algorithms for different node density and size of query area respectively. As the node density or the size of query area increases, SWIF and E^{2}STA consume more and more energy for the distribution of query message and collection of sensor readings, which leads to the growing total energy consumption of these two algorithms.

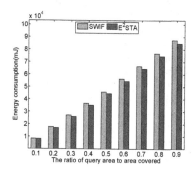

Fig. 7. Influence of query area size on energy consumption.

5   Summary and Future Work

This paper presents an energy-efficient spatio-temporal query processing algorithm E^{2}STA for wireless sensor networks. It first divides the query area into several subareas; the sink sends query messages to the coordinator node of each subarea using geographical routing protocol. Then, these coordinator nodes flood query messages to the nodes in the query area to construct several routing trees rooted at them. By these routing trees, nodes in the query area are able to send its readings to the root of their corresponding routing trees. At last these coordinator nodes send the data of their own tree back to the sink by geographic routing protocol. E^2STA organize nodes within the query area into multiple routing trees to avoid the problem of the existing algorithms that the routing path of forwarding the query results to the sink node by a single tree is too long, thus reducing the energy consumption. Theoretical and experimental results show the correctness of the conclusions.

Acknowledgments. This work is supported by the National Natural Science Foundation of China under Grant No. (61402225, 61373015, 41301407), the National Natural Science Foundation of Jiangsu Province under Grant No. BK20140832, the China Postdoctoral Science Foundation under Grant No. 2013M540447, the Jiangsu Postdoctoral Science Foundation under Grant No. 1301020C, State Key Laboratory for smart grid protection and operation control Foundation, Science and Technology Funds from National Electric Net Ltd. (The Research on Key Technologies of Distributed Parallel Database Storage and Processing based on Big Data), the Foundation of Graduate Innovation Center in NUAA under Grant No. kfjj20181608.

References

1. Belfkih, A., Duvallet, C., Sadeg, B., Amanton, L.: A real-time query processing system for WSN. In: Puliafito, A., Bruneo, D., Distefano, S., Longo, F. (eds.) ADHOC-NOW 2017. LNCS, vol. 10517, pp. 307–313. Springer, Cham (2017). https://doi.org/10.1007/978-3-319-67910-5_25
2. Chen, Y.S., Tsou, Y.T.: Compressive sensing-based adaptive top-k query over compression domain in wireless sensor networks. In: Wireless Communications and Networking Conference, pp. 1–6 (2017)
3. Cheng, S., Li, J.: Sampling based (epsilon, delta)-approximate aggregation algorithm in sensor networks. In: Proceedings of the 2009 29th IEEE International Conference on Distributed Computing Systems, pp. 273–280. IEEE Computer Society (2009). 1584555
4. Cheng, S., Li, J., Ren, Q., Yu, L.: Bernoulli sampling based (epsilon, delta)-approximate aggregation in large-scale sensor networks. In: Proceedings of the 29th Conference on Information Communications, pp. 1181–1189. IEEE Press (2010). 1833693
5. Coman, A., Nascimento, M.A., Sander, J.: A framework for spatio-temporal query processing over wireless sensor networks. In: Proceeedings of the 1st International Workshop on Data Management for Sensor Networks: in Conjunction with VLDB 2004, pp. 104–110. ACM (2004)
6. Coman, A., Sander, J., Nascimento, M.A.: Adaptive processing of historical spatial range queries in peer-to-peer sensor networks. Distrib. Parallel Databases **22**, 133–163 (2007)
7. Deligiannakis, A., Kotidis, Y., Roussopoulos, N.: Compressing historical information in sensor networks. In: Proceedings of the 2004 ACM SIGMOD International Conference on Management of Data, pp. pp. 527–538. ACM (2004)
8. Demirbas, M., Ferhatosmanoglu, H.: Peer-to-peer spatial queries in sensor networks. In: Proceedings of the 3rd International Conference on Peer-to-Peer Computing, pp. 32–39. IEEE Computer Society (2003)
9. Deshpande, A., Guestrin, C., Madden, S.R., Hellerstein, J.M., Hong, W.: Model-driven data acquisition in sensor networks. In: Proceedings of the Thirtieth International Conference on Very large Data Bases - Volume 30, pp. 588–599. VLDB Endowment (2004)

10. Deshpande, A., Guestrin, C., Wei, H., Madden, S.: Exploiting correlated attributes in acquisitional query processing. In: Proceedings of the 21st International Conference on Data Engineering, pp. 143–154. IEEE Computer Society (2005)

11. Elashry, A., Shehab, A., Riad, A.M., Aboul-Fotouh, A.: 2DPR-Tree: two-dimensional priority r-tree algorithm for spatial partitioning in spatialhadoop. ISPRS Int. J. Geo-Inf. **7**(5), 179 (2018)

12. Gandhi, S., Nath, S., Suri, S., Liu, J.: GAMPS: compressing multi sensor data by grouping and amplitude scaling. In: Proceedings of the 35th SIGMOD International Conference on Management of Data, pp. 771–784. ACM (2009)

13. Goldin, D., Song, M., Kutlu, A., Gao, H., Dave, H.: Georouting and delta-gathering: efficient data propagation techniques for geosensor networks. In: First Workshop on Geo Sensor Networks (2003)

14. Guestrin, C., Bodik, P., Thibaux, R., Paskin, M., Madden, S.: Distributed regression: an efficient framework for modeling sensor network data. In: Proceedings of the 3rd International Symposium on Information Processing in Sensor Networks, pp. 1–10. ACM (2004)

15. Huang, H., Yin, H., Min, G., Zhang, X., Zhu, W., Wu, Y.: Coordinate-assisted routing approach to bypass routing holes in wireless sensor networks. IEEE Commun. Mag. **55**(7), 180–185 (2017)

16. Karp, B., Kung, H.T.: GPSR: greedy perimeter stateless routing for wireless networks. In: Proceedings of the 6th Annual International Conference on Mobile Computing and Networking, pp. 243–254. ACM (2000)

17. Kotidis, Y.: Snapshot queries: towards data-centric sensor networks. In: Proceedings of the 21st International Conference on Data Engineering, pp. 131–142. IEEE Computer Society (2005)

18. Kumar, P., Chaturvedi, A.: Spatial-temporal aspects integrated probabilistic intervals models of query generation and sink attributes for energy efficient WSN. Wirel. Pers. Commun. **96**(2), 1849–1870 (2017)

19. Lai, Y., Gao, X., Wang, T., Lin, Z.: Efficient iceberg join processing in wireless sensor networks. Int. J. Embed. Syst. **9**(4), 365–378 (2017)

20. Li, M., Liu, Y.: Rendered path: range-free localization in anisotropic sensor networks with holes. IEEE/ACM Trans. Netw. **18**(1), 320–332 (2010)

21. Liu, Y., Li, J., Gao, H., Fang, X.: Enabling epsilon-approximate querying in sensor networks. Proc. VLDB Endow. **2**, 169–180 (2009)

22. Liu, Y., Fu, J.S., Zhang, Z.J.: k-nearest neighbors tracking in wireless sensor networks with coverage holes. Pers. Ubiquitous Comput. **20**(3), 431–446 (2016)

23. Mao, G., Fidan, B., Anderson, B.D.O.: Wireless sensor network localization techniques. Comput. Netw. **51**(10), 2529–2553 (2007)

24. Wang, Y., Wei, W., Deng, Q., Liu, W., Song, H.: An energy-efficient skyline query for massively multidimensional sensing data. Sensors **16**(1), 83–103 (2016)

25. Xu, Y., Lee, W.C., Xu, J., Mitchell, G.: Processing window queries in wireless sensor networks. In: Proceedings of the 22nd International Conference on Data Engineering, pp. 70–80. IEEE Computer Society (2006). 1129930

26. Yan, H., Al-Hoqani, N., Yang, S.H.: In-network multi-sensors query aggregation algorithm for wireless sensor networks database. In: 2018 IEEE 15th International Conference on Networking, Sensing and Control (ICNSC), pp. 1–8. IEEE (2018)

27. Yin, B., Zhou, S., Zhang, S., Gu, K., Yu, F.: On efficient processing of continuous reverse skyline queries in wireless sensor networks. KSII Trans. Internet Inf. Syst. **11**(4), 1931–1953 (2017)

Author Index

Printed in the United States
By Bookmasters